PEARSON
my World
GEOGRAPHY™

PEARSON

Boston, Massachusetts
Chandler, Arizona
Glenview, Illinois
Upper Saddle River, New Jersey

ISBN-13: 978-0-13-369162-7
ISBN-10:   0-13-369162-4
14 15 16 V011 18 17 16 15

Program Authors

Gregory H. Chu, a native of Hong Kong, is Professor and Chair of Geography at the University of Wisconsin-La Crosse and Editor of *FOCUS on Geography,* a journal published by the American Geographical Society. He earned his Ph.D. degree in geography from the University of Hawaii and has served as Program Director of Geography and Regional Science at the National Science Foundation, on the Editorial Board of *Cartographic Perspectives,* and Board of Directors of the North American Cartographic Information Society.

Susan Hardwick is a geography professor at the University of Oregon. She is an expert in the human geography of North America and is the past president of the National Council for Geographic Education. She is best known as the co-host of *The Power of Place,* an Annenberg geography series produced for public television. Professor Hardwick was awarded the Association of America's Gilbert Grosvenor Award in Geographic Education, the National Council for Geographic Education's Outstanding Mentor Award, and the statewide California Outstanding Professor Award when she taught at California State University, Chico, before moving to Oregon. She is the parent of four grown sons who all live on a west coast.

Don Holtgrieve received his Ph.D. degree in geography from the University of Oregon and was a professor of geography and environmental studies in the California State University system for 30 years. He now teaches geography and environmental planning at the University of Oregon. His attraction to geography was the interdisciplinary nature of the field and the opportunity to do research out-of-doors. Dr. Holtgrieve enjoys bringing his "real-world" experiences as a high school teacher, community planner, police officer, and consultant to government agencies into his writing and teaching.

Program Consultant

Grant Wiggins is the President of Authentic Education in Hopewell, New Jersey. He earned his Ed.D. degree from Harvard University and his B.A. from St. John's College in Annapolis, Maryland. Wiggins consults with schools, districts, and state education departments on a variety of reform matters; organizes conferences and workshops; and develops print materials and Web resources on curricular change. Over the past 20 years, Wiggins has worked on some of the most influential reform initiatives in the country, including Vermont's portfolio system and Ted Sizer's Coalition of Essential Schools. He is the coauthor, with Jay McTighe, of *Understanding by Design* and *The Understanding by Design Handbook,* the award-winning and highly successful materials on curriculum published by ASCD. He is also the author of *Educative Assessment* and *Assessing Student Performance*, both published by Jossey-Bass.

Academic Reviewers

Africa
Benjamin Ofori-Amoah
Department of Geography
Western Michigan University
Kalamazoo, Michigan

Australia and the Pacific
Christine Drake, Ph.D.
Department of Political Science
    and Geography
Old Dominion University
Norfolk, Virginia

Peter N. D. Pirie
Department of Geography
University of Hawaii at Manoa
Honolulu, Hawaii

East and Southeast Asia
Jessie P. H. Poon
Department of Geography
University of Buffalo
State University of New York
Buffalo, New York

Susan M. Walcott
Department of Geography
University of North Carolina
    at Greensboro
Greensboro, North Carolina

Europe
William H. Berentsen
Department of Geography
University of Connecticut
Storrs, Connecticut

Nancy Partner
Department of History
McGill University
Montreal, Quebec, Canada

Charles Rearick
Department of History
University of Massachusetts
Amherst, Massachusetts

Middle and South America
Connie Weil
Department of Geography
University of Minnesota
Minneapolis, Minnesota

North America
Mark Drayse
Department of Geography
California State University
Fullerton, California

South and Central Asia
Dr. Reuel R. Hanks
Department of Geography
Oklahoma State University
Stillwater, Oklahoma

Pradyumna P. Karan
Department of Geography
University of Kentucky
Lexington, Kentucky

Southwest Asia
Michael E. Bonine
School of Geography and
    Development
Department of Near Eastern
    Studies
University of Arizona
Tucson, Arizona

Shaul Cohen
Department of Geography
University of Oregon
Eugene, Oregon

Religion
Brent Isbell
Department of Religious Studies
University of Houston
Houston, Texas

Shabbir Mansuri
Munir Shaikh
Institute on Religion and
    Civic Values
Fountain Valley, California

Gordon Newby
Department of Middle Eastern
    and South Asian Studies
Emory University
Atlanta, Georgia

Robert Platzner, Ph.D.
Emeritus Professor of
Humanities and Religious
Studies
California State University
Sacramento, California

Master Teachers and Contributing Authors

George F. Sabato
Past President, California Council for
the Social Studies
Placerville Union School District
Placerville, California

Michael Yell
President, National Council for
the Social Studies
Hudson Middle School
Hudson, Wisconsin

Teacher Consultants

James F. Dowd IV
Pasadena, California

Susan M. Keane
Rochester Memorial School
Rochester, Massachusetts

Timothy T. Sprain
Lincoln Middle School
LaCrosse, Wisconsin

Marilyn Weiser
North Dakota Geographic
Alliance Coordinator
Minot State University
Minot, North Dakota

Reviewers

Carol Bacak-Egbo
Waterford Schools
Waterford, Michigan

John Brill
Bellevue School District
Bellevue, Washington

Helene Brown
Gwinnett County Public Schools
Lawrenceville, Georgia

Sherry Echols
Hartselle Junior High School
Hartselle, Alabama

MaryLynne Fillmon
George N. Smith Junior High
Mesa, Arizona

Douglas Fillmore
Bloomington Junior High School
Bloomington, Illinois

Chad Hayes
Beadle Middle School
Omaha, Nebraska

Bill Huser
Prairie Catholic Middle School
Prairie du Chien, Wisconsin

Steve Missal
Saint Peter's College
Jersey City, New Jersey

James Reed
Caledonia High School
Caledonia, Mississippi

Gina S. Rikard
Greenwood Middle School
Goldsboro, North Carolina

Chuck Schierloh
Lima City Schools
Lima, Ohio

Welcome to
my World Geography !

We hope you enjoy learning more about your world and its people. One of the most difficult parts of studying world geography is that there are nearly 7 billion people in the world. It's very difficult to think about such a large number. To make it easier, the map on these pages shows the world divided into regions. Page numbers on the map indicate where in the book you can read about each region.

This map also shows how many people would live in each region if there were only 100 people in the entire world.

We hope you enjoy your exploration of your world.

The myWorld authors

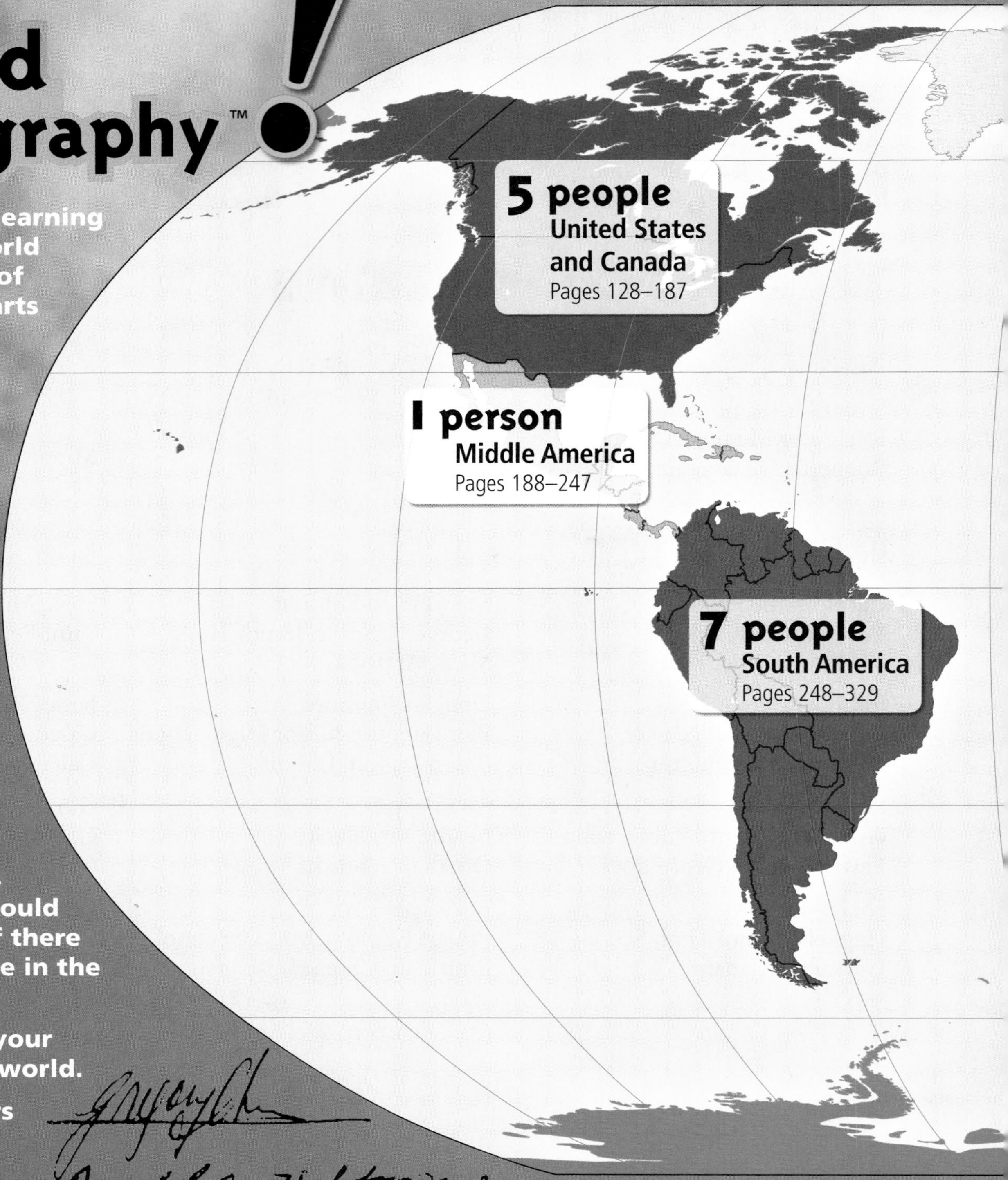

5 people
United States and Canada
Pages 128–187

1 person
Middle America
Pages 188–247

7 people
South America
Pages 248–329

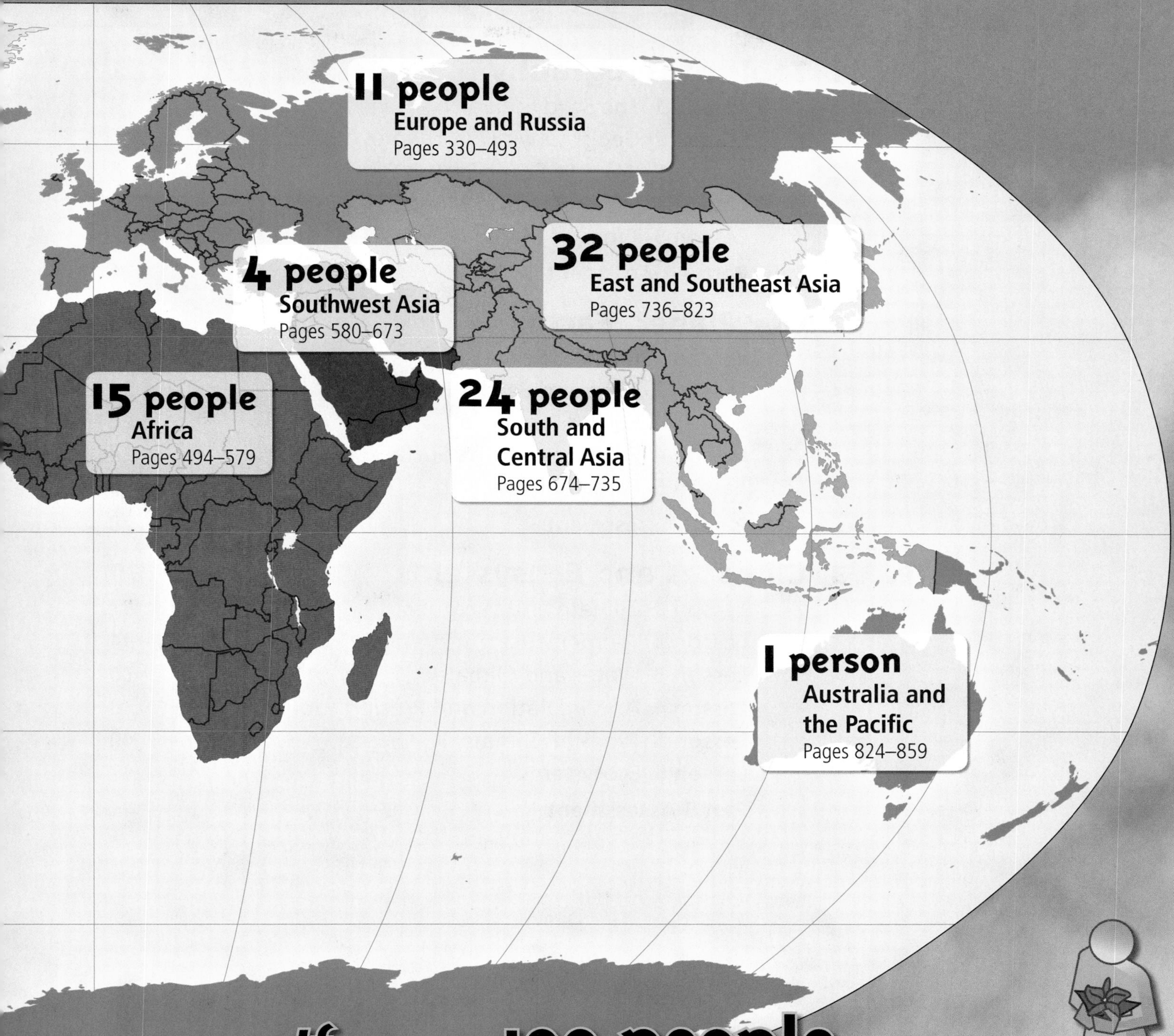

11 people
Europe and Russia
Pages 330–493

32 people
East and Southeast Asia
Pages 736–823

4 people
Southwest Asia
Pages 580–673

15 people
Africa
Pages 494–579

24 people
South and
Central Asia
Pages 674–735

1 person
Australia and
the Pacific
Pages 824–859

If there were **100 people** in the world,
where would they *live*?

Contents

Core Concepts Handbook

Part 1 Tools of Geography   **2**

Lesson 1 The Study of Earth   4

Lesson 2 Geography's Five Themes   6

Lesson 3 Ways to Show Earth's Surface   8

Lesson 4 Understanding Maps   10

Lesson 5 Types of Maps   12

Part 1 Assessment   14

Part 2 Our Planet, Earth   **16**

Lesson 1 Earth in Space   18

Lesson 2 Time and Earth's Rotation   20

Lesson 3 Earth's Structure   22

Lesson 4 Forces on Earth's Surface   24

Lesson 5 Forces Inside Earth   26

Part 2 Assessment   28

Part 3 Climates and Ecosystems   **30**

Lesson 1 Climate and Weather   32

Lesson 2 Temperature   34

Lesson 3 Water and Climate   36

Lesson 4 Air Circulation and Precipitation   38

Lesson 5 Types of Climate   40

Lesson 6 Ecosystems   42

Part 3 Assessment   44

Part 4 **Human-Environment Interaction** **46**

   Lesson 1 Environment and Resources 48

   Lesson 2 Land Use 50

   Lesson 3 People's Impact on the Environment 52

   Part 4 Assessment 54

Part 5 **Economics and Geography** **56**

   Lesson 1 Economic Basics 58

   Lesson 2 Economic Process 60

   Lesson 3 Economic Systems 62

   Lesson 4 Economic Development 64

   Lesson 5 Trade 66

   Lesson 6 Money Management 68

   Part 5 Assessment 70

Part 6 **Population and Movement** **72**

   Lesson 1 Population Growth 74

   Lesson 2 Population Distribution 76

   Lesson 3 Migration 78

   Lesson 4 Urbanization 80

   Part 6 Assessment 82

Core Concepts Handbook

Part 7 **Culture and Geography** **84**

    Lesson 1 What Is Culture?   86

    Lesson 2 Families and Societies   88

    Lesson 3 Language   90

    Lesson 4 Religion   92

    Lesson 5 Art   94

    Lesson 6 Cultural Diffusion and Change   96

    Lesson 7 Science and Technology   98

    Part 7 Assessment   100

Part 8 **Government and Citizenship** **102**

    Lesson 1 Foundations of Government   104

    Lesson 2 Political Systems   106

    Lesson 3 Political Structures   108

    Lesson 4 Conflict and Cooperation   110

    Lesson 5 Citizenship   112

    Part 8 Assessment   114

Part 9 **Tools of History** **116**

    Lesson 1 Measuring Time   118

    Lesson 2 Historical Sources   120

    Lesson 3 Archaeology and Other Sources   122

    Lesson 4 Historical Maps   124

    Part 9 Assessment   126

Unit 1 United States and Canada

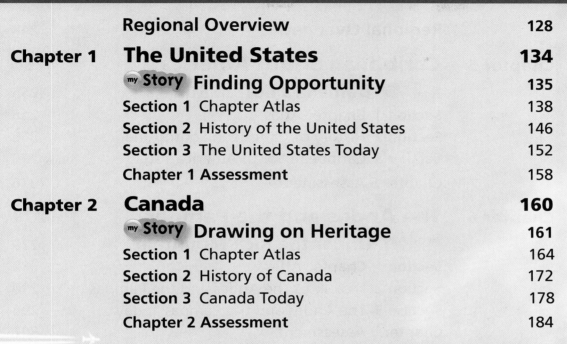

Regional Overview — 128

Chapter 1 **The United States** — **134**
my Story Finding Opportunity — 135
Section 1 Chapter Atlas — 138
Section 2 History of the United States — 146
Section 3 The United States Today — 152
Chapter 1 Assessment — 158

Chapter 2 **Canada** — **160**
my Story Drawing on Heritage — 161
Section 1 Chapter Atlas — 164
Section 2 History of Canada — 172
Section 3 Canada Today — 178
Chapter 2 Assessment — 184

Unit 2 Middle America

Regional Overview — 188

Chapter 3 **Mexico** — **194**
my Story A Long Way From Home — 195
Section 1 Chapter Atlas — 198
Section 2 History of Mexico — 206
Section 3 Mexico Today — 212
Chapter 3 Assessment — 220

Chapter 4 **Central America and the Caribbean** — 222
my Story Working for the Future — 223
Section 1 Chapter Atlas — 226
Section 2 History of Central America
and the Caribbean — 234
Section 3 Central America and the Caribbean Today — 238
Chapter 4 Assessment — 244

Unit 3 South America

Regional Overview   248

Chapter 5   **Caribbean South America**   **254**

^{my} **Story** Daniella's Coffee Run   255

Section 1   Chapter Atlas   258

Section 2   History of Caribbean South America   266

Section 3   Caribbean South America Today   270

Chapter 5 Assessment   276

Chapter 6   **The Andes and the Pampas**   **278**

^{my} **Story** Under the Rich Mountain   279

Section 1   Chapter Atlas   282

Section 2   History of the Andes and the Pampas   290

Section 3   The Andes and the Pampas Today   296

Chapter 6 Assessment   302

Chapter 7   **Brazil**   **304**

^{my} **Story** Vinicius's Game Plan   305

Section 1   Chapter Atlas   308

Section 2   History of Brazil   316

Section 3   Brazil Today   320

Chapter 7 Assessment   326

Unit 4 Europe and Russia

Regional Overview — 330

Chapter 8 Ancient and Medieval Europe — 336
my Story A Prophecy Fulfilled — 337
Section 1 Ancient Greece — 340
Section 2 Ancient Rome — 348
Section 3 Early Middle Ages — 354
Section 4 High and Late Middle Ages — 360
Chapter 8 Assessment — 368

Chapter 9 Europe in Modern Times — 370
my Story The Battle of the Spanish Armada — 371
Section 1 New Ways of Thinking — 374
Section 2 Europe Expands — 382
Section 3 An Age of Revolutions — 388
Section 4 Wars and Hardship — 394
Section 5 Rebuilding and New Challenges — 400
Chapter 9 Assessment — 408

Chapter 10 Western Europe — 410
my Story Europe at Her Doorstep — 411
Section 1 Chapter Atlas — 414
Section 2 Northwestern Europe Today — 422
Section 3 West Central Europe Today — 428
Section 4 Southern Europe Today — 434
Chapter 10 Assessment — 440

continued next page

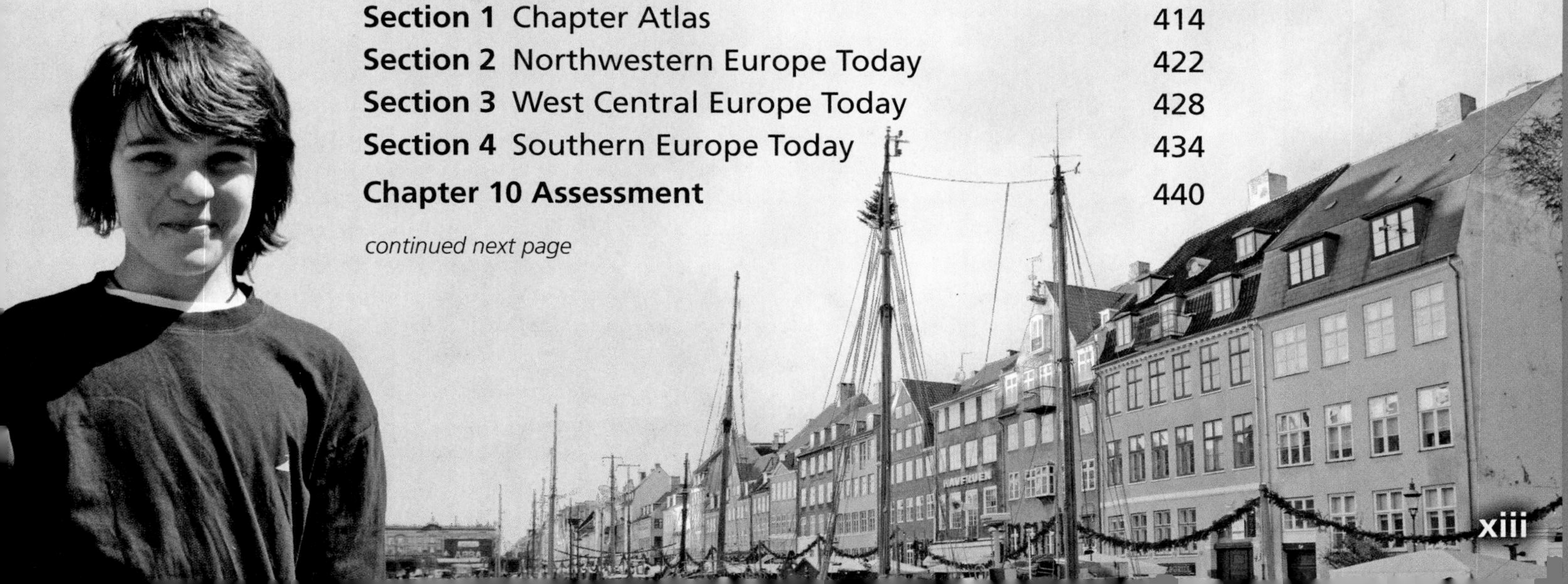

Unit 4 Europe and Russia (continued)

Chapter 11 Eastern Europe **442**

my Story Serhiy's Leap 443

Section 1 Chapter Atlas 446

Section 2 Eastern Europe Today 454

Chapter 11 Assessment 462

Chapter 12 Russia **464**

my Story Boris's Bigspin 465

Section 1 Chapter Atlas 468

Section 2 History of Russia 476

Section 3 Russia Today 484

Chapter 12 Assessment 490

Unit **5** Africa

	Regional Overview	494
Chapter 13	**West and Central Africa**	**500**
	my Story A String of Dreams	501
	Section 1 Chapter Atlas	504
	Section 2 History of West and Central Africa	512
	Section 3 West and Central Africa Today	518
	Chapter 13 Assessment	524
Chapter 14	**Southern and Eastern Africa**	**526**
	my Story A Hopeful Song	527
	Section 1 Chapter Atlas	530
	Section 2 History of Southern and Eastern Africa	538
	Section 3 Southern and Eastern Africa Today	544
	Chapter 14 Assessment	550
Chapter 15	**North Africa**	**552**
	my Story Shaimaa's Neighborhood	553
	Section 1 Chapter Atlas	556
	Section 2 History of North Africa	564
	Section 3 North Africa Today	570
	Chapter 15 Assessment	576

Unit 6 Southwest Asia

Regional Overview   580

Chapter 16   **Arabia and Iraq**   **586**

my Story **Hanan's Call to Care**   587

Section 1   Chapter Atlas   590

Section 2   History of Arabia and Iraq   598

Section 3   Arabia and Iraq Today   606

Chapter 16 Assessment   612

Chapter 17   **Israel and Its Neighbors**   **614**

my Story **Maayan and Muhammad**   615

Section 1   Chapter Atlas   618

Section 2   History of Israel and Its Neighbors   626

Section 3   Israel and Its Neighbors Today   634

Chapter 17 Assessment   642

Chapter 18   **Iran, Turkey, and Cyprus**   **644**

my Story **Bilal Looks Forward**   645

Section 1   Chapter Atlas   648

Section 2   History of Iran, Turkey, and Cyprus   656

Section 3   Iran, Turkey, and Cyprus Today   662

Chapter 18 Assessment   670

Unit 7 South and Central Asia

	Regional Overview	674
Chapter 19	**Central Asia and the Caucasus**	**680**
	^{my} Story **Askar Serves His People**	681
	Lesson 1 Chapter Atlas	684
	Section 2 History of Central Asia and the Caucasus	692
	Section 3 Central Asia and the Caucasus Today	696
	Chapter 19 Assessment	702
Chapter 20	**South Asia**	**704**
	^{my} Story **Nancy's Fruitful Loan**	705
	Section 1 Chapter Atlas	708
	Section 2 History of South Asia	716
	Section 3 South Asia Today	724
	Chapter 20 Assessment	732

UNDERSTAND

EXPERIENCE
the World in New Ways

Travel across regions and through time—without a passport. *myWorld Geography's* interactive approach using technology, student books, and classroom activities will make learning geography fun and exciting.

Take a virtual and interactive trip around the world with myWorldGeography.com.

UNDERSTAND
and "Own" Your Learning

myWorld Geography isn't just about reading content—it's about providing you with the tools so you really "get it."

Finding answers to the Essential Questions—found throughout the print, digital, and hands-on activities—helps you understand the key ideas of world geography.

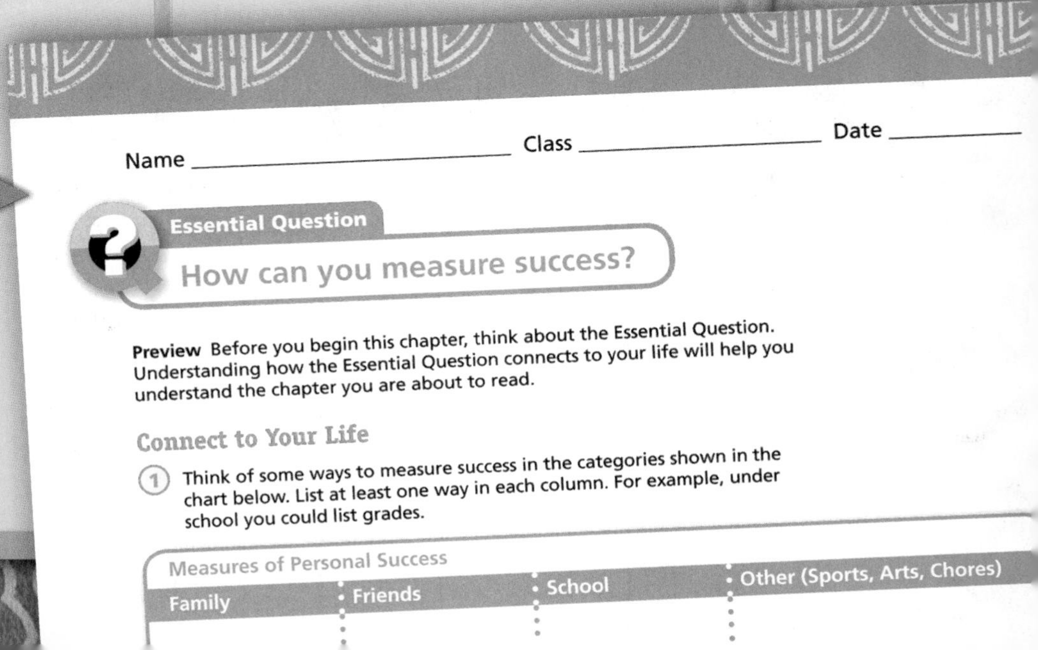

China and Its Neighbors: Population Density

KEY

Population Density

Persons per sq. mile	Persons per sq. kilometer
500	195
300	115
150	60
25	10
1	1

Urban Areas
- ☐ More than 10,000,000
- △ 5,000,000–10,000,000
- ○ Less than 5,000,000

0   400 mi
0   400 km
Lambert Conformal Conic Projection

MONGOLIA

Ulaanbaatar
Ürümqi
Kashgar
Harbin
Changchun Jilin
Shenyang
Beijing
Tianjin
Zibo
Xi'an
CHINA
Chengdu
Chongqing
Wuhan
Wuxi Shanghai
Plateau of Tibet
Lhasa
Guangzhou Shenzhen
Hong Kong
Hainan
Taipei
TAIWAN
Yellow Sea
East China Sea
South China Sea
Bay of Bengal
GOBI
TROPIC OF CANCER

Name _____   Class _____   Date _____

Essential Question

How can you measure success?

Preview Before you begin this chapter, think about the Essential Question. Understanding how the Essential Question connects to your life will help you understand the chapter you are about to read.

Connect to Your Life

① Think of some ways to measure success in the categories shown in the chart below. List at least one way in each column. For example, under school you could list grades.

Measures of Personal Success

Family	Friends	School	Other (Sports, Arts, Chores)

Core Concepts Handbook

Part
1

Part
2

Part
3

Part
4

Part
5

Tools of Geography

Learn about the study of Earth.

page 2

Our Planet, Earth

Examine the forces that affect Earth.

page 16

Climates and Ecosystems

Learn about how climate and weather affect the world and its lifeforms.

page 30

Human–Environment Interaction

Explore the ways in which people use resources and affect the environment.

page 46

Economics and Geography

Study how people make economic decisions.

page 56

Part 6

Population and Movement
Learn how and why people live in certain places.
page 72

Part 7

Culture and Geography
Understand how the practices of a people make up their culture, and how culture can change over time.
page 84

Part 8

Government and Citizenship
Learn about how people organize governments and what governments do.
page 102

Part 9

Tools of History
Examine the ways in which people study history.
page 116

Tools of Geography

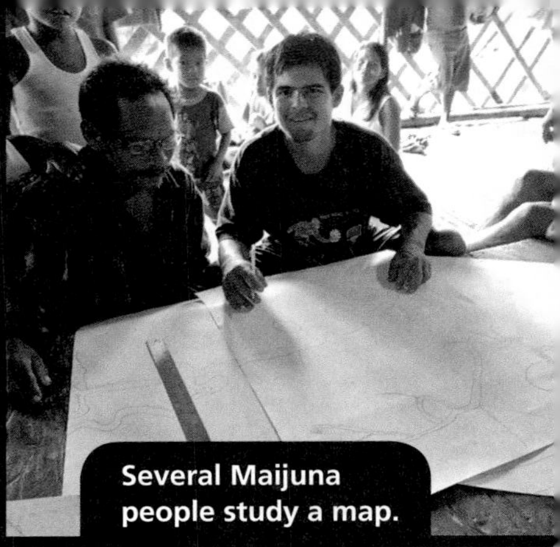

Several Maijuna people study a map.

A Peruvian toucan overlooks mountains and rain forest. The Maijuna live in a rain forest area.

Maijuna men use a GPS device.

Jason Young

Jason Maps in the Rainforest

Story by Miles Lemaire for myWorld

There were a number of things that took some getting used to for Jason Young when he first traveled to Peru. There was no electricity in the village where he was living, which meant that there was no place to charge his cell phone. The same was true for his computer, which he could not use much since there was no Internet connection.

He was alone in a foreign country, eating food that the hunters of the village provided for him. He ate toucan and piranha. "It is an entirely different world," Jason says. "The people there are living off the rainforest, so they go hunting and whatever they catch is what I eat."

Nothing about this place on the edge of the Amazon jungle felt like home to Jason. However, it was home to the people of the Maijuna (mai HU na) tribe and he was going to help them prove it.

According to Jason, the Maijuna "do not own the land where they live, and it is being threatened by things like logging. The Peruvian government wants to construct a road right through some of their traditional territory."

Fortunately, there is a way for the Maijuna to keep their land if they can prove their ownership of it. To do this, they need accurate maps of the area.

That is where Jason comes in. Jason studies geography, which deals with the human and nonhuman features of Earth. Using his geography skills, he has created maps to help the Maijuna prove their case. He used a GPS device, which uses satellites to locate places on Earth's surface.

Jason says, "I went down there and worked with them for four months over different field seasons. I worked with them to do what is called participatory mapping. It is where you have them draw what they believe is their territory on their traditional land. You use that to go out with a GPS unit and collect [data] points from each of the different spots. I actually took video interviews of them talking about the history of the spots that we went to."

Maijuna people took pictures of the spots, and Jason is working on putting them online in an interactive map. Eventually, users will be able to click on traditional sites to view videos or pictures.

"We are hoping to use that mostly as a teaching tool for safeguarding the Maijuna's traditions, as well as using it as a tool with which to speak to the government."

Jason's involvement with the Maijuna came to an end in 2009. Still, his bond with the Maijuna is so strong that he wants to revisit his new friends as often as he can. He feels that he has learned a lot from his experience.

"The level of poverty opened my eyes to how privileged I have been and how much potential I have to give back to the world," Jason says.

3

Geography: The Study of Earth

Key Ideas	• Geographers use directions to help locate points on Earth's surface.
	• Geographers have drawn imaginary lines around Earth, dividing it into parts to help pinpoint locations.

Key Terms
- geography
- degree
- cardinal direction
- hemisphere
- sphere
- longitude
- latitude

→ Visual Glossary

Geography is the study of the human and nonhuman features of Earth, our home. Geographers try to answer two basic questions: Where are things located? Why are they there? To answer these questions, geographers study oceans, plant life, landforms, countries, and cities. Geographers also study how Earth and its people affect each other.

Directions

In order to study Earth, geographers need to measure it and locate points on its surface. One way to do this is with directions. Geographers use both cardinal and intermediate directions. The **cardinal directions** are north, east, south, and west. Intermediate directions lie between the cardinal directions. For example, northwest is halfway between north and west.

Latitude

Earth is an almost perfect **sphere** (sfeer), or round-shaped body. Geographers have drawn imaginary lines around Earth to help locate places on its surface. One of these is the Equator, a line drawn around Earth halfway between the North and South Poles. The Equator is also known as the 0-degree (0°) latitude line. **Latitude** is the distance north or south of the Equator. It is measured in degrees. **Degrees** are units that measure angles. Minutes (') measure smaller units. On this map, lines are drawn every 20° of latitude.

Lines of latitude form east-west circles around the globe. Lines of latitude are also called parallels, because they are parallel to one another. That means they never cross.

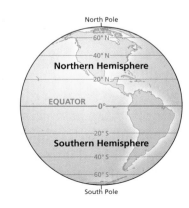

North Pole
60° N
40° N
Northern Hemisphere
20° N
EQUATOR 0°
20° S
Southern Hemisphere
40° S
60° S
South Pole

The Equator divides Earth in half. Each half of Earth is called a **hemisphere.** The half of Earth north of the Equator is known as the Northern Hemisphere. The half of Earth south of the Equator is the Southern Hemisphere.

Longitude

Geographers have also drawn imaginary north-south lines that run between the North Pole and the South Pole on Earth's surface. One of these lines is the Prime Meridian, which passes through Greenwich, England. The Prime Meridian and the other north-south lines measure **longitude,** or the distance in degrees east or west of the Prime Meridian. Lines of longitude are also called meridians.

The half of Earth east of the Prime Meridian is known as the Eastern Hemisphere. The half of Earth west of the Prime Meridian is the Western Hemisphere.

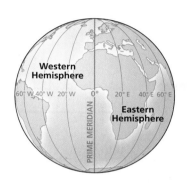

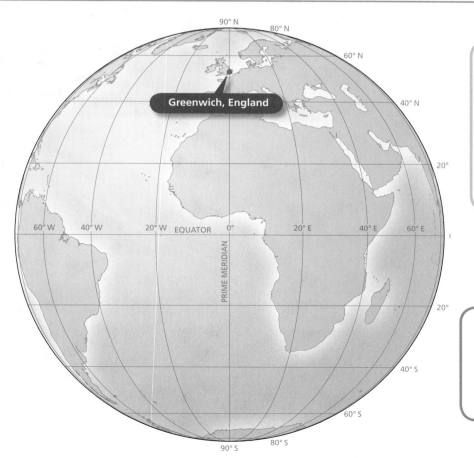

The Global Grid

Latitude and longitude form a global grid. You can describe the location of any point on Earth's surface using degrees of longitude and latitude. For example, Greenwich, England, is located at 0° longitude and about 51°29′ north latitude.

Assessment

1. What do geographers study?

2. Based on the diagrams shown here, in which two hemispheres do you live?

5

Geography's Five Themes

Key Ideas
- Using five themes can help you make sense of geography.
- The theme of location is used to describe where a place is found, while the other themes describe features of a place.

Key Terms
- absolute location
- relative location
- place
- region
- movement
- human-environment interaction

Visual Glossary

White House

1.5 miles

Washington Monument

Tidal Basin

Lincoln Memorial

Lincoln Memorial

Geographers use five different themes, or ways of thinking. These themes are location, place, region, movement, and human-environment interaction. They can help answer the geographer's two basic questions: Where are things located? Why are they there? You can see how the five themes work by looking at the example of our nation's capital, Washington, D.C.

Location

Geographers begin to study a place by finding where it is, or its location. There are two ways to talk about location. **Absolute location** describes a place's exact position on Earth in terms of longitude and latitude. Using degrees of longitude and latitude, you can pinpoint any spot on Earth. For example, the absolute location of the center of Washington, D.C., is at the intersection of the 38°54' north latitude line and the 77°2' west longitude line. **Relative location,** or the location of a place relative to another place, is another way to describe location. For example, you can say that Washington, D.C, is about 200 miles southwest of New York City.

Place

Geographers also study place. **Place** refers to the mix of human and nonhuman features at a given location. For example, you might talk about how many people live in a place and the kinds of work they do. You might mention that a place is hilly or that it has a wet climate. As a place, Washington, D.C., is on the Potomac River. It has a humid climate with cool winters and hot summers. It is a major city and the center of government for the United States.

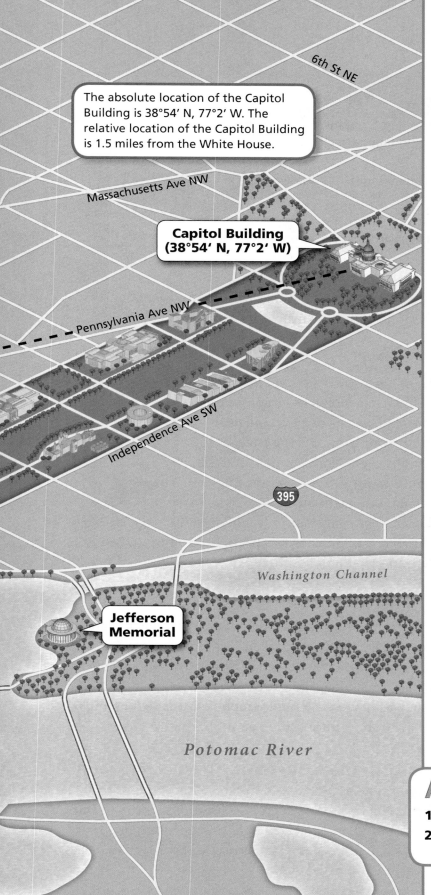

The absolute location of the Capitol Building is 38°54′ N, 77°2′ W. The relative location of the Capitol Building is 1.5 miles from the White House.

6th St NE

Massachusetts Ave NW

Capitol Building (38°54′ N, 77°2′ W)

Pennsylvania Ave NW

Independence Ave SW

395

Washington Channel

Jefferson Memorial

Potomac River

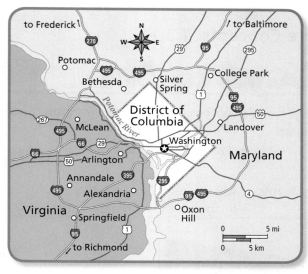

to Frederick / to Baltimore

Potomac
Bethesda
Silver Spring
College Park
Potomac River
District of Columbia
McLean
Landover
Washington
Arlington
Maryland
Annandale
Alexandria
Virginia
Springfield
Oxon Hill
to Richmond

0   5 mi
0   5 km

Region

Geographers use the theme of region to group places that have something in common. A **region** is an area with at least one unifying physical or human feature such as climate, landforms, population, or history. Washington, D.C., is part of a region called the Washington Metropolitan Area, which includes the city of Washington and its suburbs. This region shares a job market and a road and rail network. New technology, such as high-speed railroads, may give places new unifying features and connections. This can change the way people see regions.

Movement

The theme of **movement** explores how people, goods, and ideas get from one place to another. A daily movement of trucks and trains supplies the people of Washington with food, fuel, and other basic goods.

Human-Environment Interaction

The theme of **human-environment interaction** considers how people affect their environment, or their natural surroundings, and how their environment affects them. The movement of water from the Potomac River into Washington's water system is an example of human-environment interaction.

Assessment

1. What are the five themes of geography?

2. What is the difference between your hometown's location and your hometown as a place?

Ways to Show Earth's Surface

| **Key Ideas** | • Globes, photographs, computer images, and maps are all ways to show and view Earth's surface. |
| | • Each way of showing Earth's surface has advantages and disadvantages. |

Key Terms • scale • aerial photograph • satellite image • geographic information system (GIS) • distortion • projection

→ **Visual Glossary**

Geographers use a number of different models to represent Earth's surface. Each model has its own strengths and weaknesses.

Globes

A globe is a model of Earth with the same round shape as Earth itself. With a globe, geographers can show the continents and oceans of Earth much as they really are. The only difference is the **scale**, or the area a given space on the map corresponds to in the real world. For example, one inch on a globe might corespond to 600 miles on Earth's surface.

A globe would have to be hundreds of feet high to show the streets of your town. Such a globe would be impossible to carry around. Instead, people use flat maps to help them find their way.

Photographs

Geographers use photographs as well as maps. **Aerial photographs** are photographic images of Earth's surface taken from the air. **Satellite images** are pictures of Earth's surface taken from a satellite in orbit. They show Earth's surface in great detail. However, it can be hard to find specific features, such as roads, on a photograph. For this reason, maps are still the main way to show information about Earth's surface.

Geographic Information Systems

Geographic information systems (GIS) are computer-based systems that store and use information linked to geographic locations. GIS is useful not only to geographers and mapmakers but also to government agencies and businesses. It offers a way to connect information to places.

▲ An aerial photo taken in Antactica (top) and a satellite image of Antarctica (above).

Map Projections

Flat maps and photos have one major problem. Earth is round. A map or photo is flat. Can you flatten an orange peel without stretching or tearing it? There will be sections that are stretched or bent out of shape.

Showing Earth on a flat surface always brings some **distortion,** or loss of accuracy in the size or position of objects on a map. Something is going to look too large, too small, or out of place.

To show a flat image of Earth's round surface, mapmakers have come up with different **projections,** or ways to map Earth on a flat surface. A few examples show how they differ.

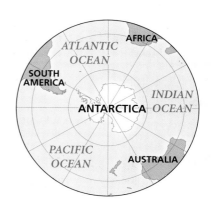

▲ This projection shows the size and shape of Antarctica nearly correctly.

HOW TO SHOW OUR ROUND EARTH ON A FLAT MAP

The Equal-Area Projection

An equal-area map shows the correct size of landmasses. However, their shapes are distorted.

The Mercator Projection

The Mercator (mur KAYT ur) projection shows correct shapes and directions but not true distances or sizes. Mercator maps make areas near the poles look bigger than they are.

The Robinson Projection

The Robinson projection shows nearly the correct size and shape of most land areas. However, even a Robinson projection has distortions, especially in areas around the edges of the map.

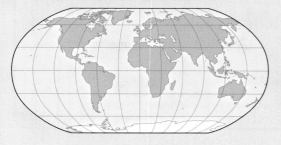

Assessment

1. How are maps different from globes?

2. What are the strengths and weaknesses of each of the three projections in showing Antarctica?

Understanding Maps

Key Ideas	• Maps have parts that help you read them.
	• Though different maps show different things about a place, you can use the same tools to help understand them.

Key Terms • key • locator map • scale bar • compass rose

Visual Glossary

Look at the maps on these two pages. One is a physical map of the state of Colorado. The other is a road map of Colorado. These maps cover the same area but show different kinds of information. Despite their differences, both maps have all of the basic parts that you should find on any map.

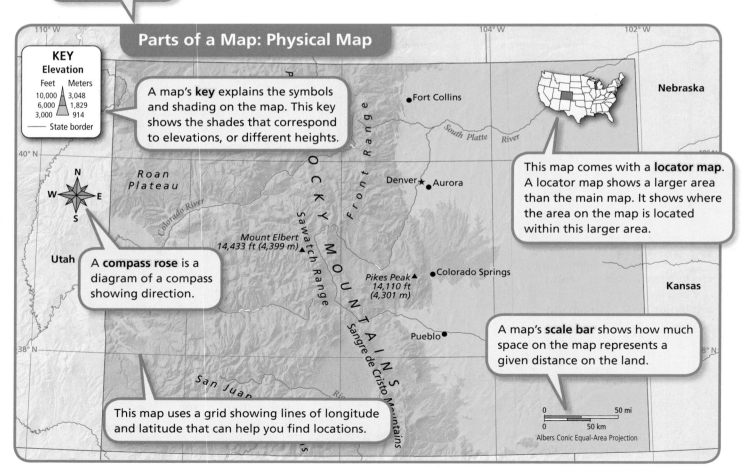

Parts of a Map: Physical Map

> The map has a title that tells you the subject of the map.

KEY
Elevation

Feet	Meters
10,000	3,048
6,000	1,829
3,000	914

—— State border

> A map's **key** explains the symbols and shading on the map. This key shows the shades that correspond to elevations, or different heights.

> This map comes with a **locator map**. A locator map shows a larger area than the main map. It shows where the area on the map is located within this larger area.

> A **compass rose** is a diagram of a compass showing direction.

> A map's **scale bar** shows how much space on the map represents a given distance on the land.

> This map uses a grid showing lines of longitude and latitude that can help you find locations.

Roan Plateau

Mount Elbert 14,433 ft (4,399 m)

Pikes Peak 14,110 ft (4,301 m)

Sawatch Range

ROCKY MOUNTAINS

Front Range

Sangre de Cristo Mountains

San Juan

Colorado River

South Platte River

Fort Collins

Denver ★ Aurora

Colorado Springs

Pueblo

Utah

Kansas

Nebraska

110° W 104° W 102° W
40° N
38° N

0   50 mi
0   50 km
Albers Conic Equal-Area Projection

Reading a Map

Look at the map below. It is a highway map of the state of Colorado. This map looks different from the physical map of Colorado that you have just studied. However, it has the same parts that can help you read it. In fact, you can read most maps using the key, scale bar, and other map tools that you have learned about.

Find the key on this map. Using the key, can you find the route number of the Interstate highway that connects Denver and Colorado Springs, Colorado? Using the scale bar, estimate the number of miles between these two cities. Using the compass rose, find the direction that you would need to travel from Denver to Colorado Springs. Now you have learned to read a highway map!

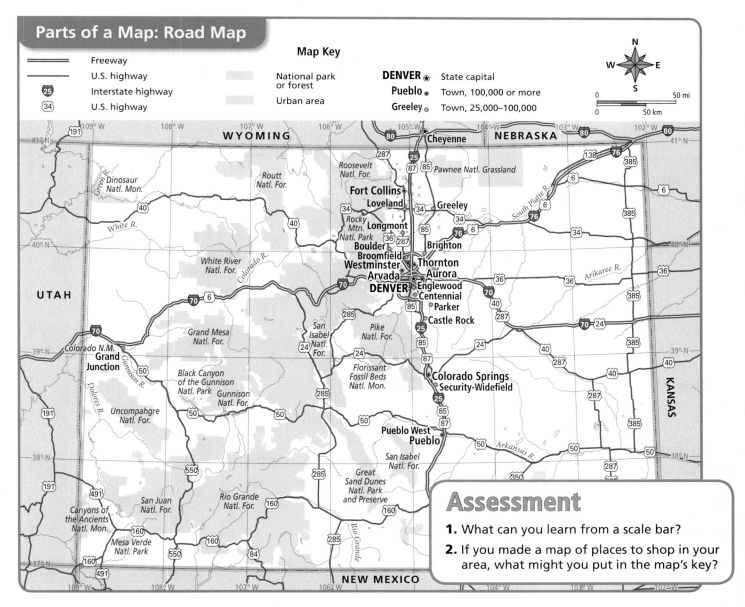

Parts of a Map: Road Map

Freeway
U.S. highway
Interstate highway
U.S. highway

Map Key

National park or forest
Urban area

DENVER   State capital
Pueblo   Town, 100,000 or more
Greeley   Town, 25,000–100,000

Assessment

1. What can you learn from a scale bar?

2. If you made a map of places to shop in your area, what might you put in the map's key?

11

Types of Maps

Key Ideas
- Maps can show many different kinds of information.
- Political, physical, and special-purpose maps are the main types of maps.

Key Terms • physical map • elevation • political map • special-purpose map

 **Visual Glossary**

The map projections, or ways to represent Earth's surface, that you have studied can be used to show different things about the area they cover. For example, they might represent the physical landscape, political boundaries, ecosystem zones, or almost any other feature of a place. People use different kinds of maps in different situations.

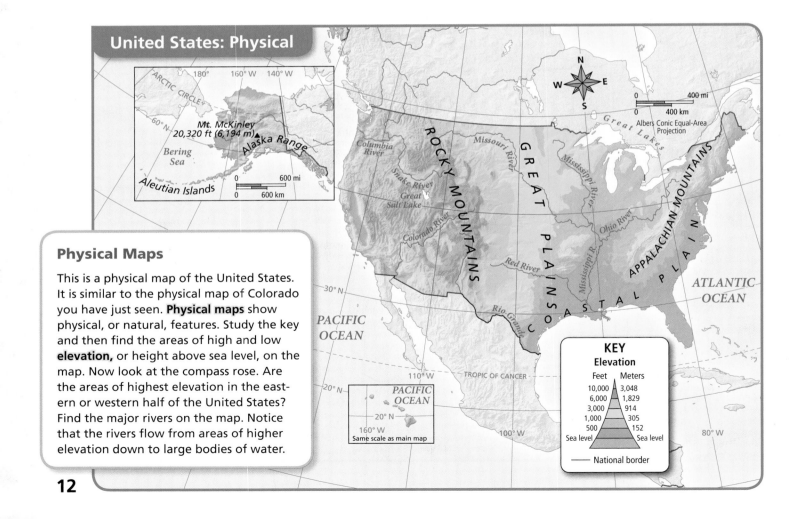

United States: Physical

Physical Maps

This is a physical map of the United States. It is similar to the physical map of Colorado you have just seen. **Physical maps** show physical, or natural, features. Study the key and then find the areas of high and low **elevation,** or height above sea level, on the map. Now look at the compass rose. Are the areas of highest elevation in the eastern or western half of the United States? Find the major rivers on the map. Notice that the rivers flow from areas of higher elevation down to large bodies of water.

KEY
Elevation

Feet	Meters
10,000	3,048
6,000	1,829
3,000	914
1,000	305
500	152
Sea level	Sea level

— National border

United States: Political

CANADA

PACIFIC OCEAN

Washington • Montana • North Dakota • Minnesota • Michigan • Vermont • Maine

Oregon • Idaho • Wyoming • South Dakota • Wisconsin • New Hampshire • Massachusetts

Nevada • Utah • Nebraska • Iowa • Pennsylvania • New York • Rhode Island • Connecticut • New Jersey

California • Colorado • Kansas • Missouri • Illinois • Indiana • Ohio • West Virginia • Virginia • Delaware • Maryland • District of Columbia

Arizona • New Mexico • Oklahoma • Arkansas • Kentucky • Tennessee • North Carolina • South Carolina

Texas • Mississippi • Alabama • Georgia • ATLANTIC OCEAN

Louisiana • Florida

ARCTIC CIRCLE • Alaska • CANADA • MEXICO

Hawaii • Same scale as main map

0 400 mi
0 400 km

Albers Conic Equal-Area Projection

TROPIC OF CANCER

Political Maps

This is a political map of the United States. **Political maps** show political units, such as countries or states. They may also show capitals of countries, or centers of government, and other major cities. Study the key and compass rose of this map. Now look at the map. Which state is directly west of Georgia? How many states border Canada?

United States: Election 2008

Washington • Montana • North Dakota • Minnesota • Michigan • Vermont • Maine

Oregon • Idaho • Wyoming • South Dakota • Wisconsin • New Hampshire • New York • Massachusetts

Nevada • Utah • Nebraska • Iowa • Pennsylvania • Rhode Island • Connecticut • New Jersey

PACIFIC OCEAN • California • Colorado • Kansas • Missouri • Illinois • Indiana • Ohio • West Virginia • Virginia • Delaware • Maryland • District of Columbia

Arizona • New Mexico • Oklahoma • Arkansas • Kentucky • Tennessee • North Carolina • South Carolina

Texas • Mississippi • Alabama • Georgia • ATLANTIC OCEAN

Louisiana • Florida

ARCTIC CIRCLE • Alaska • Hawaii • Same scale as main map

Gulf of Mexico

TROPIC OF CANCER

KEY
McCain
Obama

0 200 mi
0 200 km
Albers Conic Equal-Area Projection

Special-purpose Maps

Maps can show many different kinds of information. **Special-purpose maps** show the location or distribution of human or physical features. This map shows the results of the 2008 presidential election. A highway map is another kind of special-purpose map. Other special-purpose maps may show a region's weather patterns or other features. Study this map's key. Which presidential candidate won your home state in the 2008 election?

Assessment

1. What are the elements of a physical map?

2. What are the elements of a political map?

Tools of Geography
Part 1 Assessment

Key Terms and Ideas

1. **Compare and Contrast** What is the difference between **latitude** and **longitude**?

2. **Describe** What are some features of **place** and **region**?

3. **Analyze Cause and Effect** Why do map **projections** lead to **distortion**? Give a specific example.

4. **Discuss** What does the **scale bar** of a map show?

5. **Compare and Contrast** How do **aerial photographs** and **satellite images** show Earth's surface? What differences do you find between these types of images?

6. **Recall** What are the basic parts of a map, and what does each part show to readers?

7. **Categorize** What kind of map shows elevation?

8. **Summarize** What does a **political map** show?

Think Critically

9. **Problem Solving** Which kinds of maps could you use to choose a new city as your home? How would you use them?

10. **Decision Making** Which kinds of projections would best show the distance between your hometown and Washington, D.C., on a map of the United States? Explain.

11. **Synthesize** What can you learn from the latitude and longitude lines on a map?

12. **Categorize** Match each feature to the correct theme of geography: very flat landscape, four trains in and out of town every day, factory waste enters a local river, large Hispanic population across three states, and 42° S 147° E.

Identify

For each part of a map, write the letter from the map that shows its location.

13. title
14. compass rose
15. latitude line
16. longitude line
17. scale bar
18. key
19. What type of map is this?

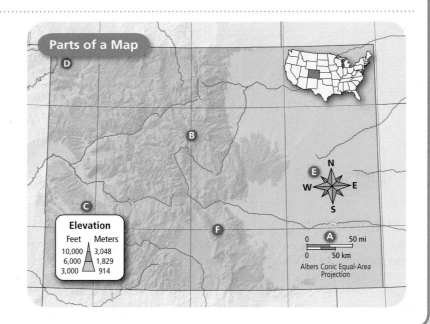

Parts of a Map

Elevation

Feet	Meters
10,000	3,048
6,000	1,829
3,000	914

0   50 mi
0   50 km
Albers Conic Equal-Area Projection

Journal Activity

Fill in the graphic organizers in your student journal.

 **Demonstrate Understanding** Complete the Sum-It-Up activity in your journal to demonstrate your understanding of the Tools of Geography. After you complete the activity, discuss your map with a partner. Be sure to support your completed map with information from the lesson.

21st Century Learning

Evaluate Web Sites

Find three different web sites that generate maps. Compare the sites and rank each according to the following criteria:
- clarity and appearance of the maps
- option to create directions for drivers or walkers
- ability to locate addresses from incomplete information

Document-Based Questions

Success Tracker™
Online at myworldgeography.com

Use your knowledge of the tools of geography and Documents A and B to answer Questions 1–3.

Document A

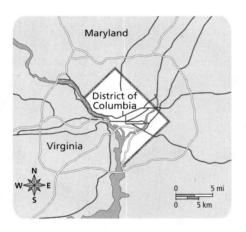

Document B

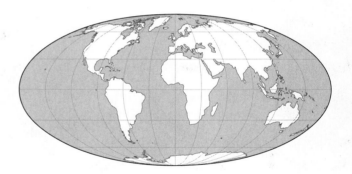

1. Which of the five themes of geography is best represented by this map?
- **A** location
- **B** place
- **C** region
- **D** human-environment interaction

2. What kind of projection does Document B show?
- **A** Mercator
- **B** equal-area
- **C** Robinson
- **D** global grid

3. **Writing Task** What are the advantages and disadvantages of the map shown in Document B? Explain your answer.

Our Planet, Earth

The volcano
Kilauea erupting

▲ Looking down into
the crater of an active
volcano, you can almost
glimpse the interior of
our planet, Earth.

16

A road destroyed by an earthquake in Indonesia

Lava flowing into the sea (left)
Tamsen Burlak (right)

Tamsen Studies a Volcano

Story by Miles Lemaire for myWorld

As 21-year-old Tamsen Burlak watched the volcano Kilauea, in Hawaii, blow lava and ash into the sky she had only one thought: "This is pretty cool."

When she was a young girl, Tamsen didn't know much about what makes up our planet, Earth, only that she loved to collect rocks during nature hikes with her parents.

"I would always pick up rocks from everywhere that we went—anything that looked cool," she says. "It was probably around middle school or high school while I was looking at the rocks that I realized I wanted to know what they were called and how they formed. So I went out and bought a bunch of those field guides, geology dictionaries for rocks. That's when I found out the field name was geology." Tamsen knew what she wanted to study.

When she went to college, Tamsen studied geology, the field of science that deals with the structure of Earth. She concentrated on volcanoes and fault lines, places where earthquakes are likely to happen. Geologists like Tamsen investigate earthquake zones to find out how likely another earthquake is, and how destructive it will be. Earthquakes sometimes occur where volcanoes are erupting.

Tamsen was able to go to Hawaii to study. The islands that make up the state of Hawaii were formed by volcanoes. Lava flowed out of volcanoes, cooled, and formed new land over millions of years. Some of the islands still have active volcanoes. Tamsen visited Kilauea, where lava has been flowing since 1983.

"The active area I went to was part of a summer course I took on the big island of Hawaii. At that time Kilauea had just started erupting, so we were there for the first days of it," Tamsen said.

"It was really exciting," she added, but not always easy, "because of the volcanic gasses in the air. That sort of stuff can itch the throat and cause irritation, but I loved every second of it!"

Tamsen, who now has a degree in geology, says that she has been studying dormant, or inactive, volcanoes and earthquake zones for years. Her experience in Hawaii is something that she and her fellow geologists dream of.

"We'd all be really excited if there was an actual earthquake that we all got to study," says Tamsen, "but we just look at faults in the area, offsets, and the different rock types, and measure how much displacement has gone on and how big a threat we think it might be."

As Tamsen learned firsthand, studying the structure of Earth can be very exciting. Geologists face down erupting volcanoes in order to learn how to predict earthquakes and save lives. Understanding Earth may someday make that possible.

Earth in Space

Key Ideas
- Planet Earth moves around the sun.
- This movement causes places on Earth's surface to receive varying amounts of sunlight from one season to the next.

Key Terms
- orbit
- axis
- solstice
- revolution
- equinox

 Visual Glossary

Earth, the sun, the planets, and the stars in the sky are all part of our galaxy, or cluster of stars. We call our galaxy the Milky Way because its stars look like a trail of spilled milk across a dark night sky. Our sun is one of its billions of stars.

Earth, the Sun, and the Seasons

Even though the sun is about 93 million miles (150 million km) away, it provides Earth with heat and light. To understand how far Earth is from the sun, consider that this distance is nearly 4,000 times the distance around Earth at the Equator.

Earth travels around the sun in an oval-shaped **orbit,** which is the path one object makes as it revolves around another. Earth takes 365 1/4 days, or one year, to make one **revolution,** or complete journey, around the sun.

Earth's **axis,** an imaginary line between the North and South Poles, is tilted relative to its orbit. Therefore, as Earth makes its revolution, the sun shines most directly on different places at different times. That is why seasons occur.

March Equinox

About March 21, the sun is directly overhead at noon on the Equator. At this point in Earth's orbit, its axis is tilted neither toward nor away from the sun. An **equinox** (EE kwih nahks) is a point at which, everywhere on Earth, days and nights are nearly equal in length. This is the spring equinox in the Northern Hemisphere and the fall equinox in the Southern Hemisphere.

June Solstice

About June 21, the North Pole is tilted closest to the sun. This brings the heat of summer to the Northern Hemisphere. This is the summer **solstice** in the Northern Hemisphere and the winter solstice in the Southern Hemisphere. A solstice (SOHL stis) is a point at which days are longest in one hemisphere and shortest in the other.

December Solstice

About December 21, the South Pole is tilted closest to the sun. The area north of the Arctic Circle is in constant darkness, while the area south of the Antarctic Circle has constant daylight. This is the winter solstice in the Northern Hemisphere and the summer solstice in the Southern Hemisphere. The lack of sunlight in the Northern Hemisphere brings the cold of winter.

September Equinox

About September 23, the sun is again directly overhead at noon on the Equator, and all of Earth has days and nights of equal length. This is the fall equinox in the Northern Hemisphere and the spring equinox in the Southern Hemisphere. Less-direct sunlight in the Northern Hemisphere brings the chill of fall.

Assessment

1. If it is summer in the Northern Hemisphere, what season is it in the Southern Hemisphere?

2. How can days be short and cold in one hemisphere when they are long and hot in another?

Time and Earth's Rotation

Key Ideas
- Earth's spinning movement causes day and night.
- This spinning also causes it to be different times in different places on Earth's surface.

Key Terms • rotation   • time zone

 Visual Glossary

You have learned that Earth revolves around the sun in an oval-shaped orbit. Earth also moves in another way. This motion explains why day and night occur.

Rotation of Earth

As Earth revolves around the sun, it is also rotating, or spinning, in space. Earth rotates around its axis. Each complete turn, or **rotation,** takes about 24 hours. At any one time, it is night on the side of Earth facing away from the sun. As Earth rotates, that side of Earth turns to face the sun, and the sun appears to rise. The sun's light shines on that side of Earth. It is daytime. Then, as that side of Earth turns away from the sun, the sun appears to set. No sunlight reaches that side of Earth. It is nighttime.

Time Zones

Because Earth rotates toward the east, the day starts earlier in the east than it does farther west. Over short distances, the time difference is small. For example, the sun rises about four minutes earlier in Beaumont, Texas, than it does in Houston, 70 miles to the west. But if every town had its own local time, people would have a hard time keeping track. So governments have agreed to divide the world into standard **time zones,** or areas sharing the same time. Times in neighboring zones are one hour apart.

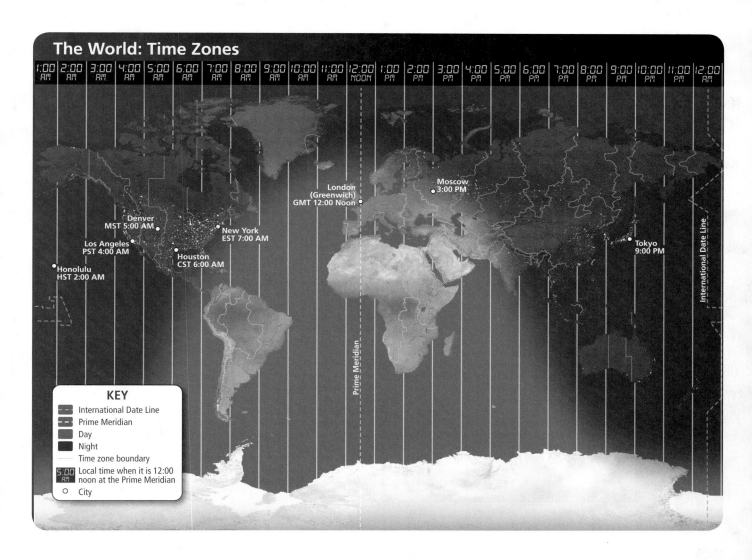

The World: Time Zones

Denver MST 5:00 AM
Los Angeles PST 4:00 AM
Honolulu HST 2:00 AM
Houston CST 6:00 AM
New York EST 7:00 AM
London (Greenwich) GMT 12:00 Noon
Moscow 3:00 PM
Tokyo 9:00 PM

International Date Line
Prime Meridian

KEY
- International Date Line
- Prime Meridian
- Day
- Night
- Time zone boundary
- 5:00 AM Local time when it is 12:00 noon at the Prime Meridian
- ○ City

The Prime Meridian

The Prime Meridian, in Greenwich, England, is at the center of one of these zones. The time in that zone is sometimes known as Greenwich Mean Time or Universal Time (UT). Other time zones are sometimes described in terms of how many hours they are behind or ahead of UT. (For example, Central Standard Time in the United States is UT – 6, or six hours behind UT.)

Assessment

1. What is the rotation of Earth?

2. If it is 8 P.M. in New York, what time is it in Los Angeles?

Earth's Structure

Key Ideas
- Earth is made up of different parts, above and below its surface.

Key Terms
- core
- atmosphere
- mantle
- landform
- crust

Visual Glossary

The diagram to the right reveals Earth's interior, or the parts beneath its surface. It also shows some of the parts above its surface. Understanding Earth's inner and outer structure will help you to understand the forces that shape the world we live in.

Earth's Core

A sphere of very hot metal at the center of Earth is called the **core**. Despite temperatures greater than 5,000°F (3,000°C), the inner core is solid because of the great pressure of the layers above it. The outer core is hot liquid metal.

Mantle

The **mantle** is a thick, rocky layer around the core. The mantle is also hot, with temperatures greater than 3,300°F (1,800°C). The mantle is solid, but its temperature makes it fluid, or able to flow. If you warm a stick of butter, you can move the top in one direction and the bottom in another. Even though the mantle is rock, its high temperature allows it to move something like a stick of warm butter.

Crust

The thin layer of rocks and minerals that surrounds the mantle is called the **crust**. The surface of the crust includes the land areas where people live as well as the ocean floor. The crust is thinnest beneath the ocean floor. It is thickest beneath high mountain ranges, such as the Himalayas, in Asia. In effect, it floats on top of the mantle. The great heat deep inside Earth and movements within the mantle help to shape Earth's crust.

Atmosphere

Above Earth's surface is the **atmosphere,** a thick layer of gases or air. It includes life-giving oxygen. Earth's atmosphere acts like a blanket. It holds in heat from the sun, which makes life possible.

Landforms

Only 25 percent of Earth's surface is land. There are many different **landforms,** or shapes and types of land. Two kinds of processes shape these landforms: processes beneath Earth's surface that push Earth's crust up, and processes on Earth's surface that wear it down.

Water

Water covers about 75 percent of Earth's surface. This water forms a layer above Earth's crust. The oceans hold about 97 percent of Earth's water. This water is salty. Most fresh water, or water without salt, is frozen in ice sheets around the North and South Poles. Only a tiny portion of Earth's water is unfrozen fresh water. People need this water for many things. Fresh water comes from lakes, rivers, and ground water, which are fed by rain and snow.

Assessment

1. What are Earth's three main layers?
2. What part of Earth's structure are oceans located on?

Forces on Earth's Surface

Key Ideas
- Forces such as wind, water, and ice shape Earth's surface.
- These forces produce a variety of different landforms.

Key Terms
- weathering
- valley
- erosion
- deposition
- plateau
- plain
- delta

Visual Glossary

Forces on Earth's surface wear down and reshape the land. Along with forces inside Earth, which you will read about later, forces on Earth's surface help create the landforms we see around us.

An eroded landscape in the southwestern United States. ▼

Wearing Away Earth's Surface

Weathering is a process that breaks rocks down into tiny pieces. There are two kinds of weathering: chemical weathering and mechanical weathering. In chemical weathering, rainwater or acids carried by rainwater dissolve rocks. In mechanical weathering, moving water, ice, or sometimes wind breaks rocks into little pieces. Mechanical weathering can happen after chemical weathering has weakened rocks.

Weathering helps create soil. Tiny pieces of rock combine with decayed animal and plant material to form soil. Soil and pieces of rock may undergo **erosion,** a process in which water, ice, or wind remove small pieces of rock. Soil is required to sustain plant and animal life, and for agriculture. Because of this, weathering is very important to human settlement patterns.

Shaping Landforms

Weathering and erosion have shaped many of Earth's landforms. These landforms include mountains and hills. Mountains are wide at the bottom and rise steeply to a narrow peak or ridge. Hills are lower than mountains and often have rounded tops. While forces within Earth create mountains, forces on Earth's surface wear them down. An area in which a certain type of landform is dominant is called a landform region.

The parts of mountains and hills that are left standing are the rocks that are hardest to wear away. Millions of years ago, the Appalachian Mountains in the eastern United States were as high as the Rocky Mountains of the western United States. Rain, snow, and wind wore the Appalachians down into much lower peaks.

Rebuilding Earth's Surface

When water, ice, and wind remove material, they deposit it farther downstream or downwind to create new landforms. **Deposition** is the process of depositing material eroded and carried by water, ice, or wind. Deposition creates landforms such as sandy beaches. **Plains,** or large areas of flat or gently rolling land, are often formed by the deposition of material carried downstream by rivers. Through deposition on the floor of the sea, rivers can create new land.

A **plateau** is a large, mostly flat area that rises above the surrounding land. At least one side of a plateau has a steep slope. At the top of this slope is usually a layer of rock that is hard to wear down.

Valleys are stretches of low land between mountains or hills. Rivers often form valleys where there are rocks that are easy to wear away.

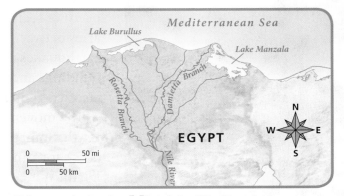

This map shows the **delta** of the Nile River in Egypt. Deltas are flat plains built on the seabed where a river fans out and deposits material over many years.

Assessment

1. How is erosion different from weathering?
2. How do plains form from the tops of worn-down mountains?

Core Concepts 2.5

Forces Inside Earth

Key Ideas
- Movements of hot, soft rock in Earth's mantle affect Earth's surface, forming volcanoes and pushing continents together or apart.

Key Terms
- plate tectonics
- plate
- magma
- fault

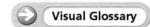 **Visual Glossary**

The volcano Kilauea in Hawaii spews molten rock. ▼

Forces deep inside Earth are constantly reshaping its surface. The theory of **plate tectonics** states that Earth's crust is made up of huge blocks called **plates.** Plates include continents or parts of continents, along with parts of the ocean floor. Earth's continental plates sit on streams of molten, nearly melted, rock called **magma.** Some scientists believe magma acts as a conveyor belt, moving the plates in different directions. Plates may move only an inch or two (a few centimeters) a year.

This movement slowly builds mountains. When two plates of crust push against each other, the pressure makes the crust bend to form steep mountains.

Earthquakes and Volcanoes

Earthquakes occur when plates slide against each other. They often occur at seams in Earth's crust called **faults**, often near the boundaries between plates. Earthquakes cause the ground to shake. Some earthquakes are too small for people to feel. But others can destroy buildings and cause great harm. For example, the 1906 San Francisco earthquake killed more than 3000 people.

The movement of continental plates creates great pressure inside Earth. Sometimes this pressure forces magma up through Earth's crust, forming volcanoes. Volcanoes spew magma from inside Earth. When magma erupts out of a volcano, it is called lava. Ash, rocks, and poisonous gasses also explode out of volcanoes during an eruption. Volcanic eruptions can be very dangerous for people. But volcanoes also serve an important purpose. When lava cools, new land forms. Undersea volcanoes even grow into islands after thousands of years of eruptions.

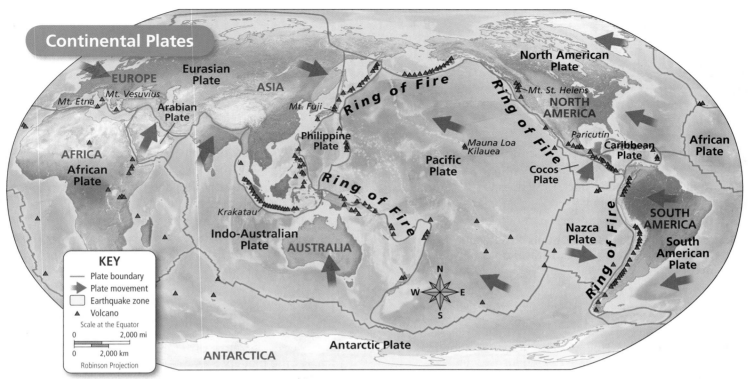

Continental Plates

KEY
- — Plate boundary
- ➤ Plate movement
- ▭ Earthquake zone
- ▲ Volcano

Scale at the Equator
0 — 2,000 mi
0 — 2,000 km
Robinson Projection

The Plates of Earth's Crust The map above shows how Earth's plates fit together today. It also shows the directions in which plates are moving. As you can see on the map, earthquakes and volcanoes occur along plate edges.

Natural Hazards

Volcanoes and earthquakes are examples of natural disasters. They are also called natural hazards, meaning dangers. Other natural hazards include hurricanes, tornados, landslides, and floods.

These events threaten lives and property. But people can take steps to prepare for natural disasters, so that damage will not be as severe when they strike. For example, architects can design buildings that will not collapse when the ground shakes. Local governments can set routes for people to leave affected areas during a hurricane. Citizens can practice what to do during an earthquake, and keep emergency supplies at home.

Preparing for a Natural Hazard
Above: Damage caused by an earthquake
Right: Students hide under their desks for an earthquake drill

Assessment

1. How do forces inside Earth shape Earth's surface?
2. What are some ways people prepare for natural hazards?

27

Our Planet, Earth

Part 2 Assessment

Key Terms and Ideas

1. **Compare and Contrast** What is the difference between an **equinox** and a **solstice**?

2. **Analyze Cause and Effect** How does Earth's **orbit** influence climate on Earth?

3. **Describe** How is Earth's **axis** part of its **rotation**?

4. **Identify Main Ideas and Details** What is sunrise? In which part of the United States does sunrise occur earliest?

5. **Categorize** Which part of Earth's structure is the thinnest? Where is this part?

6. **Summarize** How do **weathering** and **erosion** shape Earth's surface?

7. **Sequence** Describe the process that causes movement of the continents.

Think Critically

8. **Draw Inferences** How would our lives change if Earth's atmosphere were damaged? Explain.

9. **Draw Conclusions** Which parts of Earth's orbit are best for warm-weather activities in the Northern Hemisphere? For cold-weather activities? Explain using the terms *equinox* and *solstice*.

10. **Ask Questions** To choose a safe location for a new town, what questions about Earth's structure and movement would you ask? Explain.

11. **Categorize** Consider three different landforms. For each, list the main process that formed it. Was that process on the interior or exterior of Earth? How are the different processes related?

Identify

Identify the time in each location if it is noon GMT.

12. **New York, New York**
13. **Houston, Texas**
14. **Denver, Colorado**
15. **Los Angeles, California**
16. **Anchorage, Alaska**
17. **Honolulu, Hawaii**
18. Compare the time of sunrise in New York, New York, with that in Houston, Texas. Which is earlier and which is later? Are these cities in the same time zone?

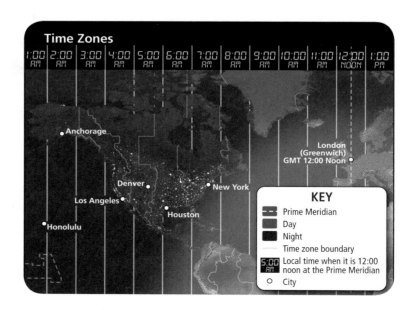

Time Zones

1:00 AM | 2:00 AM | 3:00 AM | 4:00 AM | 5:00 AM | 6:00 AM | 7:00 AM | 8:00 AM | 9:00 AM | 10:00 AM | 11:00 AM | 12:00 NOON | 1:00 PM

Anchorage

London (Greenwich) GMT 12:00 Noon

Denver

New York

Los Angeles

Houston

Honolulu

KEY
Prime Meridian
Day
Night
Time zone boundary
5:00 AM Local time when it is 12:00 noon at the Prime Meridian
○ City

Journal Activity

Fill in the graphic organizer in your Student Journal.

Demonstrate Understanding Complete the Sum-It-Up activity in your journal to demonstrate your understanding of Our Planet, Earth. After you complete the activity, discuss your diagram with your class. Be sure to support your diagram with information from the lessons.

21st Century Learning

Make a Difference

Think about earthquake or volcano safety in your community or a community like yours in an earthquake or volcano danger area. Develop ideas to raise community awareness of the dangers and the ways people can avoid them. Share your ideas on a Web page, poster, or handout.

Document-Based Questions

Success Tracker™
Online at myworldgeography.com

Use your knowledge of our planet Earth and Documents A and B to answer Questions 1–3.

Document A

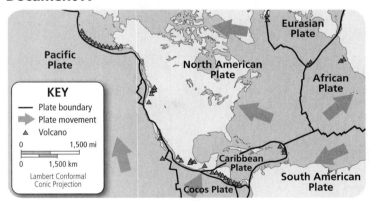

Document B

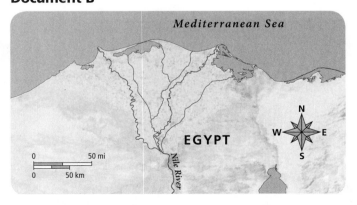

1. Why are there volcanoes where the North American Plate meets the Pacific Plate?

A Erosion breaks down the land where plates meet.

B Magma is forced through Earth's surface at plate boundaries.

C Earth's rotation causes the sun to shine directly on this area.

D Land in this area has been shaped by chemical weather.

2. How is the natural feature depicted on this map formed?

A Tectonic plates push land upward.

B A river flows into the ocean, depositing material on the seabed.

C Wind and rain wear down mountains.

D A river carves out a valley.

3. **Writing Task** Suppose a volcano forms on the ocean floor and grows thousands of feet upwards. Use that information and Document A to explain the many islands between Asia and Australia.

Climates and Ecosystems

Hurricane Katrina spins toward New Orleans.

New Orleans residents trapped by floodwaters wave for help. ▲

SOS

Katrina caused severe destruction.

Airin McGhee

HURRICANE KATRINA STRIKES

Story by Miles Lemaire for myWorld Geography

Powerful tropical storms sweep across the southeastern United States and the Gulf Coast nearly every year. At first, teenager Airin McGhee thought that Hurricane Katrina would be just like any other storm. She was wrong. Instead, Katrina was so powerful that it flooded much of Airin's city, New Orleans, Louisiana.

When weather forecasters and government officials first started warning New Orleans residents about Hurricane Katrina in late August 2005, Airin was not worried. "Every year we would get the warning and up until that point it just never happened," she said. "Nobody expected Katrina to be like it was."

Fortunately, Airin and her mother and sister decided to leave New Orleans before the storm arrived. They drove through heavy traffic to Jackson, Mississippi, a city about 190 miles north of New Orleans. While they waited for the storm to pass, they feared the worst for their home, their city, and the friends and neighbors they had left behind.

Hurricane Katrina hit New Orleans on August 29. Its powerful winds ripped buildings apart and tore trees out of the ground. Worse, Katrina's winds and rain broke the levees, or raised flood barriers, that had protected much of the area. Millions of gallons of water poured through the broken levees into the city.

After Katrina ended, Airin's family tried to get news from friends in New Orleans. "I was really devastated for a while," Airin says, "because the cell phones were really bad and I just had all these thoughts of, 'Is this person okay? Is this person okay?' For weeks all … numbers had a busy signal and it was hard to get in touch with people."

When Airin's family was finally able to return to New Orleans, they saw the results of Katrina's destructive power in person. Years later, Airin's memories of what they saw are still strong. "We had six feet of water in our house," Airin said. "We lost everything. We lost my mom's car and my car, our entire house, including all the furniture and clothes … I pretty much lost everything."

It wasn't long before Airin's family was able to find another place to live, but they still feel the effects of the storm years later.

"I'll just never forget Katrina," Airin says. "It wiped away all my memories. I lost my high school diploma, all my pictures and things that you might take for granted. I collected things like my baby teeth and blanket. All those things are just gone."

When Airin thinks about how the storm affected her, she says, "It really taught me to value sentimental things. It changed how I do certain things, because now I want to capture every moment, and I find myself taking pictures of everything."

31

Climate and Weather

Key Ideas
- Different areas of the world have different weather patterns.
- Weather and climate are described using precipitation and temperature.

Key Terms • weather   • climate   • precipitation   • temperature

 Visual Glossary

The climate of Iquitos (ee KEE tohs), Peru, is hot and wet year-round. ▼

You have learned about the powerful forces that shape Earth, including global movements, water, and sunlight. These forces also shape Earth's weather patterns. Weather patterns can vary widely from one region to another.

Weather or Climate?

Do you look outside before you choose your clothing in the morning? If so, you are checking the weather. **Weather** is the condition of the air and sky at a certain time. Or do you choose your clothing based on the normal weather for the time of year in the place where you live? If so, you dress according to your local climate. **Climate** is the average weather of a place over many years.

How you feel about today's weather may depend on your local climate. If you live in a place with a wet climate, you may be unhappy to see rainy weather, because your climate means that you get rain frequently. On the other hand, if you live in a dry climate where water is scarce, you might be very happy to see rainy weather.

Rain is a form of **precipitation,** which is water that falls to the ground as rain, snow, sleet, or hail. **Temperature** is a measure of how hot or cold the air is. Precipitation and temperature are the main ways to describe both daily weather and long-term climate.

Comparing Climates

One way to understand and compare climates is to use climate graphs. Climate graphs show the average climate for a place for each month of a year. A climate graph has a curved line that shows average temperatures. It has bars that show average monthly precipitation. The next page has two examples of climate graphs.

Chicago, Illinois

This is a climate graph of Chicago, Illinois, a city in the north central United States. It shows that Chicago has cold winters, hot summers, and moderate precipitation year-round. Notice that the line for temperature is much higher in July than it is in January. However, the heights of the bars for precipitation do not change much.

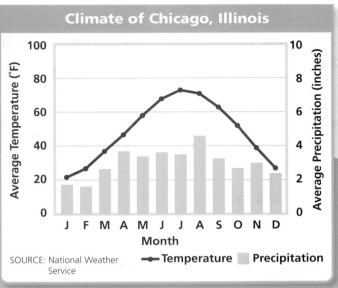

Climate of Chicago, Illinois

SOURCE: National Weather Service — Temperature ■ Precipitation

Bangalore, India

In some parts of the world, precipitation changes greatly from season to season. This is a climate graph of Bangalore, India. It shows that most of Bangalore's rain falls during a rainy season that lasts from May to October. Almost no precipitation falls from January to March.

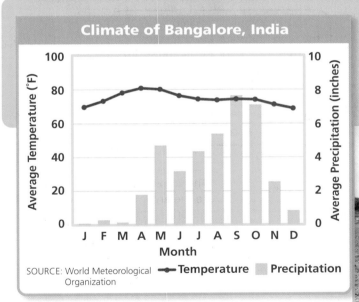

Climate of Bangalore, India

SOURCE: World Meteorological Organization — Temperature ■ Precipitation

Assessment

1. How is climate different from weather?

2. How would you describe your region's climate?

Temperature

Key Ideas
- Differences in sunlight affect temperatures at different latitudes.
- Earth's temperature patterns change from season to season.

Key Terms
- polar zone
- temperate zone
- high latitudes
- middle latitudes
- tropics
- altitude
- low latitudes

→ Visual Glossary

Zones of Latitude

Energy from the sun heats Earth. Because of the tilt of Earth's axis, different areas of the planet receive different amounts of direct sunlight. As a result, some regions are warmer than others.

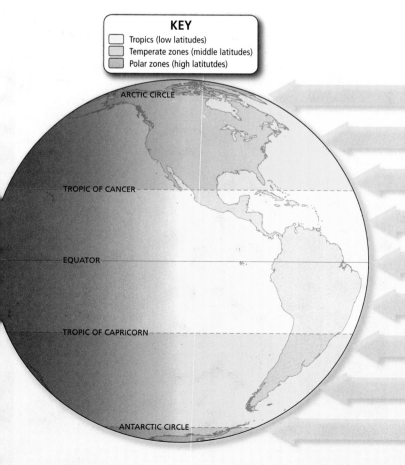

KEY
- ☐ Tropics (low latitudes)
- ☐ Temperate zones (middle latitudes)
- ☐ Polar zones (high latitutdes)

ARCTIC CIRCLE

TROPIC OF CANCER

EQUATOR

TROPIC OF CAPRICORN

ANTARCTIC CIRCLE

The **polar zones,** also known as the **high latitudes,** are the areas north of the Arctic Circle and south of the Antarctic Circle. In the polar zones, the sun is below the horizon for part of the year and near the horizon the rest of the year. Temperatures stay cool to bitterly cold.

The **tropics,** or the **low latitudes,** are the areas between the Tropic of Cancer and the Tropic of Capricorn. In the low latitudes, the sun is overhead or nearly overhead all year long. In this region, it is usually hot.

The **temperate zones,** or the **middle latitudes,** are the areas between the high and low latitudes. These areas lie between the Tropic of Cancer and the Arctic Circle in the Northern Hemisphere and between the Tropic of Capricorn and the Antarctic Circle in the Southern Hemisphere. They have a hot summer, a cold winter, and a moderate spring and fall.

Seasonal Changes in Temperature

Because of the tilt of Earth's axis, temperature patterns change from season to season. The maps below show the world's average monthly temperatures in January and July.

In January, it is winter in the Northern Hemisphere and summer in the Southern Hemisphere. In July, the seasons are reversed. Notice that temperatures are cooler year-round over western South America and other areas. The lower temperatures are due to the high altitude of these regions. **Altitude** is height above sea level. As altitude increases, temperature drops.

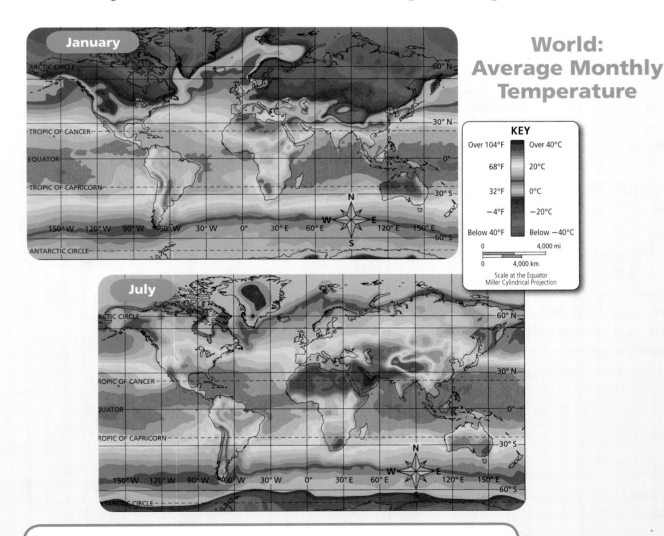

World:
Average Monthly
Temperature

KEY

Over 104°F	Over 40°C
68°F	20°C
32°F	0°C
−4°F	−20°C
Below 40°F	Below −40°C

0   4,000 mi
0   4,000 km
Scale at the Equator
Miller Cylindrical Projection

Assessment

1. Why are most of the tropics, or the low latitudes, warm all year?

2. How does the tilt of Earth's axis explain changes in temperature from one season to another in the temperate zones?

Water and Climate

Key Ideas
- Water affects climate and weather.
- Water is always moving in the process called the water cycle.

Key Terms • water cycle • evaporation

 Visual Glossary

Like plants and animals, people need fresh water to live. All fresh water comes from precipitation. As you know, precipitation is water that falls from the sky in the form of rain, snow, sleet, or hail. Water also shapes climates.

Oceans and Climate

Oceans and other large bodies of water on Earth's surface help spread Earth's heat and shape climates. Global temperature differences and wind patterns create ocean currents, which act like large rivers within the oceans. These ocean currents move across great distances. They move warm water from the tropics toward the poles. They also move cool water from the poles toward the tropics. The water's temperature affects air temperature near it. Warm water warms the air; cool water chills it.

Bodies of water affect climate in other ways, too. Water takes longer to heat or cool than land. As air and land heat up in summer, water remains cooler. Wind blowing over the cool water helps cool land nearby. So in summer, areas near an ocean or lake will be cooler than inland

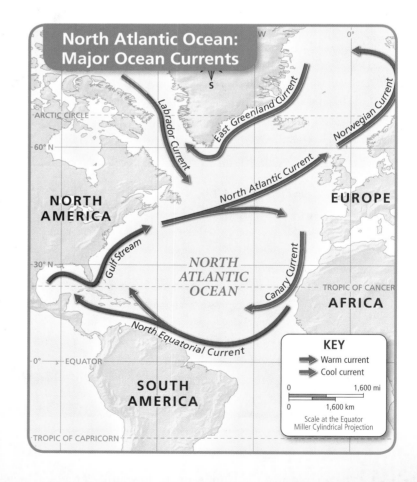

North Atlantic Ocean: Major Ocean Currents

KEY
Warm current
Cool current

0   1,600 mi
0   1,600 km
Scale at the Equator
Miller Cylindrical Projection

areas at the same latitude and altitude. In the winter, on the other hand, water remains warmer than land. So in winter, areas near oceans or lakes are warmer than inland areas.

For example, in the Atlantic Ocean, the Gulf Stream, a warm current, travels northeast from the tropics. The Gulf Stream and the North Atlantic Current carry warm water all the way to Western Europe. That warm water helps give Western Europe a much milder climate than other regions at the same latitude.

The Water Cycle

Earth's water is always moving in a process called the water cycle, shown in the illustration below. The **water cycle** is the movement of water from Earth's surface into the atmosphere and back. As water heats up, it moves from rivers, oceans, and lakes up into the air. As it cools, it falls to Earth's surface and flows back to rivers, oceans and lakes. The water cycle includes precipitation and evaporation. **Evaporation** is the process in which a liquid changes to a gas.

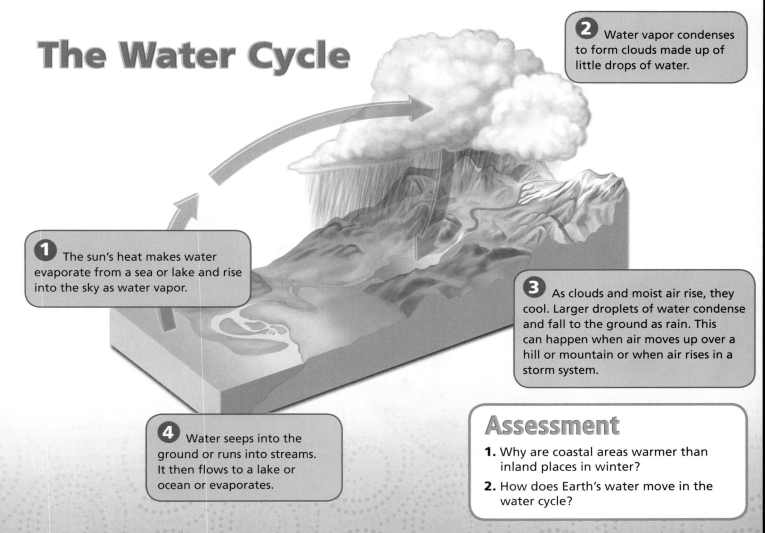

The Water Cycle

2 Water vapor condenses to form clouds made up of little drops of water.

1 The sun's heat makes water evaporate from a sea or lake and rise into the sky as water vapor.

3 As clouds and moist air rise, they cool. Larger droplets of water condense and fall to the ground as rain. This can happen when air moves up over a hill or mountain or when air rises in a storm system.

4 Water seeps into the ground or runs into streams. It then flows to a lake or ocean or evaporates.

Assessment

1. Why are coastal areas warmer than inland places in winter?

2. How does Earth's water move in the water cycle?

Air Circulation and Precipitation

Key Ideas
- Wind and air currents move heat and moisture between different parts of Earth.
- Air movement leads to precipitation and intense storms.

Key Terms
- intertropical convergence zone • tropical cyclone • hurricane
- tornado

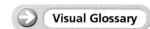 Visual Glossary

Belts of rising and sinking air form a pattern around Earth. Air rises near the Equator, sinks at the edge of the tropics, rises in the temperate zones, and sinks over the poles. The **intertropical convergence zone,** or ITCZ, is the area of rising air near the Equator.

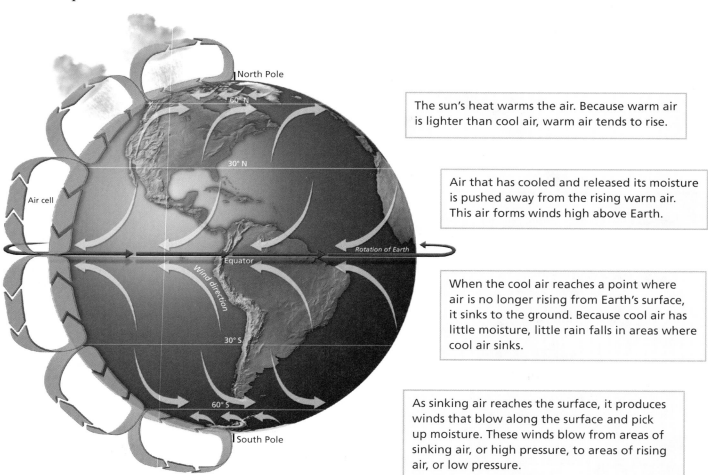

The sun's heat warms the air. Because warm air is lighter than cool air, warm air tends to rise.

Air that has cooled and released its moisture is pushed away from the rising warm air. This air forms winds high above Earth.

When the cool air reaches a point where air is no longer rising from Earth's surface, it sinks to the ground. Because cool air has little moisture, little rain falls in areas where cool air sinks.

As sinking air reaches the surface, it produces winds that blow along the surface and pick up moisture. These winds blow from areas of sinking air, or high pressure, to areas of rising air, or low pressure.

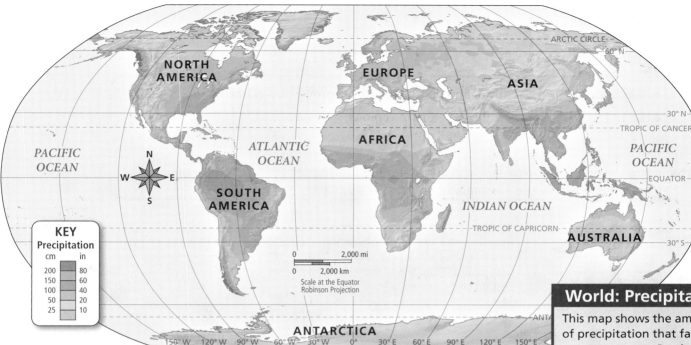

KEY
Precipitation
cm	in
200	80
150	60
100	40
50	20
25	10

0 _____ 2,000 mi
0 _____ 2,000 km
Scale at the Equator
Robinson Projection

World: Precipitation

This map shows the amount of precipitation that falls in an average year. Precipitation is heaviest near the Equator, where air usually rises. It is also heavy along coastlines, where moist air blows onshore and is forced to rise. Precipitation is lightest where cool air sinks near the poles and at the edges of the tropics, where deserts are normally found.

Raging Storms

Most storms occur when two air masses of different temperatures or moisture contents come together. Some storms bring small amounts of rain or snow, while others bring heavy wind and rain, causing great destruction.

A **tropical cyclone** is an intense rainstorm with strong winds that forms over oceans in the tropics. A **hurricane** is a cyclone that forms over the Atlantic Ocean. These storms can cause much damage. A **tornado** is a swirling funnel of wind that can reach 300 miles (500 km) per hour. Tornadoes can be more dangerous than hurricanes, but they affect smaller areas.

Most other storms are less dangerous. In winter, blizzards dump snow on parts of North America. Severe rainstorms and thunderstorms strike North America most often in spring and summer.

Assessment

1. Why is precipitation heaviest near the Equator?

2. How do physical processes such as air circulation and precipitation affect humans?

Tornadoes can cause severe damage.

Types of Climate

Key Ideas
- Temperature, precipitation, and wind interact to form global patterns.
- Earth has a number of different climate regions.

Key Terms
- tropical wet • tropical wet and dry • humid subtropical • maritime • subarctic • semiarid • arid • tundra

Visual Glossary

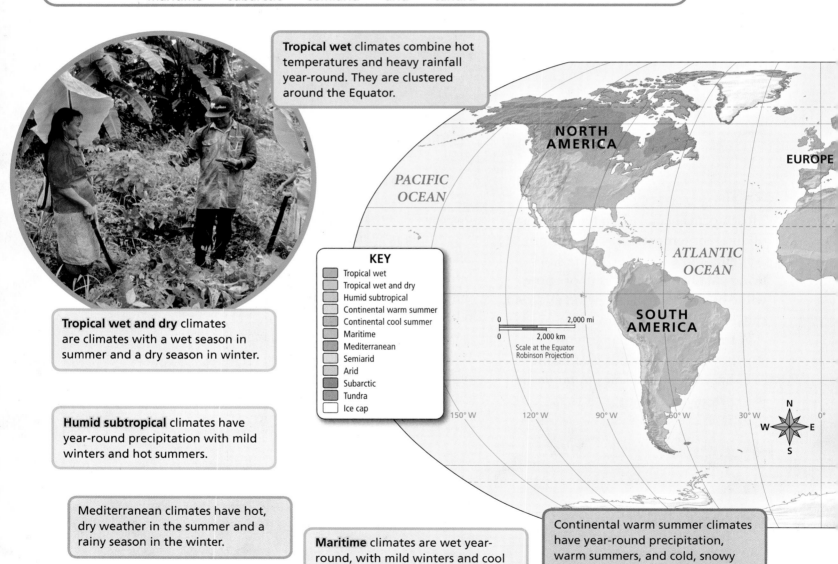

Tropical wet climates combine hot temperatures and heavy rainfall year-round. They are clustered around the Equator.

Tropical wet and dry climates are climates with a wet season in summer and a dry season in winter.

Humid subtropical climates have year-round precipitation with mild winters and hot summers.

Mediterranean climates have hot, dry weather in the summer and a rainy season in the winter.

Maritime climates are wet year-round, with mild winters and cool summers. They exist where moist winds blow onshore.

Continental warm summer climates have year-round precipitation, warm summers, and cold, snowy winters. Continental cool summer climates are similar, but they have generally lower temperatures.

KEY
- Tropical wet
- Tropical wet and dry
- Humid subtropical
- Continental warm summer
- Continental cool summer
- Maritime
- Mediterranean
- Semiarid
- Arid
- Subarctic
- Tundra
- Ice cap

NORTH AMERICA

EUROPE

PACIFIC OCEAN

ATLANTIC OCEAN

SOUTH AMERICA

0   2,000 mi
0   2,000 km
Scale at the Equator
Robinson Projection

150° W   120° W   90° W   60° W   30° W   0°

N W E S

You have already learned about the most important shapers of climate: temperature, precipitation, and wind. These factors form global patterns. For example, temperatures are warmest in and around the tropics and are coolest close to the poles. Precipitation is greatest near the Equator. These patterns of temperature and precipitation create world climate regions. Climate regions are areas that share a similar climate.

Subarctic climates have limited precipitation, cool summers, and very cold winters.

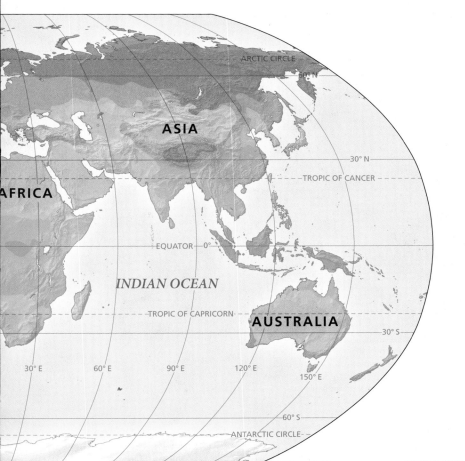

Semiarid, or dry, climates and **arid**, or very dry, desert climates occur where there is steadily sinking air.

Tundra climates have cool summers and bitterly cold, dry winters. Close to the poles, ice caps, or permanent sheets of ice covering land or sea, have bitter cold and dry climates year-round.

Assessment

1. In the winter, what kind of weather would you expect in a continental warm summer climate?
2. What factors explain the locations of Earth's tropical wet and tropical wet and dry climates?

Tropical or Subtropical Forest

Steady hot temperatures and moist air support the rich ecosystems known as tropical rain forests.

Temperate Forest

Moist temperate climates support thick forests of **deciduous trees,** or trees that lose their leaves in the fall. Some temperate forests include a mix of deciduous and evergreen trees.

Subarctic Forest

Coniferous trees are trees that produce cones to carry seeds. They also have needles. These features protect trees through the cold, dry winters of subarctic climates.

Tropical or Subtropical Grassland or Savanna

A **savanna** is a park-like landscape of grasslands with scattered trees that can survive dry spells. Savannas are found in tropical areas with dry seasons.

Temperate Grassland and Brush

Vast grasslands cover regions that get more rain than deserts but too little to support forests.

42

Core Concepts 3.6

Ecosystems

Key Idea

- An ecosystem is a network of living things that depend on one another and their environment for survival.

Key Terms

- deciduous tree
- coniferous tree
- savanna
- ecosystem

→ **Visual Glossary**

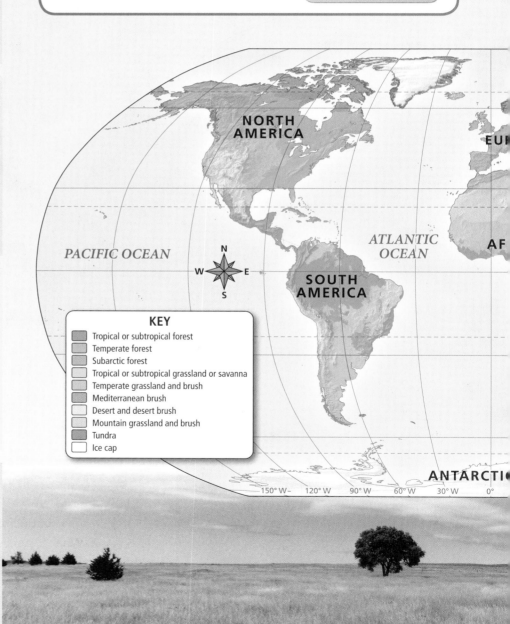

NORTH AMERICA

EU

PACIFIC OCEAN

N
W · E
S

ATLANTIC OCEAN

AF

SOUTH AMERICA

KEY
- Tropical or subtropical forest
- Temperate forest
- Subarctic forest
- Tropical or subtropical grassland or savanna
- Temperate grassland and brush
- Mediterranean brush
- Desert and desert brush
- Mountain grassland and brush
- Tundra
- Ice cap

ANTARCTIC

150° W — 120° W — 90° W — 60° W — 30° W — 0°

The connections between living things and the environment form ecosystems. An **ecosystem** is a group of plants and animals that depend on each other and their environment for survival. Ecosystems can be small or large. The map below shows Earth's major types of ecosystems.

Ecosystems can change over time due to physical processes or human activities. For example, a lack of rain in a temperate forest ecosystem might kill off many plants and animals. The building of a city is an example of a human activity that changes an original ecosystem.

Mediterranean Brush

Shrubs and other low plants in Mediterranean climates have to hold water from winter rains to survive hot, dry summers.

Desert and Desert Brush

Dry semiarid areas and deserts with some rain support animals and low-lying desert plants. These plants need little water and can live in extreme temperatures. The driest desert areas have little or no plant life.

Mountain Grassland and Brush

In mountain grassland and brush regions, vegetation depends on elevation, since temperatures drop as altitude increases.

Tundra

The tundra is an area of cold climate and low-lying plants. Here, grasses grow and low shrubs bloom during brief, cool summers. Animals of the tundra are able to live with cold temperatures and scarce food.

Ice Cap

Thick ice caps form around the poles, with their year-round climates of extreme cold. No plants can live on this ice.

ARCTIC CIRCLE
60° N
OPE
ASIA
30° N
TROPIC OF CANCER
RICA
PACIFIC OCEAN
EQUATOR 0°
INDIAN OCEAN
TROPIC OF CAPRICORN
AUSTRALIA
30° S

0   2,000 mi
0   2,000 km
Scale at the Equator
Robinson Projection
60° S
ANTARCTIC CIRCLE

A
30° E

Assessment

1. How do climate differences affect plant and animal life?
2. What features of the plants and animals in your own region let them live in your region's climate?

43

Part 3 Assessment

Key Terms and Ideas

1. **Summarize** What is a region's **weather**? What is a region's **climate**?

2. **Identify** What are the three most important factors of climate?

3. **Compare and Contrast** How do temperatures in the **low latitudes** differ from temperatures in the **middle latitudes**?

4. **Sequence** Rank these climates in terms of amount of precipitation, from most precipitation to least precipitation: **subarctic, arid, tropical wet.**

5. **Compare and Contrast** How are **deciduous trees** different from **coniferous trees**?

6. **Connect** What is the role of air temperature in the **water cycle**?

7. **Describe** How does the physical environment affect humans?

Think Critically

8. **Categorize** Explain in one sentence how today's weather is related to your region's climate.

9. **Predict** How would winter temperatures differ between two cities on the same continent at the same latitude, one on the coast and one inland?

10. **Draw Inferences** Use what you know about the amount of moisture in cool air to predict the level of precipitation in a tundra climate.

11. **Draw Conclusions** How does altitude affect temperature in different latitudes?

Identify

Answer the following questions based on the map.

12. What do the arrows on this map show?

13. In which zone of latitude is the West Wind Drift?

14. Is the North Atlantic Current warm or cool?

15. Is the California Current warm or cool?

16. Is the Brazil Current located in the Northern Hemisphere or the Southern Hemisphere?

17. Does the Benguela Current bring cool water to the polar zones or to the tropics?

18. What important parallel of latitude does the Kuroshio Current cross?

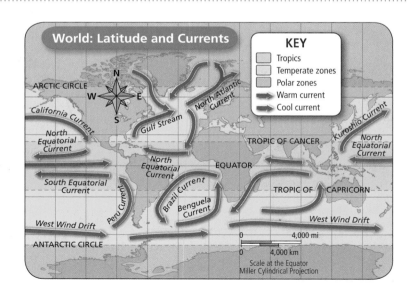

Journal Activity

Fill in the graphic organizer in your Student Journal.

Demonstrate Your Understanding Complete the Sum-It-Up activity in your journal to demonstrate your understanding of climates and ecosystems. After you complete the activity, discuss your predictions with a partner. Be sure to support your predictions with information from the lessons.

21st Century Learning

Give an Effective Presentation

Research and deliver an illustrated oral presentation on the features of one of the ecosystems described in Lesson 6. Be sure to address the following topics:
- Climate characteristics
- Effect of climate on animal and plant life
- Effect of climate on human life, including the economy

Document-Based Questions

Success Tracker™
Online at myworldgeography.com

Use your knowledge of climates and ecosystems and Documents A and B to answer Questions 1–3.

Document A

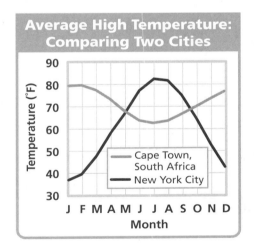

Document B

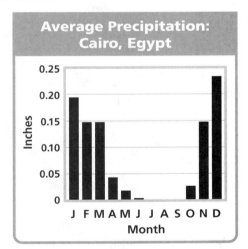

1. Examine Document A. Which of the following statements is true?

   A New York City and Cape Town are located in the same hemisphere.

   B New York City is in the Southern Hemisphere, while Cape Town is in the Northern Hemisphere.

   C New York City is in the Northern Hemisphere, while Cape Town is in the Southern Hemisphere.

   D none of the above

2. Examine Document B. Judging from the average precipitation Cairo receives, in which of the following climates is it most likely to be located?

   A tropical wet

   B maritime

   C arid

   D humid subtropical

3. **Writing Task** Using information from Document A as evidence, describe how a location's hemisphere affects its seasons.

Human–Environment Interaction

Young people support clean energy sources.

Oil leaks from an abandoned oil barrel in Alaska. ▲

Environmental workers clean up an oil spill.

Lauren Hexilon

MAKING A DIFFERENCE

Story by Miles Lemaire for myWorld Geography

Lauren Hexilon wants to save the world.
Lauren has wanted to protect the environment for as long as she can remember. After she graduated from college recently, Lauren decided to go to work for the U.S. Environmental Protection Agency (EPA).

The EPA was an obvious choice for Lauren. After all, the organization's main focus is to protect human health and the environment. Today Lauren works with people who help protect public health and the environment in many ways. Some of their work deals with hazardous waste spills around the country. Hazardous waste includes chemicals, radioactive materials, and other waste dangerous to humans, wildlife, and the environment.

Cleaning up hazardous waste can be "a very long process," Lauren says. To dispose of waste safely, she explains, "you have to follow certain rules and procedures, so it takes a while to see a project from its beginning to its end."

Lauren doesn't clean up pollution and hazardous waste herself. Still, she helps protect the environment at her job each day. She spends much of her time working with young people to teach them about environmental issues. Raising public awareness is important, she says.

Right now Lauren is working with the University of North Texas on projects that help people understand threats to the environment. She is also helping to create an environmental video conference. This conference will connect young people from countries around the world. Lauren likes these projects because they teach people to protect the environment. Plus, she says, she gets to see the results of her work quickly.

But you don't have to work for the EPA to help prevent pollution and protect the environment. Lauren says that each of us makes choices every day that have an impact on the environment, whether we realize it or not. Take conserving energy, for example. "Flipping on a light switch, that's an environmental impact," says Lauren. "If you leave the light on, you're wasting electricity."

So what does Lauren think that young people should know about human interaction with the environment? Simply this: She would like each of us to think about how our actions affect the environment. Whenever possible, Lauren says, try to make good choices about your actions. For example, consider riding a bicycle or taking public transportation instead of driving in a car.

In fact, everyone can take small steps to improve the way they interact with the environment. We should think about "all the little things" we do each day, says Lauren. As she points out, "The little things add up."

Environment and Resources

Key Ideas
- People depend on the environment for food, water, energy, and other natural resources.
- Some resources are replaced by Earth over time, but others are not.

Key Terms
- natural resource
- renewable resource
- nonrenewable resource
- fossil fuel

 Visual Glossary

Humans depend on their natural environment to survive. We need the environment to provide energy, water, food, and other materials. In prehistoric times, people lived in areas where they could hunt, gather food, and find fresh water. Later, people settled where they found pasture for their livestock or fertile soils and sufficient water for farming. Today, rapid transportation and other technologies allow people to be less dependent on their immediate environment. However, people still need access to resources.

Natural Resources

Water is just one example of a **natural resource,** or a useful material found in the environment. People depend on many kinds of natural resources. These resources can be divided into two types: renewable and nonrenewable resources.

People use many natural resources in their daily lives. Above, a young woman in Chad uses soil to build a shelter. Below, German workers use metals to build an automobile.

Major Natural Resources

Resource	Type	Formation	Major Uses
Soil	Renewable	Formed from rocks and organic material broken down by natural processes	Agriculture
Water	Renewable	Renewed through the water cycle	Drinking, agriculture, washing, transportation
Plants	Renewable	Usually grow from seeds; require water and sunlight	Food, lumber, clothing, paper
Animals	Renewable	Formed through natural reproduction; require water and food	Food, agricultural labor, transportation, clothing
Fossil fuels	Nonrenewable	Formed over millions of years from plant and animal material	Energy, plastics, chemicals
Minerals	Nonrenewable	Formed through a variety of natural geologic processes	Automobile parts, electronics, and many other human-made products

A **renewable resource** is a resource that Earth or people can replace. Examples of renewable resources include water, plants, and animals. All of these resources can be replaced over time if they are used wisely. For example, if you cut down a tree, another one can grow in its place. When dead plants decay, their nutrients increase soil fertility.

A **nonrenewable resource** is a resource that cannot be replaced in a relatively short period of time. Nonrenewable resources include nonliving things such as minerals, metal ores, and fossil fuels. **Fossil fuels** are nonrenewable resources formed over millions of years from the remains of plants and animals. Coal, natural gas, and petroleum are important fossil fuels. When nonrenewable resources such as fossil fuels are used up, they are gone.

Energy Resources

Sources of energy are important for human activity. Some sources, such as wind and sunlight, are renewable. Today, we mostly rely on nonrenewable energy resources such as coal and petroleum. Because these sources are nonrenewable, Earth will eventually run out of them.

Some countries have large supplies of petroleum and are able to export it, or sell it to other countries. Most countries, however, must buy petroleum and other energy resources from other countries.

Assessment

1. What do people need from the physical environment?
2. How are renewable and nonrenewable natural resources formed?

Land Use

Key Ideas
- People use land in different ways.
- Land use can change over time.

Key Terms • colonization   • industrialization   • suburb

The ways people use land are affected by both the natural environment and culture. In many regions, land use has changed over time.

Reasons for Land Use

How people use land depends partly on the environment. For example, people living in temperate climates with fertile soil may use land mainly for farming. People in arctic areas may use land mainly for hunting. Even in similar environments, however, people may use land differently because they have different customs and ways of life.

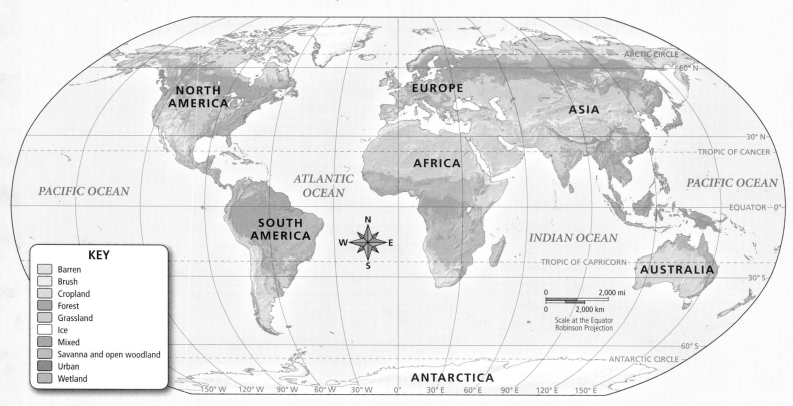

KEY
- Barren
- Brush
- Cropland
- Forest
- Grassland
- Ice
- Mixed
- Savanna and open woodland
- Urban
- Wetland

Changes in Land Use

Land use can change over time. For example, colonization has led to many changes in land use. **Colonization** is a movement of new settlers and their culture to an area. Settlers may change a region's landscape. For example, European colonists brought new crops and new ways of farming to the Americas, Africa, and Australia. These new ways led to dramatic changes in land use as Europeans cleared large areas of land for cropland and livestock pasture.

Since the 1800s, industrialization has changed landscapes in many countries. **Industrialization** is the development of machine-powered production and manufacturing. Large cities have grown around factories. Technology such as machines for clearing land and building roads has made it easier for people to change their environment. This environmental change has allowed the growth of suburbs. A **suburb** is a residential area on the edge of a city or large town.

In the United States and some other countries, most people live in cities or suburban areas. Although cities and suburbs cover a relatively small area, they are an important use of land. Land uses covering large areas include cropland, forests, and grassland.

Land use varies around the world. Above, Tokyo, Japan, is a large city with millions of residents. Below, these people from the Dominican Republic use land for agriculture.

A large portion of Rio de Janeiro, Brazil, is built on steep hills along the Atlantic Ocean. ▼

Assessment

1. How does land use vary from place to place and over time?
2. How have people adapted to and changed the environment?

51

People's Impact on the Environment

Key Ideas
- People affect the environment in many ways.
- People try to decrease the negative effects of using resources.

Key Terms • deforestation • biodiversity • pollution • spillover

 Visual Glossary

All people need food, water, clothing, and shelter. To meet these needs, people have to use materials from their environment. As a result, people have impacts on the environment in their daily lives.

Extracting Resources

People extract, or remove, many kinds of natural resources from the environment. For example, to get wood for building houses, people cut down trees. Advances in technology have allowed people to extract some resources more easily. For example, to get petroleum for fuel, people drill deep wells, sometimes far into the ocean floor.

Extracting resources can harm ecosystems and the environment. For example, cutting down too many trees can cause deforestation. **Deforestation** is the loss of forest cover in a region. Animals that live in the forest may suffer as a result. Drilling oil wells and transporting oil can lead to oil spills, which harm the land and water. Deforestation and producing oil can also reduce biodiversity. **Biodiversity** is the variety of living things in a region or ecosystem.

A bird is covered in oil from an oil spill in Spain. Oil spills and other pollution can affect land, water, and animals. ▼

Other Impacts

People also affect the environment by growing food or producing other goods and services. For example, new technology has allowed farmers to plow more land for crops. But when land is cleared, soil is loosened and can erode, or wash away.

People's activities can also produce **pollution,** or waste that makes the air, soil, or water less clean. For example, many farmers use chemicals called fertilizers and pesticides to help plants grow and to kill pests. These chemicals can help farmers produce more food. They can also harm the environment by causing pollution.

Pollution is a **spillover,** which is an effect on someone or something not involved in an activity. For example, air pollution affects everyone who breathes the polluted air, even people who did not cause the pollution.

Finding the Best Solution

People try to increase the positive and decrease the negative effects of using resources. For example, using a resource might lead to economic growth but also create pollution that needs to be reduced. Working together, people, governments, and businesses can try to use resources wisely. In some cases, governments limit land use to preserve the environment.

▲ These wind turbines in Canada convert wind energy into electricity.

Advances in technology can also help protect resources and the environment. One way of protecting the environment is for people to use vehicles that burn less fuel, such as hybrid cars. Vehicles that burn less fuel create less air pollution. People can also use clean energy sources, such as solar power and wind power. They are considered clean energy sources because they do not pollute the air.

Assessment

1. How have new technologies affected people's ability to change the environment?
2. How might future uses of technology affect Earth?

Human–Environment Interaction

Part 4 Assessment

Key Terms and Ideas

1. **Identify** List two **fossil fuels.**
2. **Recall** What is an example of a **natural resource**?
3. **Discuss** How might **colonization** affect a region?
4. **Paraphrase** In your own words, describe the causes and effects of **deforestation.**

5. **Sequence** Explain how **suburbs** develop.
6. **Summarize** How do people use natural resources?
7. **Cause and Effect** If a company pollutes a river, what is one possible **spillover**?

Think Critically

8. **Draw Inferences** Give two examples of ways technology has made people less dependent on the environment around them.
9. **Analyze Cause and Effect** Imagine that your state's supply of fossil fuels was suddenly cut in half. How might this affect daily life in your state?

10. **Solve Problems** Explain what the following statement means: *While trees are a renewable resource, it often takes human effort to make them renewable.*
11. **Synthesize** Imagine that a large factory is about to be constructed on the edge of a rain forest. How might this factory affect the region's biodiversity?

Identify

Answer the following questions based on the map.

12. India is a former British colony. Why do you think it was a valuable colony for Britain?
13. What natural resources are found in India?
14. What geographic features could also be natural resources?
15. How do you think land might be used in the Himalayas?
16. How do you think land might be used along the coast?
17. What environmental problems might use of India's natural resources cause?
18. How might altitude affect where people live in India?

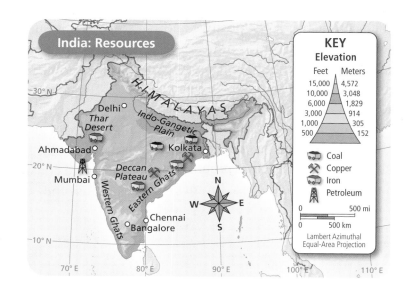

Journal Activity

Answer the questions in your Student Journal.

Demonstrate Your Understanding Complete the Sum-It-Up activity in your journal to demonstrate your understanding of human–environment interaction. After you complete the activity, discuss your answers in a small group. Be sure to support your answers with information from the lessons.

21st Century Learning

Search for Information on the Internet

Pollution can cause many harmful effects. Use online resources to research some of the effects of pollution and present your findings in a poster. When researching, remember the following:
- Use reputable Web sites, particularly those with addresses ending in *.gov* or *.edu*.
- Identify the site's author and check for bias.

Document-Based Questions

Success Tracker™
Online at myworldgeography.com

Use your knowledge of human–environment interaction and Documents A and B to answer Questions 1–3.

Document A

Pesticide Use in England and Wales, 1990–2005

SOURCE: The Environment Agency

Document B

1. **Examine** Document A. How has pesticide use changed in England and Wales in recent years?

   A It has increased.

   B It has decreased.

   C It has stopped completely.

   D It has not changed.

2. **Examine** Document B. Which of the following statements is true?

   A Major cities are spread out evenly across Massachusetts.

   B Most major cities are located far from Boston.

   C Most major cities are near Boston.

   D The location of Boston does not appear to have affected the locations of other cities.

3. **Writing Task** How might settlement and land use in Massachusetts be different if Boston were not its largest city? Explain your answer.

Economics and Geography

Surf shops are common in southern California.

Chris's childhood love of surfing helped inspire his first business.

Chris's business specializes in Web site design.

Chris Kerstner

An Extraordinary Entrepreneur

Story by Miles Lemaire for myWorld Geography

Chris Kerstner is still in his early twenties, but he has already created and successfully run four companies. In fact, Chris started his first business when he was still in middle school.

Chris is an entrepreneur, or a person who starts new businesses. "I surfed when I was a kid," Chris says, "so I'd repair surfboards for friends, and that kind of blossomed to the point where I was the main repair guy for all the local surf shops in Newport Beach [California]."

By the time he was old enough to drive, Chris had started a second business, this time on dry land: working on car stereos. This business grew quickly, Chris says. "It was like I had [an auto parts store] running out of my garage!"

Then, one night at a friend's party, Chris had an experience that led to his most successful company yet. "One of my friend's parents was talking to me about his small business and the Web designers that he had to deal with," Chris says. "He was telling me that they did great work but that they were never on time, and that he would pay anything for a Web designer who could get the work done on time. All I heard, as an entrepreneur, was 'I'll pay anything,' so immediately I turned around and said, 'Oh, yeah, I can do that. No problem!'"

The only problem was that Chris did not know anything about Web design. In fact, he did not even own a computer! But he did not let those obstacles stop him. Within a few weeks, Chris had taught himself how to design Web sites and had produced a Web site for his client.

It was this job that gave Chris the idea for his next company, which specializes in Web design and marketing. Chris created the company while attending business school at the University of Southern California. The company earned nearly $2 million during his first year of school alone. Today, Chris's business has offices in three countries. It has designed Web sites and marketing plans for many major companies.

Chris thinks that the business has been successful because of his belief in providing customers with fast, reliable service. That's the only way a company can survive in the fast-paced modern economy, he says.

So what advice would Chris give to someone else starting a business? Chris says that he loved his professors at business school, but that there was one thing he wished he had been taught in class: "Keep the customers happy. That's it! It's not complicated. … Just keep your customers happy, and that's it."

Economic Basics

Key Ideas
- People make choices about how to meet their wants and needs.
- Economies bring together people and businesses that make, sell, and buy goods and services.

Key Terms
- economics
- supply
- scarcity
- producer
- opportunity cost
- consumer
- demand
- incentive

 Visual Glossary

Economics is the study of how people meet their wants and needs. People must answer three basic economic questions:

1. What goods and services should be produced?
2. How should goods and services be produced?
3. Who uses or consumes those goods and services?

The resources people use to make goods and services are called factors of production. The three main factors are land, labor, and capital. Geographers study where the factors of production are located.

Making Choices

There is no limit to the things that people want, but there are limits to what can be created. This difference between wants and reality creates **scarcity,** or having a limited quantity of resources to meet unlimited wants. Since people have limited money and time, they have to choose

Factors of Production

Entrepreneur
A person known as an entrepreneur combines resources to create new businesses.

Land, Labor, Capital
The three main factors of production are land and resources; human labor; and capital, or human-made goods like tools and buildings.

Goods and Services
Entrepreneurs use the factors of production to produce goods and services.

what they want most. Making a choice involves an **opportunity cost,** or the cost of what you have to give up.

Economics also involves demand and supply. **Demand** is the desire for a certain good or service. **Supply** is the amount of a good or service that is available for use. Demand and supply are connected to price. As the price of a product increases, people will buy less of it. That is, demand will decrease. If the price of the product decreases, demand will increase.

Supply functions in a similar way. If the price of a product increases, companies will make more of it. If the price of the product decreases, companies will make less of it. The price at which demand equals supply is the market price, or the market-clearing price.

Basic economic choices have influenced world events. For example, high demand for resources such as gold or oil has led to exploration and colonization.

Making Goods and Services

Economies bring together producers and consumers. **Producers** are people or businesses that make and sell products. **Consumers** are people or businesses that buy, or consume, products. Producers try to win consumers' business by offering better products for lower prices than other producers. If they sell more products, they

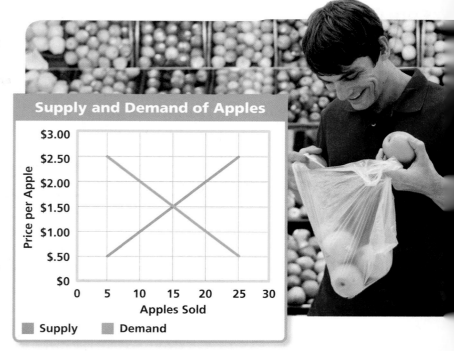

Supply and Demand of Apples

usually increase production. But producers will not make more products if the sale price is less than the marginal cost. Marginal cost is the cost of making one more unit of the product. Therefore, the marginal cost for the producer sets a minimum price for the product.

Businesses make products because of economic incentives. An **incentive** is a factor that encourages people to act in a certain way. Money is an incentive. The desire to earn money gives most producers an incentive to make and sell products. The incentive to save money leads most consumers to look for lower prices.

Assessment

1. On the line graph on this page, what is the market-clearing price?
2. How might a change in the price of one good or service lead to changes in prices of other goods or services?

Economic Process

Key Ideas

- Producers and consumers exchange goods and services in a market.
- Competition is a key part of the economic process.
- Economic activity occurs at four levels.

Key Terms
- market
- profit
- revenue
- specialization
- competition
- inflation
- recession

 Visual Glossary

The economic process is complicated, but its basic idea is simple: Producers and consumers exchange goods and services in a market. A **market** is an organized way for producers and consumers to trade goods and services.

Exchanging Goods and Services

Throughout history, people have often engaged in barter, the trading of goods and services for other goods and services. Today, the means of exchange in a market is usually money. Modern governments issue money in the form of currency, or paper bills and metal coins. Different countries use different currencies. As a result, countries must establish the relative values of their currencies in order to trade. They must also establish a system for exchanging different currencies.

Businesses and the Economic Process

Businesses want to make a profit. **Profit** is the money a company has left after subtracting the costs of doing business. To make a profit, companies try to reduce expenses and increase revenue. **Revenue** is the money earned by selling goods and services. The price of resources affects revenue and profit. If resources become more expensive, the cost of making goods with them will also increase. Businesses' profits will drop.

Companies can increase profit and revenue through **specialization,** the act of concentrating on a limited number of goods or activities. Specialization allows people and companies to use resources more efficiently and to increase production and consumption.

Companies' profits are affected by **competition,** which is the struggle among producers for consumers' money. If one company raises the price of its products, another company may sell similar goods

Economists divide economic activity into four levels, as you can see in this table. ▼

Levels of Economic Activity	
Primary Industry	Collects resources from nature. Examples: farming, mining
Secondary Industry	Uses raw materials to create new products. Example: manufacturing
Tertiary Industry	Provides services to people and secondary industries. Examples: banking, restaurants
Quaternary Industry	Focuses on research and information. Example: education

Competition in the Market

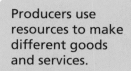

Producers use resources to make different goods and services.

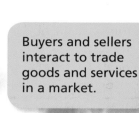

Buyers and sellers interact to trade goods and services in a market.

Competition between buyers and between sellers affects product price, quality, and marketing.

for a lower price to win more business. Companies use advertising to help increase demand for their products and to compete with other companies.

Nonprofit organizations are business-like institutions that do not seek to make a profit. Nonprofit organizations can include churches, museums, hospitals, and other bodies.

A healthy economy grows as companies produce and sell more goods and services. In a growing economy, prices may increase over time. This general increase in prices is called **inflation.**

Economies do not keep growing forever. Eventually, economic activity falls as production slows and consumers buy fewer goods and services. This lack of demand for goods and services can lead to increased unemployment. A decline in economic growth for six or more months in a row is known as a **recession.**

Assessment

1. Does a person always need money to obtain goods or services?

2. How does competition affect producers and consumers?

61

Economic Systems

Key Ideas
- Different societies have different types of economic systems.
- Most societies have economic systems with some element of government control.

Key Terms
- traditional economy
- market economy
- command economy
- mixed economy

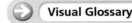 Visual Glossary

Every society has an economic system in which people make and distribute goods and services. There are four basic economic systems: traditional, market, command, and mixed. The roles of individuals, businesses, and government vary in each system. Economic goals, incentives, and government regulations can also vary.

Traditional Economies

A **traditional economy** is an economy in which people make economic decisions based on their customs and habits. They usually satisfy their needs and wants through hunting or farming, as their ancestors did. People in traditional economies usually do not want to change their basic way of life. Today, traditional economies are not common.

The Fulani people in Niger are livestock herders. ▶

Market Economies

A **market economy** is an economy in which individual consumers and producers make economic decisions. This type of economy is also called capitalism, or a free market. Market economies encourage entrepreneurs to establish new businesses by giving them economic freedom.

A consumer makes a purchase at a grocery store. ▶

Command Economies

A **command economy** is an economy in which the central government makes all economic decisions. This kind of system is also called a centrally planned economy. In a command economy, individual consumers and producers do not make basic economic decisions.

◄ In North Korea, government leaders make most economic decisions.

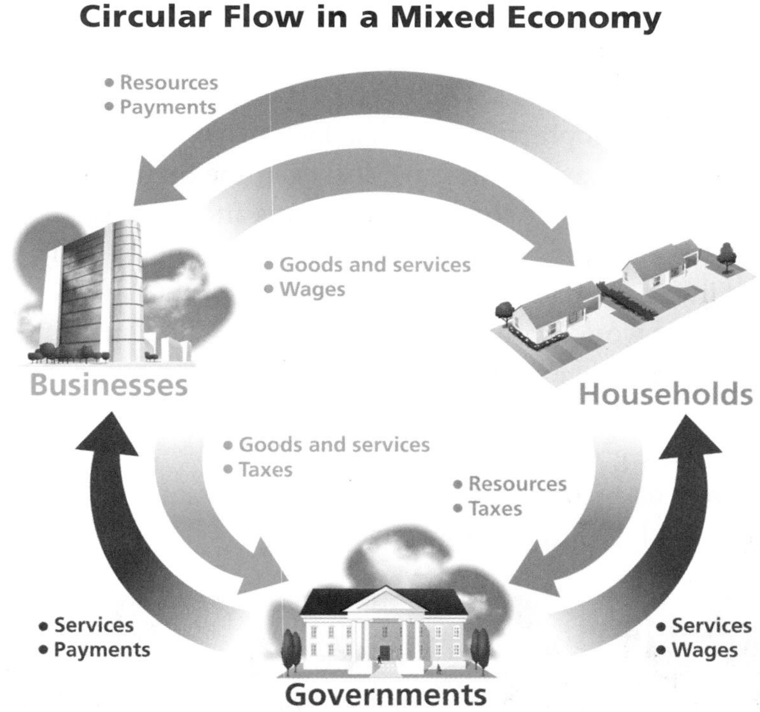

Circular Flow in a Mixed Economy

- Resources
- Payments

- Goods and services
- Wages

Businesses

Households

- Goods and services
- Taxes

- Resources
- Taxes

- Services
- Payments

- Services
- Wages

Governments

Mixed Economies

In reality, pure market or command economies do not exist. Most societies have mixed economies with varying levels of government control. A **mixed economy** is an economy that combines elements of traditional, market, and command economic systems. The diagram at left shows the circular flow of economic activity in a mixed economy.

Countries such as the United States and Australia have mixed economies that are close to pure market economies. In these countries, government makes some economic decisions. For example, government passes laws to protect consumers' rights. Government spending and taxation provide jobs and services and influence economic growth.

Countries such as North Korea and Cuba have mixed economies that are close to pure command economies. In these countries, government owns and controls most businesses.

Assessment

1. What are the differences among traditional, command, and market economies?

2. What are some possible advantages of the free-market system used in the United States and other countries?

Economic Development

Key Ideas
- The level of a country's development has direct effects on the lives of its people.
- There are many ways for a country to increase economic development.

Key Terms
- development
- developed country
- developing country
- gross domestic product (GDP)
- productivity
- technology

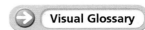
Visual Glossary

Economists use the concept of development to talk about a country's economic well-being. **Development** is economic growth or an increase in living standards.

Measuring Economic Development

When we study development, we look at factors like people's education, literacy, and life expectancy. We also examine their individual purchasing power, or their ability to buy goods and services.

A **developed country** is a country with a strong economy and a high standard of living, such as the United States or Japan. Only about 20 percent of the world's countries are developed. The remaining 80 percent are **developing countries,** or countries with less-productive economies and lower standards of living, such as Haiti or Ethiopia.

Economists use gross domestic product to measure a country's economy. **Gross domestic product (GDP)** is the total value of all goods and services produced in a country in a year.

World Population, 2008

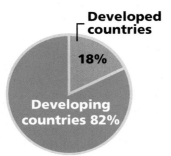

Developed countries 18%

Developing countries 82%

SOURCE: UN Population Division

People in developed countries such as Japan often work in offices. Most have access to education and healthcare.

Developing countries such as Guatemala have fewer industries. People often have lower life expectancies and literacy rates.

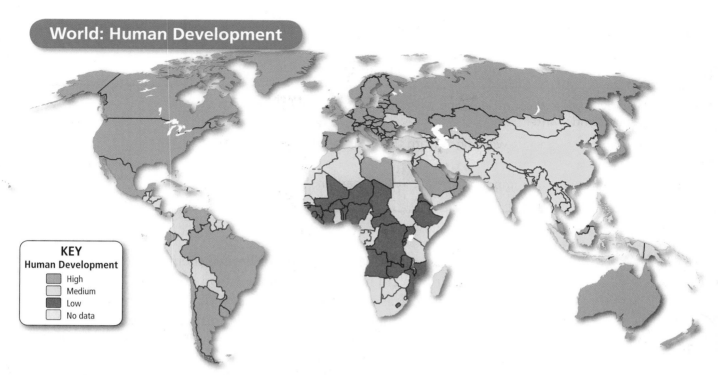

World: Human Development

KEY
Human Development
- High
- Medium
- Low
- No data

Increasing Development

A country can increase economic development in many ways. It can find more resources to use in creating products. It can invest in capital goods such as factories and equipment. It can improve education and training to increase human capital. Human capital is workers' skill and knowledge.

Highly skilled workers usually earn higher wages, or money paid for work. Wages are also affected by supply and demand. If there is a high demand for workers and a limited supply of applicants, companies must pay higher wages to attract workers.

A country can improve development by increasing **productivity,** or the amount of goods and services produced given the amount of resources used. A business that increases productivity can produce goods and services more efficiently. More productive workers often earn higher wages.

Improved technology can lead to economic growth. **Technology** is the practical application of knowledge to accomplish a task. Technological advances can create new products, such as computers. They can make it easier for people to communicate and do business. However, it can be difficult for poor countries to afford new technology.

Assessment

1. What factors do economists use to study development?

2. How might economic factors affect the use of technology in various places, cultures, and societies?

Trade

Key Ideas

- Individuals and countries trade with one another to get the things they need and want.
- Many countries are working toward the removal of trade barriers.

Key Terms • trade • export • import • tariff • trade barrier • free trade

 Visual Glossary

In the past, most people grew or hunted their own food. They made their own clothing. They built their own homes. In short, people did nearly everything for themselves. Today, however, most people depend on others to supply the goods and services they need. Our world is interdependent. That is, people and countries depend on one another for goods and services.

Trade and Geography

To get the products we need and want, we engage in trade. **Trade** is the exchange of goods and services in a market. When individuals engage in trade, they do so because they gain from that trade. In other words, trade benefits both the buyer and the seller.

Geographic location can give a country or region advantages in trade. For example, a region that is close to an ocean can more easily ship goods overseas. On the other hand, a manufacturing plant located far away from a market will need to add transportation costs to its products, making them higher in price.

Container ships, such as the ones in this photo, carry most of the world's goods from one port to another. ▼

Types of Trade

All of the buying and selling that takes place within a country is known as domestic trade. Domestic trade involves producers and consumers located inside the same country.

Domestic producers and consumers can also engage in international trade, or trade with foreign producers and consumers. International trade involves exports and imports. **Exports** are goods and services produced within a country and sold outside the country's borders. **Imports** are goods and services sold in a country that are produced in other countries. International trade requires a system for exchanging types of currency.

Trade Barriers and Free Trade

If imported goods are cheaper than domestic goods, consumers will usually buy more of them. These lower prices can harm domestic producers by reducing their sales. Governments sometimes try to protect domestic producers through tariffs. A **tariff** is a tax on imports or exports. Tariffs are an example of trade barriers. A **trade barrier** is a government policy or restriction that limits international trade.

Today, many countries are working toward **free trade,** or the removal of trade barriers. Free trade gives consumers lower prices and more choices. However, domestic producers can suffer if consumers prefer cheaper imported goods.

United States and China: Trade

Goods exported from China to the United States
- Household goods, $58.4 billion
- Computers, $53.7 billion
- Clothing and shoes, $51.5 billion

Goods exported from the United States to China
- Computers, $8.6 billion
- Aircraft, $7.5 billion
- Machinery, $7.2 billion

Assessment

1. How might geography affect the locations of economic activities?

2. How might scarcity encourage international trade and make countries interdependent?

Money Management

Key Ideas
- People must manage money to have enough for their needs and wants.
- Many people save and invest money.

Key Terms • budget • saving • interest • credit • investing • stock • bond ⊙ **Visual Glossary**

Money is anything that is generally accepted as payment for goods and services. Money is a scarce resource that people must manage to have enough for their needs and wants. Because people's needs, wants, and incomes can change, it is important to plan ahead.

Budgeting, Saving, and Lending

A key tool in money management is a budget. A **budget** is a plan that shows income and expenses over a period of time. A budget's income should be equal to or greater than its expenses. A budget should also include money reserved for saving. **Saving** is the act of setting aside money for future use. Many people save by using banks. A bank is a business that keeps money, makes loans, and offers other financial services. Credit unions are nonprofit banks owned by their members.

A man uses an automated teller machine (ATM) to access his bank account. ▼

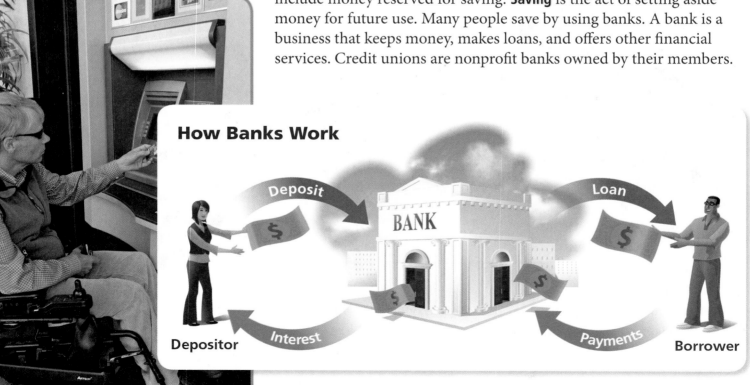

How Banks Work

Deposit
Loan
BANK
Depositor
Interest
Payments
Borrower

Many people who save money in banks do so using checking or savings accounts. Banks may pay interest on money deposited in these accounts. **Interest** is the price paid for borrowing money. Interest is an incentive for people to save money.

Banks use deposits to make loans to people and businesses around the world. These loans help people buy houses or make other large purchases. They help businesses get started or grow. As a result, banks are a big part of economic growth.

Loans are a form of credit. **Credit** is an arrangement in which a buyer can borrow to purchase something and pay for it over time, such as by using a credit card. Banks and other lending organizations charge borrowers interest on loans. As a result, it costs more for a borrower to purchase a good using credit than to pay cash for the good at the time of purchase.

Investing

Investing is the act of using money in the hope of making a future profit. Some people invest in stocks, bonds, or mutual funds. A **stock** is a share of ownership in a company. A **bond** is a certificate issued by a company or government promising to pay back borrowed money with interest. A mutual fund is a company that invests members' money in stocks, bonds, and other investments.

▲ Stockbrokers buy and sell stocks and bonds for investors at places such as the New York Stock Exchange.

Investments offer different levels of risk and return—the amount of money an investor might earn. In general, the safest investments offer the lowest rates of return. For example, a savings account is very safe, but it pays a relatively low rate of interest. Stocks are riskier but can earn a great deal of money for an investor if they increase in value. On the other hand, stocks can decline in value and become worth less than the stockholder paid. Bonds are less risky than stocks, but they usually offer a lower rate of return.

Assessment

1. How do banks function?

2. Why do people invest money in stocks, bonds, and mutual funds?

Economics and Geography
Part 5 Assessment

Key Terms and Ideas

1. **Recall** What is the most common type of economy today?

2. **Define** What is a **tariff** and why do governments sometimes use them?

3. **Paraphrase** Explain the relationship among **revenue, profit,** and the costs of doing business.

4. **Sequence** How does increased **productivity** affect business owners, employees, **consumers,** and entire nations?

5. **Explain** What is **opportunity cost**?

6. **Identify Cause and Effect** What role does risk play in investment?

7. **Identify** What level of economic activity includes mining? What level includes medical care?

Think Critically

8. **Draw Conclusions** What problems or issues might a company face if it has a shortage of one or more factors of production?

9. **Decision Making** How do societies organize and make decisions about the production of goods and services?

10. **Draw Inferences** How do factors such as location, physical features, and distribution of natural resources influence the economic development of societies?

11. **Summarize** How do government policies affect free market economies such as the U.S. economy?

Identify

Answer the following questions based on the map.

12. What kind of trade is shown on this map?

13. What is a major U.S. export?

14. What is a major U.S. import?

15. What are three goods that the United States produces?

16. What are three goods that Mexico produces?

17. What possible area of competition is shown on this map?

18. The United States and Mexico participate in free trade. What U.S. industries might free trade help or hurt?

United States and Mexico: Trade

UNITED STATES

MEXICO

U.S. exports to Mexico:
Petroleum products
Plastics
Chemicals
Automobile parts
Electronics

Mexican exports to the United States:
Petroleum
Fruits and vegetables
Electronics
Computers
Automobiles

Journal Activity

Fill in the graphic organizer in your Student Journal.

Demonstrate Your Understanding Complete the Sum-It-Up activity in your journal to demonstrate your understanding of economics and geography. After you complete the activity, discuss your answers with the class. Be sure to support your answers with information from the lessons.

21st Century Learning

Search for Information on the Internet

China had a command economy for many years, but since the 1970s the government has reduced its control over the economy. Use the Internet to research China's changing economy. Create a timeline to share your findings. Use a variety of online sources, including
- encyclopedias
- national and international newspapers
- magazines and journals

Document-Based Questions

Success Tracker™
Online at myworldgeography.com

Use your knowledge of economics and geography and Documents A and B to answer Questions 1–3.

Document A

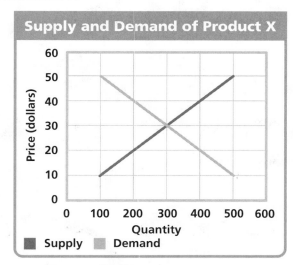

Supply and Demand of Product X

Document B

UN Human Development Index (HDI) Values, 2005	
Nation	**HDI Value**
Iceland	0.968
Samoa	0.785
Sierra Leone	0.336

SOURCE: *CIA World Factbook*

1. Examine Document A. Which of the following statements is true?

A As the price of Product X increases, demand for it decreases.

B As the price of Product X decreases, its supply increases.

C As the price of Product X increases, demand for it increases.

D As the price of Product X decreases, its supply does not change.

2. Examine Document B. The Human Development Index is a UN measure of levels of economic development and well-being in a country. Countries with higher HDI values have higher levels of development. Which of the following statements is true?

A Samoa is less developed than Sierra Leone.

B Samoa is more developed than Iceland.

C Sierra Leone and Iceland are very different in terms of development level.

D Sierra Leone is more developed than Iceland.

3. Writing Task A nation's rating in the UN Human Development Index is influenced by GDP per capita and people's education, literacy, and life expectancy. Why are these factors important to a country's development?

my worldgeography.com   Self-Test

Population and Movement

U.S. and Mexican flags

Automobiles line up to cross the busy U.S.–Mexican border. ▲

U.S. students in a classroom

Ludwig Barragan

Searching for a New Home

Story by Miles Lemaire for myWorld Geography

Anyone who has ever moved to a new place knows that it can be hard to make friends and adjust to a new school. Moving to a different country can be even more challenging. You can ask Ludwig Barragan, who moved to the United States from Mexico a few years ago.

Like many other people, Ludwig and his mother decided to move in search of more opportunities and a better life. "My position in Mexico was fine economically," says Ludwig, "but I wanted to receive an education that I knew I wouldn't be able to get in Mexico. I love my country, yet the [school] system there was not what I wanted."

Ludwig and his mother moved to McAllen, Texas, a city on the U.S.–Mexican border. He looked forward to learning more about American culture and society.

Life in McAllen was an adjustment for Ludwig and his mother. "I would say that when you live so close to the border you live in a different world," Ludwig says. "You live in a place that is neither the U.S. nor Mexico."

Ludwig found that there were a number of different cultural groups in McAllen. "The number of immigrants [in] McAllen was huge," Ludwig says, "and there was a large community in my high school that spoke only Spanish. There was a second group there that were bilingual, and they were mainly people who were born in the U.S. but had parents that were from Mexico or spoke Spanish. It was hard to relate to them because … they didn't know the Mexican culture or values that I knew, yet they were not completely incorporated into the American culture."

At first, Ludwig felt that he didn't fit in. "I knew that I had to learn the language and the values even more. I tried to get in contact with the students that spoke mostly English. That's what I did and that's what helped me a lot."

Ludwig looked for ways that he could learn about the customs of his adopted country. He eventually joined the Junior Reserve Officers Training Corps (JROTC). The JROTC is a citizenship and military program supported by the U.S. armed forces. Ludwig says that the JROTC taught him much about life in the United States.

"My friends in Mexico made fun of me because here I was, a Mexican, carrying the U.S. flag with the JROTC," remembers Ludwig. "At first I said, 'Yeah, it's kind of weird,' but then later I realized that I don't have to feel bad about it. I chose this country because I love it and it doesn't mean that I love Mexico any less. I think … the beauty of immigration is that you can learn to love both cultures. I feel honored that I had a chance to carry the U.S. flag."

Population Growth

Key Ideas
- Earth's population has grown quickly in recent years.
- Population growth can affect economic development and the environment.

Key Terms • demographer • birth rate • death rate • infant mortality rate

 Visual Glossary

Today, the world's population is around 7 billion. When people first began farming around 12,000 years ago, it was fewer than 10 million. Earth's population grew slowly, eventually reaching 1 billion by 1800. Since then, better food production and healthcare have caused a population boom.

Measuring Growth

Demographers are scientists who study human populations. They measure the rate at which a population is growing. To do this, demographers compare birth rates and death rates. The **birth rate** is the number of live births per 1,000 people in a year. The **death rate** is the number of deaths per 1,000 people in a year. When the birth rate is higher than the death rate, a population tends to grow. Population can also change when people move into or out of a region.

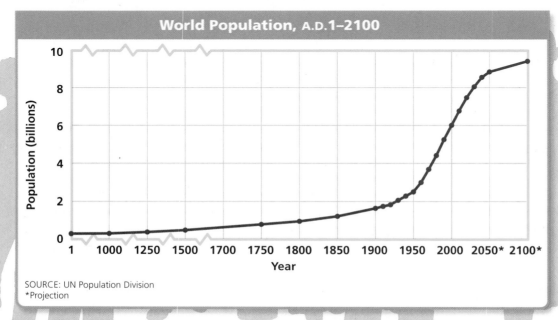

World Population, A.D.1–2100

SOURCE: UN Population Division
*Projection

Causes and Effects of Population Growth

Improvements in hygiene, such as this water purifier in Uganda, can lead to population growth.

Causes of Growth

Until about two hundred years ago, the global birth rate was only slightly higher than the death rate. As a result, the population grew slowly. Then came the Industrial Revolution, which brought many changes.

Better medical care saved many lives. Improvements in food production increased the food supply and made food healthier. Living conditions improved. These and other changes led to a much lower death rate in most regions. By 1950, the world's population had begun to soar.

In Haiti, population growth has led to to overcrowding and poor living conditions. ▼

Effects of Growth

Population growth can have positive effects. For example, a growing population can produce and consume more goods and services. This can improve a country's standard of living. However, rapid population growth can also cause problems. The population can grow faster than the supply of food, water, medicine, and other resources.

The problems caused by rapid population growth are greatest in poor developing countries. A lack of clean food and water can lead to widespread starvation and disease. In these places, the **infant mortality rate**—the number of infant deaths per 1,000 births—is high.

The environment often suffers as well, as people use up resources to survive. Pollution is common. People cut down forests for firewood or clear land for farming. This can lead to desertification, or the spread of dry desert-like conditions. A lack of fertile soil makes it even harder to grow enough food.

Assessment

1. How are the birth rate and death rate used to measure population growth?
2. If the population of your town suddenly doubled, how might your daily life change?

75

Population Distribution

Key Ideas
- The distribution of a population can vary greatly within an area.
- Population density has important effects on an area.

Key Terms • population distribution • population density

Visual Glossary

A country's population is the total number of people living within its borders. That number can be large or small. Geographers study a country's population to learn more about life in that country.

Population Distribution

Population distribution is the spreading of people over an area of land. The world's population is distributed unevenly on Earth's surface. Some places have many people. Other places are almost empty. What factors lead people to live where they do?

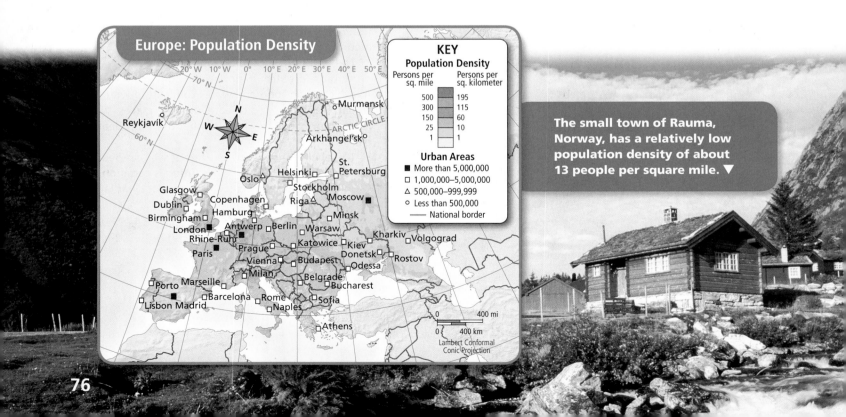

Europe: Population Density

KEY
Population Density

Persons per sq. mile	Persons per sq. kilometer
500	195
300	115
150	60
25	10
1	1

Urban Areas
- ■ More than 5,000,000
- □ 1,000,000–5,000,000
- △ 500,000–999,999
- ○ Less than 500,000
- —— National border

0   400 mi
0   400 km
Lambert Conformal
Conic Projection

The small town of Rauma, Norway, has a relatively low population density of about 13 people per square mile. ▼

People try to live in places that meet their basic needs. Natural obstacles such as oceans, mountains, and extremely cold or hot weather limit the areas where people can live easily. Throughout human history, most people have lived in areas with fertile soil, fresh water, and mild climates. Regions with good soil and plenty of water became crowded. Places that were too cold or dry for farming never developed large populations.

After about 1800, improved transportation and new ways of making a living changed things. As factories and industries grew, the ability to farm became less important. Industrial centers and large cities could develop in regions that were less suited for farming. Today, population tends to be highest in areas that were centers of early farming, industry, or trade.

Population Density

Population density is the number of people per unit of land area. It is expressed as the number of people per square mile or square kilometer. Population density gives us a way to describe how thickly settled an area is. It also lets us compare places of different sizes and populations. The density figure for any country is an average. Population density can vary greatly from one part of a country to another.

Population density has some important effects on a region. The more people there are per square mile, the more crowded a place is. Cities with high population densities tend to have crowded roads and living conditions. These places require many resources to meet people's needs. Places with low population densities tend to have more undeveloped land.

London, in the United Kingdom, has a very high population density, about 13,000 people per square mile. ▼

Assessment

1. How are population distribution and population density different?
2. How might a rapid increase in a region's population density change the region?

Core Concepts 6.3

Migration

Key Ideas
- People move from one place to another for a number of reasons.
- People may move within a country or from one country to another.

Key Terms • migration • emigrate • immigrate • push factor • pull factor

 Visual Glossary

For thousands of years, people have migrated to new places. **Migration** is the movement of people from one place to another. Scientists believe that more than 50,000 years ago, a group of early humans migrated from Africa to Asia. Over many years, their descendants spread slowly across Asia and Europe. Some crossed from Asia to the Americas.

Forms of Migration

People often migrate within a country. In modern times, this internal migration has largely been movement to cities from the countryside. People generally migrate to cities to find jobs.

In the 1800s, many people migrated from Europe to the United States in search of a better life.

People also move from one country to another. When people leave their home country, they **emigrate,** which means to migrate out of a place. To enter a new country is to **immigrate,** or to migrate into a place. Moving to another country can lead to big changes in a person's life. For example, people moving to a new country may have to learn a new language and new customs. Mass migration can greatly change a region's culture and society. Migration can also affect a region's government, economy, and environment.

Reasons for Migration

People who migrate are often looking for a better life. They may move to escape poverty, a lack of jobs, or a harsh climate. In some countries, war or other conflict forces people to migrate. These reasons for migration are known as push factors. **Push factors** are causes of migration that push people to leave their home country.

Other reasons for migration are known as pull factors. **Pull factors** pull, or attract, people to new countries. One example of a pull factor is a supply of good jobs.

People generally migrate because they choose to do so. For example, millions of Europeans chose to migrate to the United States during the 1800s and early 1900s. Some of these people were Irish, fleeing a shortage of food. Others were Jews

These immigrants to the United States become U.S. citizens at a naturalization ceremony.

escaping persecution, or mistreatment. Millions more have come from Asia and Latin America since then.

History is also full of involuntary migrations. For the most part, these involved the forced movement of enslaved people. In the late 1400s European slave traders began buying and selling captured Africans. They shipped most of these enslaved people to the Americas. As many as 10 million enslaved Africans were forced to migrate to the Americas.

Assessment

1. Why did Europeans migrate to the United States in the 1800s and early 1900s?

2. Suppose your family migrated after a flood destroyed your home. Would the flood be considered a push factor or a pull factor? Explain.

Core Concepts 6.4

Urbanization

Key Ideas
- Cities around the world have grown quickly over the last two hundred years.
- The growth of cities has created many challenges.

Key Terms • urban • rural • urbanization • slum • suburban sprawl

Visual Glossary

Panama City, Panama, had a population of 171,000 in 1950. By 2025, it is expected to grow to 2.4 million.

1950s

Panama City, Panama

Today

In many parts of the world, people are migrating to urban areas from rural areas. **Urban** areas are cities. **Rural** areas are settlements in the country. In China, for example, many new jobs have been created in cities in recent years. As a result, many rural Chinese workers have moved to cities in search of jobs. This process is known as urbanization. **Urbanization** is the movement of people from rural areas to urban areas.

The Shift from Rural to Urban

Over the last two hundred years or so, billions of people around the world have left rural agricultural areas to move to cities. In 2008, for the first time in history, more than half of the world's population lived in cities and towns.

In Europe and North America, urbanization began in the 1800s as modern industry developed. As a result, people moved to cities in search of jobs in factories and other businesses. Today, urbanization is happening most quickly in Asia and Africa. In those places, people move to cities in search of jobs, education, and better lives for their children.

Challenges of Urbanization

Rapid urbanization has created challenges for growing cities, especially those in poor countries. In some cases, cities simply have more people than they can handle. These cities cannot provide the housing, jobs, schools, hospitals, and other services that people need. One result is the spread of **slums,** or poor, overcrowded urban neighborhoods. Slums exist in cities around the world. Most people in slums live in run-down buildings or shacks. They are unable to meet their basic needs, such as enough food and clean water.

Urbanization can also create challenges in wealthy countries. Today, most large urban areas have a central core city. The core city has stores, office buildings, government buildings, and some housing. In wealthier countries, most people live in the suburbs surrounding the core city. As the population of a wealthy urban area grows, so does suburban sprawl. **Suburban sprawl** is the spread of suburbs away from the core city.

As suburbs spread, they replace farmland and other open spaces. New sewer lines, water lines, and roads must be built and maintained by the government. Because most people in suburbs use cars for transportation, suburban sprawl can increase pollution and energy use. Today, many towns and cities are working to limit sprawl.

Mumbai, India, had a population of 2.9 million in 1950. By 2025, it is expected to grow to 26.4 million.

1950s

Mumbai, India

Today

World Urbanization

30%
70%
1950

53% 47%
2000

30%
70%
2050*

■ Rural population ■ Urban population

SOURCE: UN Population Division
*Projected

Assessment

1. What are some causes of urbanization?
2. Think about living in a suburb versus living in the center of a city or town. List a few things you might like or dislike about each.

Part 6 Assessment

Key Terms and Ideas

1. **Identify** Define the terms **birth rate** and **death rate.**

2. **Summarize** Describe the process of **urbanization**.

3. **Recall** Name three negative effects of rapid population growth.

4. **Define** What is **migration**?

5. **Compare and Contrast** What is the difference between a **pull factor** and a **push factor**?

6. **Recall** What is **population density**?

7. **Explain** What factors affect **population distribution**?

Think Critically

8. **Draw Inferences** How do you think world population patterns might change in the future?

9. **Compare Viewpoints** What arguments could be made for living in an area that has a high population density or in one with a low population density? Explain your views.

10. **Synthesize** During the 1800s, millions of Europeans migrated to the United States. Identify at least one possible push factor and one possible pull factor behind this mass migration.

11. **Solve Problems** Imagine that you are a member of a city government that is trying to limit urban growth. What steps might you suggest?

Identify

Answer the following questions based on the map.

12. Describe London's population.

13. Which cities have populations between 500,000 and 1,000,000?

14. Which city is located at 0° longitude?

15. In general, where are the areas in the United Kingdom with the highest population density?

16. Describe Cardiff's population.

17. Which city is closest to 50° N latitude?

18. Which is the westernmost city shown on the map?

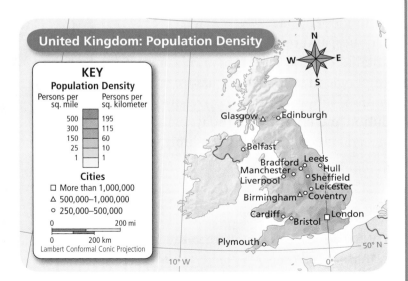

United Kingdom: Population Density

KEY

Population Density

Persons per sq. mile	Persons per sq. kilometer
500	195
300	115
150	60
25	10
1	1

Cities
□ More than 1,000,000
△ 500,000–1,000,000
○ 250,000–500,000

0   200 mi
0   200 km
Lambert Conformal Conic Projection

Journal Activity

Fill in the graphic organizer in your Student Journal.

Demonstrate Your Understanding Complete the Sum-It-Up activity in your journal to demonstrate your understanding of population and movement. After you complete the activity, discuss your predictions as a class. Be sure to support your predictions with information from the lessons.

Analyze Media Content

Find examples of recent articles about immigration to the United States. Then create a table to compare and contrast these articles. Ask yourself the following questions when reading:
- What is the main idea of each article?
- Does the author support every statement?
- Does the author show any bias?

Document-Based Questions

Success **Tracker**™
Online at myworldgeography.com

Use your knowledge of population and movement and Documents A and B to answer Questions 1–3.

Document A

Annual Birth & Death Rates in Selected Countries		
Country	Birth Rate (per 1,000 people)	Death Rate (per 1,000 people)
Austria	8.7	9.9
Chad	41.6	16.4
Pakistan	28.4	7.9
Sri Lanka	16.6	6.1
United States	14.2	8.3

SOURCE: *CIA World Factbook*

Document B

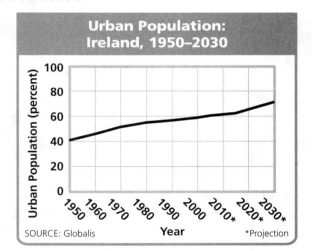

Urban Population: Ireland, 1950–2030

SOURCE: Globalis   Year   *Projection

1. Examine Document A. How does population growth in the United States most likely compare with that in Pakistan and Chad?

   A It is much faster.

   B It is much slower.

   C It is much faster than growth in Pakistan but slower than growth in Chad.

   D It is much faster than growth in Chad but slower than growth in Pakistan.

2. Examine Document B. What might be one cause for Ireland's changing rate of urbanization?

   A more dependence on agriculture

   B a higher death rate

   C growth in industry

   D housing shortages

3. **Writing Task** How do you think a graph showing urban population in Asia since 1950 might compare to Document B? Explain your answer.

Culture and Geography

Tepees at a Native American powwow

Native American dancers

Joanna Baca (at right) dances at a powwow.

Joanna Baca

Exploring Culture Through Dance

Story by Miles Lemaire for myWorld Geography

When Joanna Baca and her family moved to Las Vegas, Nevada, from the Native American Navajo reservation in Shiprock, New Mexico, she looked for things that reminded her of home—and her Navajo culture.

"Most of our family stayed back home," Joanna says. "After we first moved here [Las Vegas], we didn't think there was anyone out here that was Native American, and it actually took us a while to find someone we knew."

In an effort to make their new city feel like home, Joanna and her family looked for community organizations that promoted Native American culture. Joanna eventually discovered the Las Vegas Indian Center. Among other things, this organization helps Native American high school students apply to and get accepted at colleges.

"[The Center helps] Native American kids find out what colleges are good for them," Joanna says. "They teach us that college is possible for Native American kids, not just for the kids that live on the reservation, but for kids who live in the city, too."

The more time Joanna spent with the organization, the closer she felt to her Navajo culture. She decided that she wanted to get involved in more aspects of Native American culture, especially traditional forms of dance.

Joanna had grown up going to powwows with her family. A powwow is a gathering where Native American people dance, sing, and honor Native American cultures. "I'd just see all the dancers there and how beautiful they were," Joanna remembers. She decided that she wanted to learn more about Native American dance. "I did ballet, jazz, and hip-hop before, and I thought they were fun," she says, "but I wanted to do something cultural, because dancing is a big part of my culture."

It has been several years since Joanna first started studying and performing Native American dances. She loves how these traditional forms of dance help her connect to her culture. But she also thinks dance is a wonderful way for non-Native American people to learn more about native culture.

"We go to events where they have dancers from all over the world, and they'll have a bit of everyone's culture in this one little get-together," Joanna says. "So we shared food, we were part of the dancing there, and a lot of people were like, 'Oh that's nice, I've never seen that type of dance before, what kind is that?' We'd tell them that it's Navajo, or native and … it got them very interested. Some of those people would come to the show again just to see our part of the performance and to see what it was all about."

85

Core Concepts 7.1

What Is Culture?

Key Ideas
- Every culture has a distinctive set of cultural traits.
- Earth has thousands of different cultures.

Key Terms • culture • cultural trait • norm • culture region • cultural landscape

 **Visual Glossary**

French Quebec Culture Region

CANADA   Quebec

UNITED STATES

0   500 mi
0   500 km

Lambert Azimuthal Equal-Area Projection

120° W   110° W   100° W   90° W   80° W   70° W

50° N

40° N

30° N

N
W   E
S

Culture Regions

A **culture region** is an area in which a single culture or cultural trait is dominant. In Canada, French Canadian culture dominates much of the province of Quebec. The people of Quebec who have this culture identify themselves as French Canadian or Québécois (kay bek WAH).

All people have the same basic needs and wants, such as food, clothing, and shelter. But different cultures respond to those needs and wants in different ways. **Culture** is the beliefs, customs, practices, and behaviors of a particular nation or group of people.

Where Culture Comes From

The features that make up a culture are known as cultural traits. A **cultural trait** is an idea or way of doing things that is common in a certain culture. Cultural traits include language, laws, religion, values, food, clothing, and many other customs. Children learn cultural traits from their parents and other adults. People also learn cultural traits from the mass media and from organizations such as schools, social clubs, and religious groups. Common cultural traits are called norms. A **norm** is a behavior that is considered normal in a particular society.

Cultural Landscapes

Human activities create **cultural landscapes**, or geographic areas that have been shaped by people.

◄ Bolivia

Left, Egypt; below, Ukraine

86

Some cultural traits remain constant over many years. But culture can change over time as people adopt new cultural traits. For example, the way Americans dress today is very different from the way Americans dressed 100 years ago.

The environment can also affect culture. For example, the environment of a region influences how people live and how they earn their living. Humans can also shape their environment by creating cultural landscapes. The cultural landscape of a place reflects how its people meet their basic needs for food, clothing, and shelter. These landscapes differ from one culture to another.

Culture and Geography

Earth has thousands of different cultures and culture regions. In a specific culture region, people share cultural traits such as religion or language.

Culture regions are often different from political units. Occasionally, a culture region may cover an entire country. In Japan, for example, nearly everyone speaks the same language, eats the same food, and follows the same customs. A country may also include more than one culture region. For example, the French Canadian culture region of Quebec is one of several culture regions in Canada.

Culture regions can also extend beyond political boundaries. For example, many of the people who live in Southwest Asia and northern Africa are Arab Muslims. That is, they practice the religion of Islam. They also share other cultural traits, such as the Arabic language, foods, and other ways of life. This region of Arab Muslim culture covers several countries.

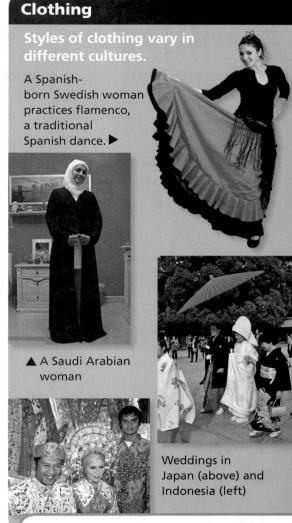

Clothing

Styles of clothing vary in different cultures.

A Spanish-born Swedish woman practices flamenco, a traditional Spanish dance. ▶

▲ A Saudi Arabian woman

Weddings in Japan (above) and Indonesia (left)

Assessment

1. Does every country form a single culture region? Explain.

2. What are some elements of the cultural landscape in the area where your school is located?

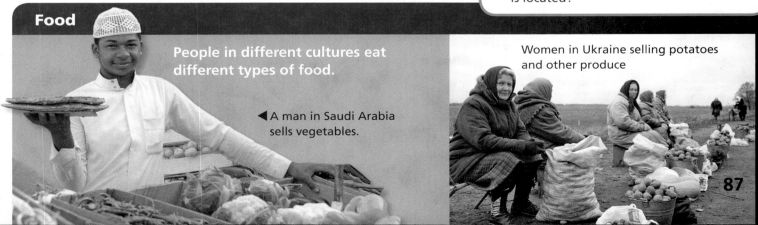

Food

People in different cultures eat different types of food.

◀ A man in Saudi Arabia sells vegetables.

Women in Ukraine selling potatoes and other produce

87

Families and Societies

Key Ideas
- The most basic unit of any society is the family.
- Family structures vary in different cultures, but every society has organized relationships among groups of people.

Key Terms • society • family • nuclear family • extended family • social structure • social class

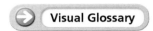
Visual Glossary

Culture, society, and family are all related. A **society** is a group of humans with a shared culture who have organized themselves to meet their basic needs. Societies can be large or small. A group of a few dozen hunter-gatherers is a society. So is a country of more than a billion people, such as India or China.

Kinds of Families

The most basic unit of any society is the family. A **family** is two or more people who are closely related by birth, marriage, or adoption. Traditionally, one person heads a family. A man has been the head of the family in many societies throughout history. Today, however, men and women often share this responsibility.

Family structures vary in different cultures. Two common family units are the nuclear family and the extended family. A **nuclear family** is a family that consists of parents and their children. An **extended family** is a family that includes parents, children, and other family members, such as grandparents, aunts, uncles, and cousins. Extended families are more common in developing countries. In some places, extended families work together on farms. In other places, relatives work separately but live together in order to share resources.

Nuclear and extended families are two kinds of family unit.

Nuclear Family

Extended Family

Kinds of Societies

Every society has a social structure. A **social structure** is a pattern of organized relationships among groups of people within a society. People interact with one another, with groups, and with institutions. For example, you have ties to friends and family members. You probably attend a school. You may also take part in a sports team or some other group. Adults have ties to coworkers and to economic institutions such as businesses and banks. Families may also have ties to religious institutions, such as a church, a synagogue, or a mosque.

Societies vary around the world and can change over time. All societies have some common institutions. These include government, religious, economic, and educational institutions.

Societies also have differences. One basic difference has to do with a society's economy. Some societies rely mainly on farming. Others depend on industry.

Industrial societies often organize members according to their social class. A **social class** is a group of people living in similar economic conditions. In modern societies, the main groupings are upper class, middle class, and lower (or working) class. The size of the world's middle class has increased greatly in recent years.

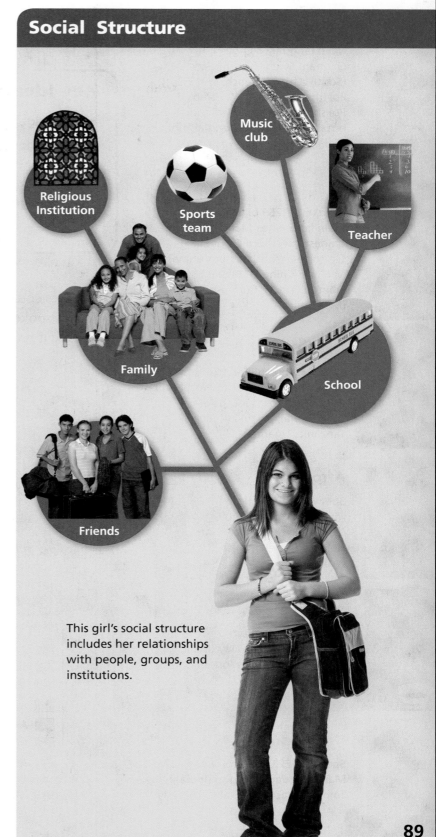

Social Structure

Religious Institution

Music club

Sports team

Teacher

Family

School

Friends

This girl's social structure includes her relationships with people, groups, and institutions.

Assessment

1. What aspects of culture do all societies share?
2. What aspects of culture differ among societies?

89

Indo-European

Speakers 2.722 billion
Main languages English, German, Swedish, Afrikaans (South Africa), French, Spanish, Portuguese, Italian, Russian, Polish, Farsi (Iran), Hindi (northern India), Bengali (Bangladesh, India), Greek

Sino-Tibetan

Speakers 1.259 billion
Main languages Mandarin Chinese (northern China), Cantonese (southeastern China), Min Nan Chinese (Taiwan), Tibetan (Tibet), Burmese (Myanmar)

Niger-Congo

Speakers 382 million
Main languages Ibo and Yoruba (Nigeria), Xhosa (South Africa), Twi (Ghana), Swahili (Kenya, Tanzania, Uganda)

Afro-Asiatic

Speakers 359 million
Main languages Arabic (Southwest Asia, North Africa), Hebrew (Israel), Hausa (West Africa)

Austronesian

Speakers 354 million
Main languages Malay (Malaysia), Javanese (Indonesia), Tagalog (Philippines), Maori (New Zealand)

Dravidian

Speakers 223 million
Main languages Telugu (India), Tamil (India, Sri Lanka)

90

Core Concepts 7.3

Language

Key Ideas

- Language provides the basis for culture.
- Language can unify people or keep them apart.

Key Term

- language

Visual Glossary

Cultures could not exist without language. **Language** is a set of spoken sounds, written symbols, or hand gestures that make it possible for people to communicate.

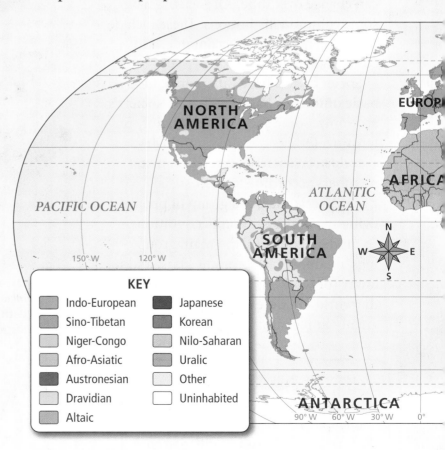

NORTH AMERICA

EUROPE

AFRICA

ATLANTIC OCEAN

PACIFIC OCEAN

SOUTH AMERICA

150° W   120° W

90° W   60° W   30° W   0°

ANTARCTICA

KEY

- Indo-European
- Sino-Tibetan
- Niger-Congo
- Afro-Asiatic
- Austronesian
- Dravidian
- Altaic
- Japanese
- Korean
- Nilo-Saharan
- Uralic
- Other
- Uninhabited

Without language, people would not be able to share information or ideas. They could not pass on cultural traits to their children.

Languages often vary from one culture to another. Within a country, differences in language can keep cultures apart and make it harder to unify the country. Language differences can also keep countries apart by preventing communication.

People who speak different languages sometimes turn to a third language in order to communicate with each other. In modern times, English has often served as the world's common language.

The map below shows the locations of the world's major language groups. Languages in each of these groups share a common ancestor. This ancestor was a language spoken so long ago that it gradually changed to become several related languages.

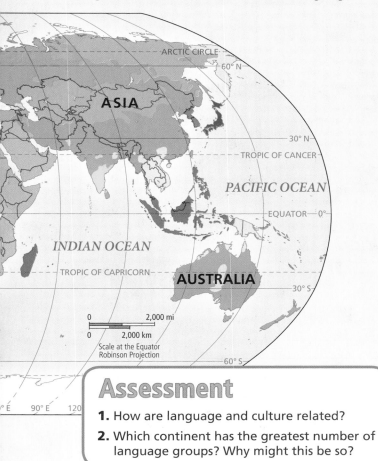

Altaic

Speakers 140 million
Main languages Turkish, Kazakh (Kazakhstan), Bashkir (Russia), Tatar (Russia), Uighur (China), Mongolian (Mongolia)

Japanese

Speakers 123 million
Spoken mainly in Japan.

Korean

Speakers 66 million
Spoken mainly in North Korea and South Korea.

Nilo-Saharan

Speakers 38 million
Main languages Luo (Kenya), Maasai (Tanzania), Kanuri (Niger)

Uralic

Speakers 21 million
Main languages Hungarian, Finnish, Estonian, Sami (Norway, Sweden, Finland), Samoyed (Russia)

Other

Speakers 394 million
These include Native American languages (North and South America), Paleosiberian languages (eastern Russia), Aboriginal languages (Australia), and languages spoken in Southeast Asia.

Assessment

1. How are language and culture related?
2. Which continent has the greatest number of language groups? Why might this be so?

Religion

Key Ideas	• Religious beliefs play an important role in shaping cultures. • The world has many different religions.

Key Terms • religion • ethics

 **Visual Glossary**

An important part of every culture is religion. **Religion** is a system of worship and belief, including belief about the nature of a god or gods. Religion can help people answer questions about the meaning of life. It can also guide people in matters of **ethics**, or standards of acceptable behavior. Religious beliefs and values help shape cultures.

Judaism

Judaism is based on a belief in one God, whose spiritual and ethical teachings are recorded in the Hebrew Bible. It began in the Middle East around 2000 B.C. By A.D. 100, Jews lived in Europe, Southwest Asia, and North Africa. The Jewish state of Israel was established in 1948. There are about 14 million Jews.

Christianity

Christianity is based on the teachings of Jesus, who Christians believe was the son of God. The Christian Bible is their sacred text. Christianity began in Southwest Asia around A.D. 30 and spread to Europe and Africa. It later spread to the rest of the world. There are about 2.07 billion Christians.

Islam

Islam is based on the Quran, a sacred text. The Quran contains what Muslims believe is the word of God as revealed to Muhammad beginning in A.D. 610. Islam spread quickly across Southwest Asia and North Africa, then to the rest of the world. There are about 1.25 billion Muslims.

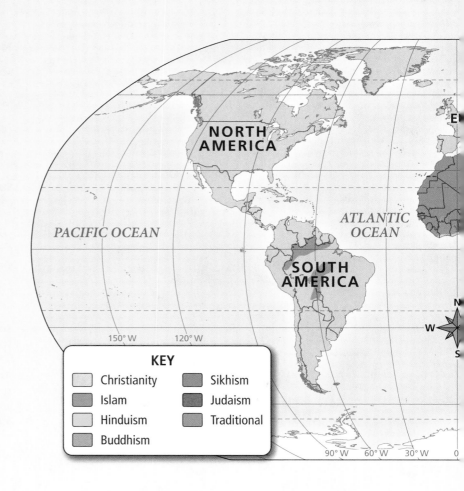

KEY

☐ Christianity	☐ Sikhism
☐ Islam	☐ Judaism
☐ Hinduism	☐ Traditional
☐ Buddhism	

The world has many religions. Jews, Christians, and Muslims believe in one God. Members of other religions may believe in several gods.

All religions have prayers and rituals. Followers also observe religious holidays. For example, Jews celebrate the world's creation on Rosh Hashanah and their escape from slavery in Egypt on Passover. On Yom Kippur, Jews seek forgiveness for their wrongdoings. Christians celebrate Jesus' birth on Christmas and his return to life on Easter. For Muslims, the holy month of Ramadan is a time to avoid food during daytime, to pray, and to read the Quran.

The world's major religions began in Asia. Hinduism, Buddhism, and Sikhism first developed in India. Judaism, Christianity, and Islam began in Southwest Asia before spreading throughout the world.

Hinduism

Hinduism evolved gradually over thousands of years in South Asia. It has several sacred texts. Hindus believe that everyone in the universe is part of a continuing cycle of birth, death, and rebirth. There are about 837 million Hindus.

Buddhism

Buddhism is based on the teachings of Siddhartha Gautama, known as the Buddha, who was born in India about 563 B.C. The Buddha's teachings include the search for enlightenment, or a true understanding of the nature of reality. There are about 373 million Buddhists.

Sikhism

Sikhism is based on the writings of several gurus, or prophets. Guru Nanak founded Sikhism about A.D. 1500 in South Asia. Sikhism's teachings include the cycle of rebirth and the search for enlightenment. There are about 24 million Sikhs.

Traditional Religions

Traditional religions include thousands of distinct religions. These religions tend to be passed down by word of mouth instead of through sacred texts. Each has its own set of beliefs. Examples include many African religions.

ARCTIC CIRCLE
60° N

ASIA

30° N
TROPIC OF CANCER

PACIFIC OCEAN

EQUATOR — 0°

INDIAN OCEAN

TROPIC OF CAPRICORN

AUSTRALIA
30° S

0   2,000 mi
0   2,000 km
Scale at the Equator
Robinson Projection
60° S

ANTARCTIC CIRCLE

ANTARCTICA
60° E   90° E   120° E   150° E

Assessment

1. How does religion help shape a culture?

2. What does the map tell you about the major religion where you live?

A print of
a fish by
Japanese artist
Katsushika
Taito, 1848

The Arts

Key Ideas
- Art is an important part of culture.
- Works of art can reveal much about society.

Key Terms
- universal theme
- visual arts
- architecture
- architect
- music
- literature

 Visual Glossary

The arts are an important aspect of culture. Works of art can reflect a society by dealing with topics or issues that are important to that society. Art can even shape society. For example, books that describe poverty or environmental problems can help win public support for solving those problems. Art can also deal with universal themes. A **universal theme** is a subject or idea that relates to the entire world. For example, the paintings of Pablo Picasso, the songs of the Beatles, and the written works of William Shakespeare deal with the universal themes of love, death, peace, and war.

Visual Arts

Art forms meant to be seen, such as painting, sculpture, and photography, are known as the **visual arts.** The visual arts can express emotions and spiritual ideas. They can also show us what life is like in other cultures and how people lived in the past. For example, a painting created in Italy in 1600 can show us how Italian people lived during this period.

Architecture

Architecture is the design and construction of buildings. A person who designs buildings is an **architect.** Architecture can show us what a society values and how it uses its resources. For example, are a society's most impressive buildings its religious buildings or its government buildings? Architectural works can be important cultural symbols.

This art museum in Bilbao, Spain, was designed by architect Frank Gehry.

Music

Music is an art form that uses sound, usually produced by instruments or voices. Music varies widely in different societies and cultures. It also changes over time as our tastes change. What one person considers beautiful music might be unpleasant noise to someone from a different place or time period. As a result, music can tell us about a society's tastes.

A Peruvian man plays a flute near the Inca ruins at Machu Picchu, Peru.

Literature

Literature is written work such as fiction, poetry, or drama. Literature can tell us what ideas a society considers important. By describing harmful things in society, literature can push for change.

A performance of Shakespeare's
A Midsummer Night's Dream

Assessment

1. What are two ways in which the arts are related to society?
2. What might a painting of a main street in your area tell a stranger about your society?

95

Cultural Diffusion and Change

Key Ideas
- Cultures change over time.
- Cultural traits can spread from one culture to another.

Key Terms • cultural hearth • cultural diffusion • diversity  Visual Glossary

Chinese people in France celebrate the Chinese New Year.

All cultures change over time. That is, their cultural traits change. In general, for a new cultural trait to be adopted by a culture, it must offer some benefit or improvement over an existing trait.

How Cultural Traits Spread

A **cultural hearth** is a place where cultural traits develop. Traits from cultural hearths spread to surrounding cultures and regions. Customs and ideas can spread in many ways, including settlement, trade, migration, and communication. **Cultural diffusion** is the spread of cultural traits from one culture to another.

In the 1500s, Spanish explorers and settlers brought horses to the Americas. Many native peoples saw the advantages of using horses for moving quickly and for hunting. Horses soon became part of some Native American cultures.

Cultural traits can also spread through trade. Traders can move among different cultures. As they travel, they carry with them elements of their own culture, such as food or religious beliefs. Traders expose people to these new traits. If people find that an unfamiliar religion or other cultural trait improves their lives, they may make it a part of their own daily lives. For example, hundreds of years ago, Muslim traders helped spread Islam from Arabia to other cultures in Asia and Africa.

In a similar way, migrants spread cultural traits. Migrants bring cultural traditions with them to their new homelands. Over time, many migrants, or immigrants, have come to the United States. Immigrants have brought with them foods, languages, music, ideas, and other cultural traits. Some of these new ways of doing things have become part of American culture.

Technology and Culture

Technology also helps spread culture. The Internet, for example, has made instant communication common. Today, Americans can find out instantly what people in places such as Peru, India, or Japan are wearing, eating, or creating. If we like some of these traits, we may borrow them and make them a part of our culture.

Rapid transportation technologies, such as airplanes, make it easier for people to move all over the world. As they travel, people may bring new cultural traits to different regions.

Cultural change has both benefits and drawbacks. If customs change too quickly, people may feel that their culture is threatened. Some people worry that rapid communication is creating a new global culture that threatens diversity. **Diversity** is cultural variety. These people fear that the things that make people and cultures unique and interesting might disappear. They worry that we might end up with only a single worldwide culture.

Assessment

1. Why do cultures change?
2. What cultural traits have you borrowed in the last few years?

Cultural Diffusion

Food

Tomatoes are native to South America and were brought to Europe by Spanish explorers. Europeans used them in recipes that immigrants later brought to the Americas.

Language

adobe (English)

dbt (Ancient Egyptian)

Adobe is brick made of sun-dried earth and straw. The word changed over several thousand years as it moved from one language to another.

adobe (Spanish)

al-tub (Arabic)

tobe (Coptic)

Clothing

Blue jeans became popular among young Americans in the 1950s and soon spread to Europe and Asia. Today blue jeans are popular worldwide.

Core Concepts 7.7

Science and Technology

Key Ideas
- Cultures often develop along with science and technology.
- Technological advances have greatly changed human life.

Key Terms • science • irrigate • standard of living

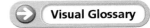 Visual Glossary

Science and technology are important parts of culture. **Science** is the active process of acquiring knowledge of the natural world. Technology is the way in which people use tools and machines.

Technology and Progress

Early humans made gradual advances in technology. About 3 million years ago, people first learned how to make tools and weapons out of stone. They later discovered how to control fire.

Technological advances changed cultures. Early humans were hunters and gatherers who traveled from place to place to find food. Later, people discovered how to grow crops. They learned how to adapt plants to make them more useful. They tamed wild animals for farming or used them as food. Over time, people began to rely on agriculture for most of their food.

Agriculture provided a steady food supply and let people settle in one place. As settlements grew and turned into cities, people began to create laws and governments. They developed writing. These advances led to the first civilizations, or societies with complex cultures, about 5,000 years ago.

The Roman empire's thousands of miles of roads let armies and trade goods move easily.

Evolution of the Wheel

The wheel transformed culture. Below, the Sumerian Standard of Ur, about 2600 B.C., showing chariots pulled by donkeys; at right, a covered wagon from the 1800s

Early civilizations developed new technologies that allowed people to grow more crops. People invented tools such as the plow to help increase food production. They built canals and ditches to **irrigate,** or supply water to, crops. Cultures that lacked writing developed more slowly. Over time, agriculture and civilization spread across the world.

Modern Technology

Beginning around 1800, people developed new technologies that used power-driven machinery. This was the Industrial Revolution. It led to the growth of cities, science, and many new businesses. Eventually, people developed even more advanced technologies such as automobiles, airplanes, computers, and space travel.

All of these advances in science and technology have greatly changed people's lives and raised their standard of living. **Standard of living** is the level of comfort enjoyed by a person or a society. Modern technology also helps to connect people, products, and ideas.

Political decisions and belief systems can affect the use of technology. For example, the Chinese government has limited Chinese citizens' use of the Internet. This is an attempt to control discussion of government policies and other issues. Many religions have used technology as part of their practices. For example, religious groups have used the printing press to print the Hebrew Bible, the Christian Bible, the Quran, and other holy writings. Today, some religious organizations use radio, television, and the Internet to broadcast their beliefs.

Technology and Culture	
Technological Advances	**Effects on Culture**
Control of fire	Allowed humans to cook food, have light, protect themselves from animals
Irrigation	Increased food production; allowed people to do jobs other than farming; led to growth of cities
Wheel	Led to improved transportation in the form of carts and carriages; eventually led to trains, cars, and other vehicles
Printing press	Allowed the mass production of books; spread knowledge and ideas, increasing the number of educated people
Steam engine	Steam-powered machines performed work once done by hand; people moved to cities to find work in factories.
Refrigeration	Kept food fresh and safe longer; allowed food to be shipped over long distances from farms to cities

Assessment

1. What are science and technology?

2. How do you think technology might change culture in the future?

Over time, wheels led to better forms of transportation. At left, a French bicycle poster from 1925; below, a car from the 1950s

Culture and Geography

Part 7 Assessment

Key Terms and Ideas

1. **Define** What is **culture**?

2. **Recall** What is **religion**?

3. **Summarize** Does migration cause **cultural diffusion**? Explain why or why not.

4. **Connect** Are all **cultural traits** also **norms**? Explain.

5. **Draw Conclusions** How can **language** both unify and divide cultures?

6. **Compare and Contrast** What is the difference between a **nuclear family** and an **extended family**?

7. **Explain** Explain the relationship between technology and a **standard of living**.

Think Critically

8. **Draw Inferences** As technology makes it easier for people to travel to different countries, how might world culture regions change?

9. **Make Decisions** What other aspects of culture might link people in a country who speak different languages?

10. **Identify Evidence** Give two examples of ways in which today's cultures are influenced by past cultures.

11. **Draw Conclusions** How do you think ethics guide a country's laws?

Identify

Answer the following questions based on the map.

12. What does this map show?

13. What is the most widely spoken dialect in China?

14. What do the two purple and pink colors represent on the map?

15. What does the color orange represent on the map?

16. Across from which island do Chinese speakers of the Min dialect live?

17. Which dialect is spoken just to the north of the largest area of the Min dialect?

18. Not including the areas shown on the map as "other dialects or languages," in what part of China are most non-Mandarin dialects spoken?

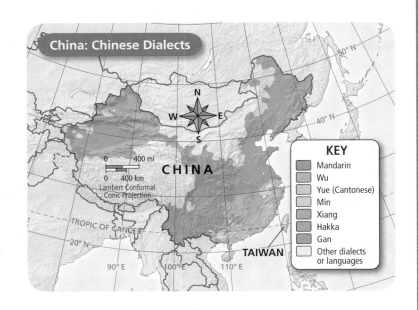

China: Chinese Dialects

KEY
- Mandarin
- Wu
- Yue (Cantonese)
- Min
- Xiang
- Hakka
- Gan
- Other dialects or languages

CHINA

TAIWAN

TROPIC OF CANCER

0   400 mi
0   400 km
Lambert Conformal Conic Projection

Journal Activity

Fill in the graphic organizer in your Student Journal.

Demonstrate Your Understanding Complete the Sum-It-Up activity in your journal to demonstrate your understanding of culture and geography. After you complete the activity, discuss your drawing with a partner. Be sure to support your answers to the questions with information from the lessons.

21st Century Learning

Work in Teams

Working with your partners, choose a country that is not familiar to anyone in your group. Then research and create an illustrated informational brochure about the country's culture. Be sure to

- provide examples of the country's art
- identify and describe the country's major religions and languages

Document-Based Questions

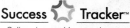

Success Tracker™
Online at myworldgeography.com

Use your knowledge of culture and geography and Documents A and B to answer Questions 1–3.

Document A

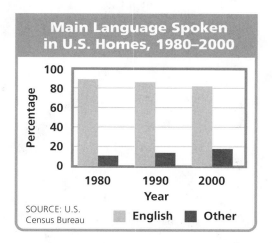

Main Language Spoken in U.S. Homes, 1980–2000
100
80
60
40
20
0
Percentage
1980
1990
2000
Year
SOURCE: U.S. Census Bureau
English
Other

Document B

"What a society [judges] important is [preserved] in its art."

—Harry Broudy

1. Examine Document A. Which of the following statements is probably true?

A Migration to and cultural diffusion to the United States are likely decreasing.

B Migration to and cultural diffusion to the United States are likely increasing.

C Migration and cultural diffusion are unrelated to the changes shown in the graph.

D Migration and cultural diffusion are no longer taking place in the United States.

2. Read Document B. Which of the following statements might Harry Broudy agree with?

A Art does not reveal clues about past societies.

B Art does not show the artist's beliefs.

C Paintings reflect culture better than music does.

D Looking at art is a good way to learn more about a society.

3. **Writing Task** Think of a favorite piece of art, such as a painting, a song, or a book. Then write one paragraph about what that piece of art reveals about your culture and beliefs.

myworldgeography.com Self-Test

Government and Citizenship

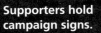
Supporters hold campaign signs.

A group of congressional interns

Voters in the 2008 presidential election

Anne Marie Sutherland

Serving Her Country

Story by Miles Lemaire for myWorld Geography

Anne Marie Sutherland has been trying to get people to vote since before she was old enough to join them at the polls.

Anne Marie is the daughter of a high school government teacher. She became interested in politics as a child. Her first experience with a political campaign was the U.S. presidential election in 1996, when she was just nine years old. "[M]y friends and I made some signs and walked up and down the street with them before the election," Anne Marie says. "We started talking to people, and we stayed up all night to see who would win."

As Anne Marie grew older, her interest in the political process increased. In 2000 and 2004, she worked as a volunteer on George W. Bush's presidential campaigns. In the 2008 presidential primaries, she helped manage candidate Mitt Romney's campaign in Atlanta, Georgia.

"We did lots of grassroots work," Anne Marie says about her work with the Romney campaign. "We were talking to different folks, getting signs out, working on some strategies for the area."

When Romney failed to win the Republican nomination for president, Anne Marie worked for 2008 Republican nominee John McCain. She looks back on her work with the Romney and McCain campaigns as a great learning experience. Most of all, she loved discussing political issues with people.

"What I took away from that opportunity was working directly with voters," Anne Marie says. "That's not something that you get to do for very long in politics [before] you move up and start taking on larger roles."

Anne Marie soon began taking on larger roles herself, winning an internship with U.S. Senator Saxby Chambliss. As part of her internship, Anne Marie helped other young people achieve their own goals. As she explains, "Every year a senator appoints a certain number of graduating [high school] seniors to the United States military academies. ... so I put most of my energy into working on that process.

"I love doing that," she says, "because what I'm able to do is [to help] prepare our future military leaders at such a young age. ... [S]ometimes when I'm working with them, I honestly think, 'This young student could really be our future president, or could be leading us in a major war, or could be the leader of any one of the branches of the military.' You never know."

Now 22 years old, Anne Marie is about to graduate from college with a degree in political science. She isn't content with helping other people achieve their dreams. "Maybe there is a campaign of my own in the future," she says. "I'd do anything I can to serve my country."

103

Foundations of Government

Key Ideas
- Governments are created to keep order in a society and provide for the people's common needs.
- A government's powers are either limited or unlimited.

Key Terms
- government
- constitution
- limited government
- unlimited government
- tyranny

 Visual Glossary

Hammurabi's Code is a set of laws created in ancient Babylon—now Iraq—around 1760 B.C. The code was carved onto a large stone slab, below. The photo at the bottom of the page shows the ruins of ancient Babylon. ▼

A **government** is a group of people who have the power to make and enforce laws for a country or area. The basic purpose of government is to keep order, to provide services, and to protect the common good, or the well-being of the people. Governments make and enforce laws to keep order. Protecting the common good can include building roads and schools or defending the country from attack. Governments also collect taxes, or required payments, from people and businesses. Governments use these taxes to pay for the goods and services they provide. The purpose of government has not changed much throughout history.

Origins of Government

Long before modern governments existed, people lived together in groups. These groups often had leaders who kept order and made decisions for the group. This was a simple form of government.

More complex governments first appeared in Southwest Asia more than 5,000 years ago. By that time, groups of people had begun to settle down. Villages grew into cities. People found that they needed an organized way to resolve problems and oversee tasks such as repairing irrigation canals and distributing food. They formed governments to manage those tasks.

Powers of Government

Today, most governments have a constitution. A **constitution** is a system of basic rules and principles by which a government is organized. A constitution also identifies the powers a government has. A government's powers are either limited or unlimited.

Limited Government

People gather in front of the U.S. Capitol.

Today, most constitutions call for limited government. **Limited government** is a government structure in which government actions are limited by law. Limited governments work to protect the common good and provide for people's needs.

In the United States, government actions are limited in order to protect people's individual freedoms. Generally, people in a limited government may gather freely to express their opinions and work to change government policies.

Unlimited Government

Chinese police arrest a protester.

Unlimited government is a government structure in which there are no effective limits on government actions. In an unlimited government such as China, a ruler or a small ruling group has the power to make all decisions for a country or society. This much power can lead to **tyranny,** which is the unjust use of power.

Unlimited governments often do not protect citizens' basic rights. They may censor, or restrict, citizens' access to the Internet and other forms of communication technology.

Assessment

1. How do constitutions limit the powers of government?

2. How do limited and unlimited governments differ?

Political Systems

Key Ideas
- Types of states have varied throughout history.
- There are many different kinds of government.

Key Terms • state • city-state • empire • democracy • nation-state • monarchy • authoritarian • communism

 Visual Glossary

A **state** is a region that shares a common government. The first real states—called city-states—developed in Southwest Asia more than 5,000 years ago. A **city-state** is an independent state consisting of a city and its surrounding territory. Later, some military leaders conquered large areas and ruled them as empires. An **empire** is a state containing several countries. Geographic features such as rivers and mountains sometimes helped governments control territory by protecting against invasion.

A man votes in Kenya's 2007 presidential election.

Democracy

Examples Direct democracy: ancient Athens; representative democracy: United States

- **Democracy** is a form of government in which citizens hold political power; citizens are the ultimate source of government power and authority.

- In a direct democracy, citizens come together to pass laws and select leaders.

- In a representative democracy, citizens elect representatives to make government decisions.

- The powers of a democratic government are usually limited.

Queen Elizabeth II of the United Kingdom

Nation-States

Today, most states are nation-states. A **nation-state** is a state that is independent of other states. The United States is an example of a nation-state. We often use the general words *nation* or *country* to refer to nation-states.

All nation-states have some common features. For example, nation-states have specific territory with clearly defined borders. Nation-states have governments, laws, and authority over citizens. Most are divided into smaller states or provinces that contain cities and towns.

Forms of Government

Each state has a government, but there are many different kinds of government. Throughout history, most states were autocracies (ruled by a single person) or oligarchies (ruled by a small group of people). Today, however, many states have some form of democracy in which citizens hold political power.

A large statue of former leader Kim Il-Sung stands above people in communist North Korea.

Monarchy

Examples Absolute monarchy: Saudi Arabia; Constitutional monarchy: United Kingdom

- A **monarchy** is a form of government in which the state is ruled by a monarch.
- A monarch is usually a king or queen.
- Power is inherited by family members.
- Absolute monarchs have unlimited power.
- Monarchs in constitutional monarchies are limited by law and share power with other branches of government.
- The powers of a monarchy can be limited or unlimited.

Authoritarian Government

Examples Nazi Germany, Cuba, North Korea

- An **authoritarian** government is one in which all power is held by a single person or a small group.
- Government may control all aspects of life.
- One of the common forms of authoritarian government is **communism**, a political and economic system in which government owns all property and makes all economic decisions.
- The powers of an authoritarian government are unlimited.

Assessment

1. What are states, city-states, and nation-states?
2. Which form of government relies most on its citizens? Explain your answer.

Political Structures

→ Visual Glossary

Key Ideas
- Political structures help governments operate in an organized way.
- The U.S. government follows basic democratic principles.

Key Terms • unitary system • federal system

Central Government

Central governments are responsible for national affairs.

U.S. Capitol

Regional Government

Regional governments include state or provincial governments.

Texas State Capitol

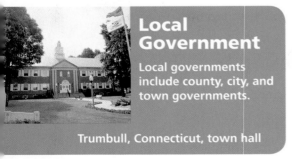

Local Government

Local governments include county, city, and town governments.

Trumbull, Connecticut, town hall

Countries distribute power between the central government and smaller units of government. We can learn more about how a government functions by examining its structure and principles.

Systems of Government

Governments can distribute power in three basic ways: the unitary system, the federal system, and the confederal system. In a **unitary system,** a central government makes all laws for the entire country. In a **federal system,** power is divided among central, regional, and local governments. In a confederal system, a group of independent states join together and give limited powers to a common government. Most countries have a unitary system. The United States and some other countries have a federal system. The confederal system is rare.

Principles of Government

Every government has basic principles that affect the way it serves its people. Authoritarian governments may seek to control all aspects of society, even people's actions and beliefs. For example, some authoritarian governments limit citizens' use of communications technology such as the Internet. Most democratic governments act to protect individual rights and the common good.

In the United States, government follows basic democratic principles. For example, government follows the rule of law. That is, government powers are defined by laws that limit its actions. Also, government decides issues by majority rule. A law cannot pass unless the majority—most—representatives vote for it. At the same time, the majority may not take away the basic rights and freedoms of minority groups or individuals. In other words, government must balance majority rule with minority rights.

Branches of Government

Under the U.S. Constitution, power is divided among the three branches of government: the legislative, executive, and judicial branches. This division is called separation of powers. The Constitution also establishes a system of checks and balances that limits each branch's power. Each branch has some power to change or cancel the actions of the other branches.

Legislative Branch

The legislative branch establishes laws. In a representative democracy like the United States, citizens elect legislative representatives to make decisions for them. The legislative branch also imposes taxes, or required payments. Taxes are used to pay for government services and public goods such as roads, parks, fire departments, and national defense. Public goods are owned by everyone in the country.

U.S. Congress

Executive Branch

The executive branch carries out, or enforces, the laws. It also provides for the country's defense, conducts foreign policy, and manages day-to-day affairs. The United States and some other countries have a presidential system with an elected president as the head of the executive branch. Other democracies, such as the United Kingdom, have a parliamentary system. In this system, the parliament, or legislative branch, chooses a prime minister as chief executive.

U.S. President Barack Obama

Judicial Branch

The judicial branch makes decisions about disputes. It does this through courts of law. These courts can range from local criminal courts to the highest court in the land. In the United States that court is called the Supreme Court. Among other things, the Supreme Court interprets the law. That is, it judges how a law should be applied and whether the law violates the Constitution.

U.S. Supreme Court

Assessment

1. What are the three branches of government?

2. What are three key democratic principles?

Conflict and Cooperation

Key Ideas
- Governments and international organizations cooperate for many reasons, including avoiding war and improving trade.
- Conflict can have serious effects on countries.

Key Terms • sovereignty • foreign policy • treaty • diplomacy

 Visual Glossary

Food being distributed in Angola. ▼

Every nation-state, or country, has clearly defined territory and sovereignty over that territory. **Sovereignty** is supreme authority, or power. Every country also has a central government. The central government takes care of matters that affect the whole country. This includes dealing with other countries' governments. Interactions between governments can take the form of conflict or cooperation.

Conflict

Most countries have a **foreign policy,** a set of goals describing how a country's government plans to interact with other countries' governments. A country's foreign policy reflects its values and intentions. Geographic factors such as location, physical features, and distribution of natural resources can influence foreign policy.

A country's foreign policy can lead to conflict with other countries. Wars and fighting begin for many reasons. Some wars begin as conflicts over control of land or resources. Others result from religious disagreements, political revolutions, or conflict between ethnic groups. Wars can lead to widespread death and destruction.

Public Health Organizations

International Red Cross and Red Crescent Movement Provides medical aid, food, and other relief services to victims of war or natural disasters

World Health Organization Fights disease, especially among the world's poor, by providing health information, medical training, and medicine

Cooperation

Many people view the world as a global community in which people should cooperate to avoid conflict and help others. This cooperation may take the form of a **treaty,** a formal agreement between two or more countries. Some treaties are agreements to help defend other countries. Other treaties are agreements to limit the harmful effects of war. For example, the Geneva Conventions list rules for the proper treatment of wounded soldiers, prisoners, and civilians.

The United Nations (UN) is the largest international organization that works for peace. Nearly every country in the world belongs to the UN. Governments send representatives to the UN to engage in diplomacy. **Diplomacy** is managing communication and relationships between countries. The UN Declaration of Human Rights lists the rights that all people should have, including life, liberty, and security. The UN works to protect these rights around the world.

Governments also cooperate for reasons other than avoiding conflict. For example, governments often work with one another to improve their countries' economies through trade. International trade can provide new goods and markets. Trade agreements involving multiple countries have become common in recent years.

This water pump in South Africa was funded by the World Bank.

Economic Organizations

World Bank Provides loans for projects aimed at promoting economic development

International Monetary Fund (IMF) Seeks to prevent and resolve economic crises by offering advice, information, technical training, and loans

Humanitarian Organizations

United Nations (UN) Seeks to encourage international cooperation and achieve world peace but sometimes faces criticism

CARE International Seeks to end world poverty through development and self-help

◄ UN peacekeeping troops in Bosnia

Assessment

1. What are some of the functions of international organizations?
2. How do governments resolve conflict and cooperate?

111

Citizenship

Key Ideas
- Citizens have basic rights, but those rights come with responsibilities.
- Rights and responsibilities can vary widely in different countries.

Key Terms
- citizen
- civic life
- civic participation
- political party
- interest group

 Visual Glossary

The United States is a representative democracy. In a democracy, all political power comes from citizens. A **citizen** is a legal member of a country. In the United States, most people become citizens by being born on U.S. territory. Immigrants to the United States can become citizens through a legal process known as naturalization.

Rights and Responsibilities

Citizens' rights and responsibilities can come from a number of sources. These sources include constitutions, cultural traditions, and religious laws.

Americans' basic rights are protected by the Bill of Rights, a part of the U.S. Constitution. The Bill of Rights and other laws protect rights such as freedom of speech and freedom of religion. If the government violates these rights, citizens can fight the injustice in court. For the most part, these rights are also guaranteed to noncitizens.

Immigrants to the United States become citizens at a naturalization ceremony. ▼

Americans also have responsibilities. For example, we have the right to speak freely, but we also have the responsibility to allow others to say things we may not agree with. Our responsibilities include a duty to participate in government and **civic life,** or activities having to do with one's society and community. Voting is both a right and a responsibility for U.S. citizens.

Rights and responsibilities can vary widely in different countries and societies. Although most democratic governments protect basic human rights, nondemocratic governments often do not. Citizens who live in autocracies or oligarchies usually cannot take part in government or express their views openly.

Citizenship Worldwide

Ideas about rights and responsibilities can change over time. Many countries have become democracies over the past 200 years. These democracies now protect basic human rights such as freedom of expression and freedom from unfair imprisonment. Some of these countries did not protect these rights in the past or did not protect these rights for all people.

Today, international trade, transportation, and communication have linked the world's people. As a result, some people think that we should consider ourselves to be citizens of a global community. They believe that we are responsible for supporting human rights and equality for all people around the world.

Assessment

1. What is the main source of American citizens' basic rights?

2. How do the roles and responsibilities of citizens vary between democratic and nondemocratic countries?

Civic Participation

Voting is one type of **civic participation**, or taking part in government. Here are some others:

- Keeping informed about local, state, and national issues
- Contacting an elected representative, such as a state legislator or member of Congress
- Voicing opinions at town meetings
- Taking part in public gatherings, protests, or demonstrations
- Signing a petition, a formal request for government to do something
- Running for public office
- Getting involved in a political party—a group that supports candidates for public offices
- Joining an interest group—a group that seeks to influence public policy on certain issues

113

Part 8 Assessment

Key Terms and Ideas

1. **Recall** There are two types of democracy: direct and representative. Which kind of **democracy** is the United States?

2. **Identify** Describe the powers of an **unlimited government.**

3. **Connect** Why did **governments** first develop thousands of years ago?

4. **Describe** How does the U.S. government balance legislative, executive, and judicial power?

5. **Compare and Contrast** How are the **unitary system** and the **federal system** similar and different?

6. **Paraphrase** Explain **diplomacy** in your own words.

7. **Identify** Name two ways American **citizens** can participate in the political process.

Think Critically

8. **Draw Inferences** Consider that you can freely read about your government's actions and policies on the Internet. How might Internet access differ in a country with an authoritarian government?

9. **Make Decisions** Do you think that people who live in a democracy should be required to fulfill their civic responsibilities?

10. **Synthesize** Imagine that a country shares its borders with three others. How do you think its geography might relate to its foreign policy?

11. **Draw Conclusions** Who do you think is more likely to speak out against the government: a citizen in a limited government or a citizen in an unlimited government? Explain.

Identify

Answer the following questions based on the map.

12. Which country is the westernmost member of the European Union?

13. Which EU members border Latvia?

14. List the EU members with territory located to the north of 60° N latitude and to the east of 0° longitude.

15. Which EU members border Slovenia?

16. How many members made up the European Union in 2009?

17. What sea do Spain and Greece border?

18. How would you describe EU membership?

European Union, 2009

KEY

☐ European Union member states

0   400 mi

0   400 km

Lambert Conformal
Conic Projection

Journal Activity

Fill in the graphic organizer in your Student Journal.

Demonstrate Your Understanding Complete the Sum-It-Up activity in your journal to demonstrate your understanding of government and citizenship. After you complete the activity, discuss your If-Then statements with a small group. Be sure to support your statements with information from the lessons.

21st Century Learning

Analyze Media Content

Authoritarian governments usually allow little media freedom. Find political news articles from authoritarian and democratic countries. Then compare and contrast them in a short essay. Remember to
- include excerpts from a variety of articles
- discuss how the government might influence what is published

Document-Based Questions

Success Tracker™
Online at myworldgeography.com

Use your knowledge of government and citizenship and Documents A and B to answer Questions 1–3.

Document A

U.S. Presidential Elections: Eligible Voter Participation, 1980–2008

Percentage of Eligible Voters

Year	Percentage
1980	54.2%
1984	55.2%
1988	52.8%
1992	58.1%
1996	51.7%
2000	54.2%
2004	60.1%
2008	61.7%

SOURCE: U.S. Election Project, George Mason University

1. Examine Document A. How has eligible voter participation changed in the time period shown?

A It has declined steadily.

B It has increased steadily.

C It has declined since 1996.

D It has increased since 1996.

Document B

" The accumulation of all powers, legislative, executive, and judiciary, in the same hands, whether of one, a few, or many … may justly be pronounced the very definition of tyranny."

—James Madison, *The Federalist,* No. 48

2. Read Document B. Which of the following statements would James Madison agree with?

A Separate branches of government are unnecessary.

B Unlimited government is not a form of tyranny.

C Separate branches of government are essential.

D A unitary system of government is ideal.

3. **Writing Task** Do you agree or disagree with James Madison? Write a short essay in which you respond to Madison's quotation. Be sure to explain your position clearly, supporting it with information from the lessons.

my worldgeography.com   Self-Test

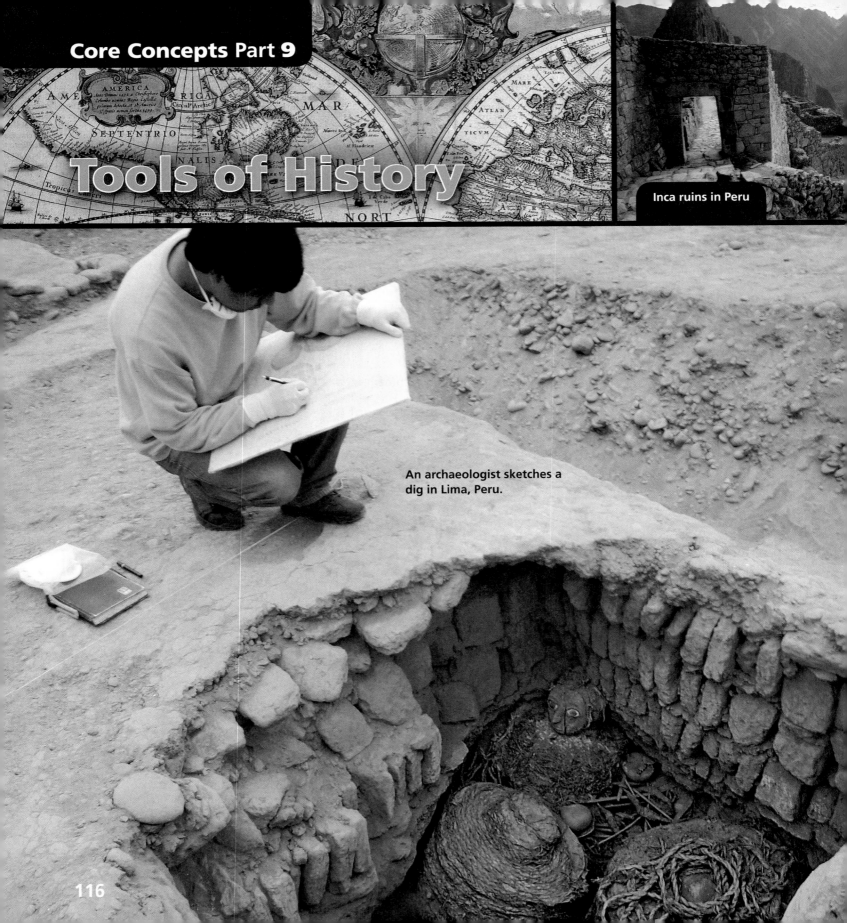

Tools of History

Inca ruins in Peru

An archaeologist sketches a dig in Lima, Peru.

Archaeologists at a dig

Brian McCray

Digging for Clues

Story by Miles Lemaire for myWorld Geography

Brian McCray likes to dig in the dirt. But Brian isn't just playing around. He's an archaeologist who has traveled around the world to dig up objects from the past and learn more about the people who made them.

Carrying out an archaeological dig isn't as simple as picking a location, grabbing a shovel, and starting to dig, Brian says. He spends weeks or months researching the history of the dig's location before a shovel goes into the ground. Brian will study maps, look at photographs, and read written descriptions of the area. He wants to know as much as possible about the site before he begins to explore it.

Once an archaeological dig begins, archaeologists like Brian carefully examine all the objects found at the site. Then they record and save the objects for future research. Keeping good records is very important. All archaeological sites are drawn and mapped carefully, with detailed information about where each object was found. It can take months or years to fully examine all of the artifacts, or objects made by people, found at an archaeological site.

"The things that are deeper in the ground are, in most cases, older than the things closer to the surface," says Brian. "We keep track of every layer of soil and what we find there."

Brian's research has allowed him to travel throughout the Americas. He has studied sites in the northern United States, the Caribbean, and western South America. Brian has worked with the Digital Archaeological Archive of Contemporary Slavery. This research has helped historians learn more about the lives of enslaved Africans in North America and the Caribbean. But his most interesting discovery was in the Andes Mountains in South America. In the Andes, Brian studied something that researchers still don't fully understand.

"It was actually what appears to be a swimming pool," Brian says. "It was constructed by the Incas at the very end of the Incan Empire." That was almost 500 years ago.

What was the "pool" used for? "Who knows?" Brian says. "It was a big sunken court with really amazing cut-stone masonry and five or six canals bringing water down into it from up the hill … It's way too cold up there for anyone to want to swim all that often."

But although Brian and his fellow archaeologists don't yet know why the Incas built this pool, you can be sure that they'll keep digging to find out the answer. Who knows? Maybe Brian will be the one to finally uncover the truth.

Core Concepts 9.1

Measuring Time

Key Ideas
- Throughout history, societies and cultures have organized time in different ways.
- People have used a number of different calendars to measure time.

Key Terms • historian • timeline • chronology • period • prehistory

 Visual Glossary

It can be hard to describe the concept of time. But **historians**—people who study events in the past—know that organizing time is important if we want to understand past events.

Using a Timeline

Historians use timelines as a tool. A **timeline** is a line marked off with a series of events and dates. Historians use timelines to put events in a **chronology,** a list of events in the order in which they occurred.

A timeline is flexible. It can cover a day, a year, a decade (ten years), a century (one hundred years), a millennium (one thousand years), or any other period in history. A **period** is a length of time singled out because of a specific event or development that happened during that time. A period is also known as an era or an epoch. Historians use periods and eras to organize and describe human activities.

The timeline on this page shows watershed events—important points in history. The period 1940–1949 is an example of a decade, or a period of ten years. Below, a Sumerian writing tablet. ▼

A.D. **1945** World War II ends.

| 1940 | 1941 | 1942 | 1943 | 1944 | 1945 | 1946 | 1947 | 1948 | 1949 |

3200 B.C. Sumerians develop the earliest known form of writing.

| **3000** B.C. | **2000** B.C. | **1000** B.C. | A.D. **1** | A.D. **1000** | A.D. **2000** |

1766 B.C. China's Shang dynasty begins.

A.D. **250** Maya Classic period begins in Mexico and Central America.

A.D. **1492** Christopher Columbus sails to the Americas.

Organizing Time

The past is often split into two parts, prehistory and history. **Prehistory** is the time before humans invented writing. *History* refers to written history, which began about 5,200 years ago.

We can also organize history by beginning with a key event from the past. Today much of the world uses the believed birthdate of Jesus as a key event. Years before that event are labeled B.C., for "before Christ," or B.C.E., for "before common era." Years after Jesus's birth are labeled A.D., meaning *anno Domini,* Latin for "in the year of our Lord." These years are also known as C.E., for "common era."

The Jewish calendar counts the years since the creation of the world, according to Jewish tradition. The Islamic calendar is dated from the year that the prophet Muhammad moved to the city of Medina.

Throughout history, societies have used different calendars. Maya and Aztec priests made calendars for farming and religious purposes. Today much of the world uses the Gregorian calendar, which has a 365- or 366-day year. It is based on the movement of Earth around the sun. The Jewish year, based on both sun and moon, varies from 353 to 385 days to adjust to the solar year. The Islamic year, however, is based on the cycles of the moon and lasts about 354 days.

Calendar Systems

Calendars are based on the movements of Earth, the moon, the stars, or a combination. Throughout history, people have used different methods to create calendars. The objects shown here were all different ways of measuring the passage of time.

Astrolabe This astrolabe was used by Muslim astronomers to calculate the positions of the sun, moon, planets, and stars. ▶

◀ **Aztec Calendar Stone** The Aztecs had two calendars: a 365-day agricultural calendar and a 260-day religious calendar.

Roman Calendar Early Roman calendars were based on the movements of the moon and had 10 months and 304 days. Later, the calendar had 12 months and 355 days. ▶

Assessment

1. How do people organize time?

2. If you created a timeline of everything you did yesterday, what would you choose to be the first event? What would be the last event? How would you decide which events are important enough to include on the timeline?

Historical Sources

Key Ideas
- Historical sources can provide important information.
- Historians must evaluate the accuracy and reliability of sources.

Key Terms • primary source • artifact • secondary source • bias

> ⊙ **Visual Glossary**

Historians try to accurately understand and describe the past. To understand past events, historians study historical sources.

Primary and Secondary Sources

A **primary source** is information that comes directly from a person who experienced an event. It consists of what the person writes, says, or creates about the event. Primary sources include letters, diaries, speeches, and photographs. Artifacts are also primary sources. An **artifact** is an object made by a human being, such as a tool or a weapon. We use primary sources to understand events from the points of view of people who lived at the time in which they happened.

Books, articles, movies, and other sources that describe or make sense of the past are secondary sources. A **secondary source** is information about an event that does not come from a person who experienced that event.

This U.S. poster created during World War II is an example of a primary source. ▼

Primary Sources

Letters written by soldiers are primary sources.

> ❝ Yesterday, December 7, 1941—a date which will live in infamy—the United States of America was suddenly and deliberately attacked by naval and air forces of the empire of Japan . . . No matter how long it may take us to overcome this premeditated [planned] invasion, the American people in their righteous might will win through to absolute victory. ❞
>
> —President Franklin D. Roosevelt, December 8, 1941

Evaluating Historical Sources

Historical sources do not always give a true account of events. Even primary sources can be wrong or misleading. An author's personal opinions may have influenced what he or she recorded. Sometimes the author may not remember the event accurately. A historian must decide what, if anything, to trust in a primary source.

A historian must also be cautious when using secondary sources. Not all secondary sources are equally reliable. For example, the Internet includes millions of well-researched articles, books, and other reliable secondary sources. However, any Internet search will also find many inaccurate Web sites.

Historians and students of history—like you—must evaluate a source to determine its reliability. When you examine primary and secondary sources, ask yourself questions like these:

- Who created the source material? A witness to an event may be more trustworthy than someone looking back at the event from a later time. However, a scholar or publication with a good reputation is also a reliable source. For example, a college professor who specializes in Chinese history would be a reliable source on China.
- Is the information fact or opinion? A fact is something that can be proved true or false. An opinion is a personal belief. Opinions are valuable not as a source of facts but as a clue to the author's judgments or feelings.
- Does the material seem to have a bias? A **bias** is an unfair preference for or dislike of something. Biased material often leaves out facts that do not support the author's point of view.

The painting and article below are secondary sources. ▼

Secondary Sources

❝ Japanese planes attacked the U.S. naval base at Pearl Harbor, Hawaii, on December 7, 1941.... This disaster caused the American public to support an immediate American entry into the war. ❞

—*History of Our World*, Prentice Hall, 2008

Assessment

1. What is a primary source?
2. Which online source will likely be more accurate, an encyclopedia or a personal journal such as a blog? Explain.

Archaeology and Other Sources

Key Idea
- Archaeology and other historical sources offer clues to what life was like in the distant past.

Key Terms
- archaeology
- anthropology
- oral tradition

→ (Visual Glossary)

Machu Picchu, Peru, is an Incan city abandoned in the 1500s and largely forgotten until the 1800s.

Archaeologists Louis and Mary Leakey found many fossil remains of human ancestors in Africa's Olduvai Gorge.

The Temple of Inscriptions in Palenque, Mexico, contains the tomb of the Maya ruler Pakal, who died in A.D. 683. ▼

Over time, much of the ancient world has disappeared. Large cities have collapsed into ruins. Buildings are buried under layers of soil and sand or covered by thick forests. The artifacts that show what life was like in ancient times are often buried or hidden. The science of archaeology aims to uncover this hidden history. **Archaeology** is the scientific study of ancient cultures through the examination of artifacts and other evidence.

Archaeologists and Anthropologists

Archaeologists are part treasure hunters and part detectives. They explore the places where people once lived and worked, searching for artifacts such as tools, weapons, and pottery. Archaeologists study the objects they find to learn more about the past.

Artifacts can help us identify the resources available to ancient people. They can help us understand how these people used technology and how they adapted to their environment.

Anthropology also helps historians understand the past. **Anthropology** is the study of humankind in all aspects, especially development and culture. Anthropologists seek to understand the origins of humans and the ways humans developed physically. This field often involves studying fossils—bones and other remains that have been preserved in rock.

Anthropologists also try to determine how human cultures formed and grew. Clues to the past can come from a culture's oral traditions. **Oral tradition** is a community's cultural and historical background, passed down in spoken stories and songs.

New Zealand's Maori people have passed down many aspects of their culture through oral tradition. ▼

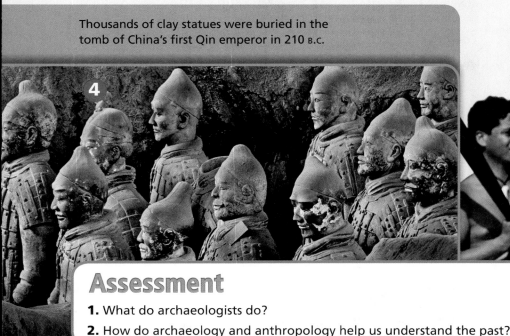

Thousands of clay statues were buried in the tomb of China's first Qin emperor in 210 B.C.

4

5

Assessment

1. What do archaeologists do?

2. How do archaeology and anthropology help us understand the past?

Historical Maps

Key Ideas
- Historical maps offer visual representations of historical information.
- Historical maps show information about places at certain times.

Key Term • historical map

 Visual Glossary

When you read about a historical event like an important battle, it can be hard to get a clear picture of what really happened. You may have to understand how landforms like rivers and hills affected the battle. Or perhaps the location of a nearby town, railroad, or road influenced the fighting. Sometimes the best way to learn about a historical event or period is by examining a historical map.

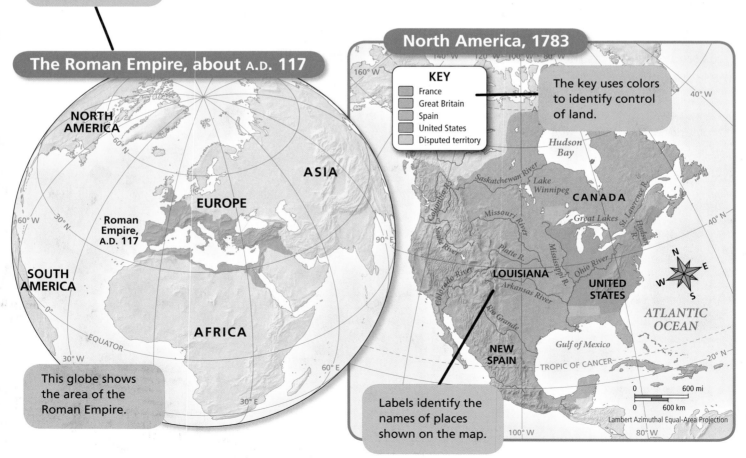

The title identifies the map's subject and time period.

The Roman Empire, about A.D. 117

NORTH AMERICA

ASIA

EUROPE

Roman Empire, A.D. 117

SOUTH AMERICA

AFRICA

EQUATOR

This globe shows the area of the Roman Empire.

North America, 1783

KEY
- France
- Great Britain
- Spain
- United States
- Disputed territory

The key uses colors to identify control of land.

Hudson Bay

Saskatchewan River

Lake Winnipeg

CANADA

Columbia R.

Missouri River

Great Lakes

St. Lawrence R.

Snake River

Platte R.

Mississippi R.

Hudson R.

Ohio River

Colorado River

LOUISIANA

Arkansas River

UNITED STATES

Rio Grande

ATLANTIC OCEAN

NEW SPAIN

TROPIC OF CANCER

Gulf of Mexico

Labels identify the names of places shown on the map.

0   600 mi

0   600 km

Lambert Azimuthal Equal-Area Projection

124

A **historical map** is a special-purpose map that provides information about a place at a certain time in history. Historical maps can show information such as migration, trade patterns, or other facts.

Historical maps have similar features. Most have a title and a key. Most use colors and symbols to show resources, movement, locations of people, or other features. Use the following four steps to become familiar with historical maps.

1. Read the title. Note the date, the time span, or other information about the subject of the map. If the map includes a locator map, examine it to see what region is shown.

2. Study the map quickly to get a general idea of what it shows. Read any place names and other labels. Note any landforms.

3. Examine the map's key. Pick out the first symbol or other entry, read what it stands for, and find an example on the map. Repeat this process for the remaining key entries until you understand them all.

4. Study the map more thoroughly. Make sure you have a clear understanding of the picture the map presents. If you need help, reread the related section of your textbook or examine the map again.

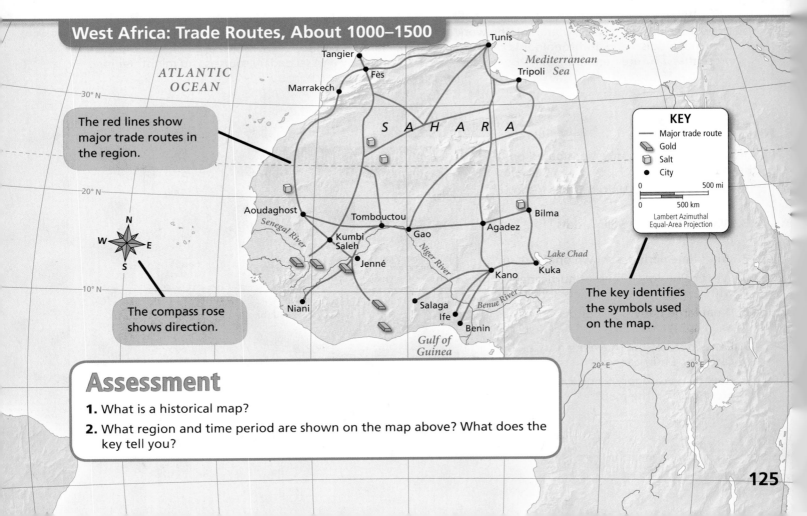

West Africa: Trade Routes, About 1000–1500

The red lines show major trade routes in the region.

The compass rose shows direction.

The key identifies the symbols used on the map.

KEY
— Major trade route
Gold
Salt
• City

0   500 mi
0   500 km

Lambert Azimuthal
Equal-Area Projection

Assessment

1. What is a historical map?

2. What region and time period are shown on the map above? What does the key tell you?

Part 9 Assessment

Key Terms and Ideas

1. **Summarize** What is **archaeology**?

2. **Identify** When a person who did not experience an event describes the event, is the description a **primary source** or a **secondary source**?

3. **Compare and Contrast** Explain the difference between history and **prehistory.**

4. **Identify Cause and Effect** What do archaeologists do with **artifacts**?

5. **Synthesize** How do **timelines** show historical events or periods?

6. **Identify** What do **historical maps** show?

7. **Recall** What three questions should you ask when evaluating a source?

Think Critically

8. **Make Decisions** Imagine that you are creating a map that will show ancient trade routes. Name three things you might include in the map's key.

9. **Draw Conclusions** How do you think the work of archaeologists and anthropologists can help present and future generations?

10. **Draw Inferences** Why do you think so many different calendars still exist today?

11. **Analyze Primary and Secondary Sources** Imagine that you are writing a biographical profile of a famous political leader. Give examples of reliable primary and secondary sources you might use in your research.

Identify

Answer the following questions based on the map.

12. What area of the United States is shown on the map?

13. What do the light yellow dots represent?

14. What time period is shown on the map?

15. What color dots represent hurricanes with the highest wind speeds?

16. What large body of water borders Texas and Louisiana?

17. List two states that have been struck by category 4 hurricanes.

18. How many category 5 hurricane strikes are shown on the map?

Southeastern United States: Hurricane Strikes, 1980–2007

KEY

Sustained winds (mph)	Category at strike
74–95	○ Category 1
96–110	○ Category 2
111–130	◑ Category 3
131–155	◐ Category 4
more than 155	● Category 5

North Carolina
South Carolina
Georgia
Mississippi
Alabama
Texas
Louisiana
Florida
ATLANTIC OCEAN
Gulf of Mexico

30° N

0   200 mi
0   200 km

Albers Conic Equal-Area Projection

TROPIC OF CANCER

Journal Activity

Fill in the graphic organizer in your Student Journal.

Demonstrate Your Understanding Complete the Sum-It-Up activity in your journal to demonstrate your understanding of the tools of history. After you complete the activity, discuss your plan for using historical resources with a small group. Be sure to support your plan with information from the lessons.

21st Century Learning

Develop Cultural Awareness

Oral tradition remains an important part of many cultures. Research a song or story still passed on by oral tradition today, either in your own culture or in another. Then share the song or story with the class. Be sure to address the following topics:
- Origins of the song or story
- Cultural significance of the song or story

Document-Based Questions

Success Tracker™
Online at myworldgeography.com

Use your knowledge of the tools of history and Documents A and B to answer Questions 1–3.

Document A

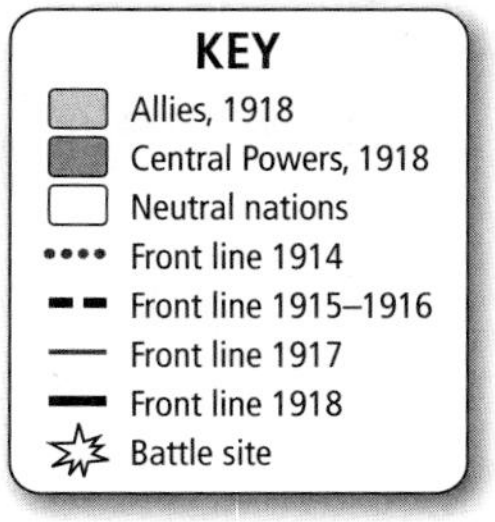

KEY
- Allies, 1918
- Central Powers, 1918
- Neutral nations
- •••• Front line 1914
- ▪ ▪ Front line 1915–1916
- ── Front line 1917
- ━━ Front line 1918
- ⚔ Battle site

Document B

" [Alexander] was only twenty years old when he succeeded to the crown, and he found the kingdom torn into pieces by dangerous [groups of people]."

— Plutarch, *Life of Alexander,* about A.D. 100

1. Document A is a key to a historical map showing Europe during World War I. What information does this map not give you?

   A location of front line in 1917

   B locations of battles

   C members of the Central Powers in 1918

   D outcome of World War I

2. Document B is an excerpt about the ancient Greek leader Alexander the Great, written by a historian about 400 years after Alexander's death. Which of the following best describes this excerpt?

   A primary source

   B secondary source

   C artifact

   D prehistoric

3. **Writing Task** Using information from Documents A and B and your knowledge of the tools of history, describe how historians use sources to understand and explain historical events.

The United States and Canada

The United States and Canada occupy the North American continent. This region has fertile plains, rugged mountains, and large metropolitan areas. The two countries share a common border and similar climates, including temperate and arctic regions.

What time is it there?

Washington, D.C.	Ottawa, Ontario
9 A.M. Monday	9 A.M. Monday

ARCTIC OCEAN

ARCTIC CIRCLE

60° N

PACIFIC OCEAN

CANADA

Ottawa

UNITED STATES

ATLANTIC OCEAN

Washington, D.C.

30° N
30° W

KEY
— National border
✪ Capital city
Orthographic Projection

TROPIC OF CANCER

Gulf of Mexico

120° W   90° W   60° W

The Unit Ahead

→ **Chapter 1** The United States

→ **Chapter 2** Canada

my worldgeography.com

Plan your trip online by doing a Data Discovery Activity and watching the myStory Videos of the region's teens.

my Story

Vy
Age: 18
Home: Texas, United States

Chapter 1

my Story

Alyssa
Age: 19
Home: Alberta, Canada

Chapter 2

Niagara Falls

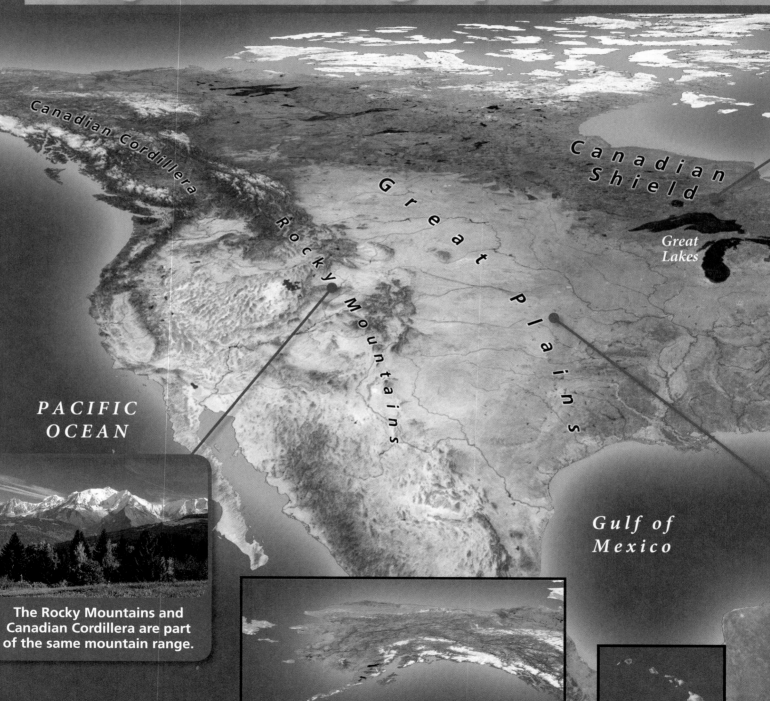

Regional Overview
Physical Geography

Canadian Cordillera

Canadian Shield

Great Lakes

Rocky Mountains

Great Plains

PACIFIC OCEAN

The Rocky Mountains and Canadian Cordillera are part of the same mountain range.

Gulf of Mexico

The Canadian Shield, with its thousands of lakes and bays, covers more than half of Canada.

Appalachian Mountains

ATLANTIC OCEAN

The Appalachian Mountains are the oldest mountain range in North America.

The Great Plains are found in the central areas of both countries and sustain farming.

Regional Flyover

Suppose you fly in an airplane across the continent of North America. If you began on the west coast of the United States, you would fly over the coastal mountain ranges, the Sierra Nevada ranges, then the Rocky Mountains. These mountain ranges extend along the entire Pacific coast of both the United States and Canada. They are part of the Canadian Cordillera, or "parallel mountain ranges."

As you traveled eastward, the Great Plains would appear, spreading across the interior of the United States and Canada. To their north, the Canadian Shield stretches to beyond the Arctic Circle. There in Canada's Arctic Region, many islands are permanently covered by snow and ice.

If you continued flying east you would cross the Mississippi River, which flows from the northern United States to the Gulf of Mexico. Soon you would arrive on the east coast of the United States. You would have flown more than 2,500 miles and covered an entire continent.

→ **In-Flight Movie**

Take flight over North America and explore the region from the air.

my worldgeography.com In-Flight Movie

131

Regional Overview
Human Geography

Where People Live

During the 1900s, large numbers of people living in the United States and Canada moved from rural areas to cities. Many were attracted to urban areas by the prospect of increased job opportunities and higher pay.

Urban Population, 1900

0 500 mi
0 500 km
Lambert Azimuthal
Equal-Area Projection

40° N
120° W
TROPIC OF CANCER
20° N
20° N
158° W 156° W
22° N
100° W

KEY
Urban Population, 1900
3,500,000
300,000
30,000
1900 U.S. Census
1901 Canadian Census

Urban Population, 2000

0 500 mi
0 500 km
Lambert Azimuthal
Equal-Area Projection

40° N
120° W
TROPIC OF CANCER
20° N
20° N
158° W 156° W
22° N
100° W

KEY
Urban Population, 2000
22,000,000
3,500,000
43,000
2000 U.S. Census
2001 Canadian Census

Immigrants arriving at Ellis Island, New York

Modern-day Toronto

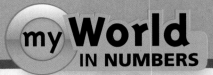

my World
IN NUMBERS

Between 1910 and 2007, many people emigrated to the United States and Canada. As you can see from the graphs, the places of origin of the people who moved to the United States changed over time.

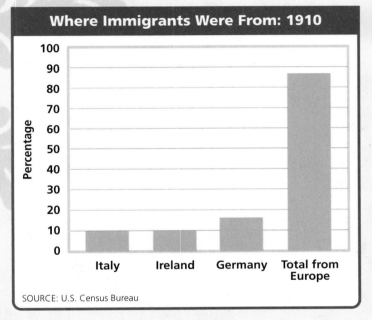

Where Immigrants Were From: 1910

Percentage (y-axis: 0 to 100)

Italy, Ireland, Germany, Total from Europe

SOURCE: U.S. Census Bureau

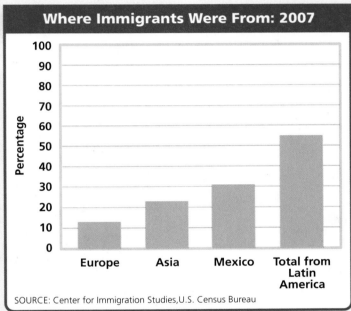

Where Immigrants Were From: 2007

Percentage (y-axis: 0 to 100)

Europe, Asia, Mexico, Total from Latin America

SOURCE: Center for Immigration Studies, U.S. Census Bureau

Put It Together

1. What physical features are common to both the United States and Canada?

2. What physical feature might keep northern Canada from being more settled?

3. Compare the places of origin of immigrants who settled in the United States in 1910 and 2007.

Data Discovery

Find your own data to make a regional data table.

Size Comparison

Including Alaska and Hawaii, the United States is two percent smaller than Canada.

my worldgeography.com Data Discovery

Chapter 1

The United States

How can you measure success?

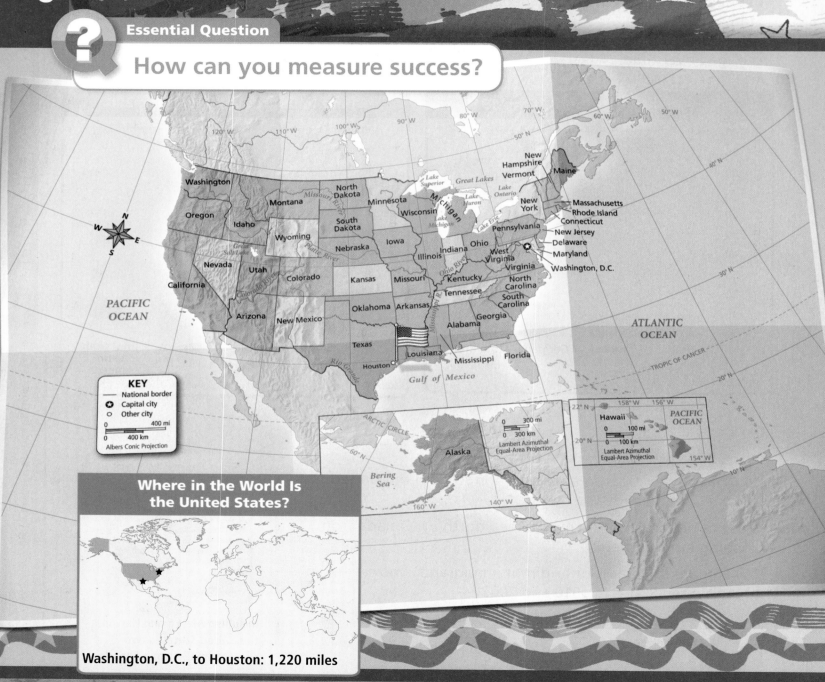

KEY
- National border
- ★ Capital city
- ○ Other city

0 — 400 mi
0 — 400 km
Albers Conic Projection

Where in the World Is the United States?

Washington, D.C., to Houston: 1,220 miles

my Story

Finding Opportunity

Explore the Essential Question
- at **my worldgeography.com**
- using the **myWorld Chapter Activity**
- with the **Student Journal**

In this section, you'll read about Vy, a young Vietnamese-American college student. What does Vy's life tell you about the opportunities immigrants have found in the United States?

Story by Jake Johnson for myWorld Geography Online

Vy is an all-American teenager. She was born in Houston, Texas, and has never faced the kind of hardships her parents and grandparents endured. Vy's parents and grandparents were born in Vietnam. They were forced to flee their native land after the fall of Saigon during the Vietnam War. Her father was only 13 when he arrived in the United States. He couldn't speak a word of English. At 18, Vy cannot speak Vietnamese.

Despite Vy's ancestry, Vietnam is a foreign and faraway place to her. She is entirely at home in the United States. Vy is one of 36,000 students who attend the University of Houston—the second-most ethnically diverse national university in the country. As a freshman, she is trying to balance academics with a job at her father's business, DI Central, a computer-related data company. She currently assists the marketing department by compiling information about customers and contacting those customers to conduct satisfaction surveys. She has yet to declare a major but thinks she might follow in her father's footsteps by focusing on business.

my worldgeography.com On Assignment

With friends, and heading home from school

Drawing comic strips

Quick to acknowledge her parents' tremendous sacrifices, Vy's greatest fear is letting them down. She feels she has been given luxuries her parents never had and should be even more successful than they've been.

Vy has her own car and her own cellphone, but she admits nothing is more important than the freedoms found in America. "I think so many people here take for granted that they can do what they want and say what they want. That's a choice not everyone gets to make in other countries," she says.

Such freedom has allowed Vy great independence. At the same time, she refuses to bury her family's roots and seems driven by her heritage. She has left behind her interest in high school sports to focus on college. Her textbooks and laptop now consume afternoons once spent at the mall. "My day starts at my dad's office at 9 a.m. and most

Vy and her sister, Ly, walk the dog.

Growing up, sports were important to Vy.

The family reconnects at dinner.

Vy working at her dad's office.

nights I don't get home until 7 or 8. I don't really have the free time that I used to." When she does have time to herself, she draws comic strips to express her feelings and plays ping-pong with her dad—a fierce opponent who, she jokes, takes the game too seriously.

Vy still lives at home. She shares a very close relationship with her two older sisters and younger brother. She credits her mother with maintaining a strong cultural bond. Her mother prepares traditional Vietnamese meals, with beef and fish dishes, and she insists the family eat together.

Three years ago, Vy took her first trip to Vietnam. Her family spent a month touring the country. The experience was bittersweet. "The cities were so dirty and so crowded, and the people seemed to have so little," says Vy. "I almost felt guilty that I had so much."

Although she still finds it impossible to imagine what her parents endured, it's a trip she says she will always treasure. Visiting Vietnam allowed Vy a unique opportunity to learn more about the land her parents call home, but she is quick to confess, "I just couldn't wait to get home and have a cheeseburger."

→ **myStory Video**

Join Vy on her trip to the city.

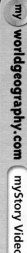
my worldgeography.com myStory Video

Meet the Journalist

Name Jake Johnson
Favorite Moment Dinner with the family

A visit to Vietnam

Essential Question

myWorld Chapter Activity

Follow your teacher's instructions to create a script for a documentary about how immigration has shaped the United States. Research major immigrant groups using the chapter activity cards and myWorld Geography online. Describe reasons people migrated, including when and where they settled, and the effect each group had on the United States.

21st Century Learning

Search for Information on the Internet

Using reliable sources online, research a civil rights leader. Using at least two resources, find and record the following information:
- Name
- Hometown
- Contribution(s) to the civil rights movement

For each source, write a sentence explaining why your source is reliable.

Document-Based Questions

Use your knowledge of the United States and Documents A and B to answer Questions 1–3.

Document A

" In the new law[s] which will be necessary for you to make, I desire you would remember the ladies. We will not hold ourselves bound by any laws in which we have no voice or representation."

—Abigail Adams to John Adams, March, 1776

" We know better than to repeal our masculine systems. [But] we are obliged to go fair and softly, and, in practice, you know we are the subjects."

—John Adams to Abigail Adams, April, 1776

Document B

" It is essential that measures be enacted aimed at unemployment relief. The first is the enrollment of workers by the federal government for public employment. The second is grants to States for relief work. The third extends to a broad public works labor-creating program."

—Franklin D. Roosevelt, March 21, 1933

1. Which statement best describes the effects of the American Revolution on women, according to Document A?

   A Women had fewer political rights.

   B Women were expected to take on new responsibilities in the government.

   C Women were encouraged to fight during the Revolutionary War.

   D John Adams and the other Founding Fathers were unwilling to allow women to vote.

2. Based on Document B, what was the most likely criticism of Roosevelt's New Deal?

   A The New Deal did not create jobs.

   B His program caused the economy to suffer.

   C The New Deal greatly expanded the federal government.

   D Roosevelt's program led us into World War II.

3. **Writing Task** Why did Roosevelt think that creating jobs was important for the economy? Explain your answer.

myworldgeography.com Self-Test

Chapter 2

Canada

Is conflict unavoidable?

KEY
- National border
- Provincial or territorial border
- ⊗ National capital
- ★ Provincial or territorial capital

0   400 mi
0   400 km

Lambert Azimuthal
Equal-Area Projection

ARCTIC OCEAN

ARCTIC CIRCLE

Baffin
Bay

Yukon

Whitehorse

Northwest
Territories

Yellowknife

Mackenzie River

Nunavut

Iqaluit

Labrador
Sea

Newfoundland and Labrador

St. John's

PACIFIC
OCEAN

Hudson
Bay

British
Columbia

Alberta

Edmonton

Saskatchewan

Saskatchewan River

Manitoba

Quebec

New
Brunswick

Prince
Edward
Island

Charlottetown

Fredericton

Halifax

Nova
Scotia

Victoria

Regina

Winnipeg

Ontario

Great Lakes

St. Lawrence
River

Quebec

Ottawa

Toronto

ATLANTIC
OCEAN

Where in the World Is Canada?

Washington, D.C., to Ottawa: 460 miles

my Story

Drawing on Heritage

In this section you'll read about Alyssa, a Canadian from the province of Ontario. What does Alyssa's story tell you about life in Canada?

? Explore the Essential Question
- at **my worldgeography.com**
- using the **myWorld Chapter Activity**
- with the **Student Journal**

Story by Jake Johnson for myWorld Geography Online

During the Spring in Ottawa, Canada, the ice melts, the grass begins to grow, and the city's waterways flow freely. Most Canadians begin to enjoy the beautiful outdoors of the nation's capital. But 20-year-old Alyssa heads north in the spring to visit her extended family in the snowy city of Iqaluit, Nunavut. In the 1950s some of Alyssa's family, including her mother Martha, were relocated from Inukjuak, in northern Quebec, to Grise Fiord, near the Arctic Circle. It is Canada's northernmost community, earning it the Inuit name of *Aujuittuq,* meaning "place that never thaws."

Canada's indigenous populations are diverse, and Alyssa is a prime example of that diversity. Her mother's family is Inuk Inuit, and her father is Cree. The Inuk Inuit people are often labeled "Eskimos." Alyssa considers the term "Eskimo" not only incorrect, but disrespectful. "Eskimo," interestingly, is a Cree word, which means "eaters of raw meat." Alyssa explains, "There is an indigenous population in Canada, and within that population there are three different groups. There are Métis, First Nations, and Inuit. Specifically, I am Inuit. The Inuit are native to Canada's northern regions.

my **worldgeography.com**

On Assignment

Alyssa and her aunt in an igloo at Iqaluit

Alyssa participates in a "Culture Circle" with younger Inuit children.

Working at Inuit Tapiriit Kanatami

Alyssa and her coworkers enjoy a lunch of traditional Inuit foods.

The First Nations are indigenous tribes that receive governmental support, and Métis are people who have mixed backgrounds of indigenous and French or Scottish heritage. It is a bit complex, eh?"

A few days later, back in Ottawa, Alyssa jumps into her work at the Inuit Tapiriit Kanatami (ITK), which means "The Inuit Brotherhood of Canada." "ITK is a national organization for Inuit, and it works on environmental, health and socio-economic issues for Inuit," says Alyssa.

On one particular day, several of Alyssa's coworkers gather in the break room. Alyssa has brought caribou, narwhal, and arctic char fish from Iqaluit. Coworkers have planned a "Country Food" luncheon. "We don't have the opportunity to do this all the time, since we live in southern Canada. So this is really nice," beams Alyssa. Her dishes are a big hit. There is plenty of bannock (Inuit fried bread), and a prized delicacy, raw narwhal skin.

Recently, Alyssa has seen a wide range of weather. In the north the weather was below freezing. Ottawa has been sunny and mild. But this morning brings powerful wind gusts and rain showers. Alyssa heads

Bannock, Inuit fried bread

Dried arctic char fish

Alyssa plays soccer.

Alyssa and her mother, Martha

to the University of Ottawa, where she is a political science major, with a minor in aboriginal studies. "I learn a lot about my traditions at school, so it helps me do my work at ITK." Today she wears a cool-weather parka. Alyssa proudly points out that her mother made the parka, complete with fox fur trim. She hurries to get out of the rain and to her next appointment.

Children await Alyssa's visit at the Ottawa Inuit Child Care Centre. Alyssa joins the children in daily rituals. Traditional songs, dancing, and language lessons bring a smile to Alyssa's face as she practices the customs of her heritage. The time goes quickly, but before she goes she joins in a friendly game of "throat singing." Women sing harsh melodic tones back and forth until one of them loses the rhythm. Alyssa loses the match, and almost loses her voice.

At the end of the workday Alyssa heads to her family's home in the countryside in Almonte, Ontario. After soccer practice with her local women's team, Alyssa goes to her parents' house where she shares video of her Iqaluit trip with her mother, Martha. Martha's face lights up at the glow of her family's campfire. "I am going up there in a few days, I can't wait," says Martha. They spend some precious minutes together and smile, united by the sights of their icy homeland. For this young Inuit woman there is a lot to smile about.

Meet the Journalist

Name Jake Johnson
Favorite Moment "When Alyssa shared with her mother the video of her trip to the north, you could see a love for their distant family and their heritage."

→ (myStory Video)

Join Alyssa in Canada.

Alyssa in the parka her mother made

Key Ideas

- There are several landform regions in Canada which affect where people live.
- Canada has impressive reserves of timber, minerals, and fresh water, and many of its industries are based on these resources.
- In economic development that has paralleled the United States, most of the Canadian population now lives in cities.

Key Terms • precipitation • tundra • permafrost • mixing zone

Visual Glossary

Reading Skill: Label an Outline Map Take notes using the outline map in your journal.

A view of downtown Vancouver

Physical Features

Canada is located immediately north of the United States. These two bordering nations have much in common. Overall, many Americans and Canadians enjoy a high standard of living. Both countries are physically large. After Russia, Canada is the second-largest country in the world in total land area.

While many people in Canada live near the United States border, Canada's geography offers many other places for people to live and work. There are several major regions in Canada. Each region is defined by its geography and its climate. The

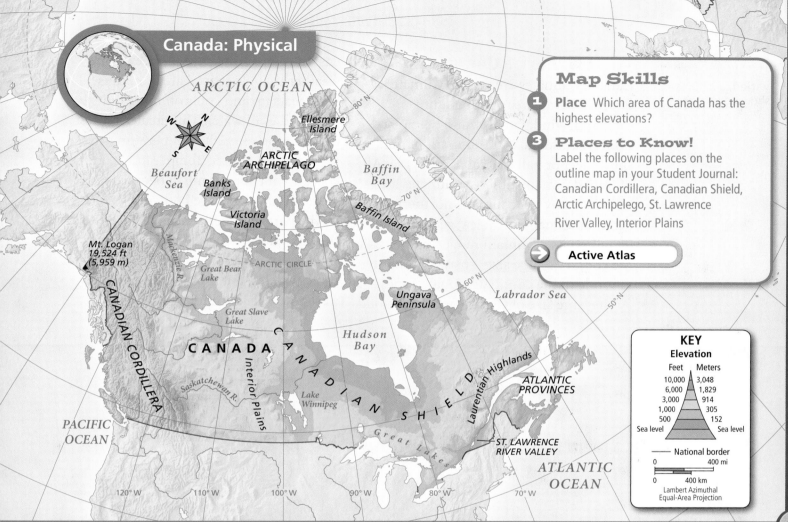

Canada: Physical

ARCTIC OCEAN

Ellesmere Island

ARCTIC ARCHIPELAGO

Baffin Bay

Beaufort Sea

Banks Island

Victoria Island

Baffin Island

Mt. Logan 19,524 ft (5,959 m)

Mackenzie R.

ARCTIC CIRCLE

Great Bear Lake

Ungava Peninsula

Labrador Sea

Great Slave Lake

Hudson Bay

CANADIAN CORDILLERA

CANADA

C A N A D I A N   S H I E L D

Interior Plains

Saskatchewan R.

Lake Winnipeg

Laurentian Highlands

ATLANTIC PROVINCES

PACIFIC OCEAN

Great Lakes

ST. LAWRENCE RIVER VALLEY

ATLANTIC OCEAN

120° W   110° W   100° W   90° W   80° W   70° W

80° N   70° N   60° N   50° N

KEY
Elevation

Feet	Meters
10,000	3,048
6,000	1,829
3,000	914
1,000	305
500	152
Sea level	Sea level

—— National border

0   400 mi

0   400 km

Lambert Azimuthal Equal-Area Projection

Map Skills

1 **Place** Which area of Canada has the highest elevations?

3 **Places to Know!**
Label the following places on the outline map in your Student Journal: Canadian Cordillera, Canadian Shield, Arctic Archipelego, St. Lawrence River Valley, Interior Plains

→ Active Atlas

Arctic region includes a chain of islands in Canada's far north called the Arctic Archipelago. Most of this region is within the Arctic Circle. Below the Arctic is the Canadian Shield, a massive, rocky area dotted with thousands of lakes. The Canadian Shield extends from Hudson Bay to the Canadian Cordillera. To the east are the Atlantic Provinces, which include the northern parts of the Appalachian Mountains. West of the Atlantic Provinces is the St. Lawrence River Valley, the most populous region in Canada. Farther west are the Interior Plains, which are part of the same geographic formation as the Great Plains in the United States. Finally, the Canadian Cordillera, the northern section of the Rocky Mountains, and the Pacific coast are in Canada's west.

Most citizens live in the southern and coastal areas of Canada. Regions like the St. Lawrence River Valley, the Atlantic Provinces, and the Southwest coast of Canada have moderate climates. In addition, these areas have <u>fertile</u> soils for farming, and other resources that help support large populations.

Reading Check What is the Canadian Shield?

fertile, *adj,* nutrient rich, well-suited for growing plants

The Effects of Climate

varied, *adj,* diverse; showing variety

Canada's climates are <u>varied</u>. Climate depends on an area's temperature, elevation, wind patterns, and precipitation. **Precipitation** is the amount of rain, snow, sleet or hail that falls in an area. All of Canada's many different climates are influenced by the country's northern location. Canada's physical geography—including its mountain ranges, as well as the country's large size—plays an important role in the country's climate zones.

The large size of Canada means that its vast interior plains have more extreme weather than its coastal areas, because land heats up and cools off more quickly than bodies of water. This creates greater extremes between the temperatures in the summer and winter. Temperatures on the coast do not vary as much because those areas are close to large bodies of water.

The part of Canada located closest to the United States has less-varied climates. It has small areas of semiarid and maritime climates, but most of the area has a continental cool summer climate.

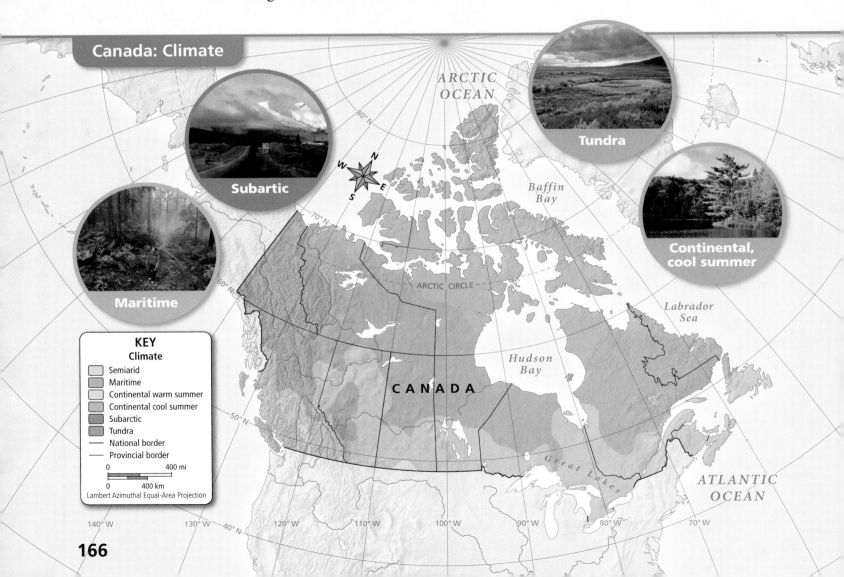

Canada: Climate

ARCTIC OCEAN

Subartic

Tundra

Maritime

Continental, cool summer

Baffin Bay

ARCTIC CIRCLE

Labrador Sea

Hudson Bay

CANADA

Great Lakes

ATLANTIC OCEAN

KEY
Climate
- Semiarid
- Maritime
- Continental warm summer
- Continental cool summer
- Subarctic
- Tundra
- National border
- Provincial border

0   400 mi
0   400 km
Lambert Azimuthal Equal-Area Projection

Summers are often hot and humid, while winters are very cold. In the maritime climate region on Canada's Pacific coast, more rain than snow falls each year and temperatures are more moderate. Northern Canada has subarctic and **tundra** climates with long, cold winters. The tundra is an area with limited vegetation, such as moss and shrubs. In this area, freezing temperatures last through the winter and summer. In the warmest weeks of the year, the temperature is rarely higher than 50 degrees Fahrenheit. In the subarctic zone, summers are generally short, cool, and rainy. Summer temperatures only reach the mid 60s to low 70s Fahrenheit.

Climate has had an important effect on where people decide to live. Outside of Canada's large cities, the country only averages about two people per square mile. This sparse population distribution is directly due to the challenges of Canada's physical geography, especially its harsh northern climates.

Reading Check What causes extreme temperature changes in the interior plains?

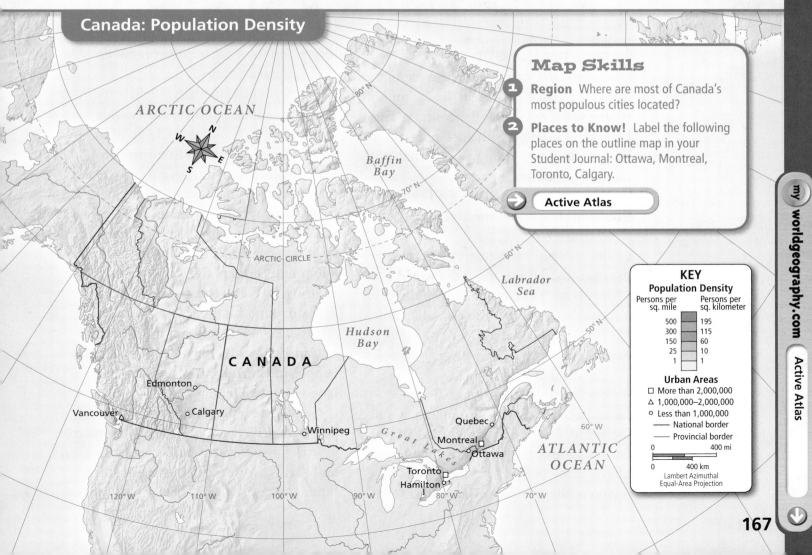

Canada: Population Density

Map Skills

1 **Region** Where are most of Canada's most populous cities located?

2 **Places to Know!** Label the following places on the outline map in your Student Journal: Ottawa, Montreal, Toronto, Calgary.

→ **Active Atlas**

ARCTIC OCEAN

Baffin Bay

ARCTIC CIRCLE

Labrador Sea

Hudson Bay

CANADA

Edmonton

Vancouver

Calgary

Winnipeg

Great Lakes

Quebec

Montreal

Ottawa

Toronto

Hamilton

ATLANTIC OCEAN

KEY
Population Density

Persons per sq. mile	Persons per sq. kilometer
500	195
300	115
150	60
25	10
1	1

Urban Areas
☐ More than 2,000,000
△ 1,000,000–2,000,000
○ Less than 1,000,000
— National border
— Provincial border

0   400 mi
0   400 km
Lambert Azimuthal Equal-Area Projection

The Continental Railroad

The St. Lawrence Seaway

Land and Resources

The largest of Canada's physical regions is called the Canadian Shield. Its 2.8 million square miles cover half the country. This huge area is dotted with ancient rocks and thousands of lakes and bays, created by the melting of glaciers, or sheets of ice formed by compacted snow. The Shield extends from Minnesota and the St. Lawrence River to the Arctic Circle.

The area produces many important minerals used throughout the world. Minerals such as copper, iron, and nickel, are vital for industry. The Canadian Shield has large deposits of lead and precious metals, such as gold and silver.

Glaciers that spread southward from the Canadian Shield created the five Great Lakes, the largest group of lakes in the world, on the Canada-United States border. One of the best-known and most dramatic features in the Great Lakes region is Niagara Falls. This waterfall is located on the Niagara River between Lake Erie and Lake Ontario.

North of the Canadian Shield is the Arctic Archipelago. This area extends into the Arctic Circle and is made up of thousands of islands such as Ellesmere and Baffin islands, that are covered by ice and snow throughout the year. While the area thaws temporarily in the summer, most of the soil remains permanently frozen. This soil that never thaws is called **permafrost.**

On both sides of the St. Lawrence River are the the St. Lawrence Lowland. The area surrounding the St. Lawrence and Great Lakes is often called the heartland of Canada because a majority of Canada's people, industries, cities, and fertile farmland is located here.

Canada has many other lakes, rivers, and bays. Rivers are used to create hydroelectric power. Dams hold the river water, and then channel it through large turbines that produce electricity. The longest and most important river in Canada is the St. Lawrence River. This river, along with a series of canals and locks, connects the Great Lakes to the Atlantic Ocean, providing an important transportation route from Canada's interior to the sea.

South of the St. Lawrence Lowlands is the Appalachian region. Here, low, rounded mountains and a rugged coastline separate the Atlantic Provinces from the rest of Canada. The Appalachians extend from Newfoundland in the north to the state of Georgia in the southern

United States. The economy in the Atlantic Provinces is similar to the northern New England states. It is based on fishing, forestry, agriculture, and tourism.

While there is fishing along both the Atlantic and Pacific coasts of Canada, one of the best-known fishing areas in the world is an area called the Grand Banks. The area is located off the Atlantic coasts of Newfoundland and Labrador. Warm waters from the Gulf Stream and cold waters from the Labrador Current meet in a **mixing zone,** an area where waters mix

myWorld Activity
Resource Attraction

Canada: Natural Resources

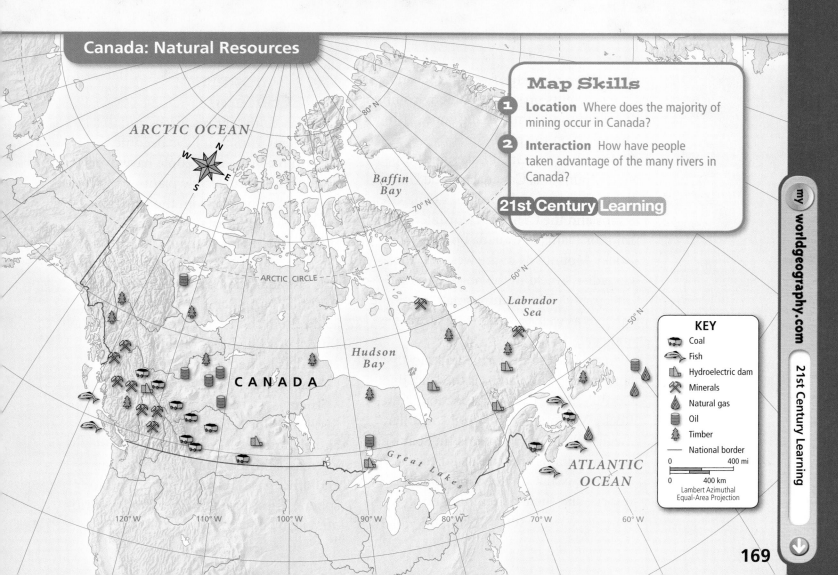

Map Skills

1 **Location** Where does the majority of mining occur in Canada?

2 **Interaction** How have people taken advantage of the many rivers in Canada?

21st Century Learning

KEY

- Coal
- Fish
- Hydroelectric dam
- Minerals
- Natural gas
- Oil
- Timber
- —— National border

0   400 mi
0   400 km
Lambert Azimuthal
Equal-Area Projection

A Changing Economy

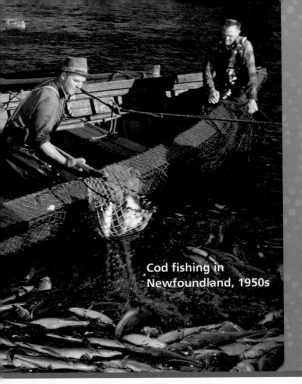

Cod fishing in Newfoundland, 1950s

Earlier in its history, Canada depended heavily on its natural resources, like cod fishing. Today, the economy is more diverse, and Canada's government regulates cod fishing to protect its natural resources.

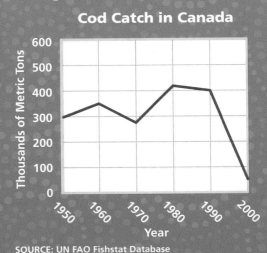

Cod Catch in Canada

Thousands of Metric Tons

SOURCE: UN FAO Fishstat Database

and stir up nutrients from the ocean floor. The nutrients provide a rich environment for plankton in the mixing zone. Fish then feed on the plankton.

As well as the Great Lakes and Appalachian Mountains, Canada and the United States share two other regions—the Great Plains and the Canadian Cordillera. The Interior Plains of Canada border the Rocky Mountains in the west and the Canadian Shield in the north and east. The grassy plains feature small farms and ranches as well as sources of natural gas and coal.

In contrast to the fertile and mostly level land in the Great Plains is the Canadian Cordillera, the Canadian portion of the Rocky Mountains. The word "cordillera" means "chain of mountains" in Spanish. The mountains are famous for their <u>dramatic</u> vistas, or views, popular ski resorts, and their rich mining history.

dramatic, *adj.,* interesting, exciting, or impressive

Reading Check **What is a mixing zone?**

The Environment: New Concerns

Canada's abundant resources and its natural environment have become threatened in recent years. People have over-developed hydroelectric plants, extracted too many minerals from the land, and have clear-cut forests.

Cleaning up air pollution in Canada requires efforts by both the United States and Canada. The Canada–United States Air Quality Agreement helped reduce acid rain in the 1990s. More recently, the Border Air Quality Strategy, passed in 2003, has helped reduce smog near the border between the two countries.

There is also concern about using fossil fuels for heating, transportation, and electricity. Using these resources increases the amount of carbon dioxide and other gases released into the atmosphere. These gases trap heat and contribute to global warming.

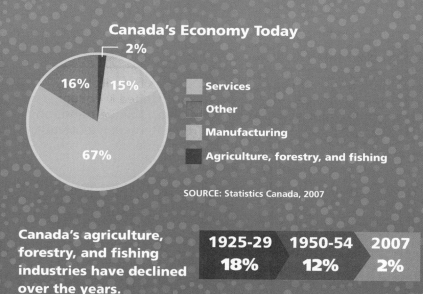

Canada's Economy Today

2%
16%
15%
67%

- Services
- Other
- Manufacturing
- Agriculture, forestry, and fishing

SOURCE: Statistics Canada, 2007

Canada's agriculture, forestry, and fishing industries have declined over the years.

1925-29	1950-54	2007
18%	12%	2%

Chart Skills

1 What is the biggest part of Canada's economy today?

2 How much have agriculture, forestry, and fishing declined since the 1925–1929 time period?

→ Data Discovery

Toronto is one of Canada's major economic centers.

Canada crafted its own Climate Change Plan in 1997. This legislation provides guidelines to help reduce global warming. Despite these efforts, however, the Arctic ice cap continues to melt, and other environmental challenges caused by global climate change continue.

The Arctic region is especially vulnerable to climate change because of its fragile environment. Damage to Arctic land and water takes years to heal. Pollution from oil and gas spills is also a dangerous threat to plants and animals in this sensitive region. As urban growth, air and water pollution, and the overextraction of its natural resources continue, Canada will face many challenges to both its environmental and its economic future.

Reading Check What has Canada done to reduce pollution and improve air quality?

my worldgeography.com   Data Discovery

Section 1 Assessment

Key Terms

1. Use these terms to describe the climate in Canada: precipitation, tundra, permafrost, mixing zone.

Key Ideas

2. Identify and describe Canada's largest landform.

3. Why are the Grand Banks ideal for fishing?

4. How has Canada's economic development been similar to that of the United States?

Think Critically

5. **Draw Conclusions** How does Canada's climate affect where people live?

6. **Analyze Cause and Effect** In what ways has economic development affected Canada's natural environment?

Essential Question

Is conflict unavoidable?

7. What agreements reflect cooperation between the United States and Canada? What environmental issues do they involve? Go to your Student Journal to record your answers.

History of Canada

Key Ideas

- Canada's natural resources have played a key role in the country's development.
- The distinct French and English populations promoted biculturalism early in Canada's history.
- Canada's historical ties to the United Kingdom outline a unique transition from interdependence to independence.

Key Terms • compromise • First Nations • New France • province • dominion

 **Visual Glossary**

 Reading Skill: Sequence Take notes using the graphic organizer in your journal.

An Iroquois man performing a ceremony in front of an Iroquois longhouse ▼

The history of Canada is unique. While native peoples have lived in Canada for thousands of years, Canada has absorbed many different kinds of people throughout its history. There has been tension among these groups of people, but Canada has usually resolved these conflicts peacefully through **compromise,** or establishing common ideas that people agree to follow.

Canada's Early History

Many thousands of years ago, people migrated across a land bridge from Asia to North America. By the 1500s, distinct groups of Native Americans lived throughout the land that is now Canada. Each group had its own culture, shaped by the geography and natural resources available to it.

Native Canadian Groups Native groups who lived south of the Arctic region in Canada are known as the **First Nations.** They shared similar lifestyles, using the available resources to build houses and make clothing, although groups developed distinct political systems, economies, and religious beliefs.

The Algonquins were skilled hunters who lived in present-day Quebec. Their birch-bark canoes and dog sleds helped them hunt large areas. The Iroquois lived in what is now southern Canada, in large farming villages. They grew corn in the milder climate, trading it for Algonquian forest products.

To the west, Plains dwellers structured their lives around hunting buffalo. Farther west, the mild climate and resources of the Pacific Coast, including salmon, whales, and forests, maintained populations such as the Yale and Yekooche people.

The Inuit people lived and continue to live in the Arctic region of the far north, and are not part of the First Nations. Inuits migrated year-round, in search of animals to hunt in their harsh climate.

Contact With Europeans Europeans first arrived off the coast of eastern Canada in the late 1400s, seeking a route from Europe to Asia, called the Northwest Passage. Although they did not find this route, they did find fish and animal furs. European fishermen stayed along the coasts, drying their catches and returning each year to Europe. European pursuit of furs had far-reaching effects for the First Nations people and for Canadian history.

As European traders made their way inland, they traded wool cloth and metal goods for Native American furs. Trading posts sprang up throughout southeastern Canada. A complex relationship developed between Europeans and Native Americans, as each sought to control the profitable fur trade. However, like the European colonists who were settling other areas, these traders carried many diseases and many native people died even as the fur trade grew in strength.

Reading Check What does the term *First Nations* describe?

France and Britain Struggle for Control

For more than 200 years France and Britain struggled to claim territory, control the fur trade, and secure Native American allies.

New France In 1534, Jacques Cartier arrived in eastern Canada and claimed it for France, giving it the name **New France.** Although French traders established a profitable fur trade in New France, it took many years for them to settle in colonies. In 1608 Samuel de Champlain established a colony at present-day Quebec City. Over the next hundred years, the French settled the region near the St. Lawrence River. For 200 years, the fur trade supported New France's economy.

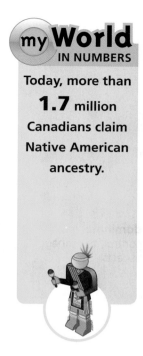

my World IN NUMBERS

Today, more than **1.7 million** Canadians claim Native American ancestry.

Trading Post in central Canada ▼

British Canada British fur traders also operated trading posts outside of New France. They learned that the best land for furs was north of New France, around Hudson Bay. In 1670 the British king granted this territory to the Hudson Bay Company.

dominate, *v.*, to control, to manage all aspects

As the French and British settled their territories, conflicts grew. Each wanted to <u>dominate</u> the fur trade. Each had native people as allies, who increasingly fought each other for influence with the Europeans. These struggles were most intense during the Seven Years' War, fought from 1756 to 1763. This war, which began in Europe and spread to America, resulted in victory for Britain. Canada became British.

Reading Check What was the Seven Years' War?

Roots of a Nation

Canada was now a colony of Britain, yet it had a history of French culture, language, and government. Also, most French Canadians were Roman Catholic, while most new British settlers in Canada were Protestant. This diversity presented Canadians with challenges as the colony became a country.

The Quebec Act When Britain took control of Canada, it wanted the colony to be British. Yet, to avoid rebellion, it knew that it had to recognize the rights of French Canadians. With the Quebec Act of 1774, Britain allowed religious freedom and French laws. The act also extended Quebec's boundaries. American colonists saw this territory as theirs, and strongly opposed the Quebec Act.

Closer Look *Conflict and Compromise*

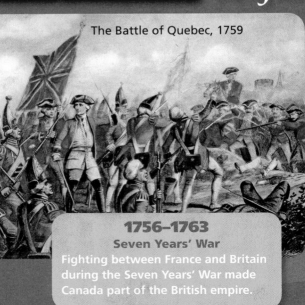

The Battle of Quebec, 1759

Britain and France fought to control early Canada. Britain won control of the area. Immediately, leaders in Canada had to balance the interests of the French and British citizens. Later, Canada won independence from Britain through negotiation and compromise, and without a revolutionary war.

THINK CRITICALLY What factors might have led Britain to negotiate with British- and French-Canadian citizens?

1756–1763
Seven Years' War
Fighting between France and Britain during the Seven Years' War made Canada part of the British empire.

1774
The Quebec Act
The Quebec Act was Parliament's first attempt at balancing the interests of both British and French citizens.

It is hereby declared, That His Majesty's Subjects professing the Religion of the Church of Rome, of, and in the said Province of Quebec, may enjoy the free Exercise of the Religion of the Church of Rome; and that the Clergy of the said Church may enjoy their accustomed Dues and Rights.

A Canadian Identity Develops The Quebec Act helped drive a wedge between Canada the other British colonies in America. After the United States won independence from Britain in 1783, Americans who had remained loyal to Britain poured into Canada. To avoid conflict between the French and the new British citizens, Britain divided the colony into Upper and Lower Canada in 1791. Both colonies would remain under British rule, but Lower Canada would retain French customs, language, and religion.

During this time, the United States felt Britain should withdraw from areas bordering the United States and Canada, such as the area that is now northern Maine.

In 1812, the United States declared war on Britain, and quickly invaded Canada.

Nearly three years later, neither Britain nor the United States won. Americans saw the war as a great victory. Canadians viewed the victory as theirs. The conflict united Canadians against a common enemy—the United States.

While Canadians felt some unity as a result of the War of 1812, hard times fell on the Canadian people. Food shortages and disease plagued Lower Canada. Groups formed to oppose British rule, and several rebellions broke out. As a result, the British granted some control to the Canadian people. The 1840 Act of Union reunited Upper and Lower Canada into one **province,** or a territory that is under the control of a larger country. Britain still maintained control over all of Canada.

Reading Check **What were Upper and Lower Canada?**

myWorld Activity
Culture Clash

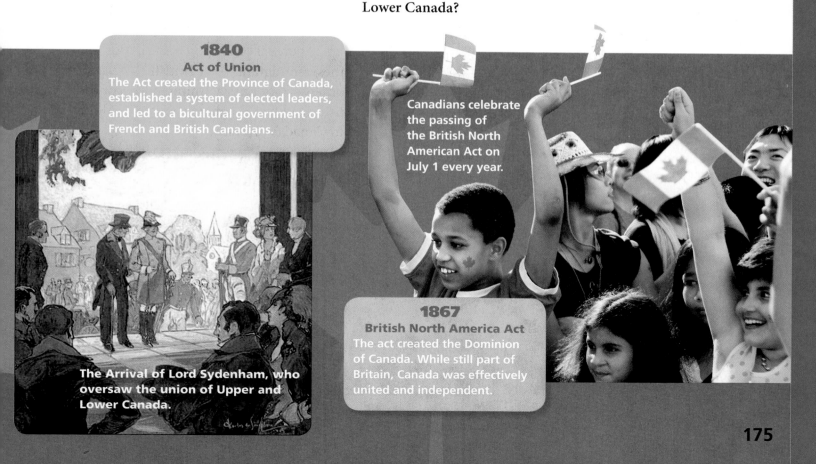

1840
Act of Union
The Act created the Province of Canada, established a system of elected leaders, and led to a bicultural government of French and British Canadians.

The Arrival of Lord Sydenham, who oversaw the union of Upper and Lower Canada.

Canadians celebrate the passing of the British North American Act on July 1 every year.

1867
British North America Act
The act created the Dominion of Canada. While still part of Britain, Canada was effectively united and independent.

175

Canada Grows

Over the next 100 years, Canada experimented with different forms of government, working out its relationship with Britain. The country expanded and <u>prospered</u>, with the help of immigrants.

prospered, *v.,* was successful

The Dominion of Canada In the 1800s, Britain feared American westward expansion. To strengthen its position, Britain passed the 1867 British North America Act, creating a new confederation called the Dominion of Canada. A **dominion** is a territory that governs itself but is still tied to its colonizing country. The Dominion of Canada included all of the provinces of British Canada except Prince Edward Island and Newfoundland. Britain would still control Canada's foreign affairs, but the country would govern itself. Like the United States, the Dominion of Canada divided its powers between national and provincial, or state, governments.

In the late 1800s, Canada had expanded its territory. By 1905, the nation had five new provinces, stretching to the Pacific coast. The First Nations people who lived in the west resisted this expansion. The Canadian government feared wars with native people similar to those in the United States. It worked to solve conflict through treaties, which resulted in many native groups being forced to move to reservations.

The Role of Immigration In the early 1900s, Canada's economy grew by leaps and bounds. New technology and better agricultural methods increased exports of Canada's main crop, wheat. The growing economy was also fueled by a growth in population, especially from immigrants, who created a strong labor force.

In the early 1900s, the Canadian government encouraged immigration to Canada, especially of farmers. From 1901 to 1911, Canada's population grew by about 34 percent. In 1901, immigrants made up 12 percent of the population. By 1911, they made up 22 percent of the population. Most of these immigrants were British, American, or Jews from Russia. Immigration continued steadily throughout the 1900s, adding to Canada's diversity.

Reading Check What was the Dominion of Canada?

British, Russian, and American immigrants in the early 1900s ▼

176

Independent Canada

In the years after the Dominion of Canada was created, Britain had less to do with governing the country. Canada began establishing itself as a world leader.

World War I Canada was still part of the British Empire when World War I began. When Great Britain entered the war in 1914, this meant Canada joined the fight as well. The war demanded many human and natural resources from Canada. The country began to collect an income tax to pay for services, which made the country less dependent on Britain. In 1918, Canada created an air force separate from Britain's. By the end of the war, Canada proved that it was ready to act as an independent nation. In 1931, Britain recognized Canada's ability to act independently of the British Empire. Canada, however, remain linked to Great Britain. Canada's courts were still tied to Britain, and the country's constitution was officially an act of Parliament.

Canada's Challenges Canada faced its first major challenge as an independent country with the Great Depression of the 1930s. As in the United States and across the world, prices for exports fell, there were widespread crop failures, and unemployment rose. New political parties formed to demand that the government do more to help people.

As in the United States, joining World War II helped lift Canada out of the Depression. Canada's economy grew rapidly to support the war. Industries and agriculture expanded, new jobs were created, and businesses developed new technologies. The economy, once dependent on agriculture, became much more diversified. This began a period of growth that carried Canada into the next century.

Reading Check What was an important effect of World War I?

▲ A bi-lingual poster recruits Canadians for World War I.

Section 2 Assessment

Essential Question

Is conflict unavoidable?

Key Terms

1. Who are the First Nations?
2. What compromise did Britain make when it took control of Canada?
3. What is the difference between a province and a dominion?

Key Ideas

4. Identify the relationship between natural resources and European settlement.
5. How did New France shape Canadian culture?
6. Describe the interdependence established between Canada and Britain in 1867.

Think Critically

7. **Summarize** What role did conflict play in Canada's early history?
8. **Analyze Cause and Effect** How did Canada's participation in World War II affect its economy?

9. How did Canada gain its independence from Britain? Go to your Student Journal to record your answer.

Canada Today

<table>
<tr><td rowspan="2">Key Ideas</td><td>● Canada's federal government reflects historical ties to Britain.</td><td>● Canada has a modern economy and is an active trade partner with many countries.</td><td>● Cultural diversity in Canada is unique, as groups maintain much of their traditions while being Canadian citizens.</td></tr>
</table>

Key Terms • cultural mosaic • constitutional monarchy • plural society

 Visual Glossary

Reading Skill: Compare and Contrast Take notes using the graphic organizer in your journal.

Queen Elizabeth visits Canada.

Although Canada and the United States have a great deal in common, the history, politics, and cultures of these two countries are distinct. As discussed in the previous chapter, the United States fought against Great Britain to win independence. Canada, on the other hand, broke away from Great Britain slowly, through political means.

Governing Canada

Today's Canadian cultural and political landscape is the result of many years of competition and compromise among the native peoples of Canada, the Europeans settlers, and the home countries of those settlers, namely France and Great Britain. While the United States is viewed as a melting pot, Canada is known as a **cultural mosaic**. Here, people from different areas retain their cultural identity. Canada is also bilingual and multicultural, with both French and English as national languages.

Historical Ties to Britain One of the major differences between Canada and the United States is Canada's long and enduring relationship with the United Kingdom. The British Queen, Elizabeth II is the Canadian head of state. As you have read, the British government first created Canada when it passed the British North America Act. More than a century later, in 1982, Canada created its own constitution. It needed to address issues that were unique to Canada such as language rights for French-speaking Quebec, financial support for regional economies, and government protection of Canada's transportation and other industries. This constitution was called the Charter of Rights and Freedoms. It serves the same function as the American Bill of Rights and it reflects Canada's slow separation from Britain.

Canada's government system is a **constitutional monarchy,** where the power of the king or queen is limited by the constitution. Canada's government is made up of three branches: the executive, legislative, and judicial. Canada also uses a federal system to balance power between the federal government in Canada's capital city, Ottawa, and the governments in each of its provinces and territories.

Heads of State Canada's executive branch of government is made up of the governor general, who represents the British monarch (currently Queen Elizabeth II of England), the prime minister, and the cabinet. The prime minister is in charge of determining government policies and steering legislation in Canada, while the Queen's role is mostly ceremonial. Since 1952, the governor general position has alternated between an English Canadian and a French Canadian. By custom, the person appointed to this position is bilingual.

The prime minister and the cabinet are elected members of the House of

legislative, *adj.,* referring to the law-making branch of Canadian government

Canada's Government

Canada is a federation—several provinces and territories are linked by a single, larger government. Canada's head of government is the prime minister, who runs the executive branch. The governor general gives the sovereign's approval to parliament bills and other actions.

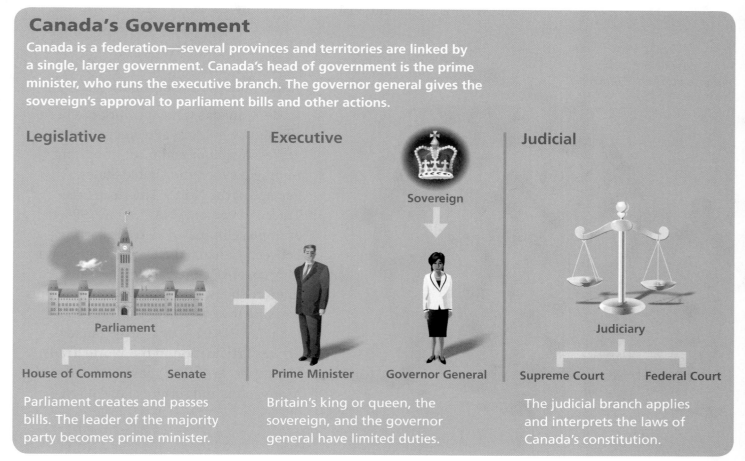

Legislative

Parliament

House of Commons — Senate

Parliament creates and passes bills. The leader of the majority party becomes prime minister.

Executive

Sovereign

Prime Minister — Governor General

Britain's king or queen, the sovereign, and the governor general have limited duties.

Judicial

Judiciary

Supreme Court — Federal Court

The judicial branch applies and interprets the laws of Canada's constitution.

179

Commons. The leader of the majority party in the House of Commons becomes prime minister. In this system there are no divisions between the executive and the legislative branches of government in Canada as there are in the United States.

The structure of Canada's government is designed to benefit its citizens. Beginning with Prime Minister Pierre Trudeau in the early 1970s, the government has continued to create programs to balance the needs of both French and English-speaking Canadians. Since then people have focused more on celebrating Canada's multiethnic, multilingual, and multicultural population.

myWorld Activity
Trade Partner Search

Reading Check **What is a constitutional monarchy?**

Many people in Quebec are proud of their French heritage. ▼

Canada's Role in the World

Canada has a growing and dynamic economy based on natural resources, well-developed services, and technology. Canada's high-end internet system and well-educated workforce are particularly important to the country's economy. Canada is currently second in the world in terms of total Internet users (despite its relatively small population), and it ranks first in the percentage of college and university graduates in its total population.

There are other reasons Canada has emerged as a world leader in economic development and trade. Along with its highly skilled population, Canada has a literacy rate of 99 percent, one of the highest in the world. Unemployment is low. Canada has developed a high quality of life, healthcare for every citizen, policies for cleaning up the environment, and a modern transportation system.

Trade Canada's trade network has been affected by political agreements with its nearest neighbor and most important trading partner, the United States. Passage of the North American Free Trade Agreement (NAFTA) in 1994, for example, eliminated all trade barriers between Canada, the United States, and Mexico. NAFTA legislation has resulted in more than one billion dollars of goods crossing the Canadian–U.S. border each day! NAFTA, as well as Canada's active participation in the World Trade Organization (WTO) has increased trade. More goods and services flow out of

Canada (exports) and more goods and services flow into Canada (imports).

Much of this international trade consists of exporting Canada's natural resources to other countries. Profits made by exporting natural resources make up one third of Canada's economic activity.

Peacekeeper Canada is known throughout the world as a peacekeeping nation. Many Canadian soldiers, sailors, and aviators today work to stop wars from developing by serving the United Nations as peacekeepers. Peacekeepers go into other countries to help guard borders and protect people—not to fight battles. Canadian soldiers have provided support for United States troops in Afghanistan and Iraq. Some peacekeepers are not in the military, but help with negotiations between groups or provide other services in conflict areas.

The United Nations (UN) was founded after World War II by fifty different countries, including Canada. Although more than seventy countries have participated in peacekeeping missions for the UN, Canada is among the leading countries in providing support to United Nations missions over the years. In addition, despite its small population, Canada is the fourth-largest contributor to the high cost of maintaining the peacekeeping efforts of the UN.

Reading Check Why is Canada known as a peacekeeping nation?

Canada as Peacekeeper

After World War II, countries looked for ways to prevent widespread war. One idea was to send troops to contain and prevent fighting. In 1956 Canada put this idea into practice. Egypt had gained control of the Suez Canal, which connects the Mediterranean and Red Sea. Britain and France wanted to control the canal, which threatened war with Egypt. Canada's Lester Pearson proposed sending United Nations troops to limit fighting and find a peaceful resolution.

Canada has participated in nearly every United Nations peacekeeping mission since 1956.

Canada has sent troops and other officials to prevent conflict in places such as Haiti, Bosnia, the Dominican Republic and Somalia.

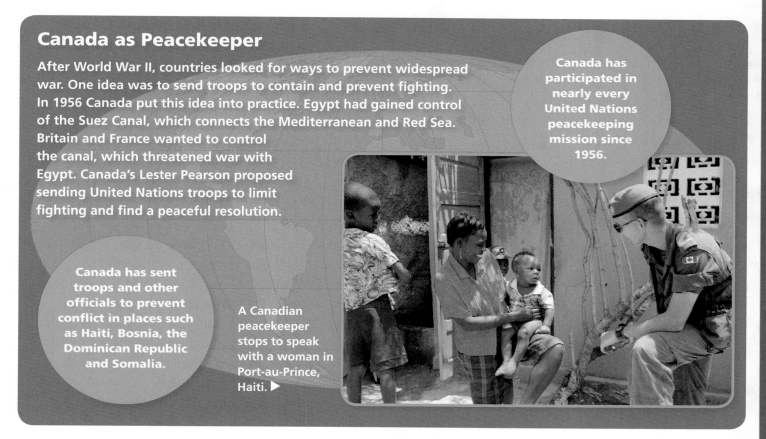

A Canadian peacekeeper stops to speak with a woman in Port-au-Prince, Haiti. ▶

French
French Canadians have maintained a distinct culture in Quebec.

→ Culture Close-up

First Peoples
First Nations people include many diverse native groups in Canada.

Chinatown
Chinese Canadians have strong communities in cities like Toronto.

Caribbean Festival
Caribbean peoples have made Canada their home more recently.

The Cultural Mosaic

As discussed earlier in this chapter, Canada's population is a mix of indigenous people, descendants of early colonizers from England and France, and immigrants from other countries. Although English and French are Canada's two official languages, Canada is a **plural society.** This means that its distinctive cultural, ethnic, and racial groups are encouraged to maintain their own identities and cultures. Canada adopted the policy of multiculturalism in the 1970s. Multiculturalism encourages Canadians to maintain the cultures and traditions of their parents and grandparents.

Canada has a long history of immigration. In the 1800s, jobs to construct railroads and the availabilty of land created opportunities for citizens. Canada's population became more diverse after the 1960s when Canada changed its immigration laws.

This increase in the racial diversity of Canada's immigrant groups has continued in recent years. In 2004, nearly half of all Canadian immigrants came from Asia and Pacific Rim countries. The presence of more people born in Asia, Latin America, and Africa has risen dramatically as economic, environmental, and political problems in the world continue.

Today, the most diverse cities in Canada are Toronto, Montreal, and Vancouver. Toronto, Canada's largest city, is one of the world's most cosmopolitan and ethnically diverse metropolitan areas. More than half of all schoolchildren in Toronto speak a language other than English at home.

Along with the descendants of earlier European settlers, this city is now home to immigrants from Asia, Africa, the Caribbean, and Latin America. Other, smaller cities also attract new immigrants.

Immigrants account for 70 percent of all labor force growth in Canada, a proportion that experts <u>project</u> will grow to 100 percent in the next ten years.

Maintaining a distinctive Canadian identity remains one of Canada's biggest challenges. American movies, television programs, and pop music flow easily into Canada and dominate its media. Efforts to curb the Americanization of Canadian culture include a law that requires that Canadian TV and radio programs contain a certain percentage of "Canadian content." There has also been an explosion of Canadian fine arts, films, television, and popular music during the past thirty years that help carry on an identity and values that are uniquely Canadian.

As Canada moves forward, its geography and the diversity of its people continue to be important to its future. Managing regional economic differences, maintaining independent foreign policies, protecting culture, and balancing trade and political relationships with the United States remain important.

project, *v.,* to calculate a thing that will occur

Reading Check **What is a plural society? How has immigration affected Canada?**

Photo Alyssa visits a culture circle at the Ottawa Inuit Child Care Center.

Section 3 Assessment

Key Terms
1. Use the following terms to describe Canada's culture: cultural mosaic, plural society.

Key Ideas
2. What position does the British monarch play in Canada's government?

3. Why is international trade important to Canada's economy?

4. What accounts for the uniqueness of Canada's cultural diversity?

Think Critically
5. Compare and Contrast How is Canada's government different from that of the United States?

6. Draw Inferences How has the government tried to balance the needs of French- and English-speaking Canadians?

Essential Question
Is conflict unavoidable?

7. Why is Canada known as a peacekeeping nation? Go to your Student Journal to record your answer.

Chapter Assessment

Key Terms and Ideas

1. **Compare and Contrast** How are a **cultural mosaic** and a **plural society** different from each other? How are they similar?

2. **Sequence** What were the major events in Canada's transition from a British colony to an independent nation?

3. **Explain** How does climate affect population distribution in Canada?

4. **Compare and Contrast** How are the **First Nations** and the Inuit different from each other?

5. **Explain** In what ways was the Quebec Act a **compromise**?

6. **Describe** During its years as a **dominion,** what was Canada's relationship with Britain?

7. **Summarize** How do natural resources contribute to Canada's economy?

Think Critically

8. **Determine Relevance** How does geography explain why it is important for Canada and the United States to address environmental issues jointly?

9. **Draw Conclusions** What were some of the lasting effects of the fur trade?

10. **Analyze Information** What geographical factors might explain why most of Canada is sparsely populated?

11. **Core Concepts: Trade** What is trade? How does Canada's economy reflect the importance of international trade?

Places to Know

For each place, write the letter from the map that shows its location.

Identify the following:

12. **Arctic Archipelago**

13. **St. Lawrence River**

14. **Canadian Shield**

15. **Ottawa**

16. **Calgary**

17. **Interior Plains**

18. **Estimate** Using the scale, estimate the distance between Ottawa and Calgary.

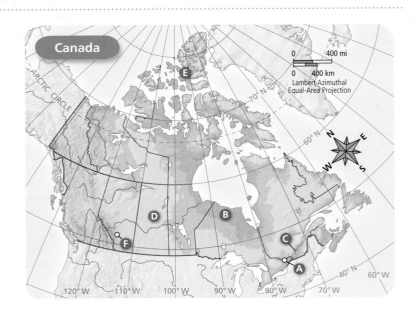

Essential Question

Chapter Transfer Activity

Follow your teacher's instructions to form groups and role-play a family moving to Canada. Review information about Canada's geographic regions and rank them by desirability. Choose an area for settlement and present your choice to the class. Compare your choice to the choices of your classmates. Then compare your choice to that of actual settlers.

21st Century Learning

Develop Cultural Awareness

Choose one of Canada's provincial flags. Do research to discover the significance of the symbols it displays. Present your findings to the class.

Document-Based Questions

Success Tracker™
Online at myworldgeography.com

Use your knowledge of Canada and Documents A and B to answer Questions 1–3.

Document A

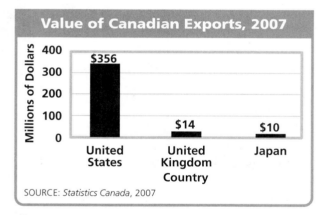

Value of Canadian Exports, 2007

Millions of Dollars

- United States: $356
- United Kingdom: $14
- Japan: $10

Country

SOURCE: *Statistics Canada*, 2007

Document B

" Construction of dams in Manitoba for the generation of electricity resulted in the decline of fishing and a significant drop in beaver and muskrat populations. Responding on behalf of his people, a First Nations chief commented, "Hydro is breaking our hearts."

—John Miswagon, Pimicikamak Chief

1. Which of the following best explains why the highest percentage of Canadian trade occurs with a single country?

   A Canada and the United States share a common language.

   B There is a high demand for Canadian products in the United States.

   C Canada and the United States share the same continent.

   D Canada and the United States have reciprocal trade agreements.

2. Which of the following best explains Miswagon's statement?

   A His people are grieving over the destruction of wildlife.

   B His people do not believe that increased generation of electricity is necessary.

   C His people are unhappy because they will not share in the profits.

   D The dams threaten his people's sustainable way of life.

3. **Writing Task** Should a nation be concerned about the environmental impact of its development? Explain your answer.

myworldgeography.com Self-Test

Road Trip:

Explore the Interstate Highway System

Your Mission You and your classmates will propose one new north–south interstate and one new east–west interstate. To gather information for your proposal, divide into four task-force teams: history, mapping, statistics, and planning.

Before the Information Superhighway, there was the Interstate Highway System. After World War II, American prosperity boomed. Everyone wanted a new car. People drove their cars to their new homes in the suburbs. In the summer, families went on driving vacations. Gradually, cars grew larger and could travel hundreds of miles on a single tank of gas. Yet, there were almost no wide, smooth roads between major cities.

Construction of the Interstate Highway System (IHS) began in 1956. The system initially called for 41,000 miles of new roads as well as uniform construction standards. By having regulations calling for uniformity on these new roads, the government could ensure greater safety for drivers. It is because of these regulations that signs along the interstate look the same anywhere in the United States.

The IHS helped make America a nation of drivers.

STEP 1

Identify Roles and Responsibilities.

Each task force must understand how its efforts will contribute to the report that is presented by the planning team. The history task force will explore the early years of the IHS and why it continues to be important today. The mapping task force will study the existing IHS and try to find regions under-served by highways. The statistics task force will research who uses the IHS and explain what these data mean. The planning task force will synthesize these data to propose new roads for the IHS.

STEP 2

Determine Your Goals.

Eack task force should focus on its specific goal. The goal of the history team is to consider how the IHS has evolved over time and what its future needs might be. The mapping task force's goal is to consider how America's changing needs affect the roadway system. The statistics task force should look for data on the IHS. The focus of the planning team is to coordinate the findings of all teams and to assemble this information in a proposal for new roads.

STEP 3

Regroup and Communicate.

Each task force member should individually research the group's topic. Some teams may choose to research together. Share ideas and respond to good points by including them in your report. Reach conclusions as a group and acknowledge the efforts of your teammates when you give your report. Keep in mind that your reports are requesting that the government spend millions of dollars but that the project will benefit the entire nation.

Middle America

Middle America is the "middle" region of the Americas, so-called because it forms a land bridge between North and South America. Caribbean island nations, including Cuba, also belong to the region. Mexico is the region's largest country. Middle America is prone to natural disasters such as hurricanes, earthquakes, and volcanic eruptions.

What time is it there?

Washington, D.C.	Mexico City, Mexico
9 A.M. Monday	8 A.M. Monday

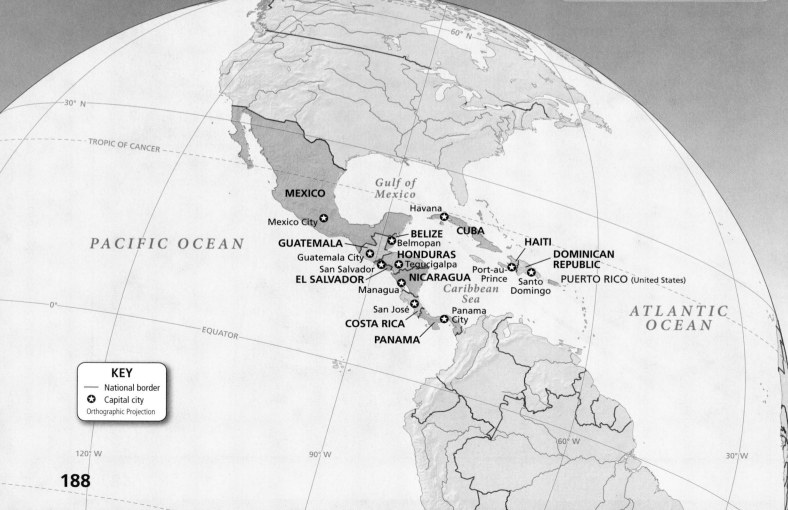

60° N

30° N

TROPIC OF CANCER

MEXICO

Mexico City ✪

Gulf of Mexico

Havana

PACIFIC OCEAN

GUATEMALA

Guatemala City ✪

San Salvador ✪

EL SALVADOR

Managua

✪ Belmopan

BELIZE

HONDURAS

✪ Tegucigalpa

NICARAGUA

CUBA

HAITI

Port-au-Prince

✪ ✪ Santo Domingo

DOMINICAN REPUBLIC

PUERTO RICO (United States)

Caribbean Sea

San José ✪

COSTA RICA

Panama ✪ City

PANAMA

ATLANTIC OCEAN

EQUATOR

0°

KEY

— National border

✪ Capital city

Orthographic Projection

60° W

120° W

90° W

30° W

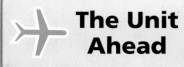

The Unit Ahead

➡ **Chapter 3** Mexico

➡ **Chapter 4** Central America and the Caribbean

my **worldgeography.com**

Plan your trip online by doing a Data Discovery Activity and watching the myStory Videos of the region's teens.

my Story

Carolina

Age: 16

Home: Tamaulipas, Mexico

Chapter 3

my Story

Luis

Age: 17

Home: Limón, Dominican Republic

Chapter 4

The Mayan ruins of Tulum, south of Cancun on the Yucatán Peninsula

Regional Overview
Physical Geography

The Sierra Madre ranges lie near both of Mexico's coasts.

Baja California

Gulf of California

Sierra Madre Occidental

Mexican Plateau

Sierra Madre Oriental

Gulf of Mexico

Yucatán Peninsula

Greater

Caribbean

PACIFIC OCEAN

Southern Mexico's rain forest supports diverse animal and plant life.

Active volcanoes dot the west coast of Nicaragua.

Cuba is the largest island in the Caribbean Sea. It belongs to a group of islands called the Greater Antilles.

ATLANTIC
OCEAN

Antilles
Sea

Lesser Antilles

Regional Flyover

Suppose you are flying in an airplane across Middle America. If you begin in the north and fly southeast, you would fly over the Sierra Madre Occidental mountain range in Mexico. Mexico's central plateau and the second range of the Sierra Madres are both to the east. As you continue flying south, you would see the lush vegetation of lower Mexico's rain forests.

East of Mexico is the Caribbean Sea and its many islands. Cuba, Jamaica, Puerto Rico, and Hispaniola, which includes both Haiti and the Dominican Republic, are part of the Greater Antilles. The Virgin Islands, Antigua, and other smaller islands make up the Lesser Antilles.

Your flight turns southwest over Central America. Soon you notice an isthmus, or a narrow land bridge between two larger land masses. The isthmus includes Costa Rica and Panama, the southernmost country of Middle America, where your flight ends.

 In-Flight Movie

Take flight over Middle America and explore the region from the air.

my worldgeography.com | In-Flight Movie

Regional Geography
Human Geography

Middle America's Economy

People who live in Middle America have a variety of jobs. In countries such as Haiti, the majority of people farm for a living. In Mexico, many people work in factories that manufacture goods for export, or for sale in other countries. In Central America and the Caribbean, many people work in the region's thriving tourism industry.

Despite the variety of economic activities, many people in this region are poor. Natural disasters, such as hurricanes, continually cause economic setbacks. Some people emigrate, or move to other countries. Many immigrants who find work in the United States send money to family members back home.

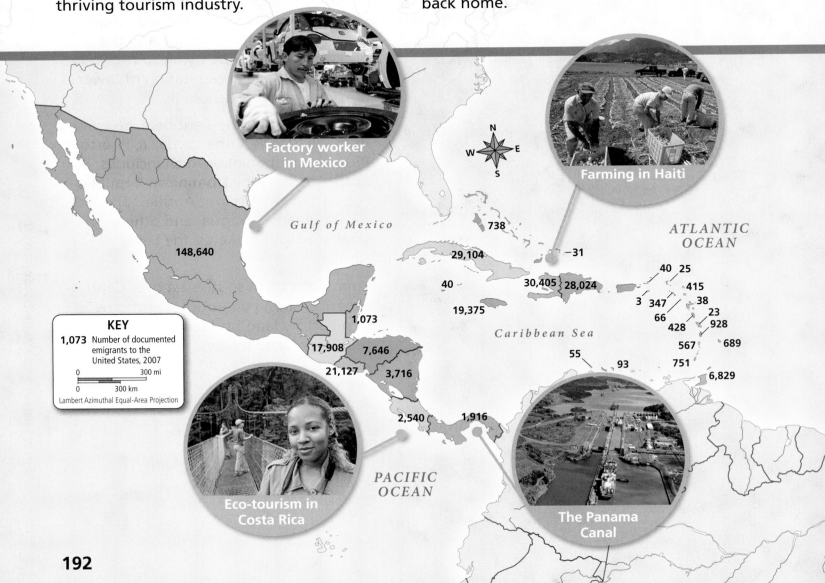

Factory worker in Mexico

Farming in Haiti

Gulf of Mexico

ATLANTIC OCEAN

148,640

738

29,104   31

40   25

40   415

30,405 28,024   3   347   38

19,375   66   23

428   928

1,073   Caribbean Sea   567   689

17,908   7,646   55   751

21,127   3,716   93   6,829

KEY

1,073 Number of documented emigrants to the United States, 2007

0   300 mi

0   300 km

Lambert Azimuthal Equal-Area Projection

Eco-tourism in Costa Rica

2,540   1,916

PACIFIC OCEAN

The Panama Canal

my World IN NUMBERS

	Mexico	Honduras	Costa Rica	Haiti
Literacy rate (15 years of age or older)	91.0%	80.0%	94.9%	52.9%
Income earned by wealthiest 10% of population	37.1%	42.2%	37.4%	47.70%
Urban population**	75.0%	46.0%	61.0%	37.0%
People employed in agriculture	15.1%	39.2%	14.0%	66.0%

SOURCE: CIA World Factbook Online, 2009

** SOURCE: Population Division of the United Nations Secretariat, 2003

Put It Together

1. What are two of Mexico's main physical features?

2. What type of natural disasters frequently occur in Middle America?

3. Compare Mexico and Haiti. What is the relationship between the percentage of urban population and the percentage of people employed in agriculture?

 Data Discovery

Find your own data to make a regional data table.

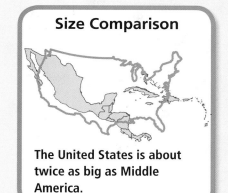

Size Comparison

The United States is about twice as big as Middle America.

my worldgeography.com   Data Discovery

Chapter 3

Mexico

Essential Question

How much does geography shape a country?

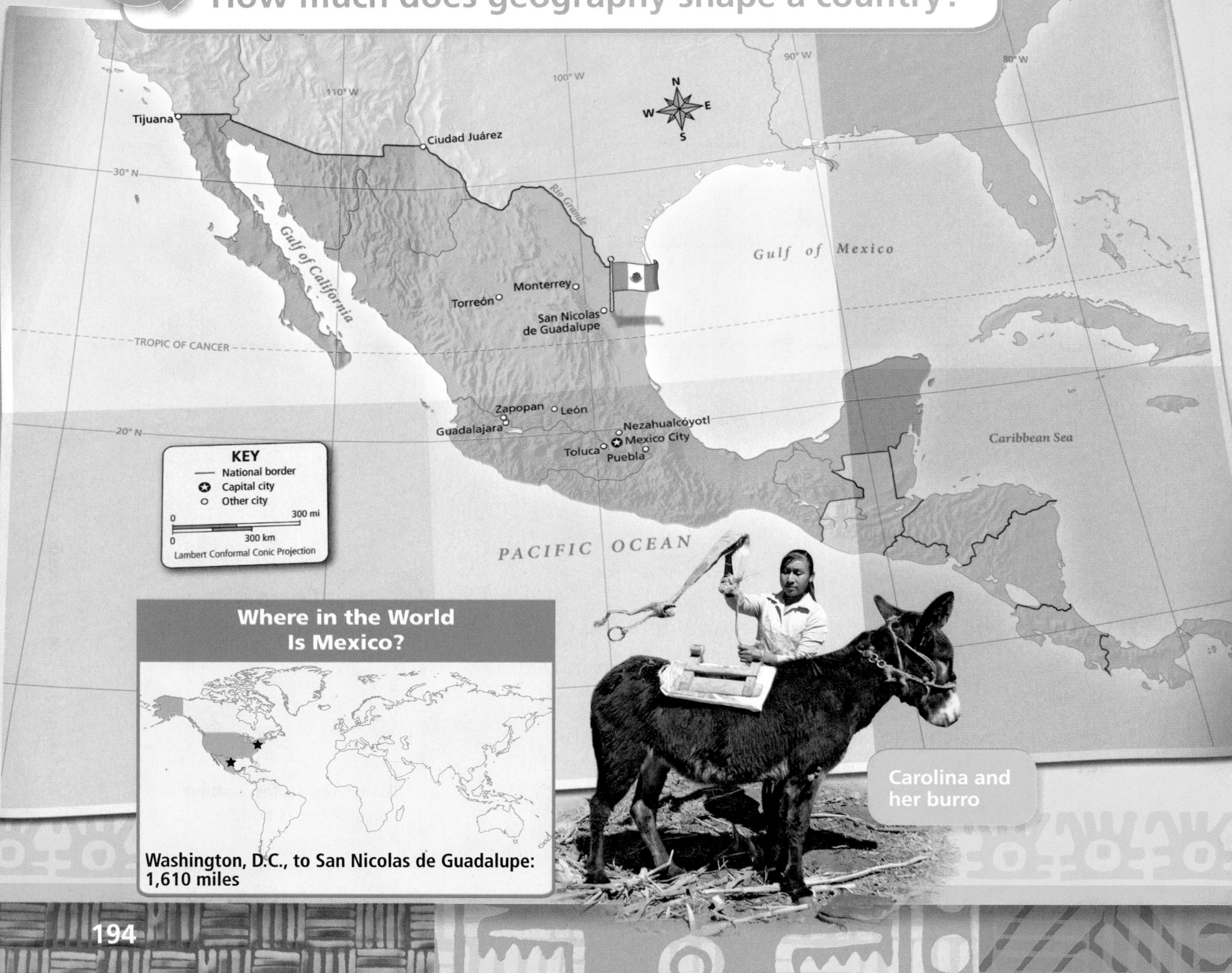

Tijuana
Ciudad Juárez
Gulf of California
Rio Grande
Monterrey
Torreón
San Nicolas de Guadalupe
Gulf of Mexico
TROPIC OF CANCER
Zapopan
León
Guadalajara
Nezahualcóyotl
Mexico City
Toluca
Puebla
Caribbean Sea
PACIFIC OCEAN
110° W
100° W
90° W
80° W
30° N
20° N
N
S
E
W
KEY
National border
Capital city
Other city
0
300 mi
0
300 km
Lambert Conformal Conic Projection

Where in the World Is Mexico?

Washington, D.C., to San Nicolas de Guadalupe: 1,610 miles

Carolina and her burro

my Story

A Long Way from Home

In this section you'll read about Carolina, a young woman from Mexico's state of Tamaulipas. What does Carolina's story tell you about life in Mexico?

Explore the Essential Question

- at my **worldgeography.com**
- using the **myWorld Chapter Activity**
- with the **Student Journal**

Story by Monica Maristain for myWorld Geography Online

During the week, Carolina rises early every day, as breakfast is served promptly at 6:30 A.M. Carolina attends Technical High School #1 in Solis, Mexico. She shares a room in a boarding house with three other girls. It hasn't been easy. Carolina's family could not pay for her to attend the school, but through hard work she was able get a scholarship that made it possible. Carolina will be the first in her family to finish her high school and preparatory school studies. "I have seen how my sisters who did not study live, and I do not want that type of life for myself," she says.

After school Carolina works in the school's computer lab until 6 P.M. and then attends a study session until 8 P.M. After dinner at 8 P.M., there is time to spend with her three roommates, or finish up any homework that still needs to be done. "We are supposed to be in bed by 10 P.M.," Carolina laughs, "but often we are still awake when they come by at 11 P.M. to check on us and turn off the lights."

Carolina knows if she wants to go to a university and get a degree she has to get good grades in school and get another scholarship. Carolina hopes to study medicine or communications in college. "Among my family and in my community there aren't too many professionals," Carolina

my worldgeography.com On Assignment

With friends at school

Eating at home

admits. "That is what I wish for the most. . . to get my diploma and to have a better future."

Each weekend Carolina travels by bus for three hours back to her home town. Along the way, she talks about how very different her life is at home. "San Nicolas de Guadalupe is a farming community full of hayfields and animals and plenty of dirt and dust," she says.

Fortunately, there are many other things that Carolina loves about her home. "The people there are very friendly," Carolina says. "When we have celebrations, everyone helps with the preparation of food and other things that need to be done."

Carolina, like most of the people in her home town, is one of the Mazahua, an indigenous group. Carolina can speak her native language in addition to Spanish, but many young people cannot. "I have cousins and if I speak to them in Mazahua, they sit there thinking, 'What did she say?' They say

Back home in San Nicholas de Guadalupe, Carolina visits a market to get ingredients for dinner. On the right, a clay table and roller are used in making tortillas.

196

Trade

Trade has become very important to Mexico's economy. Earnings from selling oil and oil products help finance the government. Manufactured goods and some crops are also major exports. Trade has brought many benefits—but also some problems.

Increased trade has allowed Mexico's economy to grow. Mexico belongs to the World Trade Organization (WTO), where it works with other countries to lower trade barriers. It has free trade agreements with more than forty other nations. Mexico's leaders hope to expand NAFTA to include more nations from Latin America in a zone called the Free Trade Area of the Americas (FTAA).

Providing Jobs Growing trade has led to more jobs in Mexico. However, Mexican workers earn less than those in the United States and Canada. Many manufacturers placed factories in Mexico to take advantage of lower wages.

Mexican workers make more than factory workers in China and other growing economies. Some Mexicans worry that more manufacturing jobs in China will lead to job loss in Mexico.

The Downside of Trade Dependence on trade has caused some problems, too. Some American companies have sold corn and apples in Mexico at lower prices than what Mexican farmers can afford to charge. As a result, Mexican farmers sell less.

Also, Mexico's great dependence on the United States means its economic success is closely linked to the United States economy. When the economy of the United States is doing well, Mexico benefits. When the United States economy slows down, Mexico also suffers. As a result, Mexico saw very slow economic growth in 2008.

Reading Check What is NAFTA, and how has it affected Mexico's economy?

my World IN NUMBERS

Mexico ranks **10th** in automobile manufacturing in the world. In 2007, Mexico produced more than **2** million vehicles.

Section 3 Assessment

Essential Question

Key Terms

1. How did the Institutional Revolutionary Party stay in power for so long?

2. How are remittances important to Mexico?

Key Ideas

3. How does Mexico's Constitution of 1917 affect the government?

4. How has the government tried to improve education for Native Americans in Mexico?

5. What steps did Mexico's government take to change the economy starting in the 1990s?

Think Critically

6. **Identify Evidence** What are two examples of ways that Mexico reveals its blended culture?

7. **Draw Conclusions** What do the names of Mexico's political parties suggest about the goals of each party?

How much does geography shape a country?

8. How has Mexico benefited from having abundant deposits of oil? Go to your Student Journal to record your answer.

Chapter Assessment

Key Terms and Ideas

1. **Recall** In what part of Mexico do **sinkholes** form?

2. **Explain** How does **irrigation** damage farmland?

3. **Compare and Contrast** What are the environmental differences between northern Mexico and southern Mexico?

4. **Sequence** Name the three major native Mexican civilizations in chronological order. Give the name of the **conquistador** who brought about the end of the native empires.

5. **Describe** What was life like for the natives during Spanish rule?

6. **Synthesize** What is the difference between the war for independence in 1810 and the **Mexican Revolution** that occurred in 1910?

7. **Explain** Why do some Mexicans go to the United States in order to send **remittances** to their families?

8. **Discuss** What recent changes have occurred in the Mexican economy, and have they resulted in economic improvement?

Think Critically

9. **Identify Evidence** Of which resources are Mexicans making good use and which resources do they need to develop further?

10. **Make Inferences** What were the problems caused by the PRI party holding power in Mexico for more than 70 years?

11. **Predict** What would happen to the Mexican economy if tourism dropped dramatically?

12. **Core Concepts: People's Impact on the Environment** What environmental problems will Mexico face during the next 10 years?

Places to Know

For each place, write the letter from the map that shows its location.

13. **Yucatán Peninsula**

14. **Sierra Madre Occidental**

15. **Mexico City**

16. **Mexican Plateau**

17. **Rio Grande River**

18. **Mérida**

19. Using the scale, estimate the distance between Mexico City and Mérida.

Mexico: Cities and Features

Essential Question

myWorld Chapter Activity

Judging Mexico's Leaders Assess the achievements of Mexico's leaders, including Montezuma, Cortés, Maximilian, Juarez, Zapata, and Calderón. Judge whether or not the leaders met their goals for Mexico and analyze the effects of the leaders' success or failure on Mexican history.

21st Century Learning

Analyze Media Content

Find three articles online about the presidential race in 2006, between Felipe Calderón and Andrés Manuel López Obrador. Analyze the articles. Is there evidence of bias, or a favoring of one view over another? Does the article suggest the election results were fair? Do supporters of Obrador or Calderón feel the results were fair? Explain your answer.

Document-Based Questions

Success Tracker™
Online at myworldgeography.com

Use your knowledge of Mexico and Documents A and B to answer Questions 1–3.

Document A

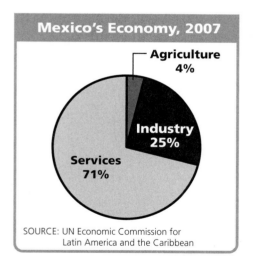

Mexico's Economy, 2007

- Agriculture 4%
- Industry 25%
- Services 71%

SOURCE: UN Economic Commission for Latin America and the Caribbean

Document B

" The mountains here are rugged and difficult, so that they can hardly be crossed, even on foot. Twice I have sent people to conquer them, but they have never been able to do anything against these Indians, who are well armed and entrenched in their mountains."

—Hernando Cortés to Charles V, 1526

1. What kind of work do most Mexican people do for a living?

   A Most people work in agriculture.

   B More than half of the people work in either agriculture or industry.

   C Most people work in the service areas of the economy.

   D More people choose to work in industry than in the service areas of the economy.

2. What was the advantage the Aztecs had that Cortés described to Charles V?

   A The Aztecs were familiar with the territory.

   B Aztec weapons were superior to Spanish weapons.

   C The Aztecs built camps in the mountains.

   D The Spanish were outnumbered.

3. **Writing Task** What does the description Cortés gives of Mexico's landscape suggest about the availability of farmland?

my worldgeography.com | Self-Test

Chapter 4

Central America and the Caribbean

? Essential Question

Is it better to be independent or interdependent?

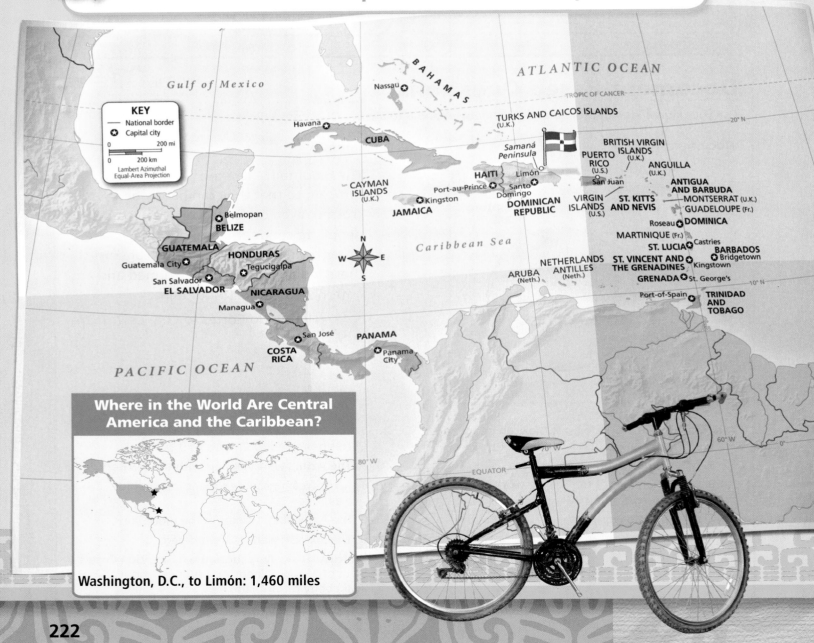

KEY
— National border
✪ Capital city

0   200 mi
0   200 km
Lambert Azimuthal
Equal-Area Projection

Gulf of Mexico

ATLANTIC OCEAN

BAHAMAS

Nassau ✪

TROPIC OF CANCER

20° N

Havana ✪

CUBA

TURKS AND CAICOS ISLANDS
(U.K.)

BRITISH VIRGIN
ISLANDS
(U.K.)

Samaná
Peninsula

PUERTO
RICO
(U.S.)

ANGUILLA
(U.K.)

CAYMAN
ISLANDS
(U.K.)

HAITI   Limón

San Juan

ANTIGUA
AND BARBUDA

Port-au-Prince ✪   Santo
Domingo

✪ Kingston

JAMAICA

DOMINICAN
REPUBLIC

VIRGIN
ISLANDS
(U.S.)

ST. KITTS
AND NEVIS

MONTSERRAT (U.K.)

GUADELOUPE (Fr.)

Roseau ✪ DOMINICA

Belmopan

BELIZE

Caribbean Sea

MARTINIQUE (Fr.)

ST. LUCIA ✪ Castries

BARBADOS
✪ Bridgetown

GUATEMALA

HONDURAS

N
W   E
S

NETHERLANDS
ANTILLES
(Neth.)

ST. VINCENT AND
THE GRENADINES

Kingstown

Guatemala City ✪

✪ Tegucigalpa

ARUBA
(Neth.)

GRENADA ✪ St. George's

San Salvador ✪

EL SALVADOR   NICARAGUA

Port-of-Spain ✪

TRINIDAD
AND
TOBAGO

Managua ✪

10° N

✪ San José   PANAMA

COSTA
RICA   ✪ Panama
City

PACIFIC OCEAN

60° W

70° W

80° W

EQUATOR

Where in the World Are Central America and the Caribbean?

Washington, D.C., to Limón: 1,460 miles

my Story

Working for the Future

Explore the Essential Question
- at **my worldgeography.com**
- using the **my World Chapter Activity**
- with the **Student Journal**

In this section, you'll read about Luis, an ambitious teenager living in a rural community in the Dominican Republic. What does Luis's story tell you about life in the Dominican Republic?

Story by César Namnúm for myWorld Geography Online

Luis's day usually begins with some chores around his house, a quick breakfast, and a bike ride to work. Luis lives in the rural town of Limón in the Dominican Republic. Limón is located on the Samaná Peninsula a few hours north of the Dominican Republic's capital city, Santo Domingo. The peninsula, shown in the photo at the top of this page, has white sandy beaches and lush tropical forests. It is home to a number of beautiful waterfalls. Perhaps the most spectacular waterfall in the region is Salto de Limón, which drops 150 feet into a deep pool of water. "A lot of tourists come to this area," Luis says, "and nearly all of them want to see the falls."

Luis knows about tourists: he works as a tour guide leading visitors to Salto de Limón. The tourists usually ride horses on the journey, while Luis walks on foot to guide them.

Salto de Limón drops 150 feet into a deep pool of water.

Luis guides tourists on horseback.

Walking with tourists to a waterfall may sound like a simple job, but it is not. Visitors to the falls must climb up a steep trail for more than an hour to reach Salto de Limón. It can be a dangerous hike during the rainy season, when the trail is wet and slippery. But Luis has made this trip more than 200 times, and he knows the way well. When he was a child, he and his friends came here to swim and hunt for fresh fruit. Now Luis is almost 17 years old, and he enjoys taking tourists to this special place.

The natural beauty of the Samaná Peninsula makes it very popular with tourists. As a result, the government and the region's people are working to protect the waterfalls and the surrounding area. A local group of tourism-based businesses helps encourage the protection of natural resources and the environment.

In Limón, Luis lives with his grandmother, Doña Graciela, and a few brothers and cousins. "My mother has been in Puerto Rico for

Luis's cousins

224

Luis lives with his grandmother.

Luis enjoys a meal with his family.

Attending school is very important to Luis.

eight years and my uncle lives in New York," he says. "My grandmother raised me."

Luis thinks of himself as an ordinary teenager. He begins a typical day by doing housework and shopping for groceries. "After my chores I like to go bike-riding," Luis says with a smile. He usually rides the mile or so to work, where he meets tourists ready to travel to Salto de Limón.

When Luis returns from leading a tour group to the falls, he is hot, tired, and often covered with mud. Then he gets ready to go to school in the afternoon. Not all Dominican children his age attend school, but Luis thinks it is important. "I want to finish my studies and get my worker's permit so I can work in the city," he says. Getting a work permit would lead to many opportunities for Luis. He wants to earn enough money to provide for his family, and he would love to be able to visit his mother in Puerto Rico.

Because it is not always tourist season in Limón, Luis also does chiripeos, or side jobs around town. Sometimes he works at construction sites. At harvest time, he helps the owner of a small organic coffee plantation pick and dry coffee beans. And, he adds, "Sometimes I go with my cousin to help with his grandmother's conuco." A conuco is a small plantation where families grow crops for their own use. Luis helps take care of the crops. Sometimes there are crops left over to sell, and Luis is able to make extra money.

No matter where you find Luis, one thing is clear: he is an extremely hardworking young man with a very bright future.

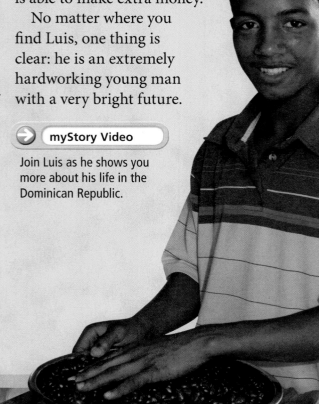

myStory Video

Join Luis as he shows you more about his life in the Dominican Republic.

Meet the Journalist

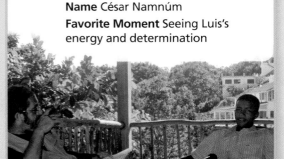

Name César Namnúm
Favorite Moment Seeing Luis's energy and determination

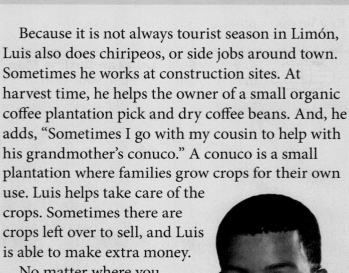

Chapter Atlas

Key Ideas

- Central America and the Caribbean are often hit by natural disasters.
- Tropical climates make agriculture and tourism vital to the region's economies.
- Plantation farming and large numbers of tourists can have negative effects on the region's environments.

Key Terms • isthmus • hurricane • biodiversity • tourism • deforestation

 Visual Glossary

 Reading Skill: Label an Outline Map Take notes using the outline map in your journal.

▼ San Pedro Volcano, Lake Atitlán, Guatemala

Two Maya girls from Guatemala share a laugh.

Physical Features

Central America connects North America and South America and separates the Atlantic Ocean from the Pacific Ocean. It includes Belize, Guatemala, El Salvador, Honduras, Nicaragua, Costa Rica, and Panama. Some geographers also include the southern portion of Mexico. Central America is an **isthmus,** or a strip of land with water on both sides that connects two larger bodies of land. The isthmus is divided by the Panama Canal, a human-made trade route between the Atlantic and the Pacific.

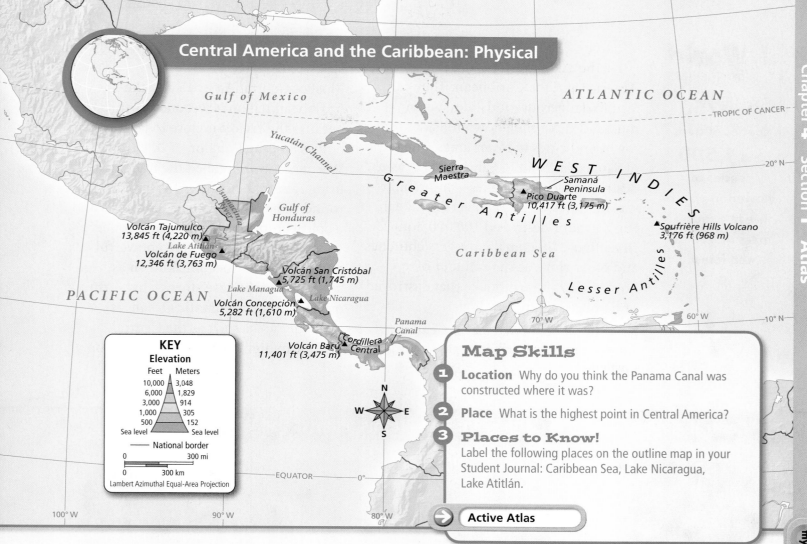

Central America and the Caribbean: Physical

Gulf of Mexico

ATLANTIC OCEAN

TROPIC OF CANCER

Yucatán Channel

Sierra Maestra

WEST INDIES

20° N

Greater Antilles

Samaná Peninsula

▲ Pico Duarte
10,417 ft (3,175 m)

▲ Soufrière Hills Volcano
3,176 ft (968 m)

Usumacinta River

Gulf of Honduras

Volcán Tajumulco
13,845 ft (4,220 m) ▲

Lake Atitlán
Volcán de Fuego
12,346 ft (3,763 m)

Volcán San Cristóbal
5,725 ft (1,745 m)

Caribbean Sea

Lesser Antilles

60° W

10° N

PACIFIC OCEAN

Lake Managua

Volcán Concepción
5,282 ft (1,610 m)

Lake Nicaragua

70° W

Panama Canal

Volcán Barú
11,401 ft (3,475 m)

Cordillera Central

KEY
Elevation

Feet	Meters
10,000	3,048
6,000	1,829
3,000	914
1,000	305
500	152
Sea level	Sea level

—— National border

0 ___ 300 mi
0 ___ 300 km
Lambert Azimuthal Equal-Area Projection

N W E S

EQUATOR

0°

80° W

100° W   90° W

Map Skills

1 Location Why do you think the Panama Canal was constructed where it was?

2 Place What is the highest point in Central America?

3 Places to Know!
Label the following places on the outline map in your Student Journal: Caribbean Sea, Lake Nicaragua, Lake Atitlán.

→ **Active Atlas**

To the east of Central America are the Caribbean Sea and hundreds of islands. Cuba, Jamaica, and Hispaniola are the largest Caribbean islands. Many smaller islands were formed by volcanoes.

Several mountain ranges divide the region. The Caribbean's highest peak is Pico Duarte in the Dominican Republic. Mexico's Sierra Madre mountains extend south into Guatemala, El Salvador, and Honduras. Some of the mountains of the Sierra Madre are high enough to be covered with snow in winter. In Panama, the Cordillera Central mountain range divides the western and eastern parts of the country. Precipitation in the Central American highlands forms important lakes and rivers, such as Lake Atitlán and the Usumacinta River.

The slow but steady movement of plates below Earth's surface makes this region physically unstable. The Central America and the Caribbean region has more than eighty active volcanoes. Volcán de Fuego in Guatemala is perhaps the most active. The Soufrière Hills Volcano in Montserrat had a <u>major</u> eruption in 1997. Today much of Montserrat is closed to people and more than half of its population has moved away.

major, *adj.,* of great importance

227

Earthquakes are common in Central America and the Caribbean. They can lead to dangerous mudslides, when mud and earth slide down hillsides onto towns and cities in lower areas. The city of San Salvador in El Salvador has been destroyed by earthquakes—and rebuilt—several times. In 2001 an earthquake in San Salvador destroyed 100,000 homes. In Antigua, Guatemala, roofless churches and other ruins are a reminder of a powerful 1773 earthquake that destroyed or damaged many buildings.

Reading Check What makes Central America and the Caribbean physically unstable?

Climate and Life

Most of Central America and the Caribbean region is wet and warm because the region is close to large water bodies and the Equator, or 0° latitude. Warm east winds called the trade winds bring rain to the region. These year-round rains provide water for forests and tropical crops like bananas and coffee. When the trade winds form powerful rainstorms, they become known as **hurricanes,** or intense storms that form over the tropical Atlantic Ocean.

Higher areas such as the Central American highlands have a dry season

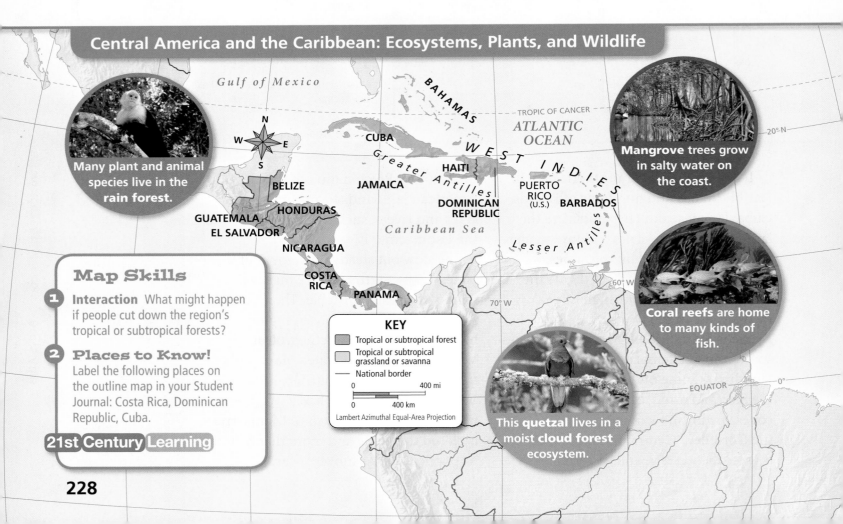

Central America and the Caribbean: Ecosystems, Plants, and Wildlife

Many plant and animal species live in the **rain forest.**

Mangrove trees grow in salty water on the coast.

Coral reefs are home to many kinds of fish.

This **quetzal** lives in a moist **cloud forest** ecosystem.

KEY
- Tropical or subtropical forest
- Tropical or subtropical grassland or savanna
- National border

0   400 mi
0   400 km
Lambert Azimuthal Equal-Area Projection

Map Skills

1 **Interaction** What might happen if people cut down the region's tropical or subtropical forests?

2 **Places to Know!** Label the following places on the outline map in your Student Journal: Costa Rica, Dominican Republic, Cuba.

21st Century Learning

and a rainy season. The area's mountains block the trade winds, leading to less rain in the winter months. The lack of rain between December and April can lead to water shortages. As a result, these areas cannot support tropical forests. They are, however, suitable for cattle ranching.

The Central American highlands have a relatively <u>dense</u> population. Most people in Central America live in the highlands because of the dry, cool highland climate. This climate allows people to grow a variety of crops.

Caribbean countries have generally lower elevations. Their climates are similar to the lower areas of Central America.

Due to the region's warm, wet weather, tropical and subtropical ecosystems cover Central America and the Caribbean. Tropical rain forests cover most areas that have not been cleared of trees. Tropical grasslands have formed in regions where people have cut down rain forests. Some countries, such as Costa Rica, have a rare ecosystem called cloud forest. Cloud forests are higher and cooler than lowland forests, with moist clouds that are near the ground. They support diverse wildlife.

Most Caribbean islands are surrounded by an underwater ecosystem known as coral reef. Reefs are largely made up of tiny organisms—coral—that produce a substance similar to limestone as they grow. Over time, coral reefs become large underwater islands that are home to a wide variety of tropical fish and other marine life. This variety of living things is called **biodiversity.**

Reading Check What is an underwater ecosystem common in the Caribbean Sea?

Hurricane Havoc

The region's unique ecosystems, warm days and nights, and beautiful beaches attract visitors from many parts of the world. However, the region's powerful hurricanes can cause great damage and keep visitors away.

Residents of Caribbean islands and coastal countries like Honduras face an average of eight hurricanes a year. Hurricanes usually occur in summer and early fall. These storms can bring several inches of rain an hour, as well as powerful 150-mile-per-hour winds that can harm many people and destroy entire towns.

myWorldActivity
Location Equation

dense, *adj.,* crowded

Hurricanes can cause serious damage in the region. ▼

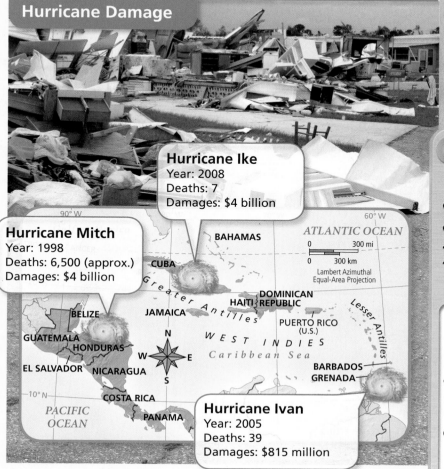

Hurricane Damage

Hurricane Ike
Year: 2008
Deaths: 7
Damages: $4 billion

Hurricane Mitch
Year: 1998
Deaths: 6,500 (approx.)
Damages: $4 billion

Hurricane Ivan
Year: 2005
Deaths: 39
Damages: $815 million

BAHAMAS

ATLANTIC OCEAN

CUBA

Greater Antilles

DOMINICAN REPUBLIC

HAITI

JAMAICA

PUERTO RICO (U.S.)

Lesser Antilles

BELIZE

GUATEMALA

HONDURAS

EL SALVADOR

NICARAGUA

WEST INDIES

Caribbean Sea

BARBADOS

GRENADA

COSTA RICA

PANAMA

PACIFIC OCEAN

0   300 mi
0   300 km
Lambert Azimuthal Equal-Area Projection

90° W   60° W   10° N

N W E S

One Region, Many Faces

Most people in Central America and the Caribbean have been influenced by a number of different cultures. The religions people practice, the art they make, and the languages they speak show how the region's people have created new cultures from many traditions.

THINK CRITICALLY **How do different cultures affect the region?**

▲ Caribbean music is known for its percussion, a tradition strongly influenced by West African music.

Haiti's official languages are French and Creole, a version of French influenced by African languages.

Native American languages are common in Guatemala. This boy speaks the Mayan language Achi.

This girl from Puerto Rico speaks Spanish and English, but she has Native American ancestors.

Like most other people from the Dominican Republic, Luis speaks Spanish.

→ Language Lesson

In Cuba, a popular religion called **Santeria** combines Catholic and West African beliefs. For example, the Santeria god Changó is a spirit from an ancient African religion. In Haiti, voodoo also includes elements of Catholic and West African beliefs. In Jamaica, Rastafarianism combines Christianity with the belief that the former emperor of Ethiopia descended from Israel's King Solomon and was divine. Trinidad has a growing number of believers in Hinduism and Islam. Recently, some Central American and Caribbean people have joined Protestant churches.

Indigenous Traditions Mestizos, or people of Spanish and indigenous background, are the largest ethnic group in Central America. In Guatemala, however, the Maya are the largest ethnic group. Most Guatemalans speak a form of Maya as their first language, although they learn Spanish in school. Many Mayas mix traditional religious rituals with European ones, such as combining the names of Catholic saints with stories about Maya gods. Most Maya women wear traditional, multicolored woven fabrics.

Going Global Many people in Central America and the Caribbean face widespread poverty. As a result, some people have migrated to North America or Europe in search of work. This spread of people from one place to many others is called a **diaspora**. After finding jobs, many immigrants send money, or remittances, to support their families.

Wherever people go, they bring their food, music, and beliefs. This leads to cultural diffusion, or the spread of cultural traits. Regional foods such as burritos and Cuban sandwiches are now popular in North America, Europe, and parts of Asia. Caribbean music has also traveled far from its roots. Salsa from Puerto Rico, merengue from the Dominican Republic, and reggae from Jamaica can be heard in many parts of the world.

Reading Check In what ways is Caribbean culture a blend of other cultures?

Government and Change

Central American and Caribbean people live in a region of change. People migrate to other countries and then return. Hurricanes can destroy crops and homes. Even governments can change quickly.

Democracy in the Region Most governments in Central America are presidential democracies in which a president is the head of government. In the Caribbean, many countries are democracies with parliamentary systems. In a parliamentary system, a prime minister is chosen from the parliament, or the legislative body of government. Most countries in the region select leaders in democratic elections. Often, citizens are legally required to vote.

Costa Rica has the region's most stable democracy. Costa Ricans have been electing their rulers since 1899. However, most of the region's democracies are less stable. Governments in poorer countries may change if voters are unhappy that leaders have failed to improve living conditions.

In fact, the lack of social services such as healthcare and education can lead to widespread anger and violence. Military takeovers and political violence are common. In Guatemala, civil war made

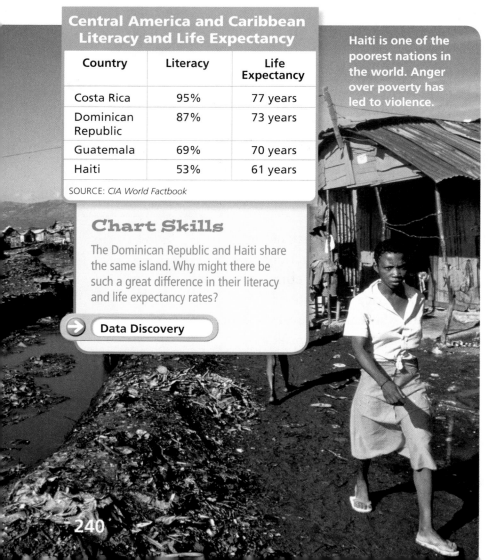

Central America and Caribbean Literacy and Life Expectancy

Country	Literacy	Life Expectancy
Costa Rica	95%	77 years
Dominican Republic	87%	73 years
Guatemala	69%	70 years
Haiti	53%	61 years

SOURCE: *CIA World Factbook*

Chart Skills

The Dominican Republic and Haiti share the same island. Why might there be such a great difference in their literacy and life expectancy rates?

Data Discovery

Haiti is one of the poorest nations in the world. Anger over poverty has led to violence.

democracy almost impossible until a 1996 peace agreement. In Haiti, 20,000 U.S. troops occupied the country to end a violent uprising in 1994. Since 2004, thousands of United Nations troops have helped keep peace in Haiti.

Dictatorship in Cuba Although most countries have removed their dictators, Cuba has not. Fidel Castro was the dictator of Cuba from 1959 to 2008, when he designated his brother Raúl to replace him. Cuba is a socialist republic with a command economy. The Communist Party is the only official political party.

Cubans cannot choose their leader, but they do vote for representatives to the National Assembly. These elections are unfair, however, since most races have only a single candidate. While Cuba <u>restricts</u> political and economic freedom, the government offers some social services that neighboring countries lack. For example, college and healthcare are practically free for Cubans.

Calls for Change Movements to improve the lives of people in the Caribbean and Central America continue. Throughout the region, there is a call to improve education and healthcare. In some places, voters have elected leaders who believe that government must help the poor and have more control over the economy. In other countries, such as the Dominican Republic, voters have turned to conservative leaders with the hope that they will be tough on crime and encourage foreign investments.

Reading Check What makes it difficult to achieve a stable democracy?

Freeing Up the Economy

One of the region's major economic goals is to increase capital investment, or investment in factories and technology. Capital investment can lead to economic growth. Government leaders often encourage foreign companies to build factories and other facilities in their countries. Countries also seek to improve human capital through education and training for workers.

Free-Trade Agreements One way the region's countries work to improve their economies is through free-trade agreements. Free trade is a system in which goods and services are traded between countries without government restrictions such as tariffs. Members of a free-trade association work to increase the amount of goods traded and to reduce taxes on products made in one member country and sold in another.

restrict, *v.,* to limit or prevent

Costa Rica has a stable government, a stable economy, and a relatively high standard of living.

241

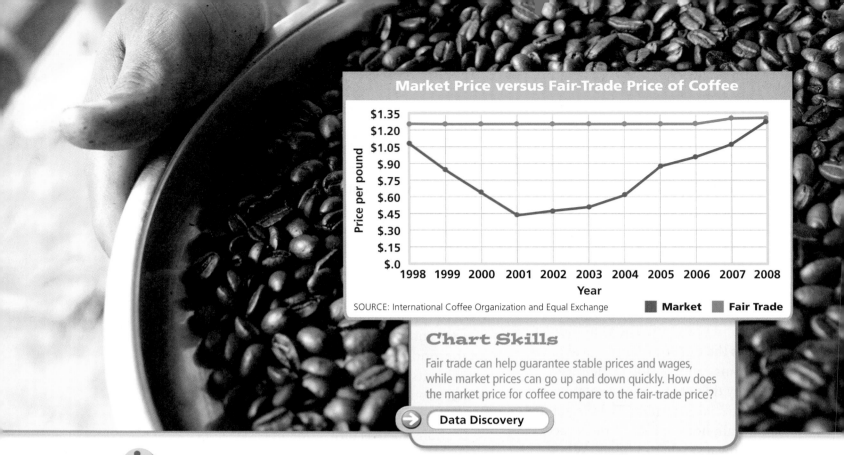

Market Price versus Fair-Trade Price of Coffee

Price per pound:
- $1.35
- $1.20
- $1.05
- $.90
- $.75
- $.60
- $.45
- $.30
- $.15
- $.0

Year: 1998, 1999, 2000, 2001, 2002, 2003, 2004, 2005, 2006, 2007, 2008

SOURCE: International Coffee Organization and Equal Exchange

■ Market ■ Fair Trade

Chart Skills

Fair trade can help guarantee stable prices and wages, while market prices can go up and down quickly. How does the market price for coffee compare to the fair-trade price?

→ Data Discovery

myWorldActivity
Is Free Fair?

One example of a free-trade association is the Caribbean Community (Caricom). Another is the Central America-Dominican Republic-United States Free Trade Association (CAFTA-DR), which also includes the United States.

Benefits and Drawbacks There are benefits and drawbacks to international free-trade agreements. Low taxes can encourage foreign businesses to build factories, creating jobs. CAFTA-DR has helped increase manufacturing in the region. However, some people worry that free trade helps wealthy countries more than poor countries. For these people, fair trade offers more benefits. Supporters of fair trade believe in paying workers fair wages and protecting the environment. They are often willing to pay more for goods that have been produced fairly.

Reforming Farms Free trade also affects farming. Farmers produce large amounts of food for free markets, and they often use a great deal of pesticides and fertilizer. This can harm the environment. In addition, most farmers do not own the crops they raise and thus cannot profit from international trade.

A few countries, such as Guatemala, have passed land-reform laws. These laws take some land from powerful landowners and divide it among poor farmers. Poor farmers can sometimes get small loans, called **microcredit,** to start their own farms. Some farmers form cooperatives, or groups of people who share the profits of their business. Many coffee and cacao growers now belong to cooperatives.

Reading Check How are people trying to improve the region's economy?

Ecotourism

Large <u>luxury</u> tourist resorts can cause environmental problems by using large amounts of resources, such as clean water. Still, tourism is an important part of the region's economy. One growing type of tourism is **ecotourism,** or tourism that focuses on the environment and seeks to minimize environmental impact. Ecotourism often involves exploring nature on foot or horseback. Tourists may sleep in simple huts or cabins. They may eat local food and require fewer imported goods to meet their needs.

Some people worry that ecotourism will change native cultures or harm natural habitats. But the Kuna Yala Reserve in Panama provides a successful example of ecotourism. In this case, the indigenous people themselves plan and manage an ecotourism program.

❝ [The Kuna Yala recognize] the importance of their natural surroundings and the need to protect their culture … [They know] how to manage the growth of tourism. ❞
—a Costa Rican travel agent

luxury, *n.,* pleasure or comfort

Reading Check What are the benefits of ecotourism?

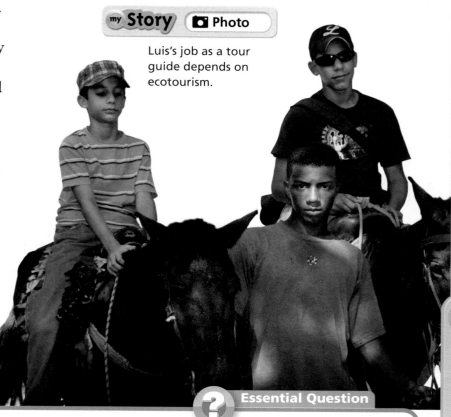

my **Story** 📷 **Photo**

Luis's job as a tour guide depends on ecotourism.

Section 3 Assessment

Key Terms

1. What are some effects of the Caribbean diaspora?

2. How has ecotourism affected Central America and the Caribbean?

Key Ideas

3. Describe the cultures in Central America and the Caribbean.

4. What causes democratic governments in the region to change frequently?

5. How might land reform, microcredit, and cooperatives affect the economy?

Think Critically

6. **Compare and Contrast** How are the governments of Cuba and Costa Rica different?

7. **Compare Viewpoints** How might a small farmer's and an American factory owner's viewpoints on CAFTA-DR differ?

? Essential Question

Is it better to be independent or interdependent?

8. In what ways are the economies of Central America and the Caribbean independent and interdependent? Go to your Student Journal to record your answer.

Chapter Assessment

Key Terms and Ideas

1. **Summarize** What are the different natural disasters that commonly affect Central America and the Caribbean?

2. **Explain** What are the geographic factors of Central America and the Caribbean that make the region well suited for **tourism**?

3. **Describe** Describe how the **Maya** civilization rose and what it accomplished.

4. **Cause and Effect** Why did the Spanish set up the **encomienda** system and what were the results of that system?

5. **Compare and Contrast** How was life in Central America and the Caribbean similar before and after **independence**?

6. **Recall** What are the main roots of Caribbean and Central American culture?

7. **Define** What does DR-CAFTA stand for and what does it allow?

Think Critically

8. **Draw Inferences** What does land ownership have to do with poverty in Central America and the Caribbean today?

9. **Sequence** Put the following terms in chronological order and explain your reasons: dictatorships, colonization, slavery, encomienda, independence.

10. **Draw Conclusions** Why might the leader of a Central American or Caribbean country find it hard to have a stable government?

11. **Core Concepts: Human-Environment Interaction** What are the benefits and drawbacks of large-scale agriculture in Central American and Caribbean countries?

Places to Know

For each place, write the letter from the map that shows its location.

12. Caribbean Sea

13. Lake Atitlán

14. Cuba

15. Costa Rica

16. Lake Nicaragua

17. Dominican Republic

18. **Estimate** Using the scale, estimate the distance between Costa Rica and the Dominican Republic.

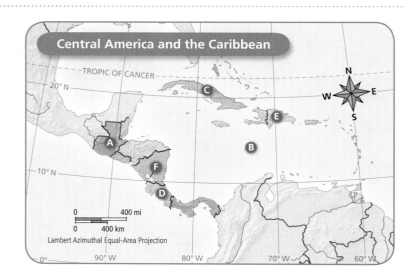

Central America and the Caribbean

TROPIC OF CANCER

20° N

10° N

0 400 mi
0 400 km
Lambert Azimuthal Equal-Area Projection

0°   90° W   80° W   70° W   60° W

Essential Question

Chapter Transfer Activity

Venturing in Nicaragua Follow your teacher's instructions to find out more about the different environments, businesses, natural hazards, and opportunities in Nicaragua. Then prepare a plan for a particular kind of tourism business that you will use to seek government or private investment funds.

21st Century Learning

Develop Cultural Awareness

Choose two cultures different from your own that are a part of your community. Then use the Internet or other sources to learn more about these cultures. Write a reflection about how what you learned might change the way you relate to someone of that culture. You might consider researching the following cultural aspects:

- food
- religious practices
- clothing
- gender roles

Document-Based Questions

Success Tracker™
Online at myworldgeography.com

Use your knowledge of Central America and the Caribbean and Documents A and B to answer Questions 1–3.

Document A

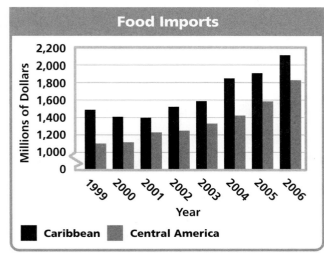

Food Imports

SOURCE: U.S. Department of Agriculture Economic Research Service and U.S. Trade Internet System

1. Which of the following best explains the change shown in Document A?

   A The Caribbean is suffering from a drought.

   B Factory workers are taking jobs on farms.

   C Free-trade laws have made it easier for food to be imported.

   D Foreign food is of better quality than Caribbean or Central American food.

Document B

" You will be engaged in subsistence agriculture in which you will be doing your own small farming … We need to ensure that our people can feel secured in obtaining not only high quality nutritious food, but it should also be at affordable prices as well … [Right now] we are importing almost everything that we eat."

—St. Kitts and Nevis Prime Minister Denzil L. Douglas, 2008

2. What slogan would best fit Prime Minister Douglas' new plan for food production?

   A Food Through Trade

   B Back to the Land

   C Worldwide Vegetables

   D Industry Rules

3. Writing Task Write a radio announcement persuading people in St. Kitts and Nevis to grow their own vegetables.

Young and Unemployed in Middle America

Your Mission Study the graphs showing education, literacy, and foreign investment in Belize, Guatemala, and Mexico. Use what you learn to propose a jobs program that helps young people find work in those countries.

In Middle America, the job market is generally weak. Finding a job is even more difficult for young people in this region. They want to work, but they may lack training or transportation. The job market also suffers when business development is slow. Finding a solution to high unemployment rates requires learning more about the factors and circumstances that have led to this situation.

Being young and unemployed in Middle America is part of the problem, but your ideas can be part of the solution.

STEP 1

Identify the Problem.

Employment is desirable not simply because it generates income. Having a job means working toward a goal, learning new skills or information, and improving one's quality of life. Belize, Guatemala, and Mexico are very different nations. They also share certain characteristics. Before you can propose an employment solution, you have to learn more about why people there are unemployed.

STEP 2

Analyze the Data.

As you analyze the graphs, recall what you read in this unit about the geography, history, and current situation in Middle America. How might factors such as education affect unemployment? Do additional research to fill in the gaps in your analysis. You might also find that newspaper articles and photographs provide helpful information about job markets in faraway countries.

STEP 3

Propose a Solution.

Working in groups, prepare a presentation based on one of the graphs provided on the next page. Explain the data in the graph and show how it relates to unemployment in all three subject nations. Integrate what you have learned into your group's final presentation on the proposed government jobs program. Your solution should be flexible enough to work in each nation, given its unique circumstances.

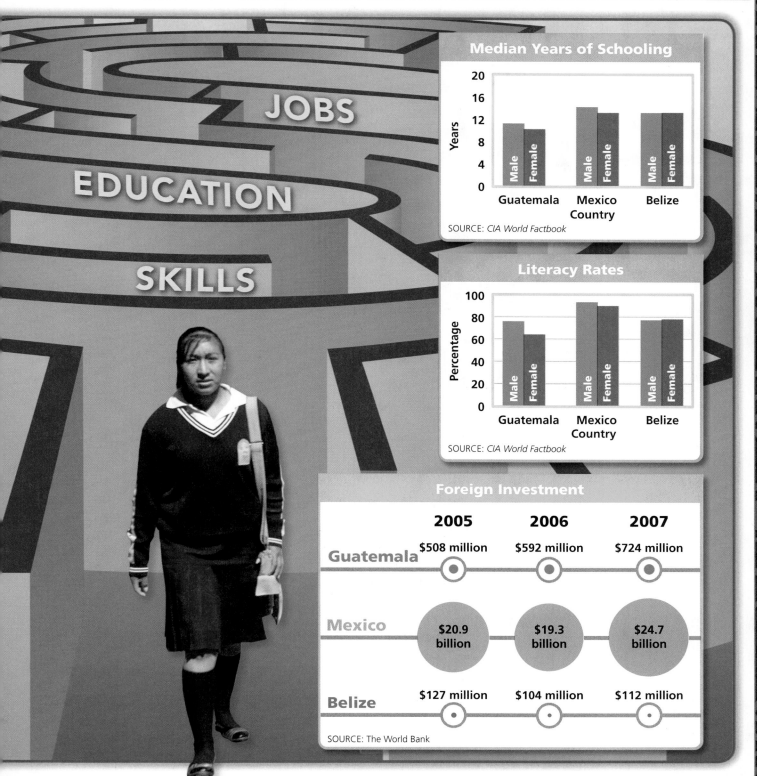

Median Years of Schooling

Years

20 | 16 | 12 | 8 | 4 | 0

Guatemala — Male, Female
Mexico — Male, Female
Belize — Male, Female

Country

SOURCE: *CIA World Factbook*

Literacy Rates

Percentage

100 | 80 | 60 | 40 | 20 | 0

Guatemala — Male, Female
Mexico — Male, Female
Belize — Male, Female

Country

SOURCE: *CIA World Factbook*

Foreign Investment

	2005	2006	2007
Guatemala	$508 million	$592 million	$724 million
Mexico	$20.9 billion	$19.3 billion	$24.7 billion
Belize	$127 million	$104 million	$112 million

SOURCE: The World Bank

South America

South America has an amazing variety of climates and landforms, including huge mountains, deserts, and rain forests. Around 371 million people live in South America. The largest country in South America is Brazil. Brazil includes most of the Amazon rain forest, a huge forest that stretches from the Andes Mountains in the west to the Atlantic Ocean in the east.

What time is it there?

Washington, D.C.	Quimbaya, Colombia
9 A.M. Monday	9 A.M. Monday

KEY
— National border
✪ Capital city
Orthographic Projection

The Unit Ahead

→ **Chapter 5** Caribbean South America

→ **Chapter 6** The Andes and the Pampas

→ **Chapter 7** Brazil

my worldgeography.com

Plan your trip online by doing a Data Discovery Activity and watching the myStory Videos of the region's teens.

Daniella
Age: 15
Home: Armenia, Colombia
Chapter 5

Omar
Age: 14
Home: Potosí, Bolivia
Chapter 6

Vinicius
Age: 16
Home: Rio de Janeiro, Brazil
Chapter 7

Mangroves on the coast of Brazil

Regional Overview
Physical Geography

PACIFIC OCEAN

The Andes are the longest range of mountains on Earth.

Amazon Basin

Mt. Aconcagua
22,834 ft (6,959 m)

Atacama Desert

Andes Mountains

Altiplano

Pampas

Rio de la Plata

The vast plains of the Pampas stretch from the Atlantic coast to the foothills of the Andes.

ATLANTIC OCEAN

Caribbean Sea

Orinoco River

Guiana Highlands

Amazon River

Brazilian Highlands

The Amazon River drains an area of about 2.7 million square miles.

Regional Flyover

Welcome aboard the fastest flight around South America ever! Your plane takes off from Bogotá, Colombia, high in the Andes. Traveling clockwise around the continent, you soon see the Brazilian rain forest—a vast green blanket veined with dark rivers flowing toward one huge river, the Amazon. This is the mighty Amazon basin, the rain forest lowlands that make up much of the continent.

As you fly down the east coast, you glimpse a river called the Rio de la Plata, flowing through the vast grasslands of the Pampas in Argentina.

When you reach the cold southern tip of the continent, your plane turns northward, following the Andes. You first see the Atacama Desert in Chile, wedged between the Andes and the Pacific Ocean, and then the Altiplano, a huge plain of level ground high up in the Bolivian Andes. After you cross the Equator in Ecuador, Colombia's parallel mountain ranges suddenly appear. As your plane lands in Bogotá, you count the number of countries you have seen—12!

 In-Flight Movie

Take flight over South America and explore the region from the air.

my **worldgeography**.com In-Flight Movie

Regional Overview
Human Geography

Origins of Diversity

South America's ethnic diversity grew from a series of migrations.

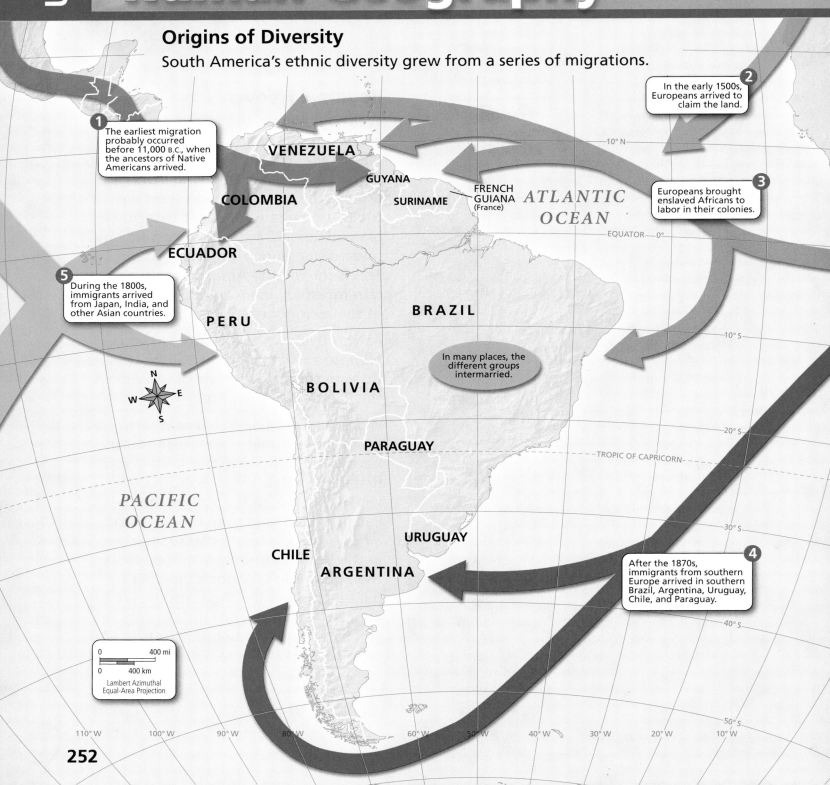

1 The earliest migration probably occurred before 11,000 B.C., when the ancestors of Native Americans arrived.

2 In the early 1500s, Europeans arrived to claim the land.

3 Europeans brought enslaved Africans to labor in their colonies.

4 After the 1870s, immigrants from southern Europe arrived in southern Brazil, Argentina, Uruguay, Chile, and Paraguay.

5 During the 1800s, immigrants arrived from Japan, India, and other Asian countries.

In many places, the different groups intermarried.

VENEZUELA
GUYANA
SURINAME
FRENCH GUIANA (France)
COLOMBIA
ECUADOR
PERU
BRAZIL
BOLIVIA
PARAGUAY
URUGUAY
CHILE
ARGENTINA

ATLANTIC OCEAN
PACIFIC OCEAN

EQUATOR — 0°
10° N
10° S
20° S — TROPIC OF CAPRICORN
30° S
40° S
50° S

110° W 100° W 90° W 80° W 70° W 60° W 50° W 40° W 30° W 20° W 10° W

N
W   E
S

0   400 mi
0   400 km
Lambert Azimuthal
Equal-Area Projection

Diversity Today

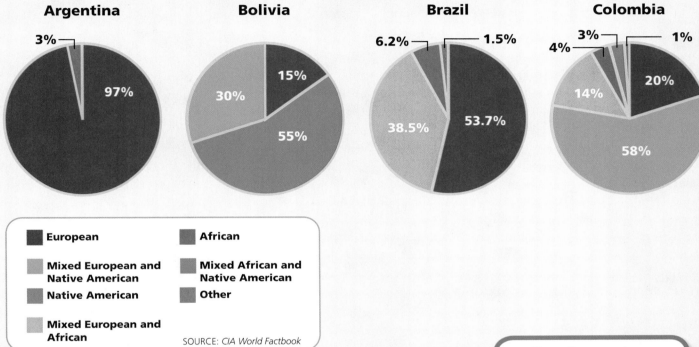

Argentina

3%

97%

Bolivia

15%

30%

55%

Brazil

6.2%   1.5%

53.7%

38.5%

Colombia

4% 3%   1%

20%

14%

58%

■ European

■ African

■ Mixed European and Native American

■ Mixed African and Native American

■ Native American

■ Other

■ Mixed European and African

SOURCE: *CIA World Factbook*

Put It Together

1. Why is South America a place of such ethnic diversity?

2. Why do some South American nations have so many people of African descent?

3. Why do you think there are more people descended from Native Americans in Bolivia than in Argentina?

Data Discovery

Find your own data to make a regional data table.

Size Comparison

South America is much bigger than the United States.

Chapter 5

Caribbean South America

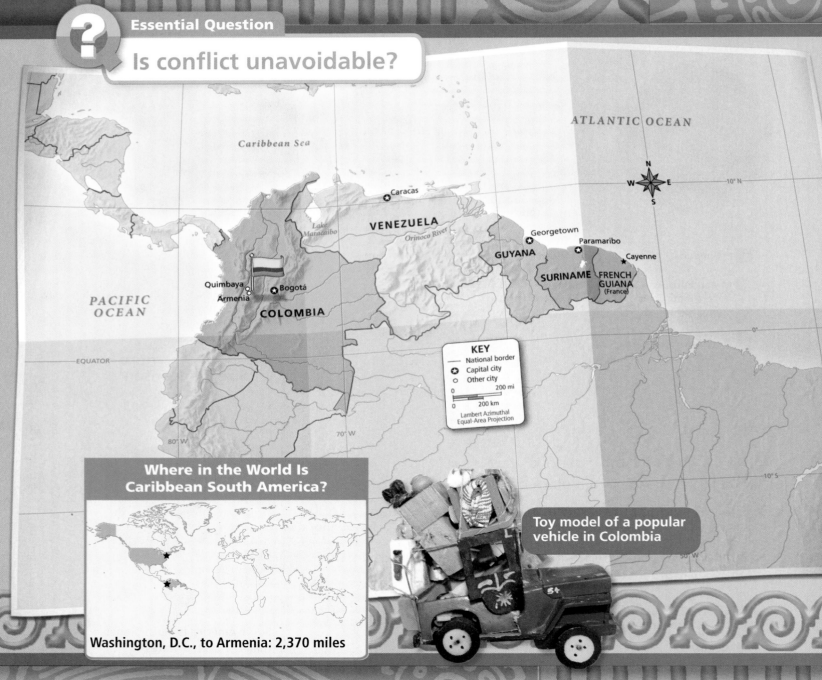

? Essential Question

Is conflict unavoidable?

ATLANTIC OCEAN

Caribbean Sea

★ Caracas

VENEZUELA

Lake Maracaibo

Orinoco River

Georgetown ●

GUYANA

Paramaribo ●

★ Cayenne

SURINAME

FRENCH GUIANA (France)

10° N

Quimbaya ○
Armenia ○ ● ★ Bogotá

COLOMBIA

PACIFIC OCEAN

EQUATOR

0°

10° S

80° W   70° W

KEY

—— National border
★ Capital city
○ Other city

0   200 mi
0   200 km

Lambert Azimuthal
Equal-Area Projection

Where in the World Is Caribbean South America?

★

★

Washington, D.C., to Armenia: 2,370 miles

Toy model of a popular vehicle in Colombia

54

my Story

Daniella's Coffee Run

In this section, you'll read about Daniella, a girl who works as a tour guide on El Carriel, her family's coffee farm in Colombia. What does Daniella's story tell you about getting along with others?

? Explore the Essential Question
- at my **worldgeography.com**
- using the **myWorld Chapter Activity**
- with the **Student Journal**

Story by Richard Rapp for myWorld Geography Online

The quiet that blankets the lush green mountains is suddenly broken by the sound of an old pickup truck starting up. Daniella, a lively fifteen-year-old from the coffee region of Colombia, rushes to the vehicle. She has just finished her weekend work as a tour guide on her family's farm. Now she and her grandfather are about to drive into town. It is the harvest season and the pair are off to Quimbaya to sell part of this year's coffee crop.

The drive into town is short, and the scenery changes quickly. The soils in this part of Colombia are volcanic, which means the ground is very rich and fertile. Plantations and farms cover the hillsides. Closer to town, the plantations dotting the hills and valleys give way to one-family houses. Soon Daniella and her grandfather have arrived in the small but bustling downtown area, and the Plaza Bolívar—the square that is the central feature of almost every Colombian town and village.

my worldgeography.com On Assignment

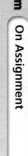

Daniella the tour guide shows visitors a coffee plant.

Tourists arriving at the farm

Daniella and her grandfather wait to be paid for the coffee bean delivery.

While in Quimbaya, Daniella draws our attention to the tourists who have brought change to her region of Colombia.

"The farm has always been for growing coffee, and not only coffee, but for other crops like plantain and beans, too," explains Daniella. "But it isn't as easy as it used to be. . . . Then tourists started to come, and most locals thought that they could help us out economically and that we could enjoy each other as well."

Over the past two years El Carriel has undergone some changes. Handed down from her grandfather to her father, the coffee farm has expanded its activities to include tourism. New cabins have been built for the visitors. Her family is even planning to build a canopy line that will carry visitors through the treetops for a bird's-eye view of the farm and its surroundings.

During the week, Daniella lives in Armenia, where she goes to school. On weekends she travels from her home to work on the farm (near Quimbaya) as a tour guide. Here she educates tourists about the coffee process and

256

During the visit to Quimbaya, the beans are tested for quality.

Daniella fits in some bowling while in Quimbaya.

daily life on the farm. Daniella enjoys the people who come to learn about her region, even though sometimes these foreigners can be difficult to understand. She explains that "Sometimes it gets complicated due to the language difference. . . . But we always try to learn from one another."

Once in the marketplace, Daniella and her grandfather open their filled coffee sacks and have the beans tested for weight and quality. Then Daniella and her grandfather consult with the merchant over the price. After a little friendly haggling, all agree and set an amount. When paid, Daniella enjoys a quick game of bowling in the Quimbaya bowling alley. Then it's back to El Carriel.

On the farm, the heat of the afternoon gives way to a starry, early evening sky. The family all drink their last cup of coffee for the day as they

chat. Daniella talks about her plans for the future. Although she hopes to become a cardiologist one day, she would still like to keep the farm in the family. Clearly enjoying the coffee produced here, she also explains why she enjoys the visitors, "We have conversations where we can learn about each other. . .besides making friends, I learn how they see things and then understand more about myself."

myStory Video

Learn more about Daniella by viewing a video about coffee farming in Colombia.

Meet the Journalist

Name Richard Rapp
Favorite Moment Waking up to the mountain view and looking forward to coffee and breakfast!

Chapter Atlas

Key Ideas

- A wide range of landforms characterizes Caribbean South America.
- Some nations in the region enjoy many natural resources, such as oil.
- Population density varies dramatically in this region of diverse ethnic groups.

Key Terms • cordillera • Llanos • ecosystem • terraced farming

 Visual Glossary

 Reading Skill: Label an Outline Map Take notes using the outline map in your journal.

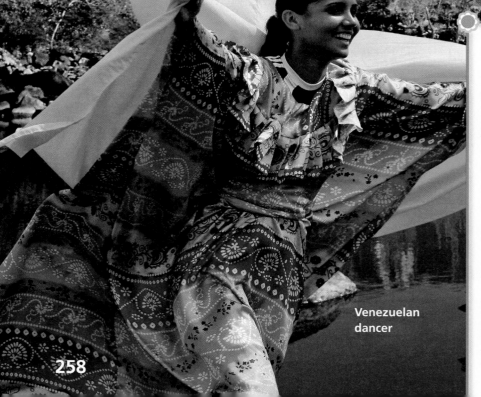

Kukenan Mountain in Venezuela

Venezuelan dancer

Physical Features

Daniella lives in a coffee-growing area of Colombia. Colombia, along with Venezuela, Guyana, Suriname, and French Guiana, all border the Caribbean Sea, along the northern coast of South America.

In Colombia, the Andes Mountains, which extend up the west coast of South America, split into three ranges, known as **cordilleras.** Because the central range is volcanic, its fertile soil is good for coffee plants.

Between the cordilleras, the Cauca and the Magdalena rivers flow north

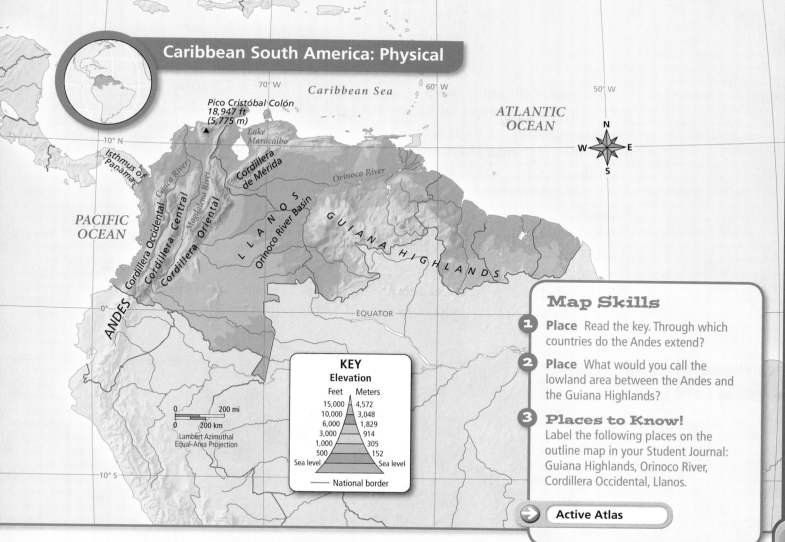

Caribbean South America: Physical

Caribbean Sea

ATLANTIC OCEAN

70° W   60° W   50° W

Pico Cristóbal Colón
18,947 ft
(5,775 m)

Lake Maracaibo

10° N

Isthmus of Panama

Cauca River

Magdalena River

Cordillera de Mérida

Orinoco River

PACIFIC OCEAN

Cordillera Occidental

Cordillera Central

Cordillera Oriental

L L A N O S

Orinoco River Basin

G U I A N A   H I G H L A N D S

ANDES

0°   EQUATOR

10° S

N W E S

0   200 mi
0   200 km
Lambert Azimuthal
Equal-Area Projection

KEY
Elevation

Feet	Meters
15,000	4,572
10,000	3,048
6,000	1,829
3,000	914
1,000	305
500	152
Sea level	Sea level

—— National border

Map Skills

1 **Place** Read the key. Through which countries do the Andes extend?

2 **Place** What would you call the lowland area between the Andes and the Guiana Highlands?

3 **Places to Know!**
Label the following places on the outline map in your Student Journal: Guiana Highlands, Orinoco River, Cordillera Occidental, Llanos.

→ **Active Atlas**

through deep valleys toward the Caribbean Sea. The Cordillera Oriental, or eastern range, extends north to form the border of Venezuela. Another branch of this range stretches deep into Venezuela. This branch, called the Cordillera de Mérida, runs past Lake Maracaibo and extends along the Caribbean coast. The northern part of the Andes is an active volcanic area. Earthquakes often shake the region.

On the eastern side of the Andes, the mountains plunge down to lowland plains, or **Llanos,** in both Colombia and Venezuela. In the southeastern corner of Colombia, the Amazon rain forest creeps over the border from Brazil. In Venezuela, savannas and tropical rain forests cover the Orinoco River basin. The Orinoco is one of the longest rivers in South America.

In the southeast of Venezuela, the ground rises again to the Guiana Highlands, which extend through Guyana, Suriname, and French Guiana. Along the eastern coastlines you might see mangrove swamps and saltwater grasses.

Reading Check How would you describe the eastern coastline of Caribbean South America?

Climate

Because part of the region is on the Equator, temperatures are hot everywhere. However, there are many different climates in the region. Hazardous weather conditions occur in some areas. Heavy rains often lead to flooding and mudslides.

Much of Colombia has a tropical wet climate, especially along the west coast and in the southeast. The northwest coast of Columbia has a tropical wet and dry climate. Most of Venezuela has a tropical wet and dry climate, which also affects southern Guyana, Suriname, and almost all of French Guiana. Here there is a wet and a dry season each year.

The northern tip of Colombia and the northwestern coast of Venezuela have a semiarid climate. In the far north of Venezuela lies an arid desert.

The climate changes in the Andes according to elevation. The higher up you go, the cooler and wetter it gets.

Reading Check What kinds of climates would you find in this region?

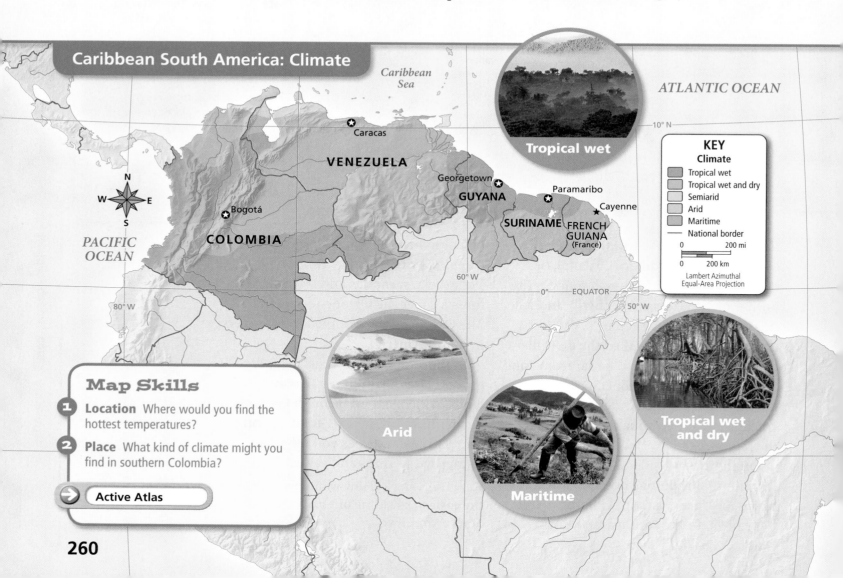

Caribbean South America: Climate

Caribbean Sea

ATLANTIC OCEAN

10° N

Tropical wet

VENEZUELA

Caracas

Georgetown

Paramaribo

GUYANA

Cayenne

SURINAME

FRENCH GUIANA
(France)

Bogotá

COLOMBIA

PACIFIC OCEAN

60° W

80° W

0°   EQUATOR

50° W

KEY
Climate
- Tropical wet
- Tropical wet and dry
- Semiarid
- Arid
- Maritime
- National border

0   200 mi
0   200 km

Lambert Azimuthal
Equal-Area Projection

Arid

Maritime

Tropical wet and dry

Map Skills

1. **Location** Where would you find the hottest temperatures?

2. **Place** What kind of climate might you find in southern Colombia?

→ **Active Atlas**

Ecosystems

If you traveled across Caribbean South America, you would pass through a variety of climate zones. You would also notice a different range of vegetation and animal life in each climate zone. The plants and animals that depend on each other and their environment for survival is called an **ecosystem.**

Along the Pacific coast of Colombia, warm temperatures and heavy rainfall have encouraged the growth of lush rain forests. Unique species of plants and animals thrive in these wet forests. Jaguars, coatimundi, giant anteaters, and tapirs hunt for food in this environment.

The Andes Mountains separate the western rain forests from one of the largest ecosystems in the region—the Llanos. Here grasslands and wetlands support many different kinds of plants and animals. Capybaras, the world's largest rodents, feed on plants along the waterways. In turn, anacondas, giant snakes that can grow to be 26 feet long, prey on the capybaras and other animals.

In the far eastern areas of the region, the Orinoco Delta supports an ecosystem that changes according to the season. During dry conditions, this area includes a mix of forests, wetlands, mangrove swamps, and grasslands. However, during the rainy season, most of the ground is flooded, providing good hunting for crocodiles and otters.

Reading Check What is an ecosystem?

unique, *adj.,* highly unusual, rare

myWorld Activity
Caribbean Cruise Stopover

Animals of the Ecosystems

Each of these animals is part of a different ecosystem in Caribbean South America.

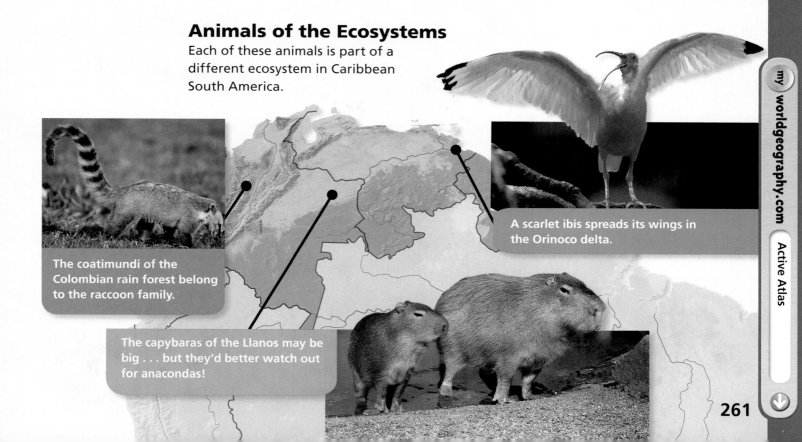

A scarlet ibis spreads its wings in the Orinoco delta.

The coatimundi of the Colombian rain forest belong to the raccoon family.

The capybaras of the Llanos may be big . . . but they'd better watch out for anacondas!

261

People and the Landscape

Human settlement and trade have always tied the region to the Caribbean world. Native Americans created a network of trade that linked the Caribbean islands to the mainland. Later, the Spanish created another economic web that connected all the lands of the Caribbean Sea.

Along the coast, Europeans established ports that prospered from the lively shipping trade. Settlers avoided areas farther inland because they feared diseases carried by insects. But the fertile soil and cooler temperatures of the highlands attracted settlement into the middle elevations.

In Colombia, European settlers reached the higher ground in the Andes by traveling through the river valleys between the cordilleras. However, east-west transportation and communication were difficult. The cordilleras isolated communities, so political unification was not easy.

Reading Check What were the main areas of European settlement in the region?

unification, *n.*, the process of uniting

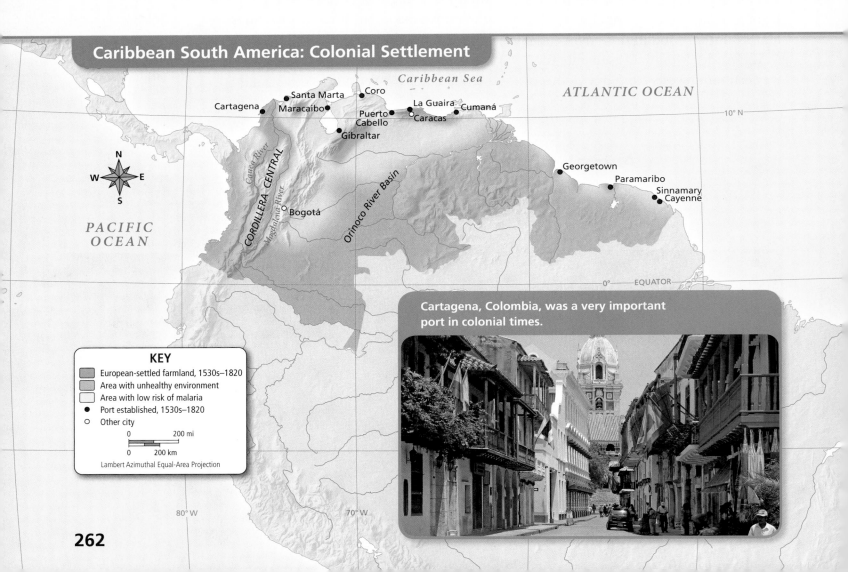

Caribbean South America: Colonial Settlement

Caribbean Sea

ATLANTIC OCEAN

Cartagena
Santa Marta   Coro
Maracaibo   La Guaira   Cumaná
              Puerto   Caracas
              Cabello
              Gibraltar
10° N

PACIFIC OCEAN

Cauca River
CORDILLERA CENTRAL
Magdalena River
Bogotá

Orinoco River Basin

Georgetown
Paramaribo
Sinnamary
Cayenne

0°   EQUATOR

KEY
- European-settled farmland, 1530s–1820
- Area with unhealthy environment
- Area with low risk of malaria
- ● Port established, 1530s–1820
- ○ Other city

0   200 mi
0   200 km
Lambert Azimuthal Equal-Area Projection

80° W   70° W

Cartagena, Colombia, was a very important port in colonial times.

Where People Live

In Colombia, 80 percent of the population lives in the higher, cooler elevations of the Andes. Colombia's three largest cities—Bogotá, Medellin, and Cali—are all located here. For the most part, Colombia's eastern border is still covered by tropical rain forest. As in colonial days, the country's Caribbean coast has many busy ports.

Caracas, the capital of Venezuela, is by far the largest city in the region. Today Venezuela has one of South America's most urban societies. In fact, nine out of ten Venezuelans live in urban areas. In recent years, the country's huge population of urban poor has become a major political force.

Most people in Guyana, Suriname, and French Guiana live in the lowlands and along the coast. Guyana, Suriname, and French Guiana have small populations, in contrast to the heavily populated countries of Colombia and Venezuela.

Reading Check **Where do most people live in the region?**

Map Skills

1. **Interaction** Look at the Colonial Settlement map on the previous page. Why did certain areas attract settlement?

2. **Place** Study the Colonial Settlement map. Why do you think there were fewer settlements in the east?

3. **Places to Know!**
Label the following places on the outline map in your Student Journal: Bogotá, Caracas, Georgetown, Cayenne.

21st Century Learning

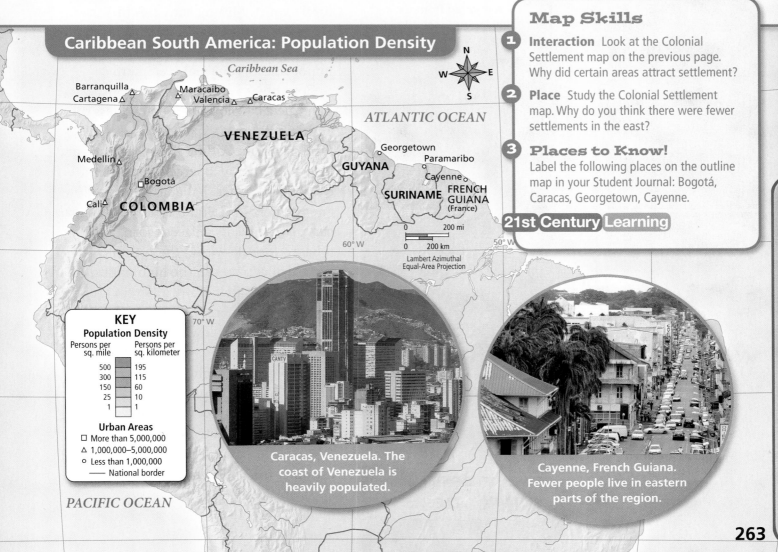

Caribbean South America: Population Density

Caribbean Sea

Barranquilla
Cartagena

Maracaibo
Valencia   Caracas

ATLANTIC OCEAN

VENEZUELA

Medellín

Georgetown
Paramaribo

GUYANA

Cayenne
FRENCH
GUIANA
(France)

Bogotá

SURINAME

Cali   COLOMBIA

0   200 mi
0   200 km

Lambert Azimuthal
Equal-Area Projection

60° W   50° W

70° W

KEY
Population Density

Persons per sq. mile	Persons per sq. kilometer
500	195
300	115
150	60
25	10
1	1

Urban Areas
□ More than 5,000,000
△ 1,000,000–5,000,000
○ Less than 1,000,000
— National border

PACIFIC OCEAN

Caracas, Venezuela. The coast of Venezuela is heavily populated.

Cayenne, French Guiana. Fewer people live in eastern parts of the region.

Coffee Production

Daniella's coffee farm is on the slopes of the Central Cordillera in Colombia. Here the combination of rich, volcanic soils and abundant rainfall is good for growing coffee. The coffee bean's journey from plant to cup is a long process.

THINK CRITICALLY Why does some of the best coffee come from Colombia?

1 The fruit of the coffee shrub is picked by hand.

2 The beans are separated from their pulp and washed.

3 The beans are dried in the sun.

4 The beans are roasted.

my **Story** 📷 **Photo**

264

How People Use Their Land

Along the coastal plains of Guyana, Suriname, and French Guiana, people grow crops for export. Large commercial farms produce sugar cane, bananas, and rice. They also export molasses, rum, and shrimp. Canals drain the soggy ground and provide fertile agricultural land.

In Venezuela, not much of the land is suitable for farming. The Orinoco River Valley floods during the wet season and is too dry at other times. Only 13 percent of Venezuela's labor force is involved in farming, and there is very little agricultural export. Mining activities in Venezuela are scattered, but oil is concentrated in and around Lake Maracaibo. Oil is very important to Venezuela's economy.

Colombia's land use differs from Venezuela's. Colombians extract less oil and minerals but export more agricultural products. Although Colombians are able to farm only 2 percent of the land, they export coffee, bananas, and cut flowers. Farmers in Colombia also grow sugar cane, cocoa beans, oilseed, corn, and tobacco for sale within the country. The variety of climates in the highlands of the Andes means that many different crops can be grown there. Bananas and sugar cane are grown at lower levels, while crops such as barley, wheat, and potatoes can grow at higher elevations. In the mountains, people gain the flat land they need through **terraced farming**—sculpting the hillside into different levels for crops.

Reading Check How does Colombia's land use differ from Venezuela's?

A Diverse Population

The region's population is ethnically and culturally diverse. Unlike many other regions of South America, Native Americans make up only a small percentage of the population. Many of the original people of the region died of European diseases. Over the centuries, the remaining population of Native Americans intermarried with Europeans. Their descendants are known as mestizos. But there was also intermarriage between Africans and Europeans as well as between Africans and Native Americans.

Although there was much intermarriage, many groups have remained ethnically distinct. Throughout the region are communities of Maroons, people descended from Africans who escaped slavery. These Africans fled into the rain forests where they joined with others for mutual protection.

After slavery ended in the 1800s, workers from around the world arrived to labor on the plantations. In Guyana and Suriname, the dominant ethnic group is made up of people descended from workers who migrated from India. There are also significant numbers of Chinese, and Javanese (from the Indonesian island of Java). In French Guiana, most of the population is of mixed European and African descent.

The variety of ethnic groups in the region has led to much cultural borrowing. In French Guiana, local dances reveal the influence of African, Indian, and French traditions. People in the former British colony of Guyana play cricket, while Venezuelans love baseball—thanks to cultural ties with the United States.

The region's location on the northern coast of South America has given it strong cultural connections with the Caribbean world. Today, this Caribbean heritage can be heard in some of the music of the region. It can also be seen in cultural traditions like Carnival. In the next section you will read how the region's unique cultural identity developed.

Reading Check What ethnic groups live in Caribbean South America?

my**World**
IN NUMBERS

If there were
100 people in the world,

Hello!

Hola!

5 would speak Spanish.

Section **1** Assessment

Key Terms

1. Use the following terms to describe the geography of Caribbean South America: cordillera, Llanos, ecosystem, terraced farming.

Key Ideas

2. What are some features shared by all nations in this region?

3. What are some natural resources in this region?

4. Where does most of the population live in Caribbean South America?

Think Critically

5. **Draw Conclusions** Look at the population map. What factors explain these settlement patterns?

6. **Identify Central Issues** Why might some nations in this region have weaker economies than others?

Essential Question

Is conflict unavoidable?

7. How might geography be a divisive force in the region? Go to your Student Journal to record your answer.

History of Caribbean South America

Key Ideas
- Colonization by European nations changed the physical and human geography of Caribbean South America.
- Simón Bolívar's campaigns liberated what are now Venezuela and Colombia.
- Political tensions and conflicts have often troubled Caribbean South America.

Key Terms • El Dorado • caudillo • paramilitary • nationalize • austerity measure

→ **Visual Glossary**

Reading Skill: Identify Main Idea and Details Take notes using the graphic organizer in your journal.

This gold figure was made in Colombia before the arrival of the Spanish. ▼

The world they had known was ending. Strange new illnesses were spreading. Tall ships patrolled the coasts. For the people of Caribbean South America, these were the first frightening signs that their lives were about to change.

For centuries, people had hunted, farmed, and fished throughout Caribbean South America. In the Andean highlands, the Chibcha had formed settled communities. In what is now Venezuela, the Arawak and Carib lived off the land and sea. Now these societies were under threat. Armored soldiers brought Spanish laws and taxes, while Christian missionaries preached a new religion. The invaders were everywhere, even in the rain forests where the Spanish hunted for treasure and a legendary gold-rich king called **El Dorado.**

Cultures Collide

Only a few years after conquering the Aztec Empire in Mexico, the Spanish were invading the lands to the south. In 1525 they settled the Colombian coast. By 1538 they had reached the Colombian highlands, where they founded Bogotá. Meanwhile, in what is now Venezuela, Spanish settlements spread through the highlands and along the coast. Rumors of El Dorado drew explorers up the Orinoco River in Venezuela. Although El Dorado was never found, the Spanish discovered plenty of gold in the highlands of Colombia.

Colonial Society The Spanish forced Native Americans to work in the gold mines and on coastal plantations that exported sugar, cacao, and tobacco. But millions of Native Americans died from mistreatment and disease. To replace them, the Spanish imported enslaved people from Africa. Many Africans did not accept a life of slavery. Some fought their masters or fled into the forests.

The Spanish had conquered such a huge empire in the Americas that they could not keep all of it under control. One of their weakest spots lay along the easternmost Caribbean coast of South America. There, English and Dutch pirates constantly threatened their shipping and their ports. In addition, rival European nations began colonizing coastal lands claimed by Spain. The Dutch, English, and French opened trading posts and settlements along the easternmost coast of the Caribbean. By the late 1700s, the British had a colony in Guyana, the Dutch controlled Suriname, and the French owned French Guiana.

Reading Check How did rival European powers gain a foothold in Spanish lands?

myWorld Activity
Shipwreck Discovery

Pirate Attacks in the Caribbean

The gold and silver of the Americas made Spain rich and filled the Caribbean with pirates. Wealthy Spanish ports suffered frequent pirate attacks in colonial times.

Culture Close-up

A pirate captain as pictured by the American illustrator Howard Pyle ▼

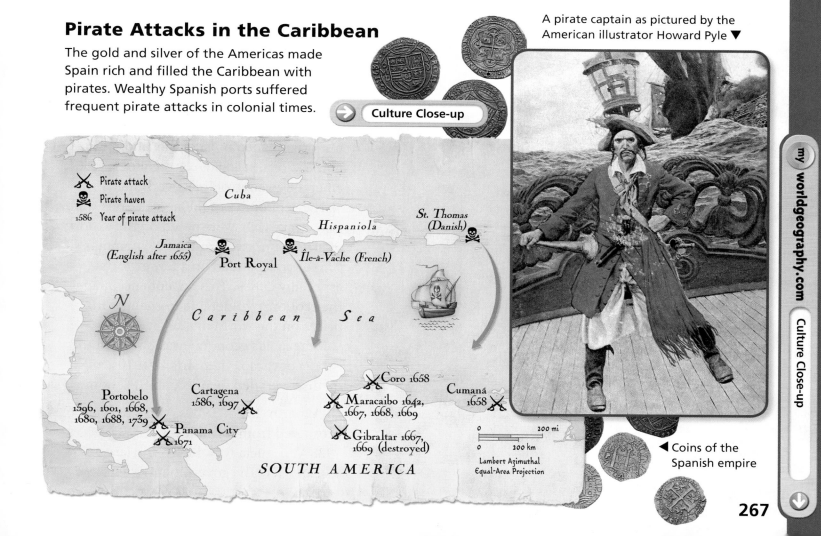

Pirate attack
Pirate haven
1586 Year of pirate attack

Cuba

Hispaniola

St. Thomas (Danish)

Jamaica (English after 1655)
Port Royal

Île-à-Vache (French)

Caribbean Sea

N

Coro 1658

Cumaná 1658

Portobelo 1596, 1601, 1668, 1680, 1688, 1739
Panama City 1671

Cartagena 1586, 1697

Maracaibo 1642, 1667, 1668, 1669

Gibraltar 1667, 1669 (destroyed)

0   200 mi
0   200 km
Lambert Azimuthal Equal-Area Projection

SOUTH AMERICA

◄ Coins of the Spanish empire

my worldgeography.com   Culture Close-up

267

The Fight for Independence

Members of the upper and middle classes were unhappy with Spanish rule. Although they owned the land, they wanted the right to trade with other nations throughout the world. They disliked being ruled by the Spanish-born peninsulares. Unlike colonial governments in North America, the Spanish colonial governments had no elected assemblies.

The rebels found a great leader in Simón Bolívar. Born in Venezuela, Bolívar dreamed of a new nation in which all people, including slaves, would be free. In 1805, he declared,

> 66 I swear before you, I swear by the God of my fathers, I swear by my fathers, I swear by my honor, I swear by my country that I will not rest body or soul until I have broken the chains with which Spanish power oppresses us. 99
> —Simón Bolívar, *Investor's Business Daily*

Bolívar kept his word. In 1811 Venezuela declared independence. Over the next decade, Bolívar fought Spanish and loyalist armies. With the help of patriots such as Colombia's Francisco de Paula Santander, Bolívar <u>liberated</u> other regions, creating several new nations.

Reading Check **Why did the colonists want independence from Spain?**

liberate, *v.,* to free

Many towns in former Spanish colonies have a statue of Simón Bolívar. ▼

After Independence

The new nations were unstable. A small minority owned most of the land. In the new nations, **caudillos,** or dictators, soon emerged to control the governments.

The economies of the new nations were also weak. They were based on the export of just one or two products. Colombia's economy depended on a few exports, especially coffee. This dependence made the economy vulnerable to changes in prices on the world market.

Venezuela's economy was based on the export of cacao. Then, in the 1910s, an oil discovery led to an economic boom.

Oil Wealth In the 1900s, Venezuela prospered from its oil revenues. By 1928 Venezuela was the world's largest oil exporter. The government used the wealth to build roads and fund social services and welfare programs. Colombia also began to expand petroleum production into a key industry.

Political Conflict Despite the wealth that came from oil, much of the region was still poor. But attempts to redistribute land to those in need largely failed and led to civil conflict. In Colombia, a wave of political violence called La Violencia ("the violence") raged from 1948 to 1957.

In the 1960s, a new wave of conflict began in Colombia. Rebel armies began to form. Later, landowners responded by supporting **paramilitaries,** armed forces that are unauthorized by the government. Rebels and paramilitaries controlled large areas and forced people to pay them taxes. Both paramilitary and rebel groups funded their wars through the illegal drug trade. Fighting continues today, although the Colombian government claims that the situation is improving.

In 1976, the government of Venezuela **nationalized,** or took ownership of, the oil industry. Oil wealth funded social programs. But the country relied too much on oil revenues. A worldwide drop in oil prices brought about an economic decline in the 1980s. In early 1989, the government of President Carlos Andrés Pérez introduced **austerity measures,** or policies meant to save money. There were huge cuts in social services. An outraged public responded with riots and strikes. The nation was ripe for the political message of Hugo Chavez in the elections of 1998.

Chavez's government took control of the oil industry and used oil revenues to fund social programs. The government provided subsidized food and free healthcare. However, Chavez's popular policies angered the business community. As he gained more power, many feared that he was becoming a dictator. In the next section you will read how political conflicts like these are changing the region today.

Reading Check How did Venezuela use its oil revenues?

my World IN NUMBERS

In 2008, **93** percent of Venezuela's export revenue (money earned from exports) came from oil.

Section 2 Assessment

? Essential Question
Is conflict unavoidable?

Key Terms

1. Use the following terms to describe the history of the region: El Dorado, caudillo, paramilitary, nationalize, austerity measure.

Key Ideas

2. What changes did Europeans bring to the region?

3. Who liberated the colonies in Caribbean South America?

4. What issues cause political tension in the countries of Caribbean South America?

Think Critically

5. **Make Inferences** Why were the liberated countries so unstable?

6. **Compare and Contrast** How did colonial governments in North America differ from those in South America?

7. What modern conflicts in Caribbean South America have their roots in colonial history? Go to your Student Journal to record your answer.

Caribbean South America Today

Key Ideas
- Caribbean South America is ethnically diverse.
- Some countries in the region have important reserves of oil and gas.
- Countries in the region struggle with environmental and political problems.

Key Terms • Latin America • subsidence • representative democracy • insurgent

 Visual Glossary

 Reading Skill: Compare and Contrast Take notes using the graphic organizer in your journal.

Daniella waves to visitors leaving her family's farm. ▼

my Story 📷 **Photo**

The solid ground around Daniella's farm sometimes trembles. The same volcanic forces that make the local soil so rich can also bring disaster. In 1999, Daniella's hometown of Armenia was destroyed by a terrible earthquake.

Like earthquakes in the Andes, political events sometimes shake the region. In Colombia, violent civil conflict has been raging for decades. In Venezuela, political changes are creating tension. Both Guyana and Suriname suffer from ethnic divisions.

Yet despite natural disasters and political conflict, Caribbean South America is a region full of energy and hope. Daniella's family, who turned to tourism for added income, is an example of how people in the region are working to improve their lives. Today, the nations of Caribbean South America are developing their economies while dealing with difficult political problems.

Diverse Cultures

Daniella lives in an area with strong Spanish influence. Yet the region of Caribbean South America as a whole is culturally quite diverse. The Spanish culture of Colombia and Venezuela differs from the culture of Guyana, Suriname, and French Guiana, where European and Asian influences mingle. Throughout the region there are also pockets of African and indigenous cultures.

Many writers have used the term **Latin America** to describe areas of the Americas influenced by the cultures of Spain, France, or Portugal—countries in which people speak languages descended from Latin. In the Caribbean countries of South America, the people of Colombia and Venezuela are overwhelmingly Catholic and speak Spanish. The population in French Guiana is mainly Catholic, and the official language is French rather than Spanish. Yet even in Latin cultures like these, music and dance are built on the <u>complex</u> rhythms of African music.

The countries that might be considered least Latin are Guyana and Suriname. The main language in Guyana is English, while in Suriname you might hear people speaking Dutch, English, or Surinamese. In both Guyana and Suriname, Hindustanis from India form the largest ethnic group, followed in number by those descended from enslaved Africans.

complex, *adj.,* complicated

Reading Check **What are the major ethnic groups in this region?**

Cultural Influences

The traditions of Caribbean South America reveal the diverse cultural influences in the region.

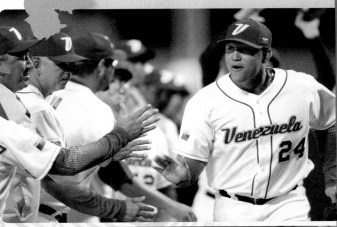

Venezuela's passion for baseball reveals the country's historical ties with the United States.

In **French Guiana,** African and French traditions merge in the carnival costumes of the Touloulous.

In **Suriname,** descendants of Indian immigrants celebrate Divali, the Hindu festival of light.

Environmental Problems

While each country in the region has different environmental challenges, all of them share one major problem—deforestation. Worldwide demand for wood products is encouraging companies to cut down trees. Large-scale commercial farming is also causing environmental damage. In this tropical region with many destructive insects, farmers are forced to use large amounts of pesticides. These pesticides are contaminating the soil and water.

Venezuela also faces another kind of pollution—contamination from the oil industry. Industrial and oil processing plants have turned Lake Maracaibo into one of the most polluted areas in the region. Since the oil deposits are located under the lake, drilling has caused numerous spills and constant leakage. Because there is only a narrow channel connecting the lake to the ocean, most of this oil-polluted water is trapped in the lake. Decades of draining the underground oilfields is also causing land **subsidence,** or sinking of the ground. With the ground sinking, severe flooding is threatening both the oilfields and the people living around the lake.

Governments are making some efforts to solve environmental problems. Venezuela has passed the Organic Law of the Environment to protect its soils, forests, and water supplies. It has also tried to restrict logging and has begun reforestation by planting trees. In Colombia, the Pacific coastal area is now a protected ecosystem. Several nature reserves have been established in Suriname to protect wildlife. In Guyana, the Kaieteur National Park has been designated a conservation area.

Reading Check **How is the oil industry affecting Venezuela's environment?**

restrict, *v.,* to limit

Air Pollution

Carbon dioxide (CO_2) is produced by the burning of coal, oil, and natural gas. Study the table to compare CO_2 emissions in the region.

Cars cause pollution in Venezuela. ▶

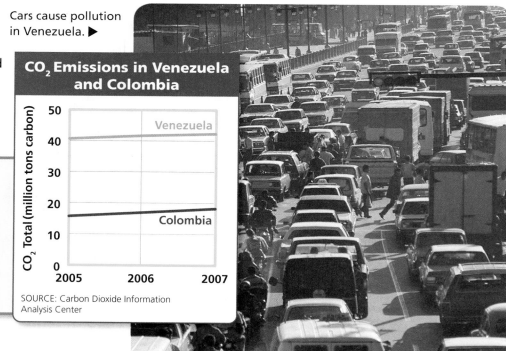

CO_2 Emissions in Venezuela and Colombia

CO_2 Total (million tons carbon)

Venezuela

Colombia

| 2005 | 2006 | 2007 |

SOURCE: Carbon Dioxide Information Analysis Center

Chart Skills

1 Which nation has higher levels of CO_2 emissions?

2 What might explain the difference in levels?

→ Data Discovery

Heads of State and Governments

Colombia

Colombia's President Álvaro Uribe Vélez presides over a bicameral (two-house) Congress: Senate and Chamber of Representatives.

Venezuela

Venezuela's President Hugo Chavez Frias presides over a unicameral (one-house) National Assembly.

Guyana

Guyana's President Bharrat Jagdeo governs with a unicameral National Assembly. The president is elected by simple majority vote.

Suriname

Suriname's President Ronald Venetiaan was elected by a unicameral National Assembly.

French Guiana

In French Guiana French President Nicolas Sarkozy is head of state. The territory sends elected representatives to the French Parliament.

▲ Some current heads of state may run for reelection in 2010 or later.

Governments and Conflicts

All the countries in Caribbean South America are independent republics except French Guiana, which is considered part of France. Most of the nations in the region suffer from various tensions and conflicts.

Varied Governments Like the United States, Colombia has executive, legislative, and judicial branches of government. The Legislature is bicameral, which means that it has two "houses"—a Senate and a Chamber of Representatives. Two parties, the Liberals and Conservatives, compete for power.

In Venezuela, the new constitution of 1999 changed the system of government. The president, Hugo Chavez Frias, reduced **representative democracy,** or democracy in which the people elect representatives to make the nation's laws. In Venezuela's new system of direct democracy, the people use referenda, or voting, to make or change laws.

Guyana is a democracy with a president and a National Assembly. The ruling party is supported by people of African descent, while the opposition party is favored by people of South Asian ancestry.

Suriname has a president and an elected National Assembly. As in Guyana, Suriname's political parties are divided along ethnic lines.

As its name suggests, French Guiana is not an independent nation. It is considered an overseas "department" of France and sends representatives to the French Parliament. Its people are French citizens who enjoy the same rights and social services as people in France.

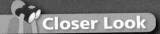

Closer Look

Politics in Venezuela

Although President Chavez is popular among the poor, many groups resent his power. Read what ordinary Venezuelans have to say about their president.

THINK CRITICALLY **Do you think that President Chavez is helping or hurting Venezuela?**

▲ Anti-Chavez demonstration

66 He is a communist and he's a disaster for Venezuela. . . . He sets the country's different groups against each other. 99

—Alicia Gomez, resident of Caracas*

▲ Demonstration in support of President Chavez

66 What other president has ever taken the time to go into the shanty towns and meet the people? . . . This country has got huge oil wealth but so many of us still live in poverty. 99

—Jose Luis Arnal, resident of Caracas*

*Quoted in "Rift in Venezuelan Society" from BBC.com

274

Conflicts and Tensions Ethnic tensions trouble the eastern parts of the region, such as Suriname and Guyana. In Suriname, warfare between South Asian and African ethnic groups has driven many Surinamese residents into neighboring French Guiana to seek refuge. In Guyana, the same two ethnic groups are also struggling for political power. The Guyanese tend to vote for public officials along racial lines.

In Colombia, the government has been fighting a civil war against **insurgents,** or rebels, for decades. The insurgents have long been able to hide in the remote forests and the mountainous terrain. Meanwhile, armed groups have formed to oppose the insurgents. Fighting between these two groups has brought suffering to civilians across the country. With military aid from the United States, the government of Colombia claims it is restoring order in this troubled land.

Political tensions are also running high in Venezuela, as the government of Hugo Chavez moves the country toward socialism. President Chavez wants to narrow the large gap between the rich and the poor. However, his political actions have angered many landowners and businesspeople. They feel they no longer have a voice in how the resources of the country should be used.

Reading Check **What are some tensions and conflicts in the region?**

myWorld Activity
Teaching Booklet

Economies

Caribbean South America is trying to diversify, or vary, its economies. The Venezuelan government is trying to create tourist and high-tech industries. However, Venezuela is still dependent on oil and natural gas exports.

President Chavez is trying to move away from a free-market economy and has begun to redirect revenues. For example, profits from oil enable the government to fund extremely low gasoline prices at the pumps. But Venezuelan oil revenues have been funding more than social programs. Since 2005, Venezuela has also been buying billions of dollars of military equipment from Russia.

Trade agreements among countries in this region are meant to eliminate tariffs and reduce unfair competition. The Organization of American States (OAS), formed in Bogotá in 1948, is one organization that promotes economic and cultural cooperation.

Although much of the region is poor, there is potential for economic growth.

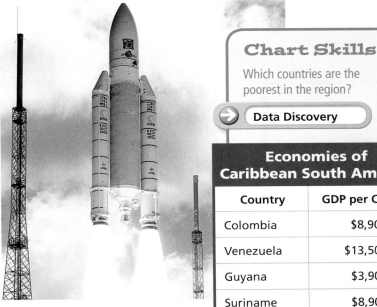

▲ A rocket launch in French Guiana

Chart Skills

Which countries are the poorest in the region?

Data Discovery

Economies of Caribbean South America

Country	GDP per Capita
Colombia	$8,900
Venezuela	$13,500
Guyana	$3,900
Suriname	$8,900

SOURCE: *CIA World Factbook*

Guyana may soon profit from offshore oil. In French Guiana, the economy is helped by the European Space Agency, which has established a rocket launch site in the nation. Venezuela has its oil fields, while Colombia has rich resources of gold, coal, oil, and emeralds.

Reading Check What industries might help Venezuela to diversify its economy?

Section 3 Assessment

Essential Question

Is conflict unavoidable?

Key Terms

1. Use the following terms to describe life in Caribbean South America today: Latin America, subsidence, representative democracy, insurgent.

Key Ideas

2. How did the region become so ethnically diverse?

3. What are some natural resources of the region, and where are they located?

4. What environmental problems trouble the region?

Think Critically

5. **Cause and Effect** What economic forces contribute to deforestation?

6. **Make Inferences** Why are many businesspeople upset by the policies of Hugo Chavez?

7. What issues fuel conflicts in Caribbean South America? Go to your Student Journal to record your answer.

Chapter Assessment

Key Terms and Ideas

1. **Recall** Through which countries do the Andes extend?

2. **Explain** How do the **cordilleras** affect transportation in Colombia?

3. **Describe** What happened to the indigenous people of the region under Spanish rule?

4. **Recall** How did the legend of **El Dorado** encourage Spanish exploration of the region?

5. **Summarize** What social problems led to conflict in Colombia?

6. **Explain** What is causing **subsidence** around Lake Maracaibo?

7. **Discuss** What natural resources could help the economies of the region?

Think Critically

8. **Make Inferences** Why is it dangerous for a nation to base its economy on only one or two exports?

9. **Draw Conclusions** What factors explain settlement patterns in the region?

10. **Analyze Information** Why are some parts of this region more urbanized than others?

11. **Core Concepts: Migration** What factors drew immigrants to Caribbean South America?

Places to Know

For each place, write the letter from the map that shows its location.

12. **Bogotá**

13. **Cordillera Occidental**

14. **Orinoco River**

15. **Cayenne**

16. **Llanos**

17. **Caracas**

18. **Estimate** Using the scale, estimate the distance from Caracas to Bogotá.

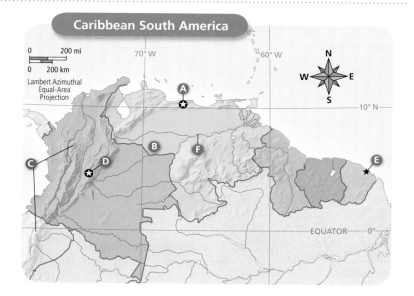

Caribbean South America

Essential Question

myWorld Chapter Activity

Hunt for Resources Follow your teacher's instructions to study the working conditions and political situation in each nation of Caribbean South America. Work with a group to choose the location of a new factory producing export goods somewhere in the region. Review the photograph and the information about the topic at each location. Then meet with your team and decide where to locate the factory. Prepare a report explaining why you have chosen this site.

21st Century Learning

Analyze Media Content

With a partner, choose one of the countries covered in this chapter. Then search online and through newspapers for articles about the political situation in that country. Discuss each article and decide whether the writer is for or against the government in power.

Document-Based Questions

Success ★ Tracker™

Online at myworldgeography.com

Use your knowledge of Caribbean South America and Documents A and B to answer Questions 1–3.

Document A

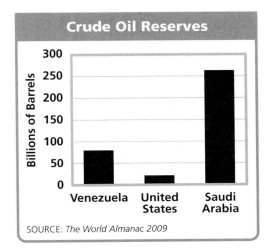

Crude Oil Reserves

Billions of Barrels

300 / 250 / 200 / 150 / 100 / 50 / 0

Venezuela / United States / Saudi Arabia

SOURCE: *The World Almanac 2009*

Document B

" Venezuela has the largest oil reserves in the world. In the future Venezuela won't have any more oil—but that's in the 22nd Century."

—President Hugo Chavez, BBC News, April 2006

1. What does the information in Document A show about Venezuela's economy?

   A why Venezuela's economy is struggling

   B why petroleum is so important to Venezuela's economy

   C why Venezuela nationalized its oil industry

   D why Venezuela hopes to diversify its economy

2. What does Document B reveal about how President Chavez regards Venezuela's oil reserves?

   A They are a resource that Venezuela can tap into forever.

   B They are a limited resource, but the country will be able to profit from them in the short term.

   C They are smaller than Saudi Arabia's.

   D They will only be useful in the next century.

3. **Writing Task** What do Documents A and B together reveal about Hugo Chavez's plans?

myworldgeography.com

Self-Test

Chapter 6

The Andes and the Pampas

Essential Question

What are the challenges of diversity?

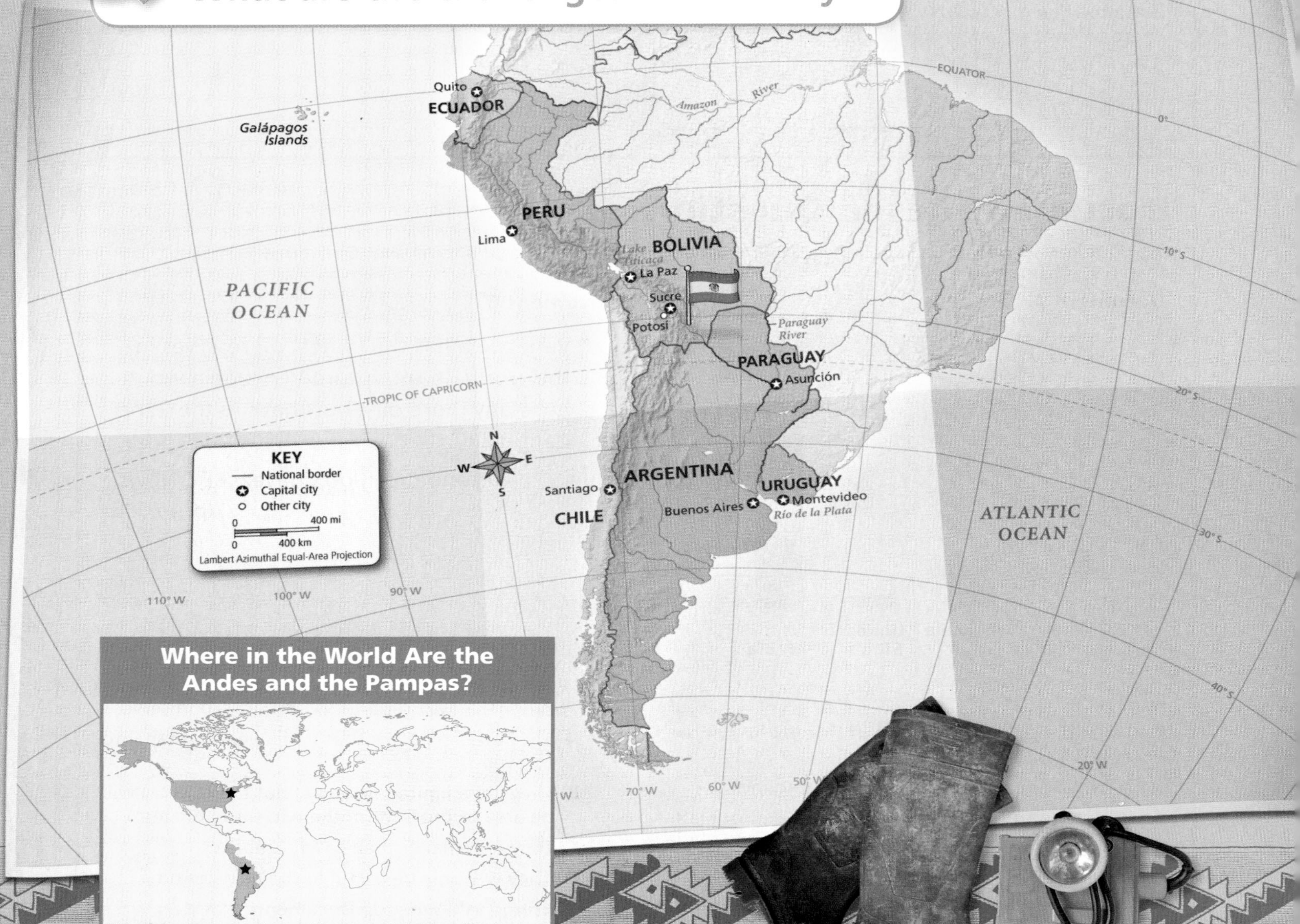

Quito
ECUADOR
Galápagos Islands
Amazon River
EQUATOR
0°
PERU
Lima
BOLIVIA
Lake Titicaca
La Paz
Sucre
Potosí
10° S
PACIFIC OCEAN
Paraguay River
PARAGUAY
Asunción
TROPIC OF CAPRICORN
20° S
KEY
National border
Capital city
Other city
0 400 mi
0 400 km
Lambert Azimuthal Equal-Area Projection
N
S
E
W
ARGENTINA
Santiago
CHILE
URUGUAY
Montevideo
Buenos Aires
Río de la Plata
ATLANTIC OCEAN
30° S
110° W
100° W
90° W
40° S
70° W
60° W
50° W
20° W

Where in the World Are the Andes and the Pampas?

Washington, D.C., to Potosí: 4,100 miles

Under the Rich Mountain

In this section, you'll learn about Omar and his struggle to earn a living under a mountain that once made an empire rich. **What does the story tell you about the diverse landforms and cultures of the Andes and the Pampas?**

Explore the Essential Question
- at **my** worldgeography.com
- using the **myWorld Chapter Activity**
- with the **Student Journal**

Story by Neville Cole for myWorld Geography Online

Most days Omar follows the same routine: rising early, making his bed, eating breakfast, and heading off to work. He is only 14 years old but, like his father and grandfather before him, Omar is a miner. Six days a week Omar digs ore in the Paylaviri mine in Potosí, Bolivia. It's a typical story around here. Three of Omar's brothers are miners; so is his cousin, Frederico. In fact, almost all the men Omar knows have been miners at one time or another. Mining has a long and terrible history in this part of Bolivia, and Omar and Frederico must work under the mountain with the longest and most terrible mining history of them all—Cerro Rico, the "Rich Mountain."

At 15,827 feet, Cerro Rico towers over the town of Potosí like a pyramid. For more than 450 years, generations of miners have dug into this mountain to extract its incredible wealth of silver and tin.

my worldgeography.com On Assignment

279

Omar at work

Omar at his father's grave

Omar and Frederico pushing an ore cart

The locals say that so many tunnels have been carved into Cerro Rico that the mountain's heart is like Swiss cheese. The mine was discovered in 1544, and by 1600 it was producing half the world's silver, much of it sent to the Spanish king. But all that wealth came at a very high cost. More than 8 million people may have died here, either from mining accidents or as a result of illnesses caused by working underground. Omar knows this all too well. His own father became sick from breathing dust in the mine and died when Omar was ten.

"I hate going down into the mine," Omar says. "Every time I go into the mine I think it is the last time. I think I won't be coming out." Fortunately, working conditions are better today than they were years ago. The miners have formed a cooperative. They work together to make conditions safer.

Omar has to work for only a few hours each day, but those few hours are far from easy. "The work inside the mine is very tough. I have to run back and forth to dig ore. I also help my brothers or my cousin, Frederico, push the ore cart. It is very hot down underground. I have to carry enough water so that I don't get thirsty. You sweat a lot in the mine. It is very difficult work. You have to dig very hard and sometimes it is dangerous, especially when you have to use dynamite."

Omar and Frederico at the market

A game of soccer in the sun

After his father died, Omar's mother had to move away to find work. Working in the mine is the only way Omar and his brothers can make enough money to survive. "I make 250 Bolivianos, which is about 30 dollars per week. That's when I am lucky. Sometimes I only make 100 Bolivianos. . . . I give my brother some of that money to buy food for the house and sometimes I buy clothes. I also send my mother money to help raise my little brother."

Omar dreams that one day soon his life will change. He goes to school each afternoon after his shift at the mine. "I would like to become an architect when I grow up," he says. "I would like to build schools so other children all over the world can go to school too."

Despite all the hard work, Omar still finds time to have fun. On this day, he and Frederico stop by a soccer court to join a game. Frederico tackles the ball and moves it quickly down the court. Without even looking up, he switches direction and passes the ball to Omar on the wing. Omar makes a move back to the inside and drives the ball past the goalkeeper. For now Omar and Frederico are just two happy cousins celebrating a goal in the sun. Yet behind them looms the peak of Cerro Rico, reminding them that tomorrow morning they will be under the mountain once more.

myStory Video

Learn more about Omar's life in the mine.

Meet the Journalist

Name Jorge Alborta
Favorite Moment Sharing Omar's good spirits despite his difficult life

Chapter Atlas

Key Ideas
- Location, climate, and natural resources have determined settlement patterns in the Andes and the Pampas.
- Throughout the region, human activity is changing the landscape.
- Population density and ethnicity vary across the region.

Key Terms • subduct • Altiplano • El Niño • vertical climate zones

 Visual Glossary

Reading Skill: Label an Outline Map Take notes using the outline map in your journal.

A horse and rider in the Andes

Physical Features

Omar lives in the Andes, the longest mountain range in the world. The Andes are the spine of South America, curving down the continent's west coast. To the west of the Andes lies the Pacific Ocean. This coast includes landforms such as the Atacama Desert. To the east of the Andes lie tropical rain forests. In the southeast, grassy plains spread out along the Rio de la Plata. These are the Pampas—vast fertile grasslands bustling with ranches and big commercial farms.

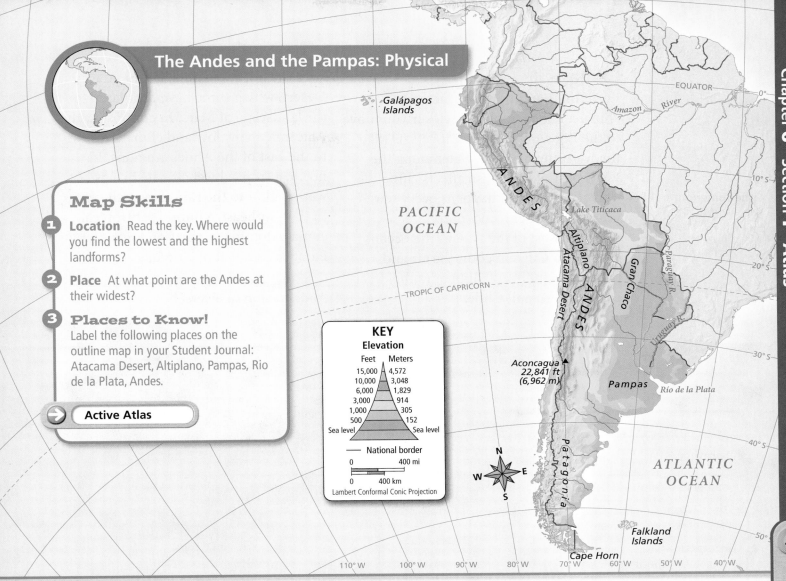

The Andes and the Pampas: Physical

Galápagos Islands

EQUATOR

Amazon River

PACIFIC OCEAN

Lake Titicaca

Altiplano

Atacama Desert

ANDES

Gran Chaco

Paraguay R.

Uruguay R.

TROPIC OF CAPRICORN

Aconcagua 22,841 ft (6,962 m)

Pampas

Río de la Plata

Patagonia

ATLANTIC OCEAN

Cape Horn

Falkland Islands

Map Skills

1 **Location** Read the key. Where would you find the lowest and the highest landforms?

2 **Place** At what point are the Andes at their widest?

3 **Places to Know!** Label the following places on the outline map in your Student Journal: Atacama Desert, Altiplano, Pampas, Rio de la Plata, Andes.

→ **Active Atlas**

KEY
Elevation

Feet	Meters
15,000	4,572
10,000	3,048
6,000	1,829
3,000	914
1,000	305
500	152
Sea level	Sea level

—— National border

0   400 mi
0   400 km

Lambert Conformal Conic Projection

The Pampas stretch for some 250,000 square miles (647,000 square kilometers). This land was once covered by ten-foot-tall grass. The grassland extended over Patagonia (southern Argentina and Chile) and most of the lowlands. Today the area is an agricultural region. It is home to most of Argentina's population.

The Andes were formed as two tectonic plates called the Nazca Plate and the South American Plate collided slowly over millions of years. As the Nazca Plate was **subducted,** or tugged under, the force buckled up the South American Plate to form the Andes.

This 80-million-year-long crash has caused volcanic eruptions and earthquakes in the nations of the Andes.

The Andes include parallel chains of mountains called cordilleras. In Peru and Bolivia cordilleras flank a high plateau called the **Altiplano,** where Potosí is located. The Altiplano is rich in metals, such as silver, zinc, tin, and lead.

Reading Check How were the Andes formed?

Climate

Location is an important factor in climate. For example, the closer you move to the Equator, the hotter it gets. **El Niño,** the warming of ocean water along the west coast of Peru, also affects climate. This <u>phenomenon</u> happens every few years and causes heavy rain.

phenomenon, *n.,* an event that can be scientifically described

To the west of the Andes, the ocean's Humboldt Current cools the air and prevents rain from falling onto the desert coast of Peru and Chile.

In the north of Chile lies the Atacama Desert, which some have compared to the landscape of Mars. In contrast to the Atacama, many lowland climate zones to the east of the Andes are rainy. In the north, a tropical wet climate brings hot, wet weather to the rain forests all year. In the southeast, a humid subtropical climate dominates parts of Argentina, Paraguay, and all of Uruguay.

Reading Check Why are climates in the Andes region so diverse?

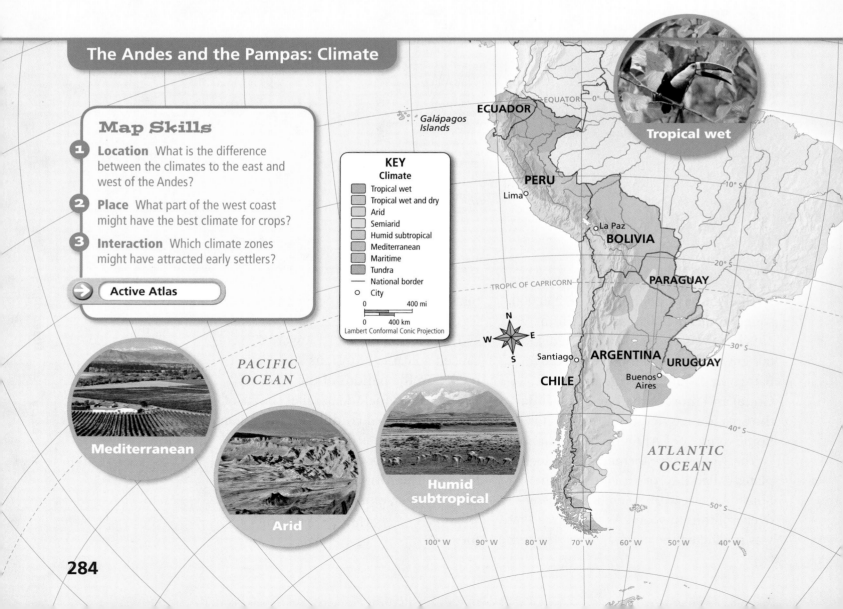

The Andes and the Pampas: Climate

Map Skills

1 **Location** What is the difference between the climates to the east and west of the Andes?

2 **Place** What part of the west coast might have the best climate for crops?

3 **Interaction** Which climate zones might have attracted early settlers?

Active Atlas

KEY
Climate
- Tropical wet
- Tropical wet and dry
- Arid
- Semiarid
- Humid subtropical
- Mediterranean
- Maritime
- Tundra
- — National border
- ○ City

0   400 mi
0   400 km
Lambert Conformal Conic Projection

Tropical wet

Mediterranean

Arid

Humid subtropical

EQUATOR — 0°
Galápagos Islands
ECUADOR
PERU
Lima
La Paz
BOLIVIA
PARAGUAY
TROPIC OF CAPRICORN
ARGENTINA
Santiago
CHILE
URUGUAY
Buenos Aires

PACIFIC OCEAN
ATLANTIC OCEAN

10° S
20° S
30° S
40° S
50° S

100° W   90° W   80° W   70° W   60° W   50° W   40° W

Ecosystems

In the Andes, climate and ecosystems vary. High rainfall in eastern Ecuador and Peru contrasts with dry conditions on the Pacific coast. In each climate zone a different ecosystem has developed. An ecosystem is the network of plant and animal life within a specific environment.

In the mountain highlands, climate is influenced by elevation as well as location. Near the Equator, the climate is hot and wet up to an altitude of 4,900 feet (1,494 meters). However, the higher up the mountains you travel, the cooler and wetter it gets. This creates a variety of ecosystems.

Temperature and rainfall determine the kind of vegetation that grows in a location. In the Andes farmers grow different crops at different elevations. The illustration that appears below shows a diagram of **vertical climate zones,** or climate zones that change according to elevation.

Reading Check Why are there so many ecosystems in the Andes?

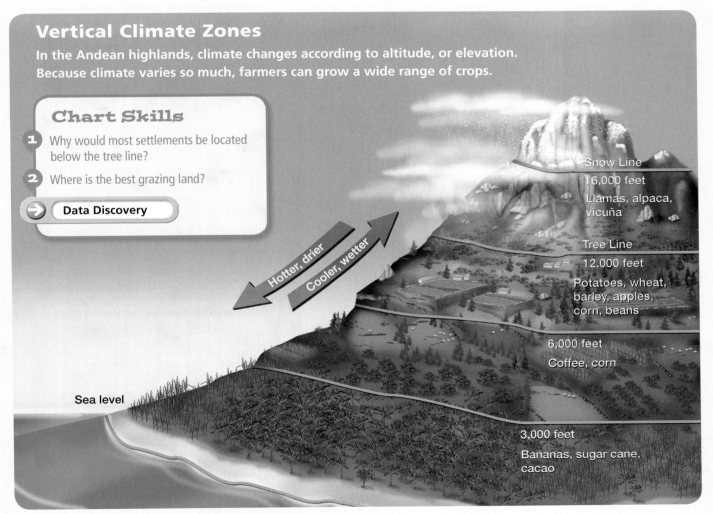

Vertical Climate Zones

In the Andean highlands, climate changes according to altitude, or elevation. Because climate varies so much, farmers can grow a wide range of crops.

Chart Skills

1 Why would most settlements be located below the tree line?

2 Where is the best grazing land?

Data Discovery

Hotter, drier

Cooler, wetter

Snow Line
16,000 feet
Llamas, alpaca, vicuña

Tree Line
12,000 feet
Potatoes, wheat, barley, apples, corn, beans

6,000 feet
Coffee, corn

3,000 feet
Bananas, sugar cane, cacao

Sea level

myWorld Activity
A Poem of the Land

Land Use and Resources

In the Andes, there is surprisingly little good farmland. Tropical rain forests cover many areas east of the Andes. The Andes themselves are too mountainous for large-scale farming.

In places where people can farm, agricultural practices differ between the Andes and the Pampas. The farmers of Andean countries have to cope with difficult landforms. For example, in the Andes there are no large areas of flat land. So farming must take place on high plateaus and in narrow mountain valleys. However, an amazing variety of crops can be grown in these vertical climate zones: wheat, coffee, corn, vegetables, many different kinds of fruit, and thousands of kinds of potatoes.

Commercial, or large-scale, farming in the Andes is limited to the western foothills and the coastal areas of Ecuador and Peru. Here the nutrient-laden Humboldt Current provides rich fishing grounds. At higher altitudes, a poorer population labors in subsistence farming—farmers grow only enough to feed themselves and their families.

The open grasslands of the Pampas are ideal for cattle ranching, which attracted early settlers to the area. In colonial times settlers exported hides from Pampas cattle. Hides were shipped to Europe, via the huge Rio de la Plata estuary, or wide river mouth. Today, Buenos Aires in Argentina and Montevideo in Uruguay are the chief ports on this estuary. The Plata Basin, which includes Uruguay, Paraguay, northern Argentina, and eastern Bolivia,

is the site of commercial farming. Here large farms grow crops such as soybeans, corn, and wheat.

Bolivia lies roughly in the geographic center of this region. Because its territory includes both the Andean highlands and the lowlands of the east, it has examples of the kinds of farming seen in both the Andes and the Pampas. Subsistence farmers can be found in the Bolivian highlands, while large commercial farms spread over the eastern lowlands.

A Subsistence farming in the Andes

B Commercial farming on the Pampas

The natural resources of the Andes have attracted settlers for centuries. The Spanish mined gold, silver, and copper in the highlands of Peru and Bolivia. The mines at Potosí, where Omar works, once supplied huge quantities of silver that made the Spanish Empire rich.

Today people are using the resources and changing the landscape of the region in other ways. Hydroelectric dams are built to produce electricity by tapping the power of falling water. These dams can cause environmental damage to delicate ecosystems. In Chile the building of dams on the Bio-Bio River is flooding river valleys. It is also forcing Native Americans from their homes.

Fortunately, some new projects are less damaging to the landscape. The La Higuera project in the San Fernando Valley of Chile <u>generates</u> hydroelectricity from the natural flow of river waters.

generate, *v.,* to produce

Reading Check **Where is the best agricultural land in the region?**

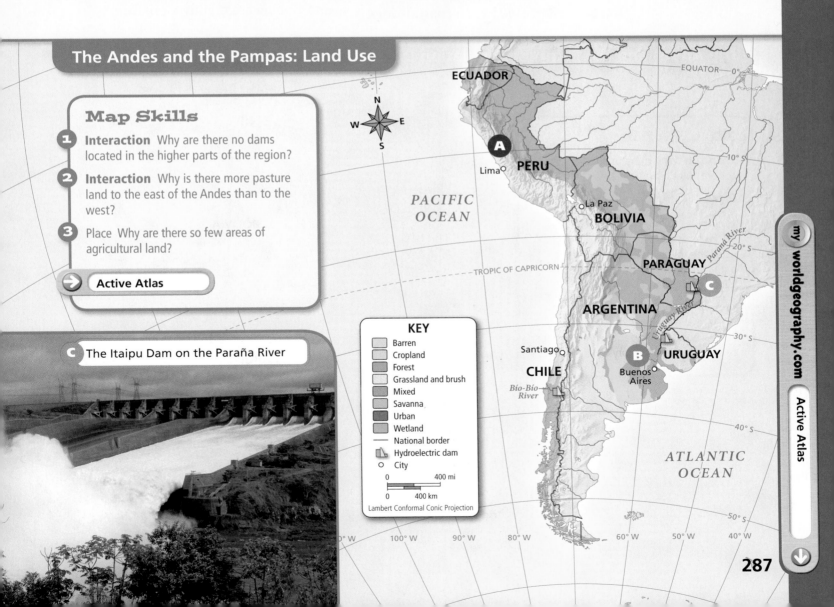

The Andes and the Pampas: Land Use

Map Skills

1 **Interaction** Why are there no dams located in the higher parts of the region?

2 **Interaction** Why is there more pasture land to the east of the Andes than to the west?

3 **Place** Why are there so few areas of agricultural land?

Active Atlas

C The Itaipu Dam on the Paraña River

KEY
- Barren
- Cropland
- Forest
- Grassland and brush
- Mixed
- Savanna
- Urban
- Wetland
- — National border
- Hydroelectric dam
- ○ City

0   400 mi
0   400 km
Lambert Conformal Conic Projection

EQUATOR — 0°

ECUADOR

PERU

Lima

PACIFIC OCEAN

La Paz

BOLIVIA

Paraná River

PARAGUAY

10° S

20° S

TROPIC OF CAPRICORN

ARGENTINA

Uruguay River

Santiago

CHILE

Bío-Bío River

Buenos Aires

URUGUAY

30° S

ATLANTIC OCEAN

40° S

50° S

100° W   90° W   80° W   70° W   60° W   50° W   40° W

my worldgeography.com   Active Atlas

287

People in the Andes and the Pampas

The region's population is unevenly distributed because of the variety of climates and landforms. There are few large cities in Paraguay, Ecuador, and Bolivia. Smaller populations live in rural areas, mountain valleys, grasslands, and in the tropical rain forests.

In earlier times settlers were attracted by the cooler temperatures and rich resources of the Andean highlands. Today most people live in coastal cities.

The largest city of the entire region is Buenos Aires, capital of Argentina, with a population of more than 12 million.

A dramatic ethnic divide exists between people in the Andes and in the Pampas. Almost all Argentina's people are of Spanish and Italian ancestry. Only 3 percent are indigenous and mestizo (people of mixed white and indigenous ancestry).

In contrast, the population of Andean countries such as Chile, Peru, Ecuador, and Bolivia are mainly a mixture

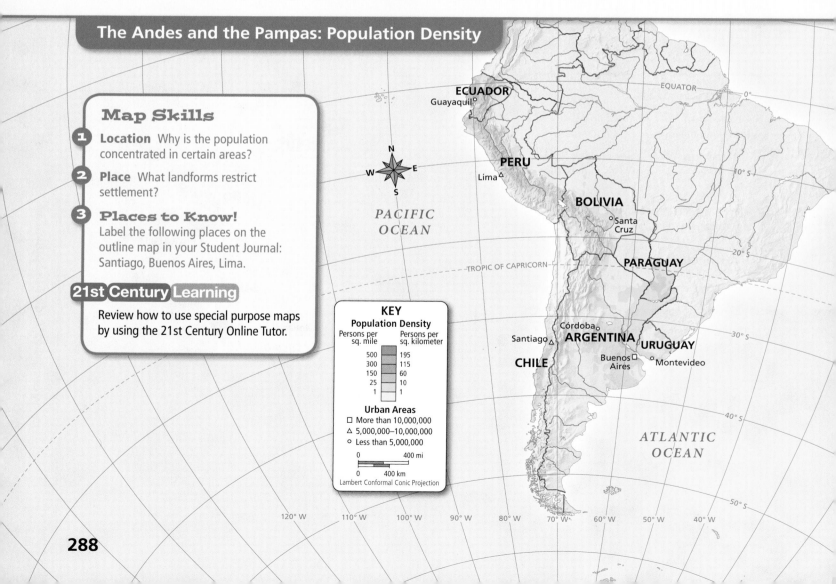

The Andes and the Pampas: Population Density

Map Skills

1 **Location** Why is the population concentrated in certain areas?

2 **Place** What landforms restrict settlement?

3 **Places to Know!** Label the following places on the outline map in your Student Journal: Santiago, Buenos Aires, Lima.

21st Century Learning

Review how to use special purpose maps by using the 21st Century Online Tutor.

KEY
Population Density

Persons per sq. mile	Persons per sq. kilometer
500	195
300	115
150	60
25	10
1	1

Urban Areas
□ More than 10,000,000
△ 5,000,000–10,000,000
○ Less than 5,000,000

0   400 mi
0   400 km
Lambert Conformal Conic Projection

of mestizos and Native Americans. However, in many places a small minority of people of Spanish descent hold on to economic and political power.

The Quechua, who are descendants of the Incas, still live on the southern Altiplano and in nearby mountains and speak the ancient Incan language. In Bolivia, indigenous people have recently won political power. This is a great achievement for groups who have suffered centuries of discrimination in their own land.

Reading Check Where do most people live in the Andes and the Pampas?

Geography and History

Physical geography has always played a central role in the history of this region. The Andes are difficult to cross. Societies and nations have always been isolated from one another. Even today, few east-west roads run through the Andes.

In the southeast, the fertile Pampas attracted settlement and helped create the wealth of Argentina. In parts of the Andes, the hot climate of the lowlands forced settlement up into the cooler highlands. It was there that the advanced civilization of the Incas developed. And it was also in the Andean highlands, in places such as Potosí, that the Spanish mined the silver that made them rich.

The Andes and the Pampas have also shaped history and culture in other ways. Just as in the American West, the wide open spaces of the Pampas bred a spirit of independence. It was the gauchos, or cowboys, of the Pampas who formed the cavalry when Argentina was fighting for independence.

The Andes also played an important part in the wars of liberation, when rebel armies climbed their heights to launch surprise attacks on royalist forces in Chile. In the next section you will read about the role geography played in the region's history.

Reading Check How has geography affected history in the Andes and the Pampas?

A gaucho on the Pampas ▼

Section 1 Assessment

Key Terms

1. Use the following terms to describe the geography of the region: subduct, Altiplano, El Niño, vertical climate zones.

Key Ideas

2. Why did the Andean highlands attract settlers?

3. In what ways are people changing the landscape today?

4. Where do most people live?

Think Critically

5. **Solve Problems** How have farmers adapted to the difficult landscape of the Andes?

6. **Draw Inferences** Why might there be many hydroelectric dams in the Andes?

? Essential Question

What are the challenges of diversity?

7. How does the geographic diversity of the region determine where people live? Go to your Student Journal to record your answer.

History of the Andes and the Pampas

Key Ideas

- A variety of societies and civilizations such as the Incas developed in the region.
- The arrival of Europeans changed the physical and human geography of the region.
- After independence the nations of the region tried to develop their economies while coping with political upheaval.

Key Terms • immunity • criollo • mestizo • mercantilism • oligarchy

 **Visual Glossary**

Reading Skill: Analyze Cause and Effect Take notes using the graphic organizer in your journal.

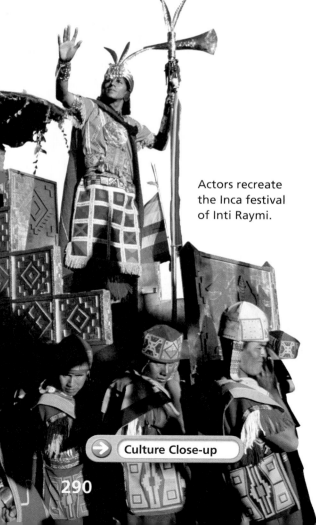

Actors recreate the Inca festival of Inti Raymi.

 Culture Close-up

In 1532 a small group of Spanish soldiers trudged up into the highlands of the Inca Empire. They were astonished by the land they had come to conquer. Here was a world full of unfamiliar plants and animals—herds of llamas, fields of potatoes, and guinea pigs bred for food. Even the air was different. Local people, who were used to breathing the thin air of the highlands, watched the invaders gasp for breath. The Spanish struggled on, driven by their hunger for treasure. It was as if they could sense the rich resources of the land under their feet.

The Spanish invasion is only one episode in the long story of the region. It is a story of trade, conquest, and the fight for the riches of the land.

Early History

Human beings have been living throughout South America for at least 11,000 years. The first people may have come from the north, crossing the Isthmus of Panama before spreading through the continent. As they settled in different areas, they adapted to their environments. Some became hunter-gatherers, like the Pampa, who gave their name to the grasslands they roamed. Others began to settle and farm the highlands of the Andes. In the mountain valleys and plateaus they built villages, and in time, cities and empires.

For thousands of years, civilizations had been developing in the Andes. Some societies adapted to the dry coastal deserts while others flourished high in the mountains. Native American communities grew different kinds of food at different altitudes. Trade routes helped distribute food. Fish from coastal settlements were traded for potatoes grown at higher levels.

In the 1400s, one Native American group began building a huge empire in the Andes. This empire was the largest in the Americas. Today these people are known as the Incas, after the title of their king, the Inca. The Inca was worshipped as a god. He ruled over a highly organized and productive society.

Reading Check **How did trade help early Andean societies survive?**

Closer Look **THE INCAS**

The Incan empire stretched from what is now Ecuador to central Chile. Paved roads tied the empire together. Careful agricultural practices ensured a plentiful food supply.

THINK CRITICALLY **How did Incan organization keep the empire running smoothly?**

The Incan Empire in 1532

Machu Picchu
Cuzco
SOUTH AMERICA
PACIFIC OCEAN
ATLANTIC OCEAN

KEY
Incan Empire

Incan gold and silver attracted the Spanish. ▶

The Incas built many cities in remote places, such as Machu Picchu, shown here.

my worldgeography.com Culture Close-up

291

The Colonial Period

In 1532, a Spanish soldier named Francisco Pizarro (frahn SEES koh pea SAHR oh) led 180 men into the Andean highlands in search of the Incas. He hoped to conquer their gold-rich empire.

Europeans Arrive The element of surprise was a key part of the Spanish plan. When Pizarro reached the Incan highlands, he tricked the Inca, Atahualpa (ah tuh WAHL puh), into visiting his camp. In a daring attack, the Spanish captured the Inca and later killed him in front of his people.

Although the Incas fought the invaders for <u>decades</u>, the conquistadors had several advantages. Their cavalry moved quickly in a land where no one had ever seen a horse. They also had deadlier weapons, such as steel swords and cannons. But the most powerful weapon that weakened the Incas was invisible. The people of South America had no **immunity,** or natural defense, against European diseases. Under these attacks, the mighty Incan Empire soon crumbled.

The Spanish divided the conquered lands into areas governed by viceroys. These viceroys ruled for Spain's king and queen. Spain's Roman Catholic Church worked to convert native peoples to Christianity. Meanwhile, the Spanish moved Native Americans from their homes and forced them to work. To expand this pool of workers, the Spanish imported enslaved people from Africa.

As the resources of the Andes created wealth for the Spanish Empire, a class system developed based on race. The Spanish who had been born in Spain, called peninsulares, were the ruling class. Spaniards born in the Americas were called **criollos**. The children of Spanish men who married indigenous women were called **mestizos**—of mixed race. At the bottom of society were Native Americans and enslaved Africans. As a result of disease and terrible working conditions, the indigenous population dropped by 90 percent by the end of the 1500s.

The Road to Revolution Spain kept a grip on the region's economy, which depended on exports to Europe. Resources such as gold and silver were shipped through the dazzling colonial capital of Lima, in what is now Peru. South American crops were also exported, including sugar and cacao.

The colonies were expected to trade only with Spain and not with one another.

decade, *n.,* a period of ten years

Spanish conquistador ▶

Manufacturing was also discouraged. This was to make sure that Spanish colonists bought manufactured products only from Spain.

Wealth was unevenly distributed in the colonies. A small number of people owned most of the land. In addition, the peninsulares would not share political power with the criollos.

The criollos believed that Spanish control limited their economies. People were also inspired by the American and French revolutions. As Spain grew weaker from war with France, many in the Spanish colonies began preparing for rebellion.

When the fight for independence began in Venezuela in 1810, Simón Bolívar (see MOHN boh LEE vahr) emerged as military leader of the rebellion. For the next 20 years, Bolívar slowly liberated countries in the north of South America.

Meanwhile, in the south, Spain struggled to defeat another rebellion. There, José de San Martín (hoh SAY deh sahn marhr TEEN) fought for Argentina's independence. He knew that Spain would try to win back Argentina, as long as Spanish forces remained in South America. So San Martín took an army over the Andes to defeat Spanish forces in Chile. After San Martín rode north to liberate Lima, Peru, Bolívar went south to defeat the remaining royalist forces. The battle of Ayacucho in 1824 freed Peru. This was the last major battle in the fight for independence from Spain.

Reading Check Why did the Spanish colonies rebel?

liberate, *v.,* to free

Mercantilism

In colonial times, Spain set up the economic system of **mercantilism**. In this system, raw materials were sent to the mother country. In return, colonists were expected to buy Spanish products. *Who benefited most from this arrangement?*

myWorld Activity
Identity Game

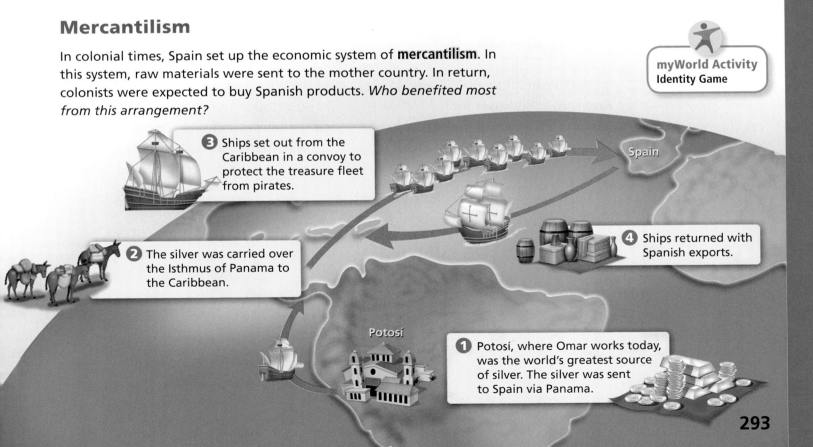

❸ Ships set out from the Caribbean in a convoy to protect the treasure fleet from pirates.

❹ Ships returned with Spanish exports.

❷ The silver was carried over the Isthmus of Panama to the Caribbean.

Spain

Potosí

❶ Potosí, where Omar works today, was the world's greatest source of silver. The silver was sent to Spain via Panama.

Essential Question

myWorld Chapter Activity

Grant Report Follow your teacher's instructions to study problems faced by each country in the region. Review photographs and information about each topic. Then meet with your team and decide what kind of grant to recommend for your country before writing your recommendation.

21st Century Learning

Give an Effective Presentation

With a partner, look back over the chapter and choose a landform that has been important in the region's history. Work together to develop a presentation on the importance of this landform. Make a checklist to evaluate each other's performance: maintain good posture, pause at important points, and use expressive body language.

Document-Based Questions

Success Tracker™
Online at myworldgeography.com

Use your knowledge of the Andes and the Pampas and Documents A and B to answer questions 1–3.

Document A

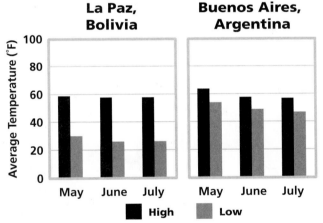

SOURCE: Weather.msn.com

Document B

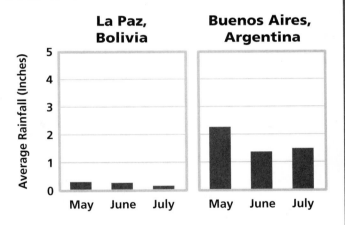

SOURCE: Weather.msn.com

1. What does document A tell you about the difference between the climates of La Paz and Buenos Aires in May, June, and July?

   A La Paz is much hotter than Buenos Aires.

   B Buenos Aires is hotter than La Paz.

   C Temperatures in La Paz vary more than temperatures in Buenos Aires.

   D Buenos Aires is much colder than La Paz.

2. Document B shows that in May, June, and July

   A La Paz is wetter than Buenos Aires.

   B Buenos Aires is wetter than La Paz.

   C La Paz receives no rain.

   D Buenos Aires receives no rain.

3. **Writing Task** Explain what the two documents tell you about the climate in the region.

myworldgeography.com Self-Test

Chapter 7

Brazil

Who should benefit from a country's resources?

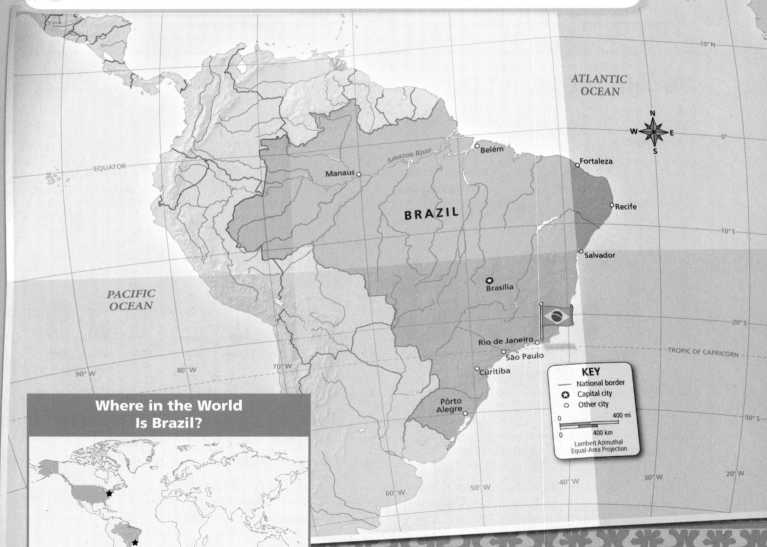

Where in the World Is Brazil?

Washington, D.C., to Rio de Janeiro: 4,790 miles

ATLANTIC OCEAN

PACIFIC OCEAN

EQUATOR

BRAZIL

Amazon River

Manaus

Belém

Fortaleza

Recife

Salvador

Brasília

Rio de Janeiro

São Paulo

Curitiba

Pôrto Alegre

TROPIC OF CAPRICORN

KEY

— National border
⊛ Capital city
○ Other city

0 — 400 mi
0 — 400 km

Lambert Azimuthal
Equal-Area Projection

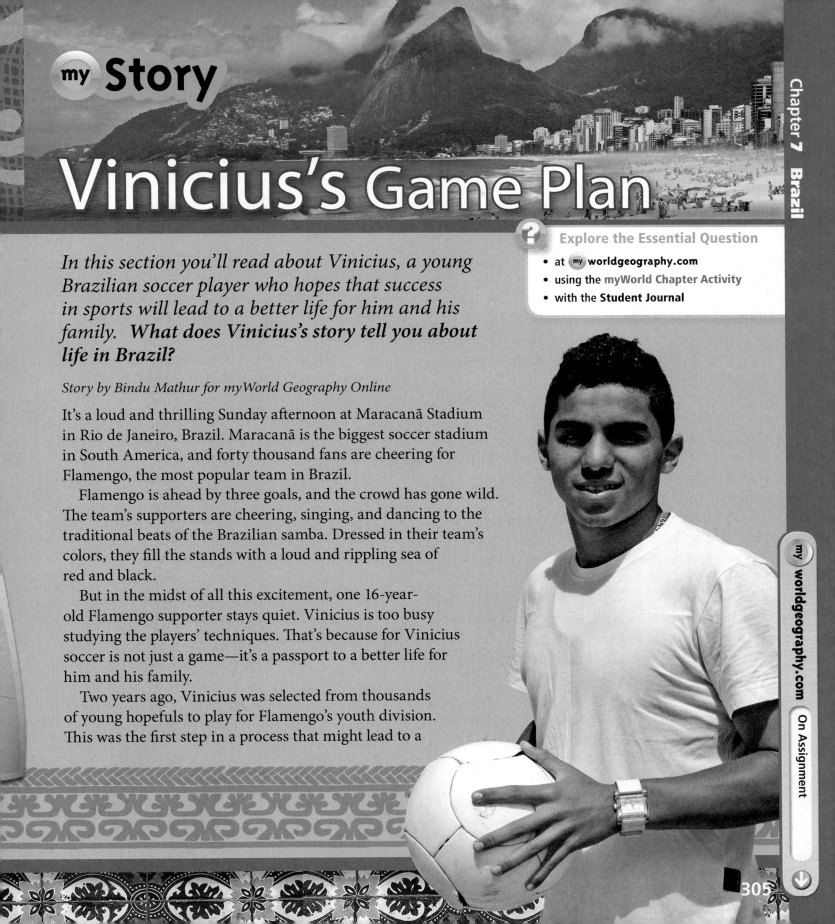

my Story

Vinicius's Game Plan

Explore the Essential Question
- at my worldgeography.com
- using the **myWorld Chapter Activity**
- with the **Student Journal**

In this section you'll read about Vinicius, a young Brazilian soccer player who hopes that success in sports will lead to a better life for him and his family. **What does Vinicius's story tell you about life in Brazil?**

Story by Bindu Mathur for myWorld Geography Online

It's a loud and thrilling Sunday afternoon at Maracanã Stadium in Rio de Janeiro, Brazil. Maracanã is the biggest soccer stadium in South America, and forty thousand fans are cheering for Flamengo, the most popular team in Brazil.

Flamengo is ahead by three goals, and the crowd has gone wild. The team's supporters are cheering, singing, and dancing to the traditional beats of the Brazilian samba. Dressed in their team's colors, they fill the stands with a loud and rippling sea of red and black.

But in the midst of all this excitement, one 16-year-old Flamengo supporter stays quiet. Vinicius is too busy studying the players' techniques. That's because for Vinicius soccer is not just a game—it's a passport to a better life for him and his family.

Two years ago, Vinicius was selected from thousands of young hopefuls to play for Flamengo's youth division. This was the first step in a process that might lead to a

Vinicius captures the spectacular landscape of Rio de Janeiro.

Vinicius strolls down the beach during his free time.

professional contract. Playing for the Flamengo team could make Vinicius a star.

Vinicius says, "It's so exciting to come to the stadium and see the professionals on the field, because I hope that will be me in the future, playing for a huge cheering crowd shouting my name. It is my ultimate dream!"

The next day, the whistle blows at the Flamengo training facility near Rio. Forty boys age 14 to 17 dressed in red and black uniforms are running drills with a coach. Vinicius is there, the only player with a Mohawk hairstyle, taking up his position as a forward on the team.

These boys were selected from all over Brazil, and here they undergo a rigorous training routine. For six days a week, physical exercise begins at seven o'clock in the morning and is followed by soccer training. Then there's time for a traditional lunch of arroz feijão (rice with black beans) and rest until the next day's practice.

For Vinicius, pursuing his dream has meant sacrifice. He moved far from his hometown of Belém, more than 1,500 miles north of Rio de Janeiro. Belém is located in the huge Amazon rain forest. He left behind his mother, who works as a secretary, and his father, a math teacher.

Vinicius loves the rain forest and regrets its ongoing destruction. "There are many green areas, trees, and rivers. But people are destroying it. There are trees that are over a hundred years old, but people are cutting the trees for wood and also polluting the rivers."

His new life away from home has not been easy. In the southeastern city of Rio de Janeiro, Vinicius has faced prejudice against people from the North, which is a poor region. "Some people called me names when I first arrived. It was upsetting," he explains. "And I really miss my family. I have cried several times, but I remember that I am here hoping to give them a better life."

Brazil is a country with widespread poverty and a huge gap between rich and poor. For young people from poorer families, success at sports is one of the few ways to achieve a more comfortable life.

For now, Rio will be his home as he waits to find out whether he will advance to the next level of the Flamengo youth team. Rio is world famous for its beaches and tourist attractions, but Vinicius doesn't

A typical Brazilian meal of chicken, rice, and black beans

Vinicius shows off some fancy footwork at training.

Flamengo supporters gather outside the stadium.

get much time to see the sights. When he's not busy training, he goes to night classes to complete his high school diploma so he can enter a university.

"Some players do sign a professional contract, but there are those who don't succeed, or who get injured, so I think it is important to have a 'Plan B.' I am thinking of studying physical education at university," he says.

Back on the soccer field, the head coach announces the selections for the following year. Some of the boys put on a brave face when they discover they haven't made the list.

But Vinicius has a big smile. Although he has not been offered a professional contract, he's been invited back for another year on the youth team and is one step closer to his dream.

"If I become professional one day, it will be worth all of this sacrifice of being far from home," he grins.

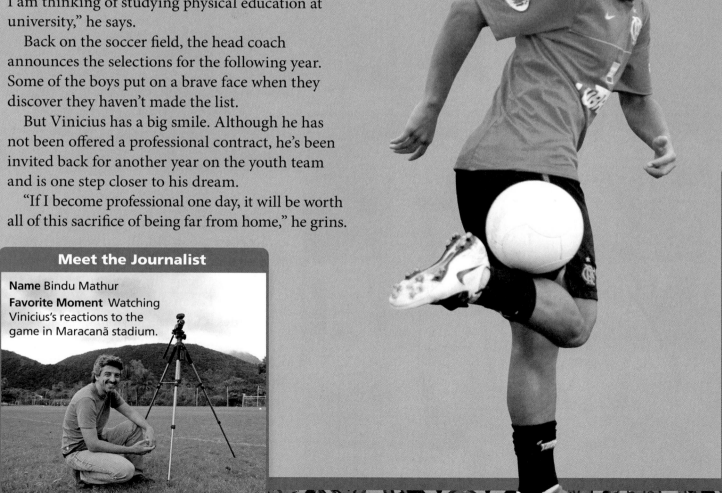

→ myStory Online

Join Vinicius as he shows you more about his life in Rio.

Meet the Journalist

Name Bindu Mathur
Favorite Moment Watching Vinicius's reactions to the game in Maracanã stadium.

my worldgeography.com myStory Video

Key Ideas
- Brazil's varied landforms contain a wealth of natural resources.
- The Amazon rain forest thrives in Brazil's climate.
- Although most Brazilians live in cities along the coast, there has been steady migration inland.

Key Terms • Amazon basin • savanna • canopy • favela

⊙ **Visual Glossary**

🌐 **Reading Skill: Label an Outline Map** Take notes using the outline map in your journal.

◄ View of Sugar Loaf Mountain and Rio de Janeiro

Boy practicing capoeira, the Brazilian dance and martial art

Physical Features

Vinicius lives in Brazil—the fifth-largest country in the world. Brazil covers nearly half of South America. It shares a border with almost every other country on the continent. Because the country is so large, it includes a wide variety of landscapes.

Brazil's best-known physical feature is the Amazon River. This mighty river flows east from the Andes for about 4,000 miles. It passes through the Amazon lowlands of northern Brazil before it empties into the Atlantic Ocean, near Vinicius's hometown of Belém. The Amazon helps drain the continent.

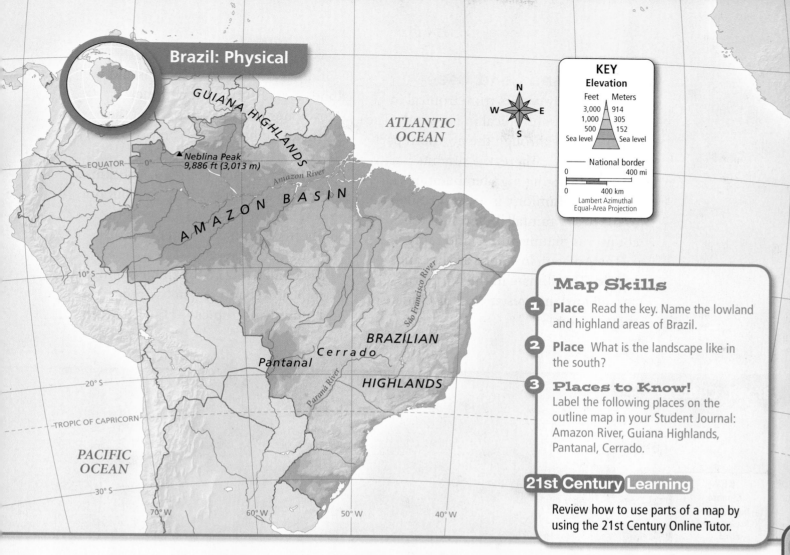

Brazil: Physical

GUIANA HIGHLANDS

ATLANTIC OCEAN

▲ Neblina Peak
9,886 ft (3,013 m)

EQUATOR 0°

Amazon River

A M A Z O N   B A S I N

São Francisco River

BRAZILIAN

Cerrado

Pantanal

HIGHLANDS

Paraná River

10° S

20° S

TROPIC OF CAPRICORN

PACIFIC OCEAN

30° S

70° W   60° W   50° W   40° W

KEY
Elevation

Feet	Meters
3,000	914
1,000	305
500	152
Sea level	Sea level

National border

0 _____ 400 mi
0 _____ 400 km
Lambert Azimuthal
Equal-Area Projection

N W E S

Map Skills

1 **Place** Read the key. Name the lowland and highland areas of Brazil.

2 **Place** What is the landscape like in the south?

3 **Places to Know!**
Label the following places on the outline map in your Student Journal: Amazon River, Guiana Highlands, Pantanal, Cerrado.

21st Century Learning

Review how to use parts of a map by using the 21st Century Online Tutor.

The Amazon carries more water than any other river in the world. It pours some 58 billion gallons of fresh water into the ocean every second. One reason for this huge flow is the size of the **Amazon basin**—the land drained by the Amazon River. The basin is 2.7 million square miles (7 million square kilometers).

The Amazon lowlands are vast. But highlands cover more of the country. North of the Amazon River are the Guiana Highlands, which include Neblina Peak, Brazil's highest point. To the south are the Brazilian Highlands. This region of plateaus and hills contains mineral resources.

The Cerrado (suh RAH doh), is located here. This area includes **savanna,** a parklike landscape of grasslands, as well as forest.

To the west of the Brazilian Highlands lies a huge wetland. Known as the Pantanal, this wetland supports many types of plants and animals.

A strip of low-lying land hugs Brazil's Atlantic coast. These Atlantic lowlands narrow farther south, where the Brazilian Highlands crowd the coast for some 1,600 miles. Still farther south, the lowland region widens again.

Reading Check Where does the Amazon River begin, and where does it end?

myWorldActivity
A Sculptor's Brazil

Climate and Land Use

Brazil's climate varies from tropical in the north to subtropical in the south. The Equator runs through the northern part of the country. There, the sun hits Earth directly, bringing high temperatures all year long. Humidity is high, too, thanks to the heavy rainfall. The rest of the country is mainly humid and rainy.

The Amazon lowlands are hot and humid. The climate in the northern coastal lowlands resembles the climate of the Amazon.

In the Northeast, heavy rains and floods arrive during the summer (November to April). In parts of the northeast, temperatures can rise above 100°F (38°C).

As you move south, the coastal climate starts to change. It is still humid but not so hot. Air from Antarctica cools the southern coast in the winter months (May to October).

The climate of the Brazilian Highlands is tropical wet and dry in the north and humid subtropical in the far south.

Brazil: Climate

KEY
Climate
- Tropical wet
- Tropical wet and dry
- Semiarid
- Humid subtropical
- Maritime
- — National border

0 — 400 mi
0 — 400 km
Lambert Azimuthal Equal-Area Projection

EQUATOR   0°

BRAZIL

10° S

60° W

20° S

TROPIC OF CAPRICORN

ATLANTIC OCEAN

30° S

50° W   40° W

Tropical wet

Tropical wet and dry

Semiarid

Humid subtropical

Map Skills

1. **Location** Why is the climate so hot in the Amazon basin?

2. **Place** How does climate differ in the south?

3. **Interaction** Which climate zone might be the poorest for crops?

→ **Active Atlas**

However, the climate also varies with elevation. Higher areas are cooler.

In the rich soil of southern and southeastern coastal areas, farmers grow a wide variety of crops such as coffee, oranges, soybeans, and other foods.

The northeast is a hot region, where rainfall is limited to the summer months. In this dry landscape, cattle ranching dominates. Drought and the growth of huge commercial farms have forced many farmers to migrate out of the region.

Ranchers raise cattle on the grasslands of the Brazilian Highlands. These highlands produce iron ore, bauxite, and gold.

Forests cover more than half the country and produce rubber, palm oil, and timber. Hardwood trees provide good lumber for furniture, flooring, and other products. As more and more roads have been built across the Amazon basin, loggers have increased their harvesting of the region's vast reserves of hardwoods.

With all the water in Brazil, it is not surprising that many hydroelectric dams have been built or planned. The largest of these is the Itaipu Dam, which generates electric power for both Brazil and Paraguay.

Some soils in the Amazon are good for farmland. The sediments washed down from the Andes enrich some areas. However, attempts to turn many other forestlands into farmland have failed. When the rain forests are cut down, the land is fertile only for a short time. Most of the nutrients in the soil come from the leaves that fall to the ground. When the trees are cut down, the soil loses fertility.

Reading Check What part of Brazil experiences drought and floods?

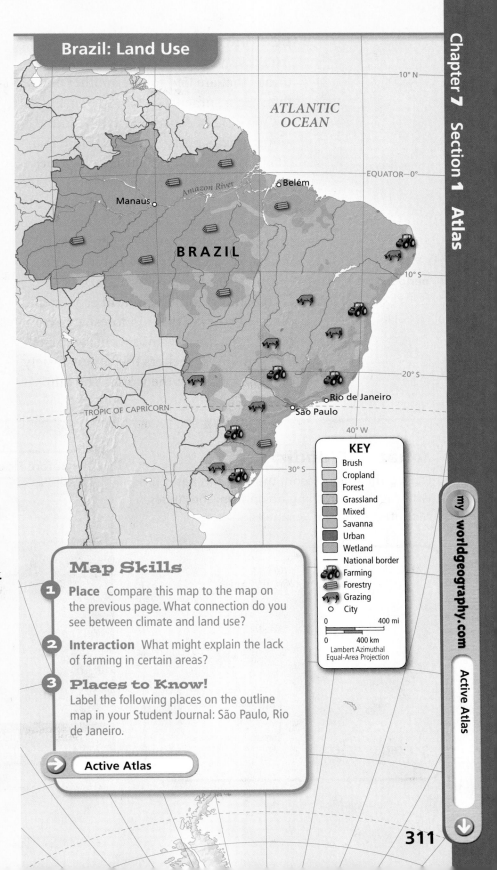

Brazil: Land Use

KEY
- Brush
- Cropland
- Forest
- Grassland
- Mixed
- Savanna
- Urban
- Wetland
- National border
- Farming
- Forestry
- Grazing
- City

0   400 mi
0   400 km
Lambert Azimuthal
Equal-Area Projection

Map Skills

1 **Place** Compare this map to the map on the previous page. What connection do you see between climate and land use?

2 **Interaction** What might explain the lack of farming in certain areas?

3 **Places to Know!** Label the following places on the outline map in your Student Journal: São Paulo, Rio de Janeiro.

Active Atlas

my**worldgeography**.com | Active Atlas

311

Ecosystems

An ecosystem is a kind of web of living things that are tied to one another and to their environment.

One kind of ecosystem can be found along Brazil's northeast coast. Here mangrove forests shelter a variety of species. In turn, sea grasses and coral reefs protect the forests from the ocean's waves.

In the semiarid northeast, rainfall is low. Here the ecosystem includes scrub vegetation and a variety of animals that can survive <u>periods</u> of drought.

In contrast to the semiarid ecosystem of the northeast, the rain forest ecosystem of the Amazon lowlands teems with life. The rain forest shelters the largest variety of plant species in the world. The rain forest is also home to an amazing number of animal species.

Most of this animal life is found high in the upper leaves of rain forest trees. This level is called the **canopy.** The canopy is like a leafy tent. It prevents most of the sun's rays from reaching the ground. The fruit that hangs in the branches of the canopy attracts animals.

Most rain forest soil is not rich. This is because most nutrients in the forest are stored in the trees. As leaves fall to the ground, heat, moisture, and insects speed up decay. Nutrients are absorbed through the tree roots and distributed to leaves and branches. In time the trees' leaves drop back to the floor. This process creates a constant cycle of growth and decay.

period, *n.,* a portion of time

Amazon Flooding

During the rainy season, the Amazon basin fills with rainwater rushing down from the Andes Mountains and the Guiana Highlands.

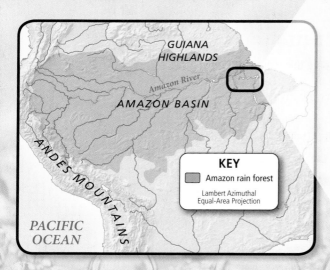

KEY

Amazon rain forest

Lambert Azimuthal Equal-Area Projection

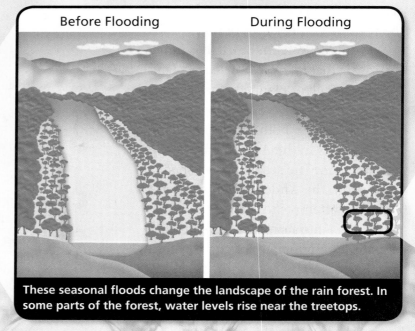

These seasonal floods change the landscape of the rain forest. In some parts of the forest, water levels rise near the treetops.

Although the Amazon lies near the Equator and does not experience great changes in seasons, many river areas are affected by seasonal flooding. When rains fall to the north and south of the Equator, waters pour into the Amazon basin. This causes land along the river to flood. Permanently flooded forests are known as igapo (ee GAP poh). Seasonally flooded forests are called varzea (VAR zee ah). As the waters rise—up to 40 feet—fish swim into areas that they would not normally visit. At such times, the ecosystems of the river and the forest merge, as trees depend on fish to eat their fruit and spread their seeds.

The igapo is full of fish such as the piranha, whose teeth can shred flesh quickly. Many animals have <u>adapted</u> to this wet landscape. The jaguar is able to climb into the canopy, swim, and it even attacks caimans, or Amazon crocodiles.

Reading Check What causes flooding in the Amazon lowlands?

adapt, *v.,* to adjust to a changed situation

Golden monkey

Blue parrot ◄

Anaconda ►

◄ River dolphin

◄ Piranha

Culture Close-up

During flooding, land and water ecosystems merge. Fish eat the fruit that falls from the trees and help spread the seeds. Animals like the river dolphin and piranha swim into areas that are normally dry.

Culture Close-up

Population Density

Today the population of Brazil is almost 200 million. However, this population is not spread evenly throughout the country. As you can see from this satellite photo, more than 80 percent of Brazilians live near the coast.

This satellite photo of Brazil at night shows the lights of settled areas.

Brazil's Declining Rural Population

SOURCE: United Nations, *World Population Prospects*

Chart Skills

What happens when great numbers of people leave the countryside?

Data Discovery

People in Brazil

Brazil has a large and diverse population. Brazil's largest city, São Paulo, has about 19 million people. Some 12 million live in the second-largest city, Rio de Janeiro.

Great Diversity Brazil is ethnically diverse. For centuries, people of European, African, and Native American ancestry have been marrying one another. Today, Brazilians share the same language and many other cultural traits.

The Cities São Paulo is in the heart of Brazil's industrial region. It is also the country's financial center. São Paulo is close to the port of Santos, which handles the highest volume of shipping in all of Latin America.

Coastal cities are overcrowded. For this reason, the government has long tried to encourage Brazilians to settle the country's vast interior. To help achieve this goal, in 1956 the government began building a brand-new capital city, called Brasília, well inland.

Manaus, with a population of 1.6 million people, is another large inland city. It is located deep in the Amazon rain forest. Manaus began as a rubber manufacturing center in the 1800s. Today, Manaus is Brazil's only free trade zone that allows the production of goods. In Manaus, foreign companies can manufacture goods without having to pay tariffs, or taxes on imports, to the government.

Rich and Poor Brazilian cities all have a similar layout. The business district and the richer neighborhoods occupy the city center. The outskirts of the city are filled with slums called **favelas.** These poor neighborhoods keep growing, as people migrate from rural to urban areas in search of jobs and a better life.

Most of the favelas are built on hillsides. Some favela houses are built of bricks. Others are built of materials gathered from waste dumps. Favelas usually have no paved roads, electricity, piped water supply, toilets, or sewers. It is estimated that more than 14 million people live in the favelas of Brazilian cities.

The gap between rich and poor in Brazil is one of the widest in the world. An estimated 10 percent of Brazilians own more than 70 percent of the land and control more than half of the country's wealth.

Since 1980, poverty has increased by 50 percent. The continued presence of poverty in such a modern country has outraged many Brazilians.

66 We have two countries here under one flag, one constitution, and one language. One part of Brazil is in the twentieth century, with high-technology computers and satellite launches. And, beside that, we have another country where people are eating lizards to survive. 99

—Wilson Braga, governor of Paraiba state, 1985

In addition to poverty, Brazilians of African ancestry often suffer from racial discrimination. However, the country is unique in the amount of racial mixing in the general population. Brazil is a new kind of society that is both multiethnic and multicultural. In the next section you will read about the events that helped create this dynamic new society.

Reading Check **Where do most Brazilians live?**

my World
IN NUMBERS

If there were **100** people in the world,

3 would live in Brazil.

Favela in
Rio de Janeiro ▼

Section 1 Assessment

Key Terms

1. Use the following terms to describe the geography of the region: Amazon basin, savanna, canopy, favela.

Key Ideas

2. What physical features have kept Brazilians from settling inland?

3. How does the climate in Brazil's northeast differ from the climate in the rest of the country?

4. In Brazil's cities, where are weathy and poor neighborhoods usually located?

Think Critically

5. Draw Inferences Road building speeds up destruction of the Amazon rain forest. Why might this be so?

6. Solve Problems What factors might persuade people to move to an inland city?

? Essential Question

Who should benefit from a country's resources?

7. Where are some of Brazil's resources located? Explain. Go to your Student Journal to record your answer.

History of Brazil

Key Ideas
- Portuguese colonization changed the human and physical geography of Brazil.
- The Portuguese introduced an export economy based on the labor of enslaved Africans.
- For most of Brazil's history, its economy has experienced a series of export booms and busts.

Key Terms • brazilwood • abolitionist • export economy • coup • boom and bust cycle

 **Visual Glossary**

→ **Reading Skill: Sequence** Take notes using the graphic organizer in your journal.

◄ Woman in traditional costume, Bahia, Brazil

→ **Language Lesson**

On March 7, 1808, the people of Rio de Janeiro awoke to an extraordinary sight. A fleet of Portuguese ships was approaching the harbor. On board were refugees from war-torn Europe. But unlike many refugees, these people were not poor. In fact, the new arrivals were members of the Portuguese royal family. For the next 13 years, Rio de Janeiro would be their home.

Rio welcomed more and more wealthy refugees as the Portuguese government and aristocracy arrived to seek safety. The arrival of the royal family changed Brazilian history. Suddenly a remote colony became the most important location in the Portuguese empire.

Brazil has always been a different kind of place. Unlike most countries in South America, Brazil was colonized by Portugal. Its people speak Portuguese rather than Spanish. In contrast to neighboring Spanish colonies, Brazil achieved independence fairly peacefully. Its history is unique for another reason as well—because for about 80 years it was the only empire in the Americas.

Cultures Meet

In A.D. 1500, Portuguese explorers first set foot on the land we know today as Brazil. This land was home to several million native people. Most of them were located along the heavily forested coast and in the Amazon basin. Native American tribes had adapted to Brazil's various environments. Some lived by hunting or fishing and gathering. Others had turned to farming.

Land Claims Portuguese explorers arrived to claim the land. In the Treaty of Tordesillas of 1494, Spain claimed all American lands west of a set line of longitude. Portugal claimed lands to the east and began colonizing Brazil.

The Portuguese first established trading posts on the northeast coast. The Portuguese traded with the Native Americans for **brazilwood,** a wood that produces a red dye. This wood gave Brazil its name. The Portuguese set up an **export economy,** an economy based on exports.

Next, the Portuguese developed another export crop, sugar. They began forcing Native Americans into slavery to work on sugar cane plantations. But native peoples either fled or died of the European diseases brought by the settlers.

Africans Arrive To replace the Native Americans, the Portuguese brought enslaved Africans to labor on sugar cane plantations and later in the gold and diamond mines of Minas Gerais.

Of the estimated 10 million enslaved Africans brought to the Americas, as many as 3 to 4 million ended up in Brazil. African culture helped shape Brazil's culture. Traditions such as capoeira, a blend of martial arts and dance, have strong African features. By the time slavery was outlawed in 1888, many Africans, Native Americans, and Portuguese had adopted one another's customs and intermarried.

Brazil's slave-based economy was part of a mercantile system. In mercantilism, colonies benefit the parent country. Brazilians were expected to export products only to Portugal. They were not allowed to trade with other countries.

An Independent Brazil The seeds of Brazil's independence were planted in 1807, when the French emperor Napoleon invaded Portugal. To escape Napoleon, Portugal's royal family fled to Brazil and governed from there.

my World IN NUMBERS

Brazil is the only country in South America where most people speak Portuguese.

Como vai?

myWorldActivity
Timeline Inquiry

The Uninvited Guests

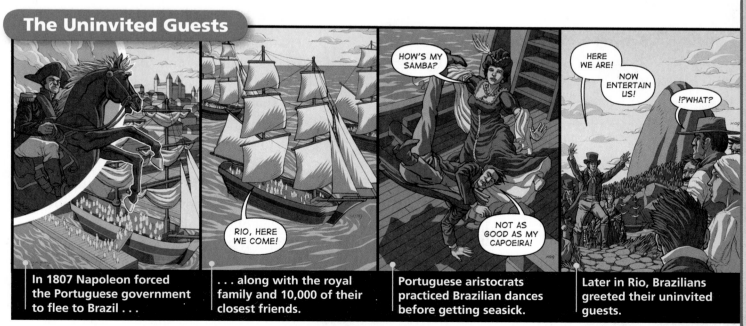

In 1807 Napoleon forced the Portuguese government to flee to Brazil . . .

. . . along with the royal family and 10,000 of their closest friends.

RIO, HERE WE COME!

Portuguese aristocrats practiced Brazilian dances before getting seasick.

HOW'S MY SAMBA?

NOT AS GOOD AS MY CAPOEIRA!

Later in Rio, Brazilians greeted their uninvited guests.

HERE WE ARE!

NOW ENTERTAIN US!

!?WHAT?

Boom and Bust

For centuries the Brazilian economy depended on one or two main export products. When foreign demand for the product was high, Brazil's economy boomed. But when demand fell, the economy suffered a decline, or a "bust."

THINK CRITICALLY **Study the timeline and the map. What export came from western Brazil and when?**

KEY
- Brazilwood
- Sugar cane
- Gold
- Diamonds
- Coffee
- Rubber

Manaus · BRAZIL · Salvador · Minas Gerais · Ouro Preto · São Paulo · Rio de Janeiro

Boom Period for Each Export

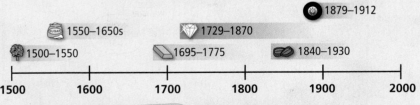

Rubber 1879–1912
Sugar 1550–1650s
Diamonds 1729–1870
Brazilwood 1500–1550
Gold 1695–1775
Coffee 1840–1930

1500 1600 1700 1800 1900 2000

Enslaved Africans worked on coffee plantations

After slavery ended, European immigrants arrived to seek work.

318

The king returned to Portugal in 1821. His son, Pedro I, stayed in Brazil. In 1822, Pedro declared that Brazil was no longer part of Portugal. He made himself emperor of an independent Brazil.

By this time, Brazilians had begun growing coffee. By the mid-1800s, coffee exports were the main source of revenue for Brazil's economy. Coffee was the latest "star" product in a **boom and bust cycle**—a period of strong economic growth followed by a period of sharp decline.

Reading Check **What three cultures came together in Brazil?**

The New Brazil

In the late 1800s, coffee had brought such wealth that coffee planters were politically powerful. They challenged the government, which was controlled by the owners of the sugar plantations. The coffee planters wanted a republic. Meanwhile, **abolitionists,** or people who wanted to end slavery, were campaigning to free the slaves.

Freedom and Republic Under pressure from republicans and abolitionists, the old Brazil was swept away. In 1888, all the slaves were freed. A year later, Brazil's military staged a **coup**—an overthrow of the government. The empire ended, and a republic took its place.

New leaders drew up a constitution. They formed a government based loosely on that of the United States. It was a federal system with an elected president.

During the republic, power shifted from the sugar plantations of the northeast to the coffee growers of the southeast. In fact, some of the first leaders of the republic were known as "coffee presidents."

Throughout the 1900s, the republic faced many challenges. Brazil's economy was hurt when demand for rubber (from the Amazon basin) declined. Coffee continued to carry the economy until the Great Depression began in 1929. Then coffee prices fell sharply in world markets.

As coffee lost its value, new groups challenged the power of the coffee elites. In 1930 Getúlio Vargas overthrew the government. Vargas appealed to the huge numbers of workers now crowding the cities. He tried to encourage manufacturing, so that Brazil would not be so dependent on foreign goods. During the 1930s his dictatorship stifled democracy but brought in many changes, such as giving women voting rights. Vargas continued to be a powerful figure in Brazilian politics for 24 years.

In the second half of the 1900s, Brazil's government was controlled mainly by dictators or the military. During this time, highways were constructed, and the new capital, Brasília, was built. By the early 1980s, Brazil had become one of the world's most important industrial nations. However, all this progress came at a terrible price for democracy. Many thousands of people were arrested for opposing government policies. Only in 1990 was democracy restored.

restore, *v.,* to bring back

Reading Check What type of government did Brazil adopt after the empire fell?

Government buildings in Brazil's futuristic capital, Brasília ▼

Section 2 Assessment

? **Essential Question**

Who should benefit from a country's resources?

Key Terms

1. Use the following key terms to explain important events in the region's history: brazilwood, boom and bust cycle, abolitionist, coup.

Key Ideas

2. What crop did enslaved Native Americans help produce?

3. Why did the Portuguese replace Native American slave labor with African slave labor?

4. What products went through periods of boom and bust?

Think Critically

5. **Draw Inferences** How might Brazil's history have been different if the coastal Indian groups had united to resist the Europeans?

6. **Synthesize** What headline might have appeared in U.S. newspapers after the coup in Brazil in 1889?

7. Did the export of sugar and other valuable resources from Brazil benefit all the people in the colony? Explain. Go to your Student Journal to record your answer.

Brazil Today

Key Ideas
- A variety of ethnic groups have contributed to Brazil's rich culture.
- Brazil's diversified economy depends on manufacturing, agriculture, and trade.
- Brazil is struggling with environmental problems, such as pollution and rain forest destruction.

Key Terms • ethanol • urban planning • market economy • social services

 Visual Glossary

Reading Skill: Summarize Take notes using the graphic organizer in your journal.

 Photo

◀ Vinicius on his tour of Rio

occer is a matter of national pride in Brazil. Brazilian soccer players are among the best in the world. The Brazilian men's team often wins the World Cup, the top international soccer tournament.

If Vinicius is offered a contract to play on the Flamengo team, he could be on the road to stardom. But Vinicius knows that for now, he has to have an alternative plan for his life. So if he doesn't make the Flamengo team, he plans to enroll in a university. Whatever happens, Vinicius is looking forward to the future with excitement. He is a good symbol of a young nation full of hope and energy.

Brazil today is a country with a lively culture, a strong economy, and rich natural resources. It is a country eager to play a leading role in the region—and in the world. However, Brazil also faces enormous challenges, such as poverty and environmental damage. Can Brazil close the gap between rich and poor? Can the country protect its rain forest and keep its economy growing?

A Rich Culture

The richness of Brazilian culture grew as different ethnic groups influenced one another's customs over the centuries. After more than 400 years of intermarriage between Africans, Europeans, Native Americans, and others, almost half of Brazil's people are of mixed racial ancestry. The long cultural exchange has also produced new kinds of religious worship as well as one of the biggest parties in the world—Carnival.

Carnival Nothing on Earth is quite like Carnival. This festival—several days of parades, music, and dance—releases the energy and creativity of Brazilian culture. Like much else in Brazil, Carnival also represents a blending of European and African traditions. The festival is held before the Christian season of Lent, a 40-day period of fasting that leads up to Easter. Traditionally, Christians hold a feast—Carnival—before beginning their fast. This European custom mingled with African music and dance and became the festival that Brazilians enjoy today.

Ethnic Groups African heritage remains strong in Brazil. This is especially true along Brazil's northeast coast, where enslaved Africans first arrived. People of European descent live throughout Brazil, although immigrants from Europe have tended to settle in the south. Native peoples, too, live in all parts of Brazil, while many Native American communities survive in the rain forests.

Religion and Family Life The Portuguese introduced Roman Catholicism to Brazil. Today, a large majority of the population remains Catholic. However, religious diversity is increasing. Various Protestant churches have gained followers in recent years. Japanese, Chinese, and Korean immigrants have brought Buddhism to Brazil. There are also small populations of Mormons, Jews, Muslims, and followers of traditional African religions.

Reading Check **What groups and traditions have shaped Brazilian culture?**

Closer Look

Carnival

Carnival combines the religious traditions of southern Europe with the music and dance of Africa and the Americas. During the festival, people dance to the music of the samba, which draws on Native American, African, and Portuguese styles of music and dance.

THINK CRITICALLY **In what ways is Carnival a multicultural event?**

The float that appears below commemorates 100 years of Japanese immigration to Brazil. ▼

Carnival costumes and floats can be dazzling.

Environmental Issues

Like all modern countries, Brazil is trying to deal with urban pollution. Vehicle exhaust and factories spew pollutants into the air and water. But Brazil's main environmental issue involves the rain forest.

The Amazon rain forest is a unique place that helps support life on Earth. Its trees absorb carbon dioxide (a major part of vehicle exhaust) and produce oxygen for all living things to breathe. The rain forest is also a vast natural pharmacy. Many modern medicines have come from tropical rain forests.

generate, *v.,* to produce

Satellite pictures of the same area show rain-forest destruction between 1990 and 2000. ▼

However, the Amazon's ecosystem is being destroyed. Humans are cutting down its trees for timber or to clear land for farms and ranches. They are mining its streams for gold and are damming its rivers to <u>generate</u> electricity.

The Amazon is a vast region, and most of it is still healthy. Today, Brazil's government is taking steps to defend the rain forest from too much development. The president has imposed fines on lawbreakers. Hundreds of federal police have been sent to stop the destruction. The government has also created large conservation areas.

Unfortunately, much of the destruction is taking place in Brazil's remote areas, or frontiers, and frontiers are always difficult to patrol. As long as there is a worldwide demand for products such as soybeans, meat, and wood, the rain forest will be under threat.

Although rain-forest destruction is a problem in the Amazon, Brazil is continously searching for other solutions. Brazil has found an alternative fuel for its cars. **Ethanol,** a fuel that can be made from sugar cane, is enabling the country to reduce its dependence on oil.

Brazil's southeastern city of Curitiba is another success story. In Curitiba, careful **urban planning**—the planning of a city— has reduced car traffic and trash while creating a parklike environment. Today Curitiba is admired throughout the world. Many consider it a new kind of "green city" that is less harmful to the environment than other cities.

Reading Check Why is it important to protect the Amazon rain forest?

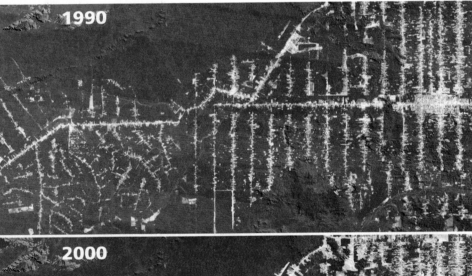
1990

2000

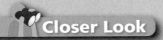 **Closer Look**

Curitiba: Green City of the Future

In the late 1900s, Curitiba's leaders realized that the city was growing too quickly. So the city adopted a plan to solve the problems of urban growth and help the environment. Curitiba's plan has been a popular success. The city has become a world-famous model of "green," or environmentally friendly, urban planning.

THINK CRITICALLY **If you were an urban planner, how would you make your own community greener?**

Problem Large populations create trash in urban centers.

Curitiba's Solution Recycling programs keep the streets clean.

Problem Increasing numbers of cars cause pollution and traffic congestion.

Curitiba's Solution Improve the public transportation system. Some streets are set aside for buses only. Other streets are set aside for pedestrians.

Problem Building on wet-lands damages habitats and worsens flooding.

Curitiba's Solution Allow only parkland and lakes along the waterways to absorb floodwaters.

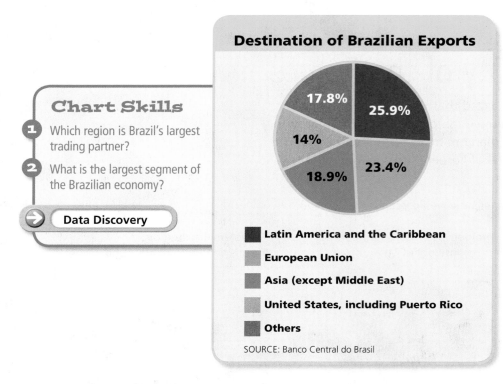

Destination of Brazilian Exports

- 25.9%
- 23.4%
- 18.9%
- 14%
- 17.8%

Legend:
- Latin America and the Caribbean
- European Union
- Asia (except Middle East)
- United States, including Puerto Rico
- Others

SOURCE: Banco Central do Brasil

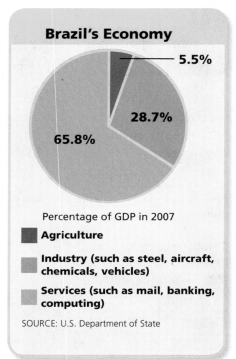

Brazil's Economy

- 5.5%
- 28.7%
- 65.8%

Percentage of GDP in 2007

Legend:
- Agriculture
- Industry (such as steel, aircraft, chemicals, vehicles)
- Services (such as mail, banking, computing)

SOURCE: U.S. Department of State

Chart Skills

1. Which region is Brazil's largest trading partner?

2. What is the largest segment of the Brazilian economy?

→ Data Discovery

A Growing Economy

Brazil has a **market economy,** in which the prices of goods are set by demand, not by the government. Brazil's economic growth is no longer dependent on a single crop or product as it was in the past. Today, the economy has diversified. Agriculture is just one part of Brazil's modern industrial economy—the largest economy in South America.

Resources and Manufacturing Brazil's geography provides a wealth of natural resources to support economic growth. Mineral resources include iron, manganese, and tin, as well as widespread oil and natural gas deposits. In addition, the Amazon basin is a source of timber, rubber, diamonds, and gold.

Brazil's main manufacturing region lies in the Southeast, between São Paulo and Rio de Janeiro. Vehicle manufacturing for the Brazilian market is a major industry. Foreign automakers have also built factories here.

Farming and Free Trade Brazil is still one of the world's major exporters of coffee. The country continues to grow a huge amount of sugar cane. Today most sugar cane is converted into ethanol, a cheaper alternative to gasoline. Recently, Brazil has also become the world's largest grower and exporter of soybeans.

Brazil is part of a trade organization that includes the nations of Argentina, Paraguay, and Uruguay. This organization is called MERCOSUR, which is short for Mercado Común del Sur, or Southern Common Market. MERCOSUR allows member countries to trade freely with one another, without tariffs.

Reading Check **How has Brazil diversified its economy?**

myWorldActivity
Challenges for Brazil

Government for the People

Brazil has been independent since 1889. But it has not always been a democracy. As you have read, starting in the 1930s Brazil was ruled by dictators or the military. However, in 1990 democracy was restored.

Branches of Government The <u>structure</u> of Brazil's national government is similar to that of the United States. A president heads the executive branch. Two houses make up the legislative branch, called the National Congress. The highest court in the judicial branch is the Federal Supreme Court. The president and members of the legislature are elected by the people. The minimum voting age is 16.

Balancing Growth and Social Needs Despite Brazil's growing economy, poverty remains widespread. Too many people in both rural and urban areas lack good housing, schools, hospitals, and police and fire protection. A wide gap exists between the poverty of the north and the wealth of the south. But dealing with problems such as these takes money. Much of that money must come from taxes.

Business owners claim that taxes slow growth. Others, like President Lula, want to redirect Brazil's oil wealth into **social services**—programs designed to help the poor. Speaking of the oil recently discovered off the coast, President Lula said,

> 66 It is the wealth of the country, it is the wealth of 190 million Brazilians, and we have to use this wealth to help the poor of the country. 99
> —President Lula da Silva, BBC News, August 5, 2008

structure, *n.,* organization

Looking Toward the Future With its newfound oil fields and its increasing production of ethanol, Brazil is on its way to energy independence. This country, which is already an industrial giant, is also becoming an agricultural superpower. But only time will tell if Brazil will use its resources wisely— lifting millions out of poverty and into a brighter future.

Reading Check What is the basic structure of Brazil's national government?

my worldgeography.com   Data Discovery

Section 3 Assessment

Essential Question

Key Terms

1. Use the following terms to describe life in Brazil today: ethanol, urban planning, market economy, social services.

Key Ideas

2. Which ethnic traditions are the main influences on Brazilian culture today?

3. What is the most serious environmental issue facing Brazil?

Think Critically

4. **Solve Problems** Why doesn't Brazil simply outlaw all development in the Amazon basin?

5. **Identify Evidence** What are some strengths of the Brazilian economy?

Who should benefit from a country's resources?

6. What is the debate in Brazil over how to use the country's oil wealth? Go to your Student Journal to record your answer.

Chapter Assessment

Key Terms and Ideas

1. **Summarize** What kind of landforms can be found in Brazil?

2. **Discuss** What causes the floods in the **Amazon basin**?

3. **Recall** What language is spoken in Brazil today?

4. **Explain** What happens during a **boom and bust cycle**?

5. **Describe** Why is Carnival a good symbol of Brazil's multicultural society?

6. **Summarize** Why is Brazil developing the fuel **ethanol** into a major industry?

7. **Discuss** In what ways has Brazil diversified its economy?

Think Critically

8. **Make Inferences** Why are Brazilian cities growing so rapidly?

9. **Draw Conclusions** What are the dangers of an export economy?

10. **Categorize** What are some of Brazil's strengths and problems?

11. **Core Concepts: Migration** How did migration help shape Brazilian culture?

Places to Know

For each place, write the letter from the map that shows its location.

12. **Guiana Highlands**

13. **Manaus**

14. **Rio de Janeiro**

15. **Amazon River**

16. **Pantanal**

17. **São Paulo**

18. **Estimate** Using the scale, estimate the distance between São Paulo and Rio de Janeiro.

Brazil

Essential Question

myWorld Chapter Activity

Job Search Follow your teacher's instructions to study the resources in each of Brazil's regions. Join a national team traveling to each location in the classroom. Review the photograph and the information about the topic at each location. Then meet with your team and decide where you would like to live. Create a résumé that presents your skills.

21st Century Learning

Search for Information on the Internet

With a partner, search for sites that give information on the Brazilian economy today. Before you begin, brainstorm the kind of key words that might help your search, such as *Brazilian trade*, *Brazilian manufacturing*, and so forth.

Success Tracker™
Online at myworldgeography.com

Document-Based Questions

Use your knowledge of Brazil and Documents A and B to answer Questions 1–3.

Document A

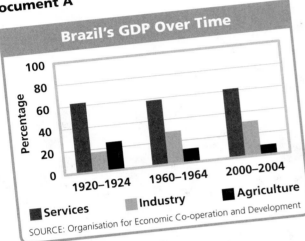

Brazil's GDP Over Time

Percentage

SOURCE: Organisation for Economic Co-operation and Development

- Services
- Industry
- Agriculture

Document B

" I come from a country and also a continent whose identity is in the making. We're a very young culture, and I think that things are not yet crystallized."

—Walter Salles, Brazilian film director

1. ... ...mation in Document A reveal

2. When Walter Salles says that things in Brazil are not yet crystallized, he means which of the ...

Closer Look

Curitiba: Green City of the Future

In the late 1900s, Curitiba's leaders realized that the city was growing too quickly. So the city adopted a plan to solve the problems of urban growth and help the environment. Curitiba's plan has been a popular success. The city has become a world-famous model of "green," or environmentally friendly, urban planning.

THINK CRITICALLY **If you were an urban planner, how would you make your own community greener?**

Problem Large populations create trash in urban centers.

Curitiba's Solution Recycling programs keep the streets clean.

Problem Increasing numbers of cars cause pollution and traffic congestion.

Curitiba's Solution Improve the public transportation system. Some streets are set aside for buses only. Other streets are set aside for pedestrians.

Problem Building on wetlands damages habitats and worsens flooding.

Curitiba's Solution Allow only parkland and lakes along the waterways to absorb floodwaters.

Mapping Life Expectancy

Your Mission Research life expectancy data on the Internet and present your findings on an annotated map and in an oral report. Divide into five teams: one mapping team and four research teams. Work together to prepare the map and report.

Do you think that you will reach the age of 100? Life expectancy depends on many factors. In general, people in developed nations live longer than people in developing nations. The factors that have a large impact on life expectancy include the quality of public health, medical care, and eating habits.

Life expectancy drops sharply in countries with high rates of infant mortality. Suppose a country has a life expectancy of 70 years for people who live past their first birthday but a 10 percent infant mortality rate. The overall life expectancy for that country would drop to 63. Life expectancy also differs for males and females.

10 years
20 years
40 years
60 year

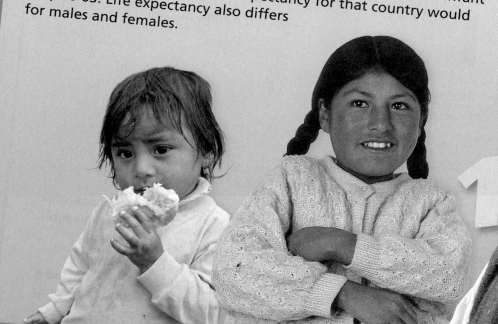

328

trading partner?

② What is the largest segment of the Brazilian economy?

→ **Data Discovery**

18.9% 23.4%

■ Latin America and the Caribbean
■ European Union
■ Asia (except Middle East)
■ United States, including Puerto Rico
■ Others

SOURCE: Banco Central do Brasil

Percentage of GDP in 2007
■ Agriculture
■ Industry (such as steel, aircraft, chemicals, vehicles)
■ Services (such as mail, banking, computing)

SOURCE: U.S. Department of State

A Growing Economy

Brazil has a **market economy,** in which the prices of goods are set by demand, not by the government. Brazil's economic growth is no longer dependent on a single crop or product as it was in the past. Today, the economy has diversified. Agriculture is just one part of Brazil's modern industrial economy—the largest economy in South America.

Resources and Manufacturing Brazil's geography provides a wealth of natural resources to support economic growth. Mineral resources include iron, manganese, and tin, as well as widespread oil and natural gas deposits. In addition, the Amazon basin is a source of timber, rubber, diamonds, and gold.

Brazil's main manufacturing region lies in the Southeast, between São Paulo and Rio de Janeiro. Vehicle manufacturing for

the Brazilian market is a major industry. Foreign automakers have also built factories here.

Farming and Free Trade Brazil is still one of the world's major exporters of coffee. The country continues to grow a huge amount of sugar cane. Today most sugar cane is converted into ethanol, a cheaper alternative to gasoline. Recently, Brazil has also become the world's largest grower and exporter of soybeans.

Brazil is part of a trade organization that includes the nations of Argentina, Paraguay, and Uruguay. This organization is called MERCOSUR, which is short for Mercado Común del Sur, or Southern Common Market. MERCOSUR allows member countries to trade freely with one another, without tariffs.

Reading Check How has Brazil diversified its economy?

myWorldActivity
Challenges for Brazil

STEP 1

Complete Specialized Tasks.

The mapping team will draw and label a large political map of South America. The four research teams should use reliable Web sites (suggested by your teacher) to find specific statistics for each country in the region. Statistics to be researched are immunization, access to clean water, infant mortality rates, and male life expectancy and female life expectancy.

STEP 2

Annotate the Map.

Each research team should discuss its findings. The teams should try to find trends or analyze the data and draw conclusions. Consider, for example, the connection between life expectancy and access to clean water. Then use captions, graphs, or photographs to annotate the political map drawn by the mapping team. Groups should cooperate as they fill in the map with their research.

STEP 3

Regroup and Prepare Oral Reports.

After the map is finished, students should return to their original teams. Each team will work together as a group to prepare an oral report summarizing the overall findings. In your report, define key terms, give your sources, and note the date of the information you found. Try to draw conclusions about why life expectancy varies among the populations of South America.

my worldgeography.com 21st Century Learning

Europe and Russia

The many countries of Europe plus Russia reach from the Atlantic Ocean to the Pacific Ocean. Russia spreads over two continents, Europe and Asia. More than 590 million people live in Europe with another 140 million in Russia. Most live in urban areas. More than 230 languages are spoken here, such as English, French, Spanish, Basque, Greek, Finnish, and Russian.

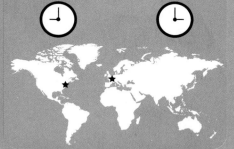

What time is it there?

Washington, D.C.	Paris, France
9 A.M. Monday	3 P.M. Monday

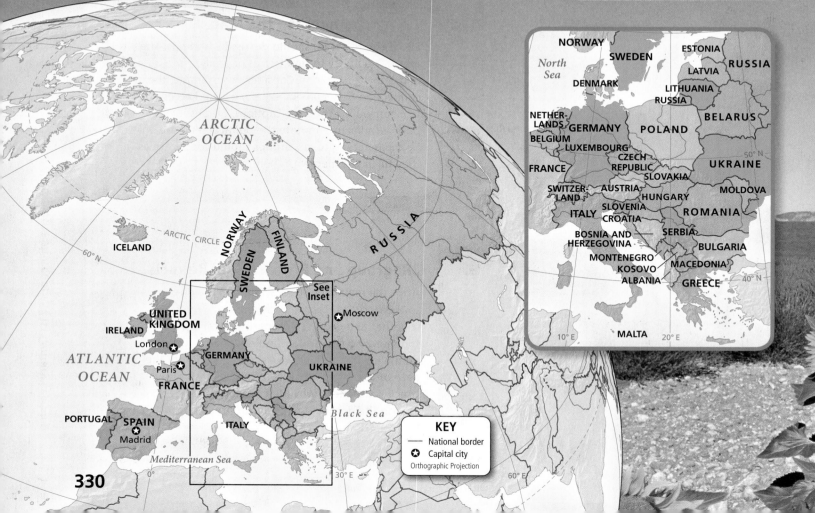

KEY

— National border
✪ Capital city

Orthographic Projection

The Unit Ahead

→ Chapter 8   Ancient and Medieval Europe   → Chapter 11   Eastern Europe

→ Chapter 9   Europe in Modern Times   → Chapter 12   Russia

→ Chapter 10   Western Europe

my worldgeography.com

Plan your trip online by doing a Data Discovery Activity and watching the myStory Videos of the region's teens.

my Story

Yasmin

Age: 18

Home: Bjärred, Sweden

Chapter 10

my Story

Serhiy

Age: 16

Home: Bezpalche, Ukraine

Chapter 11

my Story

Boris

Age: 15

Home: Moscow, Russia

Chapter 12

A field of sunflowers and lavender in France

331

Regional Overview
Physical Geography

The Alps are rugged mountains that have their own snowy climate, perfect for winter sports like skiing.

Scandinavia is a long, narrow peninsula that extends from the northernmost part of Europe.

ARCTIC OCEAN

ATLANTIC OCEAN

Ural Mountains

Northwestern Highlands

Scandinavia

Baltic Sea

North European Plain

Carpathian Mountains

Black Sea

North Sea

Alps

Balkan Peninsula

Adriatic Sea

Mont Blanc
15,774 ft (4,808 m)

Mediterranean Sea

Iberian Peninsula

Siberia

Caspian Sea

The West Siberian Plain borders the world's largest steppes region, an extensive area of cold and dry grasslands.

Regional Flyover

Suppose you fly in an airplane across Europe and Russia. If you began over the Atlantic Ocean, you would first notice that Europe is a giant peninsula stretching westward from a larger landmass. From it extend many smaller peninsulas, so that the whole continent of Europe is sometimes called the "peninsula of peninsulas."

Next, you might notice two important mountain ranges. The Alps stretch in an east-west arc through central Europe. Flying east, you would see a north–south mountain range called the Urals. These mountains form the traditional border between European Russia and Asiatic Russia.

The North European Plain sweeps east–west across Europe into European Russia. These lowlands have had both benefits and drawbacks for the region. The flat land is good for settlement and farming. It has also been a gateway for invading armies throughout history.

→ In-flight Movie

Take flight over Europe and Russia and explore the region from the air.

my worldgeography.com

In-flight Movie

333

Spartan women enjoyed more freedom than the women of Athens. They could own land and take part in business.

The city-state of Sparta was governed by an oligarchy led by the army. At the top of Spartan society were aristocrats who were also professional military men. Unlike the citizens of Athens, the people of Sparta played a much smaller part in government.

The Persian Wars War was frequent among the Greeks, but an outside threat united the city-states. That threat was the invading Persian army led by Darius, the king of Persia.

The Greek army met the Persians first at the Battle of Marathon. The Greeks surrounded the Persians, and the enemy fled to their ships in the Aegean Sea.

Darius's son Xerxes commanded the Persians in the second war with the Greeks. As allies, the Spartans joined the Greeks to stop the Persians at Thermopylae. Finally, Xerxes sailed for home after losing thousands of men and more than 200 ships in the Battle of Salamis.

Decline of the City-States In spite of their alliance, these two city-states remained enemies. War broke out between Athens and Sparta in 431 B.C. It was called the Peloponnesian War and continued off and on for 27 years. Athens was at last defeated, ending the golden age of this once-great city-state. The war also hurt other city-states around Greece, toppling governments and damaging trade. Greek culture did not end, but ongoing conflict kept it from reaching the unity or stability that had made it strong.

Spread of Greek Culture As you read at the beginning of this chapter, Alexander conquered most of the world known to the ancient Greeks. Greek culture eventually spread across southwest Asia, southern Europe, and North Africa. Today, the impact of Greek culture remains strong in democratic forms of government as well as in art and architecture.

Reading Check Which common enemy united Athens and Sparta?

As king, Alexander was popular and much loved. He died of an unknown illness at age 32. ▼

Section 1 Assessment

Key Terms

1. Use each of the following terms in a sentence: city-state, cultural hearth, direct democracy, philosophy.

Key Ideas

2. Where did most of the ancient Greeks settle?

3. Name some of the democratic reforms made during the golden age of Athens.

4. How did the Greeks defeat the Persians?

Think Critically

5. **Draw Conclusions** How were Sparta and Athens similar and different?

6. **Draw Inferences** Do you think Aristotle was influenced by Plato and Socrates? Explain why or why not.

Essential Question

What are the challenges of diversity?

7. How did the diversity of Alexander the Great's Empire affect Greek culture? Go to your Student Journal to record your answer.

Ancient Rome

Key Ideas
- The Roman empire expanded through trade and conquest.
- Roman ideas about law and government remain important today.
- Christianity arose during the Roman empire and spread throughout Europe.

Visual Glossary

Key Terms
- patrician
- plebeian
- representative democracy
- Pax Romana
- aqueduct

Reading Skill: Sequence Take notes using the graphic organizer in your journal.

◄ Livia, wife of the Roman emperor Augustus, shown as Ceres, the goddess of grains.

Historians are not sure about the origins of ancient Rome. One legend says it was founded by Aeneas, the Greek hero of Virgil's poem *The Aeneid.* Aeneas is said to have escaped after the Trojan War and traveled to Latium. There, he married a princess and founded the town that would become Rome.

We do know that by the 700s B.C., a shepherd people called the Latins lived in central Italy. From their simple villages came a great empire.

The Roman Republic

Around 1000 B.C., the Latins settled near the Tiber River in central Italy. This river gave them access to the sea. The region also had fertile soil and marble and limestone for building. The surrounding hills protected the settlement. The Latins named the village Rome.

Etruscan Influence To the north lived the Etruscans, an advanced group of artists, builders, and sailors. In their sea travels, the Etruscans had learned things from many other cultures, including the Greeks.

The Etruscans expanded into Latium, ruling with the consent of the Romans. The presence of the Etruscans added much to Roman society and its government. The Etruscans introduced a writing system that they adapted from the Greeks. This formed the basis of the Latin alphabet that we use today. In addition, the Etruscans brought a strong military tradition to Rome, including the use of the Greek phalanx formation. Roman cities were improved through Etruscan methods of paving streets and using stone arches to support heavy structures such as bridges.

From Kingdom to Republic In 509 B.C., the Romans overthrew the Etruscan kings and established a republic. A republic is a government without king or emperors.

The republic had a Senate and a citizens' assembly, which it adopted from the Etruscans. The assembly was divided into two groups: the **patricians** and the **plebeians.** The patricians were wealthy aristocrats. The plebeians were all the remaining citizens. A patrician's vote counted for more than a plebeian's vote. The assembly elected two consuls, who led the government. A group of 300 wealthy citizens were appointed to serve in the Senate, which passed the laws.

In the early 400s B.C., after many protests, the plebeians gained the right to have representatives called tribunes. A tribune could overturn the act of any public official that was unjust to any citizen. Then the plebeians were given their own assembly. Eventually, the plebeians' votes counted as much as the patricians' votes.

During a crisis, the power of government was given to a dictator. The Roman statesman Cicero describes the role of dictator.

> 66 [W]hen a serious war or civil [disagreements] arise, one man shall hold, for not longer than six months, the power which ordinarily belongs to the two consuls . . . he shall be 'master of the people.' 99

Roman Law The Romans wrote down their laws, the Twelve Tables, around 450 B.C. With written laws, people would know their rights and duties rather than rely on customs that could be ignored.

The Roman government was considered a **representative democracy,** meaning that elected representatives made the political decisions. This system prevented any one individual from gaining too much power. It differed from Athenian direct democracy. The republic of Rome influenced representative governments throughout the world, including, centuries later, that of the United States.

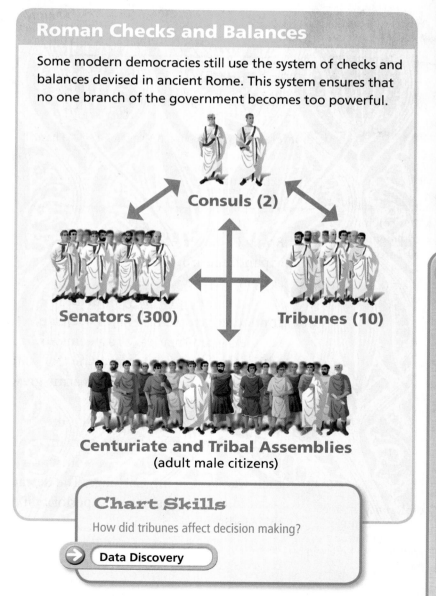

Roman Checks and Balances

Some modern democracies still use the system of checks and balances devised in ancient Rome. This system ensures that no one branch of the government becomes too powerful.

Consuls (2)

Senators (300)

Tribunes (10)

Centuriate and Tribal Assemblies
(adult male citizens)

Chart Skills

How did tribunes affect decision making?

Data Discovery

The Roman Empire

BRITAIN
London

ATLANTIC OCEAN

GAUL **GERMANY**
Danube R.
Lyon
DACIA
SPAIN **ITALY** *Black Sea*
Toledo Rome **THRACE** Byzantium
Cádiz
ASIA MINOR
Athens **MESOPOTAMIA**
MAURETANIA Carthage **GREECE** **SYRIA**
AFRICA
Mediterranean Sea **JUDEA**
Alexandria **ARABIA**
EGYPT
Red Sea

TROPIC OF CANCER

KEY
Roman Empire, A.D. 117
City
0   500 mi
0   500 km
Lambert Conformal Conic Projection

Map Skills

1 Estimate Using the scale bar, find how far the Roman Empire stretched from west to east.

2 Interaction How might the Mediterranean Sea have helped unify the empire?

➔ **Active Atlas**

▲ This column commemorates the emperor Trajan's victories in the Dacian Wars (A.D. 100–106).

diplomacy, *n.,* the art and practice of conducting negotiations between nations

Rome Expands Rome set about expanding through alliances and conquests. The Romans used military strength and <u>diplomacy</u> to turn conquered people into allies. Defeated people signed treaties, or agreements, in which they promised to provide troops to Rome. In this way, the Roman army grew to be the largest force in Italy.

During the 200s and 100s B.C., the mighty Roman army fought its main rival, Carthage, in the Punic Wars. Rome won each war, destroying Carthage. The defeat secured Rome's position of superiority in the Mediterranean region.

Reading Check What were some of the reforms gained by the plebeians?

Rome Becomes an Empire

By 100 B.C., the republic was becoming unstable. After several revolts, the republic came under the control of dictators and military leaders.

Beginnings of Empire In the 50s B.C., Julius Caesar conquered Gaul, land that is much of present-day France and Belgium. He then invaded Italy and made himself the sole ruler of Rome and its territories. Hoping to restore the republic, aristocrats assassinated Caesar.

The result was chaos and the end of the republic. Caesar's nephew Octavian eventually emerged as the victor. He took the name Augustus and became the first Roman emperor in 27 B.C.

The Empire Unifies The rule of Augustus started a period of stability known as the **Pax Romana** (Roman Peace). This period lasted for about 200 years.

Rome set up colonies in conquered areas. Many Roman citizens migrated to these colonies. Some of the people conquered by the Romans became citizens. The spread of Roman law helped to unify the empire. The empire was also united by a network of roads that helped soldiers move and keep order.

Trade along Roman roads and across the seas also stabilized the empire. The use of coins made trade easier. The empire gained wealth from trade and tributes paid by <u>provinces</u>. Tributes were a type of taxation.

Gradually, wealthy Romans came to admire Greek culture. Greek books were copied and sold widely. Learned Romans read both Latin and Greek. Greco-Roman culture was spread throughout the empire with colonies in Gaul, Spain, and North Africa. In addition to cultural influences, Roman colonists received Roman citizenship and lived under Roman law.

Reading Check **What was the result of Caesar's assassination?**

Life in Ancient Rome

The basic social unit in ancient Rome was the family. The father had complete control over the family and the home.

Roman women worked in the home. They could not vote or participate in politics. Gradually, Roman women did gain more rights. Emperors' wives, such as Livia and Julia Agrippina, also influenced politics in Rome.

Slavery in Ancient Rome About one third of the people in Rome were slaves. The economy depended on their work.

Sometimes, a slave could buy his or her freedom. Freed slaves were allowed to become citizens. Household slaves sometimes became trusted companions. Other slaves led short, brutal lives. Some worked in copper or tin mines. Gladiator slaves faced death in arena matches in the Colosseum. Slaves also worked as farmers or as rowers on Roman warships.

myWorldActivity
What's the News in Rome?

province, *n.,* country or region under control of a larger government

my
worldgeography.com
Active Atlas

One important Roman innovation was the **aqueduct,** a channel that moves water over great distances.

351

Roman Religion Romans worshiped many deities, some of whom were adopted from the Greeks and the Etruscans. In Rome, religion was tied closely to political life and emperors were sometimes worshiped as gods.

Roman Achievements Like the Greeks, Romans made statues in marble. Roman literature includes poetry by Virgil and Horace, and essays by Cicero. Architects perfected the arch and invented concrete to build temples and public buildings.

In Roman Egypt, Ptolemy (TAH luh mee) calculated the size and distance of the sun and the paths of the stars and planets across the sky. The Greek Galen discovered how parts of the body worked.

Reading Check **What elements helped to unify the Roman empire?**

Judaism and Christianity

The Jews of Judea lived in an area that came under direct Roman rule in A.D. 63. In the centuries before the Roman empire, the Jews had spread to Egypt and to other parts of southwest Asia. The Jews believed in one God. This belief is called monotheism. The Romans, who believed in many gods, did not usually force them to change their practices.

Jews Flee Harsh Rule Some Jews, however, felt Roman rule and taxes were too harsh. They rebelled. The Romans struck back harshly and destroyed the Jewish Temple in Jerusalem in A.D. 70.

The Romans killed many thousands of Jews. Other Jews left the ruined province for other parts of the empire. Many moved to Italy and other parts of Europe.

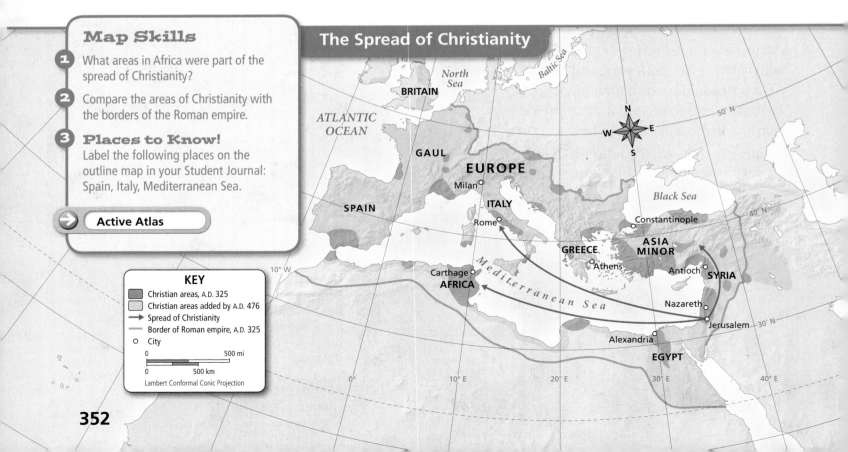

Map Skills

1. What areas in Africa were part of the spread of Christianity?

2. Compare the areas of Christianity with the borders of the Roman empire.

3. **Places to Know!** Label the following places on the outline map in your Student Journal: Spain, Italy, Mediterranean Sea.

→ **Active Atlas**

The Spread of Christianity

KEY
- Christian areas, A.D. 325
- Christian areas added by A.D. 476
- → Spread of Christianity
- Border of Roman empire, A.D. 325
- ○ City

0   500 mi
0   500 km
Lambert Conformal Conic Projection

Baltic Sea
North Sea
BRITAIN
ATLANTIC OCEAN
GAUL
EUROPE
Milan
ITALY
SPAIN
Rome
Black Sea
Constantinople
ASIA MINOR
GREECE
Athens
Antioch
SYRIA
Carthage
AFRICA
Mediterranean Sea
Nazareth
Jerusalem
Alexandria
EGYPT

10° W   0°   10° E   20° E   30° E   40° E
50° N   40° N   30° N

Birth and Spread of Christianity Around 4 B.C., a Jew named Jesus was born in Judea. He grew up in Nazareth and learned to be a carpenter.

When he was 30 years old, he became a religious teacher. Jesus preached that there was only one God. Many of his followers believed that Jesus was the Messiah. Jews believed that a leader called the Messiah would bring them freedom. The name Christ comes from the Greek word for messiah. Jesus's followers later came to be known as Christians. Jesus's teachings formed the basis for a new religion, Christianity.

Christianity gradually spread across the Roman empire and into neighboring lands. For more than 200 years, Christians faced harsh treatment from the Roman government. Then, in A.D. 312, Roman emperor Constantine I became a Christian. Over the next 100 years, Christianity spread across much of Europe, and most Romans became Christians.

Reading Check **Why did the Jews want to flee Roman rule?**

The Western Empire Falls

Historians are not sure what caused the fall of the Roman empire. One theory proposes that the Romans used so many everyday objects made of lead that people may have sickened and died from lead poisoning. Most likely the collapse came from several factors.

Instability and Division From A.D. 235 to A.D. 284, there were 60 men who declared themselves emperor. Prices increased, taxes rose, and disease reduced the population. The Roman army weakened as it came to depend more on mercenaries, or soldiers who fought for money rather than for loyalty to a leader or nation.

Diocletian eventually divided the empire into eastern and western lands to make it easier to govern. Constantine moved the capital east, renaming it Constantinople. The Eastern Roman empire went on to thrive as the Byzantine empire, while the west fell to Germanic invaders.

Reading Check **Identify one factor that led to the fall of the Roman empire.**

Invaders!

▶ **378** Visigoths defeat the Roman army.

▶ **406** Vandals attack Gaul.

▶ **410** Visigoths sack Rome.

▶ **441** Attila (above) and the Huns begin to invade the empire.

▶ **450** Angles, Saxons, Jutes invade Britain (traditional date).

▶ **476** Rome falls to the Germanic leader Odoacer.

⟳ Timeline

myworldgeography.com Timeline

Section 2 Assessment

Key Terms

1. Define each of these key terms with a complete sentence: patrician, plebeian, representative democracy, Pax Romana, aqueduct.

Key Ideas

2. Why was Julius Caesar assassinated?

3. How did the conversion of Constantine I affect religion in Europe?

4. Name three elements that led to the fall of the Roman empire.

Think Critically

5. **Compare and Contrast** How did Roman democracy differ from ancient Greek democracy?

6. **Problem Solving** If you were in charge of the Roman empire, how would you prevent it from collapsing? List at least three ways.

Essential Question

What are the challenges of diversity?

7. How did the Romans use citizenship to unify a diverse empire? Go to your Student Journal to record your answer.

Early Middle Ages

Key Ideas

- The Byzantine empire influenced the religion and writing systems of Eastern Europe.

- Charlemagne united most of Western Europe.

- Feudalism and manorialism shaped relations among medieval Europeans.

Key Terms • schism • lord • vassal • feudalism • manorialism

 **Visual Glossary**

Reading Skill: Summarize Take notes using the graphic organizer in your journal.

▼ The emperor Justinian ruled the Byzantine empire from 527 to 565.

After the fall of the Roman empire, a new age dawned in Europe. This age is often called the medieval period or Middle Ages. The word *medieval* comes from the Latin words for "middle" and "age." Historians use this term because the medieval period is beween the ancient and modern periods of European history.

The Byzantine Empire

As the Western Roman empire declined, power shifted east. The Eastern Roman empire remained strong. Its capital, Constantinople, grew rich on trade. Historians refer to the surviving eastern empire as the Byzantine empire.

Emperor Justinian's Rule Justinian ruled as an autocrat, or a single ruler with absolute power. He ruled both the empire and the Christian Church. Under Justinian, the empire expanded through conquest and trade. Justinian's wife Theodora served as his close advisor and, in effect, co-ruler. One of Justinian's greatest acts as emperor was to organize Roman laws into one code, called Justinian's Code. By the 1100s, these laws had reached Western Europe and helped monarchs unify their power. These laws remain part of many countries' laws.

Byzantine Christianity Since early Christian times, leaders called patriarchs had led the Christian churches in different regions. In the west, the head of the Church was the patriarch of Rome, known as the pope. The pope claimed the power to lead all Christians.

In the east, the highest official was the patriarch of Constantinople. This patriarch obeyed the Byzantine emperor. Unlike Christian priests in Western Europe, the Byzantine clergy had the right to marry. Greek, not Latin, was the language of the eastern Church.

A New Alphabet During Roman times, a people called the Slavs lived in what is now Poland, Belarus, and Ukraine. The Slavs had been farmers and traders for centuries. This commerce brought them in contact with the Byzantine empire.

In about 863, two Byzantine Greeks, the brothers Cyril and Methodius, traveled to Eastern Europe to bring Christianity to the Slavs. While there, they translated the Greek Bible into a Slavic language. This translation let people learn about Christianity in a language they understood. The brothers invented the Cyrillic alphabet. This alphabet combined Greek and Latin letters to express the sounds in the Slavic languages. In this way, writing and Christianity spread among the Slavic peoples. Today, people in Eastern Europe—as well as some in Russia and Mongolia—write in the Cyrillic alphabet.

Christianity Splits Gradually, the two branches of Christianity grew more divided. The Eastern church rejected the pope as leader of all Christians. Finally, the church went through an official **schism** (SIZ um), or split, called the Great Schism of 1054. The Byzantine church became the Eastern, or Greek, Orthodox church. The Western church became the Roman Catholic Church. These churches remain divided today.

The Byzantine Empire Falls By the time of the Great Schism, the Byzantine empire had begun to weaken. The emperors lost their lands to invaders such as the Arabs. Arabs conquered most of the Byzantine lands in North Africa and southwest Asia during the 600s. The Arabs were Muslims, or followers of Islam, a new religion. Like Judaism and Christianity, Islam was based on the worship of one God.

In addition, powerful merchants from the Italian city-state of Venice took control of important Byzantine trade routes. Then,

Cyril and Methodius, whom Christians revere as saints, hold religious documents writtten in Cyrillic. *How did this alphabet get its name?* ▼

in 1453, the Ottoman Turks captured Constantinople. This meant the end of the Byzantine empire. The Turks changed the city's name to Istanbul. They also introduced Islam and made Istanbul a center of Muslim culture.

Byzantine Achievements Building on Greco-Roman culture, the Byzantine empire lasted for almost 1,000 years. Its artists advanced art and architecture. Its scholars preserved ancient learning. One such scholar was Anna Comnena, the first important female historian in the west. The Byzantine <u>legacy</u> led to Europe's later cultural flowering, the Renaissance.

legacy, *n.,* something transmitted or received from a predecessor

Reading Check What did Cyril and Methodius achieve?

The Byzantine Empire

ITALY

Naples

Danube River

BALKAN PENINSULA

Black Sea

Bosporus

Constantinople

ASIA MINOR

Aegean Sea

Athens

Crete

Mediterranean Sea

Cyprus

Euphrates River

Tigris River

50° N

40° N

N W E S

10° E 20° E

KEY

Byzantine Empire, about 1020

0 400 mi

0 400 km

Miller Cylindrical Projection

Map Skills

1 **Interaction** What cultures might have influenced Constantinople?

2 **Places to Know!**
Label the following places on the outline map in your Student Journal: Asia Minor, Balkan Peninsula, Constantinople.

→ **Active Atlas**

New Kingdoms in Europe

By around A.D. 450, Germanic tribes had taken control of most of the Western Roman empire.

Germanic Tribes Take Control Different tribes controlled the various parts of the region. A Germanic tribe called the Visigoths settled in Spain. The Angles, Jutes, and Saxons—later known as the Anglo-Saxons—took over most of Britain. And the Franks set up a kingdom in Gaul, in present-day France and Belgium.

Within each of these kingdoms, people were loyal only to their local leader. As a result, the idea of a central government disappeared.

Rise of the Franks A king of the Franks named Clovis defeated the last Roman commander in 486. He then established a kingdom that stretched from the Rhine region in the east to the Pyrenees Mountains in the west. Later, this area was named France after the Franks.

After Clovis's death, his kingdom was divided into smaller kingdoms. In the early 700s, however, the Frankish ruler Charles Martel united these kingdoms.

Charlemagne During the 770s, Charles Martel's grandson, Charlemagne (742–814), became king of the Franks. He conquered much of Western Europe and expanded the Frankish empire.

Charlemagne strongly supported the Catholic Church. He believed that by converting people to Christianity all across his growing empire, he could unite and strengthen it. Pope Leo III crowned Charlemagne Holy Roman Emperor in 800.

This was important because a Christian pope had crowned a Germanic ruler as a successor to Roman emperors.

Charlemagne reestablished the rule of law, which had weakened after the fall of Rome. For example, he declared that judges should base their decisions on accepted laws. He also set up a school at his palace, though he himself could not write. This school attracted scholars from all of Europe.

After Charlemagne's death, the empire was divided among his sons. Some of these lands later became the modern countries of France and Germany.

Vikings and Magyars During the 800s and 900s, Viking invaders made terrifying raids along the coasts and rivers of Europe. The Vikings came from Scandinavia in northern Europe. They conquered parts of what are now England, Scotland, Ireland, France, and Ukraine. The Vikings who settled in France were called Normans. The Normans later conquered England.

Viking and Norman invaders also helped shape powerful kingdoms in England and in Ukraine. The kingdom in Ukraine, called Kievan Rus, adopted Eastern Christianity. The modern nations of Ukraine, Belarus, and Russia grew out of Kievan Rus.

During the 900s, a people called the Magyars conquered what is now Hungary. They made fearsome raids into Germany, Italy, and other parts of Western Europe. Around 1000, the Magyars converted to Christianity. The Magyars formed the kingdom of Hungary.

Christian Life The Christian church and its teachings were the center of medieval life. The church sent people across Europe to spread Christianity and gain new members. Gradually, most pagans in Europe converted to the Christian religion. A pagan was someone who worshiped more than one god. Although Western Europeans were divided politically, the Catholic Church united them through religion. Eastern Europeans were united through the Eastern Orthodox Church. *Orthodox* means following traditional or established beliefs.

Statue of Charlemagne ▼

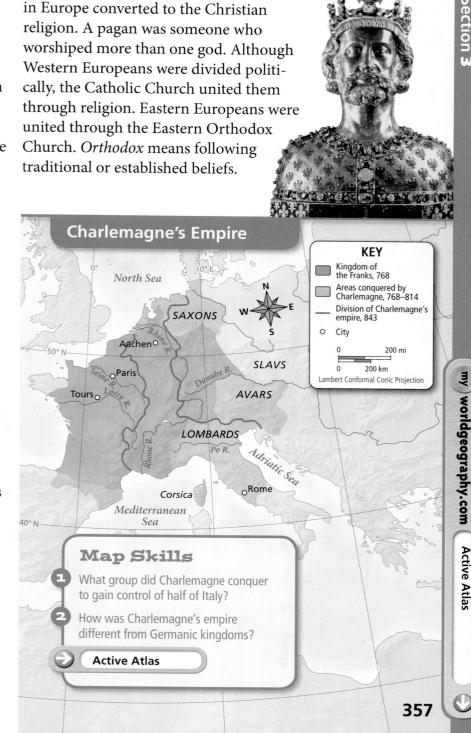

Charlemagne's Empire

KEY
- Kingdom of the Franks, 768
- Areas conquered by Charlemagne, 768–814
- Division of Charlemagne's empire, 843
- ○ City

0 — 200 mi
0 — 200 km
Lambert Conformal Conic Projection

North Sea
SAXONS
Aachen
Rhine R.
Paris
Seine R.
Tours
Loire R.
Danube R.
SLAVS
AVARS
LOMBARDS
Po R.
Rhone R.
Adriatic Sea
Corsica
Rome
Mediterranean Sea

Map Skills

1. What group did Charlemagne conquer to gain control of half of Italy?

2. How was Charlemagne's empire different from Germanic kingdoms?

→ **Active Atlas**

my worldgeography.com

Active Atlas

manuscript, *n.,* a document written by hand

Male Christian religious people called monks lived in monasteries, secluded communities focused on prayer and service. These monks made copies of the Bible and Greek and Roman works. They helped to preserve valuable <u>manuscripts</u>, many of which contained ancient learning.

Women joined religious orders as nuns. Some nuns became abbesses, or heads of female religious communities. The German abbess Hildegard of Bingen wrote poems and music inspired by her visions of God.

Reading Check What were some of Charlemagne's reforms?

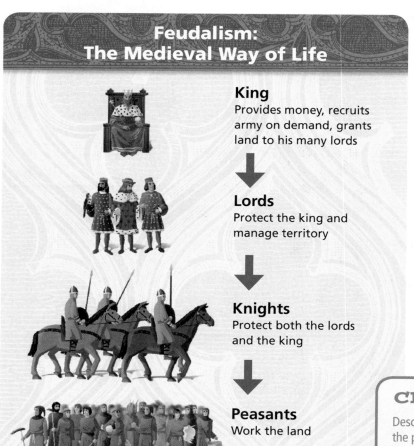

Feudalism: The Medieval Way of Life

King
Provides money, recruits army on demand, grants land to his many lords

Lords
Protect the king and manage territory

Knights
Protect both the lords and the king

Peasants
Work the land

Feudalism and Manorialism

As you have read, during the late Roman empire, people began to accept the protection and control of landowners from the nobility. In the Middle Ages, barbarians and other warriors took control of most of the land. They offered protection to the peasants, or small farmers, living on the land in return for service. Each landowning warrior pledged loyalty to a tribal leader called a **lord,** or to the king. A lord was a man who controlled large areas of land. In return for the warrior's service, the lord or king offered protection.

How Feudalism Worked As time went by, kings granted land to lords in return for service. Lords, in turn, granted land to noble soldiers called knights in return for military service. A noble who received the land was called a **vassal.** The system of rights and duties connecting lords and vassals was called **feudalism.**

The lord promised to protect his vassals. In return, the vassals provided military support and money or food for their lord. The peasants were subject to both lords and vassals. Lords and vassals also had trained warriors called knights to serve them.

Lords sometimes quarreled over territory. In these conflicts, a vassal and his knights would help their lord in battle.

Chart Skills

Describe the relationship between the king and the peasants in feudalism.

→ **Data Discovery**

By the end of the early Middle Ages, feudalism had spread across both Western and Eastern Europe. Feudalism was supported by an economic system called manorialism.

How Manorialism Worked The economic relationship that existed between lords or knights and peasants was called **manorialism.** The center of the system was the manor, a huge estate that included the lord's house or castle, farmland, pastures, peasants, and possibly a village. Many of the peasants who lived on the manor were serfs, or people who belonged to the estate as laborers. They were not slaves, but they were not free to move, marry, or buy land without the lord's permission.

Each manor was self-sufficient, supplying all the food, clothing, and shelter needed by both the lord and peasants. Peasants and their lords were thus dependent on one another.

The wife of the lord was called a lady. She attended to domestic chores and managed the servants. Literacy was not common even among noblewomen. Ladies had few rights. Some lords chose a wife for her dowry, or a payment of money and land provided at the time of marriage. In most parts of Europe, women could own land. When a woman's parents died, however, their land passed to the oldest brother in many countries.

Peasants led hard lives working from sunup to sundown. Their diets seldom varied and disease was common.

Reading Check What was the knight's role in feudalism?

Culture Close-up

▲ Peasants farmed their own plots of land as well as those of the lord.

Section 3 Assessment

my worldgeography.com   Culture Close-up

? Essential Question

Key Terms
1. Write a short paragraph showing how these key terms are related: lord, vassal, feudalism.

Key Ideas
2. What was Justinian's Code?
3. How did medieval monks preserve ancient learning?
4. What was feudalism?

Think Critically
5. **Categorize** Draw a table of three rulers who tried to unify Western Europe after the fall of the Roman empire. Under each ruler, list his ethnic group, time of rule, and accomplishments.
6. **Draw Inferences** Do you think peasants often traveled far from the manor? Explain why or why not.

What are the challenges of diversity?
7. How did cultural differences between the East and the West affect the Christian church? Go to your Student Journal to record your answer.

High and Late Middle Ages

Key Ideas

- The Crusades opened up medieval Europe to trade and new ideas.

- In the High Middle Ages, growth in trade routes led to the rise of cities.

- The Magna Carta limited the king's power and led to more democratic government.

- With the growth of cities, nation-building began in Europe.

Key Terms · Crusades · Reconquista · guild · Magna Carta

 Visual Glossary

Reading Skill: Analyze Cause and Effect Take notes using the graphic organizer in your journal.

◀ Knights wore suits of armor such as this one during the Middle Ages.

By 1000, feudalism had stabilized Europe and the population was growing. Universities formed, merchants gained power, and farming techniques improved. This period is called the High Middle Ages. It lasted until the early 1300s. During the Late Middle Ages, however, wars, disease, and famine hit Europe hard. As a result, the the feudal system weakened and collapsed.

The Crusades and the Wider World

By 1081, the Seljuk Turks had overrun much of the Byzantine empire. These people had migrated from Central Asia, and when they reached the Middle East, they converted to Islam. As they conquered new lands, they converted the defeated peoples to Islam.

The Turks also took control of Palestine. This region was sacred to Jews, Christians, and Muslims. It was known to Christians as the Holy Land. Many Christians in Europe objected to Muslim control of the Holy Land.

The Holy Wars Begin In 1095, Pope Urban II urged church leaders to organize the **Crusades,** a series of military expeditions to free the Holy Land from Muslim rule. At the Council of Clermont, named for the town in France where it was held, Pope Urban II urged people of all classes to unite to take back Jerusalem in a holy war,

❝ You common people who have been miserable sinners, become soldiers of Christ! You nobles, do not [quarrel] with one another. Use your arms in a just war! Labor for an everlasting reward. ❞

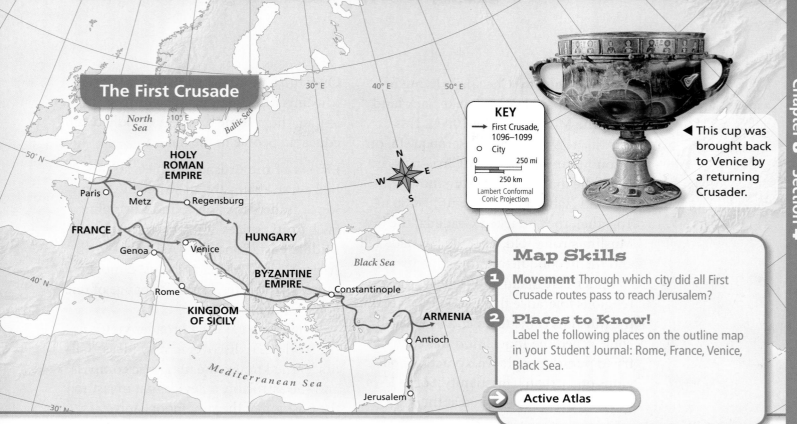

The First Crusade

KEY

→ First Crusade, 1096–1099
○ City

0   250 mi
0   250 km

Lambert Conformal Conic Projection

North Sea

Baltic Sea

HOLY ROMAN EMPIRE

Paris

Metz

Regensburg

FRANCE

Genoa

Venice

HUNGARY

Rome

BYZANTINE EMPIRE

KINGDOM OF SICILY

Black Sea

Constantinople

ARMENIA

Antioch

Mediterranean Sea

Jerusalem

◄ This cup was brought back to Venice by a returning Crusader.

Map Skills

1 **Movement** Through which city did all First Crusade routes pass to reach Jerusalem?

2 **Places to Know!**
Label the following places on the outline map in your Student Journal: Rome, France, Venice, Black Sea.

→ Active Atlas

Europeans responded to the pope's call for different reasons. Some went to war for religious reasons. They believed that God wanted the Holy Land to be Christian. Others had more worldly reasons. Some knights wanted to win new possessions in the Holy Land. Others wanted the status that came from military success. Of course, Muslims in the Holy Land wanted it to remain Muslim. They did not want foreign Christian rulers.

By the summer of 1096, a large European army had formed and headed for the Holy Land. This force captured Jerusalem, and Christian leaders divided Palestine into four states. Many Muslims in the region faced brutal treatment. Then European leaders sent a second Crusade to the Holy Land. Internal quarrels weakened this force, and Muslims defeated them.

In 1187, the Muslim leader Saladin recaptured Jerusalem. Further Crusades were attempted but failed. These conflicts led to bitter feelings between Christians and Muslims that have lasted to this day.

Muslims in Spain By 718, Muslims had conquered most of Spain. Spanish Christians controlled only a small area in northern Spain. During Muslim rule, many Spanish people converted to Islam. Muslim leaders also tolerated the practice of Judaism and Christianity.

Muslims made important advances in mathematics and medicine. They studied the learning of the ancient Greeks and Romans. In addition, they built beautiful mosques and palaces. During the 900s, Córdoba became a center of Muslim culture. Muslim influence helped shape art and literature in Christian Spain.

my worldgeography.com | Active Atlas

expel, *v.,* to force someone to leave a place

The Reconquista Christians living in northern Spain began to take back land from the Muslims in the 1000s. This was the beginning of the **Reconquista,** or reconquering of Spain by Christians. In 1469, the marriage of Ferdinand of Aragon and Isabella of Castile united Spain. Together, they attacked Granada, the last Muslim stronghold, in 1492. Granada fell and the Reconquista was complete.

Under Ferdinand and Isabella, the religious tolerance that had existed under the Muslims came to an end. A Church court called the Inquisition was set up to try to punish people who practiced religions other than Christianity. Some Jews and Muslims were burned at the stake.

Over time, more than 150,000 Jews and Muslims fled or were <u>expelled</u> from Spain, among them some of the most skilled and educated people in the nation.

Effects of the Crusades The Crusades had a lasting impact on society. Returning crusaders increased trade, bringing back exotic spices and fabrics from the Middle East (Southwest Asia and North Africa). Much of this trade used money rather than barter, or the exchange of one good for another.

People also gained a broader view of the world and discovered new ideas. Sailors learned to use the magnetic compass and the astrolabe, a device that measured the position of the sun, moon, and stars.

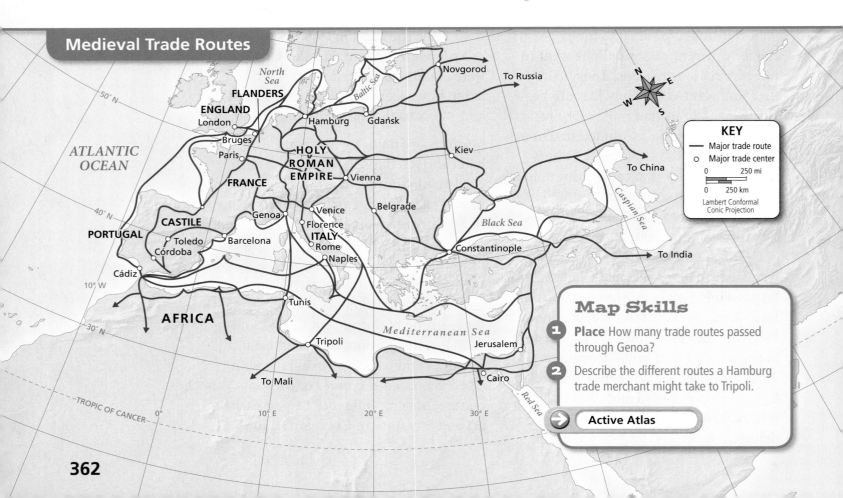

Medieval Trade Routes

KEY
— Major trade route
○ Major trade center

0   250 mi
0   250 km
Lambert Conformal Conic Projection

Map Skills

1 **Place** How many trade routes passed through Genoa?

2 Describe the different routes a Hamburg trade merchant might take to Tripoli.

Active Atlas

In this way, sailors could know their position on Earth's surface out of sight of land.

The compass and astrolabe were among the new ideas or technologies that Europe gained from contact with the Muslim world. Europeans also learned to make gunpowder and paper from Muslims, although these technologies first developed in China.

Muslims had preserved much of the learning of the ancient Greeks and Romans. Muslims also studied ancient Indian learning. Muslims drew on this ancient learning to make advances in science and mathematics. They passed this knowledge on to medieval Europeans.

Reading Check How did the Crusades increase trade?

The Rise of Cities

During the 1000s, more and more people moved from manors to cities. Many factors led to this migration.

Farming Improves During the Middle Ages, farmers found ways to improve agriculture. They gained more cropland by draining swamps and clearing forests. They also developed the horse collar and harness so horses instead of oxen could be used to plow fields. Horses plowed faster than oxen. In this way, they could plant more, harvest more, and even have surplus, or extra, crops.

As the food supply increased, people became healthier. Peasants were able to earn extra money by selling surplus crops. Some used this money to buy their freedom from their lord. Freed peasants sometimes moved to cities and towns.

Technology Develops While Europeans learned new technologies from the Muslims, they also developed new skills and products of their own. Among these were clocks, eyeglasses, and upright windmills. Military technologies like plate armor and cannons made the armies strong. Engineering advances let Europeans build soaring cathedral towers.

Commerce Begins In towns, many peasants learned special skills as craft workers. They specialized in leather goods or gold objects and sold these goods in their shops or at local markets or trade fairs.

Some merchants sold these goods along trade routes throughout Europe and Asia. They exchanged both goods and ideas. Some expanded commerce by setting up banks and issuing loans.

myWorldActivity
Trade Spices Up Life

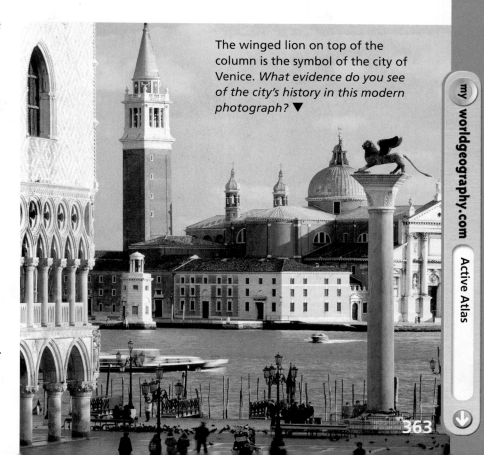

The winged lion on top of the column is the symbol of the city of Venice. *What evidence do you see of the city's history in this modern photograph?* ▼

my worldgeography.com

Active Atlas

363

The Italian Trade Centers The port of Venice was a busy place. Ships from Constantinople arrived loaded with gold, silks, and spices. Traders loaded these goods onto mules and began the trek to markets in Northern Europe.

The city-state of Venice was only one of the new commerce centers in present-day Italy. Cities such as Florence, Genoa, and Naples also served as hubs for goods coming into Europe.

The New Merchant Class As people moved to towns, many towns grew into cities. In urban areas, a person could earn a good living by working as a merchant, an artisan, or a craftsperson. As a result, the group of people who earned more than peasants grew.

Language Lesson

King John signs the Magna Carta. A copy of the original document is above.

This group became known as the middle class since they still ranked below the nobles. As their numbers increased, so did their political and economic power.

For protection, merchants and craftspeople formed **guilds.** A guild is an association of people who have a common livelihood. Guilds protected members from unfair business practices. They also set prices and wages. Women could sometimes become guild members. They often specialized in needlecraft and papermaking. Women were also active in the silk and wool trades.

City Life Develops As cities grew, they spread outward—and upward. People needed more living space and built homes with two or three stories. In the largest cities, a church called a cathedral formed the center of the city. These cathedrals became centers of learning and city life.

Weekly market stalls were replaced by permanent shops, though hawkers still rolled through the streets with their carts. There were no sewers or garbage collection, so medieval streets could be dirty as well as noisy and crowded.

Reading Check Why were medieval city craftsmen known as a middle class?

Limiting the King's Power

During the High Middle Ages, the power of kings was put to the test.

Normans Conquer England During the 1000s, England was fairly prosperous with good agricultural land. William, duke of Normandy in northern France, believed himself to be heir to the English throne.

When it was given to an Anglo-Saxon noble named Harold, William invaded England with a huge army. He defeated Harold at the Battle of Hastings in 1066. William was crowned king of England and became known as William the Conqueror.

At the time, most of the people in England were Anglo-Saxon. The Normans treated them as inferiors. Many Anglo-Saxon lords tried to revolt, but after several years, William <u>subdued</u> them. Over time, the Normans and Anglo-Saxons intermarried, becoming one people.

Magna Carta After William's death, kings often struggled with lords for control of England. During the early 1200s, King John demanded large amounts of money without consulting the lords. He also set severe penalties for minor crimes.

Lords and church leaders rebelled. Soon, they forced King John to sign a charter called the **Magna Carta.** This was a document that limited the English king's power. The Magna Carta helped lead to more democratic government in England.

By the late 1200s, King Edward I expanded his meetings with lords and church leaders to include town representatives. These meetings came to be called the Model Parliament. They were the beginning of England's Parliament, its legislative or lawmaking assembly. Royal courts made rulings based on earlier cases. The courts created a body of common law, which was applied equally in any part of a country.

Hundred Years' War In the 1330s, the French attempted to take over an English-held province in southwest France. This conflict started a series of wars between France and England known as the Hundred Years' War (1337–1453).

By 1428, the English had taken over northern France. In Orleans, a peasant girl named Joan of Arc appeared. She claimed that she had been told by God to lead the French army into battle. In desperation, the French king agreed. The 17-year-old Joan led the army to victory. However, the next year, the English captured Joan and she was burned at the stake as a witch.

New weapons developed at this time changed warfare. The English longbow launched arrows that pierced the armor of French knights. In addition, gunpowder and cannons became common. Cannons could destroy castle walls. In this way, two of the major defenses of feudal lords—knights and castles—became much less effective.

subdue, *v.,* to bring under control

At the right, the English soldiers use longbows, while the French at the left use crossbows. *How might cannons be used in this scene?* ▼

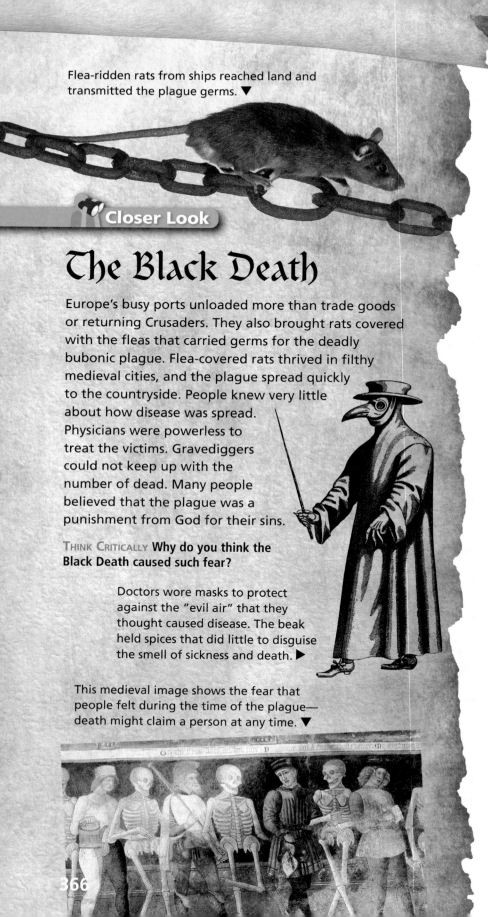

Flea-ridden rats from ships reached land and transmitted the plague germs. ▼

The Black Death

Europe's busy ports unloaded more than trade goods or returning Crusaders. They also brought rats covered with the fleas that carried germs for the deadly bubonic plague. Flea-covered rats thrived in filthy medieval cities, and the plague spread quickly to the countryside. People knew very little about how disease was spread. Physicians were powerless to treat the victims. Gravediggers could not keep up with the number of dead. Many people believed that the plague was a punishment from God for their sins.

THINK CRITICALLY **Why do you think the Black Death caused such fear?**

Doctors wore masks to protect against the "evil air" that they thought caused disease. The beak held spices that did little to disguise the smell of sickness and death. ▶

This medieval image shows the fear that people felt during the time of the plague—death might claim a person at any time. ▼

The French finally won the Hundred Years' War. The war led England and France down two different paths. The French increased the power of the monarchy. The English increased Parliament's "power of the purse," or its financial role in government.

Reading Check **What did the Magna Carta do?**

Medieval Society Weakens

Improvements in farming during the High Middle Ages caused Europe's population to grow. By the 1300s, the population had outgrown the food supply. When harvests, or crops gathered for food, were low, people experienced famines. Famines are times of hunger and starvation. Famines were just one of the hardships that increasingly weakened medieval society.

Famine Strikes In 1315, bad weather caused poor harvests in Europe. These conditions continued for two more years. By that time, many Europeans were starving. Historians estimate that about ten to fifteen percent of the population died during the winter of 1317.

The Black Death Arrives As the famines continued in later years, the constant hunger made people sickly. In 1347, Europe faced a terrible epidemic, or a widespread outbreak of disease. Because people were already weakened from poor nutrition, the epidemic was disastrous. The disease was bubonic plague, or the Black Death. Victims suffered swelling and extreme pain. Death came quickly, usually in a matter of days.

Michael Platiensis, an eyewitness, described the disease,

> Those infected felt themselves penetrated by a pain . . . Then there developed on the thighs or upper arms a boil. . . .This infected the whole body, . . . [three days later], there being no means of healing it, and then the patient expired.

Physicians had many theories about what caused the plague, all of them wrong. They tried several cures, but nothing worked. Some people falsely blamed the plague on Jews or beggars. These accusations spread, and, in some cites, thousands of Jews were tortured and killed.

By the time the Black Death ended in the early 1400s, the medieval world had begun to change. About 25 million Europeans died from the plague—from one quarter to one third of the population. The dead came from all levels of society, rich and poor. Suddenly, Europe faced a labor shortage. The disease also caused religious turmoil as many of the faithful began to have doubts.

Decline of Medieval Europe War, famine, and the Black Death changed medieval Europe profoundly. With millions of workers dead, production declined and food shortages were common. Economic uncertainty led to social upheaval. Important social structures such as manorialism and feudalism began to break down.

In manorialism, the labor of the peasant was vital. Following the plague, however, peasants began to leave the manors. In order to convince them to stay, lords offered for the first time to pay them wages. Some lords converted cropland to pastures for raising sheep. Some peasants still left the manors seeking higher wages or moving to cities.

Feudal lords found it harder to defend themselves against new weapons such as guns and cannons. In the cities, feudal influence weakened against wealthy merchants and powerful guilds. However, spurred by fresh ideas, a new age called the Renaissance was about to begin.

Reading Check **How did the Black Death change Europe?**

my World
IN NUMBERS

The Black Death killed **50,000** of **180,000** people in Paris.

Section 4 Assessment

Key Terms

1. Use each of the following terms in a sentence: Crusades, Reconquista, guild, Magna Carta.

Key Ideas

2. Why did the middle class grow during the High Middle Ages?

3. What were some of the main results of the Crusades?

4. How did the Great Famine and the Black Death lead to the decline of feudalism?

Think Critically

5. **Draw Inferences** How do you think feudal lords felt about the growth of cities? Explain.

6. **Draw Conclusions** How might the Hundred Years' War affect nation-building in France and England?

? Essential Question

What are the challenges of diversity?

7. How did diversity have both positive and negative effects on Spain? Go to your Student Journal to record your answer.

Chapter Assessment

Key Terms and Ideas

1. **Compare and Contrast** How is an **oligarchy** different from a **direct democracy**?

2. **Recall** What was the job of a tribune in the ancient Roman Republic?

3. **Compare and Contrast** What are some similarities and differences between the government of ancient Athens and that of the Roman Republic?

4. **Discuss** Did **manorialism** encourage trade? Why or why not?

5. **Describe** How did Christianity spread during the early Middle Ages?

6. **Recall** How did William the Conqueror gain the English crown?

7. **Explain** How was the **Reconquista** connected to the Spanish Inquisition?

Think Critically

8. **Determine Relevance** How did the Pax Romana lead to stability across the Roman empire?

9. **Test Conclusions** Why do you think Sparta was able to take control of the Peloponnesian Peninsula and defeat Athens? Support your answer with evidence from the chapter.

10. **Analyze Information** About 25 million Europeans died from the Black Death. Name three factors that contributed to this huge death toll.

11. **Core Concepts: Economics** How did economics contribute to the decline of feudalism?

Places to Know

For each place, write the letter from the map that show its location.

12. Athens

13. Constantinople

14. Spain

15. Venice

16. Rome

17. Sparta

18. **Estimate** Using the scale, estimate how far Constantinople was from Rome.

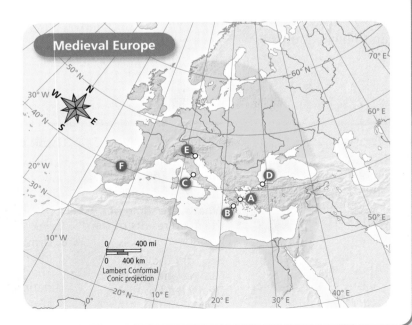

Medieval Europe

Essential Question

myWorld Chapter Activity

Piecing Together the Past Choose one image from the chapter activity cards. Follow your teacher's instructions and do your own field research to find similar objects in other European cultures. Then write a caption for each object you find, summarizing how it reflects diversity in European culture.

21st Century Learning

Generate New Ideas

Write Dialogue Write a scene in which Joan of Arc tries to convince the king to let her lead the French army into battle. Include:
- Joan's visions
- the king's desperation
- the city of Orleans
- the English army
- the French army

Document-Based Questions

Success Tracker™
Online at myworldgeography.com

Use your knowledge of the Middle Ages and Documents A and B to answer Questions 1–3.

Document A

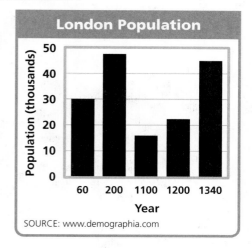

London Population

Population (thousands) / Year

SOURCE: www.demographia.com

Document B

" Each trade occupied its own quarter—butchers and tanners around the Châtelet, money-changers, goldsmiths, and drapers on the Grand Pont, scribes, illuminators, and parchment- and ink-sellers on the left bank around the University [of Paris]."

— Historian Barbara Tuchman describing Paris during the High Middle Ages

1. Which of the following might explain the drop in London's population from A.D. 200 to A.D. 1100?

   A decline of Greece, rise of feudalism

   B decline of Greece, rise of trade

   C decline of Rome, rise of feudalism

   D decline of Rome, rise of trade

2. Based on Document B, which of the following best describes Paris during the High Middle Ages?

   A an economically busy city with few craft workers

   B an economically busy city with many craft workers

   C an economically quiet city with few craft workers

   D an economically quiet city with many craft workers

3. **Writing Task** Describe details in Document B that show prosperity in medieval Paris.

my worldgeography.com | Self-Test

369

Chapter 9

Europe in Modern Times

What makes a nation?

KEY

- Austrian Habsburg territories
- Denmark and possessions
- England and possessions
- France
- Ottoman Empire
- Papal States
- Poland-Lithuania
- Portugal and possessions
- Russian Empire
- Spain and possessions
- Sweden
- United Provinces
- Venice and possessions
- —— Holy Roman Empire, 1600
- —— National border, 1600
- —— Modern border
- ○ City

0 — 400 mi
0 — 400 km
Lambert Conformal Conic Projection

Where in the World Is London, England?

Washington, D.C., to London: 3,660 miles

my Story
The Battle of the
Spanish Armada

In this section, you'll read about Queen Elizabeth I of England and the defeat of the great Spanish Armada. What does Elizabeth's story tell you about life in early modern Europe?

Explore the Essential Question ...
- at **my worldgeography.com**
- using the **myWorld Chapter Activity**
- with the **Student Journal**

By Ruth Hull Chatlien for myWorld Online

In 1588, Europe's greatest power, Spain, prepared to attack the smaller kingdom of England. The Spanish army gathered supplies and horses for an invasion. The Spanish soldiers were to travel to England on barges. At the same time, a fleet of 130 Spanish ships, the Armada, gathered to protect the barges. The Spanish Armada used massive galleons, huge ships that rode high in the water and were clumsy to maneuver. The English captains manned "race ships." These were smaller, faster, and much easier to handle.

On the English shore, the troops gathered at Tilbury to hear their queen. This was a time when few women held power, but Elizabeth had earned her people's respect. The English people also loved their queen. At Tilbury, she knew that she had to prepare the troops to meet the Spanish, the best fighters of the day.

> I know I have the body but of a weak and feeble woman, but I have the heart of a king, and of a king of England, too.

my **worldgeography.com** On Assignment

In 1587, Elizabeth's advisors convinced her to order the death of her cousin, Mary, Queen of Scotland. They saw Mary, a Catholic, as a threat to Elizabeth, a Protestant.

Elizabeth and trusted court advisors planned the strategy for the battle with the Spanish navy.

Spain's attack against England happened in a time of religious conflict between Catholics and Protestants. Catholicism had been the main religion of Western Europe until the early 1500s. At that time, some Christians left the Roman Catholic Church and started their own Protestant churches.

Spain's king, Philip II, was a very religious man who wanted to restore Catholicism to all of Europe. Elizabeth, who was a Protestant, urged Philip to let Protestants in the Netherlands practice their religion. At that time, the Netherlands was a Spanish possession.

Philip also believed that he should be king of England because he had been married to Mary I. Mary was Elizabeth's half-sister who ruled England before her death in 1558. Religious strife had shaken England ever since Henry VIII, father of Elizabeth and Mary, broke with the Catholic Church and started the Protestant Church of England.

As queen, one of Protestant Elizabeth's earliest acts was to order a compromise with Catholics. Unlike Philip, she did not want to force people to share her religion. "I have no desire to make windows into men's souls," she said. Her wise actions prevented civil war in England, although tension remained throughout her reign.

Spain and England were also rival empire-builders. England wanted an empire and colonies like those of Spain. Those colonies had brought fabulous wealth, such as gold and silver, to Spain. English ships had attacked Spanish ships and taken their gold and silver.

As the Spanish Armada set sail, the huge fleet appeared to be invincible, or unbeatable. Yet, the Spanish had several weaknesses. Besides sailing heavier ships, the Spanish captains had no maps of the coasts of Scotland or Ireland. The Spanish soldiers were brave fighters, but in the use of cannon, they lagged behind their rivals. In addition, food stores had been loaded too early and were rotting. Water barrels leaked, and cannon balls were poorly made or the wrong size. In addition, there were discipline problems on board the Spanish ships.

The Spanish were sure that they would win and saw the battle as a holy war. Philip even had the ships' sails painted with the cross of St. George, the symbol of the medieval Crusaders. In spite of the seeming advantage of the Spanish, Elizabeth predicted,

❝ Let tyrants fear. . . .We shall shortly have a famous victory over these enemies of my God, of my kingdom, and of my people. ❞

The Spanish navy had helped make Spain a wealthy global empire. But the Spanish sailed old-fashioned, slower ships. Their loss to England changed sea warfare and the fortunes of Spain.

As the Spanish Armada neared the coast of England, the English fleet moved into position. For several days, the English managed to keep the Spanish ships at a distance.

At midnight, the English sent fireships loaded with explosives into the midst of the Spanish fleet. The Spanish commanders were forced to cut the ships' anchor cables and sail out to sea to avoid catching fire. The Spanish formation became disorganized, and the English took advantage of the confusion to attack at dawn. A decisive battle took place, and the losses to Spain far outweighed those of England. Spanish domination of the seas had ended.

The English felt this victory proved that God was on their side. English admirals received a medal that said, "God blew and they were scattered." This victory at sea was one of the greatest triumphs of Elizabeth's reign.

 myStory Online

Join Elizabeth and her advisors as they plan the battle against the Spanish Armada.

my worldgeography.com myStory Online

373

New Ways of Thinking

Key Ideas
- European Renaissance thinkers and artists took a new interest in humanity and the world around them.
- Critical thinking in Renaissance Europe led to the Reformation.

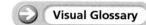
Visual Glossary

Key Terms • Renaissance • humanism • perspective • Reformation • Catholic Reformation

Reading Skill: Label an Outline Map Take notes using the graphic organizer in your journal.

Leon Battista Alberti drew on ancient models for his Renaissance church, Santa Maria Novella, in Florence, Italy.▼

The Late Middle Ages brought many changes to Europe. Feudalism came to an end. Farmers began producing more agricultural goods than they needed. Trade increased. These changes led to a new age in European history called the **Renaissance,** or "rebirth," a time of a renewed interest in art and learning.

The Italian Renaissance

Italy is a peninsula in southern Europe. Italy had been the center of the Roman Empire. This classical influence contributed to the Renaissance.

Trade Grows and Cities Compete Italian traders brought silks and spices back from Asia. They sold these in Italian cities such as Genoa, Venice, and Florence. These cities were major trade centers. In the markets, people exchanged coins of different lands. Merchants adopted a system to deposit money and write checks. These practices became the basis of modern banking.

Unlike the kingdoms of other parts of Europe, Italy was divided into city-states. These city-states were often ruled by one powerful family. In addition to ruling families, city-states were dominated by a wealthy merchant class. City-states fought often. They invented taxes on property and income and other ways to finance their wars.

Old and New Ideas Inspire Trade brought Europeans into contact with the learning of Asia and the Muslim world. For example, Muslim mathematician Al-Khwarizmi (al KWAHR iz mee) had used Hindu-Arabic numerals and developed algebra in the 700s. Muslim scholars had copied and preserved works from ancient Greece and Rome. Many of these had been lost in Europe. Europeans also learned Chinese techniques such as block printing and papermaking.

During the Renaissance, European scholars took an interest in ancient Greek and Roman ideas. This was the beginning of **humanism,** or the study of secular, or nonreligious, subjects such as history and philosophy. Humanists emphasized individual accomplishment and serving the people of this world instead of focusing on religion.

Art Copies Nature Medieval artists had focused on teaching spiritual lessons. As a result, their art was symbolic, not realistic. In contrast, the Greeks and Romans had honored nature and tried to make their art lifelike. Renaissance artists imitated the realism of classical art.

Art changed in two major ways during the Renaissance. First, artists studied the human body so that they could create lifelike statues and paintings. Second, Renaissance painters used **perspective,** a technique that allows artists to portray a three-dimensional space on a flat surface.

Artists Michelangelo and Leonardo da Vinci both created Renaissance masterpieces. Michelangelo carved sculptures, such as the statue *David*. He also painted

scenes from the Bible on the ceiling of the Sistine Chapel in Rome. Leonardo painted the famous portrait *Mona Lisa*. He also drew thousands of diagrams of ideas for inventions. Architect Filippo Brunelleschi (fee LEEP po broo nel LES kee) used classical features such as domes, columns, and arches in his buildings.

Reading Check What did humanists emphasize?

A New Perspective

For *The Last Supper* (1495–1497), Leonardo used perspective to make the painting as realistic as possible. *How did Leonardo use perspective to focus on the figure of Jesus?*

Gutenberg's Press

Gutenberg and his pressmen examine a newly printed page (above). The page at the left was copied out by hand. The page at the right was printed using movable type. *How did Gutenberg's printing press change books?*

The Northern Renaissance

A network of land and sea trade routes linked the city-states of Italy with the kingdoms and small states of Northern Europe. These northern lands included England, Germany, and Flanders (a region now divided between France and Belgium). Like Italy, Germany and Flanders were divided into small, competitive states.

Northern Cities Grow Improved ships made traveling by sea faster than traveling overland. As a result of <u>rapid</u> sea travel, trade between northern and southern Europe increased. Trade also increased within northern Europe. Some northern towns decided to form trade associations so they could have more influence over trade. For example, the Hanseatic (han see AT ik) League was a group of more than 60 towns in Germany and other lands. They worked together to improve trade among members.

Cities and countries began to specialize in the production of certain goods. The countries of England, France, and Flanders produced cloth. Northeastern Europe produced grain. Germany, Hungary, and Austria mined copper, iron, gold, and silver. Trade helped northern cities such as London, Paris, Brugge (BROOG uh), and Lyon grow. A middle class of traders and craftsmen developed. Middle-class people were wealthier than peasants and could buy more goods. This encouraged trade.

Renaissance Ideas Spread Renaissance ideas spread to northern Europe in several ways. First, traders brought the new ideas with them. Second, rulers such as King Francis I of France invited Renaissance scholars and artists to visit their courts. Third, many northern nobles and wealthy members of the middle class traveled to Italy for their education. While in Italy, they learned about Renaissance ideas.

rapid, *adj.,* fast

myWorld Activity
A Life-Changing Product

New technology helped spread knowledge. In the 1400s, German craftsman Johannes Gutenberg invented the printing press. Gutenberg made movable type, or pieces of metal formed into letters of the alphabet. He then printed pages by using a machine to squeeze paper against inked type. Before the printing press, the only way to reproduce writing was by hand. The press made it possible to create copies of books much faster than ever before. As more books became available, more people learned to read.

Renaissance ideas began to influence northern artists and writers. Flemish artist Pieter Bruegel (PEA tur BROO gel) the Elder painted lively scenes of peasant life. German artist Albrecht Dürer (AHL brekt DYOOR ur) used Italian techniques of realism and perspective to create lifelike paintings.

The English playwright William Shakespeare wrote brilliant plays seen as key works of Renaissance humanism. In his play *Hamlet*, he expressed the Renaissance view of human potential:

> 66 What a piece of work is a man, how noble in reason, how infinite in faculties, in form and moving, how express and admirable in action, how like an angel in apprehension, how like a god! 99

Shakespeare's work remains popular today, both on stage and in movies.

Some northern writers, known as Christian humanists, combined classical and religious studies. The Dutch scholar Erasmus (ih RAZ mus) studied the New Testament in its original Greek language. He suggested the Catholic Church make

changes, such as teaching in modern languages instead of Latin. The English humanist Thomas More wrote about an ideal society in his book *Utopia*. Today, we use the word *utopia* to mean a place of perfection in laws and society.

Reading Check Who spread Renaissance ideas to Northern Europe?

Above, a diagram shows the structure of the Globe Theatre.

At the right, modern actors perform a play by Shakespeare in London's Globe Theatre, an authentic replica of the theater where these plays were first performed.

377

The Protestant Reformation

During the Renaissance, humanism led Europeans like Erasmus to think critically about the Catholic Church. Some learned Europeans began to read the Bible and interpret it for themselves instead of simply following the Church's interpretation.

Criticisms of the Church Some Europeans began to believe that the Church did not uphold the Bible's teachings. Some felt that Church leaders were corrupt. Others thought that the Church had become too rich, or that it was too involved in politics.

The Inquisition also led to criticism. The Inquisition was a church court set up to try people accused of heresy, or religious belief contrary to established Church teachings. The Church gained wealth by taking property from people accused of heresy.

Early critics of the Church, such as John Wycliffe, Jan Hus (yahn hous), and Girolamo Savonarola (jee ROH lah moh sah voh nuh ROH lah), risked their lives by speaking out. Church leaders executed both Hus and Savonarola, yet the calls for reform did not end.

The printing press helped spread the desire for change. As books grew more common, more people were able to read the Bible and scholarly works. People formed their own ideas about religion. More people questioned Church teachings.

Luther Calls for Reform The Church made money by selling indulgences, or pardons for sin. A German monk named Martin Luther studied the Bible and came to believe that people could neither buy nor earn pardon for sin. In 1517, Luther drafted the 95 Theses, a list of arguments against indulgences. He sent the list to to a church official who called for an investigation of Luther's beliefs. Luther's call for reform started the **Reformation,** a religious movement in which calls for reform led to the emergence of non-Catholic, or Protestant, churches.

Comparing Catholicism and Lutheranism

	Catholicism	Lutheranism
Salvation	Faith and good works bring salvation.	Faith alone brings salvation.
Sacraments	Priests perform the seven sacraments, or rituals.	Accepts some sacraments, but rejects others because they lack Biblical grounding.
Head of the Church	The pope, together with the bishops	Elected councils
Importance of the Bible	Bible is one source of truth; Church tradition is another.	Bible alone is the source of truth.
Interpretation	Bible is interpreted by priests according to tradition and Church leadership.	People read and interpret the Bible for themselves.

Chart Skills

Note the differences in the heads of the two churches. Why was this difference important?

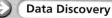 **Data Discovery**

Luther believed that religious salvation came only from faith. He also believed that the Bible—not the Church—was the only true authority for Christian life. He encouraged ordinary people to study the Bible. People began Lutheran churches based on Luther's teachings.

Other Protestants took the movement even further. In his book *Institutes of the Christian Religion*, John Calvin offered an explanation of Protestant beliefs. His main theme is the belief that God has complete control over the universe. Calvin also stressed morality and hard work.

The Reformation began a series of events in which churches continued to split up over various disagreements. One new group of Protestants, the Anabap-tists, baptized only adults. Other new churches included the Baptists, the Mennonites, and the Quakers. In the 1700s, English clergyman John Wesley founded the Methodist Church.

The Reformation and Government

During this time period, many European rulers forced their people to follow the ruler's religion. Catholics and Protestants felt certain that their own beliefs were the only correct <u>doctrines.</u> Many people did not think other views should be allowed. Sometimes, state churches punished people of other faiths. Such abuses of religious power later led the authors of the U.S. Constitution to call for the separation of church and state.

doctrine, *n.,* teaching or principle

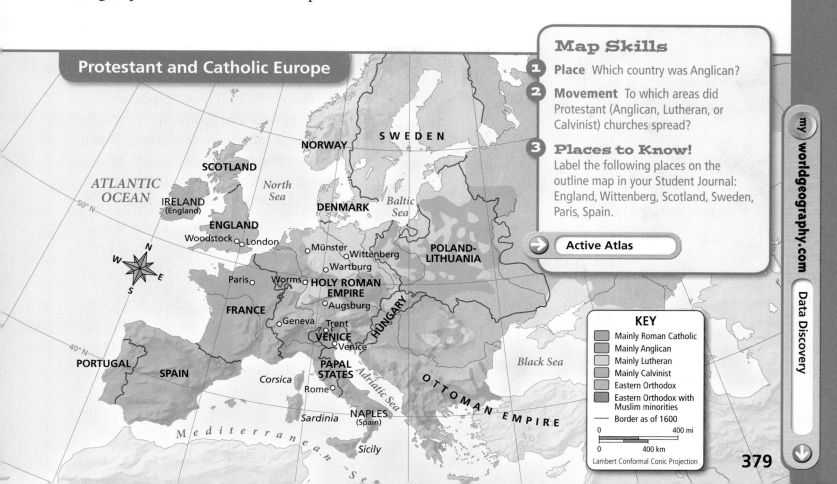

Protestant and Catholic Europe

Map Skills

1. **Place** Which country was Anglican?

2. **Movement** To which areas did Protestant (Anglican, Lutheran, or Calvinist) churches spread?

3. **Places to Know!** Label the following places on the outline map in your Student Journal: England, Wittenberg, Scotland, Sweden, Paris, Spain.

Active Atlas

my **worldgeography.com** | Data Discovery

KEY
- Mainly Roman Catholic
- Mainly Anglican
- Mainly Lutheran
- Mainly Calvinist
- Eastern Orthodox
- Eastern Orthodox with Muslim minorities
- — Border as of 1600

0   400 mi
0   400 km
Lambert Conformal Conic Projection

379

Each of the small states in Germany followed the religion of its ruler. Some German princes remained Catholic, while others became Lutheran. Religious conflict in Germany was a cause of the Thirty Years' War. The war raged in central Europe from 1618 to 1648. The fighting left Germany in ruins.

Religion in England Religion also played a major role in English politics. King Henry VIII wanted to have sons to rule after him, but he and his wife Catherine of Aragon had only one child who survived infancy—a daughter. Henry, who was Catholic, asked the pope to allow him to end his marriage. The pope refused. In response, Henry declared that England was no longer under the authority of the pope. Instead, Henry formed a new church, the Church of England. This church is also called the Anglican church. As head of the Church of England, Henry ended his marriage.

Henry went on to have five more wives, one more daughter, and one son. Each of his three children later ruled England in turn. When power changed hands, England went from Protestant to Catholic, and finally, under the rule of Elizabeth I, to Protestant again.

Reading Check How did Martin Luther begin the Reformation?

The Catholic Reformation

Even after the Protestant Reformation, millions of Europeans remained Catholic. The Catholic Church was especially strong in Italy and Spain. In response to reformers' criticisms, the Church began to make changes. These changes, which helped keep Catholicism strong, are called the **Catholic Reformation.**

The Catholic Church Responds When Luther posted his 95 Theses, Pope Leo X did not take the event very seriously. He believed that the calls for change would soon end. However, the pope did excommunicate Luther—that is, he banned Luther from the Catholic Church.

In 1545, Pope Paul III took action against the Reformation. He called Church leaders to the Council of Trent where they rejected several key Protestant beliefs.

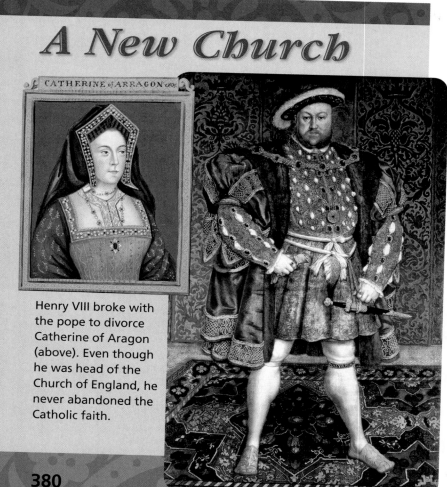

A New Church

CATHERINE of ARRAGON

Henry VIII broke with the pope to divorce Catherine of Aragon (above). Even though he was head of the Church of England, he never abandoned the Catholic faith.

First, it decided that only the Catholic Church and its leaders could interpret the Bible. Second, the council declared that Church tradition was just as important a guide for Christian life as the Bible. Third, the council decided that both faith and good deeds were needed for salvation.

The Church Renews Itself Over time, the Catholic Church ended many of the abuses that Protestants had criticized. This helped Catholics remain loyal to the faith. Also, Catholic mystics such as John of the Cross and Teresa of Avila wrote inspiring works about their faith. Mystics are people who aim to experience the presence of God. Many mystics have written about their experiences.

In addition, Ignatius (ig NAY shus) of Loyola helped the Church gain new strength. He was a Spanish soldier who became religious while recovering from war injuries. Loyola wrote a set of spiritual exercises that became the basis for the Jesuit order of priests. The Jesuits were disciplined and well trained. They became educators in Catholic schools. Many became missionaries. The Catholic Reformation and the work of Jesuits helped to spread Catholicism to European colonies around the world.

Reading Check How did Ignatius of Loyola help strengthen Catholicism?

myStory Online

Queen Elizabeth rallies the troops at Tilbury.

? Essential Question

Section 1 Assessment

Key Terms

1. Explain how the following terms affected European life in the period covered in this section: Renaissance, Reformation, Catholic Reformation.

Key Ideas

2. What cultures helped to shape the Renaissance?

3. How did the Renaissance help cause the Reformation?

4. What were two Catholic responses to the Reformation?

Think Critically

5. **Compare and Contrast** How were Italy and Germany alike and different?

6. **Synthesize** How did the printing press affect the spread of Protestantism?

7. **Analyze Cause and Effect** How did trade expand knowledge?

What makes a nation?

8. How might a desire to build a stronger nation affect a ruler's decision to become a Protestant or a Catholic? Go to your Student Journal to record your answer.

Europe Expands

<table>
<tr>
<td>Key
Ideas</td>
<td>● Renaissance ideals,
competition among rulers,
and the expansion of trade
led to an age of exploration.</td>
<td>● Exploration and a search for
wealth led European states
to create colonial empires.</td>
</tr>
</table>

Key Terms • cartography • caravel • plantation • northwest passage • triangular trade • absolutism

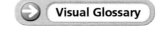 Visual Glossary

 Reading Skill: Sequence Take notes using the graphic organizer in your journal.

A modern replica of English explorer Sir Francis Drake's ship *Golden Hind*

By 1300, innovations such as navigational charts, triangular sails, and magnetic compasses had made sailing easier. These new technologies also helped Renaissance mapmakers develop **cartography,** the science of making accurate maps and globes. A new age of exploration was about to begin.

The Age of Exploration

During the 1300s, Italian merchant Marco Polo published a book about his travels in China and India. His descriptions of the wealth and wonders of Asia increased European interest in the continent.

Portugal Sets Sail Portugal led the search for a sea route to Asia. The Portuguese sailed **caravels,** small, triangular-sailed oceangoing ships. Henry the Navigator, a Portuguese prince, paid for voyages to Asia and helped train explorers in navigation.

Throughout the 1400s, Portuguese ships explored the west coast of Africa by sailing farther and farther south. In 1488, Bartolomeu Dias became the first explorer to travel around the southern tip of Africa. In 1497, Vasco da Gama reached India. During the first half of the 1500s, the Portuguese established trading centers in India, Southeast Asia, and China. They enabled Portugal to end Italy's control over trade with Asia.

Closer Look

To the Far Horizon

New tools for navigation, better maps, and tales of riches sent European explorers out on the high seas. They sailed from Portugal, Spain, England, France, and the Netherlands looking for new trade routes and new lands to claim.

Modern replicas of
Columbus's ships ▶

NORTH AMERICA

ENGLAND NETHERLANDS EUROPE
FRANCE
PORTUGAL SPAIN

ASIA

West Indies
Caribbean Sea

ATLANTIC OCEAN

AFRICA

PACIFIC OCEAN

Philippine Islands

PACIFIC OCEAN

SOUTH AMERICA

INDIAN OCEAN

East Indies

PACIFIC OCEAN

Cape of
Good Hope

KEY
Selected Early Voyages for

— Portugal
— Spain
— England
— France
— The Netherlands

0   2,000 mi
0   2,000 km
Miller Cylindrical Projection

Map Skills

1 **Movement** Which nation's explorers followed the coast of Africa to Asia?

2 **Movement** Which nation sent an explorer around the world?

3 **Region** Which nations' explorers sailed to eastern North America?

◀ Renaissance explorers used the astrolabe at left to determine their position and the compass below to find their direction.

THINK CRITICALLY **How did explorers use these tools to find their way across the oceans?**

383

Reaching the Americas Italian explorer Christopher Columbus promised to reach Asia by sailing westward across the Atlantic. Spain's rulers agreed to <u>finance</u> his voyage. They wanted to take part in the rich Asian spice trade.

In October 1492, Columbus and his crew made landfall in the Caribbean. He believed he had reached the Indies—islands in Southeast Asia—so he called the native people Indians. He later wrote:

> 66 They came to the ship in canoes, … some of them large enough to contain forty or forty-five men. 99

Columbus did not reach Asia, but he helped Spain start an empire in the Americas.

Reading Check **Why did Portugal and Spain look for water routes to Asia?**

finance, *v.,* to raise or provide funds

This painting from India shows Europeans (bottom left) bringing gifts to the Indian ruler. *Why might Europeans bring gifts?* ▼

An Age of Empires

The age of exploration was also an age of imperialism, or empire-building. European countries expanded their empires by taking over other lands as colonies. These colonies made European nations wealthy and powerful.

Spain Conquers the New World Many Spanish explorers followed Columbus to the Americas. In 1513, Vasco Nuñez de Balboa (VAHS koh NOO nyes deh bal BOH uh) became the first European to reach the Pacific Ocean from the Americas. This proved that he was not in Asia. The explorer Amerigo Vespucci (ah meh REE goh ves POOH chee) believed that explorers had found a "New World." A mapmaker at the time called the New World *America* after Vespucci.

Spain sent conquistadors, or conquerors, to the Americas to seize new lands. They used gunpowder, a Chinese invention, to help them conquer native peoples. On the Caribbean islands, the Spanish set up **plantations,** or large commercial farms.

In Mexico, Spanish troops under Hernán Cortés took control of the Aztec Empire. In Peru, troops under Francisco Pizarro conquered the Inca Empire. Spain took huge amounts of gold and silver from its American colonies. The Spanish empire covered much of the Americas.

Establishing New Colonies Explorers also searched for a **northwest passage,** a route between the Atlantic and Pacific Oceans along the northern coast of North America. They hoped to increase trade with Asia by finding a faster sea route.

The Columbian Exchange

Columbus's landing in America changed life around the world. European ships brought animals, food plants, and diseases that transformed life there. In turn, Europeans brought back new foods and other products.

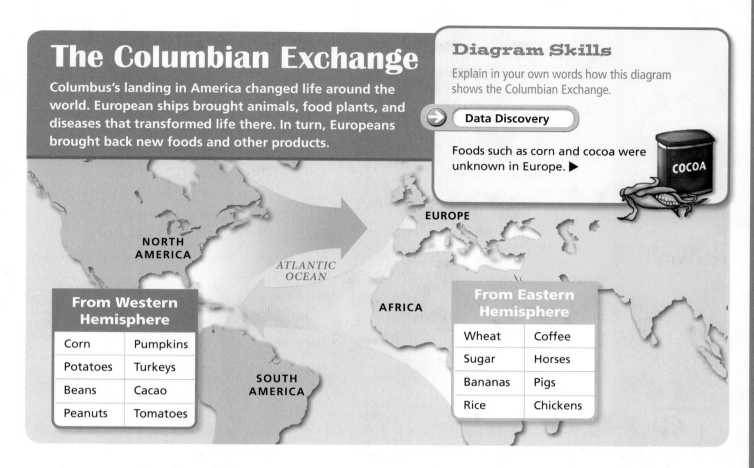

NORTH AMERICA

EUROPE

AFRICA

SOUTH AMERICA

ATLANTIC OCEAN

Diagram Skills

Explain in your own words how this diagram shows the Columbian Exchange.

→ **Data Discovery**

Foods such as corn and cocoa were unknown in Europe. ▶

COCOA

From Western Hemisphere	
Corn	Pumpkins
Potatoes	Turkeys
Beans	Cacao
Peanuts	Tomatoes

From Eastern Hemisphere	
Wheat	Coffee
Sugar	Horses
Bananas	Pigs
Rice	Chickens

Explorers never found a northwest passage, but others established new colonies in North America. Both England and France claimed lands in eastern North America. They also traded with Native Americans for furs to take back to Europe.

By the mid-1700s, England had a group of colonies stretching down the Atlantic coast of North America. Early settlements included Jamestown in Virginia and Plymouth Colony in New England. The Netherlands had also founded North American colonies, but the English took them over.

The Dutch, English, and French had colonies in other regions. The Dutch controlled land in the East Indies. England and France had additional colonies in India.

England also founded colonies in Australia during the early 1800s. Most of these colonies began as places to send people <u>convicted</u> of crimes. By the late 1800s, though, most colonists in Australia were not criminals. Those colonists went to Australia to make a living in agriculture, mining, or in Australia's growing cities.

Plantation Agriculture Plantations in the Caribbean and southeastern North America produced crops such as sugar and tobacco. Plantation agriculture required huge numbers of workers. At first, landowners used Native Americans, but they fell ill from European diseases. Europeans began to bring enslaved Africans to do this work.

convict, *v.,* to find or prove guilty

my worldgeography.com Data Discovery

myWorld Activity
Sailing for Riches

Europe in the Age of Absolutism

ICELAND (Denmark)

NORWAY (Denmark)

SWEDEN

Stockholm

SCOTLAND

North Sea

Moscow

RUSSIA

IRELAND (England)

DENMARK

NETHERLANDS

PRUSSIA (Brandenburg)

ENGLAND

BRANDENBURG

Berlin

POLAND

Warsaw

London

SPANISH NETHERLANDS (Spain)

Paris

SMALL GERMAN STATES

Prague

ZAPOROZHIA

ATLANTIC OCEAN

FRANCE

Vienna

AUSTRIA-HUNGARY

SWITZERLAND

MILAN (Spain)

VENICE

Black Sea

SMALL ITALIAN STATES

PAPAL STATES

PORTUGAL

Madrid

Rome

NAPLES (Spain)

Constantinople

OTTOMAN EMPIRE

Lisbon

SPAIN

Mediterranean Sea

MOREA (Venice)

Map Skills

1. **Location** Which large country separated Spain's possessions?

2. **Place** Why might Spain have had trouble controlling its European empire?

3. **Places to Know!** Label the following places on the outline map in your Student Journal: Paris, Constantinople, London, Poland.

→ Active Atlas

KEY

— Border as of 1700

0   400 mi

0   400 km

Lambert Conformal Conic Projection

In time, a system known as the triangular trade developed. The **triangular trade** was a three-stage pattern of Atlantic trade that carried goods and enslaved people between Europe, Africa, and the Americas. In the first stage, Europeans shipped manufactured goods from Europe to Africa. These goods were traded for slaves and gold. In the second stage, ships carried enslaved Africans to the Americas. In the third stage, ships carried sugar and other agricultural products back to Europe. Trade winds and ocean currents helped ships along this trade route.

Reading Check **Why did European nations compete for colonies?**

▲ A china vase made in the 1700s for King Augustus II the Strong, Elector of Saxony and King of Poland

An Age of Absolutism

During this time, European nations grew in size and power to become nation-states. A nation-state is a region that shares a government and is independent from other states. Monarchs during this time felt that God had chosen them to rule, a belief called the divine right of kings. They also believed in absolutism. **Absolutism** is a political system of centralized and unlimited government power.

Absolute Power in Spain Perhaps the most powerful monarch in Europe was Spain's Philip II. Philip kept firm control over the Spanish empire. As he once said, "It is best to keep an eye on everything."

Philip was a Catholic, and he used his power to back Catholicism throughout Europe. Conflict between Catholics and Protestants led to fighting in the Spanish Netherlands.

Spain also came into conflict with England. King Philip wanted to end English attacks on Spanish ships carrying gold and silver from the Americas. He also wanted to force England, a Protestant country, to return to the Catholic Church. But, as you have read, in 1588, the English navy defeated a Spanish navy fleet, called the Armada.

The Sun King Just as the sun is the center of the solar system, Louis XIV was the center of the French government. Known as the Sun King, he centralized power around the throne. In fact, Louis believed he was so important that he said "L'état, c'est moi," meaning "I am the state."

Louis wanted to make France the greatest nation in Europe. He spent years building the biggest palace in Europe at Versailles. He encouraged the growth of industry and built canals and roads. He sent the French army to build colonies in Asia and the Americas. Under Louis, France was at war almost constantly.

Prussia and Austria In 1740, Prussia seized Austrian territory in what is now Poland. That same year, Austrian Empress Maria Theresa began her 40-year rule, making Vienna a cultural center.

Although both Austrian and Prussian rulers were absolutists, Prussia practiced religious tolerance. Both struggled for years to control Central Europe.

Reading Check How did European rulers use their power?

King Louis XIV wears robes decorated with golden fleurs-de-lis, a symbol of France. ▼

Section 2 Assessment

Key Terms

1. Write complete sentences to define each of the following terms: cartography, plantation, northwest passage, triangular trade, absolutism

Key Ideas

2. Why did Spain support Columbus's voyages of exploration?

3. Which three European nations established colonies in eastern North America?

4. Why did European powers create colonies in the Americas?

Think Critically

5. **Identify Bias** What did the actions of Europeans reveal about their attitudes toward non-Europeans?

6. **Draw Inferences** How would Spain's discovery of huge quantities of silver and gold in the Americas affect relations with other European nations?

7. **Identify Evidence** How did absolutism help monarchs build power at home and abroad?

? Essential Question

What makes a nation?

8. How might wars among European powers have helped build loyalty to the new nation-states? Go to your Student Journal to record your answer.

my worldgeography.com Active Atlas

An Age of Revolutions

London's Royal Greenwich Observatory was established in the 1600s to study the stars and navigation. ▼

Medieval scholars had relied on religion and ancient writings to explain the world. But Renaissance thinkers questioned these old beliefs. Instead, they relied on logic, reason, and observation. Their ideas would transform science, government, and the economy.

A Scientific Revolution

During the Renaissance, scholars began studying the world around them. This led to the **Scientific Revolution,** a series of major advances in science during the 1500s and 1600s.

Science Changes Over time, scholars developed new ways to approach science. Francis Bacon taught that scientists should observe and interpret facts. René Descartes (ruh NAY day KAHRT) stressed the use of logic, or reason, to form scientific theories. Isaac Newton believed in testing theories using the scientific method, or controlled experiments.

Scientists Make Discoveries Medieval scientists believed that the sun, planets, and stars orbited, or circled, Earth. This theory was part of Catholic teachings. But in 1543, Polish astronomer Nicolaus Copernicus argued that the planets orbit the sun.

Italian astronomer Galileo Galilei (gal uh LAY oh gal uh LAY ee) agreed with Copernicus. Galileo published evidence that Earth circled the sun. In 1633, the Catholic Church put Galileo on trial for contradicting Church teaching. To save his life, Galileo signed a confession stating that his books were wrong.

Advances in Science

◄ Galileo sketched these phases of the moon that he saw through a telescope. In the background is a modern photograph of the moon.

The Scientific Method

Step One
State the problem.

Step Two
Gather information about the problem.

Step Three
Form a hypothesis, or educated guess.

Step Four
Experiment to test hypothesis.

Step Five
Record and analyze data.

Step Six
State a conclusion.

Step Seven
Share conclusions.

The English scientist Isaac Newton studied how the physical world worked. He described gravity and explained how objects moved in space.

Results of Discovery Scientific and technological advances improved life. Agricultural advances led to larger harvests. Inventors built instruments to measure longitude, latitude, and speed. The work of astronomers resulted in a more accurate calendar.

Thomas Newcomen and James Watt invented steam engines. Alessandro Volta and Michael Faraday conducted electrical experiments. Electricity and steam later became important energy sources.

Reading Check How did the scientific method change science?

The Enlightenment

The **Enlightenment** was a movement during the 1600s and 1700s to apply observation and reason to human affairs. The movement drew on the success of the Scientific Revolution.

Philosophers Study Society Enlightenment thinkers believed that nothing was beyond the human mind. Some studied the nature of reality. Many wrote about society and government. Thomas Hobbes believed that people were selfish and greedy and needed a strong ruler. Hobbes painted this picture of life without a strong ruler in his book *Leviathan*:

greedy, *adj.*, having a strong desire for wealth and possessions

66 There is … continual fear and danger of violent death, and the life of man [is] solitary, poor, nasty, brutish, and short. 99

389

myWorld Activity
Long Live the Revolution

consent, *n.,* agreement or approval

Other philosophers had political views that shaped modern democracy. John Locke wrote that people are born with the right to life, liberty, and property. Charles-Louis Montesquieu (MAHN tus kyoo) believed that the powers of government should be separated into branches. Jean-Jacques Rousseau (roo SOH) said that government depends on the people's <u>consent.</u> These ideas later shaped Americans' views of government.

Enlightened Rulers A few European rulers were influenced by Enlightenment ideas about government. Frederick II of Prussia improved education and outlawed torture. Joseph II of Austria ended serfdom, a system in which peasants were forced to work for a noble.

These reforms were limited. For example, Frederick II promoted religious tolerance but allowed discrimination against Jews. Frederick and other absolute monarchs kept firm control over their people. This would soon begin to change.

Reading Check How did Enlightenment thinkers shape democracy?

Democratic Revolutions

The political ideas of the Enlightenment helped shape modern government. They also led to a period of violent change.

Changes in England During the 1600s, the English Parliament gradually took power away from the monarchy. In 1628, Parliament forced King Charles I to sign the Petition of Right. This document ended illegal taxation and imprisonment.

Conflict between Parliament and the monarchy continued. A civil war began in 1642. In 1649, Parliamentary forces executed the king. England became a commonwealth, or a republic.

The English government went through many changes over the next 40 years. Charles I's sons regained the throne but had renewed conflicts with Parliament. Parliament then gave the throne to William and Mary in 1689, under the condition that they sign the English Bill of Rights. The **English Bill of Rights** was an act that limited the power of the monarch and listed the rights of Parliament and the English people. England's absolute monarchy had come to an end.

The Magna Carta Paves the Way

Magna Carta (1215)
The king and nobles must respect the law.

⬇

A Struggle for Democracy (1295–1641)
Representatives of the English people struggle with kings for power.

⬇

English Revolution and Restoration (1641–1688)
The monarchy is abolished and Parliament rules England as a republic. The monarchy is restored in 1660. Conflicts between the king and Parliament resume.

⬇

English Bill of Rights (1689)
King William and Queen Mary agree to the English Bill of Rights. The Bill of Rights ensures the superiority of Parliament over the monarchy.

⬇

American Declaration of Independence (1776)
The monarchy is abolished and replaced with a democratic government in the United States.

How does this flowchart show the changing relationship of government and the people?

390

Revolution in France In France, society was divided into three groups called estates: clergy (the First Estate), nobles (the Second Estate), and common people (the Third Estate). Most French people were in the Third Estate. They paid heavy taxes and had few rights.

Enlightenment ideas inspired some French people to demand a voice in government. However, King Louis XVI refused to give up any of his powers. On July 14, 1789, a mob stormed the Bastille, a Paris prison. This marked the start of the **French Revolution,** a political movement that removed the French king from power and formed a republic.

The Revolution took a brutal turn. During the Reign of Terror in 1793 and 1794, the republic's government killed thousands of its opponents.

Napoleon Takes Power Meanwhile, Napoleon Bonaparte rose quickly in the French army. In 1799, he took power in France as a dictator.

Napoleon wanted to create a mighty French empire. In the Napoleonic Wars, he conquered much of Europe. His invasion of Russia proved disastrous, however. The French army was weakened, and Napoleon was defeated in 1815.

Revolution Spreads French domination led to growing nationalism, or devotion to one's country. Many Europeans also wanted greater democracy. In 1848, revolutions broke out across Europe. By 1871, both Germany and Italy had become unified nations.

Reading Check What caused the French Revolution?

The Reign of Terror

The promise of the French Revolution quickly soured. What had been a revolution calling for brotherhood and liberty turned into a civil war. Respected leaders such as Robespierre became feared tyrants.

A French mob storms the Bastille. ▼

Robespierre, who sentenced hundreds to the guillotine, was executed himself in 1794. ▼

The French Republic's government used the falling blade of the guillotine (right) to silence opponents. ▶

→ Culture Close-up

my worldgeography.com Culture Close-up

391

Life in the Industrial Age

The Industrial Revolution has been chronicled in art, literature, and photography. It transformed life and society across Europe. Industrialization had both positive and negative aspects. Its innovations remain part of modern life.

- **Widespread pollution from factories**
- **Long work hours, child labor common**
- **Overcrowded living conditions**

The Industrial Revolution

Alongside these political revolutions, a different kind of revolution began. The **Industrial Revolution** was a shift from hand tools driven by animal or human power to large-scale machinery powered by fuels or natural forces. It led to a growth of cities and large organizations and to rapid changes in technology. The Industrial Revolution began in Britain but soon spread to the rest of Europe.

Technology Changes Industry Before the Industrial Revolution, most people were farmers. Others worked at home. There, they used hand tools to make cloth, leather goods, and other items.

In England in the mid-1700s, this process began to change. Fast, new machines in factories began to do much of the work once done by people in their homes. The textile industry was the first to change. Inventors developed machines for spinning thread and weaving cloth.

Transportation also changed. Coal and steampower made steamboats and locomotives possible. These ships and trains carried raw materials to factories. They brought finished goods to distant markets.

Industry Changes Landscapes

Entrepreneurs, or people who start businesses, built factories in areas that had a labor supply, resources such as coal, and good transportation. Towns without access to coal and iron or to transportation often did not industrialize.

Industrial towns grew quickly as workers moved there for jobs in factories. This rapid growth caused problems such as housing shortages. People had to live in crowded apartment buildings. Many people had no access to clean water.

Cities could not dispose adequately of waste, and coal-burning factories polluted the air. Diseases spread rapidly in these crowded, dirty conditions. Working conditions in factories were difficult. Factories and mines often hired young children to work dangerous jobs.

Trade Grows Workers in factories produced far more goods than individual workers ever had. Industrialized nations needed new places to sell these products. Many of the new markets were in European colonies in Africa and Asia. Colonies also provided raw materials for European manufacturers.

- **Better public education and social reforms**
- **Improvements in healthcare, public hygiene**
- **Advances in arts and sciences**

Positive Effects The Industrial Age also brought improvements. During this period, doctors and scientists made advances in research and medicine. Louis Pasteur and Robert Koch discovered that germs caused disease. Researchers found ways to cure or prevent illness. Cities built sewer systems to dispose of waste and prevent disease. Inventors developed ways to use electric power.

Because production was more efficient, the cost of goods went down. With the number of jobs increasing and the price of products decreasing, people could afford to buy more goods. For example, people began to wear clothing made in factories instead of at home. Middle-class families purchased new labor-saving devices, such as sewing machines. As a result, the standard of living—or the level of comfort—rose for millions of people.

Another positive change was greater access to primary school education. Where once only some boys had attended school, now girls too could receive an education.

Reading Check How did life change during the Industrial Age?

Section 3 Assessment

Key Terms

1. Using full sentences, describe how each of the following terms relates to social and political change: Scientific Revolution, Enlightenment, English Bill of Rights, French Revolution, Industrial Revolution.

Key Ideas

2. How did the Industrial Revolution transform methods of manufacturing goods?

3. What did Isaac Newton contribute to the Scientific Revolution?

4. How did the Scientific Revolution influence Enlightenment thought?

5. How did the Enlightenment affect rulers' ideas?

Think Critically

6. **Categorize** Which of the events discussed in this section would you call political revolutions and which would you call cultural revolutions?

7. **Synthesize** How did the Enlightenment change governments in Europe?

Essential Question

What makes a nation?

8. How did the Napoleonic Wars encourage nationalistic feelings in Europe? Go to your Student Journal to record your answer.

393

Section 4

Wars and Hardship

Key Ideas

- World War I resulted in defeat for Europe's multinational empires and their division into new nations.

- The Great Depression brought hardship and political unrest to Europe.

- World War II brought catastrophe for Jews and other Europeans and led to the defeat of Germany and Italy by the Allied powers.

 Visual Glossary

Key Terms • World War I • Great Depression • communism • fascism
• World War II • Holocaust

Reading Skill: Compare and Contrast Take notes using the graphic organizer in your journal.

Fighter pilots engage in a dramatic dogfight during World War I.

When the 1900s began, large multinational empires controlled central Europe. A series of alliances linked Europe's great powers into competing blocs.

The Great War: World War I

World War I (1914–1918), or the Great War, was the first modern global conflict. It involved most of Europe, the United States, Canada, and many parts of Africa and Asia.

Causes of War World War I had four main causes: nationalism, imperialism, militarism, and alliances.

- **Nationalism**—Nationalism, or devotion to one's nation or people, sometimes led to hostility toward other nations.
- **Imperialism**—European imperial powers competed to extend their empires by seizing territory to add to their colonies in Africa and Asia.
- **Militarism**—For decades, European countries had been building up military power and adopting warlike attitudes.
- **Alliances**—In a complex system of alliances, many European countries had agreed to defend one another from attack. These alliances pulled nations into the war.

War Breaks Out In June 1914, a Serbian nationalist killed the Austrian archduke. Austria-Hungary declared war on Serbia. One by one, the major European powers entered the war to support their allies. The fighting later spread overseas.

In Europe, armies fought on two fronts. On the Western Front, Germany battled the Allied Powers—France and Britain. Soldiers lived in a network of trenches dug into the earth. For years, they gained little ground. On the Eastern Front, Germany and Austria-Hungary fought Russia. But when the Russian Revolution began in 1917, Russia pulled out of the war.

In 1917, the United States entered the war on the side of the Allies. U.S. troops helped force the Germans out of France. Exhausted, Germany sought a truce, and the war ended on November 11, 1918.

Consequences of War The Allies forced Germany to sign the Treaty of Versailles. The treaty <u>humiliated</u> Germany. It made Germany give up territory and pay huge reparations, or sums for war damage.

Other treaties carved up Austria-Hungary into several new nations, ended the Ottoman Empire, and created new countries. For example, Yugoslavia was a federation of Slavic republics, including Serbia. Poland was shaped from parts of Germany, Austria-Hungary, and Russia. The maps below show these changes.

Reading Check **What were the four main causes of World War I?**

humiliate, *v.,* to embarrass or to reduce a person's feeling of self-worth

Map Skills

1. **Region** How did Europe change after World War I?
2. **Place** What areas of Europe changed the most? Why do you think this happened?

→ **Active Atlas**

Europe Before and After World War I

myWorld Activity
Runaway Prices

The Great Depression

Germany had lost land, people, and resources. At the same time, Germany owed billions of dollars in reparations. The government printed money to try to make these payments. As a result, German money lost value. The price of goods increased rapidly during a period of inflation. Many Germans lost their savings. This caused unrest and political instability in Germany.

A Global Financial Crisis Develops

During the 1920s, the American economy had grown dramatically. At same time, prices on the U.S. stock market rose.

Many Americans bought stocks, some with borrowed money, hoping to make a profit as the prices of stocks increased.

At first, stock prices soared. Then stocks leveled off and fell. Nervous lenders demanded repayment. Investors sold stocks to repay the loans. Heavy selling drove prices down quickly. In October 1929, the U.S. stock market collapsed.

Many investors lost fortunes selling their stocks for much less than they had paid. People and businesses who had borrowed money could not repay their debts. Soon, banks failed and businesses closed. As a result, millions of people were out of work. This was the beginning of the **Great Depression,** a deep, worldwide economic slump that lasted through the 1930s. It caused hardship around the world.

Europe Suffers Hard Times To protect its farmers, the United States put tariffs, or taxes, on imported farm products. These tariffs hurt European economies, so European countries imposed their own tariffs. Global trade slowed. The French and German governments lowered wages, hoping to help reduce the costs of goods. Instead, this only angered workers and increased hardship.

Banks around the world were linked by loans. As a result, U.S. banking problems spread to other nations. Some European banks failed. Most European countries had not yet recovered from World War I. These new financial troubles made hard times even harder.

Reading Check How did the Great Depression spread from the United States to Europe?

slump, *n.,*
a marked decline

A man uses German money as wallpaper. Inflation had made the money worthless.
▼

Unemployment in Europe, 1928–1938

Percentage Unemployed (y-axis: 0, 5, 10, 15, 20, 25, 30, 35)
Year (x-axis: 1928, 1929, 1930, 1931, 1932, 1933, 1934, 1935, 1936, 1937, 1938)

— Belgium
— Germany
— Norway
— Great Britain

SOURCE: *International Historical Statistics, Europe 1750–1993*

Chart Skills

In which years did each European nation on the graph experience the highest unemployment?

→ **Data Discovery**

A War of Ideas

After World War I, antidemocratic leaders took power in Italy, Germany, and other European countries. Those governments took control of daily life.

The Rise of Communism The 1917 Russian Revolution led to the formation of the communist government of the Soviet Union. **Communism** is an economic and political system in which the state, run by a Communist Party, takes over industry and farmland and controls most organizations.

Communism promised to share wealth among all workers. During the Great Depression, workers across Europe found this promise very appealing.

Fascism in Italy and Spain In Italy, nationalist pride led to fascism. **Fascism** is a political system that stresses national strength, military might, and the belief that the state is more important than individuals. Fascists use propaganda and violence to achieve goals and believe that a dictator—a leader with unlimited powers—should rule. In the 1920s, fascist Benito Mussolini took power in Italy. He promised to build a strong Italian empire. During the 1930s, fascists under Francisco Franco took control of Spain.

Nazis Take Power in Germany Many Germans resented the Treaty of Versailles and blamed it for their hardships. Some blamed Germany's democratic government for obeying the treaty.

Adolf Hitler had served in the German army during World War I. Like many other Germans, he felt that Germany had been treated unfairly after the war.

Hitler came to lead a small, fascist German political party, the Nazi Party. Hitler's ideas included extreme nationalism, racism, and anti-Semitism, or prejudice against Jews. Hitler unfairly blamed Jews for Germany's economic problems.

In 1923, the Nazis tried and failed to overthrow the government. Hitler was jailed, but worked after his release to rebuild the Nazi Party. Amid the Great Depression, the Nazis gained strength in the early 1930s. In 1932, the Nazis won more votes than any other party, but less than a majority of votes. Nonetheless, in 1933, Hitler became head of Germany's government.

Understanding Political Systems

	Democracy	Communism	Fascism
Individuals and the State	Individuals' rights are more important than government interests.	Government interests are more important than individuals' rights.	Government interests are more important than individuals' rights.
Values	Freedom, individuals' rights, justice	Obedience, discipline, economic security	Obedience, discipline, national pride, military power
Government	The people and their elected representatives make decisions; control of people's lives is minimal.	Communist party makes all decisions; extreme control of all aspects of life.	Fascist party controls all aspects of life; government is permanent and necessary for national progress.

Chart Skills

Compare the values associated with fascism to those of democracy and communism.

➜ **Data Discovery**

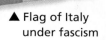

▲ Flag of Italy under fascism

▲ The Nazis forced Jewish people to wear yellow stars for identification.

Once in power, Hitler ruled as a dictator. He controlled every aspect of German life, using secret police to spy on people. Hitler imprisoned or killed his opponents. Because Germany's economy improved under the Nazis, many Germans accepted Nazi rule.

The Nazi government passed a number of laws against Jews, eliminating their rights as citizens. In 1938, Nazis led anti-Jewish riots in Germany and Austria. For 48 hours, Nazis systematically destroyed Jewish synagogues and Jewish businesses. Nazi hatred toward Jews later led to the Nazi "Final Solution," the plan to murder all Jews.

Reading Check Why were the German people attracted to the Nazi Party?

World War II

Under Adolf Hitler, Germany built a powerful army and formed an alliance with Italy and Japan. These countries were called the Axis Powers. Britain and France formed the Allied Powers, later joined by the United States and Soviet Union.

War Begins Hitler wanted to build a mighty German empire across Europe. In 1938, German troops occupied Austria and seized part of Czechoslovakia. Germany and the Soviet Union then secretly agreed to divide Poland between them. On September 1, 1939, Germany invaded Poland. Two days later, Britain and France declared war on Germany. **World War II,** the second major global conflict of the 1900s, had begun.

War in Europe By the end of 1940, Germany's powerful armies had conquered much of Europe. Italy attacked North Africa. At first, Britain fought on alone, with the help of some military aid from the United States.

The German air force repeatedly bombed British military targets and civilian areas, but the British did not give up.

Wartime Opponents, 1942

KEY
Allied territory, 1942
Axis territory, 1942
Neutral territory, 1942
— Borders as of 1938

0 — 400 mi
0 — 400 km
Lambert Conformal Conic Projection

North Sea
Baltic Sea
ATLANTIC OCEAN
Black Sea
Mediterranean Sea

60° N
50° N
10° W
40° N
40° E

Map Skills

Place Who controlled more of Europe in 1942, the Allies or the Axis Powers?

→ **Active Atlas**

British Prime Minister Winston Churchill inspired the people with stirring speeches:

66 We have before us many, many long months of struggle and of suffering. You ask, what is our policy? I will say: It is to wage war, by sea, land and air, with all our might and with all the strength that God can give us. 99

In June 1941, Germany broke its earlier agreement and invaded the Soviet Union. The Soviet Union joined the Allied Powers. Soviet resistance, brutal winter weather, and a lack of supplies finally forced Germany to retreat in 1943.

America Enters the War In late 1941, Japan bombed Pearl Harbor, a U.S. naval base in Hawaii. This pushed the United States into the war. American forces helped the Allies defeat Italy.

With U.S. help, the Allies pushed back into western Europe. On June 6, 1944, D-Day, more than 150,000 Allied troops invaded German-occupied France. The Allies slowly forced German troops back across France into Germany. At the same time, Soviet troops invaded Germany from the east. Germany surrendered on May 7, 1945. World War II ended later that year with Japan's surrender to the United States.

Effects of the War Approximately 17 million European soldiers died in World War II. Millions of civilians died as well. Many civilian deaths occurred in the **Holocaust,** the mass murder of Jews by the Nazis during World War II. The Nazis murdered 6 million Jews and another 5 million people from other groups.

After the war, Europe's cities, roads, and farms lay in ruins. Much of the continent needed to be rebuilt.

Reading Check How were the Allied forces able to win World War II?

World at War

▶ **1914** World War I begins.

▶ **1918** World War I ends.

▶ **1919** The Treaty of Versailles

▶ **1939** Germany invades Poland; France and Britain declare war on Germany. World War II begins.

▶ **1941** The United States enters the war.

▶ **1945** Germany and Japan surrender. World War II ends.

 Timeline

my worldgeography.com Timeline

Section 4 Assessment

Essential Question

What makes a nation?

Key Terms

1. Define each of the following terms using a complete sentence: World War I, Great Depression, communism, fascism, World War II, Holocaust.

Key Ideas

2. Whom did the Nazis murder during the Holocaust?

3. How did competition among nations contribute to World War I?

4. How did the Great Depression affect Europe?

5. Which nations defeated the Axis Powers in World War II?

Think Critically

6. **Problem Solving** How did Germany's situation after World War I help cause the next world war?

7. **Compare Viewpoints** How might French citizens have felt about the Treaty of Versailles? Compare their viewpoint to that of German citizens.

8. Why did so many nations gain independence after World War I? Go to your Student Journal to record your answer.

Rebuilding and New Challenges

Key Ideas

- After World War II, the Cold War divided Europe between the democratic West and the communist East.

- Western European nations joined together in the late 1900s to promote free trade and peaceful interaction.

- When communism collapsed in the Soviet Union, Eastern Europe adopted democracy and Germany reunified.

Key Terms • Cold War • Marshall Plan • Berlin Wall • European Union (EU)

 Visual Glossary

 Reading Skill: Identify Main Ideas and Details Take notes using the graphic organizer in your journal.

When World War II ended, Soviet troops occupied most of Eastern Europe. The Soviet Union set up communist governments there. U.S. troops backed democratic governments in Western Europe.

Cold War and Division

The United States and Britain wanted to stop the Soviet Union from spreading communism. The result was the **Cold War,** a long period of hostility between the Soviet Union and the democratic West.

To encourage democracy and oppose communism, the United States created the **Marshall Plan,** a U.S. recovery plan that offered money to help European countries recover from the war. This money helped Western Europe rebuild.

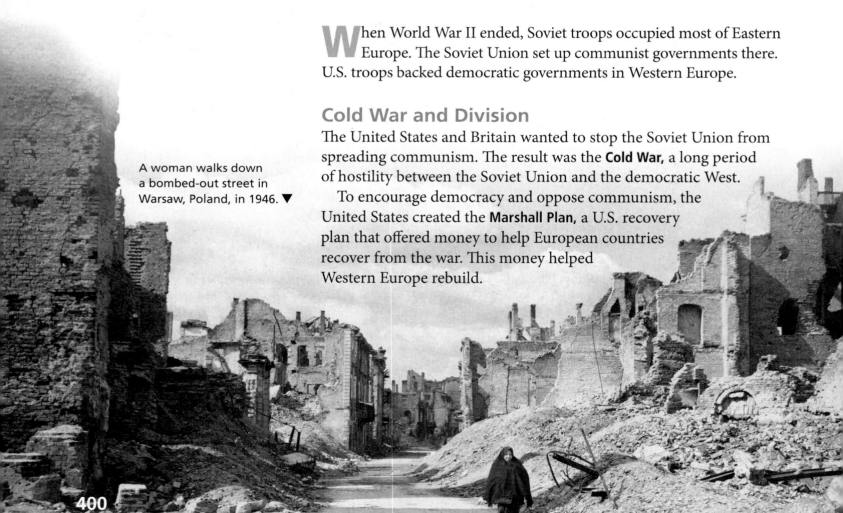

A woman walks down a bombed-out street in Warsaw, Poland, in 1946. ▼

International Cooperation After World War II, many nations joined together to form the United Nations (UN). The UN's main task was to safeguard world peace. The UN later went on to help people cope with disasters and poverty.

The Berlin Wall Goes Up The Cold War divided Europe between Soviet-controlled, communist Eastern Europe and democratic Western Europe, mostly allied with the United States. This split ran roughly along the line where the troops of the Western Allies met the Soviet troops at the end of World War II.

This dividing line ran right through the center of Germany. The Soviets occupied East Germany, which became communist. West Germany, occupied by the Western Allies, became a democracy.

The Soviets and Western Allies also divided Germany's capital, Berlin, located within East Germany. In 1948, the Soviets blocked land and sea access to West Berlin. The United States and Britain flew supplies into Berlin for 11 months until the Soviets lifted the blockade.

About 2.5 million East Germans fled to the West by crossing into West Berlin. In 1961, East Germany built a wall around West Berlin to prevent escapes. The **Berlin Wall** <u>symbolized</u> Cold War divisions.

The Democratic West Unites Helped by American aid, Western Europe's economy recovered quickly. By 1951, factories were producing more than ever. Nations such as Italy adopted democracy. Meanwhile, European nations were forced to give up their colonies. For example, Britain made India and other colonies independent.

▲ This 1962 nuclear explosion at a U.S. testing site was part of a Cold War arms race with the Soviet Union.

In 1949, the United States and Western European countries formed a military alliance called the North Atlantic Treaty Organization (NATO). The United States was NATO's strongest member. After the war, the United States and the Soviet Union became the world's dominant nations, or superpowers.

Communists Control the East The Soviet Union viewed Eastern European countries as satellites, or dependent countries. In response to NATO, the Soviet Union and its satellites formed a military alliance called the Warsaw Pact in 1955. Eastern Europe had weak, state-controlled economies.

The Soviets often used force to control Eastern Europe. In 1956, Soviet forces invaded Hungary and blocked democratic change. In 1968, Soviet troops crushed a reform movement in Czechoslovakia.

Reading Check How did the Soviet Union gain and keep control of Eastern Europe?

symbolize, *v.,* to represent or express something

Closer Look

In 1946, Winston Churchill, former British prime minister, said "[A]n iron curtain has descended across the Continent." During the Cold War, the Iron Curtain was a fortified set of defenses between the democratic west and the communist east. East of the Iron Curtain, West Berlin was surrounded by the Berlin Wall, a concrete barrier that prevented East Germans from moving to democratic West Berlin.

THINK CRITICALLY How might Germans have felt about the Iron Curtain?

Map Skills

1 **Location** What nation was divided by the Iron Curtain?

2 **Places to Know!**
Label these places on the outline map in your Student Journal: Romania, Belgium, Greece, Portugal, Italy.

KEY
- NATO, 1957
- Warsaw Pact, 1957
- Iron Curtain

0   400 mi
0   400 km
Lambert Conformal
Conic projection

ICELAND

NORWAY

SWEDEN

FINLAND

SOVIET UNION

North Sea

UNITED KINGDOM

DENMARK

Baltic Sea

IRELAND

NETHERLANDS

POLAND

BELGIUM

EAST GERMANY

ATLANTIC OCEAN

WEST GERMANY

CZECHOSLOVAKIA

LUXEMBOURG

AUSTRIA

HUNGARY

FRANCE

SWITZERLAND

ROMANIA

Black Sea

YUGOSLAVIA

BULGARIA

ITALY

PORTUGAL

SPAIN

ALBANIA

GREECE

TURKEY

Mediterranean Sea

Below, Greek children receive food supplied by the Marshall Plan. At right, construction of the Berlin Wall begins in 1961.

The European Union

Long-standing hostility between Germany and France played a role in fueling Europe's wars. After World War II, West German and French leaders searched for a way to exist in peace.

Forming a Community In 1951, France and West Germany agreed to coordinate their coal and steel production. This would tie the countries economically and help to prevent future wars. Italy, Belgium, Luxembourg, and the Netherlands also signed the agreement.

In 1957, those six countries formed the European Economic Community, or Common Market. This was a free trade zone. It let manufactured goods and services move freely among the countries. Trade increased dramatically.

Toward a Unified Europe Six more countries had joined the Common Market by 1986. The Common Market nations signed the Maastricht Treaty in 1992. This treaty created the **European Union (EU),** an economic and political partnership. Starting in 1995, an open-borders policy allowed people to move freely among many EU nations.

In 2002, most EU nations adopted a single currency called the euro. A currency is a unit of money, like the dollar. Sharing a common currency made trade easier. However, some countries rejected the euro so that they could keep control of their money. In 2003, a treaty let Eastern European countries join the EU. By 2008, the EU had grown to include 27 nations.

Reading Check Why did West Germany and France form a common market?

Democracy Spreads East

By the 1980s, communism was failing. Weak Soviet and Eastern European economies could not compete with Western market economies.

Communism Fails In Eastern Europe, government officials planned what farms should grow and what factories should produce. Officials made decisions based on the state's wishes rather than people's needs. For example, they made tanks instead of home appliances. Second, people had no motive to work hard because the government limited their pay. As a result of these two problems, communist countries often had shortages of food and consumer goods.

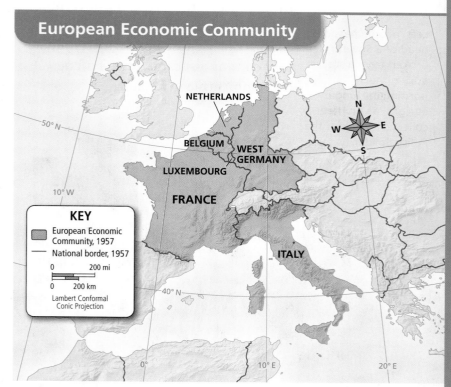

European Economic Community

NETHERLANDS
BELGIUM
WEST GERMANY
LUXEMBOURG
FRANCE
ITALY

50° N
10° W
40° N
0°
10° E
20° E

KEY
■ European Economic Community, 1957
— National border, 1957

0　　　200 mi
0　　　200 km
Lambert Conformal Conic Projection

In 1985, Mikhail Gorbachev became the new leader of the Soviet Union. Gorbachev was younger than other leaders and more open to change. In the late 1980s, Gorbachev began to loosen government control within the Soviet Union. He supported greater democracy, particularly in the Soviet satellites of Eastern Europe. Gorbachev also gave Eastern European countries more freedom to choose their own way.

A Democratic Revolution Spreads In 1980, a Polish shipyard workers' union called Solidarity went on strike. The Polish government granted some union demands and the union head, Lech Walesa (lek vah WEN suh), became a hero. Solidarity went on strike again in 1988. In response to the strike, the government agreed to hold free elections. Voters courageously chose Solidarity candidates over communist candidates, ending communist rule in Poland.

transfer, *n.,* a carrying over of something from one situation to another

myWorld Activity
Tear Down This Wall

Left, people pass the head of a Soviet ruler broken from a statue during the 1956 uprising in Hungary; at right, a volunteer collects money for the Polish Solidarity party.

Poland's example inspired other countries. In Czechoslovakia, thousands of people protested the communist government in 1989. In response to the protests, the government agreed to give up power. This peaceful <u>transfer</u> of power is known as the Velvet Revolution. In free elections later that year, Czechoslovakians elected writer Vaclav Havel (VAHTS lahv HAH vul) president. Havel described his people's experience.

> 66 People have passed through a very dark tunnel at the end of which there was a light of freedom. 99
> —Vaclav Havel, 1990

Romania overthrew its communist government in 1989, but its communist dictator killed many protesters before giving up power. Hungary's Communist Party went out of existence, and in 1990 the country elected a non-communist government. Bulgaria also held its first free elections in 1990.

Germany Reunifies During 1989, East Germans began protesting for democratic change. East Germany's communist government at first refused to make changes. The government then began to respond to some protester demands.

Finally, on November 9, 1989, East German border guards opened the gates of the Berlin Wall. East and West Germans rushed to greet each other.

Demands for reform led to free elections, which removed the communist government from power in 1989. A year later, on October 3, 1990, the two halves of Germany were reunified.

The Soviet Union Falls Nationalism and the desire for reform rocked the Soviet Union. In 1990, the Soviet republic of Lithuania demanded independence. The Soviet army invaded Lithuania.

Soviet citizens took to the streets to protest the invasion. The army refused to fight the people. In 1991, the Soviet Union broke apart into 15 new nations, including Moldova, Ukraine, Belarus, Lithuania, Latvia, and Estonia in Eastern Europe. The largest post-Soviet nation was Russia.

Reading Check How did Eastern Europe gain freedom from communism?

▲ In this 1990 political cartoon, Soviet leader Mikhail Gorbachev is pictured as Humpty Dumpty sitting on a crumbling wall with the symbol of the Soviet Union. *What does this cartoon mean?*

THE WALL COMES DOWN

During the late 1980s, communist governments across Eastern Europe followed the lead of the Soviet Union. They began to allow their opponents to speak more freely. Some scheduled free elections. East Germany's government resisted these changes. In the fall of 1989, however, East German people began to hold peaceful protests. The protesters said they wanted democracy. East German leaders knew that the Soviet Union was no longer willing to put down peaceful protests. When border guards opened the Berlin Wall on November 9, 1989, Germans on both sides began to knock it down.

❝ **We are the people!** ❞
—Chant of East German democracy protesters, 1989

405

▲ In 2004, terrorists bombed this train in Spain. In the inset, a London man reads about the 2005 terrorist bombings in that city.

Europe Faces Challenges

After reunifying, Germany struggled economically. East German factories were outdated and inefficent, and many went out of business. Unemployment soared in eastern Germany. Some citizens failed to adapt to the market economy, which required initiative and hard work.

Integrating the East After the collapse of communism, Europe worked to rebuild ties between East and West. The EU opened membership to Eastern European nations who could show that they had democratic governments and strong market economies. Most eastern nations had to make reforms before joining the EU. Even so, their economies often remained weak due to problems similar to those in eastern Germany.

Communist rule had not prepared people for democracy either. Many people in formerly communist lands did not trust their leaders. Government corruption had been widespread under communist rule and remained a problem.

International Issues In the late 1900s, a global economy developed as foreign trade and multinational corporations grew. The EU began to consider issues such as free trade with nonmember nations.

Incidents of international terrorism also scarred Europe. In 2004, the terrorist group al-Qaeda exploded bombs on commuter trains in Madrid, Spain, killing nearly 200. Afterward, European countries worked together to fight terrorism.

Immigration was another challenge. When Eastern European countries joined the EU, thousands of Eastern Europeans moved to western European countries for work. Many Western Europeans resented the newcomers. In addition, immigrants from Africa and Asia, some of them illegal, poured into Europe. Some Europeans began to fear that immigrants would take their jobs. Europeans and their leaders had to find ways to accommodate growing populations with customs and languages from outside of Europe.

Wind farms such as this one off the coast of Denmark make Europe a world leader in alternative energy sources.

Energy and the Environment Because of its industry, Europe has long fought pollution. For example, it has tried to reduce the air pollution that causes acid rain, which kills forests. The EU also signed the Kyoto Protocol, an agreement to reduce the emission of greenhouse gases that contribute to climate change.

Europe also aims to reduce its dependence on foreign oil. The EU is trying to reduce energy consumption, switch to cleaner forms of transportation, and use renewable energy such as wind and bio-fuels.

Reading Check **What economic challenges did Eastern Europe face after the collapse of communism?**

Section 5 Assessment

Key Terms

1. Using complete sentences, describe how each of the following terms relates to consequences from World War II: Cold War, Marshall Plan, Berlin Wall, European Union.

Key Ideas

2. What kind of partnership is the European Union?

3. Why did the Soviet Union set up communist states in Eastern Europe?

4. Which two countries began the movement to create a European Union and why?

5. How did change in the Soviet Union clear the way for democracy in Eastern Europe?

Think Critically

6. **Draw Conclusions** Why did Western Europe develop stronger economies than Eastern Europe?

7. **Make Decisions** What decisions do you think the German government could make to improve the economy of the former East Germany?

Essential Question

What makes a nation?

8. Why do you think East and West Germans still felt that they belonged to a single nation even after more than 40 years apart? Go to your Student Journal to record your answer.

Chapter Assessment

Key Terms and Ideas

1. **Discuss** How did **humanism** help lead to the Reformation?

2. **Summarize** In what ways did art change during the **Renaissance**?

3. **Compare and Contrast** What different routes did Portugal and Spain take when trying to find a way to reach Asia during the Age of Exploration?

4. **Recall** What Renaissance attitudes helped bring about the Scientific Revolution?

5. **Explain** How did the **Industrial Revolution** change where people lived?

6. **Compare and Contrast** What did the English Civil War and the **French Revolution** have in common?

7. **Explain** How did **World War I** change the map of central and eastern Europe?

8. **Describe** What emotions did East Germans and West Germans experience when the **Berlin Wall** was opened? How do you know?

Think Critically

9. **Draw Conclusions** How did geography contribute to Italy's role in beginning the Renaissance?

10. **Distinguish Between Fact and Opinion** Thomas Hobbes described life without strong government as "poor, nasty, brutish, and short." Is that a fact or an opinion? Explain.

11. **Identify Evidence** Use evidence from the text to describe how World War I was a global war.

12. **Drawing Inferences** How was the Cold War like a war even though the United States and the Soviet Union never engaged in battle?

13. **Problem Solving** Turn again to the last red heading in Section 5. Which of the problems described in the blue headings should be Europe's first priority? Support your answer with examples from the text.

Places to Know

For each place, write the letter from the map that shows its location.

14. Berlin

15. London

16. Rome

17. Romania

18. Belgium

19. Constantinople

20. Portugal

21. **Estimate** Using the scale bar, estimate how far fighter pilots flew between Berlin and London during World War II.

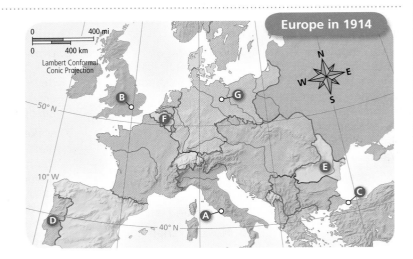

Europe in 1914

Essential Question

myWorld Chapter Activity

Technology Then and Now Follow your teacher's instructions to examine different kinds of technology that developed in early modern Europe. This technology may be related to advances in science or medicine, warfare, industry, or transportation. At the time, these inventions were cutting-edge technology. Make an illustrated poster linking these examples of past technology to current examples of technology.

21st Century Learning

Communication

Summarize Write an essay arguing for or against adding new Eastern European members to the European Union. Include
- the benefits of adding these members
- the drawbacks of adding these members
- the economic and political impact of adding these members
- your opinion
- two reasons in support of your opinion

Document-Based Questions

Success Tracker™
Online at myworldgeography.com

Use your knowledge of early modern Europe and Documents A and B to answer Questions 1–3.

Document A

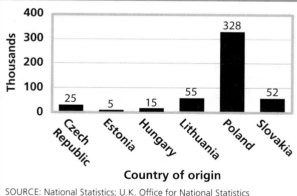

Eastern European Workers Registered in the United Kingdom, 2004–2006

Thousands (y-axis): 0, 100, 200, 300, 400

Czech Republic: 25
Estonia: 5
Hungary: 15
Lithuania: 55
Poland: 328
Slovakia: 52

Country of origin

SOURCE: National Statistics; U.K. Office for National Statistics

1. Which country shown here had the most workers registered in the United Kingdom?

A Estonia

B Latvia

C Poland

D Slovakia

Document B

" It's my dream to return to Poland, but not for 30 percent of my salary. So many have gone west [that] to return, they might not have to receive equal pay, but certainly more than now."

—Jacek Cukrowski,
"Where have all our migrants gone?
Eastern Europe wants them back,"
Christian Science Monitor

2. What would convince Cukrowski to return to Poland?

A more salary than he earns in the West

B a better salary than Polish workers earn now

C exactly the same salary that Polish workers earn

D 30 percent of the salary that he earns in the West

3. Writing Task If Eastern Europeans keep moving to Western Europe for jobs, how might Eastern Europe's economy be affected? Explain.

myworldgeography.com Self-Test

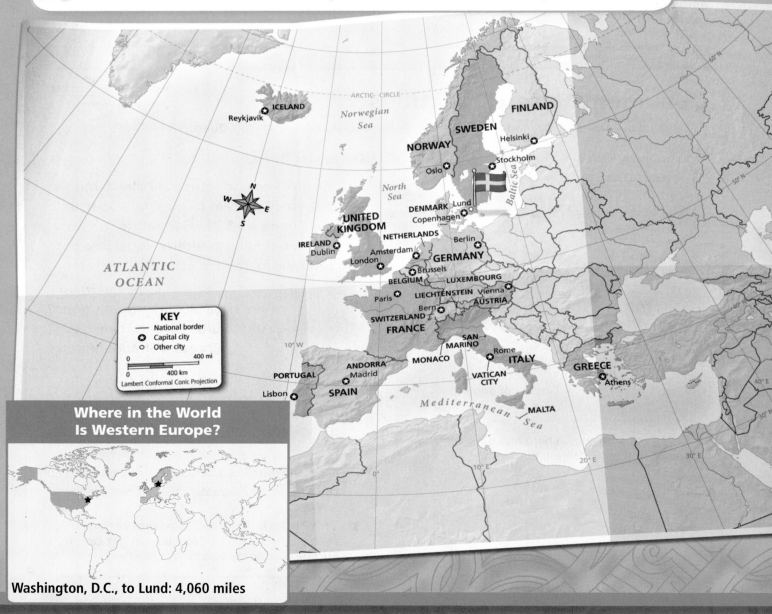

Chapter 10

Western Europe

? Essential Question

Is it better to be independent or interdependent?

ARCTIC CIRCLE

ICELAND
Reykjavík

Norwegian Sea

FINLAND

SWEDEN
Helsinki

NORWAY
Oslo   Stockholm

Baltic Sea

North Sea

DENMARK Lund
Copenhagen

UNITED
KINGDOM

IRELAND
Dublin
London

NETHERLANDS
Amsterdam
Brussels
BELGIUM

Berlin
GERMANY

LUXEMBOURG
LIECHTENSTEIN Vienna
Paris   AUSTRIA
Bern
SWITZERLAND
FRANCE

ATLANTIC
OCEAN

KEY
— National border
⊛ Capital city
○ Other city

0 _____ 400 mi
0 _____ 400 km
Lambert Conformal Conic Projection

SAN
MARINO
Rome
ANDORRA   MONACO   ITALY
Madrid   GREECE
PORTUGAL   VATICAN   Athens
CITY
Lisbon   SPAIN
Mediterranean Sea   MALTA

Where in the World Is Western Europe?

Washington, D.C., to Lund: 4,060 miles

my Story

Europe at Her Doorstep

In this section, you'll read about Yasmin, a young woman living in Sweden who has family in Spain and Pakistan. What does Yasmin's story tell you about life in Western Europe today?

Explore the Essential Question
- at **my** worldgeography.com
- using the **myWorld Chapter Activity**
- with the **Student Journal**

By Jake Johnson for myWorld Online

Yasmin straps on her dancing shoes. She glances in the mirror, adjusts her dress, and taps her way into the dance studio. With a rose in her hair and a colorful shawl stretched between her hands, Yasmin practices flamenco, a traditional Spanish dance. Inside the studio, the music makes Yasmin think of the warm Mediterranean while Sweden's winter winds blow outside.

Yasmin was born in Madrid, Spain, but she lives with her family in the coastal town of Bjärred in southern Sweden. Her father, Asif, is Pakistani and Spanish. Her mother, Monica, is Finnish and Swedish. Yasmin uses both of her parents' last names as a part of her heritage.

Yasmin's father Asif left Spain to work in Sweden in 1995. At that time, Sweden had just become a member of the European Union (EU). EU member countries allow people to move across borders without passports or complicated documents. Asif decided to try life in Sweden where more jobs were available. So, at age six Yasmin, along with her sister Sabina and brother Daniel, moved to frosty Sweden—a completely different world from Spain.

Yasmin remembers that she wasn't ready for the change in cultures. "At first, I was very different from the Swedish girls.

my worldgeography.com On Assignment

Yasmin stands in front of Lund's medieval cathedral.

Yasmin with her father and mother

In general, Swedes are much more quiet than Spaniards. I spoke very loud . . . I was a Spanish girl, and I yelled and ran around everywhere. I was more like the Swedish boys."

At home, Yasmin speaks Spanish with her father and Swedish with her mother. Everyone also speaks English. "The language that we speak is similar to the foods we eat. It is very mixed up," laughs Yasmin. She adds, "Sometimes we mix up our languages, even though our parents say we shouldn't. It's just easier to find the word you are looking for in another language. We even mix up languages within one sentence—but we all understand each other."

Even the family meal is a cultural medley. "We make it up as we go," explains Asif as he dices potatoes. He is making a Pakistani dish called alu gosht, a sort of a beef stew. Yasmin explains that this alu gosht includes Spanish olive oil, Swedish potatoes, and Chinese rice. The olive oil comes from the family's own olive trees in Spain!

Yasmin enjoys cooking and shopping at the farmers' market.

Yasmin attends classes in linguistics at Lund University.

The strait of Öresund separates Sweden from Denmark.

One of Yasmin's favorite possessions is her video camera. She has made several videos, including many that documented her trip to meet family in Pakistan. Music is also important to Yasmin, and she can play the piano, the flute, and the guitar.

Most days, Yasmin rides the bus to Lund to attend university classes. Lund is a medieval city full of gothic architecture and winding streets. Higher education is free in Sweden, so students from all over the world come to Lund University. Yasmin has many interests such as film and architecture, but she hasn't decided on a major.

One of Yasmin's new hobbies is tae kwon do, a form of martial arts that developed in Korea. At a dojo (a martial arts training school) near the university, she puts on a white uniform and her blue belt. Barefoot, Yasmin and a partner practice a complex routine designed for self-defense.

"Tae kwon do has a philosophy of peace," Yasmin says, "that teaches me to have the right mindset in order to be able to do the sport correctly."

Back in Bjärred, Yasmin walks along the beach. It's cold and windy, but beautiful. Bjärred is famous for its 500-meter pier into the strait of Öresund. It is the longest pier in the country. At the end of the pier is the Bjärred Kallbadhus (bath house). In the winter, people dive from the sauna there into the icy waters of the Öresund. Walking over the snow-covered dunes, Yasmin thinks about how much she cherishes the blazing sun of Spain. At the same time, she looks forward to ice-skating near her home in Sweden. Whether she's ice-skating, studying, or making a video, Yasmin has many choices, since Europe is at her doorstep.

Meet the Journalist

Name Jake Johnson
Favorite Moment Dinner with Yasmin's family

→ **myStory Video**

Join Yasmin as she shows you about life in her city.

413

Key Ideas

- The landmass of Eurasia includes the continents of Europe and Asia.
- The climate of Western Europe is primarily temperate, although some areas are near the Arctic Circle.
- Western Europeans are mostly urban dwellers.

Key Terms • peninsula • plain • glacier • loess • tundra • taiga • pollution

→ **Visual Glossary**

Reading Skill: Label an Outline Map Take notes using the outline map in your journal.

A hillside village on the Greek island of Santorini; below, young women from Mykonos, Greece

Physical Features

The **peninsula** of Europe is attached to Asia, a continent that lies east of the Ural Mountains. A peninsula is land almost surrounded by water but still attached to the mainland. Geographers call this huge landmass composed of Europe and Asia *Eurasia*.

The three main landforms that cover Western Europe are **plains** (flat or gently rolling lands), uplands, and mountains. Most people live on plains. The North European Plain stretches from the Atlantic Ocean to the Urals, making it one of the largest level land areas on earth.

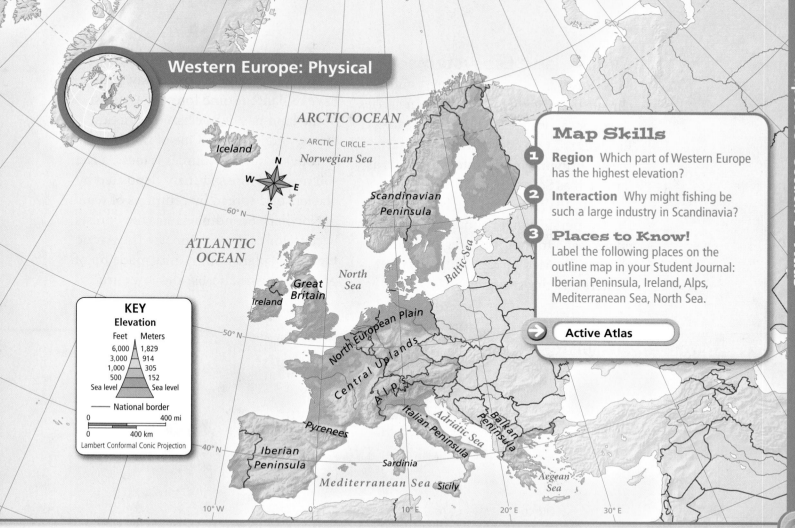

Western Europe: Physical

ARCTIC OCEAN

ARCTIC CIRCLE

Iceland

Norwegian Sea

Scandinavian Peninsula

ATLANTIC OCEAN

60° N

50° N

40° N

North Sea

Great Britain

Ireland

Baltic Sea

North European Plain

Central Uplands

Alps

Pyrenees

Iberian Peninsula

Italian Peninsula

Adriatic Sea

Balkan Peninsula

Sardinia

Sicily

Mediterranean Sea

Aegean Sea

10° W   0°   10° E   20° E   30° E

KEY
Elevation

Feet	Meters
6,000	1,829
3,000	914
1,000	305
500	152
Sea level	Sea level

—— National border

0   400 mi
0   400 km
Lambert Conformal Conic Projection

Map Skills

1 **Region** Which part of Western Europe has the highest elevation?

2 **Interaction** Why might fishing be such a large industry in Scandinavia?

3 **Places to Know!**
Label the following places on the outline map in your Student Journal: Iberian Peninsula, Ireland, Alps, Mediterranean Sea, North Sea.

→ Active Atlas

Most of northern Europe lies on the Scandinavian Peninsula, between the Arctic Ocean, the North Sea, and the Baltic Sea. The west coast of Norway features dramatic fiords, or long, narrow, deep inlets of the sea.

The Central Uplands in the center of southern Europe consist of mountains and plateaus, or raised areas of level land bordered by steep slopes.

The Alps stretch from France to Eastern Europe. Streams formed by **glaciers,** slow-moving masses of ice and snow, flow out of the Alps. These streams feed the Rhine River and the Danube River.

To the south is the warmer Mediterranean region. This region is named for the Mediterranean Sea nearby. Days are sunny and the climate is generally temperate. Here the land is mountainous peninsulas with narrow, <u>fertile</u> plains.

Active volcanoes may be found in Italy, Greece, and Iceland. At times, volcanic activity has led to earthquakes and tsunamis (tidal waves). Since ancient times, earthquakes have been widespread in the Mediterranean countries.

Reading Check What landform divides Europe from Asia?

fertile, *adj.,* rich in nutrients; able to grow many plants

Climate and Ecosystems

Most Western Europeans enjoy a mild climate because the Atlantic Ocean carries warm ocean water from the tropics to Europe's western coast. This water warms the air, bringing mild winters to places as far north as Scandinavia.

Most of Western Europe is located in the temperate zone, although its northern edges reach to the Arctic region. Land close to the Mediterranean Sea has wet winters and dry summers.

In ancient times, forests covered most of Western Europe. Today, people have replanted some forests, but most of the land has been cleared for cities, farms, and industry. One of north central Europe's natural resources is **loess,** a rich soil made of fine sediment deposited by glaciers and spread by centuries of wind.

Northern Scandinavia has few forests because of its Arctic climate. The Arctic **tundra** is a plant community made up of grasses, mosses, herbs, and low shrubs.

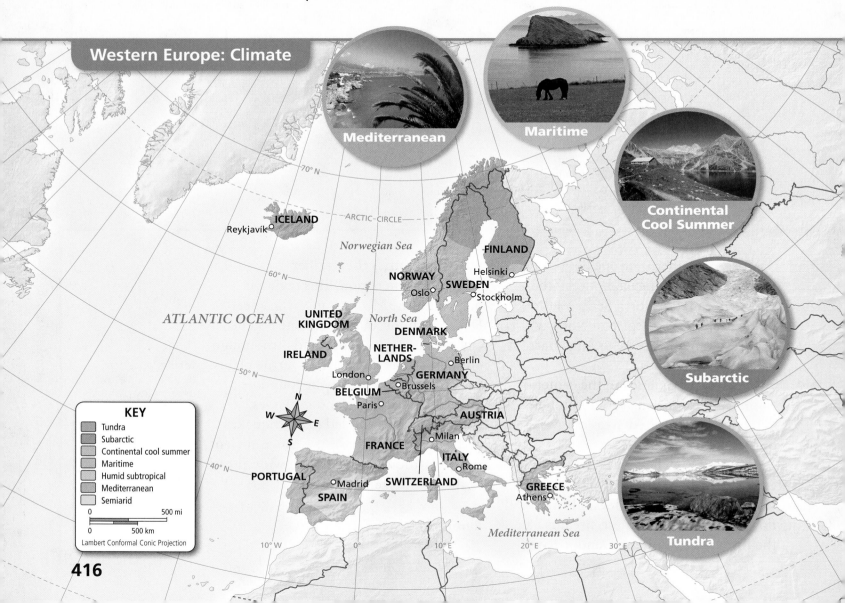

Western Europe: Climate

Mediterranean

Maritime

Continental Cool Summer

Subarctic

Tundra

ICELAND
Reykjavík

ARCTIC CIRCLE

Norwegian Sea

FINLAND

70° N

60° N

NORWAY
Oslo

SWEDEN
Stockholm

Helsinki

ATLANTIC OCEAN

UNITED KINGDOM

North Sea

DENMARK

IRELAND

NETHER-LANDS

Berlin

London

GERMANY

50° N

BELGIUM
Brussels

Paris

AUSTRIA

FRANCE

Milan

ITALY
Rome

40° N

PORTUGAL
Madrid

SWITZERLAND

GREECE
Athens

SPAIN

Mediterranean Sea

KEY
- Tundra
- Subarctic
- Continental cool summer
- Maritime
- Humid subtropical
- Mediterranean
- Semiarid

0   500 mi
0   500 km
Lambert Conformal Conic Projection

10° W   0°   10° E   20° E   30° E

416

Trees are unable to grow here because it is too cold and dry. The **taiga,** a thick forest of coniferous trees, lies south of this zone. It extends from Scandinavia east across Eurasia for thousands of miles.

Mediterranean vegetation is a mix of small trees, forests, shrubs, and grasses. Trees and shrubs here must be hardy enough to survive the dry summer season.

Reading Check Contrast taiga vegetation with that of the Mediterranean region.

A Diverse Continent

In general, the nations of Western Europe have a high standard of living. Almost all Western Europeans can read and write. This region has strong education systems. There is a direct connection between good education and a high standard of living.

Across Western Europe, people speak a variety of different languages. About half of the people in Europe speak English and their native languages or <u>dialects.</u>

dialect, *n.,* a regional variety of a language

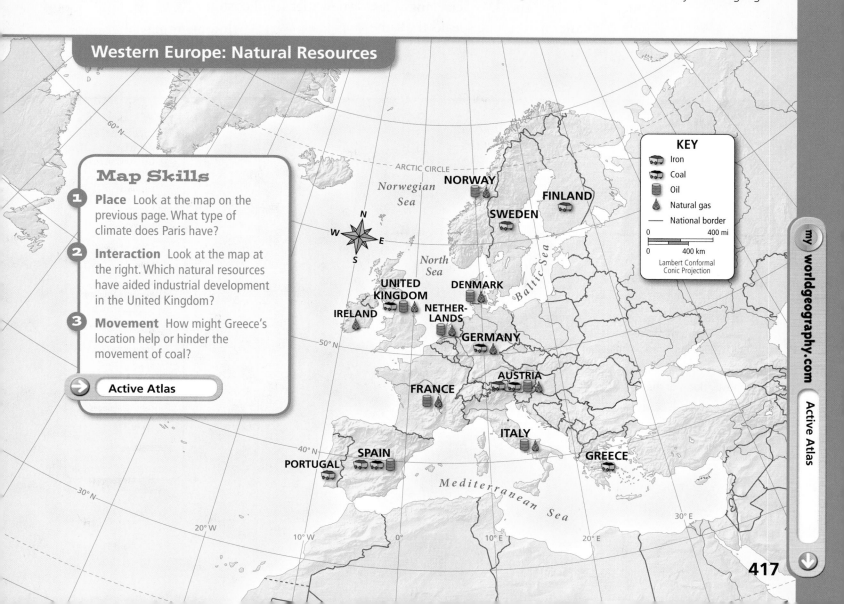

Western Europe: Natural Resources

Map Skills

1 **Place** Look at the map on the previous page. What type of climate does Paris have?

2 **Interaction** Look at the map at the right. Which natural resources have aided industrial development in the United Kingdom?

3 **Movement** How might Greece's location help or hinder the movement of coal?

Active Atlas

KEY

- Iron
- Coal
- Oil
- Natural gas
- National border

0   400 mi
0   400 km
Lambert Conformal
Conic Projection

my **worldgeography.com** Active Atlas

Language is part of culture. Sometimes, language unites those from different cultures. For example, when North Africans move to France, they encounter a different culture. But many North Africans speak French. This makes the transition to a new life a little easier.

When European Union (EU) leaders meet to discuss economics or energy policy, they often conduct business in English. This helps make discussion and decision-making easier. The European Union has 27 member nations and 23 official languages, but it is easier if everyone speaks the same language.

Europe is a region of many different cultures. For 2,000 years, Christianity has been the dominant religion. A large Jewish population has also lived there continuously. Since World War II, people from around the world have moved to Europe for jobs and education. They brought different religions, languages, and customs. When people move to a new country, they often take on parts of its cultures. At the same time, newcomers have introduced Western Europeans to new ideas and customs.

Reading Check How many official languages are there in the European Union?

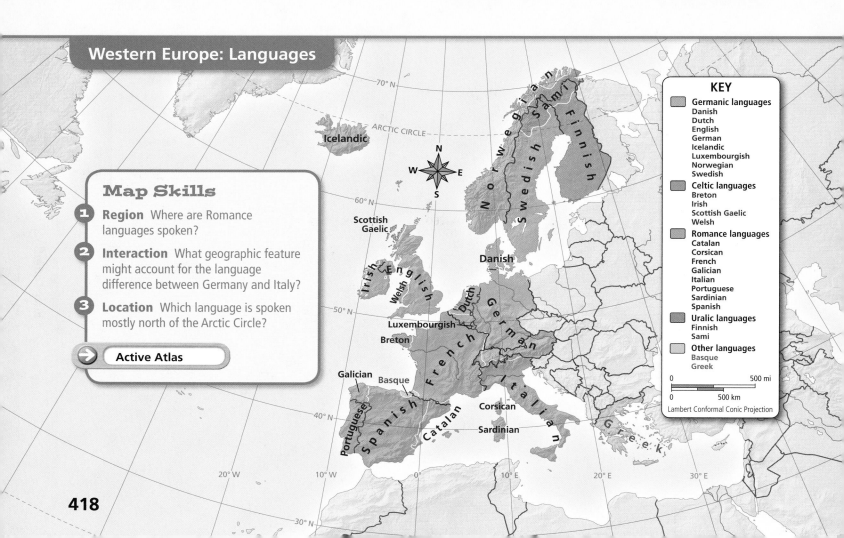

Western Europe: Languages

Map Skills

1 **Region** Where are Romance languages spoken?

2 **Interaction** What geographic feature might account for the language difference between Germany and Italy?

3 **Location** Which language is spoken mostly north of the Arctic Circle?

→ **Active Atlas**

KEY

Germanic languages
Danish
Dutch
English
German
Icelandic
Luxembourgish
Norwegian
Swedish

Celtic languages
Breton
Irish
Scottish Gaelic
Welsh

Romance languages
Catalan
Corsican
French
Galician
Italian
Portuguese
Sardinian
Spanish

Uralic languages
Finnish
Sami

Other languages
Basque
Greek

0   500 mi
0   500 km
Lambert Conformal Conic Projection

Where People Live and Work

Western Europe's geography shapes where and how people live. This region is largely urban and industrialized.

In Western Europe, most of the population lives within 100 miles of the coast. This is because being close to water offers many opportunities for trade. Europe's major rivers, the Danube and the Rhine, carry goods and people. They also carry large quantities of water. Western European highways often follow river routes to connect towns and cities that have grown along these rivers.

In northern Europe, people live near the coast. Even in Arctic climates, being near the ocean offers milder weather. Inland, <u>vast</u> empty areas separate towns and villages. Settlement is sparse because these areas are cold and dry.

In Southern and Central Europe, population is more evenly spaced. In the temperate climate of Italy, population is densest near the coast. People also live in large numbers inland as well.

In general, people do not choose to live in high mountains and marshy wetlands. Instead, they tend to settle in low, sunny, warm places close to water. Natural resources such as water, minerals, and rich farmland also attract people.

A recent report by the European Union addressed climate change trends. This report noted changes such as the melting of glaciers in the Arctic Ocean and drier conditions in the Mediterranean area of Southern Europe. Changes in climate may affect crop yields, water levels in rivers, and human health.

As a highly industrialized region, Western Europe has experienced air and water **pollution.** Pollution is harmful material released into the environment. One result of air pollution is acid rain. This occurs when exhaust from industries mixes with moisture in the air. This precipitation then falls as acid rain. It has damaged historic buildings, bridges, cathedrals, and monuments across Western Europe. Over the years, acid rain has also damaged forests and freshwater lakes.

Water pollution may result from chemical spills. A chemical spill is an accidental release of toxic or dangerous materials.

vast, *adj.,* very great in size, number, or quantity

myWorld Activity
Danube Cleanup

ENVIRONMENTAL CHALLENGES IN WALES

Over a period of 30 years, this forest has been destroyed by acid rain, due to the air pollution from nearby industrial plants.

Workers spread chemicals to clean up an oil spill on a Welsh beach. *What might be likely causes for the pollution shown in each photograph?*

my worldgeography.com Active Atlas

419

One of Western Europe's busiest waterways, the Rhine River, was once one of the region's most polluted. From the 1950s to the 1970s, industrial waste flowed into the river. Fish disappeared from it and swimmers avoided it. A cleanup effort was launched, but in 1986, a chemical spill reversed years of effort. A chemical factory fire in Switzerland led to 30 tons of toxic chemicals being washed into the river as firefighters fought the blaze. Within 10 days, the pollution traveled the length of the Rhine to the North Sea. Today, the Rhine is much cleaner and fish are returning to swim in it again.

Reading Check How have Europe's coasts and waterways affected settlement?

The Urban Continent

Europe has been called the "urban continent" because so many people live in urban areas. An urban area may include a city and its surrounding suburbs. In the United Kingdom, for example, almost nine out of ten people live in cities.

Most countries in Western Europe have dense populations clustered in small land areas. To preserve land for growing food, for forests, and for recreation, most countries set strict limits on the expansion of cities and suburbs. This means that the region's cities tend to be tightly packed with people. Very few Europeans live in single-family houses with yards. Instead, most live in apartment buildings.

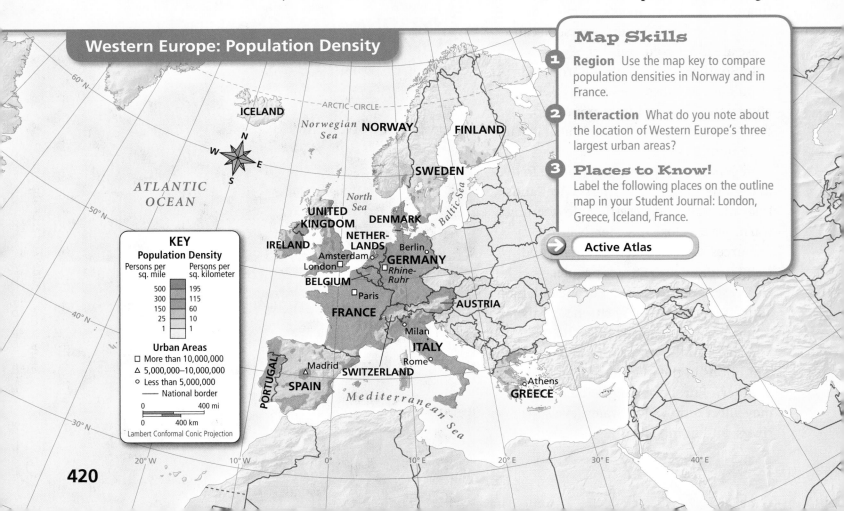

Western Europe: Population Density

KEY
Population Density

Persons per sq. mile	Persons per sq. kilometer
500	195
300	115
150	60
25	10
1	1

Urban Areas
☐ More than 10,000,000
△ 5,000,000–10,000,000
○ Less than 5,000,000
— National border

0   400 mi
0   400 km
Lambert Conformal Conic Projection

Map Skills

1 **Region** Use the map key to compare population densities in Norway and in France.

2 **Interaction** What do you note about the location of Western Europe's three largest urban areas?

3 **Places to Know!** Label the following places on the outline map in your Student Journal: London, Greece, Iceland, France.

→ **Active Atlas**

In order to reach their jobs, schools, and other activities, most Europeans use public transportation. Over time, urban areas have built up dense public transportation networks. Train, subway, trolley, and bus services connect neighborhoods and cities all over Europe.

Germany's Rhine-Ruhr region is one of Europe's largest urban areas. Five cities there have more than 500,000 inhabitants. Contrast that with Greenland, a territory of Denmark and the world's largest island. Greenland is six times as large as all of Germany, but has a population of only about 58,000 people.

European governments favor public transportation over driving by setting high taxes on gasoline. Gasoline in Europe can cost twice as much as gasoline in the United States. While most families in Western Europe have a car, they may use it only for occasional trips to the countryside or to a regional shopping center.

Reading Check Why are Europe's cities so crowded?

Germany's Rhine-Ruhr Region

KEY
- Urban area
- Autobahn
- Other highway
- Railway
- River
- ○ City

0   10 mi
0   10 km

Map Skills

The Rhine-Ruhr region is a transportation and industrial hub for the entire continent. What are the different forms of transportation available?

Active Atlas

Section 1 Assessment

Key Terms

1. Use each of the following terms in a sentence: peninsula, loess, tundra, pollution.

Key Ideas

2. What is Eurasia?

3. How does geography affect settlement patterns?

4. Why do some countries restrict urban growth?

Think Critically

5. **Compare and Contrast** Look at the physical map and the climate map in this section. Why is there more farming in France than in Scandinavia?

6. **Draw Conclusions** How does keeping a river like the Rhine clean benefit Western Europe?

Essential Question

Is it better to be independent or interdependent?

7. Look at the languages map in this section. Do you think the number of languages spoken by EU members helps or harms Western Europe? Go to your Student Journal to record your answer.

Northwestern Europe Today

Key Ideas

- The United Kingdom has a long history of democracy.
- Scandinavian nations offer a cradle-to-grave system of public services.
- Many people in Northwestern Europe favor limited ties with the European Union.

Key Terms
- constitutional monarchy
- Parliament
- cradle-to-grave system
- gross domestic product (GDP)
- cultural borrowing

 Visual Glossary

 Reading Skill: Sequence Take notes using the graphic organizer in your journal.

Beefeaters are ceremonial guards at the Tower of London. ▼

You might be surprised to learn that England has a queen, yet it also has a long history of democracy. During the summers in northern Scandinavia, there is sunshine at midnight. How can this be? The nations of Northwestern Europe are worth a closer look.

The United Kingdom and Ireland

The United Kingdom, or Britain, is an island nation made up of several regions. England, Wales, and Scotland are located on the largest island, Great Britain. Northern Ireland, on the nearby smaller island of Ireland, is also part of the United Kingdom. Most of this island is the independent nation of Ireland.

British Government You have read about King John signing the Magna Carta in 1215. This document limited the power of the king and gave rights to his people. It was the beginning of democratic government in England. Today, the British government is a **constitutional monarchy.** This means the monarch is the ceremonial leader, but Parliament makes the laws. Unlike the U.S. Constitution, the British constitution is not a single document, but a group of laws and court decisions. The symbolic head is Queen Elizabeth II, who symbolizes Britain's nationhood.

The British legislature, or **Parliament,** is located in London, England. It is made up of the House of Lords and the House of Commons. At one time, members of the House of Lords inherited their seats. Today, Parliament is moving toward a combination of elected and appointed members in both houses. These members are composed of high-ranking clergy, judges, and national leaders. The head of the majority party in the House of Commons is the prime minister, the true head of the British government.

Since the 1990s, some lawmaking power has moved from a national to a regional level. Scotland has its own Parliament and government that handles laws specific to that country. The Welsh National Assembly can pass laws that directly affect Wales. Northern Ireland also has a separate assembly with its own powers.

The official language of the United Kingdom is English. Some people also speak Welsh, Irish, or Scottish Gaelic. Thousands of immigrants come to Britain every year. Many come from countries that were once part of the British empire.

Prosperity and Partnerships Britain and Ireland both have a high standard of living and strong economies. In the past, Britain owed its wealth to iron and steel, textiles, and shipbuilding. Today, Britain is part of a global economy. The British work with international partners in finance and banking, high-technology fields, and service industries. Entrepreneurs, or people who start businesses, have had much success in Northwestern Europe.

One Nation, Four Countries

Known as the United Kingdom of Great Britain and Northern Ireland, these four countries act together on matters such as foreign policy. However, they act independently with regard to EU involvement and legal issues.

Map Skills

How might giving more power to regional governments strengthen the United Kingdom?

→ Active Atlas

SCOTLAND

NORTHERN IRELAND

WALES   ENGLAND

The United Kingdom and Ireland also benefit from being in the European Union. The European Union (EU) is an organization of European nations that promotes free movement of goods and people across borders. Ireland and Britain can trade with other member nations in an open market. There are no tariffs, or taxes, on goods imported from other member nations. Without tariffs, goods and services move freely. The EU has its own <u>currency,</u> the euro. Ireland uses the euro, but Britain does not. The British currency is the pound.

currency, *n.,* a system of money, especially the bills and coins, used in a country

A Tourist Destination Britain is the world's sixth most popular travel destination. Many people visit Britain because of their <u>heritage</u>. Americans, for example, often travel to the United Kingdom to revisit the homes of their English, Irish, Scottish, or Welsh ancestors.

Tourists flock to famous places such as London's Buckingham Palace. They also visit ancient and historic sites such as Stonehenge and Shakespeare's hometown, Stratford-upon-Avon. Ireland draws visitors to its prosperous cities and green rural areas. Fishing is popular in Scotland's rivers. History lovers visit Welsh castles and villages.

heritage, *n.,* something possessed as a result of one's natural situation or birth

Reading Check **How has EU membership promoted economic development in Britain and Ireland?**

The Scandinavian Countries

Denmark, Finland, Iceland, Norway, and Sweden make up the area known as Scandinavia. Life near the Arctic Circle is chilly, but full of variety.

Cradle-to-Grave Benefits Sweden, Norway, and Denmark are constitutional monarchies much like the United Kingdom. Each monarch is mainly a symbolic leader. Political decisions are made by an elected parliament. Finland is a democratic republic with a president. All are members of the EU except Norway. Norway has voted to remain outside the EU for several reasons. Some Norwegians feel that the EU's structure is not democratic. They also want to keep Norway's economic and political freedom.

The Cradle-to-Grave System

This system of social services originated after World War II in response to postwar hardships. Funding for the system comes from high taxes, such as payroll taxes and sales tax. These taxes fund benefits such as universal healthcare, education, and pensions.

Chart Skills

How does this diagram show advantages and disadvantages of the cradle-to-grave system?

→ **Data Discovery**

**myWorld Activity
Cradle to Grave?**

PAYCHECK

Monthly pay $5,000.00
Payroll taxes $2,600.00
TAKE HOME $2,400.00

Sales Tax

Social Services
Pensions
Healthcare
Unemployment
College tuition

The Scandinavian governments have a **cradle-to-grave system,** a system of basic services for citizens at every stage of life. It covers healthcare, education, and retirement. Benefits are funded through taxes. Because people believe this system is important, they are willing to pay high taxes for it. In Sweden, people pay on average almost 60 percent of their income in taxes. Clothing and food are also expensive due to taxes. On the other hand, healthcare costs and rents are low.

Fish, Forests, and Phones In the past, the Scandinavian countries depended on farming. Agriculture and dairy farming are still important in Denmark, where the climate is warmer. Today, the economies of these countries rely on multinational corporations, high-technology industries, and exports. Finland, for example, is a leading manufacturer of mobile telephones.

Scandinavia's geography also affects the economy. Miles of coastline and acres of forests supply the fishing and lumber industries. Oil production in the North Sea also helps this region maintain a high standard of living. Membership in the EU opens Denmark, Finland, and Sweden to free trade and global markets.

Located near the Arctic Circle, the northernmost Scandinavian cities have what are called white nights. From May to July, the sun appears on the horizon for almost 24 hours a day. This is because the northern hemisphere is tilted toward the sun at that time of year.

Reading Check Why do people in Sweden pay high taxes?

SCANDINAVIA: LAND OF THE VIKINGS

The gods, giants, and elves of ancient Scandinavian myths remain popular today. The adventures of the Norse warriors known as the Vikings left marks on territory from England to Russia. In modern times, Scandinavia has been known for its famous scientists and artists. These nations also have a long record of gender equality and human rights. *Why might people build replicas of ancient ships today?*

Danish carpenter Ole Kirk Christiansen invented one of the world's most popular children's toys. ▼

The dala horse was once a toy, but has become a symbol of Sweden. ▼

Modern-day replica of a Viking ship ▶

my worldgeography.com   Data Discovery

Life in Northwestern Europe

Aspects of daily life in northwestern Europe are changing rapidly.

Living With Technology With almost universal access to the Internet, cellphones, and television, faraway places are much nearer. Life has become more fast-paced. Technology has changed how people work in surprising ways. Danish farmers use modern technology to produce healthier food. Scientists in Norway have discovered new ways to preserve water supplies.

Finland uses more than 3 percent of its **gross domestic product** for technology research and development. Gross domestic product (GDP) is the total value of all goods and services produced and sold in a country in a year.

transportation, *n.,* a means of carrying people or goods from one place to another

In this region, finding ways to save energy is important. Due to its cold climate, Finland uses a great deal of energy for heating. One way to reduce energy use is driving cars with better gas mileage. Finland has passed a law raising taxes for cars with poor gas mileage. The owners of cars with higher gas mileage pay less in taxes.

Living in Cities Many of the large cities in this region are capital cities: London, Dublin, Copenhagen, Oslo, Stockholm, and Helsinki. These cities are centuries old and rich in history and culture.

London has museums and palaces, and Stockholm has historic city squares. In Dublin, people lunch at pubs, while in Helsinki they relax in saunas. Most people use public transportation rather than their cars for daily travels.

A United Kingdom woman paints figures for a company that exports tableware and gifts. ▼

Chart Skills

Compare Norway's GDP with the world average.

→ **Data Discovery**

GDP per Person, Northwestern Europe

GDP per Person (thousands): Iceland, Ireland, Norway, United Kingdom, World Average

SOURCE: *CIA World Factbook, 2008*

Living Together Northwestern Europe is a region of many ethnic groups due to a large immigrant population. Some immigrants have lived there for generations. Others have come more recently.

The EU's open-border policy has also let people move between nations. In this chapter's myStory, you read about how the policy lets Yasmin move easily about Europe for family trips and education.

It is common to see people from the Caribbean, India, Pakistan, Turkey, or Somalia here. These newcomers face many challenges. To find jobs, they must learn how to get around. They may have to learn a language different from their parents' language.

Some immigrants have religious beliefs that <u>conflict</u> with local customs. For example, there is a significant Muslim population in Norway. Muslims have certain religious beliefs about food preparation. These beliefs can lead to higher prices in markets and restaurants—whether or not customers are Muslim.

▲ This London restaurant owner offers food from India, where he grew up.

conflict, *v.,* to clash or to be in opposition

Immigrants may also take part in **cultural borrowing,** an exchange that takes place when groups come into contact and share ideas, language, customs—and even food. Many Londoners enjoy eating at Indian or Ethiopian restaurants. In Copenhagen, people have grown to love Turkish coffee or food that mixes traditional Danish ingredients with those of France or Japan.

Reading Check What is one way that Finland tries to reduce energy use?

Section 2 Assessment

Key Terms

1. Use the following terms to describe Northwestern Europe today: constitutional monarchy, cradle-to-grave system, cultural borrowing.

Key Ideas

2. How has a long history of democracy affected Northwestern Europe?

3. Describe how technology has changed daily life for Northwestern Europe.

4. What sorts of challenges do immigrants face in a new country?

Think Critically

5. **Draw Conclusions** How does the EU open market benefit member nations?

6. **Categorize** Name three industries that developed because of Scandinavia's geography.

? Essential Question

Is it better to be independent or interdependent?

7. What are the benefits of cultural borrowing? What might be some of the challenges? Go to your Student Journal to record your answer.

my **worldgeography.com** Data Discovery

West Central Europe Today

Key Ideas
- The countries of West Central Europe have strong international partnerships.
- The rich cultural heritage of West Central Europe makes tourism one of the region's largest industries.
- People in most of the countries in this region favor strong ties with the European Union.

Key Terms • privatization • gross national product (GNP) • polders • reunification

 **Visual Glossary**

Reading Skill: Identify Main Ideas and Details Take notes using the graphic organizer in your journal.

France's Chartres Cathedral is a masterpiece of medieval Gothic architecture. ▼

Rich in culture, the nations of West Central Europe include some of the largest and most prosperous on the continent. Most are members of the European Union, an organization that plays a major role in life in this region.

At the Center of the European Union

West Central Europe includes Austria, Belgium, France, Germany, Liechtenstein, Luxembourg, Monaco, the Netherlands, and Switzerland. All have joined the European Union (EU) except Switzerland, Liechtenstein, and Monaco. Why have some countries joined the EU while others have not?

EU membership is similar to playing on a school sports team. Each team member has different abilities or strengths, but the team works best when its members work together.

Just as not all students take part in sports, not every country in Europe is a member of the EU. Some countries do not meet certain guidelines. Some want to be members in certain ways, but not in others. Germany and France are the largest EU countries by population. They make up almost one third of the entire EU population. Some critics say that larger countries have more power in the EU government. If a country has more power, it can influence EU laws in its own favor. However, the EU has policies in place so that members work together.

Reading Check How might a larger nation influence laws in an alliance such as the European Union?

 Culture Close-up

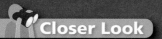

Closer Look

UNDERSTANDING THE EUROPEAN UNION

In the 1950s, European leaders wanted to ensure that world war would never happen again. In 1957, Belgium, Germany, France, Italy, Luxembourg, and the Netherlands formed the European Economic Community (EEC). Their main goal was economic unity through a single market.

The EEC later became the EU, which today consists of 27 member nations. The EU works to expand prosperity, to spread democracy, and to defend human rights and the rule of law. The EU single market system has removed trade barriers and raised standards of living. However, the EU has drawn criticism over powers given to unelected officials.

THINK CRITICALLY What are some advantages to having a single currency throughout several nations?

Council of Ministers (represents national governments)

European Union

European Parliament (represents the people)

European Commission (represents collective EU interests)

◄ The euro is the EU currency.

The European Union, 2009

KEY
- ▨ European Union member states
- ── National border
- ┄┄ Disputed border

Finland
Sweden
Estonia
Latvia
Lithuania
United Kingdom
Denmark
Ireland
Netherlands
Germany
Poland
Czech Republic
Slovakia
Belgium
Luxembourg
Austria
Hungary
France
Romania
Slovenia
Bulgaria
Italy
Portugal
Spain
Greece
Cyprus
Malta

Before France adopted the euro, signs showed prices in the national currency (French francs) as well as euro. ▶

Main Aims of the EU

- **To form a closer union among Europeans**
- **To remove trade barriers**
- **To improve the environment**
- **To fight terrorism, crime, and illegal immigration**
- **To give Europe a stronger voice in the world**

my worldgeography.com

Culture Close-up

429

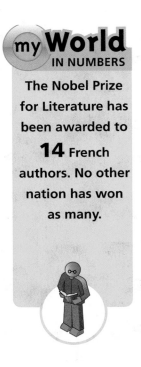
Algerian-born Zinédine Zidane (center) played for the French national soccer team, a team known for its ethnic diversity. ▼

France: History and Diversity

Known for its rich heritage, France has taken a leading role in the EU. The changing face of France presents many challenges.

The French Economy France has fertile soil, a mild climate, and large areas of level land. Its farms, dairies, and vineyards produce wines, cheeses, and grains. The EU ensures that these products reach people around the world.

However, France's largest industry is tourism. Around 75 million tourists a year come to see historic sites and scenic landscapes. French cities attract shoppers and art lovers. Some tourists come just to eat French cuisine!

France is a republic with a strong centralized government. In the past, the government owned many industries such as airlines, banks, and telecommunications. Much of that has changed due to **privatization,** or private ownership of businesses.

City of Light Paris, the capital of France, is known as the City of Light. It is the nation's cultural and economic center. Paris straddles the Seine River and is home to more than 2 million people. Its entire urban area covers around 890 square miles (2,300 square km) and is home to 12 million people.

Parisians live among Gothic churches, baroque palaces, elaborate gardens, and modern skyscrapers. Some Parisians work for the EU as their nation helps shape its policies.

The New Face of France In 2005, two North Africans youths were killed after a police chase in a Paris suburb. This event touched off riots all over France. In 2006, some French people held an anti-immigration protest, saying immigrants were changing French culture. Like the United States, France faces tough immigration issues.

More than 5 million immigrants live in France. An estimated 200,000 to 400,000 are living in the country illegally. Most immigrants come from Europe, and a large number come from North Africa and West Africa. Historically, most French practiced Catholicism. Today, 5 percent to 10 percent of the population is Muslim. Immigrants often face job discrimination and poor living conditions in France.

The French government recently added an immigration ministry. It offers immigrants money to return home. With this money, a family may be able to have a better life in its native country.

Reading Check **How have immigrants changed religious life in France?**

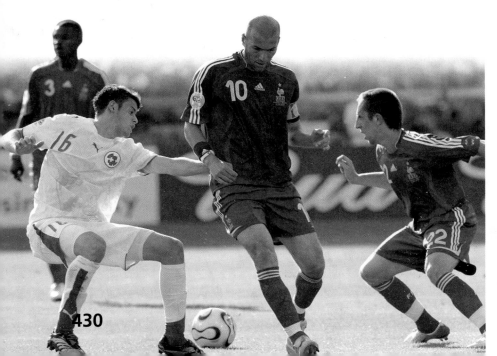

The Low Countries

Belgium, Luxembourg, and the Netherlands form the Low Countries. These countries are small in size, but they are politically and economically powerful.

Belgium: EU Headquarters Belgium serves as the political hub of Europe. Both the EU and NATO have their headquarters in the capital of Brussels. NATO is a military alliance that includes the United States, Canada, and many European nations.

Belgium is a constitutional monarchy. The country has few natural resources, so it relies on trade. It has a high standard of living and a high **gross national product (GNP),** which is the annual income of a nation's companies and residents. Almost 97 percent of Belgians live in cities.

Belgium is made up of three regions. In Flanders in the north, people speak a form of Dutch called Flemish. In Wallonia in the south, they speak French. In the third region around Brussels, people speak both French and Flemish. Periodically, some Flemish call for independence, but most Belgians prefer a united country.

Landlocked Luxembourg Luxembourg is a tiny landlocked country, one of Europe's oldest and smallest. It is a constitutional monarchy as well as a member of the EU and NATO.

Most of its citizens speak French, German, and Luxembourgish, a German dialect. Its key industries are banking and media. Because of its strict banking laws, people around the world use Luxembourg banks.

The Netherlands: A Fragile Balance The Netherlands is also known as Holland. Its people are Dutch. The Netherlands has a long history as a sea-trading nation.

More than half of the Netherlands is below sea level. For centuries, the Dutch have been working to hold back the sea. One way is to build dikes—levees or long dams—to keep out water. With dikes, the Dutch can live on **polders,** or areas of land reclaimed from lake bottoms or the seabeds. The famous Dutch windmills power pumps to drain water from land.

The Dutch live in a fragile balance with their environment. Industry and consumers produce air pollution. As the Dutch population has grown in urban areas, more rural land is needed for human use. Wildlife habitats may be threatened. Water pollution is also a concern because three of Europe's major rivers flow through the Netherlands.

Reading Check How do the Dutch use windmills?

myWorld Activity
Make a Travel Poster

fragile, *adj.,* easily broken or destroyed

The Dutch windmill aids in irrigation for farming. Some farmers also live in windmills. ▶

Germany: Industrial Giant

Germany has the largest population in the EU and Western Europe. Its economy is one of the world's largest.

A United Germany When the Berlin Wall came down in 1989, it marked the end of the split between East Germany and West Germany. **Reunification,** or the process of becoming unified again, brought many changes. Many East Germans "voted with their feet." They left the east and went west for a better life.

Germany is a member of international organizations such as the EU and NATO. Germany also joins other nations for international meetings about global economic issues. Through its membership in the Organization for Security and Co-operation in Europe (OSCE), Germany helps keep the region safe.

A Rich Culture German culture includes some of the world's finest music, art, poetry, films, and literature. Germans have also been leaders in the study of botany, mathematics, and military technology.

Modern German culture remains colored by the painful memories of World War II and the Holocaust, in which Nazis murdered six million European Jews and other innocent people. That troubled period partly resulted from excessive nationalism.

While many Germans feel proud of their nation, they want to avoid the mistakes of the past. They believe that one way to ensure a better future is through education. The country ranks high in the number of university professors, published book titles, and Nobel laureates.

Leading German Exports, 2005

Export	Percent of Total Exports	Value in Euros (billions)	Value in U.S. Dollars (billions)
1. Automobiles	17.4	155.12	183.72
2. Machinery	12.5	111.62	132.20
3. Chemicals	11.4	101.91	120.70
4. Metals	5.6	50.27	59.54
5. Electrical machinery	4.4	39.10	46.31

SOURCE: Federal Statistical Office, Federal Republic of Germany

Heat lamps are used to dry paint on a new car at a German automobile factory. ▼

Chart Skills

➔ **Data Discovery**

Compare the value of Germany's top export with its third-largest export.

Building Tolerance Like the rest of Europe, West Germany <u>recruited</u> guest workers from nearby poorer countries to address the postwar labor shortages of the 1950s. Today, immigrants still come to Germany from these same regions: Turkey, the Middle East, and Eastern Europe. Other immigrants are of German descent and are returning to Germany after generations of living in Poland or Romania.

Because of its past and its diverse population, modern Germany encourages tolerance. However, conflict still occurs. Anti-immigrant and anti-Semitic groups such as the neo-Nazis have staged violent marches. Many Turks, Germany's largest immigrant group, claim that they often encounter racism and prejudice. Even popular Turkish soccer players say they have been taunted because they are not "real Germans." German leaders continue to encourage open-mindedness.

Reading Check What are some reasons that immigrants have moved to Germany?

Austria and Switzerland

Austria shares a language as well as economic and cultural ties with Germany. Austria was once the center of the Austro-Hungarian empire. Its size was dramatically reduced during the two world wars. When Soviet occupation ended in 1955, Austria has become a prosperous democracy. Tourism is a top industry in this country, famous for its Alpine scenery and ski resorts.

Switzerland is one of the world's oldest democracies. It has a long history of neutrality, or not taking sides in wars. This neutrality has led to Switzerland's uneasy relationship with international organizations such as the United Nations. Switzerland did not formally join the UN until 2002. Some people believe joining the UN will help the nation to grow. Other worry that membership will damage Switzerland's neutrality.

Reading Check What industry contributes to the economies of both Alpine nations?

recruit, *v.*, to increase or maintain the number of

Winter sports enthusiasts keep tourism a top industry in both Austria and Switzerland. ▼

Section 3 Assessment

Key Terms

1. Write a one-sentence definition of each of the following terms: gross national product, privatization, polders.

Key Ideas

2. Most of the immigrants in France and Germany come from which regions?

3. Give some examples of the cultural heritage in West Central Europe.

Think Critically

4. **Identify Evidence** What actions of the Dutch suggest that the country has a high population density?

5. **Draw Inferences** How might Switzerland's history of neutrality have affected its history?

? Essential Question

Is it better to be independent or interdependent?

6. Why might EU membership appeal to smaller countries? Go to your Student Journal to record your answer.

Southern Europe Today

Key Ideas	• An ancient and rich history lives on in Southern Europe today.	• The nations of Southern Europe have enjoyed strong growth as members of the European Union.	• Contemporary issues facing the region include immigration and globalization.

Key Terms • Iberian Peninsula • cultural diffusion • diversify
• deportation

 Visual Glossary

Reading Skill: Analyze Cause and Effect Take notes using the graphic organizer in your journal.

The Leaning Tower of Pisa, in Italy

The nations of Southern Europe have enjoyed especially strong growth as members of the European Union. Today, these nations face some of the region's greatest challenges.

A Region of Tradition

Spain, Portugal, Italy, and Greece have an ancient history of civilization. This rich past lives on in traditions that still shape the region today.

The Legacy of Empire Although the ancient Greeks and Romans lived thousands of years ago, their legacies remain. The idea of democracy—that citizens should have a voice in government—began in ancient Greece. The protection of people's rights regardless of wealth or class began in ancient Rome. Today, the European Union (EU) assures members of its commitment to these same ideas. The 12 stars on the EU flag and the EU motto, "United in diversity," tell of the goals of fairness and solidarity, or an attitude shared by a group.

Most of the languages spoken in Southern Europe originated in ancient Greek or Latin. The **Iberian Peninsula** (Spain, Andorra, and Portugal) remains a center of culture and commerce as it has since the Age of Exploration. Farmers and shepherds here live as they have for centuries. The cities of Southern Europe have cathedrals and palaces, many of which date back to the Middles Ages or the Renaissance.

Centuries of trade have influenced the artistic traditions of Southern Europe. Pablo Picasso, a famous Spanish artist, invented a new style of painting after he saw African art for the first time. Asian music influenced Italian opera composers in the 1800s. In Spain, the beautiful Alhambra Palace is a remnant of Islamic culture in Europe.

Religious Heritage Throughout history, armies, traders, and missionaries have passed through Southern Europe. This activity resulted in religious and cultural exchanges. Historians continue to study these events, as they still have a great effect on modern society.

In Rome, Italy, the tiny country of Vatican City serves as the worldwide center of the Roman Catholic Church. Saint Peter's Basilica, one of the holiest sites for Roman Catholics, was built near the site of an ancient Roman racetrack. Athens, Greece, a center of the Greek Orthodox Church, is also home to the Parthenon, an ancient Greek temple of the goddess Athena. Granada, Spain, blends Christian, Jewish, and Muslim influences. This is an example of **cultural diffusion,** or the spread of culture, and it is visible in Granada's colorful neighborhoods and restaurants and in local customs.

Artistic Richness Many famous artists, musicians, novelists, poets, and architects have come from the nations of Southern Europe. Italian architect Renzo Piano has designed buildings in cities around the world. Maria Callas, a famous soprano from Greece, sang many memorable roles for the opera stage.

Mediterranean Culture Mix

Along the Mediterranean, the nations of Southern Europe blend cultural influences that come from centuries of immigration, trade, art, and tradition. *What different cultural influences do you see below?*

For generations, Italians have celebrated religious holidays with city-wide processions that include holy statues. ▶

The Barcelos cockerel is a symbol of Portugal. ▶

◀ Dancing the flamenco, Yasmin keeps alive art from Spanish, Roma, Arabic, Jewish, and African cultures.

435

Southern Europe is rich in both classical and modern music. Spain's many classical composers include the pianist Isaac Albéniz who first performed at age four. Rock is popular everywhere, but world music has become a new favorite. Some of this music retains ethnic or folk traditions. Fado (FAH doo), sad songs about fate or destiny, is popular in Portugal, as is the music from African nations that were once Portuguese colonies. Flamenco, a Spanish dance, incorporates Arab music and African rhythms. The largest world music festival in the world is in Ariano Irpino, Italy.

Reading Check How has cultural diffusion influenced life in Spain?

Cheese-making is one of Italy's oldest industries. ▼

Modern, Prosperous Cities

Economic growth has been strong in this region, especially from 1980 to the early 2000s. Along with this growth, there has been a rise in living standards.

Economic Changes Many of the countries of Southern Europe lived under dictatorships until relatively recently. With the end of these regimes, these nations entered a new period of freedom and prosperity. In Spain, for example, the death of Francisco Franco in 1975 allowed a peaceful transition to democracy after decades of dictatorship.

As governments became more democratic, leaders liberalized, or made less strict, the laws for running businesses. This encouraged entrepreneurs to open new businesses. Jobs increased at both large and small companies. In addition, increasing privatization made businesses stronger and lowered prices.

Modernization has also boosted economic growth in the region. In Spain, for example, factories bought new, improved machinery. Modern factories can produce better goods for less money. Modern shipping companies then make sure that these goods reach buyers more quickly.

One challenge to Southern Europe's economy has been an increase in Asian imports. These imports are often some of the same goods made in Southern Europe. Because Asian manufacturers can make these goods in larger quantities and their workers earn less, their prices are lower. As a result, many countries in this region have had to work hard to compete.

Focus on Portugal Since joining the European Union in 1986, Portugal has experienced impressive economic growth. Much of this growth is due to Portugal's efforts to **diversify,** or add variety to, its types of industries. Many service-based industries, such as telecommunications, are now centered in Portugal.

Portugal's industries had once been limited to traditional products such as textiles, footwear, cork and wood products, and porcelain. Increasingly, a large service sector has developed. This sector includes telecommunications, financial services, healthcare, and tourism. Tourism is also a major industry for Portugal, bringing in almost $10 billion per year.

Privatization has also helped Portugal's economy. Moving businesses from government control to private control has helped business owners gain <u>confidence</u> in their nation's economy. This leads to growth in trade and and more jobs.

Portugal has also benefited from joining the EU single market. Soon after Portugal adopted the euro in 2002, the nation enjoyed a spike in economic growth that has since leveled off.

Still, Portugal has not escaped economic trouble. During the years of growth, debt increased. Repaying this debt will probably slow economic growth.

Effects of EU Membership Membership in the EU made this region better off. With access to open markets and funding from richer members, EU nations generally gain stronger economies and higher living standards.

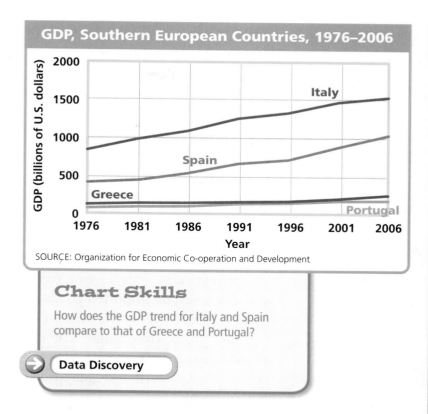

GDP, Southern European Countries, 1976–2006

GDP (billions of U.S. dollars)

Italy

Spain

Greece

Portugal

1976 1981 1986 1991 1996 2001 2006
Year

SOURCE: Organization for Economic Co-operation and Development

Chart Skills

How does the GDP trend for Italy and Spain compare to that of Greece and Portugal?

Data Discovery

Italy has long been an EU leader. Italy adopted the euro as its currency in 1999. Spain, Portugal, and Greece also experienced economic growth as EU members. This growth has slowed due to competition from Asia.

EU members sometimes find economic growth indirectly affected by the addition of new members. For example, Portugal has historically supplied Europe with low-cost labor. Recently, Portugal had its EU development funding cut by several billion euros. This happened with the entrance of new member nations such as Romania and Slovakia. Workers from these nations have begun to move to other EU countries like Portugal and are willing to work for lower wages.

Reading Check Describe one economic change in Southern Europe.

confidence, *n.,* the quality or state of being certain

crisis, *n.,* an uncertain or difficult situation, possibly heading toward disaster

myWorld Activity
Southern Europe's Neighbors

Challenges for the Region

Although Southern Europe has experienced economic growth, it still faces many challenges.

Maintaining Growth Europe is now part of a larger, global economy. This has benefits and drawbacks.

In recent years, products from China have flooded European markets. Chinese workers earn lower wages, so the products they make sell for less. To help domestic companies survive, Southern European governments have increased tariffs, or taxes, on imported goods. Increasing tariffs raises the price of imported goods while domestic goods' prices remain low. Increasing government control of the market may, however, hurt economic growth.

The worldwide financial <u>crisis</u> of 2008 also posed serious economic challenges.

The economies of Spain, Portugal, Italy, and Greece have all experienced slowdowns. Industrial production fell, leading to a decrease in GDP. Some experts think that Southern Europe's years of rapid economic growth may be at an end.

Regional Newcomers Badolato, a village in Italy, had almost disappeared when a group of Turkish Kurds arrived. The Italians welcomed these refugees, who gave new life to the village. Because Italians are no longer having large families, the population is decreasing. With fewer people to fill open jobs, many employers now rely on immigrants such as those that have come to Badolato and other cities in Southern Europe.

However, Southern Europeans don't want so much immigration that it threatens their jobs or culture. Their governments have tried to control immigration.

Facing Regional Challenges

Muslim families in Rome (left) protest against anti-immigrant violence. At right, a woman enters an employment office in Spain, where unemployment has risen dramatically. *How does each photograph show challenges faced in Southern Europe?*

In Italy, the government uses fingerprinting to monitor immigrants. Some ethnic groups, such as the Roma (formerly known as Gypsies), believe these methods lead to discrimination.

The fear of **deportation,** or being sent back to one's home country, leads many immigrants to hide from officials in their new country. Any immigrant who does not follow a country's laws may be deported. As elsewhere in Europe, immigration shows the benefits and the challenges of living in an interconnected world.

Focus on Greece Since ancient times, Greek trading ships have brought back exotic goods from foreign lands. These same traders also introduced the world to Greek art and culture and important ideas such as democracy.

Shipping is still important in Greece, and China is a major trading partner. In 2007, Greek ships carried about 60 percent of China's imports of raw materials. These commodities included

▲ Colorful shipping containers fill the busy port at Piraeus in Greece. *How does the geography of Greece contribute to its shipping industry?*

coal, oil, and iron ore. In China, those products fueled the nation's explosive growth. This trade agreement benefited both Greece and China as well as other global trading partners. Yet, when global trade began to shrink in 2008, everyone involved in this trade experienced setbacks.

Reading Check What has caused Southern Europe's economic slowdown?

Section 4 Assessment

Key Terms

1. Use each of the following terms in a complete sentence: Iberian Peninsula, cultural diffusion, diversity, deportation.

Key Ideas

2. Describe three ways in which the past still affects Southern Europe.

3. What economic advantages did EU membership bring to Southern Europe?

4. What other cultures have spread ideas to Southern Europe through cultural diffusion?

Think Critically

5. **Identify Evidence** How has Southern Europe responded to immigration?

6. **Draw Inferences** Why are countries generally more open to immigrants during economic boom times?

? Essential Question

Is it better to be independent or interdependent?

7. Has the European Union helped Southern Europe? Explain why or why not. Go to your Student Journal to record your answers.

Chapter Assessment

Key Terms and Ideas

1. **Discuss** Why does most of Western Europe have a mild climate?

2. **Describe** Where do most Western Europeans live, and why?

3. **Recall** What is a **constitutional monarchy,** and which nations have this form of government?

4. **Summarize** What does the **cradle-to-grave system** provide for citizens of Scandinavian countries?

5. **Explain** How does migration help cause **cultural borrowing** and **cultural diffusion**?

6. **Compare and Contrast** How are West Central Europe and Southern Europe similar? How are they different?

7. **Explain** What problems has Germany had to overcome since **reunification**?

8. **Recall** What cultures have influenced the artistic traditions of Southern Europe?

Think Critically

9. **Compare Viewpoints** How does the British viewpoint toward the EU compare to the viewpoint of France and Germany? Support your answer with details from the chapter.

10. **Draw Conclusions** How has immigration affected Western Europe? Explain.

11. **Predict** What long-term effect do you think EU membership will have on nationalism in Europe? Explain.

12. **Core Concepts: People's Impact on the Environment** What are some of the main causes of pollution? How has pollution affected Europe?

Places to Know

For each place, write the letter from the map that shows its location.

13. Scandinavian Peninsula

14. Italy

15. Iceland

16. France

17. Iberian Peninsula

18. Mediterranean Sea

19. Greece

20. **Estimate** Using the scale, estimate how far Iceland is from France.

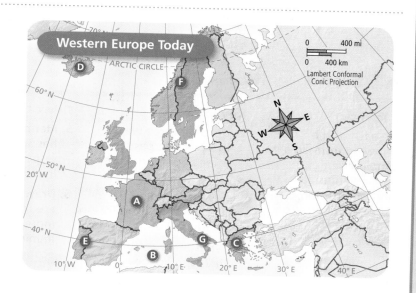

Western Europe Today

Essential Question

myWorld Chapter Activity

Norway and the European Union Follow your teacher's instructions to study data on whether or not Norway should join the European Union. Read and analyze graphs, photographs, and information about the advantages and disadvantages of EU membership for Norway. Take a stand based on your conclusions in support of your position on EU membership for Norway.

21st Century Learning

Develop Cultural Awareness

Western Europe's contact with other nations has added much to life on the continent. Make a small poster on each of the topics below to focus on cultural diffusion in Western Europe.
- Art and architecture
- Music
- Language
- Food

Document-Based Questions

Success Tracker™
Online at myworldgeography.com

Use your knowledge of Western Europe and Documents A and B to answer Questions 1–3.

Document A

Joining the Eurozone	
EU Member	**Year Euro Adopted**
Austria	1999
Belgium	1999
Finland	1999
France	1999
Germany	1999
Greece	2001
Ireland	1999
Netherlands	1999
Slovakia	2009
Spain	1999

Document B

" The people of Denmark have voted to reject membership of the single European currency. . . . The leader of the far-right, anti-Euro Danish People's Party, Pia Kjaersgaard, described the outcome as a great victory. 'This victory is a victory for Danes' wish to defend democracy, self-determination and the country's sovereignty,' she said."

—"Danes Say No to Euro,"
BBC News Online, September 28, 2000

1. Which Southern European country was last to adopt the euro?

   A Greece

   B Ireland

   C Slovakia

   D Spain

2. According to Kjaersgaard, why did the Danish people reject the euro?

   A They don't trust other EU members.

   B They are waiting to see if it succeeds.

   C They want to control their economy.

   D They have too much debt to switch.

3. **Writing Task** Explain why some Western European countries may want to have some independence from the EU.

myworldgeography.com

Self-Test

441

Chapter 11

Eastern Europe

How can you measure success?

KEY
— National border
⊙ Capital city
○ Other city

0   200 mi
0   200 km
Lambert Conformal Conic Projection

Tallinn
ESTONIA
Riga LATVIA
LITHUANIA
Vilnius
KALININGRAD (Russia)
Minsk
BELARUS
Warsaw
POLAND
Prague
CZECH REPUBLIC
SLOVAKIA
Bratislava
Budapest
HUNGARY
SLOVENIA
Ljubljana
Zagreb
CROATIA
BOSNIA AND HERZEGOVINA
Sarajevo
SERBIA
Belgrade
ROMANIA
Bucharest
MOLDOVA
Chișinău
Kiev
Bezpalche
UKRAINE
BULGARIA
Sofia
Podgorica
KOSOVO
Priština
Skopje
MONTENEGRO
MACEDONIA
Tirana
ALBANIA
Baltic Sea
Vistula River
Oder River
Dniester River
Dnieper River
Danube River
Adriatic Sea
Black Sea

Where in the World Is Eastern Europe?

Washington, D.C., to Bezpalche: 4,930 miles

my Story

Serhiy's Leap

In this section, you'll read about Serhiy, a young man who lives in the small town of Bezpalche in Ukraine. What does Serhiy's story tell you about life in Eastern Europe today?

? Explore the Essential Question
- at **my worldgeography.com**
- using the **myWorld Chapter Activity**
- with the Student Journal

Story by Mark Rachkevych for myWorld Geography Online

Serhiy lives in the historic farming hamlet of Bezpalche, located 80 miles (130 kilometers) east of the Ukrainian capital of Kiev. Its 640 people are proud of the village's roots. It was founded by Bezpalko, a famous Cossack. The Cossacks were free-roaming bands of warriors known for their expert horsemanship and fierce fighting tactics. They defended the Ukrainian frontiers from enemy attack.

Single-family brick homes with tile roofs line the village lanes. Wooden fences separate the yards. Behind the houses are small plots of land used for farming. A wooden Christian church is the tallest structure in the village. A school stands in the center of the village along an unpaved road. The village is small enough that it is easy to get around by walking.

This school is where 16-year-old Serhiy enjoys his favorite subjects of physical education, information technology, and the Ukrainian language. In his final year of study, Serhiy walks to school from home, where he lives with his parents, his older brother, and his elderly grandmother.

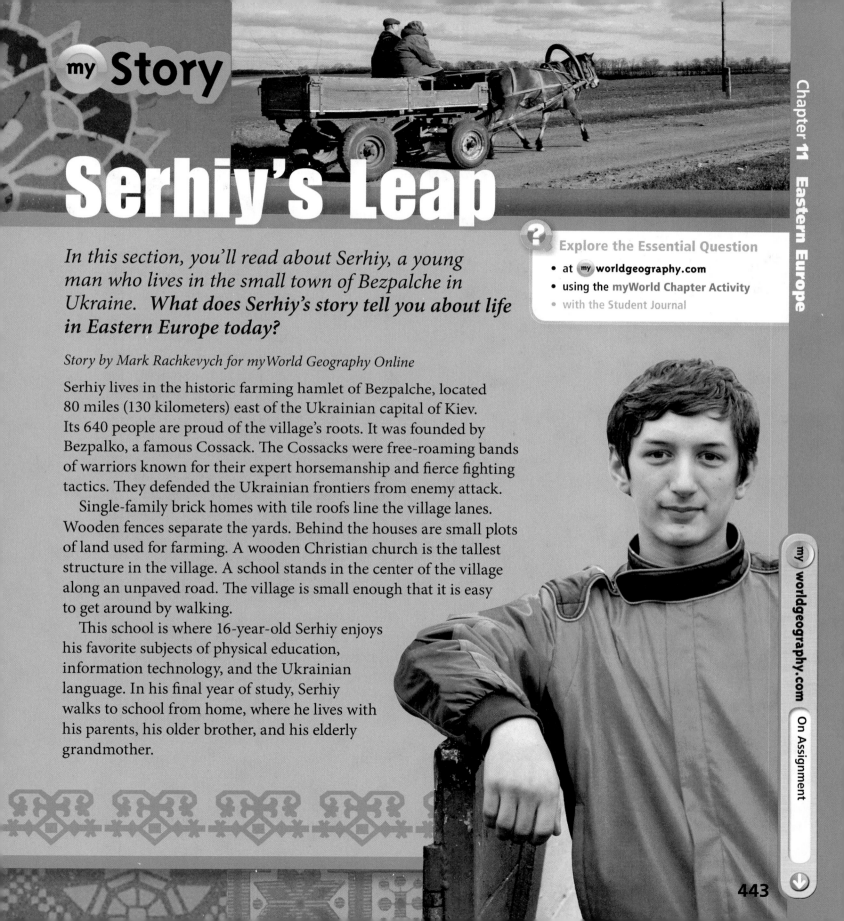

my worldgeography.com On Assignment

443

Scattering corn for the chickens is one of Serhiy's regular afternoon chores. He also must feed the family's pigs (below).

Serhiy buys bread at the only shop in Bezpalche.

His mother works a postal route three hours a day. On their small farm, his family grows beets, onions, cabbage, corn, and potatoes, and tends four pigs and three milking cows. Serhiy is personally responsible for caring for more than 40 rabbits. Small farms like this are common in Ukraine.

Ukraine used to be part of the Soviet Union. The Soviet government managed all the land in the country. Now Ukraine is an independent country. The new leadership broke up the large government farms, giving each family a small plot of land.

In villages like these, nature doesn't allow for breaks or long vacations. Serhiy rises at 6:00, feeds the livestock, and does other chores around the pens. Then he eats breakfast and heads to school for his first class, which begins at 8:30. He returns home at 2:30 and eats lunch. His favorite lunch is potatoes fried in lard and onions. His next chore is to take care of the rabbits. His grandmother pays him a small weekly allowance for this task. Then, at sunset, Serhiy starts his homework.

Short and broad-shouldered, Serhiy enjoys physical activity. He loves motorbikes and anything technical. "I even assembled a computer from scratch with a friend of mine," Serhiy says proudly, pointing at his PC, which he knows inside and out.

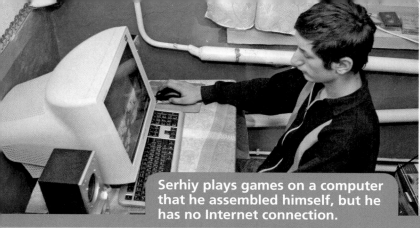

Serhiy plays games on a computer that he assembled himself, but he has no Internet connection.

The city of Kiev is about 80 miles from Serhiy's village.

But Serhiy can enjoy these hobbies only when time permits. On the weekends, his brother drives him 25 miles (40 kilometers) to the regional capital to take preparatory classes. Serhiy wants to go to the military academy in Kharkiv in eastern Ukraine. He hopes to become a pilot. But to do so, he will need to do well on the entrance exam. The prestigious and highly competitive academy accepts only one out of every four applicants.

Serhiy knows his small world and way of life will come to an end next summer when he graduates. Even if he is not accepted to the military academy, he will leave his village. The grocery store is the only real business in Bezpalche, so most young people must go elsewhere to make a living. Once his studies begin, he will not be able to take trips into the woods or drive his motorbike on country roads.

Still, Serhiy looks forward to military life. After all, could it be tougher than life in Bezpalche? Yet he worries, "Cities have wide boulevards, and I'll be a stranger among impersonal strangers."

He's willing to make the transition since he is drawn to the physical rigor of military exercises, the technical hardware and weaponry, and the challenges the regimen brings. "My family supports my decision, and my mother just worries like any other mother does," Serhiy says half-jokingly.

And if he doesn't get accepted when he applies in Kharkiv next summer, what is his backup plan? "Then I'll probably study computer programming in Cherkassy, the neighboring regional capital," Serhiy says.

How does he feel about leaving an environment where everything is familiar, where there are no surprises, and where everybody knows his name? "Well, I'm not just going to stay here," he says. "No one from my graduating class plans to remain in the village next summer, nobody."

Meet the Journalist

Name Mark Rachkevych

Favorite Moment Eating in a market and chatting with villagers in Bezpalche

→ **myStory Video**

Join Serhiy as he shows you more about his life in Ukraine.

Chapter Atlas

Key Ideas

- Glaciers have shaped the physical features of this region.
- Climate varies from the south to the north of the region.
- Eastern European countries face many environmental challenges.
- Eastern Europe has a varied religious background.

Key Terms • ice age • mechanized farming • acid rain • emigrate

→ **Visual Glossary**

Reading Skill: Label an Outline Map Take notes using the outline map in your journal.

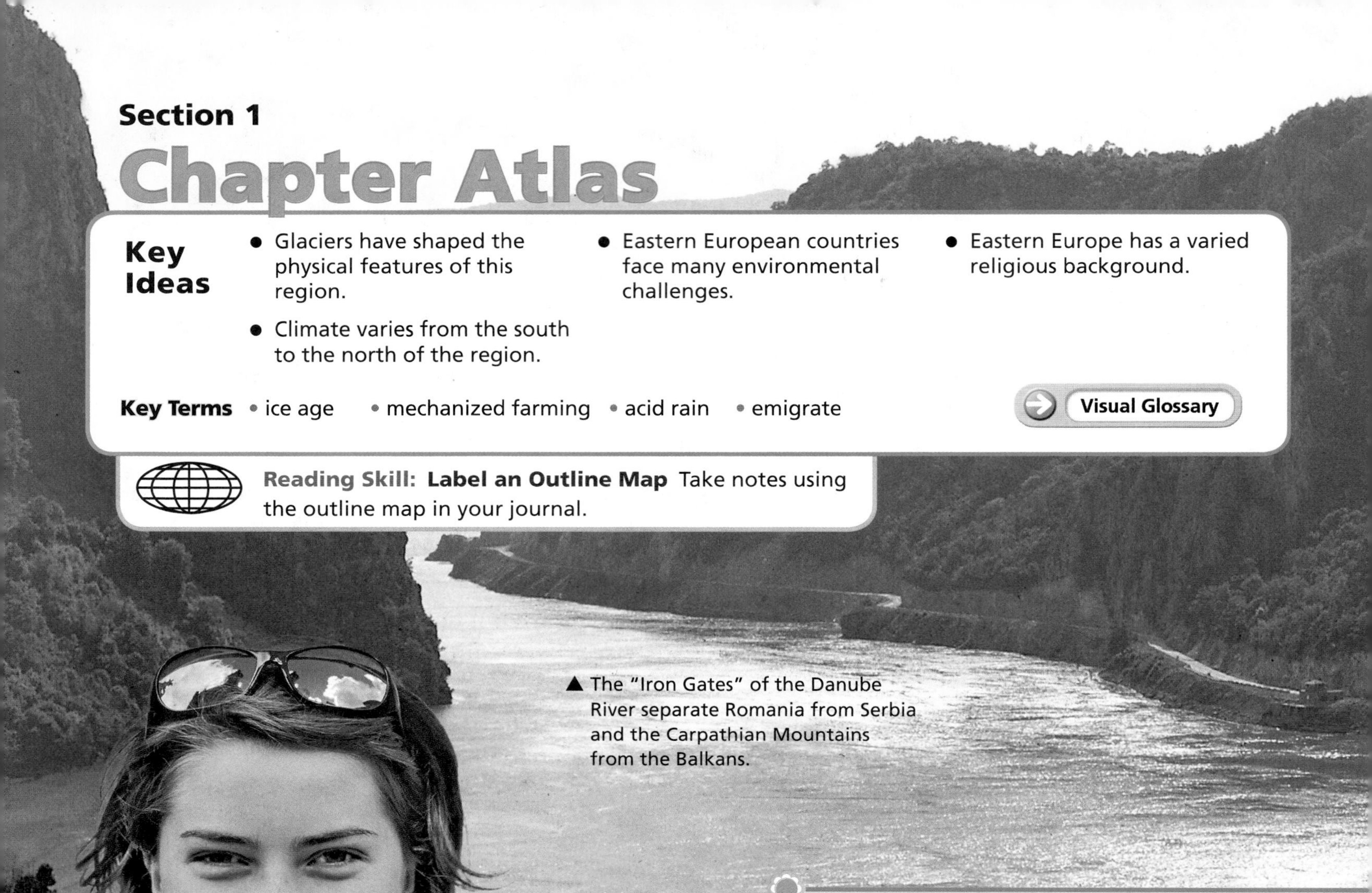

▲ The "Iron Gates" of the Danube River separate Romania from Serbia and the Carpathian Mountains from the Balkans.

◄ A young woman from Estonia

Physical Features

Eastern Europe is a region with both broad plains and high mountains. The most mountainous part of the region is the Balkan Peninsula, which juts into the Mediterranean Sea to the south. Two ranges, the Dinaric Alps and the Balkan Mountains, cover much of the peninsula.

Mountain ranges also stretch through the middle of Eastern Europe. The Carpathian Mountains begin close to the Danube River in Slovakia. They arch northeast and then bend back toward the Danube River, joining the Transylvanian Alps to the south.

Eastern Europe: Physical

Map Skills

1 **Region** What is the highest elevation in the North European Plain?

2 **Place** How does the landscape in the southwest differ from that in the northeast?

3 **Places to Know!**
Label the following places on the outline map in your Student Journal: Balkan Mountains, North European Plain, Great Hungarian Plain, Danube River

21st Century Learning

KEY
Elevation

Feet	Meters
6,000	1,829
3,000	914
1,000	305
500	152
Sea level	Sea level

— National border

0 — 200 mi
0 — 200 km
Lambert Conformal Conic Projection

Between these two groups of mountains lies the Great Hungarian Plain. Another large plain, the North European Plain, stretches from the Baltic Sea to the Black Sea. Most of the farms and cities of this region are in these broad flatlands.

The physical features of the northern part of this region were shaped by an **ice age,** or time of lower temperatures when much of the land is covered in ice. Ice piled up as deep as two miles thick. Heavy sheets of ice, called glaciers, moved slowly across the land. Glaciers scraped up rocks and soil as they moved. They then dropped these materials when they melted. This process created ridges of hills that extend for hundreds of miles across the region.

Glaciers also formed lakes and rivers. The pressure of the glacier dug pits into the land. When the ice melted, pits became lakes. Most lakes in Europe are located in glaciated areas.

In the southern part of this region, deep valleys crisscross steep mountains. The Danube river flows through the Iron Gates, one of these deep valleys.

Reading Check What effects have glaciers had on the physical features of Eastern Europe?

Climate and Agriculture

The climate varies across Eastern Europe. In particular, the climate of the northern part of the region is very different from the climate of the southern part. As a result, farmers in the north face different challenges than farmers in the south. In the north, the winters can be very harsh. In the south, the mountains make cultivating the land difficult.

Latitude is the most important factor that influences climate in Eastern Europe. In the south, a band of Mediterranean and subtropical climate extends across much of the Balkan Peninsula. Summers here are dry, while winters are rainy. The rain and snow that <u>accumulate</u> in the mountains in wet winter months are very important for agriculture. During the hot, dry months of spring and summer, melting snow flows downhill to the crops in the parched valleys below.

The continental cool summer climate covers much of the rest of Eastern Europe. In this area, winters are cold, and summers are generally mild.

Patterns of rainfall across the region vary from east to west. Each year, most of Eastern Europe receives between 20 and 40 inches of precipitation, or falling rain or snow. The amount of precipitation in the west is generally greater than the amount in the east.

Hills and mountains also have a major effect on the amount of precipitation an area receives. In general, warm air can hold more moisture than cool air. The higher air goes, the cooler it gets. When

accumulate, v., to build up over time

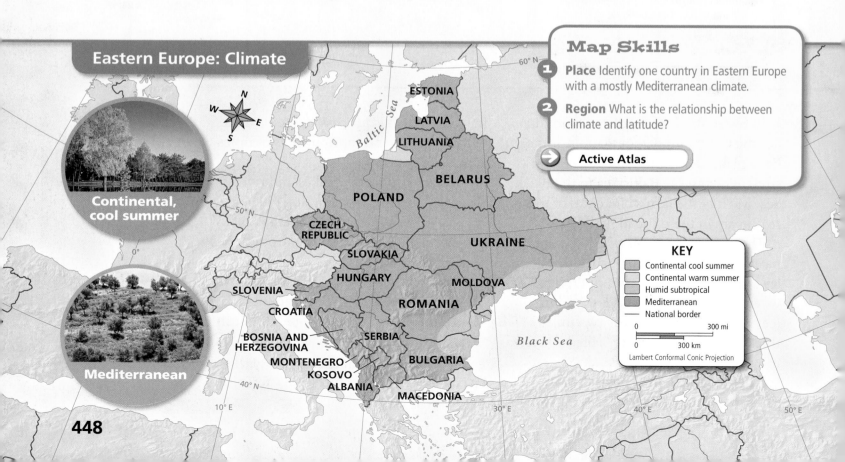

Eastern Europe: Climate

Continental, cool summer

Mediterranean

ESTONIA
LATVIA
LITHUANIA
Baltic Sea
BELARUS
POLAND
CZECH REPUBLIC
SLOVAKIA
UKRAINE
HUNGARY
SLOVENIA
MOLDOVA
CROATIA
ROMANIA
BOSNIA AND HERZEGOVINA
SERBIA
MONTENEGRO
KOSOVO
ALBANIA
BULGARIA
MACEDONIA
Black Sea

Map Skills

1 **Place** Identify one country in Eastern Europe with a mostly Mediterranean climate.

2 **Region** What is the relationship between climate and latitude?

→ **Active Atlas**

KEY
Continental cool summer
Continental warm summer
Humid subtropical
Mediterranean
National border

0   300 mi
0   300 km
Lambert Conformal Conic Projection

air cannot hold as much water, the water falls back to the earth as rain or as snow.

It is easy to see, then, how mountains affect precipitation. When wind blows against a range of mountains, the air rises and cools. Then it drops its moisture and continues over the mountains. Therefore, the side of the mountains facing the wind receives much more rain than the other side. The result is big differences in climate over small distances. Areas along the Adriatic coast, for example, receive as much as 200 inches of rainfall a year. The dry valleys on the other side of the Dinaric Alps may receive only 30 inches of rainfall during the same period of time.

The growing season on the North European Plain is shorter than the growing season farther south in the region.

Still, many people farm in this region. **Mechanized farming,** or farming with machines, is easy on the large expanses of flat land. Wheat and rye are common crops in this region. They are well suited to the cooler climate and easy to harvest with machines.

Because machines are important for agriculture here, many farms in northeastern Europe are large. Large farms are not as common in the southern part of this region. Because of the mountains, mechanized farming is more difficult. Also, more people are available to work the land. Many crops such as citrus fruits, olives, and grapes grow well in the warm climate.

Reading Check How is agriculture in the north of Eastern Europe different from that in the south?

my World IN NUMBERS

In Albania, **58%** of the labor force work on farms. Most work on small family farms.

my worldgeography.com Active Atlas

Harvesting Wheat in the North
Wheat grows best in areas without extremes of temperature. So wheat is a good crop for countries with cool summers and flat land.

Growing Olives in the South
Olive trees do well with warm, dry summers and cannot survive very cold winters. For that reason, olive growing is best suited to countries with a Mediterranean climate.

449

Coal or Nuclear:
Difficult Energy Choices

The search for energy to fuel economic growth is a major challenge in this region and across the world. Industry has developed near deposits of coal in Eastern Europe. These countries have struggled to deal with the air pollution caused by burning coal for energy. Would nuclear energy be a better choice for Eastern Europe?

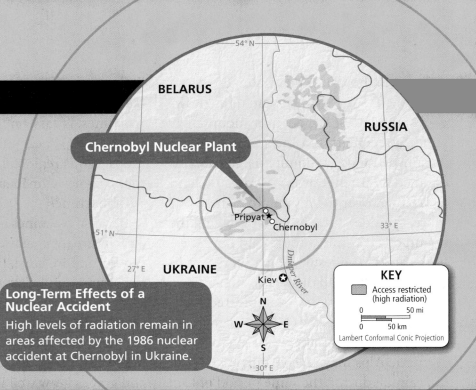

BELARUS

RUSSIA

Chernobyl Nuclear Plant

54° N

Pripyat ★
Chernobyl

33° E

51° N

27° E   UKRAINE

Kiev

Dnieper River

KEY

Access restricted (high radiation)

0   50 mi
0   50 km
Lambert Conformal Conic Projection

Long-Term Effects of a Nuclear Accident
High levels of radiation remain in areas affected by the 1986 nuclear accident at Chernobyl in Ukraine.

Coal Energy

 **Pros**

Technology to reduce coal pollution has been developed.

Large reserves of coal are readily available in parts of Eastern Europe.

 **Cons**

Mining coal is dangerous and damages the environment.

Burning coal creates pollution that causes acid rain and may contribute to climate change.

These smokestacks emit smoke from burning coal.

Nuclear Energy

 Pros

One power station creates a lot of power.

Under normal conditions, nuclear energy produces less air pollution than coal.

 Cons

A serious accident can spread radioactive pollution over a large area. People must move, and health problems continue for years.

Nuclear waste is very dangerous and must be stored for a long time.

This meter shows high radiation in the area near Chernobyl.

РАДИАН

0556.

БЕЛВАР

my Story

Boris's Bigspin

? **Explore the Essential Question**
- at my worldgeography.com
- using the **myWorld Chapter Activity**
- with the **Student Journal**

In this section, you'll read about Boris, a young skateboarder living in Moscow. What does Boris's story tell you about life in Russia today?

Story by Dmitry Saltykovskiy for myWorld Online

It's a sunny day in Moscow, and people hurry past a huge monument to the German philosopher Karl Marx. The 200-ton block of stone bears the inscription "Workers of the world, unite," a quote from Marx that became famous among communist workers. When the statue was unveiled in 1961, Russia was a communist nation, and Marx was an honored figure. Today, Russia is a very different place, and the monument to Marx is better known as a fun place for skateboarders to try tricks like the ollie or the bigspin.

Boris, a 15-year-old Russian skateboarder, loves to try jumps off of the step at the base of the monument. When the Soviet Union collapsed in 1991, Boris had not yet been born. He has never lived under communism, but he still has clear memories of hard times in Russia.

"I was born in troubled times," Boris says. "After the Soviet Union fell, people were trying to make money. It was a dangerous period with lots of crime and fighting between businesses. My father disappeared around that time. I was just four years old. He owned his own business, and he was kidnapped. We never saw him again. I am sad that I can't really remember what he looked like now."

my worldgeography.com On Assignment

Boris talks with friends after school.

Boris on a Moscow city street

Boris in front of a monument to Karl Marx

Boris goes everywhere by skateboard, including the skate park. At the indoor skate park, skaters ride curved ramps, and the clatter of decks hitting the floor fills the air.

During the Soviet era, the sport of skateboarding did not exist. Boris is one of the first young Russians to take part in paid skateboard competitions. He even has a sponsorship by a major sports brand—something else that's new in Russia.

"There was no skateboarding during Soviet times—things have changed so much since then. In those days, people couldn't travel at all outside the Soviet Union. Today, I am able to travel all over the world to participate in competitions."

"My mom was really proud when I started winning competitions," Boris recalls. "She was amazed when I managed to get a sponsorship deal. It was a really nice moment for me when I could use some of my prize money to make her birthday special."

Boris says that his mother and stepfather are proud of his skateboarding, although they worry about him being injured. They also hope that he will consider a professional career someday. "Moscow is growing so quickly that I've become interested in real estate!" Boris laughs.

Boris at the skate park in Moscow

Boris shoots basketball at the park.

Working on the computer at home

Following the 2008 Russian invasion of Georgia, Boris decided to change his last name. Georgia had once been part of the Soviet Union, but it declared its independence in 1991. Since then, relations have been tense between Russia and Georgia.

"My father was half Georgian, and he had a very un-Russian sounding last name. With all the problems between our two countries, my mom decided that we should change our name. I was really sad because I felt like I was giving away a piece of my father, but really we had no choice. Russians have become quite anti-Georgian and my name marked me as different."

The tension between Russia and Georgia also means that Boris has been unable to visit family in Georgia. "I used to go there every summer. It was really nice to get out of Moscow when the weather was hot. Now there are no airplane flights."

The wheels of Boris's deck leave the ground, and then he rolls off to the park for a game of basketball. For Boris, his skateboard is not only the best way to get around Moscow, but also a ticket to a promising future in the new Russia.

Meet the Journalist

Name Dmitry Saltykovskiy
Favorite Moment
Seeing Boris in action at the skate park

→ **myStory Online**

Skateboard along with Boris as he shows you life in his city.

467

Chapter Atlas

Key Ideas

- Russia is the world's largest country in area, reaching from Europe to the eastern edge of Asia.

- Russia has rich mineral, energy, and other resources, located mostly in Siberia.

- Most of Russia has a low population density.

Key Terms • Siberia • Ural Mountains • Lake Baikal • steppes • Kamchatka Peninsula • permafrost

 **Visual Glossary**

Reading Skill: Label an Outline Map Take notes using the outline map in your journal.

A teen in front of the Kremlin in Moscow, Russia's capital city

Physical Features

Today, a plane flight from one end of Russia to the other takes 11 hours. It took the early explorers more than a year to cross Russia's dense forests, wide plains, and high mountains as they made their way east to the Pacific Ocean. Most of the journey involved crossing **Siberia,** or the Asian part of Russia, including the vast West Siberian Plain.

Russia is the world's largest country in area. It has 11 time zones. Since there are a total of 24 one-hour time zones on Earth, this means that Russia stretches almost halfway around the world.

Russia: Physical

ARCTIC OCEAN

Chukchi Sea

Bering Sea

East Siberian Sea

Barents Sea

Kara Sea

Laptev Sea

Cherskiy Range

Kamchatka Peninsula

Baltic Sea

Kola Peninsula

RUSSIA

Sea of Okhotsk

Sakhalin Island

Kuril Islands

Russian Plain

URAL MOUNTAINS

West Siberian Plain

Central Siberian Plateau

SIBERIA

PACIFIC OCEAN

Volga River

Yenisey River

Ob' River

Lake Baikal

Lena River

Mount Elbrus 18,510ft (5,642m)

CAUCASUS MTS.

Black Sea

Caspian Sea

Sea of Japan (East Sea)

80° E

90° E

100° E

110° E

120° E

130° E

70° E

60° E

50° E

40° N

50° N

60° N

30° N

KEY
Elevation

Feet	Meters
6,000	1,829
3,000	914
1,000	305
500	152
Sea level	Sea level

0 — 600 mi

0 — 600 km

Lambert Conformal Conic Projection

N E S W

Map Skills

1 **Place** In which mountain range is Mount Elbrus?

2 **Region** Which ocean lies north of Russia?

3 **Places to Know!**
Label the following places on the outline map in your Student Journal: Siberia, Kamchatka Peninsula, Ural Mountains, Kuril Islands, Lake Baikal.

→ Active Atlas

Russia spreads across two continents, Europe and Asia. The dividing line runs along the low peaks of the **Ural Mountains,** a range that separates European Russia from Asian Russia. European Russia is located east of Latvia, Lithuania, Estonia, Belarus, and Ukraine. Asian Russia lies immediately north of China, Mongolia, and Kazakhstan.

A Vast Land

Russia has many different kinds of landforms and waterways. The Russian Plain covers much of European Russia.

It stretches east to the Ural Mountains. South of the Russian Plain are the Caucasus Mountains. These mountains run east-west between the Caspian Sea and the Black Sea. They form the southern border between European Russia and Asia.

East of the Urals is the broad West Siberian Plain. Farther east are central and eastern Siberia. This huge area consists of rugged plateaus framed by high mountains on the east and south.

spectacular, *adj.,* striking or excellent

Many of these <u>spectacular</u> mountains are volcanic in origin. Some are covered by glaciers year-round.

European Russia's longest river, the Volga, flows into the Caspian Sea. This river is famous in the songs and stories of the Russian people. Russia's European rivers also include the Don, which flows into the Black Sea, and the Dvina, which flows north to an arm of the Arctic Ocean.

In Siberia, there are many other large rivers that flow north to the Arctic Ocean. These include Russia's longest, the Yenisey, as well as the Ob and Lena. Another important Siberian river is called the Ankara. Far to the east is the mighty Amur River, which forms the border between Russia and China.

Despite its many rivers, canals, and long coastlines, Russia lacks many good harbors and ports. In European Russia, usable ports include St. Petersburg, Kaliningrad, Novorossiysk, and Sochi. In addition, there are ports in Murmansk in the far north on the Arctic Ocean and Vladivostok on the Pacific coast.

Russia: Climate

ARCTIC OCEAN

Bering Sea

East Siberian Sea

Barents Sea

Sea of Okhotsk

RUSSIA

PACIFIC OCEAN

Caspian Sea

Sea of Japan (East Sea)

KEY
- Tundra
- Subarctic
- Continental cool summer
- Continental warm summer
- Humid subtropical
- Semiarid

0   600 mi

0   600 km

Lambert Conformal Conic Projection

Semiarid

Continental, cool summer

Subarctic

Map Skills

1 **Location** Along which body of water does Russia's southernmost semiarid region lie?

2 **Region** How much of Russia's land is subarctic?

➔ Active Atlas

Russia, however, does have many large lakes and seas. Perhaps the most famous is **Lake Baikal** in the heart of Siberia. More than one mile deep, Lake Baikal holds about 20 percent of Earth's fresh water—more than all of the North American Great Lakes combined. Baikal is also home to plants and animals found nowhere else. Due to the threat of pollution from factories located along its shores, Lake Baikal was the birthplace of Russia's environmental movement.

Reading Check **Which landform separates European Russia from Asian Russia?**

Climate and Vegetation

Vast stretches of Russian lands have a subarctic climate because they lie near the Arctic Circle. North of this area is the tundra climate region, a cold, dry, treeless area covered in snow for most of the year. European Russia in the southwest has a continental climate. In cities such as Moscow and St. Petersburg, people experience long, cold winters and warm summers. Parts of southern Russia have a semiarid, or moderately dry, climate.

Russia's natural vegetation is closely tied to its climate. In the cool continental climate north of Moscow, thick coniferous forests grow. South of Moscow are temperate forests. To the east, vast areas of grasslands called **steppes** cover the land. Here, mild, moist summers and rich soils make good farmland.

In Siberia, weather and climate are more extreme than in European Russia. Here, winters are long and cold. Cold, dry conditions in parts of Siberia account for a type of low-lying vegetation called tundra. Tundra covers about one tenth of Russia and stretches all the way from the Finnish border east to the **Kamchatka Peninsula**. This peninsula in the Russian Far East is famous for its 160 volcanoes, 29 of which are active.

Near Yakutsk, Siberia, a family hauls water that they took from a hole in the ice on a local lake.

my worldgeography.com Active Atlas

471

South of the tundra is the Russian taiga, a land of dense coniferous forests. The Russian taiga covers more than four million square miles (10 million square kilometers). One of the many challenges for human settlement in northern Russia is **permafrost.** This is permanently frozen soil that often lies beneath the tundra and the taiga. It makes construction of roads, railroads, and housing difficult.

Vegetation in Russia's Far East region differs from that of the rest of the country. Because this area is close to the ocean and is located farther to the south, it is warmer and has vegetation similar to the nearby Koreas. Its animals include the Amur tiger, the world's largest cat. The eastern edge of Russia features the Kuril Islands and the Kamchatka Peninsula.

myWorld Activity
Roam Across Russia

Reading Check Where in Russia are there active volcanoes?

Russia's Resources

Russia has rich mineral and energy resources, especially in Siberia. Its resources include timber, fish, and hydroelectric power. About one third of all of Earth's coal is located in Siberia. In spite of extremes of climate and the country's massive size, vast reserves of oil and gas in West Siberia have made Russia wealthy in recent years.

Russia also has metal ores such as iron, gold, cobalt, nickel, and platinum ore. It sells these valuable minerals to many different buyers around the world for industrial use.

It can be difficult to mine Russia's rich natural resources because they are so hard to reach. Long distances and harsh climates separate resources from processing plants and markets.

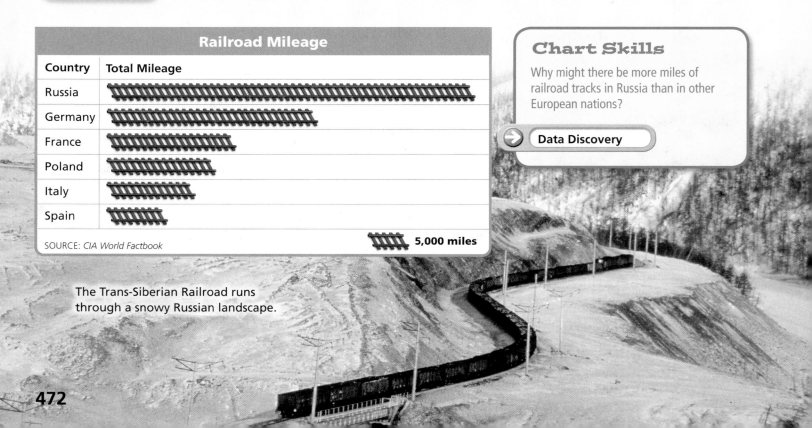

Railroad Mileage

Country	Total Mileage
Russia	
Germany	
France	
Poland	
Italy	
Spain	

SOURCE: *CIA World Factbook*

5,000 miles

The Trans-Siberian Railroad runs through a snowy Russian landscape.

Chart Skills

Why might there be more miles of railroad tracks in Russia than in other European nations?

Data Discovery

This makes it important for Russia to build and <u>maintain</u> an extensive transportation system to move products to markets. The poor quality of roads can make transport difficult. Truck drivers often find it easier to drive on frozen rivers and lakes than on Russian roads.

Many of Russia's great rivers are navigable, or passable, for only a few months of the year because they are usually blocked by ice. Underground pipelines generally transport Russia's huge reserves of oil and natural gas. An extensive railroad network moves goods to consumers.

Large-scale economic development in Siberia began only after the Trans-Siberian Railroad was completed in 1905. This famous railroad connects the city of Moscow in the west with Vladivostok on the Pacific. It also connects with rail lines running to Mongolia and China. It was built to help Russians settle the open lands of Siberia, to develop industrial centers, and to transport troops to the Pacific to protect Russia against threats of invasion by Japan and China.

Reading Check **Name two challenges Russia faces in developing its economy.**

maintain, *v.,* to keep in good condition

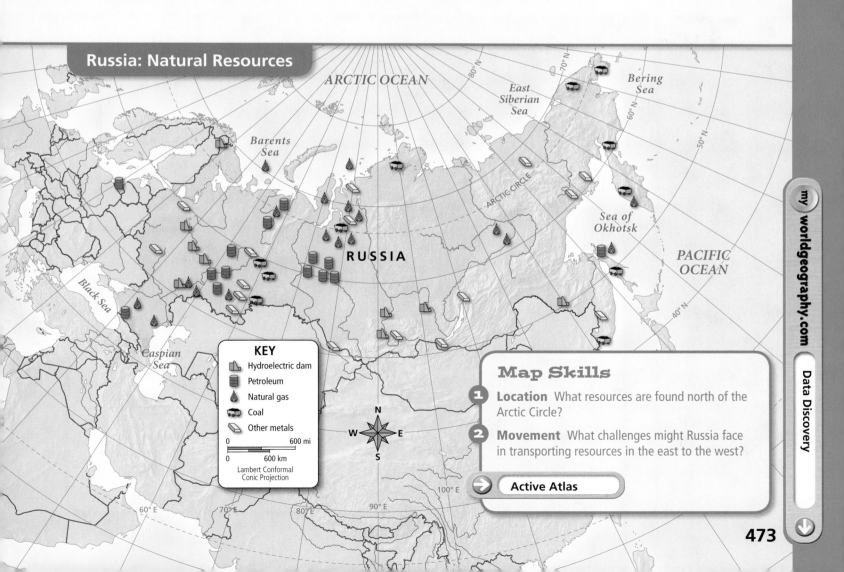

Russia: Natural Resources

ARCTIC OCEAN

Bering Sea

East Siberian Sea

Barents Sea

ARCTIC CIRCLE

RUSSIA

Sea of Okhotsk

PACIFIC OCEAN

Black Sea

Caspian Sea

KEY

- Hydroelectric dam
- Petroleum
- Natural gas
- Coal
- Other metals

0   600 mi

0   600 km

Lambert Conformal Conic Projection

N W E S

Map Skills

1 **Location** What resources are found north of the Arctic Circle?

2 **Movement** What challenges might Russia face in transporting resources in the east to the west?

→ **Active Atlas**

60° E   70° E   80° E   90° E   100° E

my **worldgeography.com**

Data Discovery

473

The People of Russia

Russia has a population of about 140 million people. Most live in the European part of the country. Russia's most densely settled areas also have the best climates and soils for agriculture. In contrast, the huge landmass of Siberia is sparsely populated, with around 20 people per square mile.

The largest cities are also located in the west, in European Russia. Moscow, the capital, is the largest metropolitan area in Russia, with more than 10 million people.

St. Petersburg, Russia's second largest city, is located on the Baltic Sea. It was called Leningrad during the Soviet era. St. Petersburg was founded by Russia's tsar, or emperor, Peter the Great, to rival the capitals of Europe.

Russia's huge population consists of many diverse ethnic groups with many languages and customs. The first Russians were East Slavs, who migrated into the area from east-central Europe. Today, about 80 percent of the population are Russian-speaking Slavs.

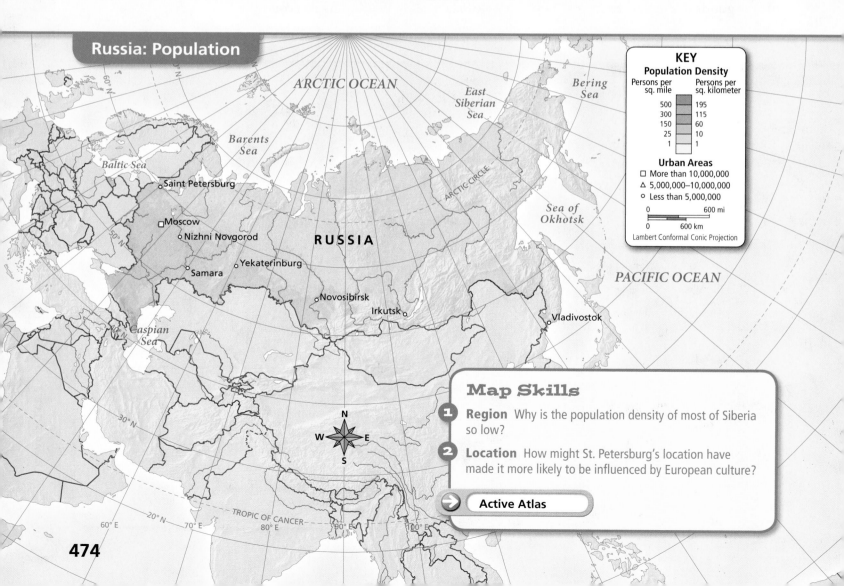

Russia: Population

KEY

Population Density

Persons per sq. mile	Persons per sq. kilometer
500	195
300	115
150	60
25	10
1	1

Urban Areas
□ More than 10,000,000
△ 5,000,000–10,000,000
○ Less than 5,000,000

0 ——— 600 mi
0 ——— 600 km
Lambert Conformal Conic Projection

Map Skills

1 **Region** Why is the population density of most of Siberia so low?

2 **Location** How might St. Petersburg's location have made it more likely to be influenced by European culture?

➔ **Active Atlas**

In Moscow, Boris (right) joins his friends to talk about sports and school. Boris participates in skateboarding competitions all over the world.

Language Lesson

This family lives in a village near Siberia's Lake Baikal. They belong to the minority Buryat nationality but also speak Russian.

Traditionally, the Slavic people who form most of the population were Russian Orthodox Christians. However, the communist rulers of the Soviet Union <u>pursued</u> a policy of discouraging religion. Today, after the collapse of the Soviet Union, more and more Russians attend Orthodox churches. Religious observance has also increased for Russia's many Muslims, Protestants, Jews, and Buddhists.

Along with Slavic Russians, there are at least 100 other ethnic and nationality groups in Russia. Each has a distinctive culture, language, and religion. Since Russian-speaking Slavs have dominated the nation for such a long time, many of these minority groups struggle to maintain their unique identities.

pursue, *v.,* to follow

Reading Check Who were the first Russians?

Section 1 Assessment

Key Terms

1. Use each of the following key terms in a complete sentence: Siberia, Ural Mountains, Lake Baikal, steppes, Kamchatka Peninsula, permafrost

Key Ideas

2. What challenges does climate present for human settlement in Russia?

3. Where are most of Russia's mineral resources found?

4. Why does the Far East region of Russia have a milder climate than most of the rest of the country?

Think Critically

5. **Identify Evidence** What facts could you use to explain why Siberia has a low population density?

6. **Solve Problems** What might minority groups do to preserve their identity in a country whose population is mostly ethnic Russian?

? Essential Question

What should governments do?

7. Look at the railroad mileage chart in this section. The Russian government paid the cost of building the Trans-Siberian Railroad. Why might governments invest in transportation systems? Go to your Student Journal to record your answer.

my **worldgeography.com** Language Lesson

History of Russia

Key Ideas
- Following centuries of invasion, Russia became an empire under the tsars.
- The Russian Revolution introduced communism and led to the establishment of the Soviet Union.
- Communism's flaws caused the Soviet Union to collapse, leading to its breakup into Russia and other republics.

Key Terms • tsar • Kremlin • serf • Bolsheviks • soviet • collectivization

 **Visual Glossary**

Reading Skill: Cause and Effect Take notes using the graphic organizer in your journal.

Russia's history spans many centuries. It is a rich story of invaders, ruthless leaders, and dramatic change that continues today.

Russia Emerges

Modern Russians are descended from East Slavs who migrated from Poland and Ukraine into western Russia in the 400s and 500s. They encountered invading Goths from Germany, along with Huns, Avars, Magyars, and Khazars from Asia.

The East Slavs The East Slavs were energetic traders. They founded trading posts along rivers that became the cities of Kiev and Novgorod. By the 800s, Scandinavian raiders and merchants, called Vikings, dominated Novgorod, Kiev, and other trading centers. They soon merged with the Slavic population.

Early Russia The Scythians, who arrived on the steppes before the East Slavs, were skilled goldsmiths. ▼

Kievan Rus Period The Viking prince Rurik and his allies invade Kiev in this medieval Russian drawing. ▶

East Slav

200   300   400   500   600   700   800

The role of Vikings in Russian history remains uncertain. Russia's *Primary Chronicle* claims that Slav and Finnish tribes invited a Viking of the Rus tribe to rule them. Some later scholars claimed that "Rus" refers to a Slav, not Viking, tribe. In any case, it was the Rus who gave their name to the first known East Slavic state: the Kievan Rus.

The Kievan Rus Forms Located in present-day Ukraine, Kiev became the region's economic and cultural center. Kiev's early rulers grew rich from trade and united the Slavic tribes. Under Vladimir, the Kievan Rus formed close ties with the Byzantine empire around the year 1000.

Vladimir adopted the Byzantines' Eastern Orthodox Christianity. He converted all of Kiev in a mass ceremony. Byzantine culture influenced Russian language, art, and music as well as the architectural style of Russian churches.

Gradually, many tribal leaders became princes. Princes were granted large areas of land, or appanages. They ruled these appanages and passed them on to family members. Competition between princes in the Kievan Rus was fierce. Some historians believe this rivalry weakened the state and invited a Mongol invasion.

In 1240, Mongol armies from Central Asia, known as the Golden Horde, took Kiev. The Kievan Rus collapsed. Russian princes now had to accept the authority of Mongol khans, or rulers.

As Kiev declined, the city of Moscow began to grow in importance. Its princes ruled an area known as Muscovy. It was a key trading center, and the Mongol khans favored its rulers. In 1328, the head of the Eastern Orthodox Church moved to Moscow, making the city even more important.

Reading Check What caused the fall of the Kievan Rus?

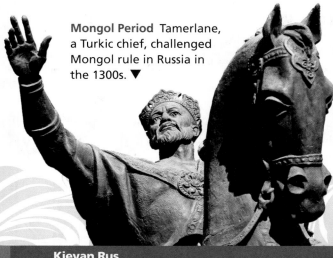

Mongol Period Tamerlane, a Turkic chief, challenged Mongol rule in Russia in the 1300s. ▼

Muscovy Period Ivan IV, or Ivan the Terrible, was the first Russian ruler to be crowned tsar. ▶

1156 Building begins at the Kremlin.

Kievan Rus			Mongol Rule			Muscovy
900	1000	1100	1200	1300	1400	1500

988 Prince Vladimir converts to Christianity.

1147 Moscow is founded.

Timeline

my worldgeography.com Timeline

However, Russia has <u>cooperated</u> with the EU on matters such as energy and climate change. These agreements include other former Soviet republics such as Ukraine, Belarus, and Kazakhstan.

Russia is a trading partner with Iran, which has poor relations with the United States. Russia has also loaned money to Iran to build nuclear reactors.

The United States has objected to this project. It is concerned that Iran will use the reactors to develop nuclear weapons. Russia's relationship with the United States has remained calm but cool.

Another foreign policy issue is Russia's relationship with China, the world's largest country in population. The Soviet Union and China had been competitors and enemies. This changed when Russia and China formed the Shanghai Cooperation Organization with several Central Asian countries in 2001. This organization has become a loose alliance. Joint military practices between Russia and China have worried Western nations.

The Future of Russia Strong post-Soviet leadership has reshaped Russia's politics and economy. Rich natural resources and continued superpower status make Russia an important player on the global stage. Whether it works together with the United States and other Western powers or takes a more hostile attitude, Russia has the world's full attention.

Reading Check What is the Shanghai Cooperation Organization?

cooperate, *v.,* to work together toward an agreed goal

Georgian soldiers run past a building bombed by Russian warplanes during the 2008 conflict. ▼

Section 3 Assessment

Essential Question

What should governments do?

Key Terms

1. Define each key term using a complete sentence: KGB, disposable income, censor, superpower.

Key Ideas

2. In what ways did the Russian government under Vladimir Putin halt democratic reform?

3. How did Russia's petroleum industry change under Putin?

4. What are some of the major health problems in Russia?

Think Critically

5. **Draw Conclusions** Why do you think Russia has opposed membership in the European Union for former Soviet republics?

6. **Draw Inferences** Why might Russia want closer relations with China?

7. Think about the life expectancy and infant mortality graphs in this section. What do you think the government can do about the health problems in Russia? Go to your Student Journal to record your answer.

myworldgeography.com

Active Atlas

Chapter Assessment

Key Terms and Ideas

1. **Recall** In what ways does **Siberia** present Russia with great advantages and great challenges?

2. **Compare and Contrast** Describe the climate and vegetation on the tundra and the **steppes.**

3. **Explain** What sort of rulers were the Russian **tsars?**

4. **Recall** How did the buildings of the **Kremlin** demonstrate power in imperial Russia?

5. **Discuss** How did communism shape the Soviet government and economy?

6. **Summarize** What was **collectivization** and how did affect the Soviet Union?

7. **Discuss** How might Putin's **KGB** background affect his beliefs about the role of government?

8. **Explain** What might prompt the Russian government to **censor** a news story?

Think Critically

9. **Draw Conclusions** Why do you think Josef Stalin took actions such as collectivization and the jailing of opponents? Explain.

10. **Compare Viewpoints** One of Stalin's officers said the Great Famine would show the peasants "who is the master. It cost millions of lives, but the collective farm system is here to stay." Do you think Stalin agreed with him? Why?

11. **Identify Evidence** What historical evidence would support the statement "Russia has a long history of autocratic government"?

12. **Drawing Inferences** Why do you think many Russians want the government to be in control of wages, pensions, and healthcare?

Places to Know

For each place, write the letter from the map that shows its location.

13. Kamchatka Peninsula

14. Yakutsk

15. Lake Baikal

16. Moscow

17. St. Petersburg

18. Ural Mountains

19. **Estimate** Using the scale, estimate the distance from Moscow to Lake Baikal.

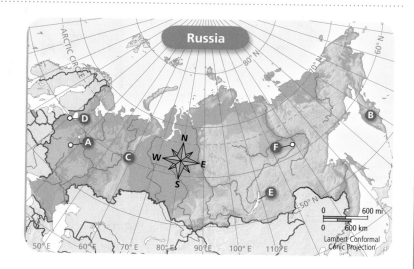

Essential Question
myWorld Chapter Activity

Memo to Russia Follow your teacher's instructions to examine information on some of the challenges facing Russia today. Consider environmental data, Russian health and crime figures, as well as the nation's international partnerships and other information as you set priorities. After your review, prepare an official government memo detailing which problem Russia should address first and why.

21st Century Learning
Search for Information on the Internet

Search for three different Web sites for additional information about the political, economic, and social challenges facing Russia. The following types of Web sites might prove helpful:
- encyclopedias or museums
- international organizations, such as the UN or World Trade Organization
- U.S. sites such as *CIA World Factbook*

Document-Based Questions

Success Tracker™
Online at myworldgeography.com

Use your knowledge of Russia and Documents A and B to answer questions 1–3.

Document A

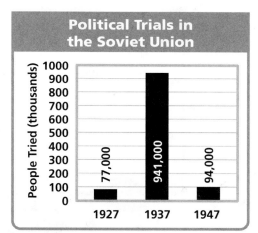

Political Trials in the Soviet Union

People Tried (thousands)

1927: 77,000
1937: 941,000
1947: 94,000

SOURCE: Open Society Archives

Document B

" You might well ask why a prisoner worked so hard for ten years in a camp. . . . In the camps they had these gangs to make the prisoners keep each other on their toes. . . . It was like this—either you all got something extra or you all starved."

—Alexander Solzhenitsyn,
One Day in the Life of Ivan Denisovich
(a book about life in a Soviet prison camp)

1. How did the number of people brought to trial change from 1927 to 1937?

   A It decreased.

   B It increased by half.

   C It increased by more than 10 times.

   D It increased by 100 times.

2. What would be the punishment if a prisoner stopped working hard?

   A The guards would whip him in front of his gang.

   B The guards would take food away from his gang.

   C He would be put into a new labor camp.

   D He would have to give his food to his gang.

3. **Writing Task** What do you think the gang would say to a prisoner who stopped working hard? Write a dialogue.

myworldgeography.com Self-Test

Media Watchdog

Your Mission Use the Media Analysis Checklist to study the poster on the facing page. Examine how the poster conveys its message. Then go online and evaluate an article or opinion piece.

Media messages are everywhere in modern society. Can you believe everything you see, hear, and read on television, in print, or on the Internet? Who keeps track of the media's honesty and objectivity? When a member of the media is accused of bias, how can you know who is right?

By understanding how to analyze media content, you can spot bias and persuasive messages. Practicing this skill will help you to evaluate whether or not public officials and news sources are telling you the truth. You can also apply these techniques to advertising, which will help you decide how to spend your money more wisely.

Media Analysis Checklist

1. Author
2. Intended audience
3. Words or phrases
4. Images and other design elements
5. Overall message
6. Persuasive techniques
7. Examples of bias, if any

STEP 1

Determine the Message.

Copy the Media Analysis Checklist at the left onto your own paper. Use it to record your observations about the poster at the right. Who published the poster, and who is its intended audience? (Hint: Look at the flag at the bottom of the poster.) Read the poster and study its visual elements, such as the use of colors or photographs. Considering the words and visuals together, what is the poster's message?

STEP 2

Check for Bias.

Next, evaluate how the poster uses persuasive techniques such as bright colors or a photograph with children. Note how the poster uses words that are short, simple, and to the point. Do these words encourage you to feel a certain way? Consider whether or not your reaction is based on facts or on opinions and feelings. Record your observations on your Media Analysis Checklist.

STEP 3

Analyze Online Media.

Make a second, blank copy of the Media Analysis Checklist. Now go online to sources suggested by your teacher. Find an article or opinion piece about Europe or Russia, and analyze it as you did the poster. Once you have completed your Media Analysis Checklist, use your findings in a class discussion.

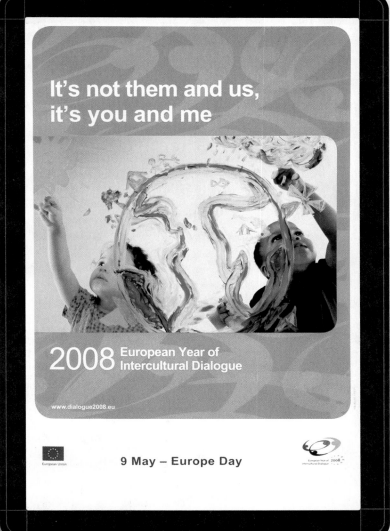

It's not them and us, it's you and me

2008 European Year of Intercultural Dialogue

www.dialogue2008.eu

European Union

9 May – Europe Day

European Year of 2008 Intercultural Dialogue

Africa

The continent of Africa is home to a wide range of climates and ecosystems, from rain forests to savannas and deserts. More than 900 million Africans live in 53 countries. They speak more than 2,000 different languages and belong to several thousand ethnic groups. Some of the countries with the largest populations are Nigeria, Democratic Republic of the Congo, South Africa, Ethiopia, Morocco, and Egypt.

What time is it there?

| Washington, D.C. | Accra, Ghana |
| 9 A.M. Monday | 2 P.M. Monday |

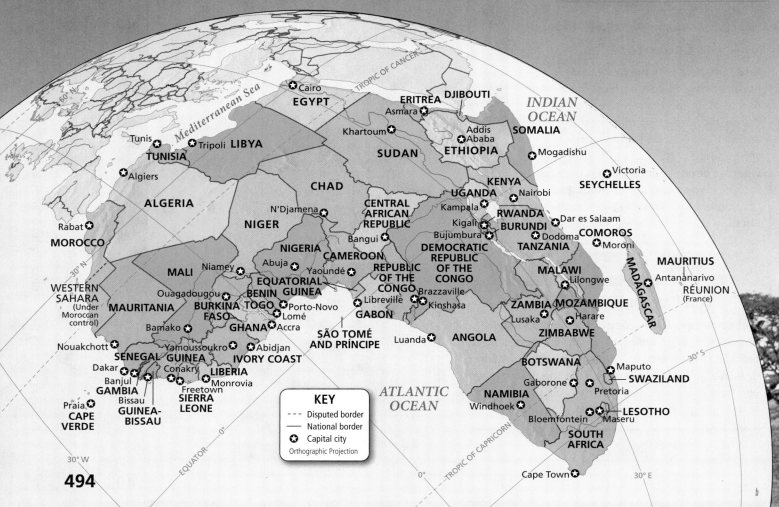

KEY
- - - Disputed border
─── National border
★ Capital city
Orthographic Projection

The Unit Ahead

➡ **Chapter 13** West and Central Africa

➡ **Chapter 14** Southern and Eastern Africa

➡ **Chapter 15** North Africa

my worldgeography.com

Plan your trip online by doing a Data Discovery Activity and watching the myStory Videos of the region's teens.

my Story

Evelyn
Age: 15
Home: Kpong, Ghana

Chapter 13

my Story

Khulekani
Age: 19
Home: Port St. Johns, South Africa

Chapter 14

my Story

Shaimaa
Age: 18
Home: Cairo, Egypt

Chapter 15

Giraffes on the savanna in Tanzania

495

Regional Overview
Physical Geography

Mediterranean Sea

Atlas Mountains

Nile River

Red Sea

S a h a r a

Niger River

Lake Chad

Blue Nile River

Volta River

S a h e l

Ethiopian Highlands

Niger Basin

White Nile River

Sudd

Great Rift Valley

Lake Albert

Congo Basin

Lake Victoria

Mt. Kenya 17,057 ft (5,199 m)

Serengeti Plain

Congo River

Mt. Kilimanjaro 19,341 ft (5,895 m)

ATLANTIC OCEAN

Lake Tanganyika

Lake Nyasa

Zambezi River

Namib Desert

Kalahari Desert

Limpopo River

Madagascar

Drakensberg

The Sahara is the largest hot desert in the world.

The Congo River Basin contains dense, lush rain forests.

The Ethiopian Highlands have a higher elevation than most of Africa.

The Serengeti plain is home to many different kinds of animals.

INDIAN OCEAN

Victoria Falls is one of Africa's most stunning natural features.

Regional Flyover

Take a trip by plane over Africa. You take off from South Africa and head north. The first thing you see is a strip of green land, and then suddenly a tall mountain range. Those mountains are the start of the high plateau on which most of Africa is located. Past the mountains, you see the Kalahari Desert.

Continuing north, the land slowly gets wetter and greener. It turns from desert into grasslands, and then dips down into the lush rain forests of the Congo River Basin. You pass the Equator. Then, the land below you slowly starts to get drier. The rain forest gives way to grassland, and then eventually to the semiarid Sahel region as you pass over Lake Chad.

Finally you cross over the Sahara, a huge desert. As your plane lands, the Mediterranean Sea is in front of you. To your east is the Nile River and to your west the Atlas Mountains. You have flown 4,600 miles and passed over 8 countries, and still you have only seen a small sample of the continent of Africa.

 In-Flight Movie

Take flight over Africa and explore the region from the air.

my worldgeography.com

In-Flight Movie

Regional Overview
Human Geography

Water

Rainfall and access to water are so important in Africa that they largely determine where its people live. Few people live in the dry deserts, but huge cities can spring up where rivers cut through them. Dense populations thrive in wetter areas. In between the deserts and rain forests, smaller groups of people live on grasslands and semiarid plains. Some countries in Africa are packed with natural resources such as gold or oil, while others are less fortunate. Although Africa contains 22 percent of Earth's land, it is home to only 14 percent of Earth's people. Each region of the continent presents a different set of challenges to its people. Africans have adapted to these challenges in different ways, giving rise to a wide variety of cultures and ways of living.

Population Density in Africa

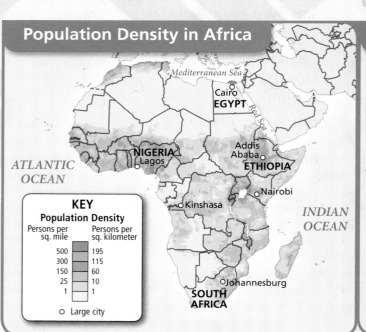

KEY
Population Density

Persons per sq. mile	Persons per sq. kilometer
500	195
300	115
150	60
25	10
1	1

○ Large city

Precipitation in Africa

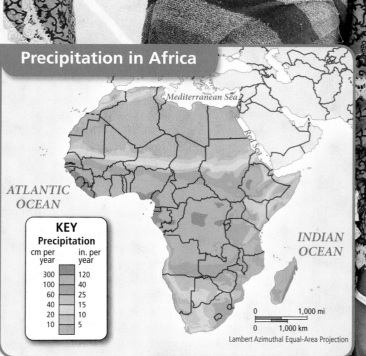

KEY
Precipitation

cm per year	in. per year
300	120
100	40
60	25
40	15
20	10
10	5

0   1,000 mi
0   1,000 km
Lambert Azimuthal Equal-Area Projection

my World IN NUMBERS

	Egypt	Ethiopia	South Africa	Nigeria	United States
Food per day per person (kcal)*	3,320	1,810	2,900	2,600	3,830
Oil production per day (barrels)	664,000	0	199,100	2,352,000	8,457,000
Gross domestic product per capita	$5,000	$700	$9,700	$2,100	$45,800
Population	82 million	83 million	49 million	146 million	304 million

SOURCE: CIA World Factbook Online, 2009
* SOURCE: UN Food and Agriculture Organization (2003)

Put It Together

1. What physical feature covers most of northern Africa?

2. Is Nigeria densely or sparsely populated?

3. How are rainfall and population density related? Why do you think this is the case?

Data Discovery

Find your own data to make a regional data table.

Size Comparison

Africa is much larger than the continental United States.

my worldgeography.com   Data Discovery

499

Chapter 13

West and Central Africa

Who should benefit from a country's resources?

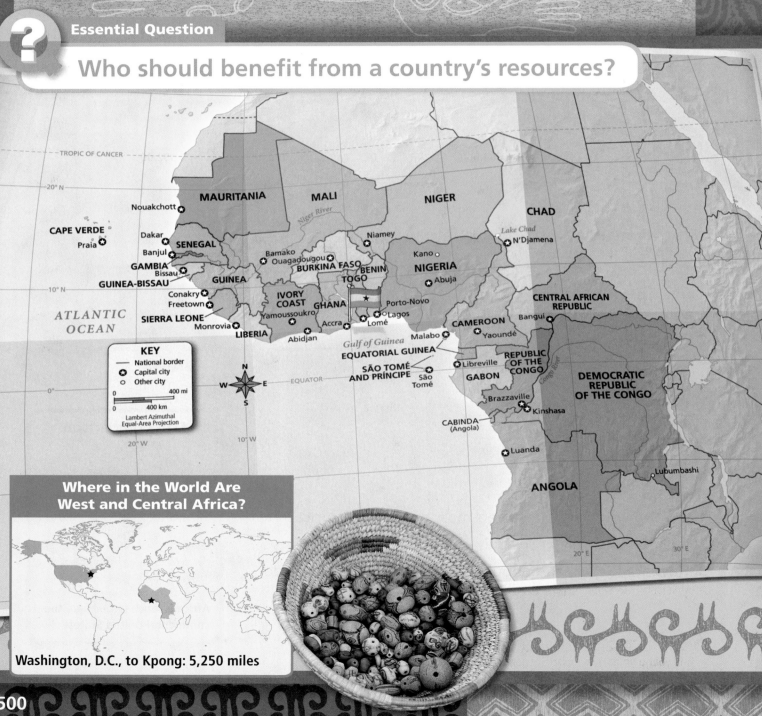

TROPIC OF CANCER

20° N

ATLANTIC OCEAN

MAURITANIA

Nouakchott

CAPE VERDE
Dakar
Praia
Banjul **SENEGAL**
GAMBIA
Bissau
GUINEA-BISSAU
Conakry
Freetown
SIERRA LEONE
Monrovia
LIBERIA
Abidjan

MALI

Niger River

Bamako
Ouagadougou
BURKINA FASO
GUINEA
IVORY COAST
Yamoussoukro
GHANA
Accra
Lomé
TOGO
BENIN
Porto-Novo
Lagos

Gulf of Guinea

NIGER

Niamey

Kano
NIGERIA
Abuja

CHAD

Lake Chad
N'Djamena

CENTRAL AFRICAN REPUBLIC

Bangui

CAMEROON
Yaoundé

EQUATORIAL GUINEA
Malabo
SÃO TOMÉ AND PRÍNCIPE
São Tomé
Libreville
GABON

REPUBLIC OF THE CONGO
Brazzaville

Congo River

DEMOCRATIC REPUBLIC OF THE CONGO
Kinshasa

CABINDA (Angola)

Luanda

Lubumbashi

ANGOLA

EQUATOR

0°

10° N

20° W

10° W

0°

20° E

30° E

KEY
— National border
⊛ Capital city
○ Other city

0   400 mi
0   400 km
Lambert Azimuthal
Equal-Area Projection

N W E S

Where in the World Are West and Central Africa?

Washington, D.C., to Kpong: 5,250 miles

my Story

A String of Dreams

In this section, you'll read about a girl from Ghana named Evelyn who works in her grandmother's bead-making business. What does Evelyn's story tell you about life in West and Central Africa?

Explore the Essential Question

- at **my** **worldgeography.com**
- using the **myWorld Chapter Activity**
- with the **Student Journal**

Story by Chrispat Okutu for myWorld Geography Online

The Kenashie Market in Accra, Ghana, is full of vendors selling everything from coconuts and chickens to textiles and furniture. Men, women, and children of all ages hustle to sell the goods balanced atop their heads or heaped in their heavy carts.

In West Africa, where Ghana is located, there is a long tradition of women trading in the marketplace. In some countries, women organize and dominate many local markets. Overall, though, women earn less than men. In Ghana, only 70 percent of women can read and write, in contrast to 84 percent of men.

Evelyn, a 15-year-old Ghanaian girl, takes part in her region's tradition of women selling goods in the marketplace. She helps her grandmother make and sell their authentic Ghanaian beads at different markets near their home village of Kpong. Kpong lies about 30 miles away from the bustling

my worldgeography.com On Assignment

501

Bottles are crushed on a stone. The glass is poured into molds that are baked in a kiln.

Members of Evelyn's family string finished beads.

markets of Accra. Kpong is Evelyn's home and where her grandmother's bead business, Adede Beads Enterprises, is located. The plantain farms and thick greenery that surround the small village of Kpong are very different from Accra.

Evelyn's grandmother, Madam Adede, is a successful entrepreneur herself. She has been running the bead business she inherited from her grandfather for more than 31 years. Adede owns a humble home where she and her family live and work. The small building in the backyard serves as her bead factory.

Evelyn crushes bottle glass to make beads. The pail blocks the glass from flying up into her eyes or spilling onto the ground.

Adede specializes in the ancient craft of bead making practiced by the Krobo people of eastern Ghana. Adede taught this craft to two daughters and six grandchildren. She expects the business to continue for many generations. Adede has chosen Evelyn to take over her business someday. Evelyn has just graduated from high school. She hopes to study accounting at a university. But the cost won't be easy for her family to afford.

Evelyn already plays an important role in the family business. It is her job to crush glass in preparation for making the beads. Today she is making transparent glass beads, which are formed from a very fine glass powder. Evelyn begins by breaking glass bottles they have collected. It is hard work, but Evelyn is accustomed to the heavy labor and stifling heat that comes with everyday life at the bead factory in Kpong.

Crushing the glass is the first of many steps necessary to produce a finished piece of clear beaded jewelry. Adede explains that they also make glazed beads and *bodom* beads. The word *bodom* means "dog" in Twi, a common language in Ghana. The bodom beads are very large, bold beads, named for their resemblance to the attention-getting bark of a dog.

The busy marketplace features many kinds of goods.

The sign for the family business

The family beads on sale at the Krobo Odumase Market

Beads, such as those made by Evelyn, are worn not only for adornment, but also to identify the various ethnic cultures of Ghana. Beads are often worn at parties, weddings, and church services.

Today the family is taking its beads to sell at the Krobo Odumase Market a few miles from Kpong. Adede's bead stand in the marketplace displays their colorful jewelry to the buyers in the market. Everyone works hard to sell as much as possible. They need money not only to support the family but also to send Evelyn to university.

For her part, Evelyn plans to pay back this kindness. Evelyn says, "After university, I'll get a job outside and help my grandma, too, because I have my siblings to take care of. It's important to have two jobs. So if one fails, you have the other one." The road ahead of Evelyn is difficult, but her family's bead business has paved the way.

Meet the Journalist

Name Travis Hamilton
Favorite Moment Seeing children play and laugh

→ **myStory Video**

Join Evelyn as she explores the Krobo Odumase Market.

Key Ideas

- Location together with wind and rainfall patterns creates a wide variety of environments in West and Central Africa.

- Climate zones vary from very dry to wet and tropical.

- Climate zones influence where and how people live in West and Central Africa.

- People have both adapted to and changed the environments of this region.

Key Terms • Sahel • savanna • arable land • desertification • deforestation • malaria

 Visual Glossary

Reading Skill: Label an Outline Map Take notes using the outline map in your journal.

A group of people travels by boat on the Niger River in Niger. ▼

Physical Features

The physical features of West and Central Africa are rich and varied. They range from vast deserts to dense rain forests. The world's largest hot desert, the Sahara, reaches down into West and Central Africa from the north. Other dry areas also occur in the far south. Between the dry areas, grasslands blend into the lush tropical rainforest at the region's center.

In contrast, the region's landforms do not have great variety. Much of the continent of Africa as a whole is a plateau. Although highland areas exist, no major mountain chains interrupt the plateau.

West and Central Africa: Physical

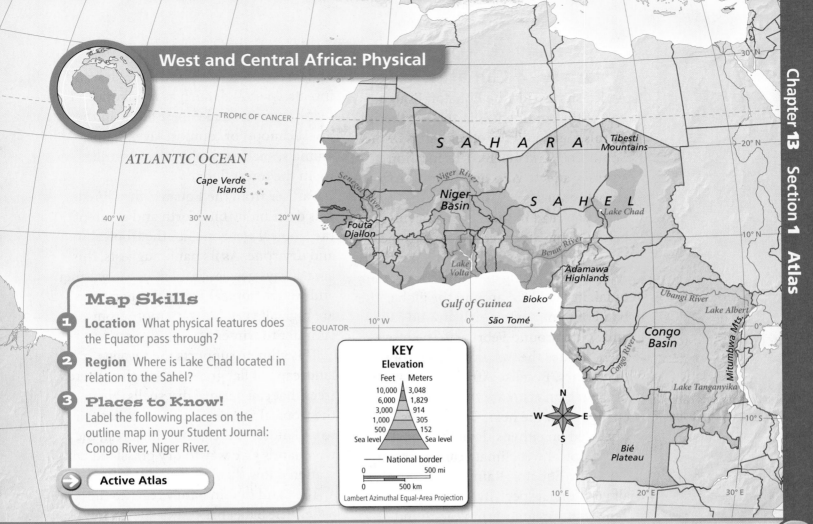

TROPIC OF CANCER

ATLANTIC OCEAN

Cape Verde Islands

40° W   30° W   20° W

SAHARA

Tibesti Mountains

Niger River

Niger Basin

SAHEL

Lake Chad

Fouta Djallon

Senegal River

Lake Volta

Benue River

Adamawa Highlands

Gulf of Guinea

Bioko

São Tomé

EQUATOR   10° W   0°

Ubangi River

Lake Albert

Congo River

Congo Basin

Mitumbwa Mts.

Lake Tanganyika

Bié Plateau

10° E   20° E   30° E

20° N
10° N
0°
10° S

Map Skills

1 Location What physical features does the Equator pass through?

2 Region Where is Lake Chad located in relation to the Sahel?

3 Places to Know!
Label the following places on the outline map in your Student Journal: Congo River, Niger River.

→ Active Atlas

KEY
Elevation

Feet	Meters
10,000	3,048
6,000	1,829
3,000	914
1,000	305
500	152
Sea level	Sea level

— National border

0   500 mi
0   500 km

Lambert Azimuthal Equal-Area Projection

The plateau has been ground down by millions of years of weathering and erosion. Low elevations in the northwest build to higher elevations in the southeast.

West and Central Africa boasts some of the largest drainage basins in the world. A drainage basin is the entire area of land from which rainfall flows into a river or lake. The Chad basin drains a huge area. At its center lies the large but shallow Lake Chad. Lake Chad is the largest body of water in the Sahel. The **Sahel** is a semiarid, fairly dry area that lies between the Sahara and regions to the south that receive more rainfall.

The Niger River basin is the largest in western Africa. More rain falls in some parts of the basin than in others. Heavy rain causes flooding at times in parts of the basin.

The huge Congo River drains most of central Africa. Heavy rainfall feeds the Congo through most of the year. In fact, the Congo basin hosts Africa's largest network of navigable rivers, or rivers that ships can pass through. However, waterfalls and rapids can make passage difficult and dangerous.

Reading Check What are two important rivers in the region?

A Variety of Climates

Africa sits astride the Equator. Roughly half of the continent is in the Northern Hemisphere, and the other half is in the Southern Hemisphere. This location strongly affects West and Central Africa's climate zones.

As you read in the Core Concepts, a belt of rising air called the intertropical convergence zone, or ITCZ, circles the Equator. The rising air causes heavy rain to fall in the ITCZ around the globe. This band of rain moves north around July and south around February. The movement creates the wet and dry seasons of the tropics. Because Africa is so flat, each of the region's climate zones gradually changes into the next. These zones are mirrored on either side of the Equator.

A tropical wet climate can be found along the Equator. Rain falls plentifully all year long, especially in spring and fall. Temperatures are warm year-round.

In West and Central Africa, dense rain forests grow in the tropical wet zone.

The forests teem with birds, reptiles, and insects. Mammals such as monkeys and flying squirrels make their home in the forest canopy, or topmost layer. Large animals, such as elephants and gorillas, roam the forest floor.

Farther from the Equator, the climate gets drier bit by bit. North and south of the tropical wet zone lies the tropical wet and dry zone. As its name suggests, this area always gets less rain than the warmer and wetter tropical areas. Temperatures are high all year, but vary more from summer to winter.

This climate supports the **savanna,** a landscape of flat grasslands with scattered trees that can survive dry spells. Near the tropical forests, the savanna has tall woodlands. Farther from the forest, the woodlands give way to dry grassland with scattered low shrubs.

The band of rain barely reaches the Sahel. The Sahel has only a short rainy season of at most three months. Less rain falls than on the savanna. Daily temperatures are high. As in a desert, evening temperatures can dip very low.

Beyond the bands of precipitation lie the arid zones. These desert regions get little rainfall. Brutally hot days contrast with very cold nights. Not surprisingly, fewer animal species live in the drier regions, especially in the desert, where vegetation is sparse. Small mammals, such as rats and hares, are found along with gazelles, hyenas, and ostriches.

Reading Check How is a tropical wet climate different from a tropical wet and dry climate?

A man herds cattle in the semiarid Sahel. ▼

myWorld Activity
Compare Climates

West and Central Africa: Climate

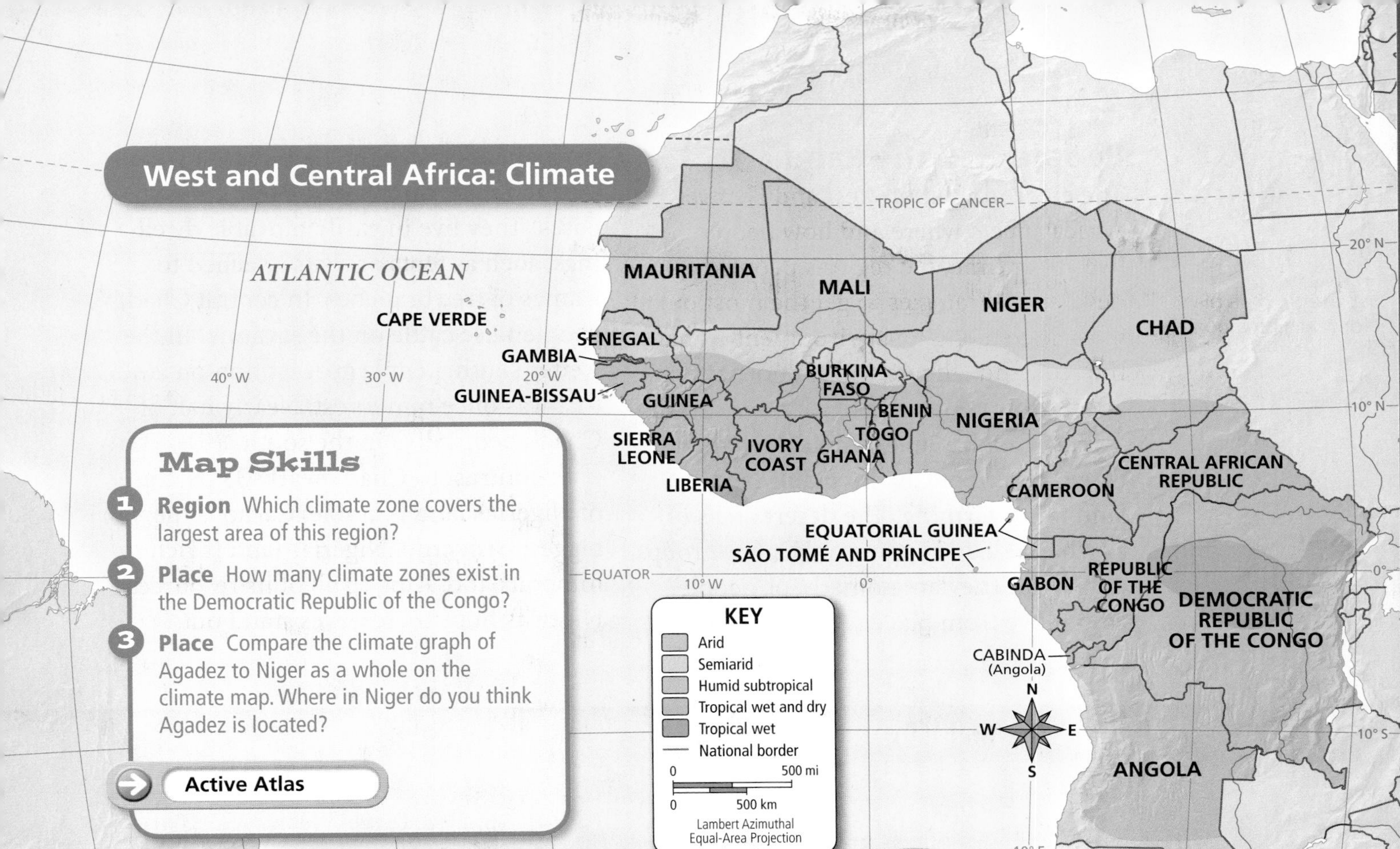
ATLANTIC OCEAN
MAURITANIA
MALI
NIGER
CHAD
CAPE VERDE
SENEGAL
GAMBIA
GUINEA-BISSAU
GUINEA
BURKINA FASO
BENIN
TOGO
NIGERIA
SIERRA LEONE
IVORY COAST
GHANA
LIBERIA
CENTRAL AFRICAN REPUBLIC
CAMEROON
EQUATORIAL GUINEA
SÃO TOMÉ AND PRÍNCIPE
GABON
REPUBLIC OF THE CONGO
DEMOCRATIC REPUBLIC OF THE CONGO
CABINDA (Angola)
ANGOLA
TROPIC OF CANCER
EQUATOR
40° W
30° W
20° W
10° W
0°
10° E
20° E
30° E
20° N
10° N
10° S
20° S
N
S
E
W
KEY
Arid
Semiarid
Humid subtropical
Tropical wet and dry
Tropical wet
National border
0
500 mi
0
500 km
Lambert Azimuthal Equal-Area Projection

Map Skills

1. **Region** Which climate zone covers the largest area of this region?
2. **Place** How many climate zones exist in the Democratic Republic of the Congo?
3. **Place** Compare the climate graph of Agadez to Niger as a whole on the climate map. Where in Niger do you think Agadez is located?

Active Atlas

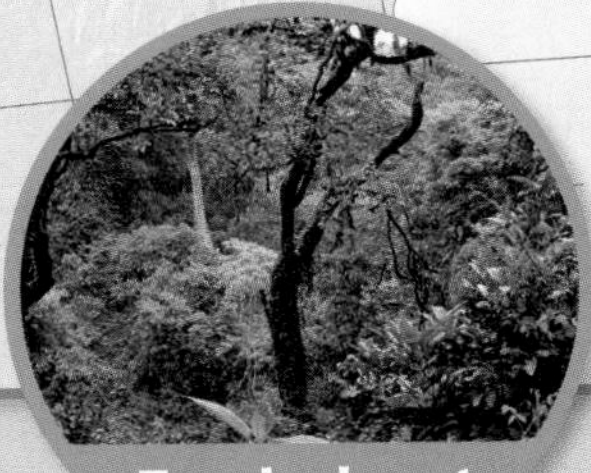
Tropical wet

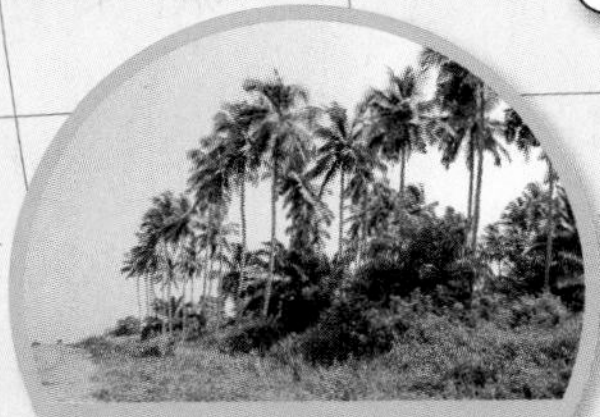
Tropical wet and dry

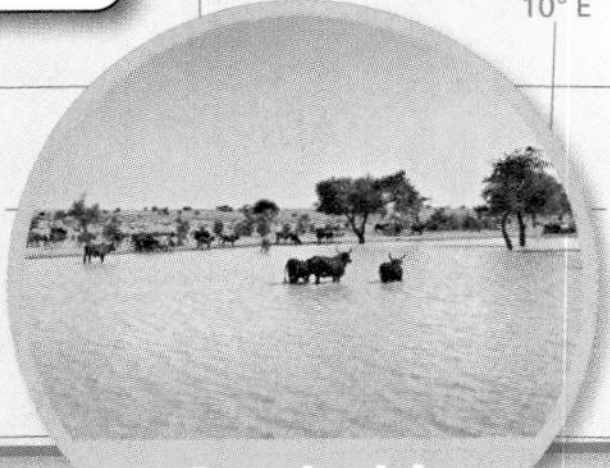
Semiarid

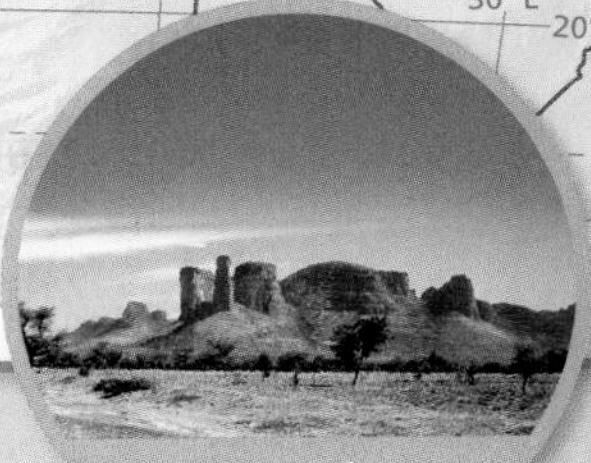
Arid

Climate of Kinshasa, Democratic Republic of the Congo

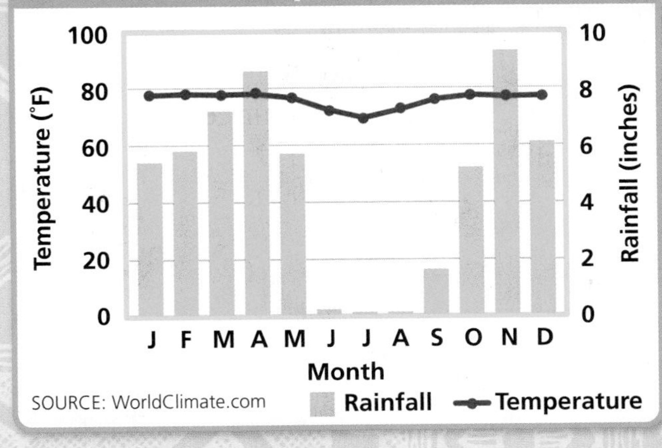
100
80
60
40
20
0
Temperature (°F)
10
8
6
4
2
0
Rainfall (inches)
J F M A M J J A S O N D
Month
Rainfall
Temperature

SOURCE: WorldClimate.com

Climate of Agadez, Niger

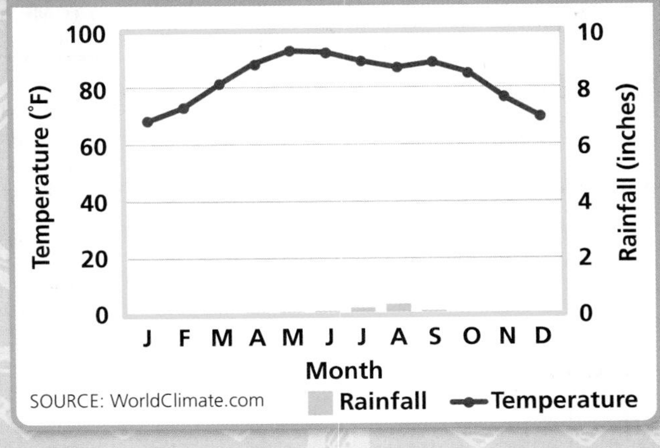
100
80
60
40
20
0
Temperature (°F)
10
8
6
4
2
0
Rainfall (inches)
J F M A M J J A S O N D
Month
Rainfall
Temperature

SOURCE: WorldClimate.com

my worldgeography.com Active Atlas

People and the Land

The environment of West and Central Africa affects where and how people live. Over time, the region's people have developed <u>strategies</u> to get the most out of their challenging environment. What the land and climate will support often affects how people make a living.

Take Chad as an example. Less than three percent of Chad is **arable land,** or land fit for farming. The desert areas of northern Chad support only a few groups of people. They are nomads, or people who move from place to place without a permanent home. The nomads who live in Chad raise camels and a few crops in oases. They live in easily movable dwellings, such as tents or mats attached to frames of tree branches. In central Chad, people raise cattle on the savanna. In the wetter south, people grow cotton on land that was once rain forest. Nearly half of Chad's people live in the south.

In contrast to Chad, nearly 33 percent of Nigeria's land is arable. Cacao is the biggest cash crop. Nigeria's land is rich in minerals, too. Among all of its resources, Nigeria's huge oil reserves stand out.

strategy, *n.,* a plan for reaching a goal

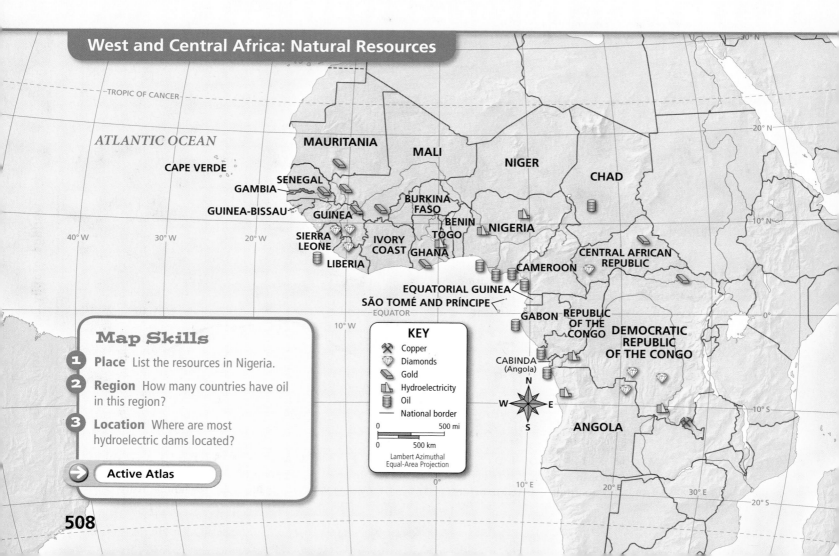

West and Central Africa: Natural Resources

Map Skills

1 **Place** List the resources in Nigeria.

2 **Region** How many countries have oil in this region?

3 **Location** Where are most hydroelectric dams located?

→ **Active Atlas**

KEY

- ⚒ Copper
- ◇ Diamonds
- ⬙ Gold
- ⬠ Hydroelectricity
- ▮ Oil
- — National border

0   500 mi

0   500 km

Lambert Azimuthal Equal-Area Projection

Tapping this resource, however, hurts Nigeria's environment. An estimated 1.5 million tons of oil have dripped from leaky pipelines into the Niger Delta over the past 50 years. Oil seeps into wetlands, forests, and farmlands. It pollutes air and water and causes fires.

Many countries in this region have rich natural resources. Like Nigeria, Angola, Cameroon, Chad, and other countries also have oil reserves. The Democratic Republic of the Congo has deposits of copper, diamonds, uranium, and other minerals. Liberia and Sierra Leone have diamond fields. These natural resources have the potential to bring great wealth to the region. As you will read, they have also often caused conflict.

Many people in the region use land to farm and graze animals. Although not always harmful, this use of land can hurt the environment. During dry periods in the Sahel, herders allow too many of their animals to graze. In addition, people also chop down trees for firewood or to sell.

These uses, combined with drought, have caused parts of the Sahel to dry out and become desert. This change from arable land to desert is called **desertification.** Chad and other Sahel nations are working on ways to stop desertification.

The Ivory Coast (also called Côte d'Ivoire) gets plentiful rain. Even so, desertification threatens this nation as well. The main culprit is deforestation. **Deforestation** is the loss of forest cover that occurs when the trees in a forest are removed faster than they can grow back. The soil dries out without the shade of trees to protect it from the hot sun.

The Ivory Coast has a very high rate of deforestation. More than 90 percent of its forests have been cleared by the timber industry in the past few <u>decades.</u> Foreign-owned companies have done much of the harvesting of this raw material for their industries. Deforestation is also a problem in the Democratic Republic of the Congo.

Reading Check What causes desertification?

decade, *n.,* a period of ten years

Deforestation

1 People cut down trees to burn as firewood, to sell as lumber, or to clear land for farms or houses.

2 After trees are gone, soil bakes in the sun and falls apart. No longer held in place by tree roots, it is blown away by the wind or washed away by heavy rains.

my worldgeography.com | Active Atlas

509

Population

Just as the environment affects what people do for a living, it also affects where they live. As you have read, Nigeria has plenty of land that is good for farming. Not surprisingly, it also has the largest population in the region. In fact, it is the most populous nation in all of Africa, with 148 million people. In contrast, fewer people live in countries that are in desert regions. For instance, Mauritania is home to only about 3.3 million people.

People often think of Africans as rural farmers. In this region of Africa, many people do still farm or raise livestock. However, more and more people are moving to cities such as Lagos in Nigeria or Accra in Ghana.

People may move to cities to look for work because a season's crops have failed. Conflict forces others from their homes. Some move away from the Sahel because of desertification. The desert spreads to where they raise animals or crops.

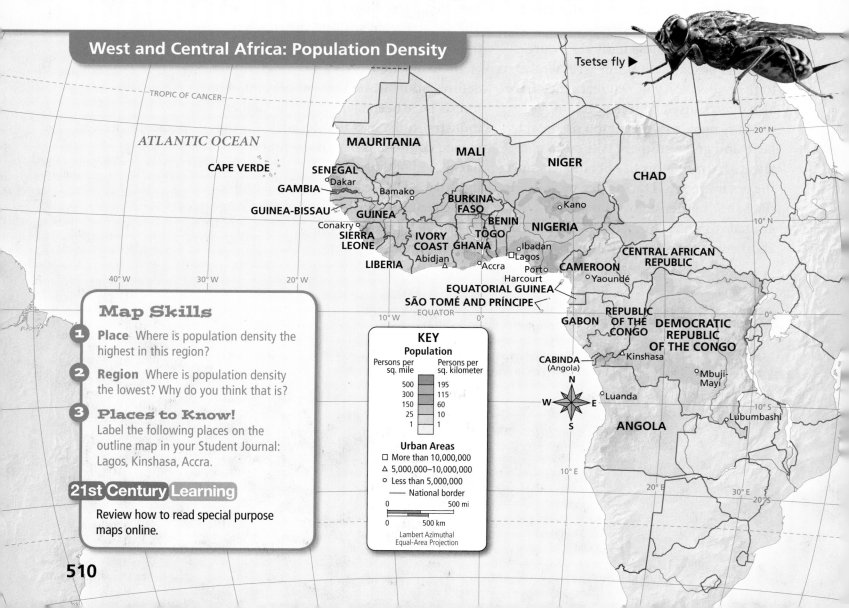

West and Central Africa: Population Density

Tsetse fly ▶

ATLANTIC OCEAN

TROPIC OF CANCER

MAURITANIA
CAPE VERDE
SENEGAL
°Dakar
GAMBIA
Bamako°
GUINEA-BISSAU
GUINEA
Conakry°
SIERRA
LEONE
LIBERIA
IVORY
COAST GHANA
Abidjan △
MALI
BURKINA
FASO
BENIN
TOGO
NIGER
°Kano
NIGERIA
°Ibadan
□Lagos
°Accra Porto
Harcourt
EQUATORIAL GUINEA
SÃO TOMÉ AND PRÍNCIPE
EQUATOR
CHAD
CENTRAL AFRICAN
REPUBLIC
CAMEROON
°Yaoundé
GABON
REPUBLIC
OF THE
CONGO
DEMOCRATIC
REPUBLIC
OF THE CONGO
CABINDA
(Angola)
°Kinshasa
°Luanda
°Mbuji-
Mayi
°Lubumbashi
ANGOLA

40° W   30° W   20° W

20° N
10° N
10° W   0°
0°
10° S
10° E
20° E   30° E
20° S

Map Skills

1 **Place** Where is population density the highest in this region?

2 **Region** Where is population density the lowest? Why do you think that is?

3 **Places to Know!**
Label the following places on the outline map in your Student Journal: Lagos, Kinshasa, Accra.

21st Century Learning

Review how to read special purpose maps online.

KEY
Population

Persons per sq. mile	Persons per sq. kilometer
500	195
300	115
150	60
25	10
1	1

Urban Areas
□ More than 10,000,000
△ 5,000,000–10,000,000
○ Less than 5,000,000
— National border

0   500 mi
0   500 km

Lambert Azimuthal
Equal-Area Projection

N
W   E
S

510

Unfortunately, the city doesn't always hold a better life for them. Because the cities are growing so quickly, they are overcrowded. There are shortages of good housing and good jobs.

Reading Check How are West and Central Africa's populations changing?

The Problem of Disease

Some big environmental challenges in West and Central Africa come in very small packages: insects. Insects carry parasites, or small organisms that live off of a larger organism. The tsetse (TEE tsee) fly spreads a parasite that causes a disease known as sleeping sickness. It is fatal to both humans and cattle. The disease is widespread. The presence of the tsetse fly limits where cattle can be raised, and where people can live.

Mosquitoes spread **malaria**, another life-threatening disease caused by parasites. Mosquitoes thrive in environments that are hot and wet. Therefore, malaria is common throughout the tropical and subtropical regions of Africa. Ninety percent of deaths from malaria occur in these regions.

Some diseases are both treatable and preventable. Sadly, many people in this region cannot afford to take even the simplest measures to protect themselves. Nigerian doctor Emmanuel Miri visits rural villages to educate communities on disease prevention and treatment.

66 Most people in rural areas are farmers, and when you have a disease like Guinea worm [a parasite], you are incapacitated, unable to continue with your work. By preventing the hundreds of thousands of cases that we do each year, we are freeing up that many more people to farm so that they will have food and be able to take care of their families. 99

—Emmanuel Miri

Local education programs like Miri's are helping to combat many diseases.

Reading Check How does malaria spread?

my World IN NUMBERS

Mosquito nets treated with insecticide help prevent malaria. Yet, in 2007, only **6%** of households in the Ivory Coast owned one.

Section 1 Assessment

Essential Question

Key Terms

1. Use the following terms to describe the challenging environment of West and Central Africa: deforestation, desertification, malaria.

Key Ideas

2. What are some ways in which the Sahel is different from the tropical wet zone?

3. Why do so few of Chad's people live in the north of the country and so many in the south?

4. What is one problem oil production causes in Nigeria?

Think Critically

5. **Summarize** Why are people in West and Central Africa moving from the countryside to the city?

6. **Draw Inferences** Use what you have learned in this section to explain why Ghana has a higher percentage of arable land than Mali.

Who should benefit from a country's resources?

7. How might not having abundant farmland or natural resources affect a country? Go to your Student Journal to record your answer.

History of West and Central Africa

Key Ideas	● The people of West Africa traded with each other from an early date, leading to well-developed trading kingdoms.	● The Atlantic slave trade, beginning in the 1500s, followed by European colonization in the 1800s, disrupted life in the region.	● Most West and Central African countries gained independence in the 1960s, but deeply rooted problems remain.

Key Terms • salt trade • Atlantic slave trade • middle passage • colonialism • imperialism • Pan-Africanism

 **Visual Glossary**

Reading Skill: Sequence Take notes using the graphic organizer in your journal.

Geography shaped life in early West and Central Africa in many ways. The people turned to trade to cope with a challenging environment. The natural resources and location of the area encouraged trade.

Trade in Early West and Central Africa

During ancient times in the savannas and forests of West Africa, people grew crops and raised animals. Sometimes, a community produced more food than it needed. In this case, the farmers or herders eagerly traded their products at local markets. In time, small kingdoms arose to guide and direct this local trade.

Empire of Ghana
Arab traders traded salt like this for gold. Gold had little value south of the Sahara but was prized by Arab traders.

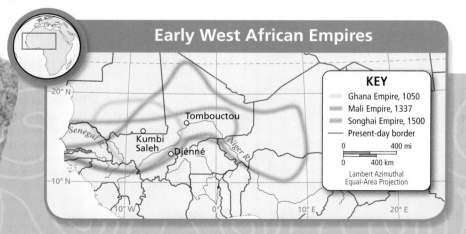

Early West African Empires

KEY
Ghana Empire, 1050
Mali Empire, 1337
Songhai Empire, 1500
Present-day border

0   400 mi
0   400 km

Lambert Azimuthal
Equal-Area Projection

20° N

Tombouctou
Senegal   Kumbi Saleh
Djénné   Niger R.

10° N

10° W   0°   10° E   20° E

512

Salt for Gold Beginning around A.D. 750, these kingdoms began to develop a long-distance trade with Arab traders who lived in North Africa. They exchanged all sorts of goods with their neighbors. The bestsellers were gold and salt. Unlike today, salt was rare and expensive. West Africans traded gold for the Arabs' salt in what was called the **salt trade.**

Arab trading partners brought more than salt to the region. They also carried scholarship, law, and the religion of Islam to West Africa. The trade networks gave birth to new cities. Rulers gained power by collecting taxes and tribute.

Three great trading empires arose in West Africa between 600 and the mid-1600s. Each had its days of glory. Each fell due to a combination of factors.

Ghana Leads the Way Ghana, the first of the great empires, flourished between 600 and 1200. The modern country of Ghana took its name from this empire. However, the empire of Ghana ruled over much of present-day Mali and Mauritania. It did not include present-day Ghana.

Success led to a larger population, which strained resources. Then, around 1050, power struggles with peoples to the north weakened Ghana. In 1240, the leader of a newer empire called Mali attacked Ghana's last strongholds. Soon Mali swallowed up the old empire.

Mali Makes an Impression Mali's greatest emperor, Mansa Musa, ruled from about 1312 to 1337. He practiced Islam. He made a spectacular pilgrimage, or religious journey, to the Arabian city of Mecca in 1324. The trip strengthened Mali's ties with North Africa. It drew the world's attention to the empire. However, Mali, too, weakened and <u>declined.</u>

Songhai's Glory In the mid-1400s, the empire of Songhai took over from Mali. It became the largest empire in African history. Songhai took over the great trading cities of Tombouctou (also spelled Timbuktu) and Djenné. Tombouctou flourished as the center of the salt trade and of Islamic learning and culture in West Africa. But by the early 1600s, the empire had split into smaller states.

Reading Check What was the effect of Mansa Musa's pilgrimage to Mecca?

decline, *v.,* to get weaker

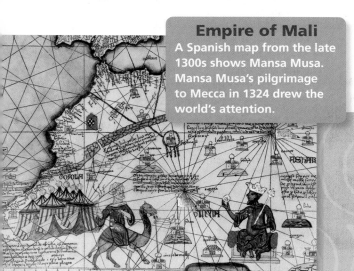

Empire of Mali
A Spanish map from the late 1300s shows Mansa Musa. Mansa Musa's pilgrimage to Mecca in 1324 drew the world's attention.

Songhai Empire
At its height, Songhai controlled a region roughly the size of the United States. The Great Mosque at Djenné (right) was rebuilt in the 1900s.

my worldgeography.com

Timeline

→ Timeline

Europeans in the Region

In the late 1400s, West and Central Africans began trading with new partners, Europeans. Like Arab traders, gold drew Europeans to West and Central Africa. Soon, they became involved in the slave trade.

Trading in enslaved people was not new in Africa. Various forms of slavery existed before European contact. Slaves were part of the trans-Saharan trade. However, the Europeans' slave trade affected many more people. It had more serious effects on African society.

The Atlantic Slave Trade Begins

In the 1500s, Europeans began to colonize the Americas. They brought enslaved Africans across the Atlantic Ocean to work on colonial plantations. This trade is called the **Atlantic slave trade**. It was part of the triangular trade between Europe, its American colonies, and Africa. African traders sold slaves for manufactured goods from Europe, such as cloth and guns. Thousands of the captives died during the grueling **middle passage,** the voyage across the Atlantic that formed the middle leg of the triangle.

Effects of the Trade

The Atlantic slave trade was the largest forced migration in history. Perhaps 13 million people left Africa in slave ships. This migration had several effects.

Some scholars believe that the slave trade changed the relationship between African states in the region. Stronger states attacked weaker ones to get slaves to trade. These wars hurt governance and economies in the region.

Africans who went to North America, the Caribbean, and South America brought their cultures with them. Their traditions influenced religion, music, and other ways of life in the Americas.

Colonialism

Slavery was outlawed in the United States and Europe in the early 1800s. But European interference was far from over. In the late 1800s, European countries looked to Africa for more colonies. **Colonialism** is a policy by which one country seeks to rule other areas. The policy of creating an empire by taking over other areas is also often called **imperialism**. European countries had colonized nearly all of Africa by 1900.

Reading Check What was the triangular trade?

This model of a slave ship from 1790 shows the cruel way slave traders packed their ships with as much human cargo as possible. The captives were locked in these positions for six weeks or more. ▼

Closer Look

EUROPEAN COLONIZATION IN AFRICA

In the 1880s, European powers made a mad dash for territory in Africa. This rush is known as the "Scramble for Africa." Africans resisted the start of European rule. But they couldn't stand against the Europeans' powerful new weapons, such as the Maxim machine gun. From the 1880s until the 1960s, European powers ruled almost every part of Africa. Some of colonization's damaging effects are still being felt today.

THINK CRITICALLY What did European powers want from the colonies?

Poster showing Africa as a market for British goods ▲

CAUSES European nations wanted colonies
- to win prestige.
- to get natural resources needed to produce industrial goods in Europe.
- as markets for goods made in factories.

EVENT Europeans got colonies

In 1884, European leaders met and divided up Africa among themselves. No African leaders took part. Before long, Europe controlled nearly the entire continent.

EFFECTS Colonial powers hurt Africa
- by ignoring the location of ethnic groups when drawing borders.
- by not developing colonial economies beyond their own aims.
- by forcing Africans to extract resources or grow cash crops.

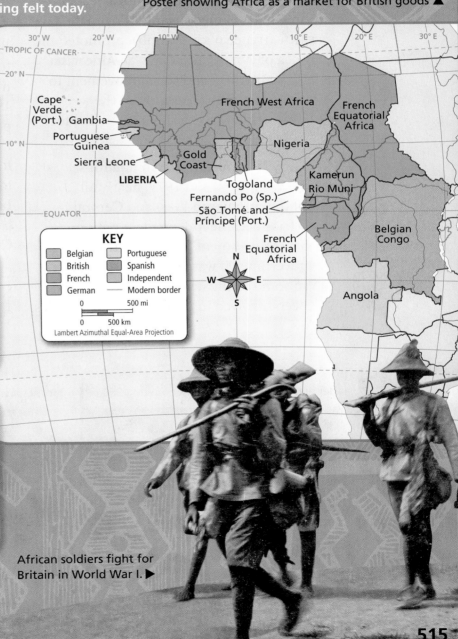

KEY
- Belgian
- British
- French
- German
- Portuguese
- Spanish
- Independent
- Modern border

0 — 500 mi
0 — 500 km
Lambert Azimuthal Equal-Area Projection

30° W 20° W 10° W 0° 10° E 20° E 30° E
TROPIC OF CANCER
20° N
10° N
EQUATOR

Cape Verde (Port.) Gambia
Portuguese Guinea
Sierra Leone
LIBERIA
Gold Coast
Togoland
Fernando Po (Sp.)
São Tomé and Príncipe (Port.)
French West Africa
French Equatorial Africa
Nigeria
Kamerun
Rio Muni
French Equatorial Africa
Belgian Congo
Angola

African soldiers fight for Britain in World War I. ▶

**myWorld Activity
The Promise of
Independence**

Independence and Beyond

Most Africans did not take part in colonial government. Some colonies, however, did ask a small number of Africans to help run their governments. As these Africans became educated, leaders emerged. They grew frustrated with the unfair rule of colonial powers. After World War II, a political leader in Ghana named Kwame Nkrumah (KWAH mee n KROO muh), promoted the idea of Pan-Africanism. **Pan-Africanism** was a political and social movement to unite black Africans around the world. Throughout Africa, Africans called for independence.

Early Dreams and Harsh Realities

Between 1960 and 1975, nearly all of the colonies in West and Central Africa became independent nations. The <u>transition</u> of power to African governments was mostly peaceful. But in some countries, the people had not been involved in government for decades.

transition, *n.,* movement from one condition to another

Also, Europeans still controlled many economic structures. The borders of the countries were drawn without regard to ethnic and language groups.

Despite bright hopes, the new nations soon ran into problems. Groups within countries fought one another. Governments banned opposition parties. Military dictators often led these governments.

Trouble in the Congo For example, Belgium abruptly granted independence to the Belgian Congo in 1960. Within months, the new nation was in chaos. In 1965, army leader Joseph Mobutu seized power. Mobutu renamed the country Zaire (zah EER) after a traditional name for the Congo River. He claimed to want to restore the nation's cultural identity. Instead, he ruled as a dictator for 32 years of incredible corruption. Meanwhile, Congo's people suffered.

Civil War in Nigeria In the 1940s, Nigerian leaders united more than 40 ethnic groups to oppose British rule.

A happy crowd greets the news of independence in the Belgian Congo in 1960.

By 1965, the dictator Joseph Mobutu (middle left) controlled the Congo, using violence to maintain power.

Everyone from soldiers to market women joined the call for freedom. Nigeria became independent in 1960.

However, ethnic unity did not last long. In 1967, three eastern states that were controlled by the Igbo (ig boh, also called Ibo) ethnic group attempted to leave Nigeria. They wanted to secede, or formally break away, and form their own country. The new country would be called the Republic of Biafra. One reason behind the move was that Igbos had been the victims of ethnic fighting in northern Nigeria.

Another reason was that Biafra was rich in oil. A bloody civil war followed. An estimated 500,000 to several million people died before Biafra rejoined Nigeria.

Economic Dependence and Dictatorship The new nations often continued relationships with their former colonial rulers. They stayed loyal to their former rulers in return for technical advice and loans. This arrangement tended to keep their economies focused on exporting cash crops and natural resources that mainly benefited European nations. As a result, homegrown manufacturing and businesses grew slowly. Taking on foreign loans created huge debts.

From 1945 until 1989, the United States and the Soviet Union carried on a rivalry called the Cold War. African nations were caught in the middle. To further their ends, both sides often supported dictators that were friendly to their point of view.

When the Cold War ended, so too did some of the support from Cold War powers. This paved the way for a new push for democracy throughout the region. By the early 1990s, most nations in the region had reestablished some form of elected government. Some of these democracies have been successful. Others have remained unstable.

Reading Check What happened after Nigeria gained independence?

▲ In 1960, Nigeria's first president, Nnamdi Azikiwe (NUM dee ah ZEE kway) said, "The past is gone with all its bitterness." But soon Nigeria plunged into conflict.

Section 2 Assessment

Key Terms

1. Use the following words to explain how outsiders have affected West and Central Africa throughout history: salt trade, Atlantic slave trade, middle passage, colonialism, imperialism, Pan-Africanism.

Key Ideas

2. How were the West African trading empires able to grow and become wealthy?

3. Describe the effects of the Atlantic slave trade.

4. What are some reasons why European powers created African colonies?

Think Critically

5. **Compare Viewpoints** How might Nnamdi Azikiwe's view of the future in 1960 be different from that of someone who fought in Nigeria's civil war in later years?

6. **Summarize** How did Cold War rivalries affect West and Central Africa?

? Essential Question

Who should benefit from a country's resources?

7. What role did natural resources play in the history of West and Central Africa? Go to your Student Journal to record your answer.

West and Central Africa Today

Key Ideas
- Many West and Central African countries have struggled to build their economies.
- Some of the nations in the region still experience violent upheaval.
- The people of the region enjoy rich, varied cultures.
- West and Central Africans search for solutions to economic problems, disease, and violence.

Key Terms • infrastructure • corruption • griot • African Union • microcredit

 Visual Glossary

Reading Skill: Identify Main Ideas and Details Take notes using the graphic organizer in your journal.

Traffic moves slowly along a rough road in Lagos, Nigeria.

After independence, many countries in West and Central Africa struggled to establish strong economies and stable governments. Today, West and Central Africans still struggle with poverty and unrest. They seek ways to solve continuing problems.

Economic Challenges

The nations of West and Central Africa are among the poorest in the world. Even nations with rich natural resources have struggled to build and maintain healthy economies.

Legacies of Colonialism Colonial powers did little to foster the economies of their colonies. When they gained independence, the new nations of West and Central Africa did not have strong infrastructures. **Infrastructure** is the body of public works, such as roads, bridges, and hospitals, that a country needs to support a modern economy. To build infrastructure, nations borrowed money from other countries. Many now owe huge debts.

Some of the nations in this region still depend on exporting one or two products. This dependence is risky because the price of products can go up and down drastically. In return for raw materials, West and Central Africans import manufactured goods. They often spend more on imports than they earn with exports. This situation is called a negative balance of trade.

Corruption **Corruption,** or the use of power for personal gain, is common in this region. International observers consider Nigeria to be one of the most corrupt nations in the world. The country is in the top ten of the world's largest oil exporters. Yet, around 70 percent of Nigerians live on less than one dollar per day. Corruption and poor management of money by the government both play a role in keeping most Nigerians poor.

Oil is a very capital-intensive business. In other words, it requires a large investment of money to buy machinery. Often, businesses from other countries have made this investment and, in turn, gained huge profits. Nigerians living near the oil fields resent the fact that oil profits often benefit only foreigners and corrupt officials. This resentment has led to violence that has hurt the country as a whole.

Subsistence Farming Another challenge in this region is that the majority of people are subsistence farmers. For example, about 80 percent of people in Mali survive by growing food to eat. Many parts of West and Central Africa lack good farmland, so farming is a difficult way of life. Since they don't make money by selling goods, many farmers cannot afford equipment that would make their farms more profitable.

Children often work on the family farm. Sending them to school is a sacrifice for the family. Many parents make the sacrifice because they know education will improve the lives of their children.

Reading Check **How have many nations in the region paid for infrastructure?**

Political Challenges

When the colonies of West and Central Africa became independent, they faced many political problems. As you have read, the borders that new nations inherited cut across ethnic groups. Also, poverty and weak economies meant that vital goods were scarce, or hard to find. Competition over scarce necessities and rich natural resources caused tension.

In many nations, violence between ethnic groups raged in civil wars. Years of warfare damaged economies and hurt the formation of strong democratic governments. Some countries still struggle with poor economies and bad leadership, leading to more violence.

A Country in Turmoil: The Democratic Republic of the Congo As you have read, the greedy dictator Joseph Mobutu ruled the Democratic Republic of the Congo (which he called Zaire) for more than 30 years. In 1997, rebels led by Laurent Kabila caused Mobutu to fall from power.

myWorld Activity
Two Economies

A farmer in Nigeria uses a hand tool to tend to his field. ▼

519

In the Democratic Republic of the Congo, rebel forces have recruited children in their teens, sometimes by force, to fight.

In Ghana, citizens vote to elect their president and legislative representatives, as do citizens in the United States.

Kabila renamed the country the Democratic Republic of the Congo. But he did little to restore democracy. Former Mobutu supporters, with the aid of Uganda and Rwanda, rebelled in 1998. Uganda and Rwanda supported the rebels to continue their own ethnic conflicts. Angola, Namibia, and Zimbabwe joined the war on the side of the Kabila government. The conflict continued despite a <u>ceasefire</u> in 1999.

In 2001, Joseph Kabila came to power when his father was assassinated. With help from the United Nations, his government and the rebels reached a peace agreement in 2002. However, real peace has been slow in coming. Rebel forces still fight in the eastern part of the country. The fighting goes on in part because various groups want to control the rich mineral resources of that area.

The fighting has left the nation in shambles. Since 1998, an estimated 5 million people have died because of the war or the poor conditions brought about by the war.

ceasefire, *n.,* an agreement to stop fighting temporarily

Ghana, Back From the Brink Compared to other nations in the region, Ghana, where Evelyn lives, was in good shape upon independence. Still, it has had its problems. Ghana's first president was the independence movement leader Kwame Nkrumah. As he worked to build Ghana's economy, he also became a dictator. He fell from power in a coup, or sudden overthrow, in 1966.

Ghana then suffered several coups until air force officer Jerry Rawlings seized power in 1981. He restored constitutional democracy and won election as Ghana's president in 1992. Since that time, Ghana has been fairly stable.

Rawlings introduced several economic reforms. By the 1990s, Ghana had one of the fastest-growing economies in Africa. Its greatest income comes from gold and cacao production. In the future, Ghana plans to diversify exports and improve the status of women. It also aims to promote good governance.

Reading Check How did Ghana come to achieve stability?

The Cultures of the Region

There are many rich and varied cultures in West and Central Africa. Traditional and modern ways exist side by side, often blending to form new traditions.

Religion Before contact with the outside world, ethnic groups throughout the region developed their own religions. Then new religions were introduced through trading networks. Islam spread south from the Sahara. Mali, for example, has an overwhelmingly Muslim population. Next, Europeans brought Christianity to the region. For example, in Angola, many ethnic groups practiced religions based on ancestor worship and local deities. After the arrival of the Portuguese in the 1400s, many people adopted Christianity.

The Arts In West and Central Africa today, people enjoy both traditional dance and modern ballet. Modern music reflects traditional rhythms and styles. Even when it comes to sports, fans flock to both traditional and newer games. In Senegal, for example, the two most popular sports are soccer and traditional wrestling.

Stories are told through both oral tradition and literature. In West Africa, musician-storytellers called **griots** use music to track their heritage and record history as well as to entertain. Many see hip-hop artists as modern griots. Writers and filmmakers use literature and the cinema to explore Africa's cultural heritage as well as issues facing Africa today.

Reading Check How do griots preserve traditions in West Africa?

▲ West and Central Africans have created ceremonial masks for centuries.

A Nigerian girl reads from the Quran. ▼

Culture Close-up

In Senegal, a griot plays the kora, a traditional instrument. ▼

▲ A dancer wears a traditional mask and costume in Central Africa.

my worldgeography.com Culture Close-up

521

Hope for Change in the Future

Violence, poverty, and disease threaten daily existence for many in this region. Many countries are searching for <u>innovative</u> solutions to their problems. They seek to create better opportunities for the next generation of West and Central Africans.

innovative, *adj.,* fresh, new, or original

The Cost of Warfare Political instability and ethnic conflict threaten the safety of young people in this region. In some places, children are the victims of violence. For example, an estimated 10,000 child soldiers fought in Sierra Leone's ten-year civil war. In addition, thousands of people are forced to flee their homes to escape violence. In the Democratic Republic of the Congo alone, nearly 1.5 million people were internally displaced in 2007.

Poverty and Disease Poverty is another challenge faced by people in this region. Most people do not get to enjoy the benefits of the region's rich natural resources. Conflict, bad government, weak economies, and other factors lead to people being undernourished. A person who is undernourished does not have enough food to make a healthy diet. In West Africa, around 15 percent of the population is undernourished. In Central Africa, more than 50 percent of the population is undernourished.

Undernourishment makes people more vulnerable to diseases. Malaria and sleeping sickness affect millions of people every year. Another disease, acquired immunodeficiency syndrome (AIDS) is an epidemic in the continent of Africa south of the Sahara. Southern Africa has been hit the hardest. Still, many people in West and Central Africa suffer from this illness or know someone who does.

The African Union In 2002, an organization called the **African Union** was formed to promote unity among African states and to foster development and end poverty. The African Union continues the work of an earlier group called the Organization of African Unity, which was established in 1963. In recent years, the African Union has sent peacekeepers to several countries. It also works with international organizations to develop economic programs.

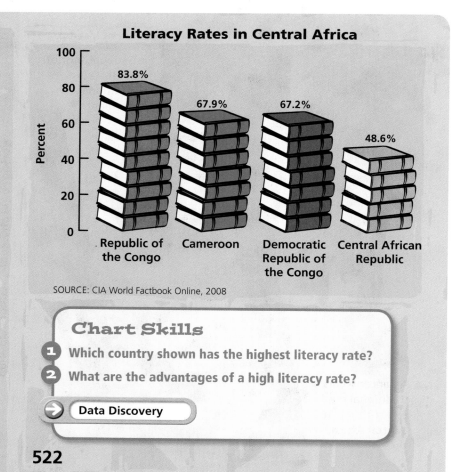

Literacy Rates in Central Africa

Republic of the Congo: 83.8%
Cameroon: 67.9%
Democratic Republic of the Congo: 67.2%
Central African Republic: 48.6%

SOURCE: CIA World Factbook Online, 2008

Chart Skills

1. Which country shown has the highest literacy rate?
2. What are the advantages of a high literacy rate?

→ Data Discovery

An Eye Toward the Future The African Union, along with many foreign aid agencies, has identified these key factors in getting rid of poverty and promoting development in Africa:

- democracy
- women's rights
- development of infrastructure
- development of social services (such as education and healthcare)

The people of the region are working toward these goals by investing locally. Giving **microcredit,** or small loans usually less than $200, to individuals to fund their own businesses is a growing practice. Women use microcredit to start and run small businesses similar to Adede's bead business. The region is also investing in people by building new universities.

On a larger scale, others are developing new ways to meet people's needs. New technologies aim to improve lives without harming the environment. For example, many nations in the region have a huge potential for generating hydroelectricity.

Angola gets around 75 percent of its electricity from water power.

In all these ways, West and Central Africans are working to meet the challenges of their daily lives. The filmmaker Ousmane Sembene of Senegal sums up the hope for the future this way:

> 66 Forty years ago, we had nothing—no doctors, no engineers, no writers. We had no university. We thought a flag and a national anthem were enough for independence. . . .That is now a thing of the past. One has to count on the people. And despite all the problems, success for us is a certainty. Every day we're working hard, because we're dreaming of a better quality of life. 99
>
> —Ousmane Sembene

Reading Check How are West and Central Africans working to make their lives better?

  Story **Photo**

Evelyn looks forward to going to a university. ▶

Section **3** Assessment

? **Essential Question**

Who should benefit from a country's resources?

Key Terms

1. Use the following terms to describe the obstacles standing in the way of progress in West and Central Africa, and how they might be overcome: infrastructure, microcredit, corruption.

Key Ideas

2. Describe how subsistence farming weakens economies.

3. How have neighboring countries made the Democratic Republic of the Congo's problems worse?

4. What health problems does undernourishment lead to?

Think Critically

5. **Analyze Cause and Effect** How do corruption and undemocratic governments contribute to poverty in West and Central Africa?

6. **Draw Inferences** How might other nations learn from the progress Ghana has made?

7. How does unequal access to oil wealth affect the lives of Nigeria's people? Go to your Student Journal to record your answer.

Chapter Assessment

Key Terms and Ideas

1. **Summarize** What produces the different climate zones of West and Central Africa?

2. **Compare and Contrast** How are the **Sahel** and **savanna** different from each other?

3. **Sequence** How does **deforestation** lead to **desertification**?

4. **Describe** In what ways did **imperialism** affect West and Central African countries?

5. **Explain** What do subsistence farmers do to make a living?

6. **Identify** What is a **griot**?

7. **Describe** What are some effects of disease on West and Central African people?

Think Critically

8. **Draw Inferences** Why has the Democratic Republic of the Congo been so unstable since independence?

9. **Draw Conclusions** What are some of the lasting effects of European colonialism?

10. **Categorize** Which religions were brought to West and Central Africa from other regions?

11. **Core Concepts: Five Themes of Geography** What are the five themes of geography? How would geographers use these themes to describe West and Central Africa?

Places to Know

For each place, write the letter from the map that shows its location.

Identify the following:

12. **Niger River**

13. **Congo River**

14. **Accra**

15. **Lagos**

16. **Kinshasa**

17. **Estimate** Using the scale, estimate the distance between Accra and Lagos.

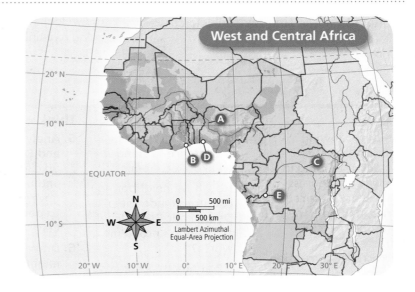

West and Central Africa

myWorld Chapter Activity

To Drill or Not To Drill? Follow your teacher's instructions to prepare advice for the president of a fictional African country that has just discovered oil deposits within its borders. Review evidence to see if you think developing the resource is a good idea or not. Prepare a report for the president recommending or advising against developing oil resources in your country.

21st Century Learning

Make a Difference

Research an aid organization in your community that helps people in West and Central Africa. Find out three things that you could do to help that organization. Present your findings to the class.

Document-Based Questions

Success ☆ Tracker™
Online at myworldgeography.com

Use your knowledge of West and Central Africa and Documents A and B to answer Questions 1–3.

Document A

Infant Mortality in Selected Countries

Average Deaths per 1,000 Live Births

100	
80	
60	
40	
20	
0	

Democratic Republic of the Congo   Ghana   United States

SOURCE: CIA World Factbook Online, 2008

Document B

" We spent three days running from the rebels. We went 60 km [kilometers], walking in the day and sleeping in the bush at night. We ran with nothing. I saw so many people being killed that I just left without collecting my things. Even children are being killed."

—Woman in the Democratic Republic of the Congo

1. What did you learn in this chapter that explains the difference in infant mortality in the Democratic Republic of the Congo, Ghana, and the United States as shown in Document A?

   A Ghana has been very unstable in recent years.

   B The Democratic Republic of the Congo has an efficient healthcare system.

   C The United States is very diverse.

   D Conflict in the Democratic Republic of the Congo makes good healthcare impossible.

2. Who do you think the woman quoted in Document B is most afraid of?

   A the government of the Democratic Republic of the Congo

   B the rebel army

   C African Union peacekeepers

   D Belgian colonists

3. **Writing Task** How does civil violence affect a country and its people? Explain your answer.

myworldgeography.com   Self-Test

Southern and Eastern Africa

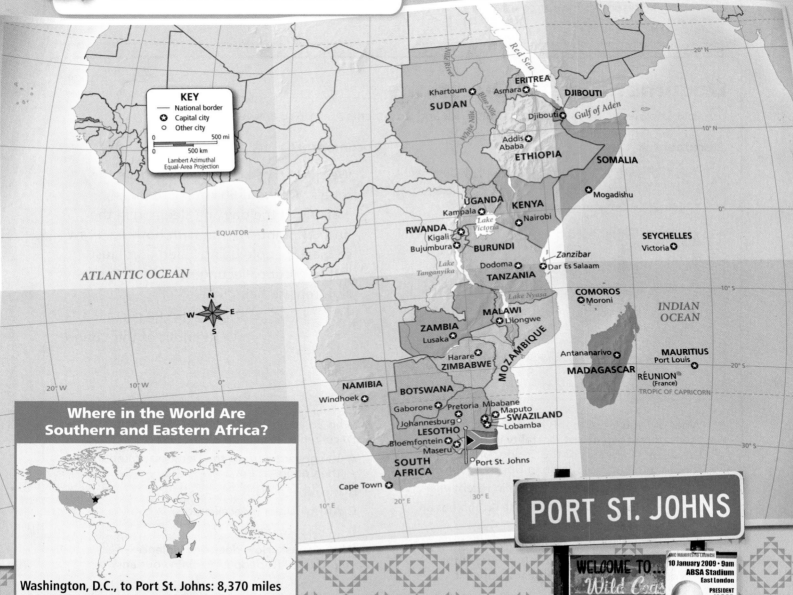

? Essential Question

Is conflict unavoidable?

Where in the World Are Southern and Eastern Africa?

Washington, D.C., to Port St. Johns: 8,370 miles

KEY
— National border
✪ Capital city
○ Other city

0 — 500 mi
0 — 500 km
Lambert Azimuthal Equal-Area Projection

PORT ST. JOHNS

WELCOME TO...
Wild Coast
GUEST HOUS
(247) BEAU-ORD

10 January 2009 · 9am
ABSA Stadium
East London
PRESIDENT
JACOB
ZUMA
SPEAKS
ANC

my Story

A Hopeful Song

In this section, you'll read about Khulekani, a young South African man who lives in Port Saint Johns. What does Khulekani's story tell you about life in Southern and Eastern Africa today?

? Explore the Essential Question

- at **my worldgeography.com**
- using the **myWorld Chapter Activity**
- with the **Student Journal**

Story by Greg Fell for myWorld Geography Online

At 19, Khulekani is a young man with strong principles and big dreams. Khulekani is a member of the Xhosa (кон sah) people, the second-largest ethnic group in South Africa. His parents passed away ten years ago. Now he lives with his aunt and his sister.

Khulekani lives in a settlement called Nonyevu, on a hill that overlooks the town of Port Saint Johns, in the Transkei region of South Africa. Behind the town is the mighty Umzimvubu River. From Khulekani's home, the view of the lush, tropical landscape is spectacular. Still, life can be difficult for Khulekani and his family.

"We have no water or electricity in Nonyevu. This is a problem for me because I often get homework that requires me to watch television. Without electricity I cannot watch television. When my school shirt gets dirty and there is no rainwater I have to use water from the tap in town, and this water is not clean enough for washing."

Along with water and electricity, healthcare is also lacking in parts of Transkei. The HIV/AIDS epidemic has taken a heavy toll in this area.

my worldgeography.com On Assignment

Khulekani doing the laundry

Filling a water jug to bring home

Cooking breakfast

Until 1994, the apartheid system oppressed black South Africans. Under apartheid, white South Africans controlled the country, even though black South Africans are a majority. Since the fall of apartheid, South Africans of all races have shared power. The racial divide is slowly healing. Like most young South Africans today, Khulekani has moved past the racial divisions of the past.

"You see, now everything is right," he says, "because we are equal. White people can help black people if they are suffering. Black men have also oppressed other black men, so all in all, it just depends on how good or nice you are, rather than your skin color. Either way you are equal."

Still, like all South Africans, Khulekani is aware of the huge gap between developed and undeveloped areas in his country. He and his family struggle to get by, but many South Africans, mostly white, live more comfortable lives.

On a a typical morning, Khulekani wakes up at 6 A.M. and boils water on his gas stove for a bath. He makes his breakfast, usually bread and tea. Then it's time to go to school. Khulekani walks to school, where he is in 11th grade. When he finishes school next year, he hopes to study at a nearby university. His goal is to graduate and become an accountant.

An assembly at school

Khulekani meets his friends in town.

Having breakfast and rushing off to school are things teenagers do all over the world. But because Khulekani's family is so poor, everyday routines can be challenging. For example, just to have enough water for drinking, cooking, and washing, Khulekani must carry six-gallon jugs of water more than a half a mile. He is responsible for carrying all the water his family needs.

"You must not waste things like water and just throw them away. I don't have the means to get new things so I must look after what I have. The things we have must only be used in the right way in order to survive."

Despite the challenges he faces, Khulekani remains positive, "Yes, things like carrying water from town and doing homework without electricity can affect my schoolwork but I can work past those things."

Today, being involved at school helps Khulekani enjoy his life. He runs a local youth leadership group, for example. "I like to be involved with the youth group. I like to do positive things."

Khulekani is also a part of the school choir. He is optimistic about the choir. He tells us it is the highlight of his day, "The reason why I want to sing in the choir is because I want to take advantage of my opportunities. I want to learn how to do everything in life."

They sing mostly Xhosa hymns, and Khulekani finds joy when he is singing with the choir.

"I like to be happy, and singing with other kids makes me happy. It's very nice. It takes away the worries."

Khulekani believes in his future and the future of South Africa. He believes that once he has made his own way in the world, he can come back and help fix the problems in his town.

Meet the Journalist

Name Greg Fell
Favorite Moment Choir practice: everything that Khulekani had said to us about the joy singing brought him was true.

myStory Online

Join Khulekani as he shows you more about his life in South Africa.

Choir practice

Chapter Atlas

◀ Mount Kilimanjaro, Africa's highest mountain

◀ A woman from Tanzania

Remarkable Land and Water

Southern and Eastern Africa, where Khulekani lives, are home to diverse and impressive physical features. From the huge desert of the Sahara to Africa's great lakes, this region has some of Earth's most breathtaking landscapes and wildlife.

One of Southern and Eastern Africa's unique features is the **Great Rift Valley.** This is a long, unusually flat area of land between areas of higher ground in Eastern Africa. It was formed when two of Earth's plates moved away from each other. This movement caused the land in between them to sink and form a valley.

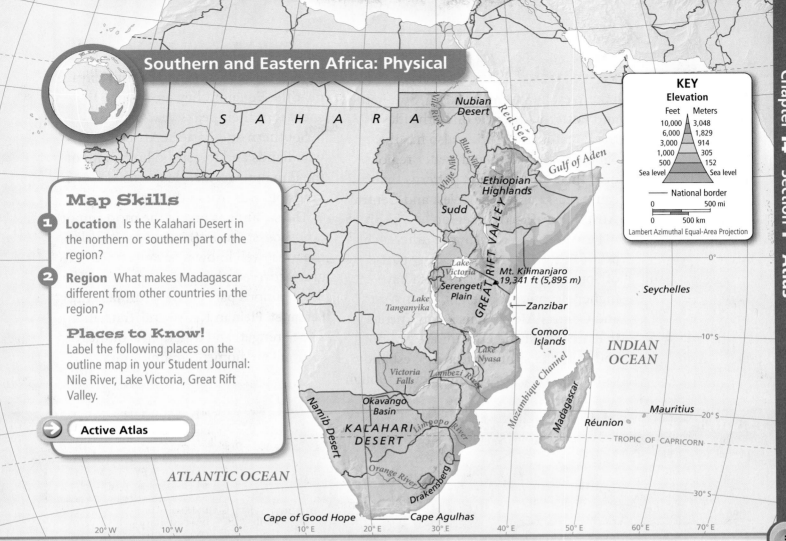

Southern and Eastern Africa: Physical

Map Skills

1 **Location** Is the Kalahari Desert in the northern or southern part of the region?

2 **Region** What makes Madagascar different from other countries in the region?

Places to Know!
Label the following places on the outline map in your Student Journal: Nile River, Lake Victoria, Great Rift Valley.

Active Atlas

KEY
Elevation

Feet	Meters
10,000	3,048
6,000	1,829
3,000	914
1,000	305
500	152
Sea level	Sea level

National border

0   500 mi
0   500 km

Lambert Azimuthal Equal-Area Projection

SAHARA

Nubian Desert

Nile River

Red Sea

Gulf of Aden

White Nile

Blue Nile

Ethiopian Highlands

Sudd

GREAT RIFT VALLEY

Lake Victoria

Mt. Kilimanjaro
19,341 ft (5,895 m)

Serengeti Plain

Zanzibar

Lake Tanganyika

Seychelles

Comoro Islands

INDIAN OCEAN

Lake Nyasa

Victoria Falls

Zambezi River

Mozambique Channel

Madagascar

Mauritius

Réunion

TROPIC OF CAPRICORN

Okavango Basin

Namib Desert

KALAHARI DESERT

Limpopo River

Orange River

Drakensberg

ATLANTIC OCEAN

Cape of Good Hope — Cape Agulhas

20° W   10° W   0°   10° E   20° E   30° E   40° E   50° E   60° E   70° E

0°

10° S

20° S

30° S

The valley's sides rise steeply into mountains and high plateaus. Africa's highest point, Mount Kilimanjaro, sits along the Great Rift Valley. There are also large plains between mountain ranges.

Near the Great Rift Valley lie a group of large and beautiful lakes. One of these, Lake Victoria, is the largest lake in Africa. Africa's great lakes support plant, animal, and human life in areas around them. So do the large rivers that originate, or start, in this region. The Nile, the Zambezi, the Orange, and the Limpopo are the largest. A spectacular waterfall called Victoria Falls is on the Zambezi River.

Rivers serve as a <u>transportation</u> network. But the Sudd swamps block movement between East Africa and Egypt, in North Africa. In the Sudd, floating mats of vegetation and tall papyrus reeds make it difficult for ships to pass.

Parts of Southern and Eastern Africa are very dry. Deserts ring the region: the Sahara, Nubian, Kalahari, and Namib. The Namib Desert, along the coast of Namibia, has some of the world's tallest sand dunes.

Reading Check How do lakes and rivers affect plant, animal, and human life in Southern and Eastern Africa?

transportation, *n.,* system used to move people or things

Patterns of Ecosystems

Like West and Central Africa, Southern and Eastern Africa lie on both sides of the Equator. This region also has the Sahara in the north and wetter regions near the Equator. Wind patterns that cause seasonal rains in West and Central Africa also affect this region.

However, there is a major difference between the two regions. Many parts of Southern and Eastern Africa have a higher elevation, or height, than West and Central Africa. This height means that areas near the Equator are less hot and wet than similar areas in West and Central Africa. For example, even though Mount Kilimanjaro and Mount Kenya are near the Equator, they are so high that snow caps their peaks year-round.

Southern and Eastern Africa have woodlands and forests on both sides of the Equator. Gorillas, leopards, and many kinds of birds live in these areas.

The savanna is one of the most important ecosystems in this region. It is also the most well known. Savannas are flat, grass-covered plains with few trees. The most famous part of the savanna is the **Serengeti Plain** in Kenya and Tanzania. The Serengeti and other parts of the savanna are home to many animals.

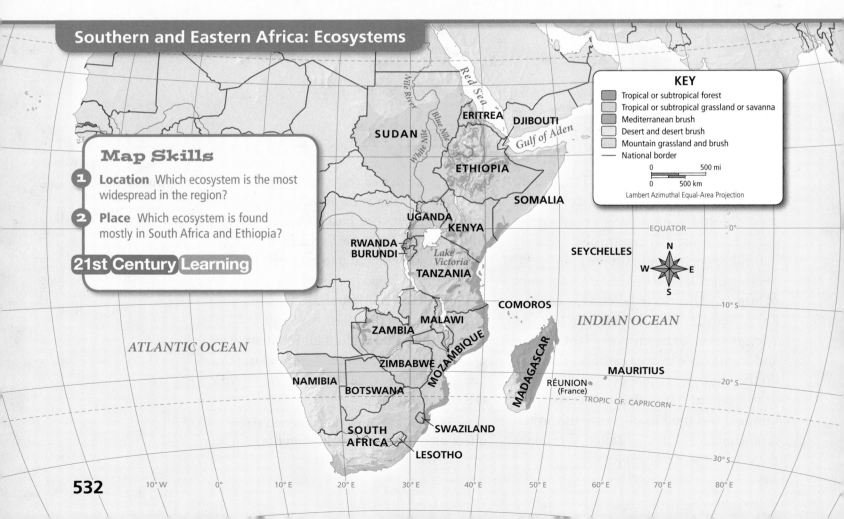

Southern and Eastern Africa: Ecosystems

Map Skills

1. **Location** Which ecosystem is the most widespread in the region?
2. **Place** Which ecosystem is found mostly in South Africa and Ethiopia?

21st Century Learning

KEY

- Tropical or subtropical forest
- Tropical or subtropical grassland or savanna
- Mediterranean brush
- Desert and desert brush
- Mountain grassland and brush
- National border

0   500 mi
0   500 km
Lambert Azimuthal Equal-Area Projection

Large herds of elephants, lions, wildebeests, zebras, giraffes, gazelles, and other animals live on the plains. This wildlife shapes the way people see the region. Still, many Africans live in towns and cities and may never see one of these animals in the wild.

Many African animals have become endangered. This can happen because they are hunted too much or because people move into places they live. Governments have tried to protect the animals. However, **poaching,** or illegal hunting, is still a problem. Kenya, South Africa, and other countries have set up national parks to protect animals. At the same time, these countries promote **ecotourism**. This is a kind of tourism in which people learn about conservation and try to do little or no harm to the environment.

As in West and Central Africa, the trees in many forested areas in Southern and Eastern Africa have been cut down. Cleared land is used for farmland or mining. South Africa, Madagascar, Kenya, and other countries in the region are trying to grow new forests in some areas.

Reading Check **What type of ecosystem supports zebras and lions?**

my**World**
IN NUMBERS

150,000 gazelles and **3,000** lions live in Tanzania's Serengeti National Park.

Chapter 14 Section 1 Atlas

Mountain gorillas live in high tropical woodlands in Rwanda, Uganda, and neighboring countries.

Gazelles, lions, elephants, zebras, and many other animals thrive on the wide-open plains of the savanna.

Culture Close-up

my worldgeography.com Culture Close-up

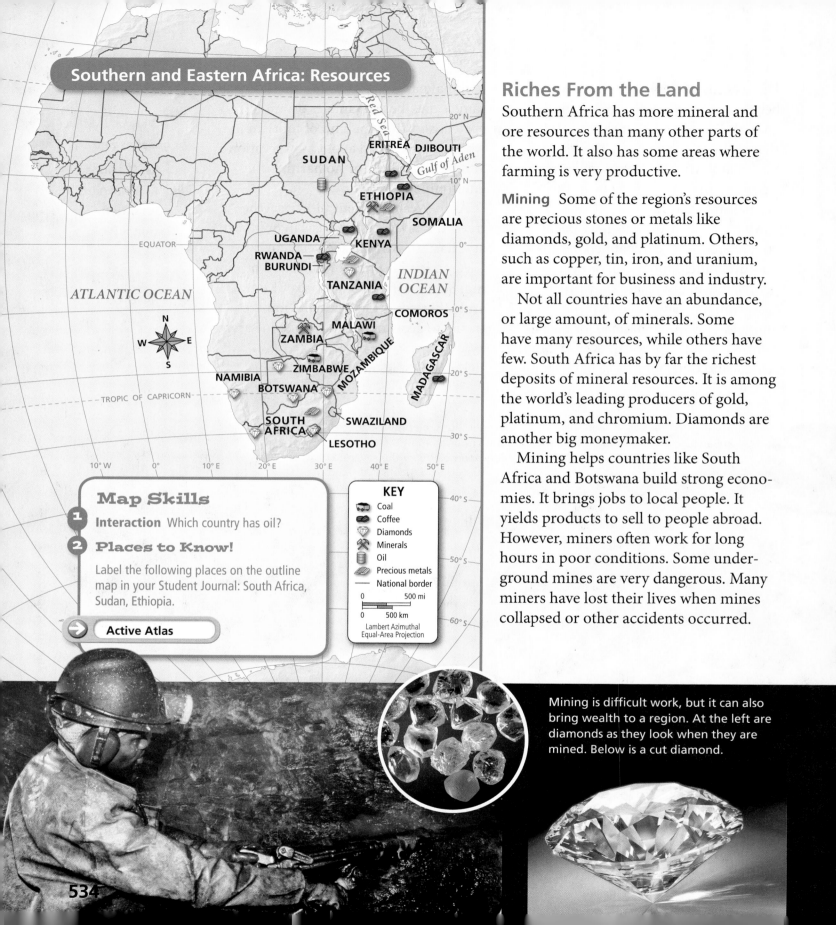

Southern and Eastern Africa: Resources

Red Sea

SUDAN

ERITREA DJIBOUTI

Gulf of Aden

ETHIOPIA

SOMALIA

UGANDA

KENYA

RWANDA
BURUNDI

TANZANIA

INDIAN OCEAN

COMOROS

MALAWI

ZAMBIA

ATLANTIC OCEAN

ZIMBABWE

MOZAMBIQUE

MADAGASCAR

NAMIBIA

BOTSWANA

SOUTH AFRICA

SWAZILAND

LESOTHO

EQUATOR

TROPIC OF CAPRICORN

20° N

10° N

0°

10° S

20° S

30° S

10° W   0°   10° E   20° E   30° E   40° E   50° E

Map Skills

1 **Interaction** Which country has oil?

2 **Places to Know!**

Label the following places on the outline map in your Student Journal: South Africa, Sudan, Ethiopia.

→ **Active Atlas**

KEY

- Coal
- Coffee
- Diamonds
- Minerals
- Oil
- Precious metals
- — National border

40° S

50° S

60° S

0 ___ 500 mi
0 ___ 500 km

Lambert Azimuthal
Equal-Area Projection

Riches From the Land

Southern Africa has more mineral and ore resources than many other parts of the world. It also has some areas where farming is very productive.

Mining Some of the region's resources are precious stones or metals like diamonds, gold, and platinum. Others, such as copper, tin, iron, and uranium, are important for business and industry.

Not all countries have an abundance, or large amount, of minerals. Some have many resources, while others have few. South Africa has by far the richest deposits of mineral resources. It is among the world's leading producers of gold, platinum, and chromium. Diamonds are another big moneymaker.

Mining helps countries like South Africa and Botswana build strong economies. It brings jobs to local people. It yields products to sell to people abroad. However, miners often work for long hours in poor conditions. Some underground mines are very dangerous. Many miners have lost their lives when mines collapsed or other accidents occurred.

Mining is difficult work, but it can also bring wealth to a region. At the left are diamonds as they look when they are mined. Below is a cut diamond.

Mining can also hurt the environment. Some types of mining leave large scars on the land. Mining can cause pollution. Air and water can be polluted when minerals are processed and when fuel is burned to run drills.

Farming People also use the land in this region to farm and raise animals. Farmlands can be found in most of the countries in the region. But there are many areas that are very dry. These places cannot rely on regular rainfall for crops. Sudan, Ethiopia, Somalia, and Namibia struggle to find enough water to grow their crops.

Because so much of the region is dry, many farmers <u>irrigate</u> their land. Cotton, tobacco, and tea are grown in irrigated areas. People also raise cattle and other livestock in drier parts of the region. In some of these areas, wild animals are a threat to the herds. Herders must defend their animals at night.

Some of the region has very fertile land. In South Africa and other countries, people grow many crops. They run large commercial farms or plantations. These farms grow crops such as sugar cane, cotton, avocados, and tropical fruits. They often export their crops.

Coffee is Ethiopia's most important export. In fact, the plant was probably first grown in Ethiopia's highlands. The word *coffee* may even come from the Kaffa region of Ethiopia, where the crop is grown.

Reading Check **What are the advantages and disadvantages of diamond mining?**

irrigate, *v.,* to bring water to an area

Coffee is Ethiopia's largest export. Red coffee berries are grown on plantations like this one. Ethiopian coffee is enjoyed around the world. *Can you think of some other products from Africa that you might be able to find in your hometown?*

535

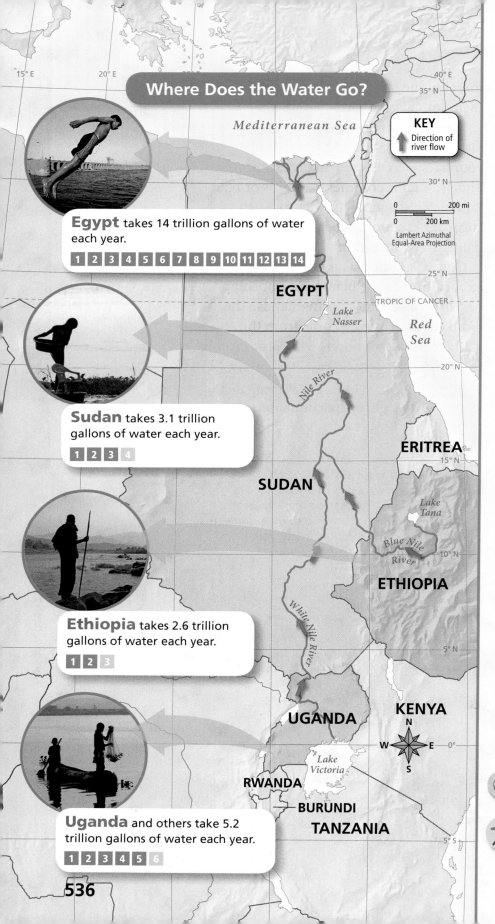

Where Does the Water Go?

Mediterranean Sea

KEY

↑ Direction of river flow

Egypt takes 14 trillion gallons of water each year.

| 1 | 2 | 3 | 4 | 5 | 6 | 7 | 8 | 9 | 10 | 11 | 12 | 13 | 14 |

EGYPT

Lake Nasser

Red Sea

TROPIC OF CANCER

Sudan takes 3.1 trillion gallons of water each year.

| 1 | 2 | 3 | 4 |

SUDAN

ERITREA

Lake Tana

Blue Nile River

ETHIOPIA

Nile River

Ethiopia takes 2.6 trillion gallons of water each year.

| 1 | 2 | 3 |

White Nile River

KENYA

UGANDA

Lake Victoria

RWANDA

Uganda and others take 5.2 trillion gallons of water each year.

| 1 | 2 | 3 | 4 | 5 | 6 |

BURUNDI

TANZANIA

200 mi

200 km

Lambert Azimuthal Equal-Area Projection

N W E S

536

Challenges of the Environment

Water—who has it and who doesn't—is a huge challenge for countries in this region. Countries that have enough water resources have a better chance of feeding their populations. Countries that do not have enough water struggle to support their populations. Lack of water and good farmland leads to famine, or a shortage of food. Sudan and Ethiopia receive more food aid than many other countries in the world for this reason.

The region's many rivers provide a valuable benefit to some countries. Dams have been built along major rivers to generate hydroelectricity. They also provide water for nearby farms.

But these dams can cause conflict. For example, the Nile flows through Sudan and other countries before reaching Egypt. Dams built in Uganda take water away from Sudan. Who gets to decide how much water each country can take?

Reading Check What are the advantages and disadvantages of building dams?

Map Skills

This map shows the amounts of water taken from the Nile River by different countries each year.

Interaction What might happen if Uganda took more water? How would this affect Sudan?

→ **Active Atlas**

🏃 **myWorld Activity** **Cause-and-Effect Pairs**

Disease

As in West and Central Africa, disease causes many problems in Southern and Eastern Africa. Some diseases stem from the environment. Just as mosquitoes carry malaria, tsetse flies carry sleeping sickness. The flies live in many areas between the Sahara and the Kalahari Desert. These areas are known as the tsetse belt.

Sleeping sickness can be deadly to both people and the cattle they raise. The disease makes it impossible to raise cattle in the tsetse belt.

Many people in Southern and Eastern Africa do not have access to clean water, and so they contract diseases carried by water. For example, cholera and river blindness have crippled and killed many Southern and Eastern Africans.

AIDS, which does not stem from the environment, has reached epidemic proportions in this region. You will read more about AIDS later.

Reading Check What harm does the tsetse fly cause?

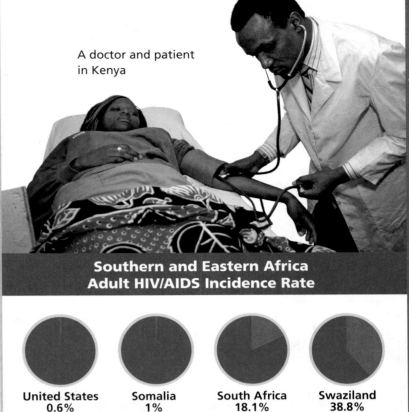

A doctor and patient in Kenya

Southern and Eastern Africa Adult HIV/AIDS Incidence Rate

| United States 0.6% | Somalia 1% | South Africa 18.1% | Swaziland 38.8% |

■ People with HIV/AIDS   ■ People without HIV/AIDS

SOURCE: *CIA World Factbook*, 2009

Chart Skills

The United States population is 307,000,000. Swaziland has 1,123,000 people. Which country has more people living with HIV/AIDS?

 Data Discovery

Section 1 Assessment

Key Terms

1. How was the Great Rift Valley formed?

2. How do ecotourism and poaching affect the environment?

3. In which nations is the Serengeti Plain located?

Key Ideas

4. What are some animals that live on the savanna?

5. What resources help make countries like South Africa more prosperous than others?

6. Why might a dam in Uganda cause trouble in Sudan?

Think Critically

7. **Compare Viewpoints** Why do some people believe mining helps people in the region while others say it is harmful? Give evidence.

8. **Compare and Contrast** Somalia and Botswana have different resources. How might this difference affect the lives of their people?

Essential Question

Is conflict unavoidable?

9. How do you think the lack of resources in some countries might cause conflict? How might the abundance of resources in other countries cause conflict? Go to your Student Journal to record your answers.

my worldgeography.com

Data Discovery

537

Section 2

History of Southern and Eastern Africa

Key Ideas
- Earth's first people lived in Africa.
- Humans settled throughout Africa, creating societies, states, and trade networks.
- Contact with Arabs and Europeans influenced the culture, religions, and ethnic makeup of the region.
- In the 1800s, Europeans colonized and settled in the region, but African nations gained independence in the 1900s.

Key Terms • fossil • Boers • ethnocentrism • Mau Mau • apartheid • African National Congress

 Visual Glossary

 Reading Skill: Sequence Take notes using the graphic organizer in your journal.

Southern and Eastern Africa may have been home to the earliest humans. From ancient times to the present, many different cultures and civilizations have left their mark on the region.

Early Humans and Great Civilizations

The first humans may have lived in Africa two million years ago. In particular, the remains of early humans have been found in countries such as Ethiopia and Tanzania.

Earth's First People Scientists have found fossils of early human beings in Eastern Africa. **Fossils** are the remains of ancient humans or animals. Most early humans lived in warm places. They moved around in search of food. One kind of early human called *Homo erectus* lived in Africa between 1 and 2 million years ago. Early humans spread out from Africa to other continents.

▲ Scientists searching for fossils
◄ The skull of an early ancestor of human beings who lived in South Africa 2.5 million years ago

Nubia and Aksum The first civilization in this part of Africa was in Nubia. Nubia is a region in modern-day Sudan. It was home to the states of Kush and Meroë. Civilization in Nubia grew from around 2000 B.C. Nubia became a center of trade. It traded with its neighbor, Egypt. Skills and technologies from Egypt were introduced into Nubia. Nubians passed these on to other parts of Africa. The most important technology was iron-making.

The kingdom of Aksum was located in what is today Ethiopia. Aksum had a port on the Red Sea. This location helped make Aksum a center for trade in and beyond Africa. Aksum's traders sold gold, ivory, and other goods. They traded with Rome and India. Roman traders may have brought Christianity to Aksum. It became a Christian kingdom. Ethiopia still is mostly Christian today.

The Bantu Migrations Around A.D. 500 the population of the Bantu people in western Africa grew until their land could not accommodate them. They left their homeland and migrated across Southern Africa. This migration spread the Bantu language. The Bantu brought with them their farming methods, including the raising of cattle. They also spread their knowledge of iron tools. Many groups the Bantu met adopted their language. They began raise to cattle and make iron.

Great Zimbabwe In Southern Africa, Great Zimbabwe thrived in the 1400s. It was a large trading city founded by Bantu speakers. Great Zimbabwe's traders took gold and ivory to Africa's east coast ports. There they traded for goods from China, India, and Southeast Asia.

Arab Influence Traders who spoke Arabic came to Eastern Africa by sea and across the Sahara. They practiced Islam. Some settled in the region, mostly along the eastern coast and on the island of Zanzibar. Zanzibar and coastal areas were tied into a large trading network. It included the Mediterranean, India, and Southeast Asia. Arab traders widened East Africa's slave trade. They brought their language, religion, and cultural influence to the region. Arab merchants also founded cities, including Mogadishu in modern-day Somalia.

Reading Check How did early civilizations spread ideas in Africa?

This doorway from Zanzibar shows the artistic influence of Arab merchants who lived and traded in the region.

▼ This large enclosure is one of the most impressive remains of the city of Great Zimbabwe. *What can you infer about the culture that built it?*

Europeans in Southern and Eastern Africa

In the 1400s, Europeans began to come to Southern and Eastern Africa. They came first to trade and later to set up colonies.

First Meetings and the Slave Trade

Portugal began to trade with Eastern Africa in the 1400s. Around 1500, the Portuguese took control of parts of Eastern Africa. They wanted to control trade along the Eastern African coast. They expanded the slave trade.

Southern and Eastern Africans, like the West and Central Africans, suffered from the effects of the trans-Atlantic slave trade. <u>Constant</u> warfare and loss of population weakened their societies. They became vulnerable to European empires.

constant, *adj.,* continuing; not stopping

European Rule

Many European nations spread their empires into Africa in the late 1800s. As in West and Central Africa, Europeans traded and conquered territory in Southern and Eastern Africa. They also founded colonies of settlers there. By around 1900, European nations ruled most of Africa.

Some European colonies were founded by trading companies. These companies needed to send supplies to traders traveling to Asia. They sent settlers to build supply posts. For example, the Dutch East India Company started a settlement in South Africa. It was called Cape Town. Over many years, Dutch settlers spread out to create the Cape Colony. Many farmers from the Netherlands, France, and other European countries settled there. They became known as **Boers,** which is Dutch for "farmers." More European settlers came, especially when gold and diamonds were discovered. Great Britain took the colony from the Dutch in 1795. British settlers also moved to modern-day Kenya and Zimbabwe.

Colonial Impact

Many Southern and Eastern Africans hated colonial rule. Europeans often took Africans' lands. They forced Africans to work for little or no pay. Europeans held high positions.

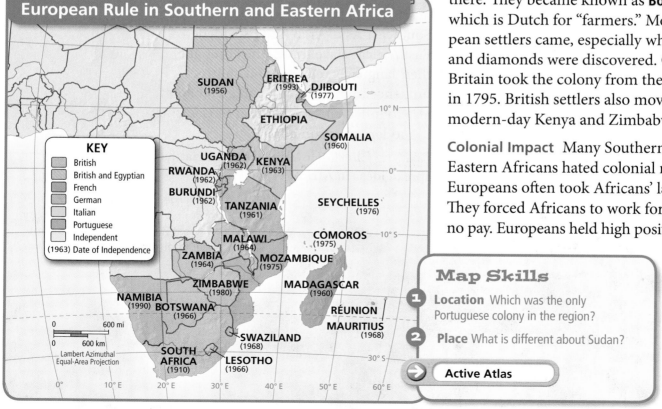

European Rule in Southern and Eastern Africa

KEY
- British
- British and Egyptian
- French
- German
- Italian
- Portuguese
- Independent

(1963) Date of Independence

SUDAN (1956)
ERITREA (1993)
DJIBOUTI (1977)
ETHIOPIA
SOMALIA (1960)
UGANDA (1962)
KENYA (1963)
RWANDA (1962)
BURUNDI (1962)
TANZANIA (1961)
SEYCHELLES (1976)
MALAWI (1964)
COMOROS (1975)
ZAMBIA (1964)
MOZAMBIQUE (1975)
ZIMBABWE (1980)
MADAGASCAR (1960)
NAMIBIA (1990)
BOTSWANA (1966)
RÉUNION
MAURITIUS (1968)
SWAZILAND (1968)
SOUTH AFRICA (1910)
LESOTHO (1966)

0   600 mi
0   600 km
Lambert Azimuthal Equal-Area Projection

10° N
0°
10° S
30° S
0°   10° E   20° E   30° E   40° E   50° E   60° E

Map Skills

1 Location Which was the only Portuguese colony in the region?

2 Place What is different about Sudan?

→ **Active Atlas**

Colonialism: Positive and Negative

▼ Europeans built up Southern and Eastern Africa's infrastructure, including railways. This helped Africans, although Europeans built them for their own purposes.

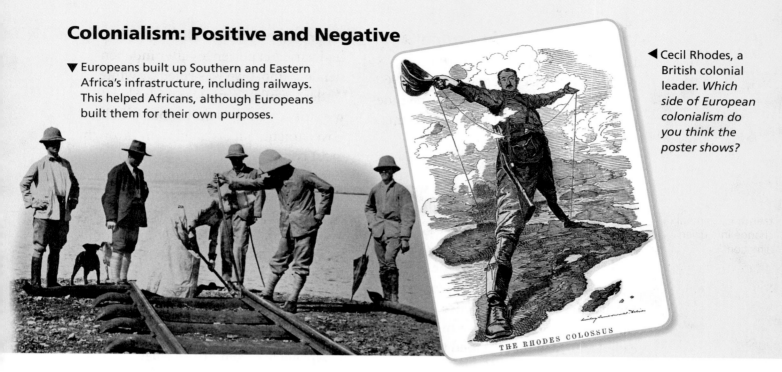

◀ Cecil Rhodes, a British colonial leader. *Which side of European colonialism do you think the poster shows?*

THE RHODES COLOSSUS

But Africans had little political power. Many Europeans also looked down on African cultures. They believed their own cultures were superior, an attitude called **ethnocentrism.** For example, colonial leader Cecil Rhodes believed that British people were better than others.

> 66 I contend that we are the first race in the world, and that the more of the world we inhabit the better it is for the human race. 99
>
> —Cecil Rhodes

However, not everything European colonialists did was negative. Though the British had held African slaves for centuries, they outlawed slavery in 1833. They then helped fight the slave trade across Africa. Europeans brought modern healthcare to Southern and Eastern Africa. They built up infrastructure to access resources.

This infrastructure also helped Africans. Europeans built schools. More Africans had access to education. With that education, Africans felt ready to take charge of the governments of their own countries.

Reading Check How was the first colony in South Africa founded?

◀ Haile Selassie, the Emperor of Ethiopia from 1930 to 1974, resisted European aggression. He fought the Italian army, which invaded his country in the 1930s. Ethiopia was never colonized by Europeans.

541

Winning Independence

In 1900, almost every country in the region was under colonial rule. By 1960, many African nations had become independent. But the road to independence was very bumpy.

Trouble in Kenya The Kikuyu (kee KOO yoo) people of Kenya were one group that opposed colonial rule. The British had taken much of their land, and British ethnocentrism made good relations difficult. In the 1940s, the Kikuyu started a political party that worked toward Kenya's independence. Change came slowly. Some began a movement called **Mau Mau** that decided to use force to end British rule in Kenya more quickly. The British and the Mau Mau fought for four years. Finally, Kenya gained independence in 1963. Kikuyu leader Jomo Kenyatta led the new nation.

trend, *n.,* general change in a given direction

British soldiers guard Kenyan villagers while looking for Mau Mau fighters.

After Independence Different countries had varied experiences after independence. Zimbabwe was ruled by white settlers, while Kenya was under black majority control. Namibia had a stable government, but Somalia went through great conflict.

In Kenya, as in other countries such as South Africa, urbanization and industrialization were important <u>trends</u> after independence. Factories were built in major cities. Rural people left farms behind to find work in factories. These trends made Kenya and South Africa richer but hurt traditional rural life.

Reading Check **Why did the Kikuyu want independence from British rule?**

The Rise and Fall of Apartheid

South Africa gained independence from Britain in 1910. However, the white minority kept political and economic power for themselves.

South Africa Under Apartheid In 1948, the white minority in South Africa adopted **apartheid,** an official government policy of keeping white and black South Africans apart. It was similar to American segregation in many ways. Apartheid laws secured power for white South Africans. Black people could only live and work in certain places, and harsh laws made travel difficult. Schools and hospitals were segregated. Black people could not vote. The Prohibition of Mixed Marriages Act made marriage between people of different races illegal.

Mandela and the End of Apartheid Many people inside and beyond South Africa believed apartheid was wrong. Black South Africans organized and protested. White police all too often responded with violence. The government banned groups like the **African National Congress** (ANC), a political party that worked for black civil rights. Many ANC leaders were jailed. Other nations criticized South Africa sharply. Some refused to trade with South Africa. That hurt its economy.

One man who played a key role in ending apartheid was Nelson Mandela. He was an ANC leader who was jailed in 1962. He continued to protest from his prison on Robben Island. Another man who played a role was F. W. de Klerk, South Africa's president from 1989 to 1994. Although he was white, de Klerk realized that apartheid was destroying South Africa. In 1990, he released Nelson Mandela from prison. Together, Mandela and de Klerk worked to end apartheid. In 1994, South Africans of all races voted together. Mandela became president. South Africa was truly independent.

Reading Check Who were two people who helped end apartheid?

myWorld Activity
Where I'm From

◄ Nelson Rolihlahla Mandela led the struggle against apartheid and became South Africa's president. He shared a Nobel Peace Prize with F. W. de Klerk in 1993.

Section **2** Assessment

Essential Question

Is conflict unavoidable?

Key Terms

1. What is ethnocentrism?

2. Who were the Boers? What does the word *boer* mean and what language does it come from?

3. What system did the African National Congress fight?

Key Ideas

4. Where do scientists believe the first human beings came from?

5. What were some effects of the Bantu migrations?

6. How did contact with Arabs influence Southern and Eastern Africa?

7. How did apartheid hurt black South Africans?

Think Critically

8. Analyze Cause and Effect What caused Kenyans to fight British rule?

9. Compare and Contrast How was Kenya's path to independence different from South Africa's?

10. Apartheid in South Africa ended without civil war or large-scale ethnic conflict. What do you think made this possible? Go to your Student Journal to record your answer.

Southern and Eastern Africa Today

◀ Kenyan runners have won many Olympic gold medals.

Southern and Eastern Africa have a wealth of natural resources. But the region also faces unique and serious challenges. Some of its nations have had more success than others in building peace and prosperity.

A Variety of Ethnic Groups and Religions

Most people in Southern and Eastern Africa are **indigenous,** or native, to the region. There are many different groups of people in the region. They belong to hundreds of different ethnic groups, speak different languages, and practice different religions.

Ethnic Groups Some ethnic groups live in a single country. Others stretch across borders. Few countries are made up of a single ethnic group. Some of the largest groups are the Zulu and Xhosa, who live in South Africa; the Kikuyu in Kenya; and the Hutu and Tutsi in Rwanda. In the past, different ethnic groups lived different lifestyles. For example, the Maasai, in Kenya and Tanzania, herded cattle. The Baganda in Uganda farmed and lived in large villages. However, today many people in the region live in cities. They no longer make a living in the ways that their ancestors did.

Religions Practiced in Southern and Eastern Africa

2%
14%
24%
60%

- Christianity
- Islam
- Indigenous religions
- Other

SOURCE: Association of Religion Data Archives (ARDA)

A procession of Ethiopian Christians

Chart Skills

1 Which two religions are most widely practiced in this area?

2 What percentage of people practice Islam?

→ **Data Discovery**

Languages The diverse people of Southern and Eastern Africa speak many different languages. Most belong to the Bantu language family. This fact is a legacy of the Bantu migrations. Languages from outside the region have also made inroads. English is spoken as a second language in countries that were once part of the British Empire. In South Africa, Afrikaans (af rih KAHNZ) is widely spoken. It comes from the Dutch spoken by early colonists.

Arab influence is widespread throughout the region. Arabic is spoken in Sudan. It also helped create the Swahili language. **Swahili** is a Bantu language. It is unique because it has many Arabic elements and words from other languages. For example, when you count from one to ten in Swahili, three of the numbers come from Arabic, while seven are Bantu. Swahili developed because of trade between Eastern Africa and Arab countries. It is now used as a common language throughout much of Eastern Africa.

Religions Many people in Southern and Eastern Africa practice indigenous African religions. Others practice Islam or Christianity. Some mix their indigenous religions with one or the other. Christianity is strongest in the southern part of the region. Islam is mostly practiced in northern parts of the region. Although Islamic countries surround Ethiopia, it has been a center of Christianity for many centuries.

Reading Check **What are three indigenous groups in Southern and Eastern Africa?**

Ndebele (un duh BEE lee) people from South Africa paint their homes in bright colors. ▶

myworldgeography.com

Data Discovery

545

Conflict in Southern and Eastern Africa Today

As Europeans carved up Africa and then left their colonies, they created many new countries. They often drew borders without regard to where different <u>ethnic</u> groups lived. Sometimes one ethnic group was divided between two different countries. In other places, opposing ethnic groups were included in the same country. These ethnic groups fought for power after Europeans left. Some of these conflicts are still going on. Two of the most deadly conflicts in recent years have taken place in Sudan and Rwanda.

ethnic, *adj.,* group of people with the same nationality, language, or religion

myWorld Activity
Analyze Conflicts

Conflicts in Sudan Sudan is divided among many different ethnic groups. In the north, most people are Arabs and practice Islam. In the south, most people belong to other ethnic groups and are not Muslims. After independence, northerners dominated the country. Southerners rebelled twice. This led to two civil wars between north and south. The wars continued until 2005 and killed several million people.

Since 2003, Darfur has been the scene of another bloody conflict. Darfur is a region in the west of Sudan. Black farmers have fought Arab herders over scarce water resources. The herders support the Sudanese government, while the farmers oppose it. Militias of herders with government backing have attacked civilian farmers. Hundreds of thousands of people, mostly black farmers, have been killed. Many more have been forced to flee their homes. Many people call the Darfur conflict a **genocide,** or an attempt to destroy a whole people.

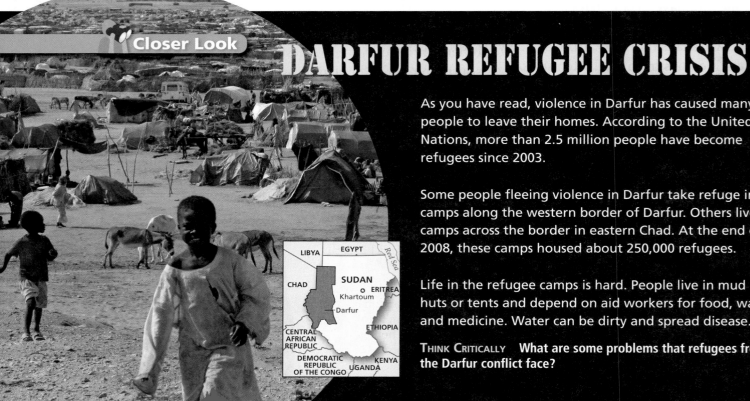

Closer Look

DARFUR REFUGEE CRISIS

As you have read, violence in Darfur has caused many people to leave their homes. According to the United Nations, more than 2.5 million people have become refugees since 2003.

Some people fleeing violence in Darfur take refuge in camps along the western border of Darfur. Others live in camps across the border in eastern Chad. At the end of 2008, these camps housed about 250,000 refugees.

Life in the refugee camps is hard. People live in mud huts or tents and depend on aid workers for food, water, and medicine. Water can be dirty and spread disease.

THINK CRITICALLY   What are some problems that refugees from the Darfur conflict face?

Genocide in Rwanda Rwanda has had a troubled history since the colonial period. The country is divided between two ethnic groups, the majority Hutu and the minority Tutsi. Before Belgium colonized the region, the Tutsi formed an elite class that ruled the Hutu. The Belgians favored the Tutsis and used them to keep control of the Hutus. After independence, violence flared up against the Tutsi and the Hutu took control. Further fighting and struggles for power between the groups continued.

Eventually the situation exploded into a horrible genocide. During a few months in 1994, Hutu military and militia groups killed an estimated 800,000 to 1 million Tutsis. The United Nations sent French, Canadian, and other troops to Rwanda to stop the killings. However, they were not effective. The murders stopped when the Tutsi once again came to power. Millions of Hutus fled the country to neighboring Zaire, today called the Democratic Republic of the Congo. Fighting between the two groups continues in that country.

Many people abroad regret that foreign countries could not or did not do more to stop the killing. Kofi Annan, former Secretary General of the UN and a high UN official during the genocide, believes more should have been done to stop it.

> 66 The international community failed Rwanda and that must leave us always with a sense of bitter regret. 99
> —Kofi Annan

Reading Check How did colonialism lead to conflicts in Southern and Eastern Africa?

Governing the Region

Southern and Eastern African countries have many different forms of government. Some are democratic, while others are ruled by dictators.

Democracy Today, one of the most democratic governments in the region is South Africa. Since the end of apartheid, fair and free elections have produced a stable government. Citizens participate in their government and can freely join voluntary organizations. But the new multiracial democracy has experienced growing pains as it tries to integrate and improve South African society. The lingering legacy of apartheid is that black South Africans are still, on average, much poorer than white South Africans. Inequalities remain in areas such as healthcare, unemployment, education, and landownership.

Dictatorship Unlike South Africa, Sudan is a dictatorship. Though the country calls itself a republic, President Omar al-Bashir rules by force. People cannot participate in the government or choose their leaders.

Zimbabwe has also been a dictatorship. A single political party has held on to power for more than 28 years. Even though there is a constitution, President Robert Mugabe has ruled like a dictator. Corruption and oppression have become common. Failed policies have led to economic collapse. Millions of people from Zimbabwe have fled to South Africa.

Reading Check What is a major social problem in South Africa after apartheid?

integrate, *v.,* bring together, particularly people from different groups

Problems and Potential

Serious obstacles stand in the way of economic development in the region. Political violence hurts economic growth. Poor transportation systems and low literacy rates also hold back development. On the other hand, the region possesses rich natural resources. It could one day use them to build up economies. Countries like Kenya and South Africa have proved that progress is possible in Southern and Eastern Africa.

Barriers to Development One major obstacle to development is the lack of stable governments in some countries. Somalia, for example is ruled by competing militias and warlords. Without a government, theft and violence are common. Piracy has become a serious problem. Gunmen off the Somali coast have attacked ships, seizing cargoes and holding crews for ransom.

Another obstacle to development is the lack of resources in some countries. For example, frequent droughts have helped keep Ethiopia among the world's poorest

African Union Peacekeepers
Former South African President Thabo Mbeki reviews African Union peacekeeping troops.

countries. Corruption also hurts development, because corrupt countries are unreliable places to do business. Corrupt leaders also steal foreign aid. Lack of education is another serious obstacle. Many families in the region cannot afford to send their children to school. Boys often have more access to education than girls. This makes it difficult for women to get better jobs and improve their situation.

Another problem is disease. Of all the regions in the world, Southern and Eastern Africa have been hit hardest by HIV and AIDS. **AIDS** is an often-deadly disease caused by the HIV virus. It attacks the immune system. It kills about 1.5 million people in this region each year, and that number is rising. Many countries are too poor to properly treat the sick. Also, when so many people get sick or die, work that is necessary to the economy does not get done. This holds back development and hurts everybody.

Hope for the Future While Southern and Eastern Africa have difficult obstacles to overcome, there are positive signs for the future. Governments are

Piracy in Somalia
Pirates in small, fast boats attack larger, slower cargo ships.

548

making serious efforts to fight AIDS. For example, the Ugandan government sends text messages on mobile phones to educate people about the epidemic. Globalization makes international trade faster and easier. It lets countries like Kenya and South Africa ship more export goods and improve their economies.

Foreign governments and **nongovernmental organizations (NGOs),** groups that operate with private funding, are helping to deal with environmental problems, poverty, disease, and conflict. They also help provide more opportunities for education, especially for women. Nations in the region have formed different organizations to cooperate in solving common problems. The African Union (AU) is the most important. Recently, it has sent peacekeeping troops to Sudan and Somalia.

Reading Check What are some barriers to development in this region?

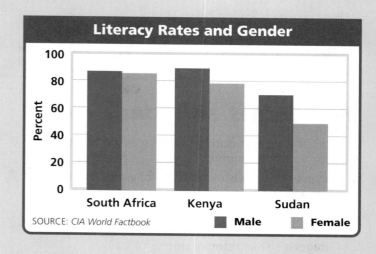

Literacy Rates and Gender

Percent

SOURCE: *CIA World Factbook*

■ Male ■ Female

Chart Skills

1 In which country are literacy rates most similar for men and women?

2 Do you think boys and girls have equal access to education in all of these countries? Explain.

→ **Data Discovery**

Section 3 Assessment

Key Terms

1. Name one example of a genocide from this region.

2. What part of the body does the HIV virus attack?

3. How do NGOs (nongovernmental organizations) help improve life in Southern and Eastern Africa?

Key Ideas

4. How does HIV/AIDS hold back development?

5. Which groups are fighting in Darfur, and what are they fighting about?

6. Describe some of the successes and failures of South Africa since the fall of apartheid.

Think Critically

7. **Compare and Contrast** How are the recent histories of Rwanda and South Africa similar? How are they different?

8. **Solve Problems** What do you think are the most effective ways Southern and Eastern Africans are improving their region? Why do you think these are the most effective?

Essential Question

Is conflict unavoidable?

9. In the countries of Sudan, Rwanda, Kenya, and South Africa, what has caused ethnic violence? Go to your Student Journal to record your answer.

Chapter Assessment

Key Terms and Ideas

1. **Discuss** Why do Southern and Eastern Africans clear forests for mining?

2. **Summarize** Why is the location of water resources so important in Southern and Eastern Africa?

3. **Recall** Where did the Bantu come from and where did they migrate to?

4. **Categorize** Give three examples of early civilizations in the region and name a feature of each.

5. **Analyze Cause and Effect** How did European control change Southern and Eastern Africa?

6. **Summarize** What have been some of the main consequences of **apartheid** in South Africa?

7. **Synthesize** Given the challenges that the region's people and governments face, why are **nongovernmental organizations (NGOs)** important in Southern and Eastern Africa?

Think Critically

8. **Solve Problems** Economic progress has been slow for the nations of this region. What geographic and human factors contribute to the problem? What factors allow or contribute to progress?

9. **Compare and Contrast** How is the role of citizens in Sudan today different from their role in the United States?

10. **Compare Viewpoints** During the apartheid era in South Africa, what main views were held and by whom?

11. **Core Concepts: Cultural Diffusion and Change** How has the movement of people influenced religion, culture, and language in Southern and Eastern Africa?

Places to Know

For each place, write the letter from the map that shows its location.

12. **South Africa**

13. **Madagascar**

14. **Kenya**

15. **Lake Victoria**

16. **Khartoum**

17. **Kalahari Desert**

18. **Draw Inferences** What might be some geographic reasons for South Africa being the region's economic superpower?

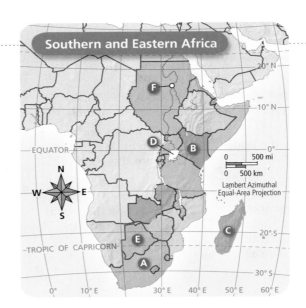

Southern and Eastern Africa

550

Essential Question

myWorld Chapter Activity

Agents of Change Follow your teacher's instructions to participate in a community group meeting attended by important individuals involved in the fall of apartheid in South Africa. Learn how different individuals helped take down apartheid. Think about ways that different groups of people can live together peacefully, and about what causes conflicts to occur.

21st Century Learning

Analyze Media Content

Using reliable sources in the library or online, research an ethnic conflict in the region. Find three examples and create a report card for each.
- type of media (print, online, TV, or radio)
- accuracy in describing conflict and participant views
- reliability (Is the source objective?)

Document-Based Questions

Success ★ Tracker™
Online at myworldgeography.com

Use your knowledge of Southern and Eastern Africa, as well as Documents A and B, to answer Questions 1–3.

Document A

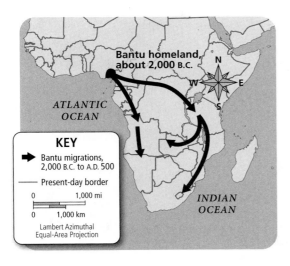

Document B

Bantu Genes		
Country or Region	Number of People Tested for Gene Type	Number of People With Bantu Gene Type
Kenya	227	223
Tanzania	41	41
Mozambique	4	2
Southern Africa	23	20

SOURCE: *Genetics and Molecular Biology,* volume 24 (1998), no. 4

1. Where was the Bantu people's original homeland?
   A Europe
   B North Africa
   C West Africa
   D Southern Africa

2. Which of the following can you conclude from Document B?
   A Very few Tanzanians are of Bantu heritage.
   B Most Kenyans are of Bantu heritage.
   C Most Mozambicans are of European heritage.
   D Most people in the world are of Bantu heritage.

3. **Writing Task** Based on what you have learned from the chapter and the documents above, explain the information presented in Document B.

Chapter 15

North Africa

? Essential Question

How much does geography shape a country?

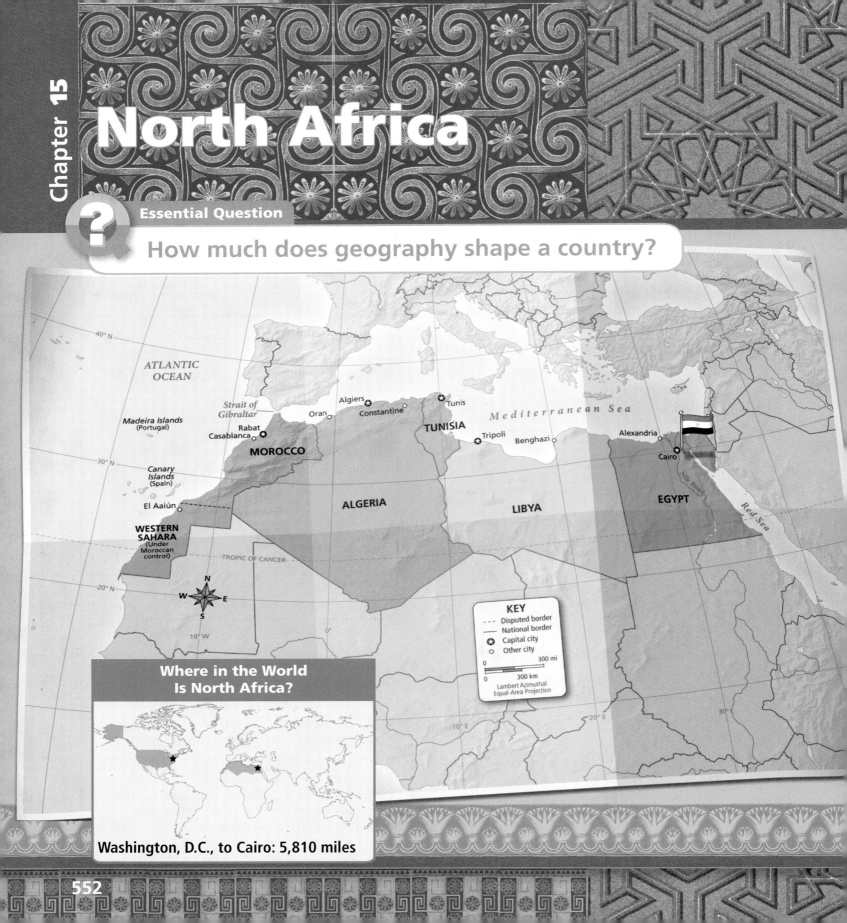

KEY
- - - Disputed border
— National border
✪ Capital city
○ Other city

0 ——— 300 mi
0 ——— 300 km
Lambert Azimuthal
Equal-Area Projection

Where in the World Is North Africa?

Washington, D.C., to Cairo: 5,810 miles

my Story

SHAIMAA'S NEIGHBORHOOD

In this section, you'll read about Shaimaa, a young Egyptian woman who lives in Cairo. **What does Shaimaa's story tell you about life in North Africa today?**

? Explore the Essential Question
- at **my worldgeography.com**
- using the **myWorld Chapter Activity**
- with the **Student Journal**

Story by Oliver Wilkins for myWorld Geography Online

Sitting on the top of Cairo's medieval city wall, 18-year-old Shaimaa is focused on her sketchbook. Pencil in hand, she traces the domes and towers that make up the skyline of Darb al-Ahmar, the neighborhood where she was born and raised. Her spot overlooks a large park, and the sound of birds fills the air. For Shaimaa, it seems a million miles away from the hustle and bustle of the crowded neighborhood below where she lives with her family.

"I have four sisters. We all sleep in the same room. My older sister Asmaa got married. They had to leave the area because they couldn't afford an apartment."

Shaimaa's parents, like many in the neighborhood, moved here from the countryside. They originally came from a village in southern Egypt. They moved to Cairo to find a new life.

Shaimaa's apartment is located in one of the hundreds of small alleys that make up Darb al-Ahmar. The neighborhood lies in the shadow of the citadel, or fortress. The citadel was once home to Cairo's rulers and its wealthiest families lived in Darb al-Ahmar.

my worldgeography.com On Assignment

Shaimaa at a market

Laundry drying in Darb al-Ahmar

The neighborhood was very prosperous. Its wealthy residents built beautiful mosques.

But later, the area fell on hard times. For many years the beautiful buildings crumbled. As the population mushroomed, the area became overcrowded. Like many parts of Cairo today, Shaimaa's neighborhood is struggling to support a growing population.

Every weekday Shaimaa leaves her house at 9 A.M. and makes her way through the bustling market to catch a bus to school in downtown Cairo. She is studying computer science and hopes to continue at a university at the end of the year.

However, Shaimaa's real passion is to help restore her neighborhood. Most days after school she volunteers at a community center to do her part.

With hammer in hand, Shaimaa nails together a wooden backdrop, painted with the minarets and domes of Darb al-Ahmar's distinctive skyline. Today she is helping a group of children

Two puppets and a backdrop showing the skyline of Darb al-Ahmar

The puppet show

Shaimaa on the city wall

to prepare a puppet show on the history of their neighborhood. Puppet shows are a traditional form of entertainment. Shaimaa hopes that by bringing these old stories to life, she may be able to encourage a sense of pride in the neighborhood.

"We are trying to tell the people about this neighborhood through the program. We are trying to make people proud of Darb al-Ahmar by reminding them about their history, trying to revive the heritage and the folklore of the neighborhood."

In the courtyard of the school, the children rehearse the puppet show. In two weeks they will be performing it in the park by the city wall. It's hard to believe now, but the park was a garbage dump until a few years ago. After centuries of people throwing their trash over the wall, the dump grew into a hill, Shaima recalls.

"I remember before it was a park, it was a dusty hill. We were frightened to go in there because the wild dogs would chase us."

Sketching on the top of the wall, Shaimaa gazes down on her neighborhood. She points out the buildings that are undergoing restoration.

"Here, each house is like a piece of art from the past. After being restored, each house regains its sense of history. "

Shaimaa is optimistic about the future of her neighborhood. "I hope that I'll have more chances to represent the habits and traditions of my neighborhood and to let other people know more about Darb al-Ahmar."

→ **myStory Video**

Join Shaimaa as she shows you more about her life in North Africa.

my worldgeography.com   myStory Video

Meet the Journalist

Name Oliver Wilkins
Favorite Moment Watching Shaimaa teach her mother to write.

Chapter Atlas

Key Ideas

- North Africa is very dry, especially in the vast desert called the Sahara.

- People settle where rivers or rainfall provide water.

- More and more North Africans are moving to cities.

- People in the region have altered their environment with both positive and negative consequences.

Key Terms • oasis • delta • nomad • urbanization

 Visual Glossary

Reading Skill: Label an Outline Map Take notes using the outline map in your journal.

▲ The Atlas Mountains in Morocco.

◀ A Tunisian woman ▶

Physical Features

The five countries of North Africa lie along the Mediterranean coast from Morocco in the west to Egypt, Shaimaa's home, in the east. The region is very dry. In fact, most of North Africa is desert.

The world's largest hot desert, the Sahara, covers much of North Africa. Conditions in the Sahara are harsh. In some places it does not rain for years at a time. Sandstorms are common. Temperatures can be extremely high during the day but cool or even cold at night. Life in the Sahara centers around oases. An **oasis**

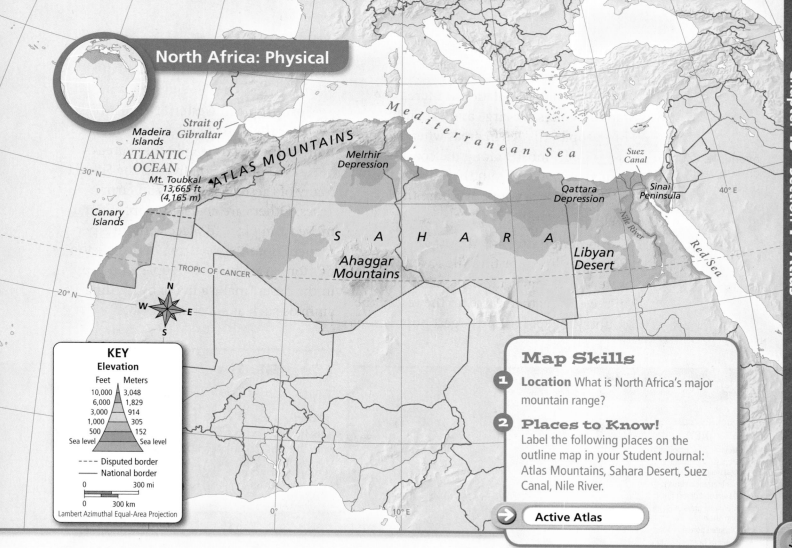

North Africa: Physical

ATLANTIC OCEAN

Madeira Islands

Strait of Gibraltar

Mt. Toubkal 13,665 ft (4,165 m)

ATLAS MOUNTAINS

Canary Islands

Melrhir Depression

Mediterranean Sea

Suez Canal

Sinai Peninsula

Qattara Depression

Nile River

S A H A R A

Red Sea

Libyan Desert

Ahaggar Mountains

30° N

20° N

TROPIC OF CANCER

40° E

0°   10° E

N W E S

KEY
Elevation

Feet	Meters
10,000	3,048
6,000	1,829
3,000	914
1,000	305
500	152
Sea level	Sea level

- - - - Disputed border
——— National border

0   300 mi
0   300 km

Lambert Azimuthal Equal-Area Projection

Map Skills

1 **Location** What is North Africa's major mountain range?

2 **Places to Know!**
Label the following places on the outline map in your Student Journal: Atlas Mountains, Sahara Desert, Suez Canal, Nile River.

Active Atlas

is a place in a desert where water can be found.

The Atlas Mountains run through Morocco, Algeria, and Tunisia. They sit between the desert and the sea. Clouds move in from the west and drop their rain as they rise over the mountains. That gives more rainfall to the slopes of the mountains facing the coast and to areas north of the mountains.

The country of Egypt gets almost no rain. It is about 96 <u>percent</u> desert. But the remaining land is green and lush thanks to the Nile River. The Nile travels through its valley north from eastern Africa and

Sudan to the Mediterranean Sea, splitting Egypt in two. It brings water to a strip of land along its banks and to its triangle-shaped delta. A **delta** is a flat plain formed on the seabed where a river deposits material over many years. Until a dam was built on the Nile, the river flooded every year, coating its banks in rich soil.

One part of this region, Egypt's Sinai Peninsula, sits between Asia and Africa. The peninsula is a mountainous desert separated from Africa by the Suez Canal.

Reading Check What is an oasis, and why would people live near one?

percent, *n.,* one part out of one hundred

Living in a Dry Place

North Africa's population is increasing rapidly. Cities are large and expanding. But people still live in areas where water is <u>available</u>, mostly along the coasts or near rivers. Away from these areas, the land is too dry to support more than a handful of people.

Settlement Patterns Almost all Egyptians live near the Nile River, where water makes agriculture possible. Few live in the deserts that make up the rest of the country. Egypt has the largest population in the region. In fact, almost half of all North Africans are Egyptians.

Most people in western North Africa live near the coast or in the mountains. Rain supports farming in these areas.

A small population lives in the Sahara. Many of these people live and farm in oases. Others are **nomads,** people who move from place to place without a permanent home. Away from oases it is too dry for agriculture, so people who live in the desert make a living by herding animals such as sheep and goats.

available, *adj.,* present, ready to be used

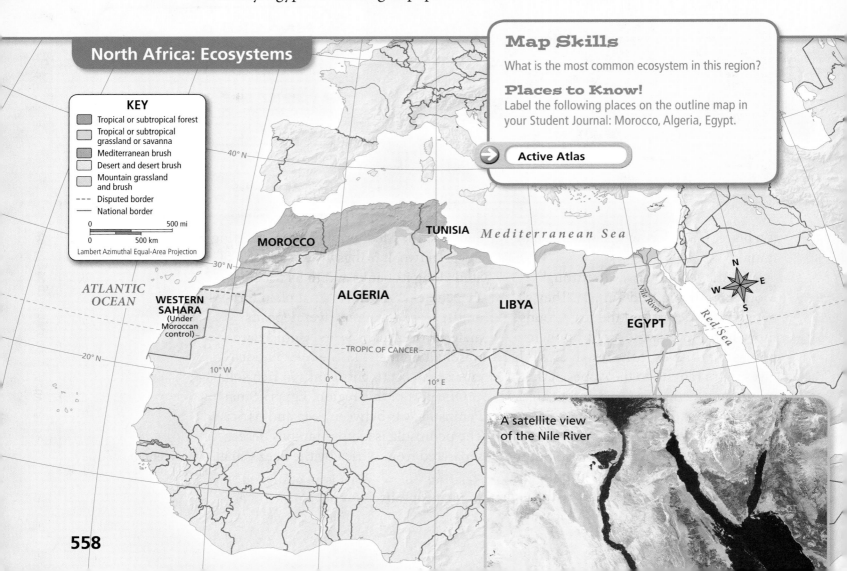

North Africa: Ecosystems

KEY
- Tropical or subtropical forest
- Tropical or subtropical grassland or savanna
- Mediterranean brush
- Desert and desert brush
- Mountain grassland and brush
- - - - Disputed border
- ——— National border

0   500 mi
0   500 km
Lambert Azimuthal Equal-Area Projection

Map Skills

What is the most common ecosystem in this region?

Places to Know!
Label the following places on the outline map in your Student Journal: Morocco, Algeria, Egypt.

→ **Active Atlas**

ATLANTIC OCEAN

MOROCCO
TUNISIA
Mediterranean Sea
WESTERN SAHARA (Under Moroccan control)
ALGERIA
LIBYA
EGYPT
Nile River
Red Sea
TROPIC OF CANCER

40° N
30° N
20° N
10° W
0°
10° E

A satellite view of the Nile River

Cities Slightly more than half of all North Africans live in cities. Over the past century, farmers across the region have left their villages and migrated to urban areas in search of jobs and a higher standard of living. North Africa is experiencing urbanization. **Urbanization** happens when people in an area move into cities and those cities grow larger.

Cairo, the capital of Egypt, is the largest city in Africa and home to more than one in five Egyptians. It is Egypt's economic, political, and educational center. That makes it a magnet for poor people from the countryside, like Shaimaa's parents, who have moved there in large numbers.

The trend of urbanization is even stronger in the western part of the region. More than half of all Moroccans, Tunisians, and Algerians live in cities, as do more than three quarters of Libyans.

Rapidly growing urban populations can cause problems. Cities have trouble providing services like drinking water to so many people. Many cities are severely overcrowded. Still, people keep moving to the cities to find new opportunities.

Reading Check **Why do people in North Africa move to cities?**

myWorld Activity
On the Move

The Nile River, Egypt. Many of Egypt's people live in rural areas near the Nile.

Marrakech, Morocco. Urban North Africans visit cafes and souqs, or markets.

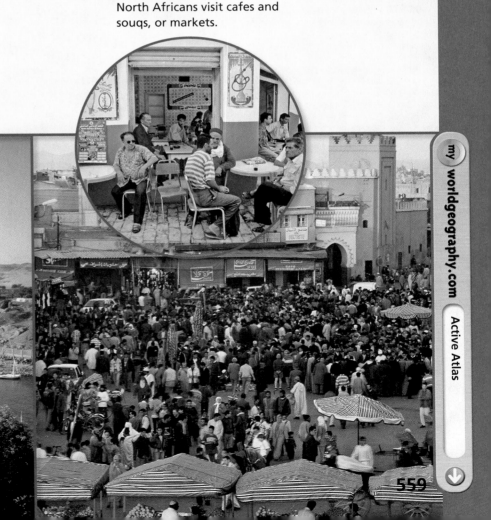

my worldgeography.com Active Atlas

THE FLOODING OF LAKE NASSER

→ **Culture Close-up**

The Aswan High Dam helped Egypt but the large lake it created flooded many ancient monuments (above).

The ancient Egyptian temples at Abu Simbel (below) were cut into pieces and moved to a location away from the new lake. They are now a tourist attraction.

The temples at Abu Simbel were cut into **20**-ton blocks and moved **213** feet up and **820** feet back.

North Africa's Environment

Human beings have changed the environment of North Africa. These changes have made life easier, but they sometimes have had negative side effects.

In 1964, the Egyptian government built a dam across the Nile River called the Aswan High Dam. Building the dam allowed people to use water more efficiently, irrigate more land, and grow more crops. It also stopped dangerous flooding, and it produces electricity.

Unfortunately, the dam has also had negative effects on Egypt's environment and people. Before the dam was built, Egyptian farmers relied on annual floods to bring fertile soil to their fields. Since the river no longer floods, farmers must use chemical fertilizers to keep their land productive. These fertilizers eventually wash back into the river and through it into the sea. That pollutes water, killing fish and hurting people who fish for a living. Fortunately, fish stocks have recovered in recent years to near what they were before the dam was built.

As water collected behind the dam, it formed a giant lake called Lake Nasser. It is now a habitat for malaria-carrying mosquitoes. The creation of Lake Nasser forced 100,000 people out of their homes.

Like Egypt, Libya has also made serious changes to its environment. As you have read, Libya gets very little rain. However, there are large underground reserves of water deep in the Sahara. The Libyan government has built pipelines to carry water to the coast. The water is used to irrigate farmland and support growing coastal cities, where four out of every five Libyans now live.

Across this region and other parts of Africa, desertification is a major environmental problem. You learned already that this can happen when people cut down forests. It can also happen in regions such as North Africa that have few forests to begin with.

One way desertification happens is through overgrazing. Herders allow their goats to eat the grass in an area down to the roots. Without those roots, there is nothing left to hold the soil in place. Wind then blows top away, leaving barren desert behind. So much of North Africa is desert already that the region cannot afford to create more.

However, desertification can be slowed or even <u>reversed</u>. When land that is at risk is set aside and herds of sheep or goats are kept away from it, desertification can be reversed and plant life can return. People can also prevent the spread of deserts by planting a "green wall." This is a belt of trees and other vegetation planted along the edges of the desert. The trees and other plants hold soil in place and protect the land.

Algeria pioneered this technique in the 1970s. Since then, belts of forest have been planted along the edges of deserts in other parts of Africa and in different countries around the world.

Reading Check What are two environmental issues in North Africa?

reverse, *v.,* turn back, turn in the opposite direction

A landscape in Morocco that shows the effects of desertification. Overgrazing can cause desertification.

Resources and Trade

Water and oil are the most important natural resources in North Africa. The Nile River flows through several countries before it reaches Egypt. As you read in Southern and Eastern Africa, deciding who gets to use that water is a difficult issue. If other countries take too much water, Egypt could face shortages.

The Nile River in Egypt, and rainfall in the western part of the region, allow farming. Cotton, olives, citrus fruits, and other crops are important exports.

Oil Although North Africa does not produce as much oil as parts of Southwest Asia, every nation in the region has enough to satisfy its own needs and to export, or sell abroad. Algeria and Libya have the largest reserves by far.

Most of North Africa's oil and natural gas reserves are found inland, in the heart of the Sahara. Governments and international companies have built pipelines. They transport oil and gas to the coast, where they are shipped around the world.

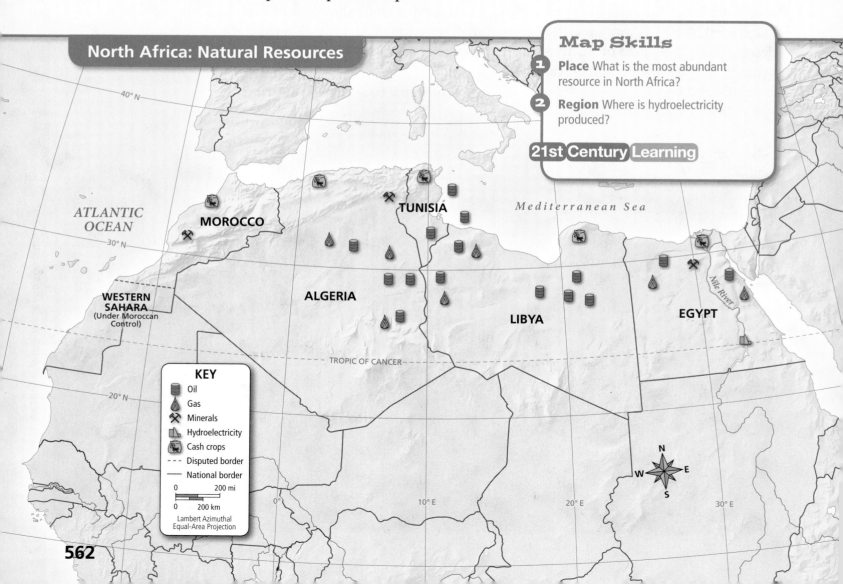

North Africa: Natural Resources

Map Skills

1 **Place** What is the most abundant resource in North Africa?

2 **Region** Where is hydroelectricity produced?

21st Century Learning

ATLANTIC OCEAN

MOROCCO

WESTERN SAHARA (Under Moroccan Control)

ALGERIA

TUNISIA

Mediterranean Sea

LIBYA

EGYPT

Nile River

TROPIC OF CANCER

KEY

- Oil
- Gas
- Minerals
- Hydroelectricity
- Cash crops
- - - Disputed border
- — National border

0   200 mi
0   200 km

Lambert Azimuthal Equal-Area Projection

The Suez Canal The canal was built in Egypt in 1869. It allows large ships to pass from the Mediterranean to the Red Sea. The canal makes traveling by sea between Asia and Europe shorter by thousands of miles. Ships do not have to go around the entire continent of Africa. That makes the cost of transportation cheaper. Businesses can pass the money they save on transportation on to consumers in the form of lower prices.

One of the most important goods that passes through the Suez Canal today is oil. More than 3,000 oil tankers use the canal every year.

Because of its role in world trade, the Suez Canal affects people around the world. The canal is good for Egypt, too, since it collects a fee from each ship that passes through.

Reading Check Which two North African countries have the largest oil reserves?

Crossroads of Continents

North Africa's closeness to Europe, Asia, and Africa south of the Sahara has helped shape life there for thousands of years.

The Sahara made travel between North Africa and other parts of Africa difficult in the past. However, it was not an impassable barrier. People, ideas, and goods have long moved across it.

North Africa and Southern Europe have had connections across the Mediterranean for thousands of years. Today European languages, especially French, are often spoken as second languages in parts of the region. Millions of North African immigrants also live in Europe.

The country of Israel, in Southwest Asia, shares a land border with Egypt. North Africa's majority religion and language both came from Southwest Asia.

Reading Check How did Southwest Asia change North Africa?

my **World** IN NUMBERS

In 2007, **20,384** ships passed through the Suez Canal. They carried **710** million tons of cargo.

Section 1 Assessment

Essential Question

How much does geography shape a country?

Key Terms

1. Use the following words to describe life in the Sahara: nomad, oasis.

2. How are deltas formed?

3. What is urbanization?

Key Ideas

4. What single factor most affects where people in North Africa live?

5. What have been the positive and negative changes caused by the Aswan High Dam?

6. How has urbanization affected North Africa?

7. How does the Suez Canal affect world trade?

Think Critically

8. **Compare and Contrast** Compare the Egyptian desert to the Nile River Valley. Which of these areas occupies more space? Which is home to more Egyptians?

9. **Identify Main Ideas** What do you think is the most important environmental problem facing North Africa?

10. How does water shape human settlement patterns in North Africa? Go to your student journal to record your answers.

History of North Africa

The Great Sphinx in Egypt ▼

North Africa produced one of the world's first civilizations. The ancient Egyptians took advantage of their country's fertile river valley and built a wealthy and sophisticated society. Ancient Egypt's achievements influenced other cultures. In fact, ancient Egypt is considered a cultural hearth, or one of the places where human civilization began.

Ancient Egypt

About 5,000 years ago the civilization of ancient Egypt developed in the Nile River Valley. It endured for almost 3,000 years.

Ancient Egypt Develops An ancient Greek writer called Egypt "the gift of the river." The Nile River made Egyptian civilization possible. The river was like an oasis surrounded by desert. Every summer it brought great floods. They left behind deposits of silt, a rich soil, along the river's banks. Plants and animals thrived in this environment. In ancient times, nomads lived around the river. They survived by hunting, gathering, and fishing.

Fertile soil made the river valley a perfect place for agriculture, which spread into Egypt from Southwest Asia. Societies that farm are different from fishing and hunting-gathering societies. Farming produces more food than hunting and gathering or fishing. It allows the population to expand. Small villages grow into towns and then cities.

By about 3,000 B.C., as many as one million people may have lived along the Nile. They shared a language, a culture, and religious beliefs.

Early on, Egypt developed a powerful government ruled by a **pharaoh,** or king of ancient Egypt. The Nile River and the need to use it for irrigation encouraged powerful central government in Egypt. A single ruler could direct the people's labor to build irrigation canals. Canals changed Egypt's environment. They brought water to fields far from the river. They also helped control floods. Pharaohs taxed the people to pay for building the canals or forced people to work part of the year for no pay. Pharaohs also used these methods to build temples and tombs.

The pharaoh was not just a political leader. Egyptians also believed he was like a god and worshipped him after his death. That belief made Egypt a **theocracy,** a government based on religion.

Egypt's strong central government made it different from ancient civilizations in Iraq and India. They were often politically divided. Egypt was more like China, which unified at an early date.

Egyptian Culture The Egyptians were among the first people to study mathematics, astronomy, engineering, and other scientific fields. They built trade networks into Eastern Africa and other regions. Egyptian culture influenced other parts of the world.

The Egyptians invented **hieroglyphics,** a system of writing using pictures and other symbols. Hieroglyphics were used to help the government keep records and to write about history and religion. Egyptians also invented papyrus, the first paper, which they made from reeds that grew along the banks of the Nile River.

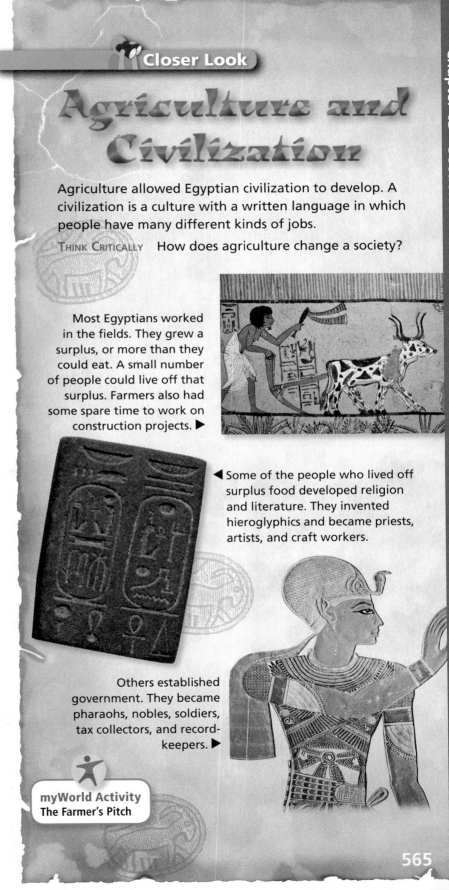

Closer Look

Agriculture and Civilization

Agriculture allowed Egyptian civilization to develop. A civilization is a culture with a written language in which people have many different kinds of jobs.

THINK CRITICALLY   How does agriculture change a society?

Most Egyptians worked in the fields. They grew a surplus, or more than they could eat. A small number of people could live off that surplus. Farmers also had some spare time to work on construction projects. ▶

◀ Some of the people who lived off surplus food developed religion and literature. They invented hieroglyphics and became priests, artists, and craft workers.

Others established government. They became pharaohs, nobles, soldiers, tax collectors, and record-keepers. ▶

myWorld Activity
The Farmer's Pitch

565

Egyptian Religion Ancient Egyptians believed in hundreds of gods that controlled all places and things. They also believed in an afterlife, life after death. Pharaohs and the very rich were buried with valuables, favorite pets, food, and even boats to take them to the afterlife.

Many pharaohs built elaborate tombs. In fact, the famous pyramids of Giza are tombs. Each has rooms on the inside to hold the pharaoh's body and possessions.

Some Egyptians had their bodies mummified, or turned into mummies after death. A **mummy** is a body that has been preserved so it will not decompose. The corpse's internal organs were removed and the brain pulled through the nose with a hook. Then the body was

◄ An ancient Egyptian mummy

dried and wrapped in sheets of linen to preserve it. Much of what we know about ancient Egypt comes from its tombs.

Greek and Roman North Africa After more than 2,000 years of rule by pharaohs, Egypt was conquered by Persians and then Greeks. Greeks ruled Egypt for 302 years. The famous Queen Cleopatra VII was the last Greek ruler of Egypt. Around 800 B.C, Phoenicians from modern-day Lebanon built the powerful city of Carthage in what is now Tunisia. Eventually the whole region fell under Roman rule. By the A.D. 400s most North Africans had converted to Christianity.

Reading Check Why was Ancient Egypt called the "gift of the Nile"?

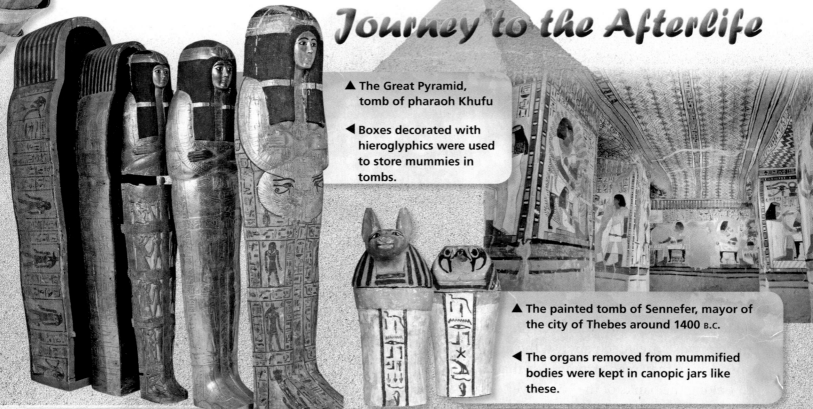

Journey to the Afterlife

▲ The Great Pyramid, tomb of pharaoh Khufu

◄ Boxes decorated with hieroglyphics were used to store mummies in tombs.

▲ The painted tomb of Sennefer, mayor of the city of Thebes around 1400 B.C.

◄ The organs removed from mummified bodies were kept in canopic jars like these.

Arab North Africa

With the arrival of Arab Muslims from Southwest Asia, North Africa's religion, language, and culture were <u>transformed</u>.

The Arab Conquest In the A.D. 600s, the religion of Islam was first preached in Arabia. Followers of Islam are called Muslims. The first Muslims were Arabs. Arab Muslim armies built an empire that stretched from Spain to Iran. North Africa was part of this empire.

Religious leaders and merchants followed the army, building trading centers and mosques, or Islamic houses of worship. Then many Arab migrants came. They spread Islam to Egyptians and **Berbers,** the indigenous people of western North Africa. These migrants also helped spread the Arabic language throughout the region. Most North Africans converted to Islam, although many Jews and Christians continued to live in the region.

North Africa became one of the most culturally productive parts of the Islamic world. Arab rulers founded cities such as Kairouan in Tunisia and Cairo in Egypt. Both grew into major centers of religion and learning. Cairo became one of the largest cities in the world. Art and literature flourished under Arab rule.

Trade in Arab North Africa While earlier conquerors saw the Sahara as a barrier, the Arabs saw it as an opportunity. They quickly came to control the trans-Saharan caravan routes that linked Africa south of the Sahara with North Africa. Merchants spread Arabic and Islam to peoples they traded with in the Sahara and beyond.

Reading Check **How did the Arabs change North Africa?**

transform, *v.*, change into a new form or appearance

Painted tiles are often used to make decorative geometric shapes in Arab architecture. ▼

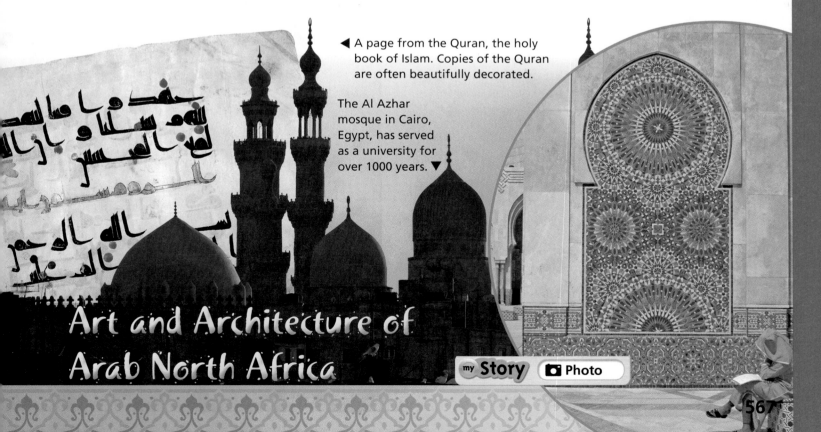

◀ A page from the Quran, the holy book of Islam. Copies of the Quran are often beautifully decorated.

The Al Azhar mosque in Cairo, Egypt, has served as a university for over 1000 years. ▼

Art and Architecture of Arab North Africa

my **Story** 📷 **Photo**

567

European Rule and Independence

The united Arab empire did not last long. Various states gained and lost power in the region over time.

European Colonization During the 1800s, European powers came to rule North Africa. They wanted to control the region's resources, to guard important trade routes, or to force local rulers to pay debts they owed to European lenders. Britain took control of Egypt, while France ruled most of western North Africa. Spain and Italy governed other parts of this region.

majority, *n.,* a group with more than half of a population

The Struggle for Independence
Resistance to European rule began immediately and grew into nationalism. North Africans resented that they did not get a say in their own government. Many protested European rule. Most of the region gained independence in the 1950s.

Algeria had a longer road to travel. Around one million Europeans had settled in Algeria. Many argued that Algeria was a part of France. Some Algerians agreed and wanted to be more like the French. But the <u>majority</u> disagreed. They argued that Algeria had a different culture, language, and religion from France. According to a nationalist,

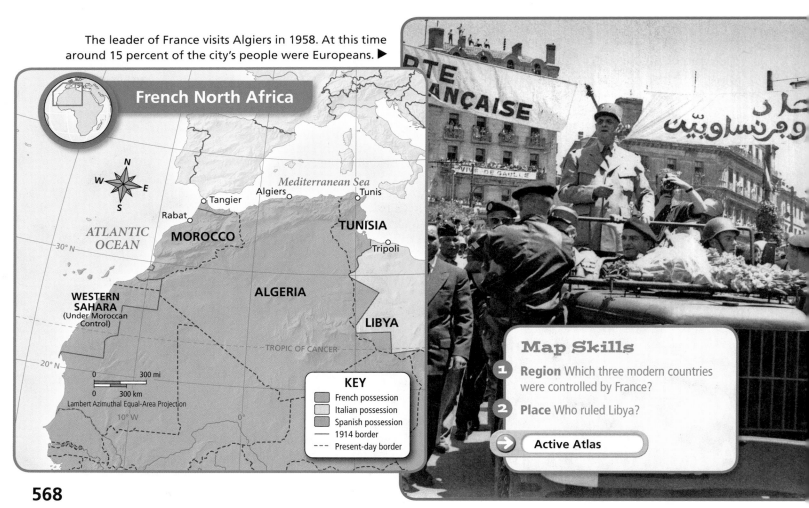

The leader of France visits Algiers in 1958. At this time around 15 percent of the city's people were Europeans. ▶

French North Africa

Mediterranean Sea
Algiers • Tunis
Tangier
Rabat
ATLANTIC OCEAN
MOROCCO
TUNISIA
Tripoli
WESTERN SAHARA (Under Moroccan Control)
ALGERIA
LIBYA
TROPIC OF CANCER

0   300 mi
0   300 km
Lambert Azimuthal Equal-Area Projection

KEY
- French possession
- Italian possession
- Spanish possession
- — 1914 border
- --- Present-day border

Map Skills

1. **Region** Which three modern countries were controlled by France?

2. **Place** Who ruled Libya?

→ **Active Atlas**

> 66 Islam is our religion, Arabic our language, Algeria our fatherland. 99

—Ben Badis

It took eight years of bloody war for the country to win independence. In 1962, French troops left. Most Europeans in Algeria fled the country.

Egypt Since Independence Egypt gained its formal independence in 1922, but Britain continued to quietly control the country for many years. In 1952, a group of military officers led by Gamal Abdel Nasser overthrew the government and seized control of Egypt. Nasser ruled like a dictator.

Nasser tried to modernize and strengthen Egypt. In 1956, he seized control of the Suez Canal from its British and French owners. Britain, France, and Israel responded by attacking Egypt, but the United States and the United Nations forced them to withdraw. As a result, Egypt gained control of the canal.

This event, the Suez Crisis, was seen as a major success of Nasser's rule. Arabs in other countries admired him for standing up to European powers and for building the Aswan High Dam. He was a leader of the Pan-Arab movement. **Pan-Arabism** is the idea that all Arabic-speaking peoples should unite into one country.

In another area, Nasser was less successful. He opposed the existence of the country of Israel and tried to fight it. In 1967, Israel defeated Egypt and its allies Jordan and Syria. Israel took the Sinai Peninsula from Egypt. Nasser's successor, Anwar Sadat, failed to take the Sinai back when he went to war with Israel in 1973. Egypt only regained the Sinai when it signed a peace agreement with Israel in 1979.

Reading Check What happened to the Sinai Peninsula in 1967 and 1979?

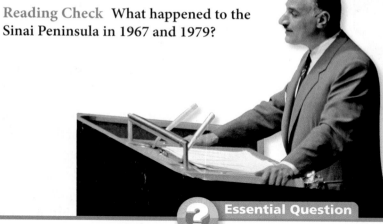

Gamal Abdel Nasser, Egypt's president from 1956 to 1970 ▼

Section 2 Assessment

Key Terms

1. Use the following words to describe ancient Egyptian religion and government: pharaoh, theocracy, mummy, hieroglyphics.

2. Who are the Berbers?

3. What do people who support Pan-Arabism believe?

Key Ideas

4. How did the Arab-Islamic conquest of North Africa change the region?

5. What were two of Gamal Abdel Nasser's major achievements?

Think Critically

6. **Analyze Cause and Effect** Why was the development of agriculture important for ancient Egypt? What did agriculture allow?

7. **Compare and Contrast** How were independence struggles in Algeria and Egypt different?

? Essential Question

How much does geography shape a country?

8. How did physical geography shape the development of ancient Egypt? Go to your student journal to record your answers.

North Africa Today

Key Ideas
- Islam and the Arabic language dominate North Africa, but there are minority groups and significant outside influences.
- North Africa is more developed than other parts of the continent, but its people still struggle to make a living.
- Tensions between Islamism and secularism have complicated the region's politics.

Key Terms • Copts • gross domestic product • gross domestic product per capita
• human development Index • secularism • Muslim Brotherhood

 Visual Glossary

Reading Skill: Identify Main Idea and Details Take notes using the graphic organizer in your journal.

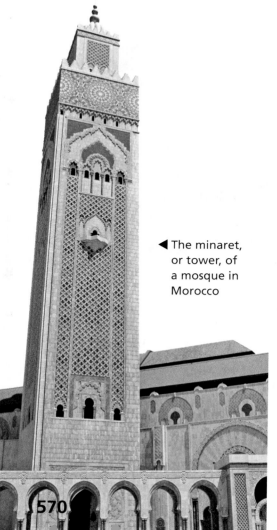

◀ The minaret, or tower, of a mosque in Morocco

North Africa is today the most developed region on the continent. It benefits from large oil deposits and a more peaceful recent history than other regions. North Africa's culture links it closely to Southwest Asia, while trade and migration tie it to Europe.

North African Culture

Most North Africans practice Islam and speak Arabic. These traits tie the region to Southwest Asia and to other parts of the Islamic world.

North Africa and the Middle East Arabic is the most widely spoken language in North Africa and much of Southwest Asia. As in North Africa, most people in Southwest Asia practice Islam. North Africa and Southwest Asia together are often called the Middle East.

The term *Middle East* can have different meanings. It usually includes Egypt but not always other countries in North Africa. It includes Israel, where Islam is not the majority religion. It may also include Iran and Turkey, where Arabic is not generally spoken. It does not include mostly Muslim countries like Indonesia or Nigeria, which are outside of Southwest Asia and North Africa.

People in the Arabic-speaking world from Morocco to Iraq are bound together by their common language and religion. Arabic-speaking countries form a culture region. That means that they share many aspects of their culture with one another.

Egypt has the largest population of any Arabic-speaking country. It produces many of the most popular books, films, and television shows in Arabic. An Egyptian writer says of Egypt's film industry,

> 66 With a scale of production unequalled anywhere else in the Arab world, and with its Egyptian-Arab cultural appeal, it became the commercial cinema for all Arab countries. 99

—Samir Farid

Raï (rah EE) music is originally from Algeria, but it appeals to Arabic-speaking people from many different countries. Raï blends traditional and modern styles and deals with current issues.

Minority Groups Ethnic and religious minorities also live in North Africa. The Berbers are the largest ethnic minority. They speak their own language, Tamazight, and live in the western part of the region. Berbers have worked to preserve their culture. Today, Tamazight is an official language in two countries.

The **Copts** are a minority group in Egypt. They practice Christianity. Coptic Christianity has been practiced in Egypt since ancient times. Copts are generally tolerated by the Muslim majority but are sometimes treated as second-class citizens. The Copts are the largest Christian population in the Middle East.

Large Jewish populations lived in the region from ancient times until the 1900s. Most now live in Israel, but small numbers remain, particularly in Morocco.

Reading Check What regions are often considered part of the Middle East?

North African Life

A woman prepares couscous, a common dish in western North Africa. ▶

◀ Berber men in Algeria enjoy a cup of tea.

◀ Algerian raï singer Rachid Taha gives a performance.

571

Economy and Development

North Africa is the wealthiest and most developed region in Africa. It benefits from large oil reserves, trade with Europe, good educational systems, and relatively <u>stable</u> governments.

stable, *adj.,* firm, likely to last, well established

Living Conditions The standard of living in North Africa is generally higher than in other parts of Africa. But, it is not as high as in Europe or North America. Many North Africans live in poverty. Water shortages and urban problems such as overcrowding are serious issues.

One way to compare living conditions from place to place is to compare life expectancy, or how long an average person lives. High life expectancy is a sign that a country has a good healthcare system and enough food. Libya has the highest life expectancy in Africa.

You can also compare different countries by their **gross domestic product (GDP).** Gross domestic product is the total value of all goods and services produced in a country over a single year. Bigger countries often have bigger GDPs. For example, Algeria has more people than Libya, and it has a higher GDP.

But GDP does not show how real Algerians or Libyans live. In a big country, all those goods and services are shared among more people. The **gross domestic product (GDP) per capita** gives a better picture of conditions. It is a country's GDP divided by the number of people in the country. Libya has a higher GDP per capita than Algeria. That means that on average, a Libyan

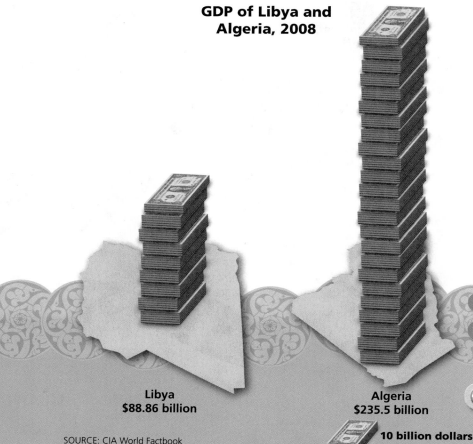

GDP of Libya and Algeria, 2008

Libya
$88.86 billion

Algeria
$235.5 billion

10 billion dollars

SOURCE: CIA World Factbook

Chart Skills

1 What is Algeria's gross domestic product?

2 Does this graph show that, on average, an Algerian earns more than a Libyan? Explain your answer.

→ **Data Discovery**

has a higher income than an Algerian. On average, a Libyan has more purchasing power, meaning he or she can afford more things, than an Algerian. The problem with this measure is that it does not show inequality. Some people earn more than others but the GDP per capita does not reflect this difference.

The **human development index,** or HDI, takes more into account. An HDI is a number that reflects a country's average life expectancy, education, income, and other factors. HDI values are shown as decimals. For example, Egypt's HDI is 0.7. The closer a country's HDI is to one, the higher its standard of living.

Looking at the literacy rate, or the percentage of adults who can read, is also helpful. A high literacy rate suggests that country has a good education system. Tunisia's literacy rate is 74.3 percent. The United States' is 99.9 percent. Educated workers are more productive, so education can improve a country's economy.

North Africa's Economies Oil production is the most important primary industry in North Africa. A primary industry <u>extracts</u> natural resources. Agriculture is also an important primary industry. Secondary industries make finished products from raw materials. Food processing, textile production, and crafts such as making leather goods or jewelry are important secondary industries in North Africa.

Oil, food, and manufactured goods are all exported from North Africa to Europe. In this trade, Europeans buy needed products, and North Africans receive the money they need. Voluntary trade like this can benefit both sides.

Tourism brings a great deal of business into the region. Tourists flock to North Africa for its historic sites and warm winters. Tourists spend money at hotels and restaurants. These services are called tertiary, or third-level, industries. Fourth-level or quaternary industries, such as scientific research, produce knowledge. They are less important in North Africa than in more developed regions.

Despite its advantages, the region still suffers from economic problems. For example, corruption and unemployment are serious issues.

Reading Check What are three factors that the human development index measures?

myWorld Activity
Human Bar Graph

extract, *v.,* to get, take out, remove

A silversmith's shop in a market in Tunisia ▼

myworldgeography.com

Data Discovery

▲ Muslim Brotherhood members protest against the Egyptian government.

Different Forms of Government

Each nation in North Africa has its own form of government. All are different from the American system of government, with different methods of selecting leaders and making laws. For example, many political parties compete for office in Morocco, while political parties are banned in Libya.

Egypt: Secularism and Islamism Egypt is not a democracy, but its people have some say in their government. A single party has ruled Egypt since the 1950s. It controls the newspapers, television, and radio. The government of long time president Hosni Mubarak imprisons many of its opponents. Corruption is common, and the police regularly abuse people they arrest. Egyptians elect members of parliament, but the largest

opposition party is not allowed to run for office. The government has not been able to greatly improve Egyptians' standard of living. Rapid population growth makes this problem even more difficult.

Because of these problems, many Egyptians oppose the government. But it is the issue of religion and politics that most divides Egyptians. The government is based on **secularism,** the idea that religion and government should be separate. However, many Egyptians are Islamists. They believe that the government should be run according to Islamic law.

The **Muslim Brotherhood** is an Islamist party. It is the largest group that opposes the Egyptian government. It also opposes the policies of the United States, and the country Israel. In addition to supporting Islamism, the brotherhood pushes for a more democratic Egypt and against corruption. The party generally does not use violence to achieve its goals. However, small groups of Islamic extremists in Egypt have comitted terrorist attacks that target foreign tourists.

Algeria: An Unstable Government As a republic, Algeria has a constitution. However, the country is politically unstable, and elections have been manipulated or rigged.

As in Egypt, Algeria's rulers are secular, and there is a moderate Islamist opposition. However, violent Islamic extremists are more powerful in Algeria than elsewhere in the region. They fought a civil war with the government from 1991 to 2002. Even after the end of the civil war, terrorism remains a problem.

Morocco: A Constitutional Monarchy Morocco is the only nation in North Africa still ruled by a king, Mohammed VI. The king is very powerful but does not completely control the government. A written constitution limits his power. An elected parliament plays a role in government.

In recent years, Morocco has taken steps to increase women's equality. People have more rights than ever before, but the government restricts some civil liberties such as complete freedom of speech.

Morocco has also been criticized for its decades-long occupation of neighboring Western Sahara. This occupation has complicated relations with neighboring countries and with the African Union. Still, Morocco has made greater strides towards full democracy than most other North African nations.

Reading Check How is secularism different from Islamism?

Members attend a meeting of the Moroccan parliament. After the 2007 election, control of parliament changed peacefully from one political party to another. An opposition party won the election, and the head of that party became the prime minister. *How does this fact show that Morocco is different from Egypt?*

Section **3** Assessment

Key Terms

1. Use the following terms to describe Egypt's government and its interaction with religion: secularism, Muslim Brotherhood.

2. How are the gross domestic product and the gross domestic product per capita different?

Key Ideas

3. What is a culture region, and which culture regions is North Africa a part of?

4. What are some ways to measure and describe North Africa's standard of living?

5. What religion do the Copts practice, and where do they live?

Think Critically

6. **Compare and Contrast** How is Morocco's system of government similar to Egypt's? How is it different?

7. **Compare and Contrast** What aspects of culture link North Africa and Southwest Asia? What aspects might divide societies?

? Essential Question

How much does geography shape a country?

8. How has oil affected life in North Africa today? How has geography affected standards of living in different North African countries? Go to your Student Journal to record your answers.

Chapter Assessment

Key Terms and Ideas

1. **Describe** How was ancient Egyptian religion related to government?

2. **Summarize** What is **secularism,** and how is it different from Islamism?

3. **Recall** What effect do the Atlas Mountains have on rainfall?

4. **Categorize** How do North Africa and much of Southwest Asia form a culture region?

5. **Analyze Cause and Effect** What is a major cause of desertification in North Africa?

6. **Summarize** How was ancient Egypt different from other ancient civilizations?

7. **Synthesize** How do countries in North Africa treat minority groups? Compare the situations of the **Berbers** and the **Copts**.

Think Critically

8. **Analyze Primary and Secondary Sources** What does Ben Badis's statement in Section 2 tell you about Algerian nationalism?

9. **Problem Solving** What are some steps that governments can take to slow down or reverse desertification?

10. **Identify Evidence** What aspects of modern North African culture demonstrate that Arab Muslims conquered the region in the A.D. 600s?

11. **Core Concepts: Economic Development** What are three different ways to measure a country's level of economic development?

Places to Know

For each place, write the letter from the map that shows its location.

12. Algiers

13. Rabat

14. Nile River

15. Sinai Peninsula

16. Cairo

17. Atlas Mountains

18. **Estimate** Using the scale, estimate the distance between Cairo and Algiers.

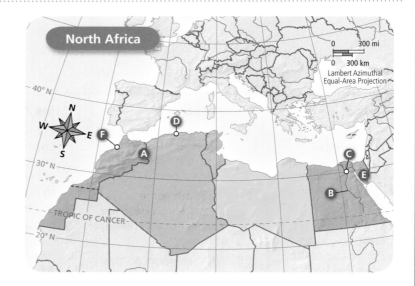

North Africa

Essential Question
myWorld Chapter Activity

National Crest Follow your teacher's instructions to draw a national crest for a North African country that represents its physical geography, history, government, and economy. Consider how the physical geography of your country affects everything else about it.

21st Century Learning

Search for Information on the Internet

Using reliable online sources, research a pharaoh of your choosing. Using at least two sources, find and record the following information:
• name
• dates of reign
• major accomplishments

For each of your sources, write a sentence explaining why you believe it is trustworthy.

Document-Based Questions

Online at myworldgeography.com

Use your knowledge of North Africa, as well as Documents A and B, to answer Questions 1–3.

Document A

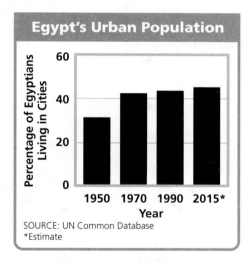

SOURCE: UN Common Database
*Estimate

Document B

" In a city where the streets were designed to accommodate half a million cars more than three million daily cross the capital. Cairo is now home to 20 percent of Egypt's population. The streets are packed. . . . Pollution levels have soared."

—Dena Rashed, "To Salvage a City"

1. Which of the following describes the change seen in Document A?

A corruption

B desertification

C urbanization

D Islamization

2. Which of the following does Document B suggest?

A Cairo is well governed.

B Cairo is overcrowded.

C Cairo is a medium-sized city.

D Cairo is Egypt's cultural capital.

3. Writing Task Why do you think so much of Egypt's population lives in Cairo?

577

Come to Africa

PLAN A TOURISM CAMPAIGN

Your Mission Your group has just been asked to investigate tourism for the African Union. Your job is to increase the number of people who come to the continent, visiting landmarks, going on tours, staying in hotels, and eating in restaurants.

If you had a chance to travel to Africa, what would you do on your trip? Would you want to see the monuments of past civilizations, visit the habitat of wild animals, or explore the vegetation of the rain forest? Would you want to learn about African music and arts? Whatever your interests, you would probably begin by researching places in Africa, reading tour books, or visiting tourism Web sites.

Your impressions of Africa would probably be influenced by tourism books or Web sites. You would find that the best tourism campaign finds a way to combine the uniqueness of a place with the expectations that visitors have for travel there. A trip that is called "the vacation of a lifetime" makes you want to travel! To reach visitors and persuade them to travel, a good tourism campaign should also be innovative. It should generate interest by conveying its message in an exciting and intriguing way.

STEP 1

Research Your Country.

Decide with your teacher whether your group will design a tourism campaign for Botswana, Egypt, Ethiopia, Ghana, Kenya, Mali, Republic of the Congo, Uganda, or Tanzania. Research the geography, economy, history, and culture of your country. Study photographs and tourism information to learn what makes these countries appealing to tourists.

STEP 2

Choose Your Specialty.

Based on your country's strengths, determine the special focus of your tourism campaign. You might choose to appeal to people interested in historic sites, ecotourism, wildlife habitats, photo safaris, culture, or sports. Decide what kind of marketing campaign (print or multimedia) will attract the attention of tourists interested in one of those areas.

STEP 3

Plan Your Marketing Campaign.

Develop a proposal for your marketing campaign. Explain who your target audience is, how you will portray the country, and what persuasive techniques you will use. Your campaign may take the form of a Web site, an illustrated brochure, a television commercial, or a video. Write a memo to the head of the tourism ministry that describes your proposal in detail.

Regional Overview

Southwest Asia

Southwest Asia is a region of towering mountains in the north and vast deserts in the south. It is a continental crossroads that connects Asia to Europe and Africa. The region includes the world's most important oil producer, Saudi Arabia, and several other oil-rich nations. Southwest Asia is also the birthplace of three great world religions: Judaism, Christianity, and Islam.

What time is it there?

Washington, D.C.	Jidda, Saudi Arabia
9 A.M. Monday	5 P.M. Monday

60° N

ARCTIC CIRCLE

30° N

Black Sea

Mediterranean Sea

Ankara ✪
TURKEY

Nicosia ✪
CYPRUS
Beirut ✪
LEBANON
Jerusalem ✪✪ Amman

Caspian Sea

✪ Damascus
SYRIA
Baghdad ✪
IRAQ

Tehran ✪
IRAN

TROPIC OF CANCER

ISRAEL
JORDAN

KUWAIT
Kuwait ✪

SAUDI ARABIA
Riyadh ✪

Red Sea

BAHRAIN
Doha ✪
✪ Abu Dhabi

QATAR

UNITED ARAB EMIRATES

Masqat ✪
OMAN

Sanaa ✪
YEMEN

Arabian Sea

KEY
— National border
✪ Capital city
Orthographic Projection

0°

EQUATOR

30° E

INDIAN OCEAN

60° E

90° E

The Unit Ahead

➡ **Chapter 16** Arabia and Iraq

➡ **Chapter 17** Israel and Its Neighbors

➡ **Chapter 18** Iran, Turkey, and Cyprus

my **worldgeography.com**

Plan your trip online with a Data Discovery Activity and the myStory Videos of the region's young people.

my Story

Hanan
Age: 20
Home: Jidda, Saudi Arabia
Chapter 16

my Story

Maayan
Age: 18
Home: Adi, Israel
Chapter 17

my Story

Muhammad
Age: 15
Home: Jerusalem, Israel
Chapter 17

my Story

Bilal
Age: 18
Home: Urfa, Turkey
Chapter 18

Dry mountains rise above fertile plains in eastern Turkey.

Black Sea

Anatolia

Taurus Mountains

Caspian Sea

Mediterranean Sea

Tigris River

Zagros

Mesopotamia

Euphrates River

Syrian Desert

Elburz Mountains

Iranian Plateau

Mountains

Persian Gulf

Hejaz

Red Sea

Arabian Peninsula

Asir

Ruб' al-Khali

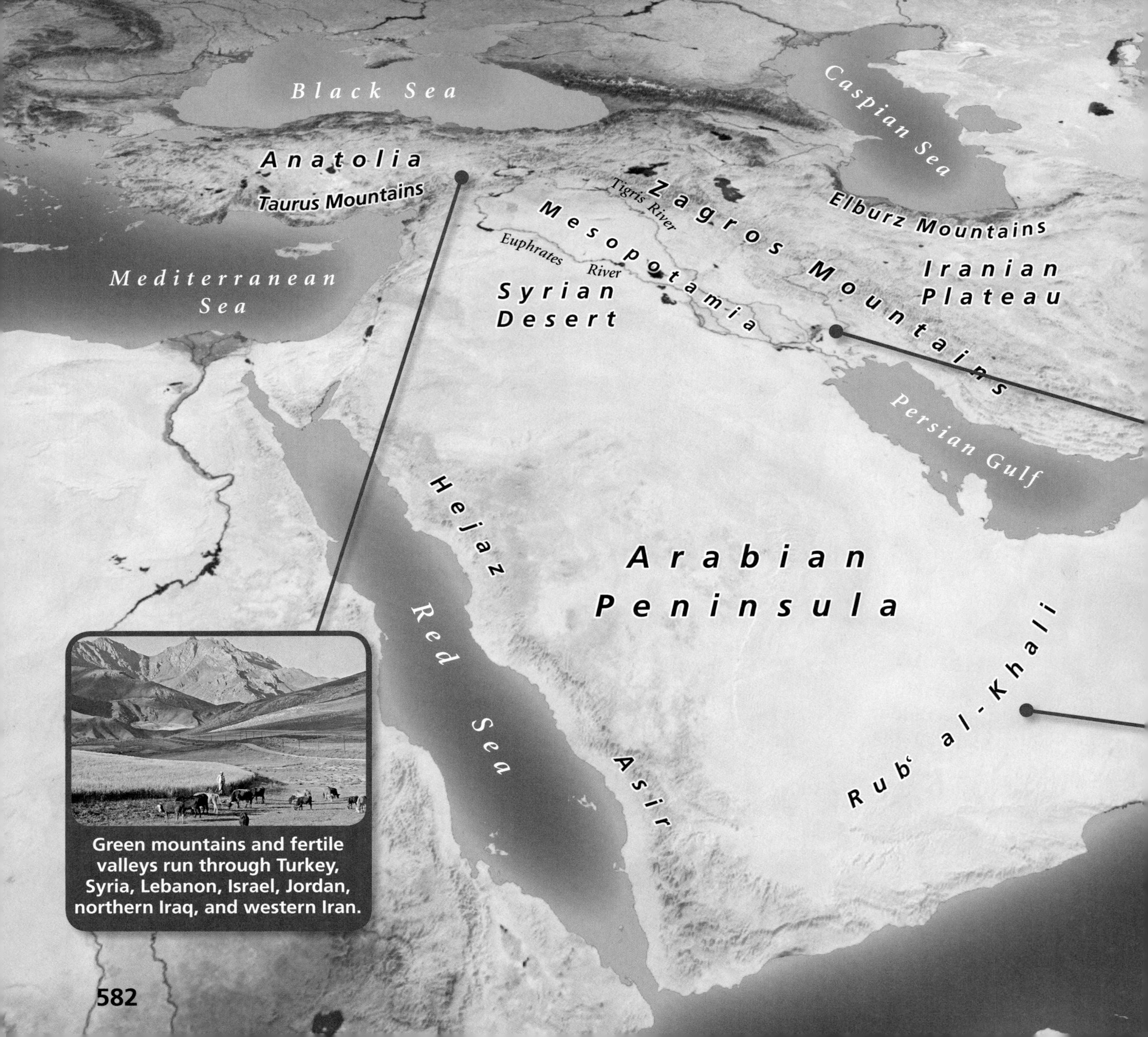

Green mountains and fertile valleys run through Turkey, Syria, Lebanon, Israel, Jordan, northern Iraq, and western Iran.

582

The Tigris and Euphrates rivers bring life to the dry lowlands of Iraq.

Arabian Sea

Not much grows in the vast deserts of the Arabian Peninsula.

INDIAN OCEAN

Regional Flyover

Suppose that you are in an airplane flying toward Southwest Asia. Flying east from Europe, you come to Turkey, whose mountains and plains lie between the Black Sea and the Mediterranean Sea. To its south is the Mediterranean island country of Cyprus.

Along the eastern shore of the Mediterranean lies a range of hills that runs through Syria, Lebanon, Jordan, and Israel. Next, you come to the flat valley of the Tigris and Euphrates rivers in Iraq. Farther east, you come to the high plateaus and mountains of Iran.

Turning south from Iran, you fly across the Persian Gulf, surrounded by oil wells and refineries. Across the Persian Gulf lies the Arabian Peninsula. Vast deserts stretch across this peninsula. Small countries line the coast of the peninsula. These are Kuwait, Bahrain, Qatar, the United Arab Emirates, Oman, and Yemen. You fly across Saudi Arabia, which covers most of the peninsula. In Saudi Arabia, your plane lands in Jidda.

my worldgeography.com In-Flight Movie

→ **In-Flight Movie**

Take flight over Southwest Asia and explore the region from the air.

583

Regional Geography
Human Geography

A Diverse Region

Southwest Asia is home to different peoples and religions. Arabs are the main ethnic group in most countries. However, Turks are the dominant group in Turkey, Persians are the dominant group in Iran, and Jews are the dominant group in Israel. A people called the Kurds are spread across several countries. Most people in the region are Muslims, or people who follow the religion of Islam. However, the region's Muslims belong to different branches of Islam. Most follow either Sunni or Shia Islam. There are also Christians and other religious minorities and a Jewish majority in Israel.

Judaism
This Jewish man is worshiping at the Western Wall in Jerusalem.

Christianity
This Christian man is worshiping at a shrine in Lebanon.

Islam
This Muslim man is reading from the Quran, Islam's holy book.

my World IN NUMBERS

Southwest Asia has a rich variety of ethnic groups and religions. Arab Muslims dominate most countries in the region, but they follow different branches of Islam. Turkish Muslims dominate Turkey, Persian Muslims dominate Iran, and Israeli Jews dominate Israel. Each country has many minority groups.

Southwest Asia: Religion

KEY
- Christianity
- Druze
- Ibadism
- Judaism
- Shiism
- Sunnism
- Yezidi
- Zoroastrianism
- Sparsely populated

Lambert Conformal Conic Projection

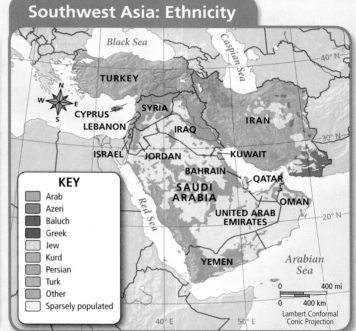

Southwest Asia: Ethnicity

KEY
- Arab
- Azeri
- Baluch
- Greek
- Jew
- Kurd
- Persian
- Turk
- Other
- Sparsely populated

Lambert Conformal Conic Projection

Put It Together

1. What physical features cause parts of this region to be sparsely populated?

2. In which country do most of the region's Jewish people live?

3. In which countries do the Kurds live?

Data Discovery

Find your own data to make a regional data table.

Size Comparison

Southwest Asia is slightly smaller in area than the United States.

myworldgeography.com

Data Discovery

585

Chapter 16

Arabia and Iraq

How much does geography shape a country?

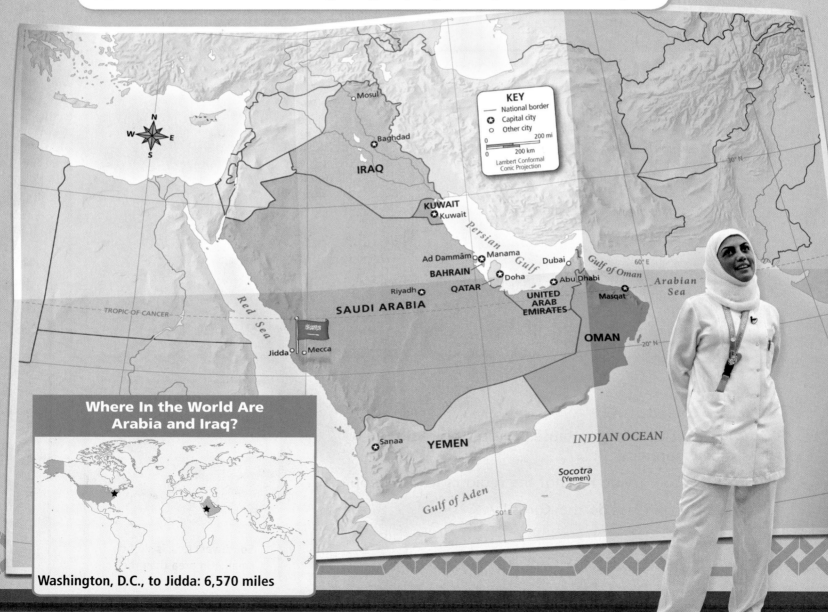

KEY
- National border
- ⊛ Capital city
- ○ Other city

0   200 mi
0   200 km
Lambert Conformal Conic Projection

Mosul

Baghdad

IRAQ

KUWAIT
⊛ Kuwait

Ad Dammām ○ ⊛ Manama   ○ Dubai
BAHRAIN   ⊛ Doha
Riyadh ⊛   **QATAR**   ○ Abu Dhabi   Masqat
SAUDI ARABIA   **UNITED ARAB EMIRATES**

OMAN

Jidda ○ ⊛ Mecca

Red Sea

Persian Gulf

Gulf of Oman

Arabian Sea

TROPIC OF CANCER

60° E
30° N
20° N

⊛ Sanaa   **YEMEN**   **INDIAN OCEAN**

Socotra (Yemen)

Gulf of Aden
50° E

Where In the World Are Arabia and Iraq?

Washington, D.C., to Jidda: 6,570 miles

my Story

Hanan's Call to Care

In this section, you'll read about Hanan, a young Saudi woman who has become a professional in a country where women face many difficulties. What does Hanan's story tell you about life in Arabia and Iraq today?

? Explore the Essential Question
- at **my worldgeography.com**
- using the **my World Chapter Activity**
- with the **Student Journal**

Story by Danya M. Alhamrani for myWorld Geography Online

In the darkness of the early morning, Hanan awakes to the sound of adhan. This is the Islamic call to prayer, sung out by a muezzin, often from the minaret, or high tower, of an Islamic house of worship called a mosque. The adhan call tells the faithful that it is time to begin their daily prayer rituals. They will perform these rituals five times over the course of the day.

As the muezzin's voice drifts through the warm stillness remaining from the night, it is joined by another, then another, and yet another voice calling out the prayer, in Arabic: "Allahu akbar. Hayya alal sala. Hayya alal falah." That is Arabic for "God is most great. Come to prayer. Come to success."

The calling continues as Hanan walks to the bathroom to make her wudu, her ritual washing before beginning prayer. She covers herself from head to toe with her sharshaf, a long, traditional robe, and joins her mother for the first prayer of the day.

my worldgeography.com On Assignment

587

Hanan's driver drives her to work.

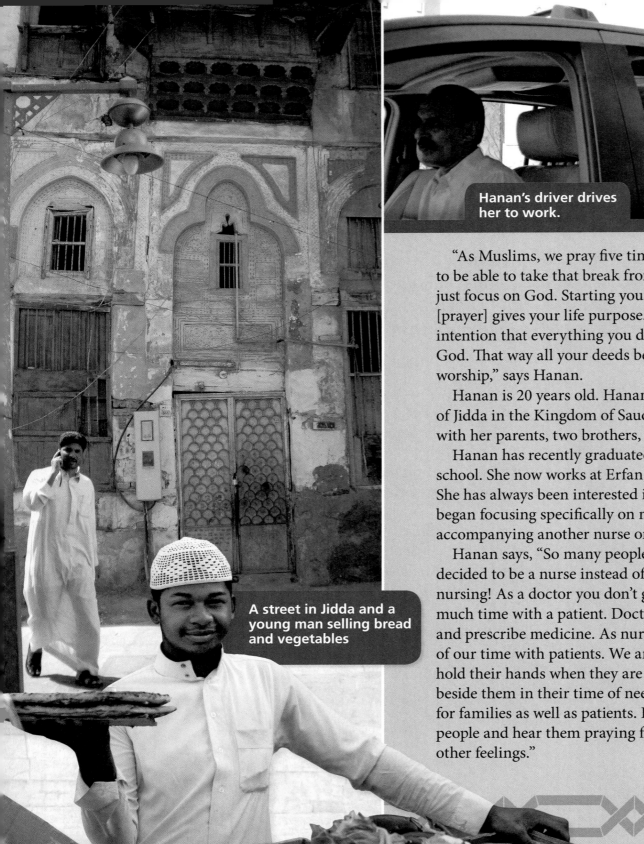
A street in Jidda and a young man selling bread and vegetables

"As Muslims, we pray five times a day. It is great to be able to take that break from everything and just focus on God. Starting your day with sala [prayer] gives your life purpose. You make your intention that everything you do that day is for God. That way all your deeds become a form of worship," says Hanan.

Hanan is 20 years old. Hanan lives in the city of Jidda in the Kingdom of Saudi Arabia. She lives with her parents, two brothers, and one sister.

Hanan has recently graduated from nursing school. She now works at Erfan hospital in Jidda. She has always been interested in medicine but began focusing specifically on nursing after accompanying another nurse on the job one day.

Hanan says, "So many people ask me why I decided to be a nurse instead of a doctor. I love nursing! As a doctor you don't get to spend that much time with a patient. Doctors mostly diagnose and prescribe medicine. As nurses, we spend most of our time with patients. We are the ones who hold their hands when they are scared and stand beside them in their time of need. We are there for families as well as patients. Being able to help people and hear them praying for me surpasses all other feelings."

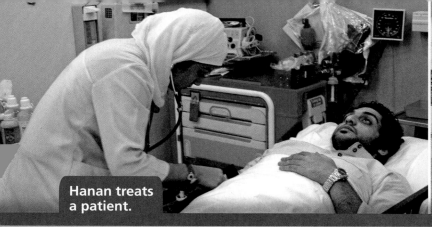

Hanan treats a patient.

Hanan's family in their living room

Many nurses in Saudi Arabia come from other countries, but the number of Saudi nurses is growing. Nursing, however, is not a typical profession for Saudi women.

In fact, few Saudi women work outside the home. Saudi law and culture place many restrictions on the lives of women. For example, Saudi women are not legally allowed to drive cars. They may not travel abroad without the permission of their husband or a male relative.

Saudi culture strongly encourages women to stay home and take care of their families rather than work. Because of these cultural and legal restrictions it is difficult for them to hold jobs. Still, 20 percent of Saudi women work outside their homes.

Restrictions aside, Hanan's biggest headache is her hectic schedule. The necessity of working around-the-clock in shifts takes a toll on family life.

"Nursing is a tough profession," Hanan says. "People who want to go into this line of work need to have patience and endurance. I end up missing a lot of family gatherings due to long working hours. I sometimes stay at home on my days off just to get some rest."

Despite the hardships she sometimes faces, Hanan loves her job and looks forward to a long career in her chosen field of nursing.

 myStory Video

Join Hanan as she shows you more about life in her city.

Meet the Journalist

Name Camilo Moreno
Favorite Moment Watching families pray together at the beach

Hanan and her mother praying together

my worldgeography.com myStory Video

Chapter Atlas

Key Ideas
- Physical geography has made much of this region rich in oil and natural gas.
- The climate of Arabia and Iraq makes water scarce.
- The region is home to different ethnic and religious groups.

Key Terms
- plate
- fossil fuel
- desalination
- urbanized
- majority

 **Visual Glossary**

 Reading Skill: Label an Outline Map Take notes using the outline map in your journal.

◄ A Yemeni woman. Her hands are painted with henna.
Behind her is the Rub' al-Khali desert in Oman. Its name means "the empty quarter" in Arabic.

Physical Features

Arabia, or the Arabian Peninsula, is surrounded on three sides by water. To the west, the Red Sea separates the peninsula from Africa. To the south are the Gulf of Aden and the Arabian Sea. The Persian Gulf and the Gulf of Oman to the east separate the peninsula from the rest of Asia. All of these bodies of water are arms of the Indian Ocean.

North of the Arabian Peninsula are the nation of Iraq and other parts of Southwest Asia. Arabia and Iraq are part of the continent of Asia.

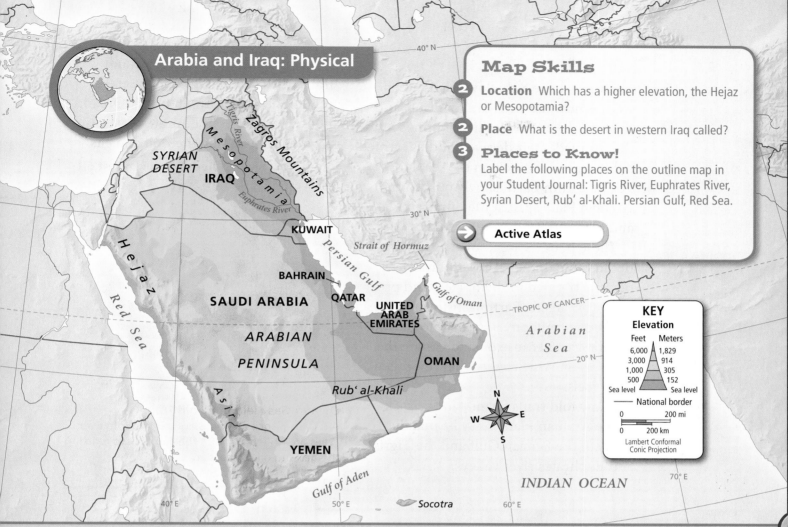

Arabia and Iraq: Physical

SYRIAN DESERT

Tigris River

Zagros Mountains

Mesopotamia

IRAQ

Euphrates River

KUWAIT

Persian Gulf

Strait of Hormuz

BAHRAIN

Hejaz

QATAR

SAUDI ARABIA

UNITED ARAB EMIRATES

Gulf of Oman

Red Sea

ARABIAN PENINSULA

Arabian Sea

OMAN

TROPIC OF CANCER

Asir

Rub' al-Khali

YEMEN

Gulf of Aden

Socotra

INDIAN OCEAN

Map Skills

2 **Location** Which has a higher elevation, the Hejaz or Mesopotamia?

2 **Place** What is the desert in western Iraq called?

3 **Places to Know!**
Label the following places on the outline map in your Student Journal: Tigris River, Euphrates River, Syrian Desert, Rub' al-Khali. Persian Gulf, Red Sea.

Active Atlas

KEY
Elevation

Feet	Meters
6,000	1,829
3,000	914
1,000	305
500	152
Sea level	Sea level

— National border

0 — 200 mi
0 — 200 km

Lambert Conformal Conic Projection

As you read in the Core Concepts Handbook, Earth's crust consists of separate **plates,** or blocks of rock and soil. Most of Arabia and Iraq are on the Arabian Plate. Mountains rise sharply from the Red Sea and Gulf of Aden to form the plate's southeastern and western edges. The Arabian Plate is, in effect, a plateau, or raised flat area, that slopes gradually toward the east.

Near the eastern edge of the Arabian Plate, the plate's rocks bend downward to form a long, broad depression, or dip. In the south, the Persian Gulf also lies within this depression.

The Tigris (TY gris) and Euphrates (you FRAY teez) river valleys also lie within this depression. These rivers provide fresh water to a region that is mostly desert. They are the only major rivers in the region.

The eastern edge of the Arabian Plate presses against the Eurasian Plate. The pressure has pushed up rocks to form mountains in northeastern Iraq and in the southeastern corner of the Arabian Peninsula, in the nation of Oman.

Reading Check Which major rivers flow through Iraq?

my worldgeography.com Active Atlas

Oil and Gas Riches

There was once a shallow sea between what is now the Arabian Peninsula and the rest of Asia. When living things in the sea died, their decayed bodies formed a thick layer of muck on the sea floor. Forces within Earth slowly pushed the Arabian Plate against the Eurasian Plate and bent it downward into folds.

These pockets are known as fold traps because the undersea layer of muck became trapped in them. Heat and pressure from inside Earth transformed the muck over millions of years into oil and natural gas. Because oil and gas are the remains of living things, they are called **fossil fuels.**

Many fold traps formed in the rock of the Arabian Plate. They lie mainly beneath the Persian Gulf and the Tigris and Euphrates river valleys.

These fold traps have given Saudi Arabia the world's largest oil reserves and output. Iraq, Kuwait, Qatar, Oman, and the United Arab Emirates have also grown rich by selling their oil and gas.

Reading Check **Where are the largest oil reserves?**

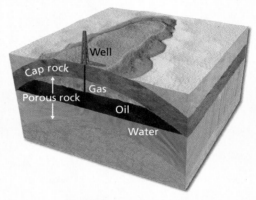

Oil and Gas Field in a Fold Trap
A hard cap rock traps gas and oil in a fold trap. Wells are drilled through the cap rock to reach the gas and oil beneath it.

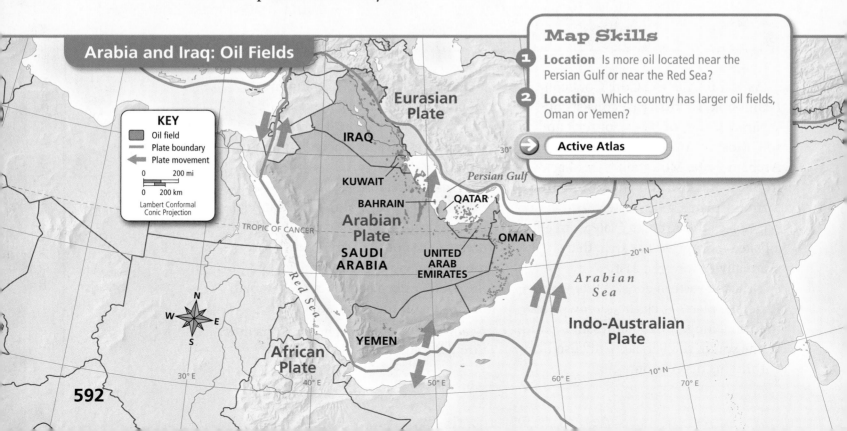

Arabia and Iraq: Oil Fields

KEY
- Oil field
- Plate boundary
- Plate movement

0   200 mi

0   200 km

Lambert Conformal Conic Projection

Eurasian Plate

IRAQ

KUWAIT

BAHRAIN

QATAR

Arabian Plate

SAUDI ARABIA

UNITED ARAB EMIRATES

OMAN

Persian Gulf

TROPIC OF CANCER

Red Sea

YEMEN

African Plate

Arabian Sea

Indo-Australian Plate

N
W   E
S

30° N

20° N

10° N

30° E   40° E   50° E   60° E   70° E

Map Skills

1 **Location** Is more oil located near the Persian Gulf or near the Red Sea?

2 **Location** Which country has larger oil fields, Oman or Yemen?

→ **Active Atlas**

592

Living on Oil

Iraq and most countries in Arabia rely on oil and natural gas to pay for nearly all of their needs.

The Importance of Oil Because these countries lack water, they use money from oil and gas sales to build water facilities. Even so, most countries in the region do not have enough water to grow their own food. They use money from oil and gas sales to pay for food grown in other regions.

The countries of Arabia also rely on millions of foreign workers, paid with oil money, to keep their economies running.

Arabia and Iraq produce more than one fourth of the world's oil. People in other parts of the world use oil to power their cars, to heat their homes, and for other purposes. As a result, the rest of the world is very dependent on this region's oil supplies. Any disruption of oil exports from this region creates shortages of oil and sends oil prices soaring.

In the long run, prospects are uncertain for the nations rich in oil and gas. These nations are slowly using up their oil and gas reserves, and it will take millions of years for more oil and gas to form.

Oil and the Environment Oil production has sometimes harmed the region's environment. Oil spills in the Persian Gulf have killed sea life and polluted shorelines. Oil production and processing create toxic chemicals that have polluted the soil, and the rivers of Iraq.

Reading Check Why is oil so important to Arabia and Iraq?

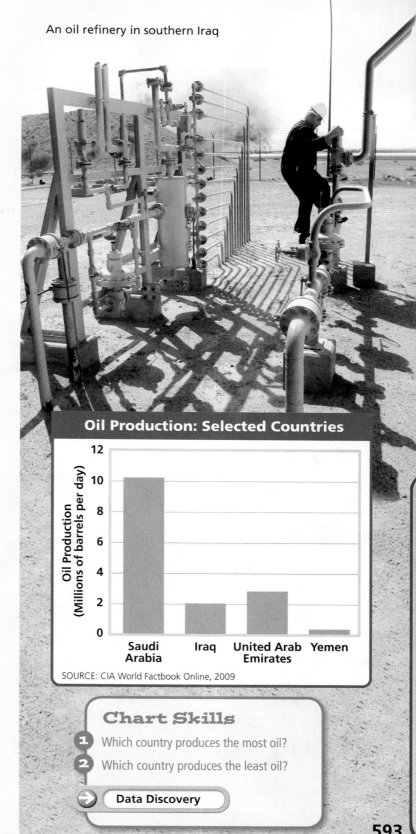

An oil refinery in southern Iraq

Oil Production: Selected Countries

SOURCE: CIA World Factbook Online, 2009

Chart Skills

1. Which country produces the most oil?
2. Which country produces the least oil?

Data Discovery

my **worldgeography.com** Data Discovery

Vast Deserts and Scarce Water

Most of Arabia and Iraq is desert, or an area that receives very little rainfall or snowfall. You read in the Core Concepts Handbook that a belt of deserts circles the subtropical latitudes. Most of the region lies in this subtropical desert belt.

The main ecosystems across the region are desert and desert scrub. Deserts have few plants and animals. Desert scrub has some plants. Camels, which can live without much water, live in the desert and were used by people to cross it.

The region's deserts are dry, but the hills and mountains of northern and eastern Iraq are slightly <u>moister.</u> They get some rainfall. Moist air comes from the Mediterranean Sea in the west. In the summer, moist air from the Indian Ocean drops rain in the mountains of Yemen.

moist, *adj.,* slightly wet

Farming is possible only where there is enough water. The mountains of Yemen and Iraq receive enough rainfall to support some farming. Elsewhere, farming depends on water taken from rivers or oases in the desert. The most important rivers in the region are the Tigris and the Euphrates in Iraq. The water from these rivers nurtured one of the world's first civilizations thousands of years ago. Most people in Iraq live in the valleys around these rivers. Their water is crucial to the country. It supports Iraq's population, which is by far the largest in the region.

The driest countries in the region, such as Saudi Arabia, Kuwait, and the United Arab Emirates, depend on **desalination,** or the removal of salt from seawater. These countries have large desalination plants.

Reading Check Which parts of Arabia and Iraq get seasonal precipitation?

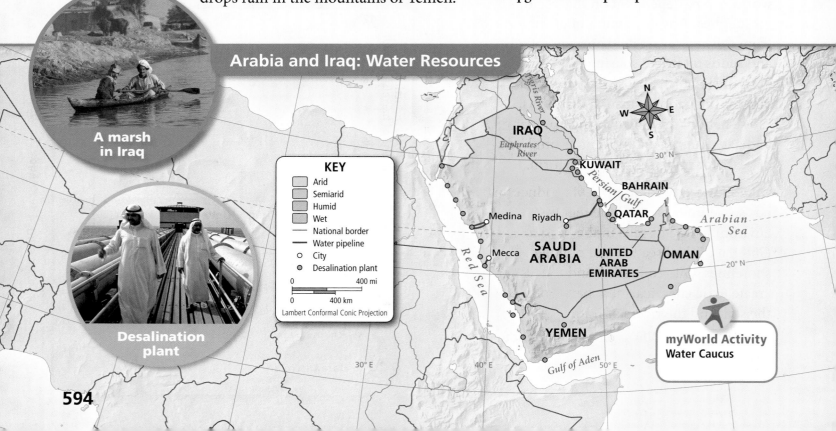

Arabia and Iraq: Water Resources

A marsh in Iraq

Desalination plant

KEY
- Arid
- Semiarid
- Humid
- Wet
- National border
- Water pipeline
- ○ City
- ● Desalination plant

0   400 mi
0   400 km
Lambert Conformal Conic Projection

IRAQ
Euphrates River
Tigris River
KUWAIT
Persian Gulf
BAHRAIN
QATAR
Medina   Riyadh
Mecca
SAUDI ARABIA
UNITED ARAB EMIRATES
OMAN
Red Sea
Arabian Sea
YEMEN
Gulf of Aden
30° N
20° N
30° E
40° E
50° E

myWorld Activity
Water Caucus

Population Patterns

People cannot live without water. Because water is very scarce in most of the region, its people cluster where there is water for drinking and cleaning.

As a result, the region's population has clustered for centuries in the places with the most water. These places include the mountains of Iraq and Yemen, near the Tigris and Euphrates rivers of Iraq, and desert oases on the Arabian Peninsula.

As you just read, some nations in the region have used money from oil and gas sales to to build desalination plants. These plants provide fresh water for growing populations. As a result, people in these countries depend on water from desalination. Countries usually build desalination plants near their cities.

Except for Yemen, the countries of the region are heavily **urbanized.** This means that most of their people live in cities.

Money from oil and natural gas sales has helped these countries develop jobs in construction and services. These kinds of jobs are usually found in cities. Many people from outside the region have also moved to oil-producing areas in search of jobs. They generally settle in the cities.

Arabia and Iraq have some of the highest rates of population growth in the world. These high rates of growth result from both migration and high birth rates. Local customs and religious traditions practiced in many parts of the region favor large families. When most women have many children, populations grow quickly. This high rate of population growth poses challenges for the region. The growing population will need more jobs, water, education, and other services.

Reading Check **Why are populations growing in this region?**

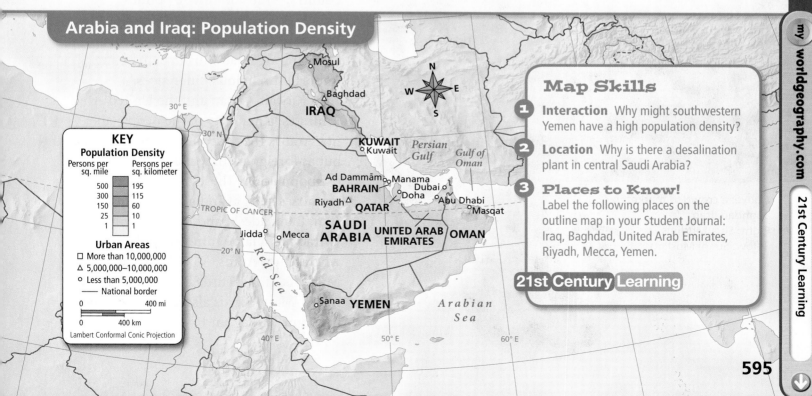

Arabia and Iraq: Population Density

KEY

Population Density

Persons per sq. mile	Persons per sq. kilometer
500	195
300	115
150	60
25	10
1	1

Urban Areas

☐ More than 10,000,000
△ 5,000,000–10,000,000
○ Less than 5,000,000
— National border

0 _____ 400 mi
0 _____ 400 km
Lambert Conformal Conic Projection

Map Skills

1 **Interaction** Why might southwestern Yemen have a high population density?

2 **Location** Why is there a desalination plant in central Saudi Arabia?

3 **Places to Know!** Label the following places on the outline map in your Student Journal: Iraq, Baghdad, United Arab Emirates, Riyadh, Mecca, Yemen.

21st Century Learning

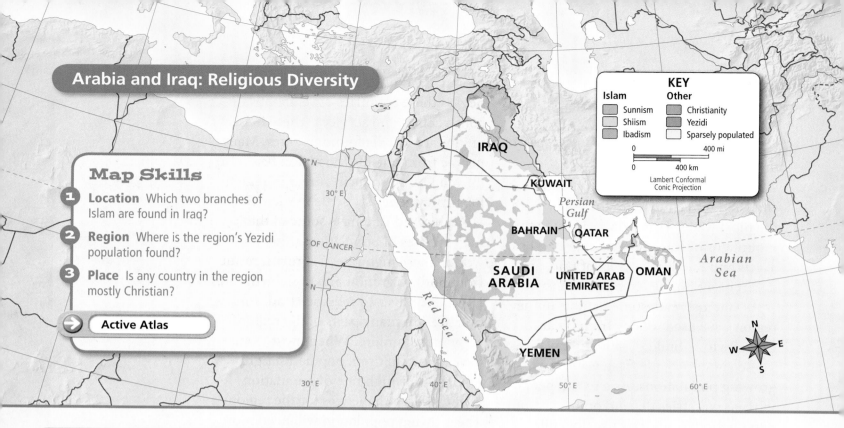

Arabia and Iraq: Religious Diversity

Map Skills

1 **Location** Which two branches of Islam are found in Iraq?

2 **Region** Where is the region's Yezidi population found?

3 **Place** Is any country in the region mostly Christian?

→ **Active Atlas**

KEY

Islam
- Sunnism
- Shiism
- Ibadism

Other
- Christianity
- Yezidi
- Sparsely populated

0   400 mi
0   400 km
Lambert Conformal
Conic Projection

IRAQ

KUWAIT

Persian Gulf

BAHRAIN   QATAR

SAUDI ARABIA   UNITED ARAB EMIRATES   OMAN

Arabian Sea

Red Sea

YEMEN

OF CANCER

Above: a crowded market in Baghdad, Iraq
Right: Shia Muslims
Below: Sunni Muslims

A Diverse Region

In most countries of Arabia and Iraq, Arab Muslims form a **majority,** or more than half, of the population. In every country, Arabs dominate politics. However, most countries in Arabia and Iraq have large non-Arab minorities. Even among Arab Muslims, there are important religious differences.

In Kuwait, Qatar, and the United Arab Emirates, a majority of the people are not Arabs. These people are not citizens, but as foreigners they make up most of the population. These people come from countries such as India, Sri Lanka, Pakistan, Bangladesh, and the Philippines.

Iraq has a large minority of Kurds, who are not Arabs. Most Kurds are Sunni Muslims. Iraq's Kurds live mainly in the north. Many Kurds also live in neighboring Iran, Turkey, and Syria.

Iraqi Kurds suffered brutal treatment under Saddam Hussein. In recent years, they have <u>created</u> a self-governing area in northern Iraq.

The vast majority of the people of Arabia and Iraq follow Islam. However, there are important differences within Islam. Long ago, the religion split into two main groups—the Sunnis and the Shias. Most people in Oman follow a third branch of Islam, called Ibadism.

The majority of the region's people are Sunnis, even though Shias are the majority in some places. Most Iraqis are Shia Arabs. Since the elections of 2005, Shias took power in Iraq for the first time.

Most of the citizens of Bahrain are Shia, but their ruler is a Sunni. Sunnis rule Kuwait, Saudi Arabia, and Yemen. However, large Shia minorities live in all three of these countries.

In Iraq, a three-way civil conflict developed among Sunni Arabs, Shia Arabs, and Kurds after U.S.-led forces overthrew Iraq's secular, Sunni-led dictatorship in 2003. Tensions among these groups could lead to conflict in the future.

The region also has small non-Muslim religious minorities. Iraq's Christians are an ancient community. Most practice eastern forms of Christianity that are different from Eastern Orthodox, Roman Catholic, or Protestant Christianity.

From ancient times to the recent past, Iraq and Yemen had important Jewish communities. However, 180,000 Jews fled, mostly to Israel, because of discrimination in the mid-1900s. Only a few hundred Jewish people remain in the region today.

Iraq's Yezidis are Kurdish speakers who practice a religion that combines Islam with more ancient religions. Finally, while most foreign workers in the Persian Gulf countries are Muslims, there are also Christians, Hindus, and Buddhists.

Reading Check **What are some differences among Muslims in this region?**

create, *v.*, form, cause to exist

Section 1 Assessment

Key Terms

1. What are fossil fuels?

2. Use the word desalination in a sentence.

Key Ideas

3. Describe the fossil fuel resources of Arabia and Iraq.

4. What are some natural sources of water in Arabia and Iraq, and where are they located?

5. Describe the region's religious diversity.

Think Critically

6. Draw Conclusions What might happen to Arabia and Iraq if they began to use up their oil reserves?

7. Compare and Contrast In what ways has the urban population in the region changed in recent years? Give reasons for the changes.

? Essential Question

How much does geography shape a country?

8. What features of Arabia and Iraq depend on the region's geography? What features do not depend on its geography? Go to your Student Journal to record your answers.

History of Arabia and Iraq

Key Ideas

- Civilization developed along the rivers of Mesopotamia.
- Islam arose in Arabia and spread to other regions in the early Middle Ages.
- Britain controlled parts of the region and redrew borders in the early 1900s.
- The region gained independence and oil wealth, but some countries faced dictatorship and war.

Key Terms • civilization • monotheism • Quran • caliph • mosque • minority • dictator

 Visual Glossary

Reading Skill: Summarize Take notes using the graphic organizer in your journal.

Reconstructed gates of the ancient city of Babylon ▼

Arabia and Iraq have played a key role in world history. This region was one of the places where **civilization** began. A civilization is a culture that has a written language and in which people have many different kinds of jobs. Writing first developed in this region. The world's first known empires also developed in what is now Iraq. Later, Arabia was the birthplace of Islam, one of the world's major religions. Over the centuries, foreign powers controlled much of this region. In modern times, Arabia and Iraq became the world's most important source of oil, a fuel that every country in the world needs.

3000 B.C. The Sumerians

The figure at the left shows a Sumerian man. The Sumerians invented cuneiform. This kind of writing uses wedge-shaped marks on clay tablets. The name comes from the Latin word for wedge.

Early Civilizations and Empires

Mesopotamia means "between the rivers" in Greek. It refers to the valley of the Tigris and Euphrates rivers. This region is mainly in present-day Iraq.

In Mesopotamia, people developed a new way of life. For thousands of years, people lived by hunting, fishing, and gathering wild plants. About 10,000 years ago, people in Southwest Asia began to plant crops and raise animals. These farmers produced plenty of food for everyone. Some people were now free to do other work. They became potters and weavers and merchants.

Farmers and others had to pay taxes. These taxes supported priests and government officials. Populations grew. By 4000 B.C., the first cities appeared.

A Birthplace of Civilization Sumer was a region in southern Mesopotamia. Sumerians developed a civilization. Around 3000 B.C. they created the world's first writing system, which is called cuneiform (kyoo NEE uh form). They built irrigation canals and invented mathematics and the potter's wheel.

331–129 B.C. Greek Rule

After Alexander conquered Mesopotamia in 331 B.C., Greeks ruled the region for 200 years. Later, Romans and Persians fought over the region.

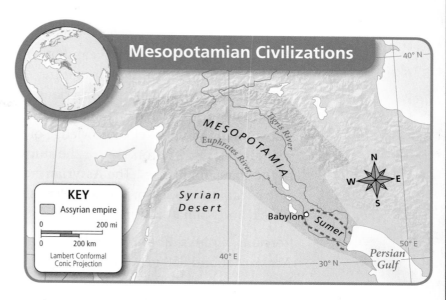

Mesopotamian Civilizations

We can learn about the Sumerians from the Epic of Gilgamesh. This is one of the world's oldest written stories. The story is based on a real Sumerian king, Gilgamesh, who lived around 2700 B.C.

> 66 Surpassing all kings, powerful and tall beyond all others, violent, splendid, a wild bull of a man . . . huge, handsome, radiant, perfect. 99
> —The Epic of Gilgamesh

The most complete version of this story appears on cuneiform tablets.

The First Empires Sumerian cities grew into the first city-states. Each was a small country, focused on a single city. Around 2270 B.C., King Sargon from the city of Akkad conquered Sumer and other parts of Mesopotamia to found the first known empire. Later, around 1700 B.C., the city-state of Babylon built an empire that included all of Mesopotamia.

The Assyrian people built an even larger empire. Assyria was an area in northern Mesopotamia. By around 900 B.C., Assyria had defeated Babylon.

Assyria brought Mesopotamia and other areas, including Egypt, into its empire.

Both the Babylonians and Assyrians contributed to world civilization. The Babylonians added to our knowledge of mathematics and astronomy, or the study of the stars and planets. The Assyrian empire became a model for the later Persian, Greek, and Roman empires.

Persians, Greeks, Romans, and Arabs Around 550 B.C., Mesopotamia became part of the Persian empire, based in modern Iran. The Persian empire stretched from North Africa to India.

Alexander the Great defeated the Persian Empire in 331 B.C. When he died, his Greek empire split apart. But Alexander's influence <u>persisted.</u> He had founded dozens of new cities and spread Greek culture far and wide. Mesopotamia remained under Greek rule for 200 years.

The Roman Empire eventually took over the western parts of Alexander's empire. After 235 B.C., Persians regained power in the east. Persians fought with the Roman Empire for control of the fertile lands of Mesopotamia. For several centuries they continued to fight with the Eastern Roman empire, which was also called the Byzantine empire.

Through trade, Greeks, Romans, and Persians met the Arab tribes of the Arabian Peninsula. Many Arabs were nomads. They had no permanent homes. They herded sheep, goats, and camels. Nomads visited oases for food and water. Oases were centers for trade.

Reading Check Which civilization first developed writing?

▲ A copy of the Quran, the holy book of Islam

persist, *v.,* to continue, often in spite of setbacks

A New Religion

One important oasis was the city of Mecca. It was a trading and religious center. People throughout the Arabian Peninsula traveled to Mecca. They went to worship at a shrine called the Kaaba. Many worshiped more than one god. In the A.D. 600s, however, this changed.

A man named Muhammad made Mecca a center for the new religion of Islam. Its believers are called Muslims. Like Jews and Christians, Muslims worship only one god, whom they consider the Creator, or God. Worshiping only one god is called **monotheism.**

The Birth of Islam Muhammad was born in Mecca. One day, he was meditating in a cave. There, Muslims believe, he saw the angel Gabriel, who brought him a message from God. Muhammad later received more messages.

Muhammad shared these messages with the people of Mecca. Some people began to follow the ideas Muhammad spread. They believed that Muhammad was bringing messages from the God recognized by Jews and Christians. These messages were collected and preserved in the **Quran,** the holy book of Islam.

The wealthy people of Mecca wanted visitors to keep coming to the Kaaba. They knew that most of these visitors worshiped many gods. They opposed Muhammad's teachings. Muhammad and his followers had to leave Mecca.

In A.D. 622 they moved to the city of Medina. When Mecca attacked the Muslims in Medina, the Muslims won.

Muhammad returned to Mecca in 632. He made the Kaaba a place of worship for Islam before dying later that year.

Muhammad's followers argued over how to choose leaders to follow him. One group believed that Muhammad had chosen his son-in-law, Ali, and his heirs, as leaders. This group became known as the Shia. Another group, known as the Sunnis, wanted Muhammad's father-in-law, Abu Bakr, as the next leader.

Muhammad's Sunni followers chose Abu Bakr to be the new leader. He became their first **caliph**. The caliph was the Muslims' political and religious leader.

Over time, differences in belief grew between Sunni and Shia Muslims. Today, about 15 percent of all Muslims are Shia. In some parts of Arabia and Iraq, however, most Muslims are Shia.

The Beliefs of Islam The word *Islam* means "submission" in Arabic. This term comes from the idea of submitting one's will to God. Muslims believe that the will of God lies in the words of the Quran.

Like Judaism and Christianity, Islam stresses the importance of family, community, and social justice. Many Muslims turn to the Quran and Muhammad's teachings to help them make good choices. The Quran, Muhammad's teachings, and the traditions of the Muslim community form the basis for Islamic law.

Reading Check **Why did Sunni and Shia Muslims split?**

myWorld Activity
Comparing Religions

Muslims circle around the Kaaba, in Mecca, as part of their pilgrimage to that city. ▶

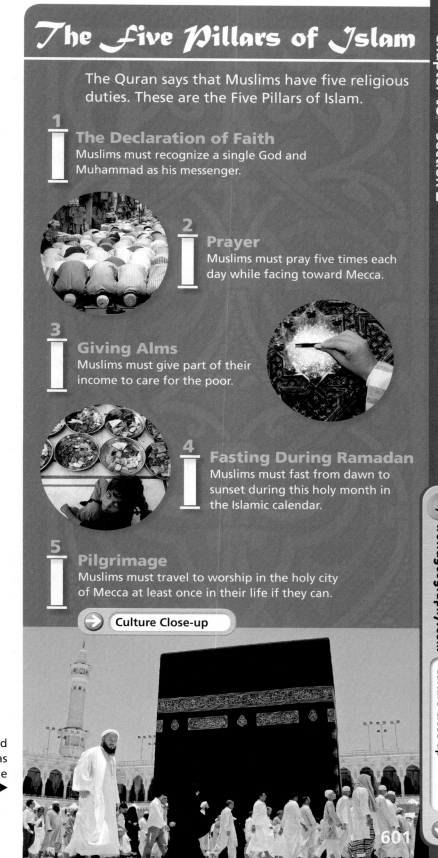

The Five Pillars of Islam

The Quran says that Muslims have five religious duties. These are the Five Pillars of Islam.

1 **The Declaration of Faith**
Muslims must recognize a single God and Muhammad as his messenger.

2 **Prayer**
Muslims must pray five times each day while facing toward Mecca.

3 **Giving Alms**
Muslims must give part of their income to care for the poor.

4 **Fasting During Ramadan**
Muslims must fast from dawn to sunset during this holy month in the Islamic calendar.

5 **Pilgrimage**
Muslims must travel to worship in the holy city of Mecca at least once in their life if they can.

→ Culture Close-up

myworldgeography.com Culture Close-up

601

Muslim Civilization

Within 10 years of Muhammad's death, Muslims under the first caliphs had conquered all of Arabia and Iraq. Within 100 years of Muhammad's death, the caliphs ruled a vast empire, stretching from India to Spain. Arabia and Iraq were at the center of a rich civilization. Muslim civilization made great advances in science, mathematics, and the arts.

A Muslim Empire During the 600s and 700s, the Muslims conquered all of the Persian Empire, much of the Byzantine Empire, North Africa, Spain, and parts of India and Central Asia. In 762, the caliphs founded Baghdad, in present-day Iraq, as the capital of their empire.

The Muslim Empire controlled key trade routes between Asia, Africa, and Europe. One of these was the Silk Road to China. Sea routes from Eastern Africa brought goods, as well as many enslaved Africans, to Arabia and Iraq.

The caliph's control allowed merchants to travel more safely. The empire grew prosperous from trade. Cities grew along busy trade routes. Baghdad became the largest and one of the richest cities in the world. In the empire's cities, people from distant lands came together to trade.

A Center of Learning Travel and trade brought the Muslim Empire into contact with ideas from around the world. Muslim scholars learned about Greek science and philosophy through contact with the Byzantine Empire. They learned about advances in mathematics and astronomy made in India.

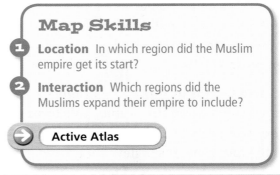

Map Skills

1. **Location** In which region did the Muslim empire get its start?

2. **Interaction** Which regions did the Muslims expand their empire to include?

→ **Active Atlas**

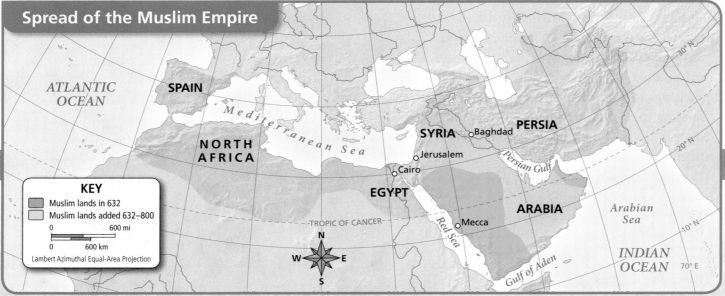

Spread of the Muslim Empire

ATLANTIC OCEAN

SPAIN

Mediterranean Sea

NORTH AFRICA

SYRIA · Baghdad · PERSIA

Jerusalem

Cairo

EGYPT

ARABIA

Persian Gulf

Arabian Sea

KEY
- Muslim lands in 632
- Muslim lands added 632–800

0 — 600 mi
0 — 600 km
Lambert Azimuthal Equal-Area Projection

TROPIC OF CANCER

Red Sea

Mecca

Gulf of Aden

INDIAN OCEAN

30° N
20° N
10° N
70° E

N W E S

Baghdad became more than a center of Muslim culture and trade. It became a center of learning. Literature and other arts blossomed. Muslim architects built beautiful **mosques,** or Islamic houses of worship. Muslim scientists and mathematicians built on the work of the Greeks and Indians. Their work formed a basis for modern chemistry, physics, and medicine. They also developed algebra. Our own system of numerals came to us from India by way of Arab Muslims.

The Ottoman Empire After the 900s, the Muslim Empire fell apart into several states. These states were partly independent. The last caliph in Baghdad was defeated by Mongol invaders in 1258. In the 1500s, Ottoman Turks conquered much of the region. The Ottoman Empire, centered in Turkey, included Iraq and much of the Arabian Peninsula. At its height it included most of Southwest Asia outside of Persia. The Ottomans remained in control until World War I ended in 1918.

Reading Check **How did trade advance Muslim learning?**

The Persian Gulf in Modern Times

World War I brought much of the region under European control. The region's countries gained independence later in the 1900s. Still, foreign powers continued to play a role.

British Domination By World War I, the British dominated several countries on the Arabian Peninsula. These countries were Bahrain, the United Arab Emirates, Oman, Qatar, Kuwait, and part of Yemen.

Britain defeated the Ottoman Empire in World War I. After the war, Britain and the League of Nations created Iraq from part of the Ottoman empire, ignoring divisions in the new country.

Within Iraq's borders were Shia Arabs in the south, Sunni Arabs in the west, and non-Arab Kurds in the north. There were also Turks, Assyrian Christians, and Jews. Until 2003, the Sunni Arab **minority**—a group with less than half of the population—dominated the country. Their rule led to conflicts with the other groups.

Timeline

622 Muhammad and his followers establish the first Islamic community in Medina.

762 Caliphs make Baghdad the center of a vast Muslim Empire.

1258 Mongol invaders conquer Iraq and destroy Baghdad.

1500s Ottoman Turks make Iraq and much of Arabia part of their empire.

1918 Britain defeats Ottoman Turks and occupies Iraq and parts of Arabia.

| 500 | 750 | 1000 | 1250 | 1500 | 1750 | 2000 |

my worldgeography.com Timeline

603

Oil was discovered in Iraq in 1927 and in Saudi Arabia and Kuwait in 1938. The region became a <u>vital</u> source of fuel for the world's growing energy needs.

In 1930, Saudi Arabia, Oman, and northern Yemen were the only independent countries in the region. Saudi Arabia controlled much of the Arabian Peninsula, including Mecca. Saudi Arabia is an absolute monarchy. This means that its king has total control over the country. There is no elected government.

Independent Iraq Britain controlled Iraq and Kuwait. However, Iraqis fought to end British rule. In 1921, Britain put King Faisal, an Arab, into power. Iraq gained independence in 1932. Still, King Faisal kept close ties with Britain. He let a British company take control of Iraq's oil.

In 1958, Iraqi army officers forced King Faisal out of power. This caused a period of disorder during which Iraq's Kurds rebelled. In 1963, the Baath Party took power. It took over the oil industry. It used oil income to improve people's lives, but became oppressive. Baath leader Saddam Hussein took control in 1979.

◀ Ibn Saud, king of Saudi Arabia 1932-1963

British troops in the 1910s
British troops occupied Iraq during the World War I Mesopotamian campaign.

Under Baath rule, Iraq became a one-party government. When elections were held, Iraqis had no choice of parties. The Baath leader had total control over the country. Under Saddam Hussein, Iraq became a dictatorship, a country under the control of a dictator. A **dictator** is a leader who seizes power undemocratically and has complete control over a country.

The Gulf Monarchies The smaller Persian Gulf states—Kuwait, Bahrain, Qatar, the United Arab Emirates, and Oman—are all monarchies like Saudi Arabia. These smaller countries gained full independence from Britain only in the 1960s and 1970s. Some monarchs have complete control, but others have more limited power.

In 1960, Saudi Arabia, Iraq, and Kuwait joined Iran and Venezuela to form OPEC, the Organization of the Petroleum Exporting Countries. Qatar and the United Arab Emirates joined OPEC later. This organization helps members agree on a shared oil policy. Often members agree to limit oil production. This keeps the price of oil high and increases their income.

American troops in the 1990s
American troops in Saudi Arabia in 1991 prepare to free Kuwait from Iraqi control.

Persian Gulf Conflicts In 1980, under Saddam Hussein, Iraq invaded Iran's oil-rich lands. Iraq had the open support of Saudi Arabia, Kuwait, and other Arab states. The United States also quietly supported Iraq. The Iran–Iraq War dragged on for eight years at a high cost. It ended without a clear winner in 1988.

Then Iraq invaded Kuwait in 1990. The United States and other nations went to war with Iraq. The United States and its allies wanted to defend Kuwait's independence. They also wanted to protect the world's oil supplies. These countries quickly defeated Iraq in 1991. They drove Iraqi troops out of Kuwait.

In 2003, U.S. President George W. Bush claimed that Iraq was a threat to the region and the world. He claimed that Iraq had weapons of mass destruction.

Later that year, the United States and some allies again went to war with Iraq. U.S.-led forces quickly removed Saddam Hussein from power. No weapons of mass destruction were found.

Some Iraqis resisted U.S.-led forces. Fighting also broke out among Iraq's Kurds, Sunni Arabs, and Shia Arabs. The United States and its allies supported the creation of a democratic Iraqi government in 2005. Additional US troops were sent to Iraq in 2007 to support the Iraqi government. US and other foreign troops were still in Iraq in 2009.

Reading Check What form of government does Saudi Arabia have?

Section 2 Assessment

Key Terms

1. Use the following terms to describe religion in Arabia and Iraq: monotheism, Quran, mosque, caliph.

Key Ideas

2. Describe the importance of the Sumerians to world history.

3. What are the main beliefs of Muslims?

4. What role did the United States play in the history of Arabia and Iraq?

Think Critically

5. **Draw Conclusions** Use what you know about history in Arabia and Iraq to explain how trade contributed to the region's rich cultural heritage. Give examples.

6. **Categorize** Identify different groups within Islam and explain their role in modern Iraq.

? Essential Question

How much does geography shape a country?

7. How has geography shaped the history of Arabia and Iraq? Are there parts of its history that did not depend on its geography? Go to your Student Journal to record your answers.

Arabia and Iraq Today

Key Ideas

- Regional traditions and modern global culture have shaped the region's culture.
- Many oil-rich countries in the region have worked to make their economies less dependent on oil.

Key Terms • fundamentalism • Islamism • jihad • terrorism • entrepreneurship • hijab

 Visual Glossary

Reading Skill: Analyze Cause and Effect Take notes using the graphic organizer in your journal.

▼ A luxury hotel in Dubai, United Arab Emirates

Islam and other traditions have shaped the cultures of Arabia and Iraq. So have the rich oil and natural gas reserves that come with the region's geography. Oil has brought wealth and contact with outside cultures. The region's people have worked to balance tradition and modern culture.

Religious Traditions

The people of Arabia and Iraq value their cultural traditions. Islam is a very important source of tradition. Most people in the region are Muslims who follow the five pillars of Islam. Islam shapes many parts of daily life.

Although most people in the region share a religion, they have different ideas about politics and cultural activities. For example, some Muslims believe that women should not mix with men in public. Others believe that Islam allows unrelated men and women to work together. There are many cultural traditions as well. Some traditions concern the foods that people like to eat, or the importance of tribal membership. Others concern how to welcome guests, treat elders with respect, or give gifts.

Fundamentalism One powerful <u>tradition</u> in the region is a branch of Sunni Islam called Wahhabism, which was founded in the 1700s. Wahhabis believe in returning to the original teachings of Islam, interpreting the Quran literally, and rejecting all modern interpretations of Islamic scripture. Wahhabism is a form of **fundamentalism,** or the belief that holy books should be taken literally, or word for word. Fundamentalist Muslims believe the Quran provides clear meanings that do not need to be debated.

Wahhabis also believe that government should be based on the original teachings of Islam. It is a form of **Islamism,** or the belief that politics and society should follow Islamic teachings. The rulers of Saudi Arabia are Wahhabis. Wahhabism determines much of the kingdom's politics. Most Muslims in the region are neither Wahhabis nor Islamists.

While Wahhabis are both fundamentalist and Islamist, the two beliefs do not always coincide. Many fundamentalists are Islamists, because they believe that Islamic scripture calls for Islamic government. However, not all Islamists are fundamentalists. Some Islamists, like other Muslims, accept less literal interpretations of Islam.

Islamism and Jihad A small number of Muslims in the region see European and American influence as a threat. They have adopted a form of Islamism that draws on the tradition of **jihad.** The word *jihad* in Arabic simply means "struggle." It can refer to the struggle to be a better person.

However, some groups use the word to mean violent struggle. Some of the region's Islamists believe in violent jihad. This small minority supports the use of violence to attack Westerners or Muslims with different approaches to Islam. Those calling for violence include groups such as al Qaeda. Al Qaeda is a group of radical Islamists led by Osama bin Laden, who came from Saudi Arabia. Al Qaeda practices **terrorism.** Terrorism is the use of violence against innocent civilians to create fear for political reasons. In fact, the holy writings of Islam call on Muslims to avoid violence toward innocent people. Most Muslims reject violent jihad and terrorism.

Reading Check **Are all Islamists fundamentalists?**

tradition, *n.,* practices handed down from one generation to the next

Students study the Quran at an Islamic school in Medina, Saudi Arabia. ▶

A Region Built on Oil

The world today depends on oil to power cars, trucks, and other vehicles; as a fuel for industries; for heating homes; and as a raw material for plastics and other products. Oil is one of the world's most important products. It is also a vital source of income for this oil-rich region.

One-Track Economies Oil and natural gas were found in the region in the 1920s and 1930s. Every country in the region but oil-poor Yemen had an oil boom, or rapid growth in jobs, construction, and income due to oil production. From then on, the economies of the oil-rich countries specialized in oil production. Specialization led to trade. The region sold oil to other countries. It bought many basic goods, such as food, from other countries. Income from oil allows the region to buy goods that it cannot grow or make.

Oil sales have made some governments in the region wealthy. Many give cash or free services directly to citizens, even if they do not work. As a result, the region's businesses can hire millions of foreign workers. These workers do jobs that citizens are unwilling or unable to do.

Economic growth depends on four conditions: natural resources, educated workers, investment in local businesses, and **entrepreneurship** (ahn truh pruh NUR ship). Entrepreneurship is the willingness to take the risks of starting a business.

The region's oil and gas are great natural resources. However, money from oil sales lets the region get by without meeting the other three conditions for economic growth. Until recently, education in the region has failed to prepare its people—especially its women—for many available jobs. There has been little investment outside the oil industry. There has also been little entrepreneurship. As a result, the region has depended largely on oil sales.

Foreign workers
Like these construction workers, foreign workers hold lower-paying jobs.

Saudi workers
Like these investment bankers, Saudis usually hold higher-paying jobs.

Trying to Diversify In recent years, leaders in the region have seen the need to diversify their economies. To diversify is to go from just one or two sources of income, such as oil and gas, to many sources. To help diversify, many countries in the region have improved education for the whole population, including women. They have encouraged investment and entrepreneurship.

Two parts of the region have built economies that depend less on oil. Bahrain, and Dubai, a state in the United Arab Emirates, have become regional financial centers. Their economies have diversified away from reliance on oil. They now rely more on services.

Banks from Bahrain, Dubai, and elsewhere have provided finance to other parts of the region. The region's banks keep the savings of people in the region who have made money from oil. The banks invest this money in new businesses that help diversify the region's economy. The countries' governments have also used government money saved from oil earnings. They have invested these savings in construction projects. Some of these have strengthened the region's economy.

These projects include desalination plants that provide water to many parts of the region. According to a Saudi prince,

> 66 Currently, Saudi Arabia is the largest producer of desalinated water in the world, and the kingdom continues to invest in research and development to make access to fresh water more affordable. 99
> —Prince Dr. Turki Al Saud Al Faisal, from ibm.com

Governments have also invested in education, so that their people can compete in the global economy in areas other than the oil industry.

Reading Check Why are there so many foreign workers in Arabia?

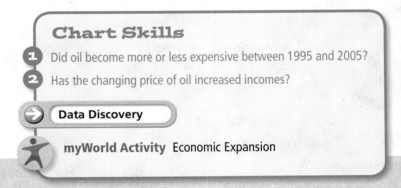

Chart Skills

1. Did oil become more or less expensive between 1995 and 2005?
2. Has the changing price of oil increased incomes?

→ Data Discovery

🕺 **myWorld Activity** Economic Expansion

Oil, Population, and Income

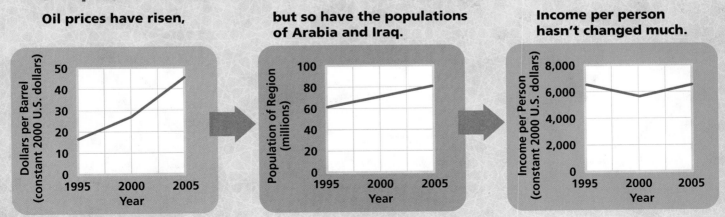

Oil prices have risen,

Dollars per Barrel (constant 2000 U.S. dollars) — Year (1995, 2000, 2005)

but so have the populations of Arabia and Iraq.

Population of Region (millions) — Year (1995, 2000, 2005)

Income per person hasn't changed much.

Income per Person (constant 2000 U.S. dollars) — Year (1995, 2000, 2005)

SOURCE: *CIA World FactBook, BP Statistical Review*

Arab Culture, Old and New

Culture in Arabia and Iraq today is a mix of modern and traditional elements. One traditional art form is Arabic calligraphy, or decorative writing. Most Muslims believe that depicting humans or animals in art is forbidden by Islam. Because of this, art forms that show letters and geometric designs are highly developed in the Islamic world.

Contemporary music of the region uses more modern elements as well as traditional styles. Arabia has long been famous for its poetry. Many modern Arabic songs use traditional poems, but back them up with synthesizers instead of the instruments that would have been used in the past.

THINK CRITICALLY Why is calligraphy an important art form in Islamic societies?

Tradition These artists are decorating the covering that will go over the Kaaba in Mecca. They are using Arabic calligraphy.

Cultural Change A piece of calligraphy used as a background for modern dance. ▼

Below is modern Iraqi singer Shatha Hassoun.

Arabia and Iraq in the Modern World

Income from oil changed society in the region. From the mid-1900s, elite people in the region met Westerners working in the oil industry. They bought televisions and computers. They traveled to foreign countries and sent their children to study there. They were <u>exposed</u> to Western and global culture.

The Pull of Global Culture Modern, foreign culture appealed to many people in the region. They have adopted some aspects of modern global culture. Some of the region's people work for Western firms. Others work for local firms using Western business practices. The region has become part of the modern world. However, not all people in the region are comfortable with this change.

The Place of Women Traditionally, women in the Arab world have had to obey men. In much of Arabia, they cannot travel without the permission of a father, husband, or other male relative.

In most of the region, women are expected to cover their heads and hair by wearing **hijab.** They are expected to wear concealing, baggy garments.

Despite the pull of global culture, tradition still shapes the lives of men and especially women in this region. In most countries, women face more restrictions than in the United States or other Western countries. The most restricted country is Saudi Arabia, where women are forbidden to drive cars or ride bicycles. They cannot legally meet with unrelated men in public. Many Saudi women cannot pursue certain careers, since that would mean working with unrelated men.

However, attitudes are changing. In some countries, such as Iraq, women are free to work outside the home. Some can dress as they wish. Even in Saudi Arabia, women like Hanan are finding ways to pursue careers.

Reading Check How is life changing for women in Arabia and Iraq?

expose, *v.,* to show, make aware of, uncover

▲ Hanan at work

Section 3 Assessment

Essential Question

Key Terms

1. Explain the different meanings of the word jihad.

2. What is entrepreneurship, and why is it important?

Key Ideas

3. How are some Islamic traditions regarding women different from those in modern Western culture?

4. Why do leaders in Arabia and Iraq want to diversify their countries' economies?

Think Critically

5. **Analyze Cause and Effect** How have Islamic traditions shaped lives in this region?

6. **Categorize** What benefits and problems have resulted from Western involvement in Arabia and Iraq?

How much does geography shape a country?

7. What are some challenges the region's nations could face if oil and gas reserves run out? Go to your Student Journal to record your answer.

Chapter Assessment

Key Terms and Ideas

1. **Draw Conclusions** How do the physical features of Arabia and Iraq, such as desert oases, affect where people live in the region?

2. **Summarize** Why are **fossil fuels** important to Arabia and Iraq?

3. **Recall** What are some important accomplishments of early **civilizations** in Arabia and Iraq?

4. **Categorize** What are some features of the religion of Islam? Make sure you include the Five Pillars of Islam.

5. **Analyze Cause and Effect** How did British control change Arabia and Iraq after World War I?

6. **Compare and Contrast** Compare and contrast **Islamism** and **fundamentalism** in their beliefs and their influence on modern society in Arabia and Iraq. Is there any overlap between the two? Give examples in your explanation.

7. **Synthesize** Why do many countries in Arabia and Iraq want to boost **entrepreneurship** to lessen their dependence on oil?

Think Critically

8. **Problem Solving** Water and oil are both important to Arabia and Iraq. How are the region's supplies of these two resources related? How can the region use a wealth of one resource to take care of a shortage of the other?

9. **Make Inferences** Since World War I, Iraq has overthrown its king and fought several wars. What role did oil play in these conflicts? How might oil and instability be linked? Explain.

10. **Compare Viewpoints** How do traditional Islamic cultures in the region view the role of women in society? How do these views differ from those held in most Western nations?

11. **Core Concepts: Culture and Geography** What role has religion, especially religious differences, played in the history of Arabia and Iraq?

Places to Know

For each place, write the letter from the map that shows the place's location.

12. **Persian Gulf**

13. **Mecca**

14. **Euphrates River**

15. **United Arab Emirates**

16. **Yemen**

17. **Iraq**

18. **Draw Inferences** Which of these countries does not have a coastline on the Persian Gulf?

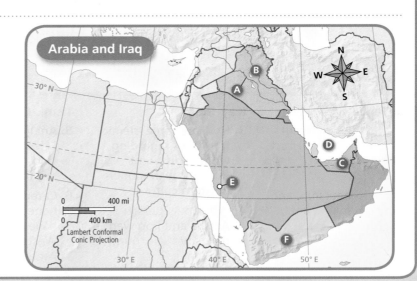

Arabia and Iraq

Essential Question

How much does geography shape a country?

Water for Arabia and Iraq Follow your teacher's instructions to participate in a regional meeting on water scarcity and oil dependency in Arabia and Iraq. Remember to consider how one nation's needs interact with the needs of other nations in the region.

21st Century Learning

Develop Cultural Awareness

Using reliable sources in the library or online, research an ethnic group in the region. Create a Venn diagram that includes the regional ethnic group's culture and your own culture. List information such as the following:
- main religious views
- foods
- language

Document-Based Questions

Success Tracker™
Online at myworldgeography.com

Use your knowledge of Arabia and Iraq, as well as Documents A and B, to answer Questions 1–3.

Document A

" Brother Osama: How much blood has been spilled? How many innocent children, women, and old people have been killed, maimed, and expelled from their homes in the name of "al-Qaeda"? …
This religion of ours comes to defense of the life of a sparrow. It can never accept the murder of innocent people, regardless of what supposed justification is given for it."

—Sheikh Salman al-Oadah, Islamic religious leader from Saudi Arabia

Document B

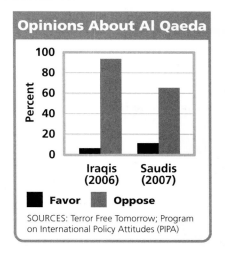

Opinions About Al Qaeda

Favor ■ Oppose ■

SOURCES: Terror Free Tomorrow; Program on International Policy Attitudes (PIPA)

1. Which of the following sums up the main idea of Document A?
   A Islam calls for violent jihad.
   B Al Qaeda's killings are justified
   C Islam opposes the killing of innocent people.
   D This leader sees Osama bin Laden as his brother.

2. Which of the following can you conclude from Document B?
   A Saudis support only 10% of al Qaeda's actions.
   B Large majorities in Iraq and Saudi Arabia oppose al Qaeda.
   C Only 10% of Iraqis support al Qaeda.
   D Al Qaeda is most popular in Iraq.

3. **Writing Task** Based on what you have learned from the chapter and the documents above, explain the information presented in Document B.

myworldgeography.com Self-Test

Chapter 17

Israel and Its Neighbors

Essential Question

Is conflict unavoidable?

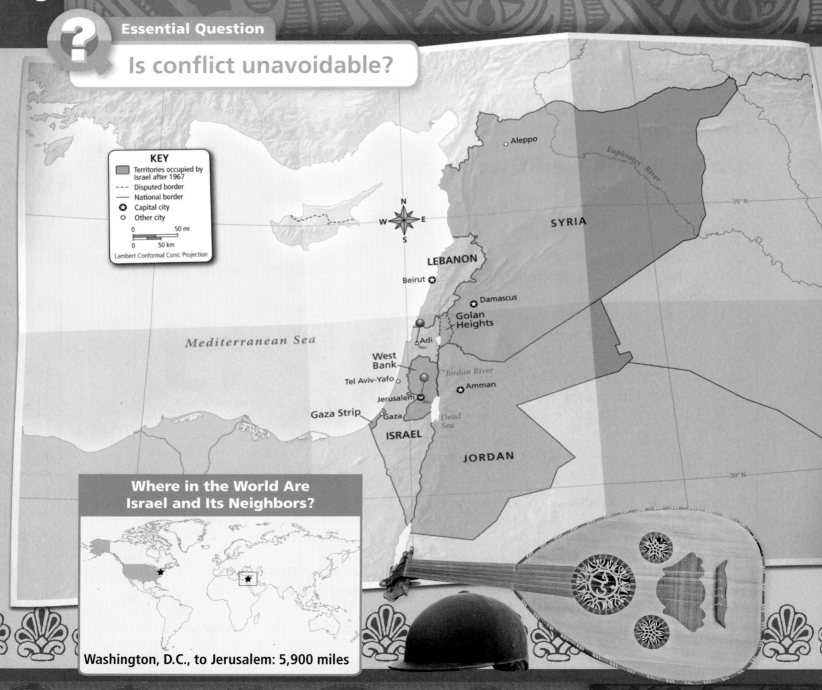

KEY

- Territories occupied by Israel after 1967
- Disputed border
- National border
- ✪ Capital city
- ○ Other city

0 — 50 mi
0 — 50 km

Lambert Conformal Conic Projection

Aleppo

Euphrates River

SYRIA

35° N

LEBANON

Beirut ✪

Damascus ●

Golan Heights

Mediterranean Sea

Adi

West Bank

Jordan River

Tel Aviv-Yafo ○

Amman ●

Jerusalem ✪

Gaza Strip — Gaza

Dead Sea

ISRAEL

JORDAN

30° N

Where in the World Are Israel and Its Neighbors?

★

★

Washington, D.C., to Jerusalem: 5,900 miles

my Story

Maayan and Muhammad

Explore the Essential Question
• at my worldgeography.com
• using the myWorld Chapter Activity
• with the Student Journal

In this section, you'll read about Maayan, a young Jewish Israeli woman, and Muhammad, an Israeli Arab boy. What do Maayan's and Muhammad's stories tell you about life in this region today?

Story by Hila Baroz for myWorld Geography Online

Maayan is an 18-year-old Israeli woman from Adi, a small community in northern Israel. She decided to put off her required military service in order to volunteer in Magen David Adom (MDA). MDA is Israel's equivalent to the Red Cross. Maayan is a paramedic giving first-aid treatment to injured and sick patients.

Maayan studied in an agricultural school near her home. The school has a dairy barn and a horse ranch. Maayan completed the school's horse care program and she enjoys riding horses. She loves the landscapes of her childhood, and does not think she would like to live in the city. Still, not everything is peaceful and quiet in the region where she grew up. Israel faces the threat of terrorist attacks.

"MDA is a reflection of the country we live in. At any given moment, something might happen, and you must always be prepared. I've learned to save lives in a place where life is not taken for granted."

my worldgeography.com On Assignment

Maayan practices first aid at MDA.

Maayan's family eating together

Talking about her first-aid work, Maayan says, "The first few seconds are the most critical. Whatever mistake you make during those seconds, even the most sophisticated hospital equipment could not put right. It gives you a sense of mission."

"I remember how we once [revived] a 48-year-old woman. It took us an hour and a half. Eventually, we managed to bring her back to life. . . . After this case, I felt tremendous pride and satisfaction."

When Maayan returns home from MDA, she drives past Arab villages. "My ignorance is so great. I see these houses, but I don't know anything about the people who live in them. There's this huge cultural gap, and there's also fear. Sometimes when I take the bus and I see an Arab sitting inside I'm afraid the bus might blow up. I wish we didn't live in a conflict, but you have to learn a lot about the other side and get to know it."

Fifteen-year-old Muhammad likes to walk the narrow streets of the Old City of Jerusalem where he was born. Muhammad lives in a Jerusalem neighborhood called Beit Safafa. His family has been living here for many generations. It was built by two large families, or clans, and Muhammad's is one of them. Like Maayan, Muhammad enjoys horseback riding. "I particularly like to ride my cousins' horses. . . . I am sure I'd like to spend the rest of my life in Beit Safafa."

Muhammad is a Muslim living in Israel as part of its Arab minority. Both he and his family have many Arab Palestinian friends and acquaintances living in the Israeli-controlled West Bank.

Seven years ago, Israel built a wall near Muhammad's home—part of the West Bank security barrier—to try to prevent terrorist attacks on Israel.

616

The old city of Jerusalem

Muhammad practices playing the oud.

Muhammad's father prepares coffee.

Muhammad doesn't like the barrier, because security restrictions make it difficult or impossible to cross. Those who do cross may have difficulty returning. Muhammad says, "I still remember how we used to walk to Bethlehem, which is only two miles away. . . . Some people in my neighborhood are Israeli Arabs whose partners are Palestinian. Because of the barrier, they cannot meet now."

Muhammad is learning to play the oud (ood), a traditional pear-shaped wooden stringed instrument, in a music school not far from the Old City. Both Arabs and Jews attend this school. Muhammad plays traditional Arab music. In the school, he joined a Jewish-Arab youth orchestra, with 25 musicians. They play original adaptations of traditional Arab music and combinations of eastern and western musical styles.

"I don't really care about the conflict. Only human beings are important to me. In music, there are no Arabs or Jews, only people playing together and getting to know each other. In our music school, there are both Jewish and Arab teachers. This orchestra is proof we can coexist."

→ **myStory Video**

Join Maayan and Muhammad as they show you more about life in their hometowns.

Meet the Journalist

Name Hila Baroz

Favorite moment Interacting with a video crew made up of a Jew, a Christian, and a Muslim

617

Chapter Atlas

Key Ideas

- Israel and its neighbors are a continental crossroads, near the points where Europe, Asia, and Africa meet.
- Water is a scarce but vital resource for Israel and its neighbors.
- The region has a complex pattern of ethnic and religious differences.

Key Terms
- Fertile Crescent
- Druze
- rain shadow
- Alawite
- aquifer

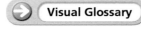 **Visual Glossary**

 Reading Skill: Label an Outline Map Take notes using the outline map in your journal.

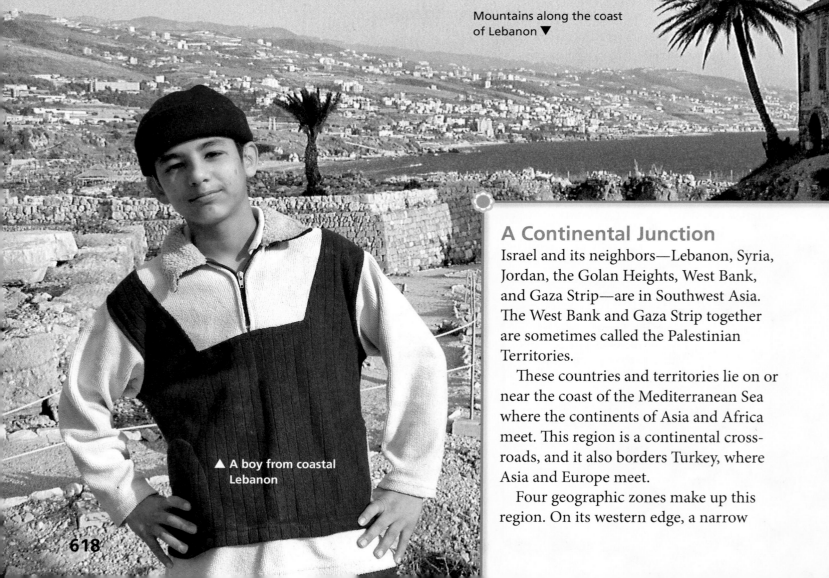

Mountains along the coast of Lebanon ▼

▲ A boy from coastal Lebanon

A Continental Junction

Israel and its neighbors—Lebanon, Syria, Jordan, the Golan Heights, West Bank, and Gaza Strip—are in Southwest Asia. The West Bank and Gaza Strip together are sometimes called the Palestinian Territories.

These countries and territories lie on or near the coast of the Mediterranean Sea where the continents of Asia and Africa meet. This region is a continental cross-roads, and it also borders Turkey, where Asia and Europe meet.

Four geographic zones make up this region. On its western edge, a narrow

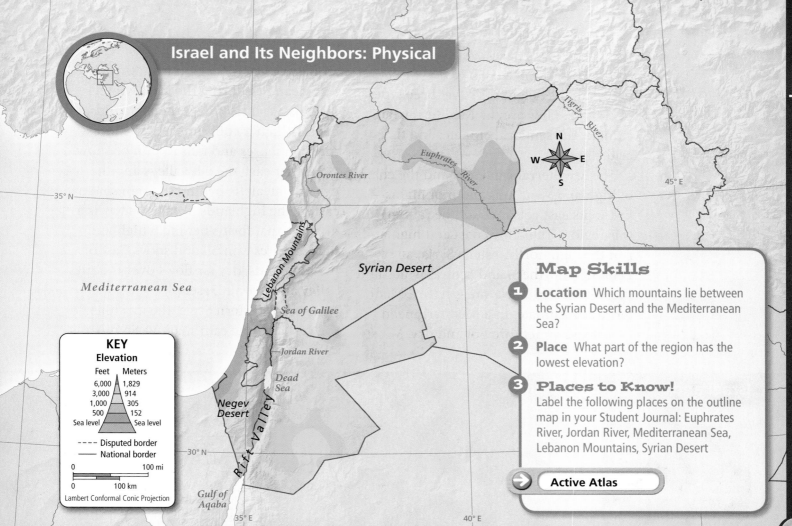

Israel and Its Neighbors: Physical

Orontes River

Euphrates River

Tigris River

Syrian Desert

Lebanon Mountains

Mediterranean Sea

Sea of Galilee

Jordan River

Dead Sea

Negev Desert

Rift Valley

Gulf of Aqaba

N W E S

35° N

45° E

30° N

35° E

40° E

KEY

Elevation

Feet	Meters
6,000	1,829
3,000	914
1,000	305
500	152
Sea level	Sea level

- - - - Disputed border
——— National border

0   100 mi
0   100 km
Lambert Conformal Conic Projection

Map Skills

1 **Location** Which mountains lie between the Syrian Desert and the Mediterranean Sea?

2 **Place** What part of the region has the lowest elevation?

3 **Places to Know!** Label the following places on the outline map in your Student Journal: Euphrates River, Jordan River, Mediterranean Sea, Lebanon Mountains, Syrian Desert

➡ Active Atlas

coastal plain runs along the Mediterranean Sea. Just east of this plain is a chain of hills and mountains. Farther east is a branch of the Great African Rift Valleys. This chain of valleys runs from Africa through the Red Sea into Israel and its neighbors. Above these valleys to the east is a vast desert plateau. The Syrian Desert covers much of this plateau.

Flowing through one of the rift valleys is the Jordan River. Its water flows from Syria and Lebanon into the freshwater Sea of Galilee. It then flows south from this lake to the Dead Sea, also in this rift valley. The Dead Sea shoreline is the lowest land on Earth, at 1,378 feet (420 meters) below sea level.

The Euphrates River flows from the rainy mountains of Turkey, through eastern Syria, and across the Syrian Desert into Iraq. These river valleys and the relatively rainy Mediterranean coast and highlands are part of the Fertile Crescent. The **Fertile Crescent** is a region that stretches from the Mediterranean coast east through Mesopotamia (modern Iraq) to the Persian Gulf. It has good conditions for growing crops.

Reading Check Which three continents meet in or near this region?

my worldgeography.com   Active Atlas

Wet and Dry Climates

Israel and its neighbors have three types of climate. They are the Mediterranean climate, the semiarid climate, and the arid climate.

The Mediterranean coast and the chain of highlands—or hills and mountains—just to its east gets most of the rainfall in this region. The rainy coast and highlands run through northwestern Syria, all of Lebanon, northern and central Israel, and the West Bank. These areas have a Mediterranean climate. In a Mediterranean climate, summers are hot and dry. Moist air flows over this region from the Mediterranean Sea during the mild winter months. As it rises over the highlands, it cools. When it cools, most of the moisture condenses and falls as rain or snow.

Farther east, the rift valleys and the desert plateau lie behind the rain shadow cast by the highlands. A **rain shadow** is a dry area that forms behind a highland that captures rainfall and snow. East of the highlands, dry air flows over the rift valley and Syrian Desert.

In northwestern Syria, the low hills do not cast a strong rain shadow. So most

condense, *v.,* to become denser, change from a gas to a liquid

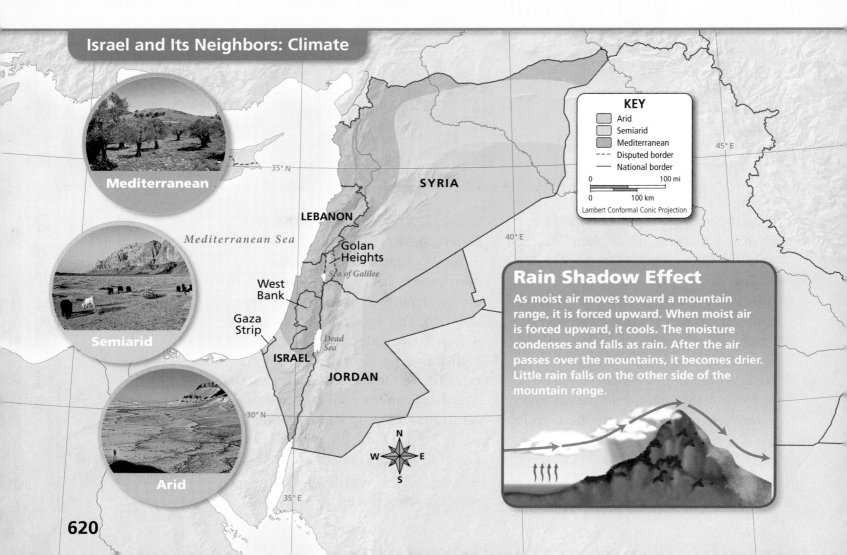

Israel and Its Neighbors: Climate

Mediterranean

Semiarid

Arid

SYRIA

LEBANON

Golan Heights

Mediterranean Sea

Sea of Galilee

West Bank

Gaza Strip

Dead Sea

ISRAEL

JORDAN

35° N

35° E

30° N

40° E

45° E

KEY

Arid
Semiarid
Mediterranean
- - - Disputed border
— National border

0   100 mi
0   100 km
Lambert Conformal Conic Projection

N W E S

Rain Shadow Effect

As moist air moves toward a mountain range, it is forced upward. When moist air is forced upward, it cools. The moisture condenses and falls as rain. After the air passes over the mountains, it becomes drier. Little rain falls on the other side of the mountain range.

of northern Syria has a semiarid climate. This is a dry climate, but with enough rainfall for some animals and plants, such as wheat. The semiarid climate stretches through central Syria to western Jordan.

Southeastern Syria and eastern Jordan have an arid, or desert, climate. This area is behind the rain shadow cast by the hills around the rift valleys. Very little moisture reaches the plateau. Few plants or animals can live in the desert.

Southern Israel and Jordan also have an arid climate, with a belt of semiarid climate just to its north. In the semiarid zone, low hills cause the air to lose some moisture during winter.

The desert to the south is part of the belt of subtropical deserts that stretches around the world. These deserts include the Sahara and the deserts of Arabia. As you learned in the Core Concepts Handbook, cool, dry air tends to sink over this belt of deserts. This sinking air keeps moist air from flowing in from the Mediterranean Sea. It also keeps air from rising and dropping rain or snow.

Reading Check Why is the climate of eastern Jordan so dry?

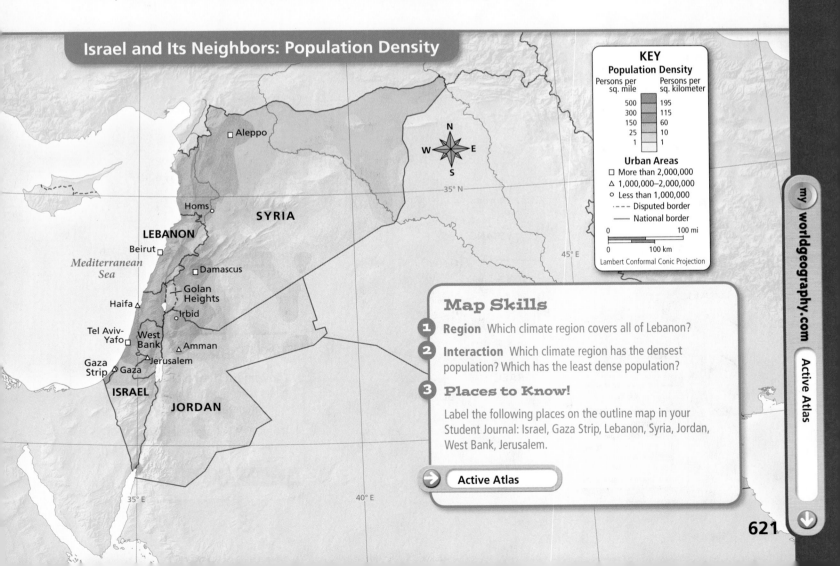

Israel and Its Neighbors: Population Density

KEY

Population Density

Persons per sq. mile	Persons per sq. kilometer
500	195
300	115
150	60
25	10
1	1

Urban Areas

☐ More than 2,000,000
△ 1,000,000–2,000,000
○ Less than 1,000,000
---- Disputed border
—— National border

0   100 mi
0   100 km

Lambert Conformal Conic Projection

Map Skills

1 **Region** Which climate region covers all of Lebanon?

2 **Interaction** Which climate region has the densest population? Which has the least dense population?

3 **Places to Know!**

Label the following places on the outline map in your Student Journal: Israel, Gaza Strip, Lebanon, Syria, Jordan, West Bank, Jerusalem.

Active Atlas

my **worldgeography.com** Active Atlas

621

Water for a Thirsty Region

Israel and its neighbors get little rain outside the winter rainy season. Fresh water is a scarce resource here.

Many of the region's streams run only during the rainy winter or shrink to a trickle in the summer. People need year-round sources of fresh water.

Main Water Sources Some of the most important sources of water for Israel and its neighbors are their aquifers. **Aquifers** are underground layers of rock where water collects. Wells and pumps can bring this water to the surface for use. However, the region's population and water use have grown faster than these aquifers can refill. Some are slowly running out of water. This makes wells run dry. Desalination plants are another possible source of fresh water for this region. However, they are expensive.

Lebanon is the only country in the region with plenty of fresh water. Syria, on the other hand, has a water shortage. Few rivers run year-round. An exception is the Euphrates River, which flows across eastern Syria. The Euphrates is a major

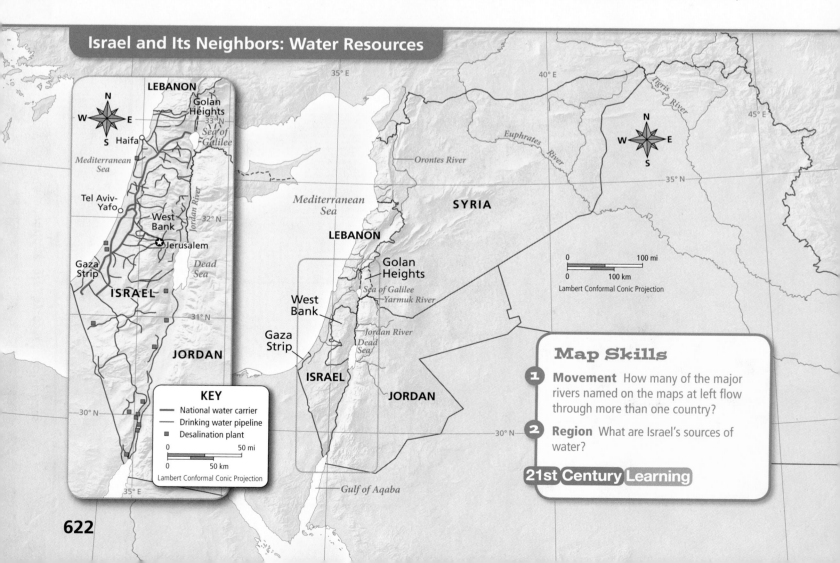

Israel and Its Neighbors: Water Resources

KEY
— National water carrier
— Drinking water pipeline
■ Desalination plant
0   50 mi
0   50 km
Lambert Conformal Conic Projection

0   100 mi
0   100 km
Lambert Conformal Conic Projection

Map Skills

1 **Movement** How many of the major rivers named on the maps at left flow through more than one country?

2 **Region** What are Israel's sources of water?

21st Century Learning

source of water for Syria. Syria also uses water from aquifers, but some wells have run dry.

Conflicts Over Water Competition over the Euphrates has brought tensions. The river flows from Turkey through Syria to Iraq. Turkey takes water from the Euphrates. This reduces the supply for Syria and Iraq.

Jordan has the region's most serious shortage of water. It shares the Jordan and Yarmuk rivers with Israel and Syria. Jordan has had disagreements with its neighbors over these rivers.

Israel depends on two main water sources. It gets surface water from the Jordan River and the Sea of Galilee. The Sea of Galilee is the largest body of fresh water in the region. Israel also takes water from underground aquifers.

Israel also has had tensions with its neighbors over water. The Jordan River flows from the Golan Heights, an area that Syria claims and that Israel has <u>occupied</u> since 1967. Water also flows into the Jordan River from southern Lebanon and from the country of Jordan.

Israel also uses aquifers that lie partly under the West Bank, which is home to many Palestinians. Some Palestinians complain about Israel's use of these aquifers. Because the aquifers are limited, both sides fear a loss of their water. However, Israel has made agreements with Jordan and with the Palestinians over water use.

An Israeli water expert has warned that disagreements over water with other countries in the region could lead to war:

> 66 I can promise that if there is not sufficient water in our region, if there is scarcity of water, if people remain thirsty for water, then we shall doubtless face war. 99
>
> —Meir Ben Meir,
> Israel's former Water Commissioner

Reading Check What river does Israel share with three other countries?

occupy, *v.*, to take or hold, especially by military force

myWorld Activity
Water Rules

An Israeli farmer watering crops

623

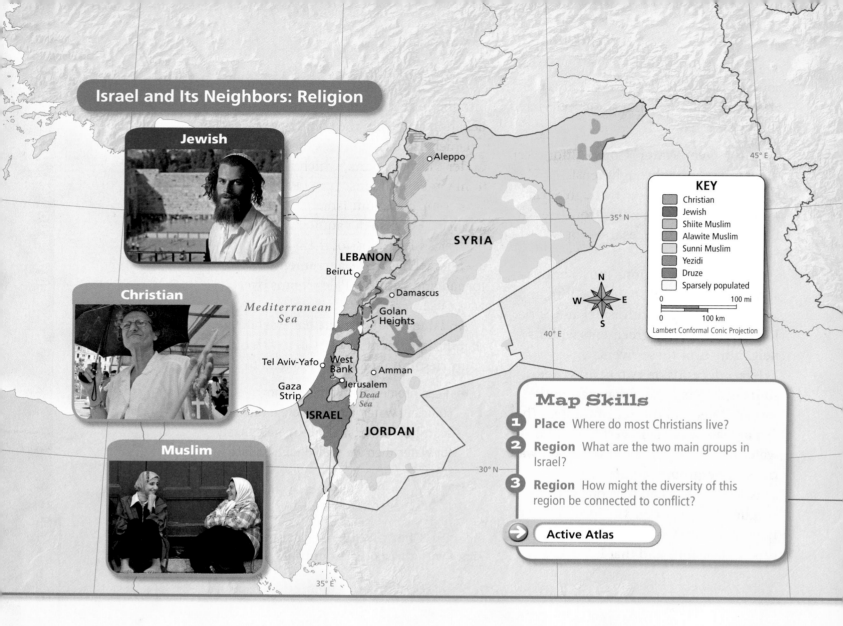

Israel and Its Neighbors: Religion

Jewish

Christian

Muslim

Aleppo

SYRIA

LEBANON

Beirut

Mediterranean Sea

Damascus

Golan Heights

Tel Aviv-Yafo

West Bank

Amman

Gaza Strip

Jerusalem

Dead Sea

ISRAEL

JORDAN

45° E

35° N

40° E

30° N

35° E

KEY

Christian
Jewish
Shiite Muslim
Alawite Muslim
Sunni Muslim
Yezidi
Druze
Sparsely populated

0   100 mi
0   100 km
Lambert Conformal Conic Projection

Map Skills

1 **Place** Where do most Christians live?

2 **Region** What are the two main groups in Israel?

3 **Region** How might the diversity of this region be connected to conflict?

→ **Active Atlas**

A Region of Many Peoples and Religions

Most of the people of Israel and its neighbors fall into two broad ethnic groups, or groups sharing a language and an identity. These groups are the Jews and the Arabs. Most of Israel's people are Jews. Most Israeli Jews speak Hebrew.

Arabs speak Arabic. Arabs make up a large majority of the people in the Palestinian Territories, Jordan, Lebanon, and Syria. Arabs also make up a minority of the population of Israel. Syria has an important Kurdish minority in the northeast. Syria also has much smaller Turkish and Armenian minorities.

Differences Among Jews Most people in Israel are Jewish. Some Israeli Jews strictly follow the rules of Judaism, while others are less strict. Most Israeli Jews, even if they are not religious, identify with the culture and history of Judaism. This is a cornerstone of their identity.

Israel's Jews have ancestors from many parts of the world. Some families have lived in the area for thousands of years. Other families immigrated from neighboring countries or other areas in Southwest Asia and North Africa. Still others came from Europe, Russia, North America, Ethiopia, and elsewhere. These immigrants have brought different customs from their former homes.

Differences Among Arabs The Arabs of the region share an ethnic identity, but they follow several different religions. Most Arabs here are Sunni Muslims, but some are Shia Muslim, Alawite Muslim, Christian, or Druze. The **Druze** follow a religion that combines Islam with other teachings. The **Alawites** follow a form of Islam similar to Shia Islam.

Most Arabs of Israel, the West Bank, and the Gaza Strip are Sunni Muslim. Some are Christian. Many Israeli Arabs consider themselves Palestinian, like the Arabs of the West Bank and Gaza Strip.

In Lebanon, almost all of the people are Arabs, but no one religious group has a majority. The two largest groups of Lebanese are the Shia Muslims and Christians. There are also Sunni Muslims and Druze in Lebanon.

Most Syrians, including Syria's Kurds, are Sunni Muslims. However, some are Christians. Others are Shia or Alawite Muslims. Smaller numbers are Druze. Syria's rulers for the past 40 years belong to a family of Alawites.

A large majority of Jordanians are Sunni Muslim Arabs. Jordan has a small Christian population and smaller groups of Shia Muslims and Druze.

Tensions among ethnic and religious groups in this region have led to conflicts within and between its countries. For example, Israel and its Arab neighbors have fought several wars. Lebanon suffered through years of war among its Christian, Druze, and Muslim groups.

Reading Check Which ethnic group lives in every country of this region?

my World IN NUMBERS

This region's population is **13%** Jewish, **10%** Christian, **73%** Muslim, and **4%** Druze or another religion.

Section 1 Assessment

Key Terms

1. Use the terms *rain shadow* and *aquifers* to describe where water can be found in Israel and its neighbors.

2. What is the Fertile Crescent?

Key Ideas

3. How does the climate change from the coast to inland areas?

4. What is the most important resource for Israel and its neighbors? Explain.

5. How would you describe ethnic and religious patterns in this region?

Think Critically

6. **Draw Inferences** How might religious patterns in the region contribute to conflict?

7. **Analyze Cause and Effect** How has water affected the relationships among Israel and its neighbors?

? Essential Question

Is conflict unavoidable?

8. Describe steps that Israel and its neighbors have taken to reduce conflict over water resources. Go to your Student Journal to record your answer.

Section 2
History of Israel and Its Neighbors

Key Ideas	• Judaism is the oldest monotheistic religion, and its idea of justice remains important around the world.	• Nearly 2,000 years ago, the religion of Christianity developed in this region. • During the Middle Ages, the region became mainly Muslim and Arabic-speaking.	• Seeking safety from persecution, Jews founded the state of Israel in 1948, but conflict between Jews and Arabs continues.

Key Terms • agriculture • prophet • ethics • messiah • Trinity • Crusades • anti-Semitism • Zionism

 Visual Glossary

Reading Skill: Compare and Contrast Take notes using the graphic organizer in your journal.

A jar made in Canaan around 1500 B.C. ▼

Israel and its neighbors are part of the Fertile Crescent. The first people in the Fertile Crescent were hunters and gatherers. Then, about 10,000 years ago, they began to practice **agriculture,** or the raising of plants and animals. These early farmers built permanent villages. They developed new tools for farming, such as plows.

A Cradle of Civilization

Villages grew into towns. One of the world's oldest towns, Jericho, still exists today in what is now the West Bank. It was settled about 9,000 years ago.

Present-day Israel and the Palestinian Territories were once called Canaan. North of Canaan, in modern Lebanon and Syria, was a region called Phoenicia. The Phoenicians invented an alphabet. Through trade, the Phoenicians spread their alphabet, which is the basis for our own. The Canaanites—the people of Canaan—and the Phoenicians were pagan. That is, they worshiped more than one god.

After 2000 B.C., a people known as Israelites moved into the region. Unlike the Canaanites, the Israelites worshiped only one God. Their religion came to be known as Judaism.

Reading Check When was Jericho settled?

626

The Origins of Judaism

The Israelites practiced monotheism, the belief in a single God. They rejected the gods of the Canaanites.

Abraham's Covenant According to the Hebrew, or Jewish, Bible, Abraham was the father of the Jewish people. According to the Bible, God promised that Abraham would found a great nation in Canaan. In return, Abraham and his people had to obey God. God's agreement with Abraham is called a covenant. Abraham's grandson Jacob, later called Israel, had twelve sons. Their families grew to form the people known as the Israelites.

Escape From Slavery Famine drove the Israelites to Egypt, where the Egyptians enslaved them. According to the Bible, God chose an Israelite named Moses to lead his people out of Egypt. Moses was later known as a **prophet,** a messenger of God. The pharaoh, or Egyptian king, refused to let the Israelites go. God then caused Egypt to suffer until the pharaoh freed the Israelites. Moses then led his people out of Egypt to the edge of Canaan. The Jewish holiday of Passover commemorates this event.

During this time, according to the Bible, God gave Moses a law code including the Ten Commandments. The Ten Commandments are ten rules for good behavior. The Israelites took control in Canaan and established first the kingdom of Israel and later the kingdom of Judah. In 587 B.C., however, the Babylonian empire conquered the Israelite kingdom of Judah.

Captivity, Return, and Diaspora The Babylonians destroyed the great Temple of Jerusalem and carried away many people from Judah as captives. However, the people of Judah preserved their religion. They came to be known as Jews, a name derived from *Judah*. Captivity in Babylonia was the start of the Jewish Diaspora, or scattering. After the Persians conquered Babylonia, the Persian king allowed Jews to return to Judah. The Jews rebuilt their Temple in Jerusalem.

The region eventually came under Roman rule as the province of Judea. The Romans demanded heavy taxes and outlawed parts of the Jewish religion. Jews rebelled against Rome twice. The Romans destroyed the Temple in A.D. 70 and later killed thousands of Jews. Many Jews fled the region, and the Romans banned Jews from Jerusalem.

Reading Check What was the Diaspora?

Moses leading his people out of Egypt in a scene from the Hebrew Bible ▼

627

The Beliefs of Judaism

Judaism developed a system of **ethics**—or beliefs about what is right and wrong. Judaism also developed a tradition of acting responsibly within a community. These traditions are guidelines for living a just and righteous life.

Faith in One God At the core of Judaism lies the belief that there is a single God who created the universe and has always existed. This God does not take a physical form. Most Jews refer to God as *He*. However, for Jews, God is neither male nor female. God knows the thoughts and actions of people. He rewards the good

▼ A jeweled Torah cover, with wrapped Torah scrolls below and to the right

▲ Israeli Jewish worshipers

and punishes the evil. Jews believe that they carry on the Israelites' covenant with God. They believe that God chose them to bear the responsibility of upholding his laws and serving as an example of justice to other peoples.

The Holy Scriptures The scriptures, or religious writings, of Judaism include the Hebrew Bible, known as the Tanakh. The Tanakh has three parts: the Torah, the Nevi'im, and the Ketuvim. The Torah, or Law, tells the story of the Israelites from God's creation of the world until the death of Moses. It provides the basis for Jewish ethics and religious practice. The Nevi'im, or Prophets, contains the teachings of the many prophets of Judaism. The Ketuvim, or Writings, includes psalms (sacred poems or songs) and proverbs (writings of wisdom). Another Jewish religious text, not part of the Tanakh, is the Talmud. This text explains and interprets the Torah.

The Ten Commandments and Justice Jews' covenant with God includes rules that form a system of ethics. According to the Bible, God gave rules to Moses on the journey from Egypt to Canaan. They include the Ten Commandments. These are guidelines for acting justly and fairly that are meant to create a stable and peaceful society. Judaism calls on people to follow the righteous example of God. Jewish ideas of justice form a basis for democracies, legal systems, and ethics in many parts of the modern world.

Reading Check **Why is justice important to Jews?**

The Birth of Christianity

Around A.D. 35, a new religion arose in the Roman province of Judea. This religion, based on Jewish traditions, was Christianity.

Jewish Roots Judaism included a belief in a **messiah**—a leader chosen by God. This messiah would restore the Jewish nation and help create God's kingdom in the world. For Christians, this messiah was Jesus.

As with Abraham, what we know of Jesus comes mainly from scripture. According to the Christian Bible, Jesus was a Jew born in Judea. He grew up in the town of Nazareth. As an adult, Jesus began to preach about Jewish beliefs and ethics. He preached forgiveness, compassion for the poor, and trust in God. He attracted many followers.

According to scripture, the Roman governor of Judea put Jesus to death by crucifixion, or nailing to a cross. The cross became an important Christian symbol.

The Story of the Resurrection According to the Christian Bible, two days after Jesus' death, some of his followers went to his tomb and found it empty. Jesus then appeared to many followers. God, they believed, had raised Jesus from the dead, or resurrected him.

Unlike other Jews, Jesus' followers believed that his resurrection proved that he was the messiah. Jesus' followers called him "Christ," which was a Greek translation of the word *messiah*. His followers became known as Christians.

The Early Church and Its Spread At first, most Christians came from a Jewish background. However, one of Jesus' followers, Paul—known to Christians as Saint Paul—began preaching Christian beliefs to non-Jews. Gradually, non-Jewish Christians began to outnumber Christians with a Jewish background. For hundreds of years, Christians faced harsh treatment in the Roman Empire.

In 312, however, Roman Emperor Constantine became a Christian, and the religion spread throughout the Roman world. Today it is the most practiced religion in the world. There are more than 2 billion Christians today.

Reading Check Why is the resurrection important to Christians?

▼ An early Christian painting of Jesus

Beliefs of Christianity

The beliefs of Christianity are based on the life and teachings of Jesus, as described in the Christian Bible. Christians believe that Jesus was more than a wise man, like Abraham or Moses. They believe that he was God in human form. They see Jesus' death as proof of his humanity and his resurrection as proof that he is the son of God.

concept, *n.,* an idea about how something is or should be

For Christians, the resurrection is also God's promise of eternal life. The resurrection shows that God controls life and death. For Christians, belief in Jesus can lead to a rewarding life after death. Christians believe that Jesus died on the cross because of people's sins, or evil actions. They believe that Jesus' resurrection, with its promise of eternal life, is proof of God's forgiveness.

The Christian Bible The Tanakh, or Hebrew Bible, makes up most of the Christian Bible. Christians refer to the writings from the Tanakh as the Old Testament. In addition to the Old Testament, the Christian Bible contains the New Testament. The New Testament contains writings about the life and teachings of Jesus and the writings of early Christian leaders.

The Trinity The **Trinity** is one of the most complex <u>concepts</u> of Christianity. Most Christians believe that God exists in three forms, or persons. Together, these three persons form the Trinity. These three persons are God the Father, the creator; God the Son, or Jesus; and the Holy Spirit. The Holy Spirit (also known as the Holy Ghost) is sometimes described as the power of God as experienced on Earth. The idea of the Trinity separates Christianity from the other two monotheistic religions. Judaism and Islam do not recognize the Trinity.

Reading Check **What are the two main parts of the Christian Bible?**

A Christian religious procession in Lebanon ▼

A Crossroads of Empires and New Religions

Over the centuries, armies from different empires conquered the region that is now Israel and its neighbors. Some of these conquests brought new religions to the region or re-established old religions.

Life Under the Romans and Byzantines
After the Jewish revolt of A.D. 135, the Romans changed the name of the region from Judea (or land of the Jews) to Palestine as punishment for the revolt.

After his conversion in 312, Roman Emperor Constantine made the region a center of Christian worship. Palestine and Syria were part of the Eastern Roman, or Byzantine, empire. In Byzantine times, most people in the region were Christian.

Arab Conquest and Islam Between 614 and 629, the Byzantine empire lost control of Syria and Palestine to the Persian empire. The weakened Byzantine empire recovered the province in 629. However, Muslim Arabs attacked the region just five years later. The Byzantines were too weak to hold back the Arabs.

By 640, the Arabs had conquered the entire region. In 661, Damascus became the capital of a Muslim empire. Muslims recognize Abraham and Jesus as prophets. However, they believe that Muhammad was God's last and most important prophet. Muslims believe that Muhammad traveled to heaven from Jerusalem.

Because of its importance to Muhammad and earlier prophets, Muslims consider Jerusalem a holy city. There they built an important mosque in 705.

Islamic law favored Muslims but tolerated Christians and Jews. By the 800s, most people in the region had converted to Islam, and Arabic was the main language.

Crusaders and Muslim Rule Beginning in the late 1000s, Christian soldiers from western Europe attacked Palestine in religious wars called the **Crusades.** They aimed to stop the spread of Islam and to take control of Palestine from the Muslims.

Around 1100, Crusaders established Christian kingdoms in Palestine. Muslims and Jews suffered brutal treatment under the Crusaders. In 1187, however, Muslim forces reconquered Jerusalem.

In 1517, the Muslim Ottoman Turks conquered the entire region. The Ottoman Turks ruled until the early 1900s.

Reading Check Why is Jerusalem a holy city for Muslims?

myWorld Activity
Diversity Mosaic

The Dome of the Rock, a Muslim shrine built in Jerusalem in 691 ▼

Culture Close-up

my worldgeography.com

Culture Close-up

Independence and Conflict

Britain, France, and other European nations defeated the Ottoman empire in 1918, at the end of World War I. This defeat ended Ottoman rule.

European Mandates After World War I, most of the world's nations joined to form the League of Nations. The League of Nations created mandates for areas conquered during the war. Mandates were territories placed under the control of powerful nations with a promise of future independence. Syria (including modern Lebanon) became a French mandate. Palestine (modern Israel and Jordan) became a British mandate.

Zionism and Jewish Settlement In Europe, Jews faced cruel and sometimes violent anti-Semitism. **Anti-Semitism** is <u>discrimination</u> against Jews. In the late 1800s, Jews in Europe formed a movement called Zionism. **Zionism** aimed to create a Jewish state in Palestine because of Jews' historic connection to the region. A Jewish state would allow Jews to create a safe homeland. Jews from the Diaspora began to move to Palestine, where an ancient Jewish community already existed.

discrimination, *n.,* unfair treatment of a person or group

Independence Anti-Semitism in Europe grew and led to the Holocaust during World War II. This pushed more Jews to migrate to the Palestine Mandate.

Meanwhile, the mandates gained independence: Lebanon in 1943 and Syria and Jordan in 1946. Thousands of Jews migrated from Europe to Palestine after the end of World War II in 1945. Tensions mounted between the Arab majority and Jews over the future of Palestine.

In 1947, the United Nations created a plan to partition, or divide, Palestine into two separate states—an Arab state and a Jewish state. Arabs rejected the UN plan, which Jews accepted. Israel declared independence as a Jewish state in 1948.

Arab-Israeli Conflicts Tensions erupted into violence. Neighboring Arab states attacked Israel. During the Arab-Israeli War of 1948, half of the Arab people in the land that came under Israeli control fled as refugees. Israel gained more territory than under the UN plan. Arab states took control of the West Bank and Gaza Strip. Many Jewish refugees from Arab countries came to Israel. Israel and Egypt fought a second war in 1956.

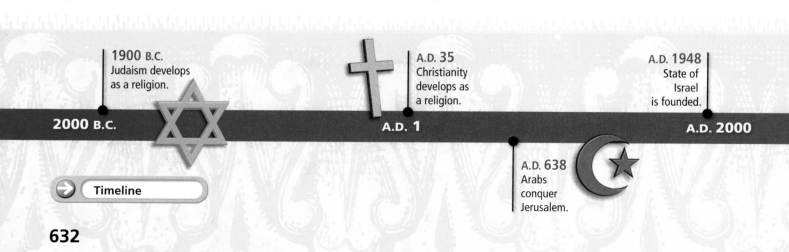

1900 B.C.
Judaism develops as a religion.

A.D. 35
Christianity develops as a religion.

A.D. 1948
State of Israel is founded.

2000 B.C.

A.D. 1

A.D. 2000

A.D. 638
Arabs conquer Jerusalem.

Timeline

In 1967, Syria, Jordan and Egypt massed troops on Israel's border and threatened to attack. Israel then attacked Syrian, Jordanian, and Egyptian territory. After six days, Israel controlled the West Bank of the Jordan River and East Jerusalem—both of which Jordan had controlled. Israel also gained control of the Sinai Peninsula and the Gaza Strip from Egypt and the Golan Heights from Syria. Egypt and Syria attacked Israel in 1973, hoping to regain their lost territories. However, Israel defeated them.

In 1979, the United States helped Egypt and Israel reach a peace agreement. Under this agreement, Israel returned the Sinai Peninsula to Egypt. Israel and Jordan signed a peace treaty in 1994.

War in Lebanon When Lebanon gained independence, Christians were the largest group and held the most power. After Palestinian Arabs fled Israel, Muslims

▲ Israeli artillery in the Syrian Desert in 1973

became the largest group and demanded more power. In 1975, civil war broke out between Muslims and Christians. Syrian troops invaded Lebanon in response. In 1982, Israel invaded to stop terrorist attacks from Lebanon. War continued until 1990. Peace during the 1990s allowed Lebanon to rebuild. Israeli and Syrian troops had left by 2005. However, tensions among Lebanese groups remained.

Reading Check What are some reasons for the conflict between Jews and Arabs?

Section 2 Assessment

Key Terms

1. Use the term *ethics* to describe Jewish beliefs.

2. Explain the meaning of the term *Trinity* in Christianity.

3. Describe how anti-Semitism and Zionism affected the founding of Israel.

Key Ideas

4. In what historical order did religions influence the region of Israel and its neighbors?

5. How do the scriptures of Judaism and Christianity show that these religions have common roots?

6. What conflict between Arabs and Jews followed the United Nations plan to divide the Palestine Mandate?

Think Critically

7. **Compare Viewpoints** Why are ethics so important to Judaism and Christianity?

8. **Analyze Cause and Effect** How did conquest bring a new religion and culture to the region of Israel and its neighbors?

Essential Question

Is conflict unavoidable?

9. Give an example of a conflict in the region. Could it be avoided? If so, explain how. Go to your Student Journal to record your answers.

Israel and Its Neighbors Today

Key Ideas

- Political systems in the region include democracy, autocracy, and monarchy.

- Standards of living vary widely across the region.

- Israelis and Palestinian Arabs have been fighting over land and security.

- The region is important to the world because it is sacred to Judaism, Christianity, and Islam and is located at a crossroads for trade.

Key Terms
- parliamentary democracy
- capital
- hereditary monarch
- Israeli settlement
- autocracy
- Intifada

Visual Glossary

Reading Skill: Summarize Take notes using the graphic organizer in your journal.

This Israeli man is voting in an election, a key feature of a democracy. ▼

As you have learned, the region of Israel and its neighbors contains sites sacred to three great religions: Judaism, Christianity, and Islam. Followers of each of these religions live in the region. Tensions among religious groups have led to conflict here. However, there are many differences among the region's countries besides religion.

Different Political Systems

There are great differences among the political systems of Israel and its neighbors. These systems range from Israel's strong democracy to Syria's autocracy.

Democratic Footholds Israel has a **parliamentary democracy,** or a democracy in which parliament chooses the government. Its parliament is called the Knesset. The Knesset elects the prime minister, who runs the government. Like Britain, the nation has no written constitution. Instead, its basic laws and practices function as an unwritten constitution. All citizens 18 and older—including both Jews and Arabs—may vote in elections to choose Knesset members.

The Palestinian Authority (PA) was established to govern the Gaza Strip and West Bank, which remain subject to Israeli control. According to its constitution, the PA is also a democracy. Since 2006, however, a conflict between the two main Palestinian parties—Hamas and Fatah—has divided the PA. In 2007, armed fighters from Hamas seized control of the Gaza Strip. At the same time, Fatah took control in the parts of the West Bank governed by the PA.

Lebanon also has a democracy. However, its constitution requires that its leaders belong to specific religious groups. For example, the president must be a Christian and the prime minister must be a Sunni Muslim.

Seats in Lebanon's parliament are reserved for religious groups in a way that no longer reflects their populations. Tensions among the religious groups have made it hard for them to govern together.

A Constitutional Monarchy Jordan's King Abdullah II is a **hereditary monarch,** a ruler who is the son or younger relative of the previous ruler. The king is more powerful than most presidents, but a constitution limits his power somewhat. A two-chamber legislature passes laws. The king appoints members of one chamber. Citizens freely elect members of the other.

A Family Autocracy Syria has an autocracy. An **autocracy** is a government controlled by one person who has not won a free election. In Syria, that person is President Bashar al-Assad. He took office when his father died, so power stayed in the family. His family controls the only legal party, the Ba'ath Party. Syria has been under a state of emergency since 1963. The state of emergency <u>suspends</u> protections for Syria's people and most of the powers of parliament.

suspend, *n.,* to call off, cancel, or remove

Reading Check What is the Knesset?

Political Systems

Parliamentary Democracy
Lebanon's elected parliament, shown below, makes laws for the country.

Monarchy
The king of Jordan and his sister, shown below, are both members of the royal family.

Autocracy
Bashar al-Assad is the president of Syria, an autocracy. He relies on the support of the army to hold power.

Different Standards of Living

Standards of living vary throughout the region. Israel has a higher standard of living than its neighbors. Israel's neighbors are poor by comparison.

A Land of Opportunity Israelis enjoy a high standard of living, even though Israel has few resources and faces ongoing conflict. Most Israelis are employed in the service sector. Israel also has a large industrial sector.

Israel's success is partly due to its strong schools and universities. Israel offers its citizens more educational opportunities than its neighbors. As a result, it has highly skilled workers. These skilled workers produce valuable products that allow them to earn high incomes.

Israel's skilled workforce has also attracted capital from other countries. **Capital** is money or goods that are used to make products. Israel's large supply of capital has created a strong economy. Foreign aid from the United States also helps boost Israel's economy.

Because Israel has few natural resources of its own, it benefits from trade. Israel trades its people's skill for resources by selling its goods and services and buying natural resources.

Barriers to Success Israel's neighbors lack these strengths. Some earn money from limited supplies of mineral resources. However, most have relatively poor schools and universities. In many Arab countries, women have fewer opportunities for education. Ongoing tension and conflict in Lebanon and the Palestinian Territories have also discouraged the creation of capital and jobs. Corruption has also weakened the economies of some Arab countries.

Different Outcomes Because Israel's Arab neighbors have weak economies, most people in these countries are relatively poor. The middle class is small compared to Israel's. However, a small number are rich. In Lebanon, the rich often belong to families that have been wealthy for many years. In other Arab countries, wealthy people often have government connections and benefit from corruption. In these economies, the poor earn little.

Reading Check How has education helped Israel?

Like these people waiting for food in Jordan, many Arabs are poor.

A few Arabs in this region enjoy great wealth, like these Lebanese people.

636

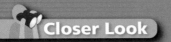

Closer Look

THE ECONOMIES
of Israel and Its Neighbors

Israel's economy is different from those of its neighbors. Israel's workers make products that require advanced skills and technology. Neighboring economies depend mainly on activities that require less skill and technology. As a result, Israelis tend to have higher incomes than their neighbors.

THINK CRITICALLY If education improved in countries neighboring Israel, how might that affect their economies?

Workers preparing medicines in Israel

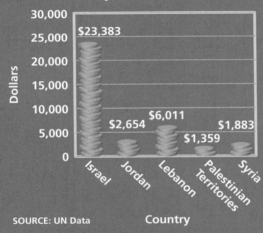

Per Capita GDP, 2007

Dollars / Country

$23,383 — Israel
$2,654 — Jordan
$6,011 — Lebanon
$1,359 — Palestinian Territories
$1,883 — Syria

SOURCE: UN Data

Farmers delivering wheat in Syria

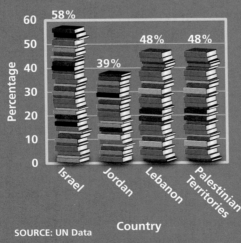

College Enrollment

Percentage / Country

58% — Israel
39% — Jordan
48% — Lebanon
48% — Palestinian Territories

SOURCE: UN Data

Shoppers at an outdoor market in Jordan

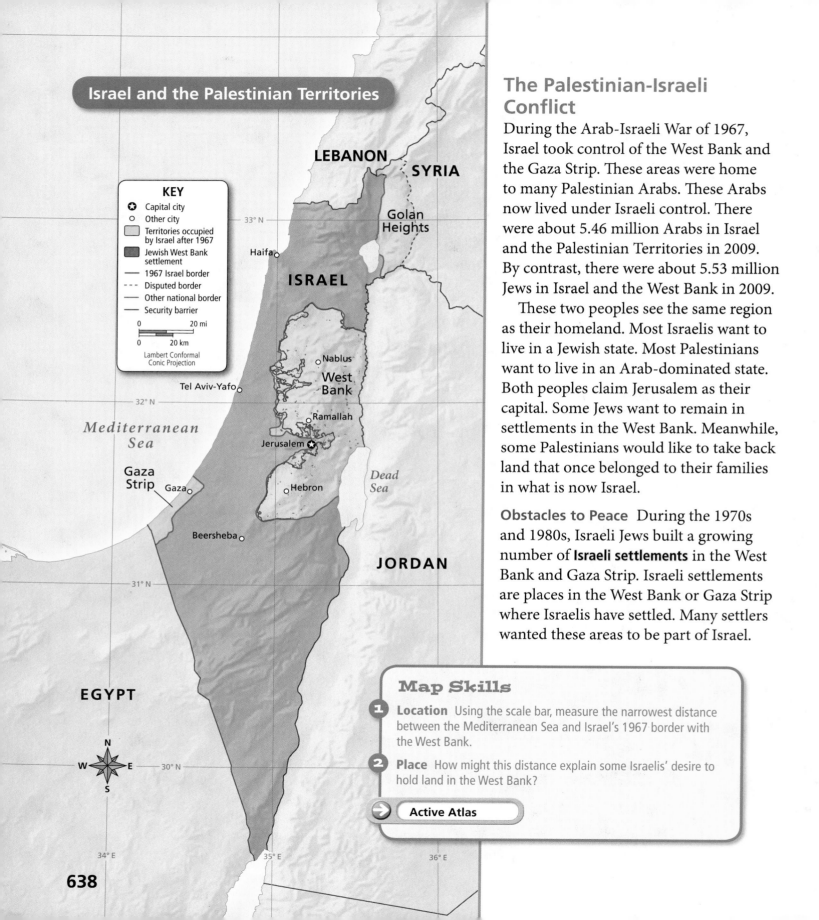

Israel and the Palestinian Territories

KEY

- ⊛ Capital city
- ○ Other city
- ▢ Territories occupied by Israel after 1967
- ▪ Jewish West Bank settlement
- — 1967 Israel border
- --- Disputed border
- — Other national border
- — Security barrier

0   20 mi
0   20 km
Lambert Conformal
Conic Projection

LEBANON

SYRIA

Golan
Heights

Haifa

ISRAEL

Nablus

West
Bank

Tel Aviv-Yafo

Ramallah

Jerusalem

*Mediterranean
Sea*

Gaza
Strip

Gaza

Hebron

*Dead
Sea*

Beersheba

JORDAN

EGYPT

N
W   E
S

The Palestinian-Israeli Conflict

During the Arab-Israeli War of 1967, Israel took control of the West Bank and the Gaza Strip. These areas were home to many Palestinian Arabs. These Arabs now lived under Israeli control. There were about 5.46 million Arabs in Israel and the Palestinian Territories in 2009. By contrast, there were about 5.53 million Jews in Israel and the West Bank in 2009.

These two peoples see the same region as their homeland. Most Israelis want to live in a Jewish state. Most Palestinians want to live in an Arab-dominated state. Both peoples claim Jerusalem as their capital. Some Jews want to remain in settlements in the West Bank. Meanwhile, some Palestinians would like to take back land that once belonged to their families in what is now Israel.

Obstacles to Peace During the 1970s and 1980s, Israeli Jews built a growing number of **Israeli settlements** in the West Bank and Gaza Strip. Israeli settlements are places in the West Bank or Gaza Strip where Israelis have settled. Many settlers wanted these areas to be part of Israel.

Map Skills

1 **Location** Using the scale bar, measure the narrowest distance between the Mediterranean Sea and Israel's 1967 border with the West Bank.

2 **Place** How might this distance explain some Israelis' desire to hold land in the West Bank?

→ **Active Atlas**

By 1988, Israel controlled more than half of the land in the West Bank, although Israelis made up less than one tenth of the West Bank's population. Some Israelis think it was wrong to build the Israeli settlements. Most other nations have opposed the settlements.

During this time, Palestinians living in Arab countries had launched repeated terrorist attacks against Israel. Many attacks <u>targeted</u> Israeli civilians. Civilians are people other than soldiers.

In the late 1980s, some Palestinians began the Intifada. The **Intifada** was a campaign of violent resistance against Israeli control. Israeli troops fought the Intifada. More than 1,000 people died, mainly young Palestinians.

A Peace Plan Frustrated In 1994, Israel agreed to a peace plan with the Palestine Liberation Organization, or PLO, which represented Palestinians. This plan created the Palestinian Authority to rule the parts of the West Bank and Gaza Strip

not controlled by Israel. Israel agreed to remove settlers from the Gaza Strip and parts of the West Bank. The PLO recognized Israel's right to exist and agreed to end terrorist attacks on Israel.

However, each side accused the other of violating the peace plan, and the plan failed. In 2000, Palestinians launched a second Intifada. Terrorists also attacked civilians inside Israel. These attacks brought the peace process to a halt, and Israel again fought back. The fighting died down around 2005 when Israel removed its settlers from the Gaza Strip.

Israel built security barriers around the Gaza Strip and the West Bank in the 1990s and 2000s. The West Bank barrier separated Arab from Jewish areas to prevent attacks on Israel. It also separated some Palestinian villages from each other and blocked some Palestinians' access to their farmland. The barriers succeeded in reducing attacks on Israel but made life more difficult for Palestinians.

target, *v.,* to aim for, make a target

Palestinians at a checkpoint along Israel's security barrier ▼

639

myWorld Activity
Peace Conference

Ongoing Conflict and Hopes for Peace
In 2006, a Palestinian political party called Hamas won the most seats in the Palestinian parliament. Hamas has stated that it wants to eliminate the state of Israel. Hamas fighters took control of the Gaza Strip in 2007. Israel then imposed a blockade on the Gaza Strip, blocking all traffic by air, sea, or land. Hamas began shooting rockets into Israel. These rockets killed more than a dozen Israeli civilians.

In response, Israel bombed the Gaza Strip in 2008 and 2009 and sent troops to kill or capture Hamas fighters. Hundreds of Palestinian civilians were killed, as were hundreds of Hamas fighters.

Most Palestinians and Israelis want peace. Many support creating an independent Palestinian state in the Palestinian Territories alongside Israel. However, violence from both sides will need to end for this solution to work.

Reading Check Which city do both Israelis and Palestinians claim as their capital?

A Region of Worldwide Importance

Israel contains sites holy to three major world religions. The region lies along key trade routes linking three continents.

A Region Sacred to Three Religions
Jews, Christians, and Muslims all believe that they worship the God who made a covenant with Abraham. This region is the Jewish Holy Land and the land where Jesus lived and died. According to Islamic tradition, Jerusalem is the place where the prophet Muhammad rose to heaven. Jews, Christians, and Muslims retain an intense interest in this region.

At the Intersection of Three Continents Israel and its neighbors sit at a continental crossroads. Throughout history, many peoples passed through the region. Ancient trade routes through the region connect Africa, Europe, and Asia.

Bombing in Israel
A bus in Israel blown up by Palestinian suicide bombers

Bombing in the Palestinian Territories
A neighborhood in the Gaza Strip damaged by Israeli bombing

640

A Gateway to Vital Oil Supplies

Southwest Asia has the world's largest oil reserves. Most of these reserves surround the Persian Gulf to the east of Israel and its neighbors. Israel, Jordan, and Lebanon have almost no oil reserves, while Syria has only small reserves.

Still, Europe and other parts of the world depend on oil that must pass through or past Israel and its neighbors. It is difficult to reach the Persian Gulf by air from the United States or Europe without flying over this region.

For this reason, Israel and its neighbors have great economic and military importance. Regional conflicts could disrupt the flow of oil from the Persian Gulf. Thus, tensions within the region can drive up oil prices. For military as well as cultural reasons, the United States and other nations have a strong interest in Israel and its neighbors.

Reading Check Why is this region so important for trade?

myStory   **Photo**

Jerusalem is a city sacred to three religions: Judaism, Christianity, and Islam. In this photograph, Jews worship at Jerusalem's Western Wall, a sacred Jewish site and a remnant of the Jewish Temple. Both Christian and Muslim holy sites lie close by.

Section 3 Assessment

Key Terms

1. Use the terms *parliamentary democracy* and *autocracy* to describe governments in the region.

2. Define the terms *Intifada* and *Israeli settlement*.

3. Describe the role of capital in Israel's economy.

Key Ideas

4. Describe differences in standards of living in the region.

5. What are the main reasons for the conflict beween the Israelis and the Palestinians?

6. How does the location of oil make Israel and its neighbors important to the rest of the world?

Think Critically

7. **Draw Inferences** Israelis and Palestinians agreed to a peace plan in 1994. Why do you think both sides accused the other of breaking its promises?

8. **Compare and Contrast** How are the democracies in the region the same and different?

? Essential Question

Is conflict unavoidable?

9. What evidence from this chapter—including the myStory in the chapter opener—shows how Arabs and Jews might avoid conflict? Go to your Student Journal to record your answers.

Chapter Assessment

Key Terms and Ideas

1. **Analyze Cause and Effect** How does the region's location help explain the many conflicts it has suffered?

2. **Summarize** Why did Palestinians begin the **Intifada?**

3. **Synthesize** How do **rain shadows** create deserts?

4. **Draw Conclusions** How are **ethics** important to the religion of Judaism?

5. **Categorize** What are the core beliefs of Christianity, including the **Trinity**?

6. **Compare and Contrast** What is life like for most Arabs in the region? Most Israelis? All people in the region?

7. **Draw Inferences** Why is the future of **aquifers** so important to the people of the region?

Think Critically

8. **Analyze Cause and Effect** How are Arabs in the region different from one another? How are they all different from most Israelis? How have differences within the groups led to greater conflict in the region?

9. **Identify Evidence** Defend the statement that if the region had more water, there would be less conflict. Use evidence from this chapter.

10. **Compare and Contrast** How are the conflicts within Lebanon similar to and different from the Palestinian-Israeli conflict?

11. **Core Concepts: Culture and Geography** What role has religion played in the history of Israel and its neighbors?

Places to Know

For each place, write the letter from the map that shows its location.

12. Syria
13. Jordan River
14. Euphrates River
15. Jerusalem
16. Lebanon
17. Gaza Strip
18. **Estimate** Using the scale, estimate the distance between Jerusalem and the Gaza Strip.

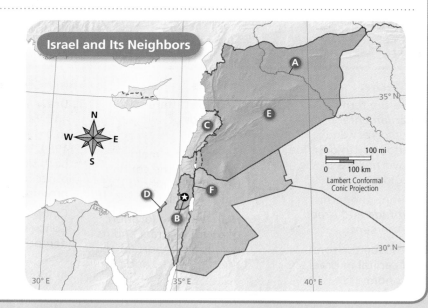

Israel and Its Neighbors

Essential Question

myWorld Chapter Activity

History Museum Tour You want to teach other people about the history of Israel and its neighbors. Develop a stop on a history museum tour to tell about one time period. Present your tour stop and view other tour stops, then join a discussion about the entire tour.

21st Century Learning

Analyze Media Content

Find three articles about conflicts between Israelis and Palestinians. Using what you know from the chapter, analyze the articles. How accurate are the facts? Is there evidence of bias, or a favoring of one view over another? Does the article clearly explain the current conflict and connect it to the larger conflicts in the region?

Document-Based Questions

Success Tracker™
Online at myworldgeography.com

Use your knowledge of Israel and its neighbors, as well as Documents A and B, to answer questions 1–3.

Document A

Peace and Prosperity in Israel and the Palestinian Territories

How important is peace to economic prosperity?

■ % very ■ % somewhat ■ % not very

Israel: 78% very, 12% somewhat, 8% not very
Palestinian Territories: 83% very, 12% somewhat, 4% not very

SOURCE: Gallup Poll, December, 2007

Document B

"Today, many policy makers [call for] a total separation between Israel and the Palestinians. But the [Palestinians] cannot develop a prosperous economy . . . in economic isolation. Separation will result in economic ruin. . . . The fates of Israelis and Palestinians are economically intertwined."

—Daniel Doron, "Mideast Peace Can Start with Economic Growth," Wall Street Journal, March 12, 2009

1. In 2007, what percentage of Israelis felt that peace was very important to their country's economic future?

A 70%

B 77%

C 78%

D 83%

2. According to Document B, what must Israeli and Palestinian economies do?

A The Israeli economy must control the Palestinian economy.

B The Palestinian economy must control that of Israel.

C The two economies should work together.

D The two economies should separate entirely.

3. Writing Task Do you think the views expressed in Document A support the views expressed in Document B? Explain.

Chapter 18

Iran, Turkey, and Cyprus

What are the challenges of diversity?

KEY
— National border
--- Disputed border
⊛ Capital city
○ Other city

0   200 mi
0   200 km
Lambert Conformal Conic Projection

Black Sea

Istanbul

Ankara

TURKEY

Izmir

Urfa

Nicosia

CYPRUS

Mediterranean Sea

Caspian Sea

Tabriz

Mashhad

Tehran

I R A N

Esfahan

Shiraz

Persian Gulf

Gulf of Oman

Arabian Sea

TROPIC OF CANCER

40° N

30° N

60° E

Where in the World Are Iran, Turkey, and Cyprus?

Washington, D.C., to Urfa: 5,780 miles

← Belediye

↑ Eyyüp Peygamber

↑ Harran

↑ Havaalanı ✈

Akçakale ↗

my Story

Bilal Looks Forward

Explore the Essential Question

- at **my** **worldgeography.com**
- using the **myWorld Chapter Activity**
- with the **Student Journal**

In this section, you'll read about Bilal, a young Kurdish man from Turkey who lives in Urfa. What does Bilal's story tell you about life in Iran, Turkey, and Cyprus today?

Story by Can Ertür for myWorld Geography Online

Looking out over the rooftops of Urfa, 18-year-old Bilal is proud of his town. This town, located in southeastern Turkey, has been home to Bilal and his family for most of his life.

"Urfa has a very rich history. I want people to come to see Urfa. It is a beautiful place," says Bilal.

The city of Urfa is several thousand years old. It was once called Edessa, and was one of the most important cities in the area in ancient times. Like most of Urfa's people, Bilal is a member of the Kurdish ethnic group. He is proud to be both a Kurd and a citizen of the Republic of Turkey.

Kurdish people are a minority in Turkey. For many years, the Turkish government tried to suppress Kurdish culture. Kurds were not allowed to speak the Kurdish language or even give their children Kurdish names. Many Kurds fought the Turkish government because of this. Some still do, although today the government treats Kurdish people better.

Bilal believes that Turks and Kurds are getting along well in Turkey today. "Kurds have been living here for many years. Turks and Kurds have fought in wars together side by side. There are no

my worldgeography.com On Assignment

Feeding the fish in the courtyard of a famous mosque in Urfa.

Bilal hard at work serving tea

problems between the Kurds and Turks."

Bilal speaks Kurdish with his parents and Turkish with his four brothers and two sisters.

"Turkish has become so widespread," he explains. "Older Kurds did not speak much Turkish, but today we speak more Turkish than Kurdish. Turkish is much more useful."

Bilal has been working since he was nine years old. He goes to school as well. "I work and go to school because it is necessary. In the morning I work in the tea house of a hospital. I serve tea. I go to school in the afternoon."

Bilal's father works day jobs during the winter and grows pistachios in the summer. "There are a lot of pistachios grown in this part of Turkey," Bilal adds with a smile. "I work on the farm all summer when I am not at school."

Bilal's family has only a small plot of land, so they mainly work in his uncle's field. Lack of water is a constant problem on the farm and across Turkey.

"Turkey is surrounded by sea, but salt water is useless," Bilal notes. "Drinking water is scarce. There will be conflict over water.

A statue of the founder of modern Turkey in Bilal's hometown

HAYATTA
EN HAKİKİ MÜRŞİT
İLİMDİR

K. ATATÜRK

Bilal in class

Bilal and his family at dinner

Something must be done about that."

Bilal is concerned about some of the things that lie ahead for his country. He follows current events closely by reading newspapers on the Internet.

"I read the Internet every day," he says. "If we want to see ahead, we have to learn from mistakes and try not repeat them."

Though Bilal worries about the future, he is encouraged by the progress he has already seen. Urfa's new mayor has brought about many changes to the city, according to Bilal.

"The roads here were awful. My younger brothers and sisters always would come home covered in mud. The mayor fixed the roads. He built new green parks and gardens. I believe he will win again next time around."

Bilal really looks forward to his weekends. "I spend most of my time playing soccer. Like everyone else, everywhere, we like to listen to music and play football." A few years ago, Bilal even made plans to move to Istanbul and become a professional soccer player.

"Back then I thought I wanted to be a soccer player," he laughs. "But as time goes by people change. At one time I wanted to become an engineer, but it was not possible. Now I would like to be a historian. As you investigate the distant past, eventually you come to the recent past. When you study the recent past, you can use it to see ahead."

 myStory Video

Join Bilal as he shows you more about his life in Turkey.

Meet the Journalist

Name Can Ertür
Favorite Moment Bilal's description of the peaceful world he hopes to live in

A group of young children from Urfa ▼

647

Chapter Atlas

Key Ideas

- Mountains cover much of this region and have a major effect on rainfall patterns and climate.

- The location of water resources is important to land use and settlement patterns.

- Oil and natural gas are important to Iran's economy.

- A variety of ethnic and religious groups call this region home.

Key Terms • strait • shamal • qanat • Zoroastrianism **Visual Glossary**

 Reading Skill: Label an Outline Map Take notes using the outline map in your journal.

▲ Mount Ericyes, in central Turkey

A young Turkish woman ▶

Physical Features

Iran and Turkey form a broad band stretching from the Mediterranean Sea to Afghanistan. South of Turkey, in the Mediterranean, lies the island of Cyprus. Much of this region is mountainous.

Mountains and Seas Turkey is located on two continents, Europe and Asia. Most of Turkey is made up of the peninsula of Anatolia, in Asia. Anatolia is bordered by the Black Sea to the north, the Mediterranean to the south, and a narrow waterway connecting the two seas.

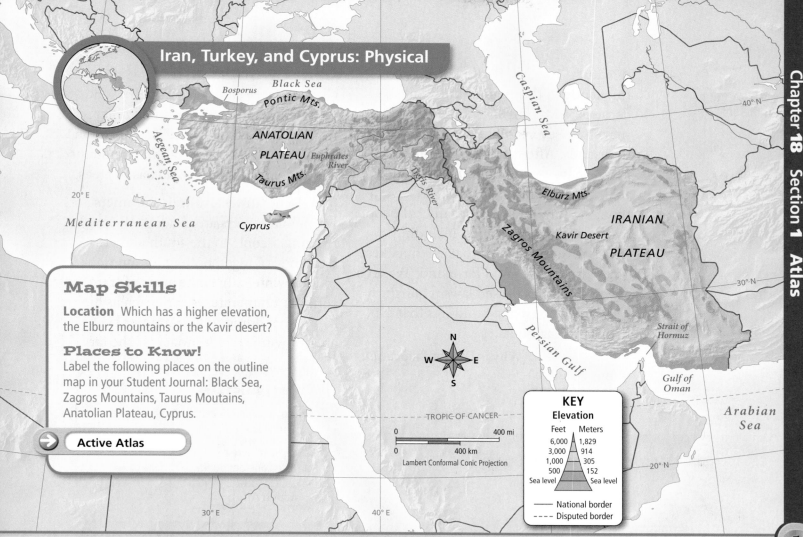

Iran, Turkey, and Cyprus: Physical

Bosporus

Black Sea

Pontic Mts.

Caspian Sea

40° N

ANATOLIAN

PLATEAU *Euphrates River*

Aegean Sea

Taurus Mts.

Tigris River

Elburz Mts.

20° E

IRANIAN

Kavir Desert

PLATEAU

Zagros Mountains

Mediterranean Sea

Cyprus

30° N

Persian Gulf

Strait of Hormuz

Map Skills

Location Which has a higher elevation, the Elburz mountains or the Kavir desert?

Places to Know!

Label the following places on the outline map in your Student Journal: Black Sea, Zagros Mountains, Taurus Moutains, Anatolian Plateau, Cyprus.

→ **Active Atlas**

N
W E
S

Gulf of Oman

20° N

Arabian Sea

-TROPIC OF CANCER-

0 _____ 400 mi

0 _____ 400 km

Lambert Conformal Conic Projection

KEY
Elevation

Feet	Meters
6,000	1,829
3,000	914
1,000	305
500	152
Sea level	Sea level

—— National border
- - - - Disputed border

30° E   40° E

A smaller part of Turkey is in Europe. It is divided from Asia by water. The city of Istanbul is split between the two continents. It guards a part of the waterway between the Mediterranean Sea and the Black Sea, a strait called the Bosporus. A **strait** is a narrow body of water that cuts through land, connecting two larger bodies of water. Because of its location on the Bosporus strait, Istanbul has been a major port and trading center for nearly two thousand years.

Two bands of mountains extend across Turkey from east to west along the northern and southern edges of the country.

These mountains join in eastern Turkey, where they form a rugged a landscape. The mountains surround the high Anatolian plateau. Narrow plains lie along the coasts.

Like Turkey, Iran is ringed by mountains. They surround a central plateau. Iran's plateau is larger and flatter than Turkey's. It is mostly covered by desert. Iran also has lowlands in the northwest, along the shores of the Caspian Sea, and to the south, along the Persian Gulf.

Similarly, two bands of mountains run across the north and south of Cyprus. Between them lies a highland plateau.

myWorld Activity
Trade Talk for Turkey

my worldgeography.com Active Atlas

649

vary, *v.,* to be different

A Natural Hazard Earthquakes occur frequently in this region. In recent decades, both Iran and Turkey have been shaken by severe quakes that have killed thousands. After these earthquakes, people have rebuilt buildings or added wall supports. Most do not move away, though. Hundreds of thousands of people live in quake-prone cities, including Istanbul. Some regions that earthquakes often strike have good farmland. Turkey's government has passed laws requiring builders to construct buildings that can withstand earthquakes.

Reading Check Why is Istanbul's location so important?

Climate and Rainfall

Climates <u>vary</u> across Iran and Turkey. Both temperatures and rainfall differ from one area to another. This variation is in large part because of the mountains and the mix of inland and coastal areas.

Iran In northwestern Iran, summers are warm but winters are generally below freezing. People to the south and east have much longer, hotter summers and milder winters. In some areas of Iran, summer temperatures can reach as high as 110°F. Adding to the summer heat are dry winds that blow across the far

Map Skills

1. **Place** Why might central Turkey have a semiarid climate?

2. **Region** Where can the humid subtropical climate zone be found?

→ **Active Atlas**

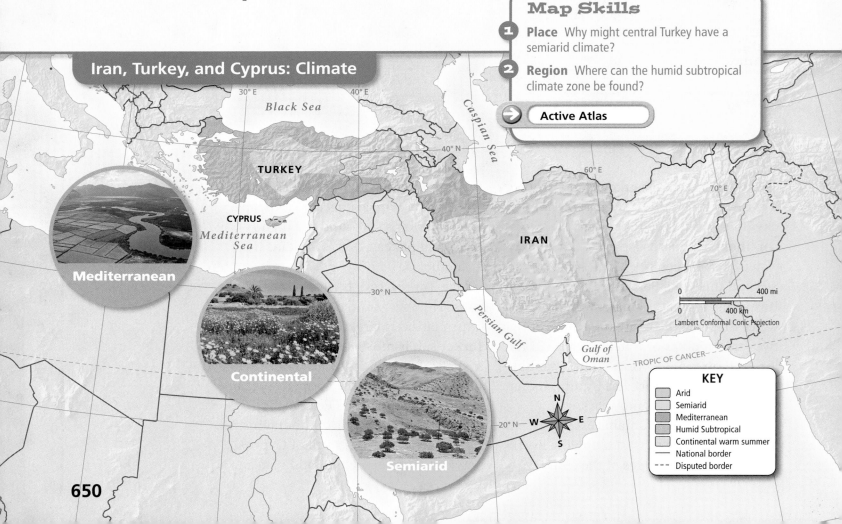

Iran, Turkey, and Cyprus: Climate

Black Sea

30° E   40° E

40° N

TURKEY

CYPRUS

Caspian Sea

Mediterranean Sea

60° E

70° E

IRAN

Mediterranean

30° N

Continental

0   400 mi
0   400 km
Lambert Conformal Conic Projection

Persian Gulf

Gulf of Oman

TROPIC OF CANCER

Semiarid

20° N

N
W   E
S

KEY
- Arid
- Semiarid
- Mediterranean
- Humid Subtropical
- Continental warm summer
- —— National border
- - - - Disputed border

western part of Iran from northwest to southeast. These winds are called the **shamal.** The shamal and other winds blow almost constantly during the summer. They can start powerful dust storms.

Rainfall in different parts of Iran varies. The wettest area is along the shore of the Caspian Sea. There, moist winds blowing over the sea strike the Elburz Mountains. As the air rises, it cools and drops its moisture on the coastal plain. Areas on the other side of the mountains are a desert that receives little or no rain.

Cyprus and Turkey Cyprus has a Mediterranean climate. Hot, dry summers are followed by milder, rainier winters. Farmers depend on the autumn and winter rains for their crops.

Parts of Turkey also have a typical Mediterranean climate like that of Greece or Lebanon. But seas on three sides and high mountains change climate patterns. Coastal areas tend to have milder winters than interior regions. Winter temperatures can remain around freezing in the central plateau and plunge well below freezing in the eastern mountains.

Coastal areas in Turkey receive more rain than the central plateau or the mountains—32 or more inches a year on the shores of the Black Sea and 24 to 32 inches along the western coast. As in Iran, the mountains create a rain shadow. As a result, the central plateau receives only about 16 inches a year.

Reading Check Why does the central plateau in Turkey receive little rain?

A salt flat in Iran's Kavir desert ▶

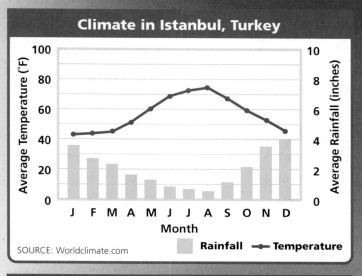

Climate in Istanbul, Turkey

SOURCE: Worldclimate.com Rainfall ▬ Temperature

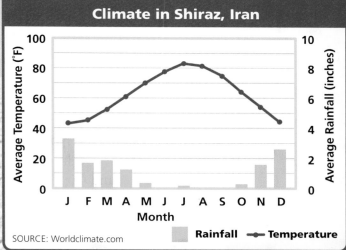

Climate in Shiraz, Iran

SOURCE: Worldclimate.com Rainfall ▬ Temperature

Chart Skills

1 What is the average temperature in Istanbul in November?

2 Do you think Shiraz is located in a semiarid or in a continental climate zone?

→ **Data Discovery**

my worldgeography.com Data Discovery

651

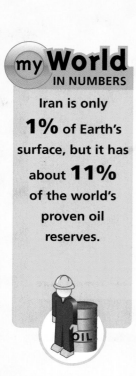
Land Use and Energy

Landforms and climate patterns affect where people live in Iran, Turkey, and Cyprus. Rainfall is especially important.

Settlement Patterns Few people live in the high mountains or in the driest areas of this region. For example, settlements are sparse in Iran's desert interior. Those few people who do live in the desert cluster around oases, where water comes from below the ground to the surface. Most of Iran's people live in the rainier western and northern parts of the country, including the capital Tehran.

In Turkey, more than half of the people live along the narrow coastal plains, especially in the milder and wetter north. The hotter southern coast has fewer people, as does the interior. Similarly, most people in Cyprus live along the coastal plains.

Iran, Turkey, and Cyprus receive more rainfall than most other countries in Southwest Asia, but water is still scarce. In ancient times, the people of Iran developed a clever method for bringing water to their homes and fields. First, they looked in the foothills of mountains for aquifers, or underground sources of water. Then they built tunnels from the aquifers to their villages. These tunnels, called **qanats,** channeled water to their villages. They used the water to irrigate their fields.

The qanat system has an advantage over irrigation channels on the surface. Because most of the channel is below the ground, the water does not dry up, or evaporate, even in Iran's hot climate.

Although qanats are still used today, wells and above-ground irrigation are also widely practiced in Iran. They account for most of the country's water usage. But some people argue that this change has been a mistake. According to one Iranian urban planner and architect,

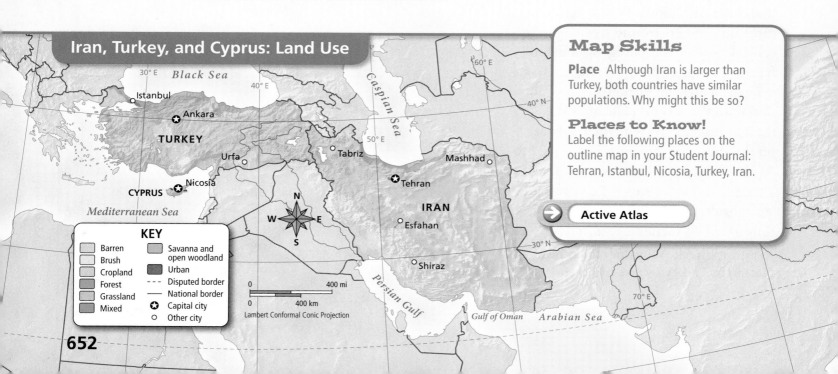

Iran, Turkey, and Cyprus: Land Use

Black Sea
Istanbul
Ankara
TURKEY
Urfa
Nicosia
CYPRUS
Mediterranean Sea
Tabriz
Caspian Sea
Mashhad
Tehran
IRAN
Esfahan
Shiraz
Persian Gulf
Gulf of Oman   Arabian Sea

KEY
Barren
Brush
Cropland
Forest
Grassland
Mixed
Savanna and open woodland
Urban
- - - Disputed border
——— National border
✪ Capital city
○ Other city

0   400 mi
0   400 km
Lambert Conformal Conic Projection

Map Skills

Place Although Iran is larger than Turkey, both countries have similar populations. Why might this be so?

Places to Know!

Label the following places on the outline map in your Student Journal: Tehran, Istanbul, Nicosia, Turkey, Iran.

Active Atlas

❝ in comparison to qanats, wells have a shorter life span (that is between 20–50 years), whereas qanats hold good for centuries. Excavation of such wells in the past half a century has further led to the drying up of wells and qanats both, contributing to drought and increasing water shortages ❞

—Mohammad Reza Haeri

Oil and Natural Gas In today's world, oil and natural gas are also precious resources. Iran has large deposits of both fuels. It has more oil than all but four countries, and has 10 percent of the world's natural gas. Iran's oil is a vital source of national income. Oil sales provide more than 85 percent of the government's income.

Turkey has very little oil and must import most of its fuel. It does have coal and generates hydroelectric power from mountain rivers. Cyprus has few energy resources but uses its sunny climate to make solar power.

Reading Check What important resources are plentiful in Iran?

An oil refinery in Iran. Oil is by far Iran's most important export.

Iran's Exports

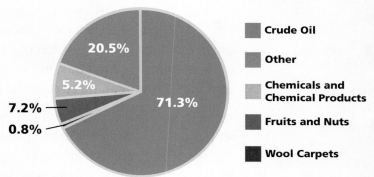

- 20.5%
- 5.2%
- 7.2%
- 0.8%
- 71.3%

- Crude Oil
- Other
- Chemicals and Chemical Products
- Fruits and Nuts
- Wool Carpets

SOURCE: *Time Almanac*, 2009

Chart Skills

What percentage of Iran's exports does crude oil make up?

→ **Data Discovery**

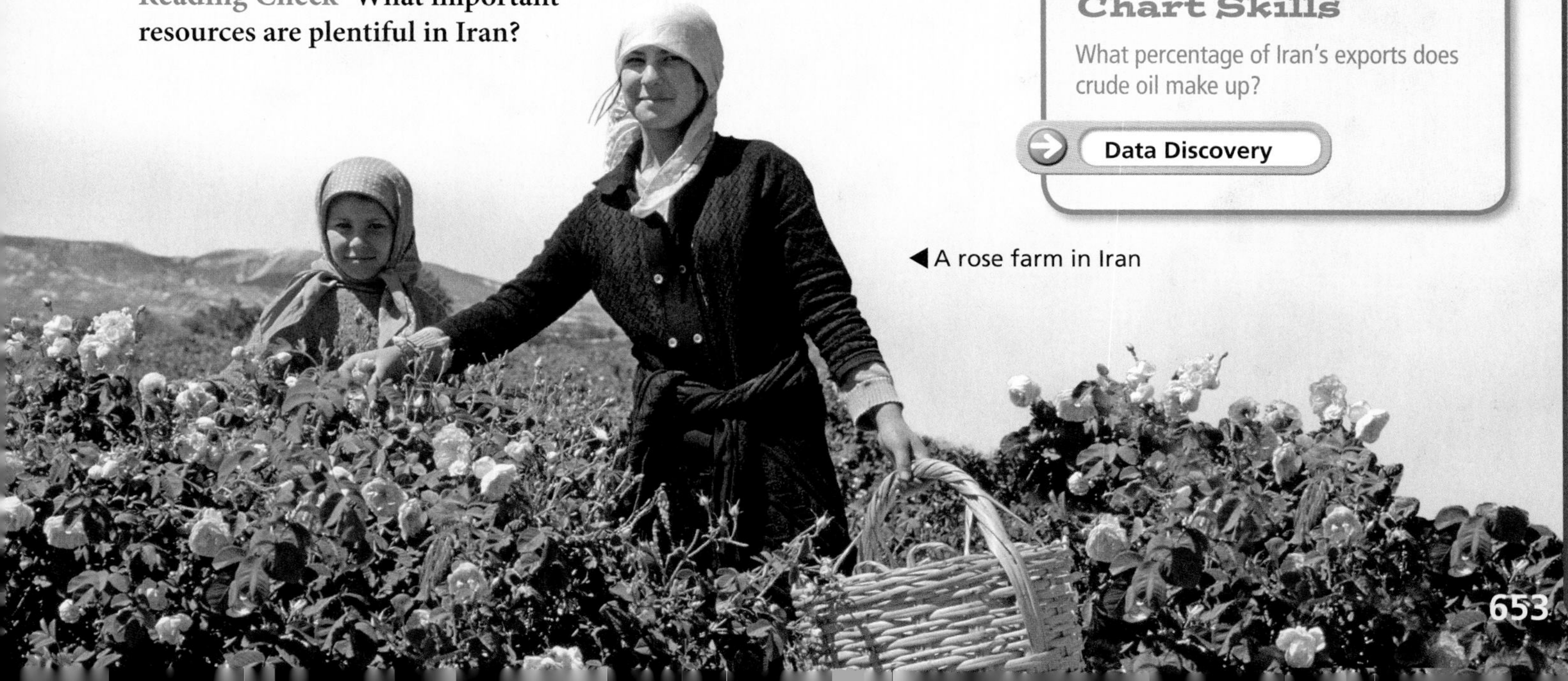

◀ A rose farm in Iran

653

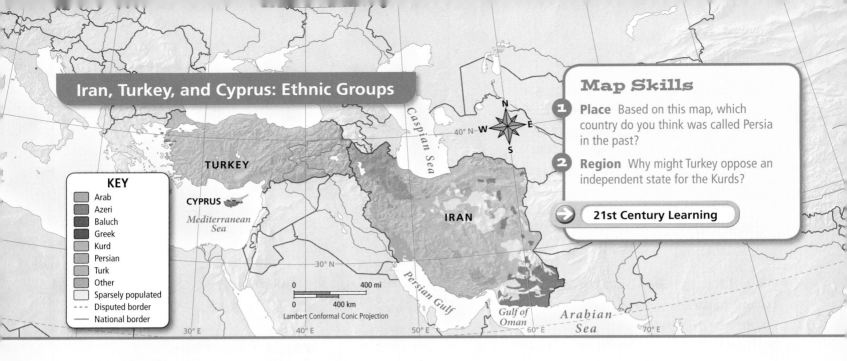

Iran, Turkey, and Cyprus: Ethnic Groups

KEY
- Arab
- Azeri
- Baluch
- Greek
- Kurd
- Persian
- Turk
- Other
- Sparsely populated
- - - Disputed border
- — National border

TURKEY

CYPRUS

IRAN

Mediterranean Sea

Caspian Sea

Persian Gulf

Gulf of Oman

Arabian Sea

40° N

30° N

30° E   40° E   50° E   60° E   70° E

0   400 mi
0   400 km
Lambert Conformal Conic Projection

Map Skills

1 **Place** Based on this map, which country do you think was called Persia in the past?

2 **Region** Why might Turkey oppose an independent state for the Kurds?

→ **21st Century Learning**

Ethnicity and Religion

Iran, Turkey, and Cyprus are ethnically diverse. More than 97 percent of people in this region are Muslims, but religious minorities live in all three countries.

Turkey The Turkish government defines all people in Turkey as Turks. It does not recognize separate ethnic groups. But there are large ethnic minorities in Turkey. About 80 percent of the people in Turkey are ethnic Turks, while about 20 percent are Kurds. Small numbers of people from other ethnic groups, such as Arabs and Greeks, also live in Turkey.

The Kurdish people live in a region that is split among Iran, Turkey, Iraq, and Syria. Many Kurds in these countries seek independence or self-government.

A Christian priest in Cyprus ▼

Muslim worshipers in Turkey ▼

654

In the past, Turkey banned all expressions of Kurdish culture. The government fought Kurdish rebels who wanted their own independent country. Recently, Turkey has given the Kurds more rights and the situation has improved.

Most people in Turkey are Sunni Muslims. About a quarter are Alevis, who practice a form of Shia Islam. Smaller groups include Christian Greeks and Armenians, along with Jews.

Iran In the past Iran was called Persia. Today just over half of Iranians are ethnic Persians. About a quarter of people in Iran are Azeris. They live mainly near neighboring Azerbaijan, a mostly Azeri country. Several million Kurds also live in Iran.

Nearly all people in Iran are Muslims. Almost 9 in 10 practice Shia Islam. Sunnis are a minority. Jews and Christians, who have lived in Iran since ancient times, form much smaller minorities. Today, more Jews live in Iran and Turkey

◄ A Zoroastrian fire temple in Iran

than in any other Muslim countries.

A very small number of Iranians practice **Zoroastrianism,** an Iranian religion that dates back to ancient times. Many more practice the Baha'i faith, which was founded in Iran in the 1800s.

Cyprus People who live in Cyprus are called Cypriots. About three quarters of Cypriots are Greek-speaking Christians. The rest are Turkish-speaking Muslims. Conflict between these groups has occurred in recent decades.

decade, *n.,* period of ten years

Reading Check Which large minority group is found in both Iran and Turkey?

Section **1** Assessment

Essential Question

Key Terms

1. How does the rain shadow affect climate in Iran and Turkey?

2. What are qanats, and why are they important?

Key Ideas

3. How do people in Turkey adapt to living in an earthquake-prone area?

4. How have landforms and climate influenced where people live in these countries?

5. How does the religious makeup of Iran show the long history of this region?

Think Critically

6. **Compare and Contrast** How are the landforms of Turkey and Iran similar? How are they different?

7. **Analyze Cause and Effect** Why do these countries have ethnic diversity?

What are the challenges of diversity?

8. What political issues have arisen from the ethnic diversity of these countries? Go to your Student Journal to record your answer.

History of Iran, Turkey, and Cyprus

| **Key Ideas** | • The countries in this region are at a cultural crossroads, blending influences from many different regions and peoples. | • Civilizations of this region have made important contributions to world culture. | • In the 1900s, empires in this region fell and were replaced by modern nations. |

Key Terms • satrap • millet • shah • Armenian genocide
• Ataturk • Ayatollah

 **Visual Glossary**

Reading Skill: Sequence Take notes using the graphic organizer in your journal.

The Persian emperor Darius ▼

As you have read, Iran used to be called Persia. Ancient Persia was influenced by Mesopotamian civilization, in modern-day Iraq.

The Persian Empire

Around 550 B.C., the Persian king Cyrus the Great conquered the Babylonian empire, in Mesopotamia, and many other lands. He created the Persian empire.

Cyrus and the rulers who followed him spread Persian control from modern Pakistan and Afghanistan in the east to modern Turkey, Cyprus, and Egypt in the west. This empire lasted about two hundred years. A Persian ruler was called the King of Kings, or the Great King.

◄ An image of archers painted on the wall in Darius' palace at Susa

Government and Trade To control their empire, Persian rulers sent a governor, called a **satrap,** to run each province. A general commanded the army in each area. A third official collected taxes. By splitting power, rulers made sure no satrap grew too powerful. They also regularly sent inspectors to observe these officials and report back to the king.

The Persians built a system of roads to improve communication across their empire. The roads made travel faster for soldiers and messengers sent by the government. They also made it easier for merchants to carry goods.

To help people from far-away regions trade fairly with one another, the Persians created a system of weights and measures. They also minted, or produced, coins that could be used across the empire.

Life in the Persian Empire Although they were feared conquerors, the Persians were not overly harsh rulers. They respected local traditions, though at the same time they were willing to crush revolts brutally.

Art flourished under Persian rule. Kings brought artists and craftspeople to their capital. They built large palaces decorated with sculptures and jewels.

Conquest by Alexander the Great The Persian empire met its match in Alexander the Great. In the 330s B.C., Alexander led armies from Greece into Persia. He conquered the Persian empire.

Alexander adopted some customs of Persian rulers. For example, he wore Persian-style clothing. Alexander planned to

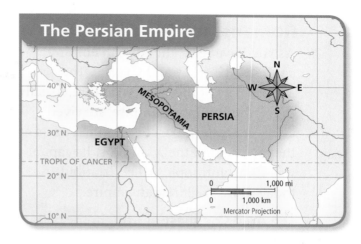

The Persian Empire

MESOPOTAMIA
PERSIA
EGYPT
TROPIC OF CANCER

0   1,000 mi
0   1,000 km
Mercator Projection

rule with Persian help. However, after his sudden death, his empire broke up into smaller kingdoms ruled by Greek kings.

These kingdoms spread Greek culture in the region. Much of modern-day Turkey became Greek-speaking. Eventually these Greek kingdoms fell too.

A new Persian empire, called the Sassanian empire, took their place. That empire dominated Iran for four hundred years. The Sassanian rulers made Zoroastrianism their official religion, though many Jews and Christians lived under their rule.

Reading Check How did the Persians govern their empire?

A gold model of a chariot from the Persian empire ▼

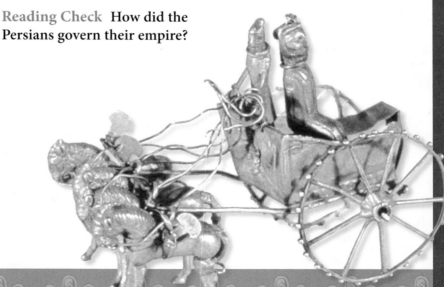

Romans, Arabs, and Turks

As you have read, the Roman empire conquered Turkey and Cyprus. The eastern part of the Roman empire, usually called the Byzantine empire, survived after the western part fell. It ruled parts of the region until the A.D 1400s. Its capital was Constantinople, called Istanbul today. It was a Christian empire.

The Arab Conquest of Iran In the 600s, Muhammad began to preach Islam in Arabia. His followers spread Islam in many regions. They defeated the Sassanian empire and conquered Iran.

Over time, most Iranians converted to Islam. Iran became a vital part of Muslim economic and cultural life. The first madrassas, or Islamic religious schools, were founded there in the 900s before spreading to other areas. However, ethnic pride remained strong in Iran. Its native language and culture survived.

The Ottoman Empire In the 1000s, Muslim Turks from Central Asia migrated into Turkey and Iran and began to gain power. They spread their language and culture. They gave the country of Turkey its name.

The Turks <u>established</u> kingdoms in the region. By the 1400s, the kingdom of the Turkish Ottoman family became the most powerful. The Ottomans claimed to be caliphs, or religious leaders of all Muslims. They captured Constantinople, and ended the Byzantine empire, in 1453. The Ottomans made Constantinople, now called Istanbul, their capital. They built an

establish, *v.,* to found or build

Map Skills

1. **Place** Which empire ruled the Islamic holy cities of Mecca and Medina?
2. **Region** Which empire was based in Persia?

→ **Active Atlas**

The Ottoman and Safavid Empires

KEY
- Ottoman empire, 1566
- Safavid empire, 1629
- ○ City

0   400 mi
0   400 km
Miller Cylindrical Projection

empire that spread over three continents.

The Muslim Ottomans ruled over many Jews and Christians. They allowed their subjects to practice their own religions. Some Jews and Christians rose to high positions in the government. Religious groups were organized into **millets,** or self-governing religious communities. Millets had their own laws and leaders.

Perhaps the greatest Ottoman ruler was Suleiman the Magnificent, who conquered much of southeastern Europe. In the 1500s, Suleiman was probably the richest ruler in the world, and one of the most powerful. He built mosques, schools, and libraries. His court was a center of art and culture.

The Safavids In the 1500s, the Safavid empire rose in Iran. It fought several large wars with the Ottomans. The Safavid ruler was called a **shah,** the Persian word for king. The Safavids made Shia Islam the official religion of Iran. This set Iran apart from its Sunni neighbors.

Iranian art and architecture reached new heights under Safavid rule. The Safavids built a magnificent capital in Esfahan. It was famous for its dazzling mosques and beautiful flower gardens.

Reading Check **What religion did the Ottomans practice?**

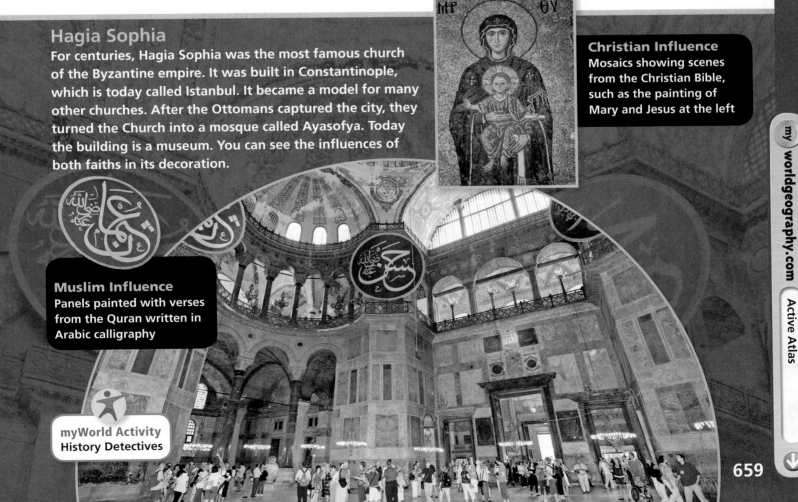

Hagia Sophia

For centuries, Hagia Sophia was the most famous church of the Byzantine empire. It was built in Constantinople, which is today called Istanbul. It became a model for many other churches. After the Ottomans captured the city, they turned the Church into a mosque called Ayasofya. Today the building is a museum. You can see the influences of both faiths in its decoration.

Christian Influence
Mosaics showing scenes from the Christian Bible, such as the painting of Mary and Jesus at the left

Muslim Influence
Panels painted with verses from the Quran written in Arabic calligraphy

myWorld Activity
History Detectives

my worldgeography.com

Active Atlas

659

Empires Collapse in the Modern Age

By the 1800s, old empires in Turkey and Iran were losing power rapidly. European countries began to influence affairs in the region. But nationalists in Turkey and Iran opposed them.

deny, *v.,* to say something is not true

Last Days of the Ottoman Empire In the early 1900s, a group of army officers called the Young Turks took power in the Ottoman empire. They wanted to create a secular nation, like those of Europe. They sided with Germany in World War I.

Though the Ottoman empire was mostly tolerant of minorities, Armenian Christians faced persecution before World War I. During the war, when some Armenians sided with Russia, the empire's enemy, Turkish soldiers forced large numbers of Armenian civilians from their homes onto long marches. The soldiers killed many, and caused the death of others from starvation and disease. Between 600,000 and 1,500,000 Armenians died. The killing of Armenians by Turkish leaders from 1915 to 1918 is called the **Armenian genocide**. The leaders of modern Turkey do not use this term. They deny the Turkish government's responsibility for the killings.

Turkey Forms After the Ottoman empire and its allies lost World War I, the empire collapsed. European powers took control of some of its lands. They tried to take control of Turkey itself, too. But a Turkish army officer named Mustafa Kemal led forces to save Turkey's independence.

Under Kemal's rule, Turkey became a republic. Kemal tried to modernize Turkey and to westernize it, or to make it more European. Kemal made Turkey a secular state. That is, government was strictly separated from religion. Women were given more rights. People were encouraged to wear European clothes. Language and writing were reformed.

Kemal ruled using undemocratic methods. Still, many of his reforms won great respect from the Turkish people. He called himself **Ataturk,** which means "Father of the Turks." Most Turks today consider him a national hero.

A New Iran Around the beginning of the 1900s, the dynasty that ruled Iran was in trouble. It had run out of money. Russia and Britain controlled Iran's oil resources and influenced the government. Many Iranians resented this situation.

In the 1920s, a military leader named Reza Pahlavi overthrew the government

A Turkish Republic Day parade ▼

Mustafa Kemal Ataturk ▼

660

of Iran. He made himself shah. He tried to modernize and westernize Iran.

After 1941, his son, Mohammad Reza Pahlavi, continued this work. He became a close ally of the United States. In 1953, an elected government threw out the shah, but he returned with American help. The shah became a more oppressive ruler. He created a powerful secret police force that arrested or killed critics of his rule.

Revolution in Iran The shah's repressive policies created opposition. One leading critic of the shah was a Shia religious leader named Ayatollah Ruhollah Khomeini. **Ayatollah** is a title for high-ranking Shia leaders in Iran. Khomeini opposed the shah's efforts to make Iran more like western countries. He wanted Iran to follow Islamic law and traditions. The shah forced Khomeini to leave Iran, but the Ayatollah's attacks continued.

In 1978, a revolution broke out. Iranians took to the streets to protest the shah's rule. When the shah ordered troops to attack the protestors, this

◀ Protesters hold a poster of Khomeini during the Iranian Revolution.

provoked even more protests. Eventually, the shah and his family fled, and his government collapsed. In February 1979, Khomeini returned and took power.

Reading Check What happened to the shah's government?

Section 2 Assessment

Essential Question

What are the challenges of diversity?

Key Terms

1. What is a satrap? What function did satraps perform?

2. What is a secular state?

Key Ideas

3. How did the rulers of the Persian empire encourage trade?

4. How did Iran contribute to Muslim cultural life?

5. What were the goals of Mustafa Kemal Ataturk's reforms?

Think Critically

6. **Analyze Cause and Effect** What effect did Alexander's conquest have on the culture of the region?

7. **Compare and Contrast** How were the new governments formed in Turkey and Iran in the early 1900s similar? How were they different?

8. What role did national feeling play in the creation of modern Turkey and Iran? Go to your Student Journal to record your answer.

Iran, Turkey, and Cyprus Today

Key Ideas
- Iran's government is a theocracy, while Turkey and Cyprus are democracies.
- Turkey's culture is split between tradition and modernity while it seeks greater economic ties with Europe.
- The island of Cyprus has been divided by conflict between Greeks and Turks.

Key Terms • Majlis • cleric • brain drain • coup

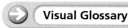 Visual Glossary

Reading Skill: Identify Main Ideas Take notes using the graphic organizer in your journal.

▼ Ayatollah Ali Khamenei, Supreme Leader of Iran

After the 1979 Iranian revolution, a government that was dedicated to following Islamic law took power. The people of Iran have some say in their government, but lack many important rights.

The Islamic Republic of Iran

Iran's government is a theocracy in which religious leaders hold great power. Laws must follow Islam as it is interpreted by these leaders.

Structure of Iran's Theocracy The head of Iran's government is a religious figure called the Supreme Leader. He must approve all major government policies. He is the head of the military. Revolutionary leader Ayatollah Ruhollah Khomeini was the first Supreme Leader.

Iran's voters elect a president and a legislature, called the **Majlis.** The Majlis passes the laws for the president to carry out. The president is sometimes better known outside Iran than the Supreme Leader, but the Supreme Leader is more powerful.

The Supreme Leader names six of the twelve members of a body called the Guardian Council. All members of the council are **clerics,** or religious leaders. The Council reviews all laws passed by the Majlis. It vetoes any that it believes violate Islamic law. The Guardian Council also decides who can run for office. It uses this power to block candidates who want to change the system of government.

Rights and Restrictions on Citizens
Iranians have the right to vote. The constitution guarantees other rights as well. However, Iran's government places many limits on people's freedom. It restricts freedom of speech and freedom of the press, or newspapers and other media. The government can close newspapers and imprison journalists. It also sometimes imprisons or executes people who oppose the government.

As well, Iranian women and men do not have fully equal rights. Harsh punishments can be applied to people who violate certain moral codes established by the government.

Reform and Opposition Many Iranians are unhappy with their government. Even some clerics oppose government policies. They work within the current system to reform it. One reformist cleric, Mohammed Khatami, was elected president by a large majority in 1997. He carried out some changes, but many of his reforms were stopped by the Supreme Leader and Guardian Council. Iranians who supported reform were disappointed.

> 66 We thought that Mr. Khatami's victory was a victory for us as well. The election of a more democratic government seemed to be a bright new beginning . . . But within less than a year of the election, the journalists, reformists and intellectuals began to be persecuted by hard-liners in the judiciary and Intelligence Ministry . . . 99
> —Camella Entekhabifard, "Tehran's Eternal Youth," *The New York Times*

Some Iranians hold public protests, risking imprisonment or death. In 1999 and 2003, many students protested. In 2009, reformists claimed that an election had been rigged against their candidate. They held the largest street protests since the revolution. The government used violence against the protesters, killing many.

Reading Check **Does the Supreme Leader or the president of Iran have more power?**

◄ Iranian students protest against their government's restriction of the press.

Iran and the United States

Iran has had difficult relations with the United States. After the revolution, many Iranians were angry with the United States for supporting the shah. Iranian students attacked the American embassy and held Americans inside hostage for 444 days. Relations between the two countries have been tense ever since.

Another issue has been Iran's nuclear program. Iran says it needs nuclear energy. But the United States and other countries fear it is trying to develop nuclear weapons. The United States has tried to convince other countries to stop trading with Iran until it shows that it is not building nuclear weapons.

The United States government also accuses Iran of supporting groups that have attacked both Israel and United States troops in Iraq.

Reading Check **Why do some countries object to Iran's nuclear energy program?**

The Economy of Iran

Iran's economy is dominated by oil. Money from oil sales brings in most of the government's income. But the economy is still weak.

Economic Problems Unemployment is a major problem in Iran. In 2008, one in every eight workers was out of work. High rates of population growth contribute to unemployment. The economy has not grown fast enough to provide jobs for all of Iran's people.

In recent years, inflation, or the rise in prices from year to year, has been another problem. Rising prices mean that people can buy fewer goods with their money.

The lack of freedom and economic opportunity in Iran have a cost. Perhaps as many as 1.5 million Iranians have left their country since the 1979 revolution. Many of them are highly educated. Educated people leaving a place is called a **brain drain**. These migrants hope to find more opportunity and freedom in other places. Iranian immigrants have built prosperous communities in other countries, including the United States.

Industries A major industry in Iran is the petrochemical industry, which turns crude oil into different products. Iran also makes automobiles, appliances, steel, paper and rubber, medicines, and textiles. For centuries, craft workers in Iran have been famous for their skill in making beautiful hand-woven rugs. Weavers carry on that traditional work today.

Reading Check **Why do many educated Iranians leave their country?**

A poor neighborhood on the outskirts of Tehran, Iran.

Iranian Art and Architecture

A scene from the Iranian movie
Children of Heaven

The Imam Mosque in Esfahan ▼

Iranians today are proud of the beautiful art Iran has produced throughout the ages. Iranian culture has had a large influence on the cultures of neighboring countries. For example, Iranian architecture has been widely imitated in Central and South Asia, while Iranian painting influenced Ottoman art. Today, Iranian movies receive international praise and win prestigious awards, as do movies made by Iranians living abroad.

THINK CRITICALLY   **How did Iranian culture influence the cultures of other countries?**

A man painting in a traditional style ▼

665

Turkey: Connections to Europe and the Middle East

Turkey bridges Southwest Asia and Europe. It is a mostly Muslim country with strong connections to Europe.

Turkey's Democracy Turkey is a democracy led by a president and prime minister. Its constitution forbids discrimination and guarantees important human rights for all Turkish citizens.

Voters elect the 550 members of the legislature, which passes laws. The president can challenge laws. He or she can also send laws to the constitutional court for review. If the judges of that court believe a law <u>violates</u> the constitution, they can strike down the law.

violate, v., to break a rule or law

One issue in Turkish democracy is the power of the military. The army is a very important institution in Turkish society. It has overthrown four civilian governments since the Turkish Republic was founded in 1923. When the military uses force to overthrow a government, it is called a **coup.**

Another issue is a law that makes it a crime to "insult the Turkish nation." This law is opposed by human rights activists.

Some people who write about subjects that offend the government have been put on trial under this law. Turkish nationalism remains a very strong force in society.

A Secular State Turkey's constitution separates the nation's government from Islam. The military is strongly in favor of secularism, or nonreligious government. It helped force out a government it did not consider secular enough in 1997.

In recent years, a political party that embraces Islam more closely has grown popular. It is called the Justice and Development Party. Its initials are AKP in Turkish. In 2003, an AKP member became prime minister. Some feared that the military would overthrow the AKP government.

AKP leaders have promised they will keep Turkey a secular state. Some Turks are not convinced. In 2008, the party passed a controversial law that allowed women who wear traditional headscarves to attend universities, which the government runs. In the past the scarves had been banned at universities because they were thought to violate the government's secular character.

Istanbul Today

With more than twelve million people, Istanbul is Turkey's largest city. Istanbul and its suburbs span two continents. ▼

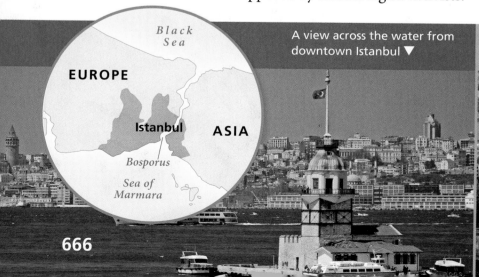

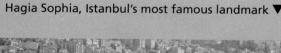

A view across the water from downtown Istanbul ▼

Hagia Sophia, Istanbul's most famous landmark ▼

Some Turks strongly opposed the law. One opposition leader even challenged the AKP in Turkey's constitutional court. He said that the party should be banned because it is not secular. The court disagreed and the AKP continued to govern.

Turkey's Culture Today Turkey's culture shows European and Asian influences. Most urban men and women, and most rural men, for instance, wear Western-style clothing. Rural women often wear traditional Middle Eastern clothes.

Women's roles in Turkish society show similar differences. In rural areas women generally do not work outside of their homes. In cities, women can be found in many occupations. A woman was Turkey's prime minister in the 1990s.

Life in Istanbul is very different from life in rural Turkey. Istanbul today is a modern city with skyscrapers and a busy port, though there are also traditional areas. Many people have moved to Istanbul from the countryside in search of jobs and a higher standard of living.

Reading Check What role does Turkey's military play in its government?

Turkey's Economy

Unlike Iran, Turkey does not have large deposits of oil that it can sell to bring in money. It has a more mixed economy, with agriculture, industry, and services all playing important roles.

Development For many decades, Turkey has lagged behind European nations economically. One reason is that agriculture has been a large sector in the economy, and farming does not usually lead to high incomes. In addition, the government used to run many industries. These industries were not very productive. Turkey also set up barriers to trade with other nations. These barriers prevented Turks from importing low-cost goods to improve their standard of living.

Starting in the 1980s, Turkey made changes. It removed trade barriers and became more active in importing and exporting goods. It cut the government's role in the economy and made it easier for private companies to form. As a result, the economy has grown rapidly in most recent years. People are more productive and enjoy higher incomes.

occupation, *n.,* job or profession

my worldgeography.com

Culture Close-up

A traditional crafts market in Istanbul ▼

Modern Istanbul's business district ▼

Turkey's Trade Partners

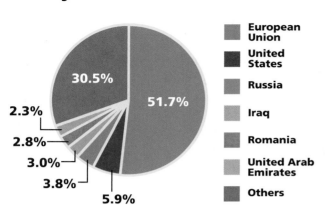

- 51.7% European Union
- 30.5%
- 2.3%
- 2.8%
- 3.0%
- 3.8%
- 5.9%

Legend:
- European Union
- United States
- Russia
- Iraq
- Romania
- United Arab Emirates
- Others

SOURCE: European Commission

A woman weaving a decorated textile in Turkey. Textiles are one of Turkey's major exports.

Chart Skills

1. Does Turkey trade more with Russia or the United Arab Emirates?

2. Based on this graph, do you think Turkey's economy is more closely tied to Europe or to Southwest Asia?

→ Data Discovery

myWorld Activity
To Join or Not
To Join

The European Union Turkey's government has attempted to join the European Union (EU). Turks who support this argue that it will improve the economy by allowing Turkey to trade more freely with Europe. But not all members of the EU are willing to admit Turkey. Some criticize Turkey's record on human rights, especially its treatment of Kurds and its role in Cyprus. Many Turks resent this criticism. Some fear that joining the EU will force Turkey to change its policies. Still, Turkey continues to move slowly towards EU membership.

Reading Check **Why do some EU nations object to admitting Turkey?**

Divided Cyprus

Conflict between Greeks and Turks has been a problem on Cyprus for decades.

Violence and Invasion Cyprus gained its independence from Great Britain in 1960. The new republic faced difficulties from the start. Many people in the Greek majority wanted Cyprus to become a part of Greece. Turkish Cypriots feared Greece would not protect their rights. They opposed unification. They also resented Greek domination of the government of Cyprus. Greeks and Turks fought bitterly.

Events came to a boil in 1974. At that time a dictatorship held power in Greece. It sponsored an attempt to overthrow the government of Cyprus so that the island would join with Greece.

In response, Turkey invaded the island and soon controlled its northern third. The Greek-dominated Republic of Cyprus held the rest. During and after the invasion, tens of thousands of Greek and Turkish Cypriots were forced from their

Divided Cyprus

KEY
- Greek Cypriot-administered area
- Turkish Cypriot-administered area
- British Sovereign Base Area
- United Nations buffer zone

Mediterranean Sea

TURKISH REPUBLIC OF NORTHERN CYPRUS
★ Nicosia

REPUBLIC OF CYPRUS

0 — 20 mi
0 — 20 km
Lambert Conformal Conic Projection

34° E
35° N
32° E
33° E

Mediterranean Sea

A border guard surveys Nicosia, the divided capital of Cyprus.

homes. About one third of all people in Cyprus were displaced.

Continuing Divisions In 1983, Turkish Cypriots declared independence. They formed the Turkish Republic of Northern Cyprus. Turkey is the only nation in the world that recognizes this government.

Turkish troops remain in the northern part of the island. UN peacekeepers patrol a buffer zone that separates the two parts of the island. Movement between them was closed off until 2003.

Many efforts have been made to reunite the island. These have not yet succeeded. In 2004, Turkish Cypriots voted in favor of a reunification plan, but Greek Cypriots voted against it. Cyprus joined the EU without the Turkish north.

Reading Check How is Cyprus divided?

Section 3 Assessment

Key Terms

1. What is the role of clerics in Iran's government?

2. What happens during a military coup?

Key Ideas

3. Is Iran's government an example of rule by many, by few, or a combination? Explain your answer.

4. Why was the AKP challenged in court, and what was the result?

5. What new economic policies did Turkey adopt in the 1980s?

Think Critically

6. **Analyze Cause and Effect** What has caused Iran's brain drain?

7. **Compare and Contrast** How do women's rights compare in Iran and Turkey?

Essential Question

What are the challenges of diversity?

8. What political conflict has arisen in Turkey as a result of different views about religion? Go to your Student Journal to record your answer.

Chapter Assessment

Key Terms and Ideas

1. **Summarize** How does the location of water resources affect settlement patterns in Iran, Turkey, and Cyprus?

2. **Compare and Contrast** How is Iran's government today different than the government before the Revolution of 1979?

3. **Recall** What resources are most important to Iran's economy?

4. **Describe** Has Iran's **brain drain** been good or bad for the country?

5. **Recall** List the majority ethnic and religious group in each of Iran, Turkey, and Cyprus.

6. **Describe** How did the founding of modern Turkey affect that country's laws and culture?

7. **Explain** Why is Cyprus divided and how did the division happen?

Think Critically

8. **Compare and Contrast** What are some aspects of Turkey's government that could be considered more democratic and less democratic?

9. **Make Inferences** Why might the United States and other countries be worried by Iran seeking nuclear weapons?

10. **Solve Problems** What did the Turkish government do in the 1980s to improve its economy?

11. **Core Concepts: Cultural Diffusion and Change** How did the ancient Persians and later Arab Muslims change the region's culture?

Places to Know

For each place, write the letter from the map that shows its location.

12. **Cyprus**
13. **Istanbul**
14. **Turkey**
15. **Iran**
16. **Tehran**
17. **Black Sea**
18. **Estimate** Using the scale, estimate the distance between Istanbul and Tehran.

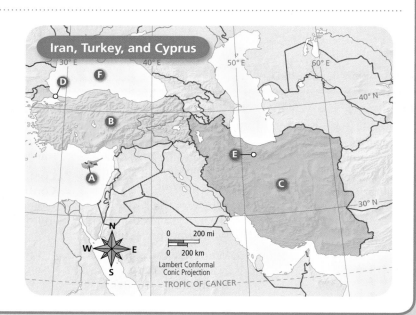

Iran, Turkey, and Cyprus

Lambert Conformal Conic Projection

TROPIC OF CANCER

Essential Question

What are the challenges of diversity?

Regional Ethnic Cooperation Conference
Suppose you represent either an ethnic group or a government in Turkey, Iran, or Cyprus. You will attend a United Nations conference to exchange ideas and present a plan of action for addressing common problems.

21st Century Learning

Solve Problems

Suppose you are working to help people in Cyprus end their conflict. Develop a list of questions you could ask people you meet in Cyprus. Focus your questions on helping those you interview to identify actions or changes in attitude that they feel would lead Greek and Turkish Cypriots to more effective efforts at peace.

Document-Based Question

Online at myworldgeography.com

Use your knowledge of Iran, Turkey, and Cyprus, as well as Documents A and B to answer Questions 1–3.

Document A

Individual Freedom		
Country	Individual Freedom Rank*	Government Type
Israel	29	Democracy
Turkey	61	Democracy
Iran	125	Theocracy
Saudi Arabia	130	Absolute monarchy

SOURCE: The State of World Liberty Project
* The freest country in the world is ranked 1.
  The least free is ranked 159.

Document B

" There are two countries in the Middle East that offer models for the future: the democratic Republic of Turkey and the Islamic Republic of Iran."

—Bernard Lewis,
Middle East historian

1. According to the table, which country provides its citizens with the least individual freedom?

   A Saudi Arabia

   B Iran

   C Turkey

   D Israel

2. Which statement best restates the views in Document B?

   A Turkey and Iran have similar governments.

   B Turkey is a theocracy and Iran is a monarchy.

   C Turkish democracy and Iranian theocracy are two paths other countries might follow.

   D Iran gives citizens more freedom than Turkey.

3. **Writing Task** Write a paragraph comparing the governments of Iran, Turkey, and one other country in Southwest Asia that you have studied.

my worldgeography.com | Self-Test

Sharing the Wealth:

How the Oil Rich Can Help the Oil Poor

Your Mission Divide into at least two groups. Research and develop a proposal for ways that oil-rich countries can help oil-poor countries. Each group should listen to the other groups' proposals. Together, the groups then develop one proposal that everyone can accept.

Imagine a group of friends in which half the people receive very large allowances and the other half receive hardly any allowance at all. The friends who have money would be able to do activities and buy things that the others can't afford. Resentments might build up over time. Keeping friendships intact in such a group might be difficult.

Southwest Asia faces a similar situation. Several of the nations earn enormous wealth from exporting oil, while other nations in the region have much lower incomes. Because of this economic gap, the nations of this region develop at different rates. Such a situation could lead to instability in the region.

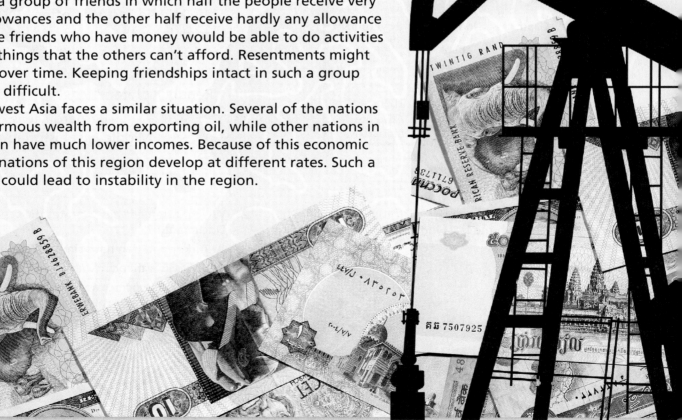

An oil refinery in
Saudi Arabia ▼

Oil Production: Jordan and Saudi Arabia

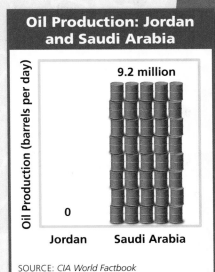

Oil Production (barrels per day)

9.2 million

0

Jordan   Saudi Arabia

SOURCE: *CIA World Factbook*

STEP 1

Research the Problem.

Identify which countries in Southwest Asia are oil-poor (OP) and which are oil-rich (OR). If your group represents an OP country, research the economic and social conditions there. Consider how an OP nation might expand existing resources or attract foreign investment. If your group represents an OR country, research how you might use your nation's advantages to help a neighbor with fewer resources. Discuss ways in which helping your neighbor will also benefit you.

STEP 2

Make a Decision.

After both groups have made their presentations, discuss the two sets of ideas. The research and the proposals from the two groups may not agree. However, before you reject a proposal entirely, think about how you might use certain elements and work them into a new solution that benefits both OP and OR nations. Remember that part of your task as a combined group is to come up with a compromise plan that both sides can accept. Discuss how to present the new proposal.

STEP 3

Present Your Ideas.

After you have finished your research and discussion, prepare a presentation with the new plan. Your presentation should explain your group's ideas about how OR countries can help OP countries. Use graphs, charts, photographs, maps, diagrams, and quotations to support your proposal. When you are ready to make your presentation, your teacher will pair OP representatives with OR representatives. The paired groups should then make their presentations to each other.

South and Central Asia

South and Central Asia are regions of grasslands, deserts, huge lakes, and mountains. The mountainous Himalayas dominate the area. Extremes of climate characterize these regions, with heavy monsoon rains in South Asia and desert climates in Central Asia.

What time is it there?

Washington, D.C.	Palampur, India
9 A.M. Monday	7:30 P.M. Monday

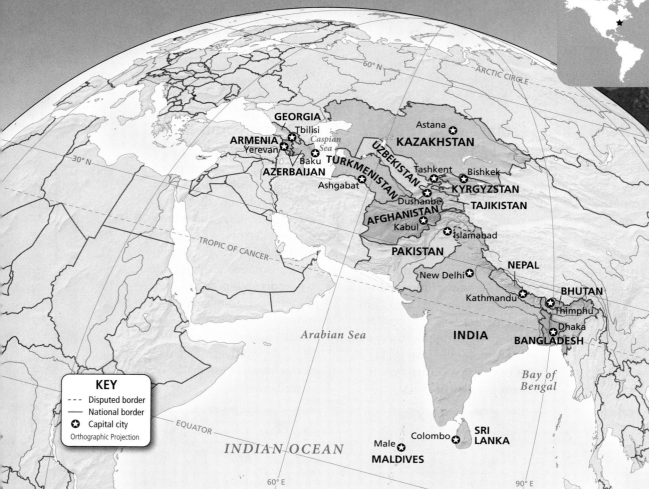

GEORGIA
Tbilisi
Caspian Sea
ARMENIA
Yerevan
Baku
AZERBAIJAN
TURKMENISTAN
Ashgabat
UZBEKISTAN
Tashkent
Astana
KAZAKHSTAN
Bishkek
KYRGYZSTAN
Dushanbe
TAJIKISTAN
AFGHANISTAN
Kabul
Islamabad
PAKISTAN
New Delhi
NEPAL
Kathmandu
BHUTAN
Thimphu
Dhaka
INDIA
BANGLADESH
Arabian Sea
Bay of Bengal
Colombo
SRI LANKA
Male
MALDIVES
INDIAN OCEAN

60° N
ARCTIC CIRCLE
30° N
TROPIC OF CANCER
EQUATOR
60° E
90° E
120° E

KEY
--- Disputed border
— National border
✪ Capital city
Orthographic Projection

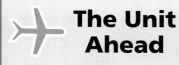

The Unit Ahead

➡️ **Chapter 19** Central Asia and the Caucasus

➡️ **Chapter 20** South Asia

my **worldgeography.com**

Plan your trip online by doing a Data Discovery Activity and watching the myStory Videos of the region's teens.

my Story

Askar

Age: 15

Home: Naryn, Kyrgyzstan

Chapter 19

my Story

Nancy

Age: 18

Home: Palampur, India

Chapter 20

View of the Himalayas

Applying for a loan at the bank

Nancy at work

need to make a down payment of 15 percent of the total cost of the project. The rest of the project will be financed by the bank. Loans for things such as seeds or fertilizer require a 7-percent down payment. The money involved may not seem like much by Western standards, but the average annual income in the region is only about $300 a year.

Nancy is proud to be involved in the process and excited about helping to set up a new plantation. The older women are glad to have Nancy in the group as well. They know she is high-spirited, hardworking, and intelligent.

Later, Nancy and her mother prepare for a week-long sales trip. They fill the sales van with their products and set off. Their first stop is just outside Palampur itself, but they will also travel to several other towns before returning home.

Nancy works hard to sell as much as she can. She knows that the money they make will not only help

pay for the new loan but also provide income for her family. Some of the money will be set aside to educate Nancy and her brother. "Right now I am planning to study computer science," Nancy says. "But if there is a chance for me to join the police then I will do that. I want to serve my country."

The Samriddhi has done more for this village than just make money; it has provided hope for the future. By working together to manage the land and grow a business, the Samriddhi has brought the community together. Sometime soon they hope to see fruit growing on the new plantation that Nancy and the microcredit loan help set up. That will be something for everyone to enjoy!

Meet the Journalist

Name Sachin Singh
Favorite Moment Watching Nancy climb trees to harvest the fruit

myStory Video

Join Nancy as she shows you more about her life.

Key Ideas
- Landforms and resources have influenced settlement in South Asia.
- People have adapted to a range of climates in South Asia.
- Physical geography plays a divisive role in South Asia.

Key Terms
- Indian subcontinent
- Green Revolution
- subsistence farming
- flood plain

 Visual Glossary

Reading Skill: Label an Outline Map Take notes using the outline map in your journal.

The Himalayas

Dancer in Rajasthan, India

Physical Features

Nancy lives in the highlands of Himalchal Pradesh (huh MAHL chul pruh DESH), which are part of the massive mountain range known as the Himalayas (hi muh LAY uz). The land to the south of the Himalayas is called the **Indian subcontinent.** In the distant past, the subcontinent was connected to Africa. Then around 90 million years ago, this huge chunk of land broke away and drifted to the northeast. As the landmass collided with Asia, pressure caused the ground to buckle up. This process created the Himalayas—the highest mountains on Earth.

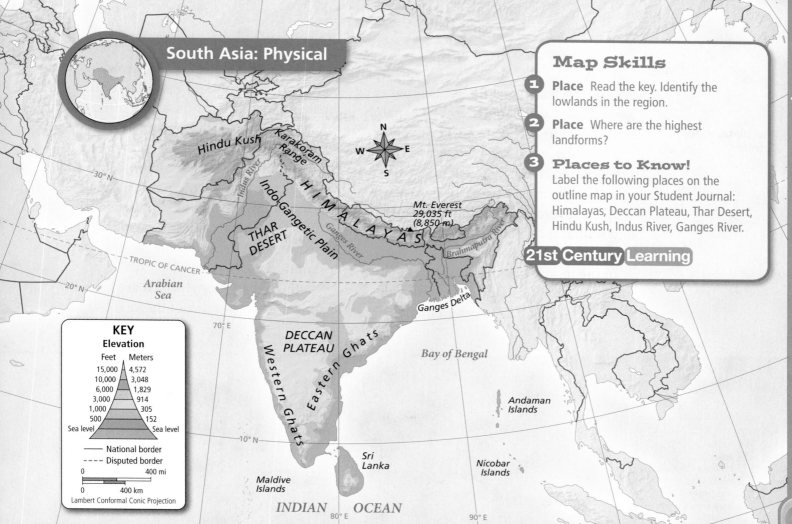

South Asia: Physical

Hindu Kush
Karakoram Range
Indus River
Indo-Gangetic Plain
THAR DESERT
H I M A L A Y A S
Ganges River
Mt. Everest 29,035 ft (8,850 m)
Brahmaputra River
Ganges Delta
DECCAN PLATEAU
Western Ghats
Eastern Ghats
Arabian Sea
TROPIC OF CANCER
30° N
20° N
70° E
10° N
80° E
90° E
Bay of Bengal
Andaman Islands
Nicobar Islands
Sri Lanka
Maldive Islands
INDIAN OCEAN

KEY
Elevation

Feet	Meters
15,000	4,572
10,000	3,048
6,000	1,829
3,000	914
1,000	305
500	152
Sea level	Sea level

—— National border
- - - Disputed border

0 ———— 400 mi
0 ———— 400 km
Lambert Conformal Conic Projection

Map Skills

1. **Place** Read the key. Identify the lowlands in the region.

2. **Place** Where are the highest landforms?

3. **Places to Know!** Label the following places on the outline map in your Student Journal: Himalayas, Deccan Plateau, Thar Desert, Hindu Kush, Indus River, Ganges River.

21st Century Learning

The Himalayas form India's northern border. They surround nearly all of Nepal and Bhutan. Smaller ranges, such as the Hindu Kush, extend this wall of mountains into western Pakistan and central Afghanistan.

Large rivers drain the melting snows of the mountains. To the south of the Himalayas, the Ganges (GAN jeez) River runs across India's northern plains and meets the Brahmaputra (brah muh POO truh) River in the heart of Bangladesh. In the west, the Indus River flows through the dry plains of Pakistan.

The southern part of South Asia is a peninsula that juts into the Indian Ocean. Much of this peninsula is a fairly flat highland area called the Deccan Plateau. It is bordered by two coastal mountain ranges known as the Western Ghats and the Eastern Ghats.

Off the southern tip of India lies the island nation of Sri Lanka. To the southwest are the Maldives, a chain of 1,190 islands formed from coral.

Reading Check What physical feature forms the northern border of India?

Climate

South Asia has many different climate zones. India and Bangladesh have mainly humid subtropical or tropical wet and dry climates. Daytime high temperatures can reach 80°F, even in the coolest months. The most intense heat, in May, can average more than 100°F. Arid and semiarid climates run through the countries of Afghanistan and Pakistan.

In the mountains of the west and far north, the high peaks are covered with snow year-round. Glaciers fill many valleys. But this area is not all snow and ice. The mountains and foothills contain fertile valleys, grasslands, and forests.

The Himalayas help to <u>regulate</u> the region's climate. They block much of the cold, dry air that would otherwise stream into South Asia from the north in winter. The mountains also draw moisture out of the warm, humid summer winds. The moisture falls as snow in the mountains and rain to the south.

South Asia's seasonal winds are known as monsoons. For most of the year the

regulate, v., to control

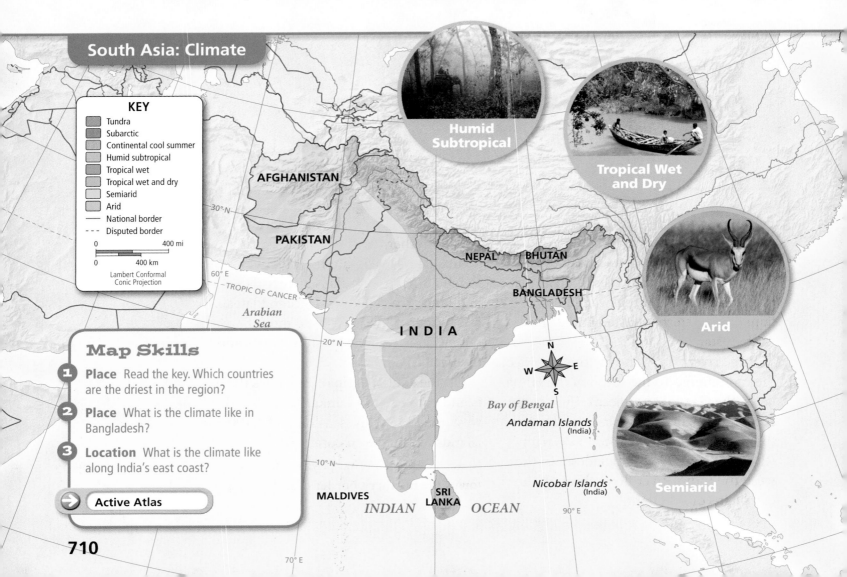

South Asia: Climate

KEY
- Tundra
- Subarctic
- Continental cool summer
- Humid subtropical
- Tropical wet
- Tropical wet and dry
- Semiarid
- Arid
- — National border
- --- Disputed border

0 — 400 mi
0 — 400 km
Lambert Conformal Conic Projection

AFGHANISTAN

PAKISTAN

30° N

60° E

TROPIC OF CANCER

Arabian Sea

NEPAL   BHUTAN

BANGLADESH

INDIA

20° N

Bay of Bengal

Andaman Islands (India)

N
W   E
S

10° N

Nicobar Islands (India)

MALDIVES

SRI LANKA

INDIAN OCEAN

90° E

70° E

Humid Subtropical

Tropical Wet and Dry

Arid

Semiarid

Map Skills

1. **Place** Read the key. Which countries are the driest in the region?

2. **Place** What is the climate like in Bangladesh?

3. **Location** What is the climate like along India's east coast?

→ Active Atlas

710

monsoon blows from the northeast and brings dry air. During the wet season, lasting from June to September, the southwest winds bring drenching rain.

The warm wind of the southwest monsoon picks up moisture from the Indian Ocean. It dumps heavy rain on India's western coast, the northern plains, and the northeast. On the west coast of India, the Western Ghats block this moisture, so the land to the east of the Ghats has a semiarid climate.

The southwest monsoon can bring <u>intense</u> storms and floods. In 1988, the flooding of the Ganges and other rivers washed away crops and livestock in Bangladesh and killed some 2,000 people. A quarter of the population was left homeless.

In Afghanistan, much of the land stays dry year-round. The southwest monsoon does not penetrate far into this area.

Reading Check **How do the mountains affect climate?**

intense, *adj.,* very strong

Closer Look

Climate and Culture

People in South Asia have adapted to their environments in many ways. Their houses are well suited to local climates.

THINK CRITICALLY Where on the climate map might you find each of these buildings? Study each house and read the description for clues.

This haveli, or mansion, was built for a rich merchant. Its balconies and screens allow breezes to pass through the house—a relief in the hot dry area where it was built.

This stilt house is well adapted to its lowland delta environment. It can easily withstand the seasonal floods, as long as they don't get too high!

Mud brick houses with flat roofs are a common sight in areas that do not get much rain.

In cold climates, farmhouses must shelter people, animals, and grain. In this house, grain and produce are kept in the attic. Farm animals are kept on the ground floor.

my worldgeography.com

Active Atlas

Land Use and Resources

Most South Asians work in agriculture. Farms tend to be rather small. Their owners engage mainly in **subsistence farming**, which means they use the crops they grow to feed themselves, but have little left over to send to market.

In the mid-1960s, technology created a **Green Revolution**, an increase in agricultural production. This produced more food for growing populations.

However, in some places, farmers overused chemical fertilizers and pesticides. They pumped too much water out of the ground to irrigate crops. Farming practices like these poisoned the soil, fouled rivers, and dried up wells.

The region is also rich in resources. Rivers provide hydroelectric power. Mines in the plateaus and mountains produce iron ore, bauxite, copper, and coal. Petroleum and natural gas are found in the plateaus and mountains, as well as offshore. These resources support manufacturing in India and Pakistan.

Reading Check Why are rivers an important resource?

◀ A farmworker sprays pesticides on his rice fields.

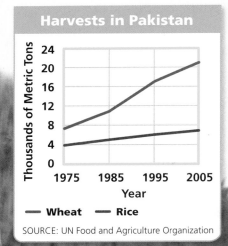

Harvests in Pakistan

Thousands of Metric Tons

— Wheat — Rice

SOURCE: UN Food and Agriculture Organization

Land Use Issues
in South Asia

The Green Revolution has helped feed South Asia's growing population. However, new research shows that the use of pesticides is causing medical problems among local people.

Chart Skills

Which crop produces more?

→ Data Discovery

Population Explosion

South Asia suffers from two related problems: high population growth and poverty. Nearly half the world's poor live in this region.

The size of South Asia's population is one of the main problems. The region contains three of the ten most populous countries in the world—India, Pakistan, and Bangladesh. Just meeting people's basic needs—food, clothing, and shelter—is a monumental task.

About half of South Asia's population is located on the Indo-Gangetic plain, in the valleys of the Ganges and Brahmaputra rivers. Most of the people of this region live in rural areas.

India, for example, is only 29 percent urban, but its urban population has grown steadily. Much of this increase is made up of rural families moving to cities to improve their lives. Many Indian migrants, however, are forced to live in urban slums or on the streets.

Reading Check **Which countries are the most populous in the region?**

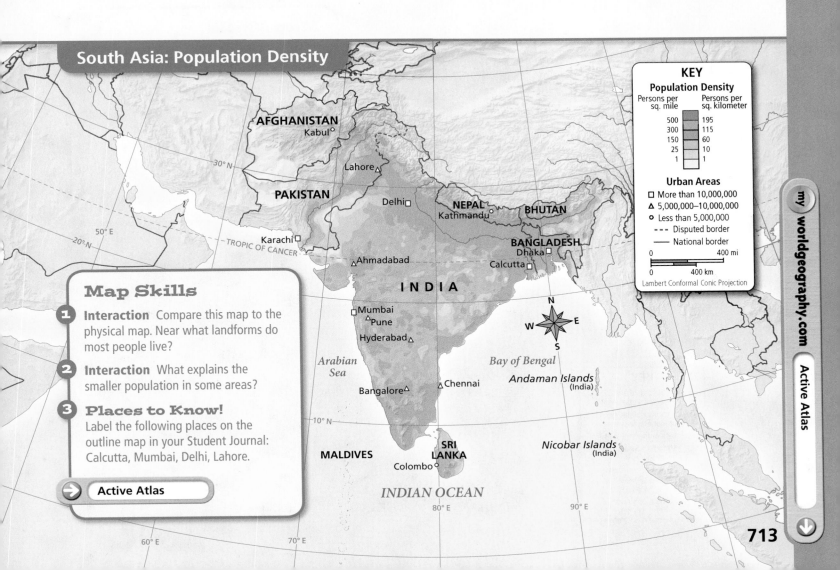

South Asia: Population Density

KEY
Population Density

Persons per sq. mile	Persons per sq. kilometer
500	195
300	115
150	60
25	10
1	1

Urban Areas
- ☐ More than 10,000,000
- △ 5,000,000–10,000,000
- ○ Less than 5,000,000
- --- Disputed border
- — National border

0   400 mi
0   400 km
Lambert Conformal Conic Projection

Map Skills

1 **Interaction** Compare this map to the physical map. Near what landforms do most people live?

2 **Interaction** What explains the smaller population in some areas?

3 **Places to Know!**
Label the following places on the outline map in your Student Journal: Calcutta, Mumbai, Delhi, Lahore.

→ Active Atlas

my worldgeography.com Active Atlas

Geography Shapes History

Since prehistoric times, people have migrated to the rich **flood plains**—the flat lands along the rivers. When snows melt in the mountains, rich soil is washed down onto the lowlands of the Indo-Gangetic plain. This fertile plain attracted early settlers. In time, civilization developed and rich cities arose.

The wealth of the cities attracted invaders. Although the Himalayas were too high for armies to cross, newcomers found their way into the subcontinent through mountain gorges such as the famous Khyber Pass.

Other landforms continue to shape the region's history. For example, the mountain landscapes of Afghanistan and Pakistan have always isolated communities. In both countries, fiercely independent tribes have long resisted government interference in their affairs. Today, governments struggle with rebel forces in these same tribal areas.

Reading Check How did invaders reach the rich lowlands of India?

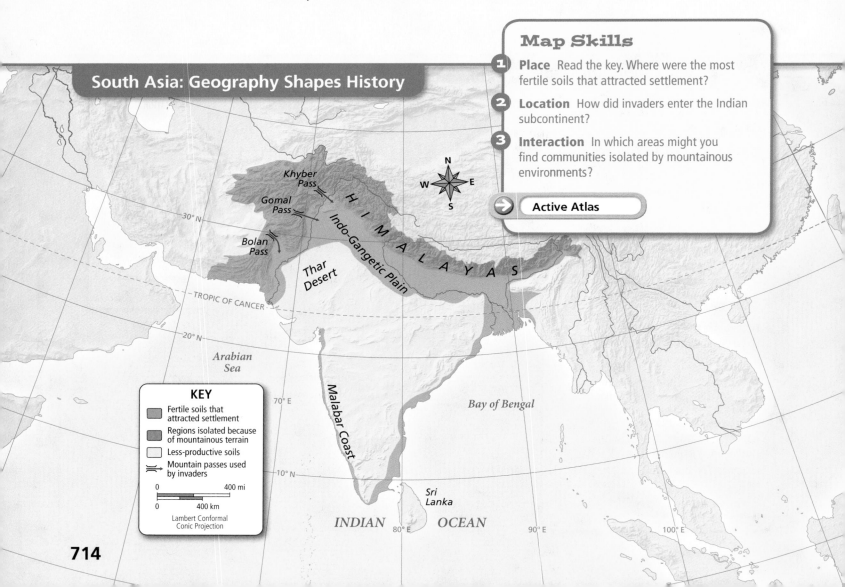

South Asia: Geography Shapes History

Khyber Pass

Gomal Pass

Bolan Pass

HIMALAYAS

Indo-Gangetic Plain

Thar Desert

30° N

TROPIC OF CANCER

20° N

Arabian Sea

Malabar Coast

Bay of Bengal

70° E

10° N

Sri Lanka

INDIAN OCEAN

80° E

90° E

100° E

KEY
- Fertile soils that attracted settlement
- Regions isolated because of mountainous terrain
- Less-productive soils
- Mountain passes used by invaders

0 — 400 mi
0 — 400 km

Lambert Conformal Conic Projection

Map Skills

1. **Place** Read the key. Where were the most fertile soils that attracted settlement?

2. **Location** How did invaders enter the Indian subcontinent?

3. **Interaction** In which areas might you find communities isolated by mountainous environments?

→ **Active Atlas**

Crossroads of Culture

While some parts of South Asia were isolated by mountains, other areas have always been in contact with the wider world. Goods and ideas traveled from China to Europe along the Silk Road, which passed through northern Afghanistan. Farther south, India lay at the center of the international sea trade routes.

These trade routes brought immense wealth to the region. Indian cotton, pearls, and pepper from the Malabar coast were in worldwide demand. Sri Lanka exported cinnamon. Ancient Greek traders used the monsoon winds to sail quickly across the Arabian Sea to reach these goods. Merchants from distant lands sometimes settled in the trading ports. Meanwhile, South Asian merchants helped spread the religions and culture of South Asia to China and Southeast Asia.

As you have read, the Himalayas did not stop invaders from entering the region. Some of these invaders came to raid and others to conquer. Each set of newcomers changed the history of the Indian subcontinent. In turn, these newcomers were changed by the regions they invaded. A cultural exchange began that continues today.

The Muslim invasions brought the religion of Islam to South Asia. They also brought cultural influences from Persia and the Arab world.

Despite much peaceful cultural interaction, growing diversity also created tensions. This is a region of multiple faiths, ethnic groups, and languages. At times the tension between different groups has led to violence. However, the people of South Asia have also enjoyed periods of religious tolerance and cultural exchange. In the next section you will read how a complex and rich civilization developed in this crossroads of culture.

Reading Check How did the region become a crossroads of culture?

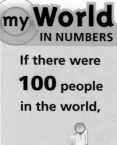

my World
IN NUMBERS

If there were **100** people in the world,

17 would live in India.

Section 1 Assessment

Key Terms

1. Use the following terms to describe the geography of South Asia: Indian subcontinent, subsistence farming, Green Revolution, flood plain.

Key Ideas

2. Identify three roles that the northern mountains play in South Asia's geography.

3. What is the southwest monsoon, and how does it affect South Asia?

4. Where are the most fertile farmlands in South Asia located?

Think Critically

5. **Categorize** Some people categorize South Asia as a hot and humid region. Is that accurate? Explain.

6. **Draw Conclusions** Why are the river valleys among the most densely populated areas of South Asia?

? Essential Question

What makes a nation?

7. How does the geography of a nation help create a common bond among its people and help shape its national identity? Go to your Student Journal to record your answer.

History of South Asia

Key Ideas
- A series of migrations mark the history of South Asia.
- Religious diversity developed early and increased over time.
- Britain slowly gained political control of most of the region.
- After India gained independence, new nations and conflicts emerged.

Key Terms
- cultural hearth
- Buddhism
- caste system
- partition
- Hinduism
- nonalignment
- nirvana

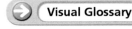 Visual Glossary

Reading Skill: Analyze Cause and Effect Take notes using the graphic organizer in your journal.

◀ A dancing Shiva, Hindu god of creation and destruction

In ancient times, an advanced civilization developed in the Indus River Valley, in what is now Pakistan. Cities such as Mohenjo Daro and Harappa were amazingly sophisticated and well planned. Brick houses, two to three stories high, lined streets laid out on a grid pattern. The people of these cities had plumbing and clean water. They used a writing system and traded with other parts of the world.

Early History

Indus Valley civilization developed around 2500 B.C. and lasted for almost a thousand years. Its cities were spread over a huge area in the fertile Indus River basin. Here, as in other parts of the world, resources attracted settlement. Farmers in the fertile Indus flood plain grew wheat, barley, rice, cotton, and other crops. Traders set up networks to exchange goods. Soon Indus Valley products, goods, and ideas reached people in less-advanced areas. In this way, the Indus Valley served as a **cultural hearth**—a place where civilization began and spread.

Around 1900 B.C., the Indus Valley civilization went into a mysterious decline. Some believe that earthquakes or climate change may

◀ Jain temples on Mount Girnar, a mountain that attracts Jain, Hindu, and Muslim pilgrims

have disrupted the food supply. But even though its cities collapsed and were abandoned, aspects of its culture survived.

A Culture Forms Around 1700 B.C., a massive migration changed the history of the region. Migrants entered the subcontinent through the mountain passes. They spread across the northern plains of the Indus and the Ganges. The newcomers blended with local peoples, forming a group we call Aryans (AYR ee unz). Out of this union came a new culture, religion, and social system.

Social Divisions The Aryan **caste system** divided society into four main groups: priests, warriors, farmers, and laborers. Priests formed the highest caste. Those in the lowest caste were scorned and considered unclean.

Reading Check **What is the caste system?**

New Religions

In South Asia the Aryans' faith merged with local beliefs. The result was **Hinduism,** the religion of most people in India today.

Hindu Beliefs The sacred texts of Hinduism are called the Vedas, a collection of hymns and instructions. The Vedic texts may date to about 1200 B.C. Later, between the years 300 B.C. and A.D. 300, great poems, known as epics, were also composed. The *Mahabharata* is the world's longest epic poem. It deals with a conflict between royal cousins.

Hindus believe in one spirit that lives in all things. In Hindu belief, this spirit, called Brahman, also takes the form of

▲ Hindu procession in Mumbai

lesser gods and goddesses. More than thirty gods are mentioned in the Rig Veda hymns.

Another principle of Hinduism is the idea that the human soul is eternal. According to Hindus, when the body dies, the soul passes into a new body. This process, known as reincarnation, can occur again and again, in an endless cycle. For believers, reincarnation is also affected by karma, the collection of good and bad deeds of a person's life. Karma determines the kind of life that will follow when the soul has been reborn.

To escape this cycle of rebirth many became ascetics—people who give up the luxuries of the world in order to try to live a spiritual life. The goal of the ascetic was to achieve salvation by uniting the individual soul with the universal soul, the Brahman.

Buddhism The Hindu search for salvation encouraged the development of a new religion. In the 500s B.C., a man named Siddhartha Gautama (sih DAHR tuh gow TUH muh) taught that all suffering is caused by desire. In other words, human beings become unhappy when they cannot get what they want. In order to overcome desire, people must follow a code of conduct. According to Gautama, their goal should be to achieve **nirvana,** a state of understanding that releases the soul from the cycle of rebirth.

Gautama became known as the Buddha, or Enlightened One. His teachings developed into a religion known as **Buddhism.** Traders and Buddhist monks spread this new religion throughout Asia.

Another religion, Jainism, also emerged in South Asia. The followers of Jainism, called Jains, believed that the soul can be perfected and purified in this world. One of the ways to reach this perfection is to practice ahimsa, or nonviolence toward all living beings.

Reading Check **According to Buddhist teachings, what makes people unhappy?**

Early Empires

In 327 B.C., the kingdoms of South Asia were threatened by Greek armies under Alexander the Great.

The Greek Invasion Alexander, king of Macedon, had built a huge empire over Greece and parts of Africa and Asia. His Greek army fought their way into the northern Indus Valley. Alexander's army was exhausted. Faced with a long march across the Ganges plain in monsoon rains, the soldiers forced Alexander to head home.

Shortly after Alexander's retreat, one South Asian state took control of much of the region. That state became known as the Mauryan empire. Its most famous leader was Asoka (uh SOH kuh).

Religious Tolerance Asoka led several campaigns against his enemies in the first dozen years of his reign. But after one especially brutal battle he rejected violence and adopted Buddhist beliefs. Under Asoka, Buddhism spread through the Mauryan empire.

Not long after Asoka's death, the Mauryan empire declined and smaller kingdoms arose once more. Then, around A.D. 320, a state located on the Ganges plain expanded its power to form the Gupta empire. This empire ruled territory

The Mauryan Empire

Indus R.
Ganges R.
Pataliputra ⊛
30° N
20° N
Arabian Sea
60° E
70° E
Bay of Bengal
10° N
90° E

KEY

Mauryan empire, 250 B.C.
Present-day border

0   600 mi
0   600 km
Lambert Conformal
Conic Projection

Map Skills

1 **Interaction** Look back at the maps in Section 1. What factors might explain the location of the Mauryan capital?

2 **Place** What modern nations occupy land that was once part of the Mauryan empire?

➔ Active Atlas

from the Himalayas south to the Deccan Plateau. The two centuries of Gupta rule were a golden age of culture. Great advances were also made in science and mathematics. Gupta mathematicians developed the concept of zero. By A.D. 600, Indians were using a system of numbering that uses place value and numerals to represent numbers. Arab traders carried this system to Southwest Asia and Europe. Today, this system, called the Hindu-Arabic system, is used worldwide.

Reading Check Which South Asian religion did Asoka embrace?

Islam Arrives

Because India was such an important part of the international trade routes, new ideas and religions were spread by travelers and merchants. This is how Islam first entered the subcontinent.

Trade and Conquest Islam arrived in India in waves. The first came in the early 700s, when Arab traders introduced Islam to South Asia. The new faith spread throughout what is now Pakistan. Then, in the 900s, Turkish Muslim kingdoms began to spread through Afghanistan. Afghan kings launched raids into India to seize the wealth that was stored in the Hindu temples.

In the 1200s, one group of Muslim invaders established the Delhi Sultanate. This was a kingdom centered on the city of Delhi and led by a Muslim ruler called a sultan. Muslims would rule much of South Asia for the next 600 years. However, Hindu rajas, or rulers, controlled kingdoms in south India.

The arrival of Islam in a mainly Hindu region changed the history of South Asia. Hindus and Muslims were often rivals. Despite religious differences, there was a great deal of cultural exchange.

As Islam spread in the north, a new religion called Sikhism was born. Most followers of this religion, the Sikhs, live in an area of north India called the Punjab.

The Mughals In 1526, a Muslim from Central Asia named Babur founded the powerful Mughal empire. His grandson, Akbar, was a wise and tolerant ruler. Akbar extended Mughal control over much of South Asia. Akbar included Hindus in his army and government and protected other religions. He supported the arts and learning.

Muslim worshipers at a mosque in Lahore, Pakistan ▼

worldgeography.com

Active Atlas

has also signed trade agreements with other countries in South Asia. Trade has helped give India one of the world's fastest-growing economies. Today, about 100 million Indians can afford goods like televisions and washing machines.

In the 1990s, the government began building software technology parks. Here, workers create computer software for worldwide export.

India is also providing software services to companies all over the world. For example, companies in Europe and the United States have found it cheaper to send many computer-related tasks to workers outside the company. This practice is called **outsourcing.** India's economy and its skilled workforce have benefited from this practice.

India has put its high-tech skills to work in another area—space. The country has launched many satellites into orbit around Earth for many nations. In 2008,

India successfully landed a space probe on the moon.

▲ India has a highly skilled technology workforce.

Reading Check In which South Asian country do citizens have the most democratic freedoms?

my **worldgeography.com** Data Discovery

Section 3 Assessment

? **Essential Question**

Key Terms

1. Use the following terms to describe life in South Asia today: epic, Bollywood, secular democracy, outsourcing.

Key Ideas

2. What are the two most commonly practiced religions in South Asia?

3. Why is Kashmir one of the main trouble spots in South Asia?

4. What actions by India's government opened up trade with the rest of the world?

Think Critically

5. **Draw Inferences** What is the connection between dense population, poverty, and environmental problems?

6. **Summarize** How is India's economy tied to the world economy?

What makes a nation?

7. What problems threaten the national unity of each nation in South Asia? Go to your Student Journal to record your answer.

Chapter Assessment

Key Terms and Ideas

1. **Recall** What areas in South Asia have good soil and why?

2. **Describe** What benefits has the **Green Revolution** brought to South Asia?

3. **Recall** What religions first emerged in South Asia?

4. **Explain** Why did **partition** take place in India?

5. **Describe** What problems are caused by South Asia's growing population?

6. **Compare and Contrast** What is the difference between the **secular democracy** of India and the Islamic republics of Pakistan and Afghanistan?

7. **Summarize** What are some hopeful signs of economic growth in South Asia?

Think Critically

8. **Draw Conclusions** Why are some areas of South Asia more populated than others?

9. **Synthesize** What factors help slow economic growth in South Asia?

10. **Compare Viewpoints** Why did Gandhi want the British to leave India?

11. **Core Concepts: Human–Environment Interaction** How does South Asia's population growth affect the environment?

Places to Know

For each place, write the letter from the map that shows its location.

12. **Ganges River**

13. **Kabul**

14. **Himalayas**

15. **Lahore**

16. **Indus River**

17. **Sri Lanka**

18. **Estimate** Using the scale, estimate the distance between Kabul and Lahore.

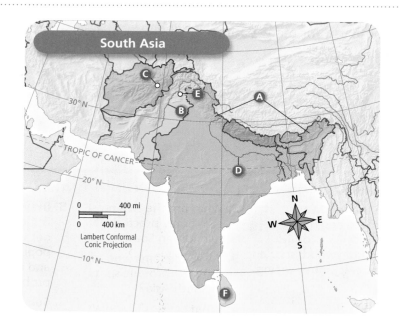

Essential Question

myWorld Chapter Activity

Microloan Assessment Follow your teacher's instructions to study the countries of South Asia in order to recommend a microloan to a group in need. Discuss your findings and decide who should get the loan. Then write a proposal that includes your reasons for granting the loan.

21st Century Learning

Search for Information on the Internet

With a partner, search for sites that give information on the economies of South Asia today. You may want to select three countries before you begin your search. Then do a Web search about each country's trade, manufacturing, exports, and so on.

Document-Based Questions

Success Tracker™
Online at myworldgeography.com

Use your knowledge of South Asia and Documents A and B to answer Questions 1–3.

Document A

Arable Land	
Country	**Arable Land**
Pakistan	24.44%
India	48.33%
Afghanistan	12.13%

SOURCE: *CIA World Factbook*

Document B

" India has become a key market for many information communication technology products made in the U.S., while the U.S. is an important consumer of Indian [information technology]-enabled services."

—U.S. State Department

1. Which of the following best describes the information about the three countries shown in Document A?

   A Afghanistan has the highest percentage of land that can be farmed.

   B Pakistan has less farmland than Afghanistan.

   C India has the highest percentage of farmland.

   D Afghanistan has more farmland than Pakistan.

2. Which of the following best describes the meaning of the quote in Document B?

   A India buys products made in South Asia.

   B India and the United States have an important economic relationship.

   C The United States does not use Indian products.

   D The United States buys Indian products.

3. **Writing Task** Compare the economic strengths of India and Pakistan, using Documents A and B.

Getting to the Truth:
Fact or *Opinion?*

Your Mission In groups, research Web sites for information on one South or Central Asian nation. As you read, look for examples of facts and opinions and develop a presentation evaluating the Web sites you have visited.

When researching on the Internet, it is important to be able to evaluate the reliability of Web sites. One way to do this is to be able to distinguish between facts and opinions. Facts are claims that can be confirmed by evidence.

Opinions are claims that cannot be confirmed by evidence, even if you agree with them. Your friend may say that basketball is better than baseball, but that claim cannot be confirmed by evidence as it is merely your friend's opinion.

Web sites can present facts, opinions, or both. When researching, learn to spot the differences by evaluating the evidence that is presented to support any claims.

It's raining.

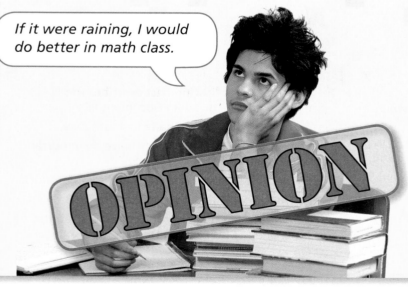

If it were raining, I would do better in math class.

STEP 1

Break It Down.

First, break down the different elements of your group's task. You will investigate information about your nation in order to make a presentation. As you do so, note where you find information. Then, check another site for the same data and note any discrepancies. For example, India's population figures might differ between two sites. Why might this be? As you research, look for clues to whether or not the Web site is reliable and the data on it are based on fact or based on opinion.

STEP 2

Look for Clues.

Think about the purpose of the Web site. Consider how the site functions. Is it easy to use? Look for the author of the site and how often the site is updated. Also, try to determine if the site has any affiliations. Some sites share content or republish content without reviewing it. Errors may be transferred from site to site in this way. As you read, you should also be aware that Web sites may have certain points of view and are designed to reinforce certain attitudes.

STEP 3

What's the Truth Factor?

Focus your group's presentation on the reliability of the information you found on the sites you visited. As you present your nation's data, discuss what the data mean as well as any conflicting information you discovered. Read aloud at least one quote from each of the news Web sites you visited. Point out specific word clues that led you to believe the quote was fact or opinion. Also, discuss your overall impression of the reliability of the content on these sites.

East and Southeast Asia

East and Southeast Asia are regions of rugged mountains, vast plains, dense forests, and crowded coastlines. These regions are heavily populated. The largest country in these regions is China, which has more inhabitants than any other country on Earth.

What time is it there?

Washington, D.C.	**Wuxi, China**
9 A.M. Monday	10 P.M. Monday

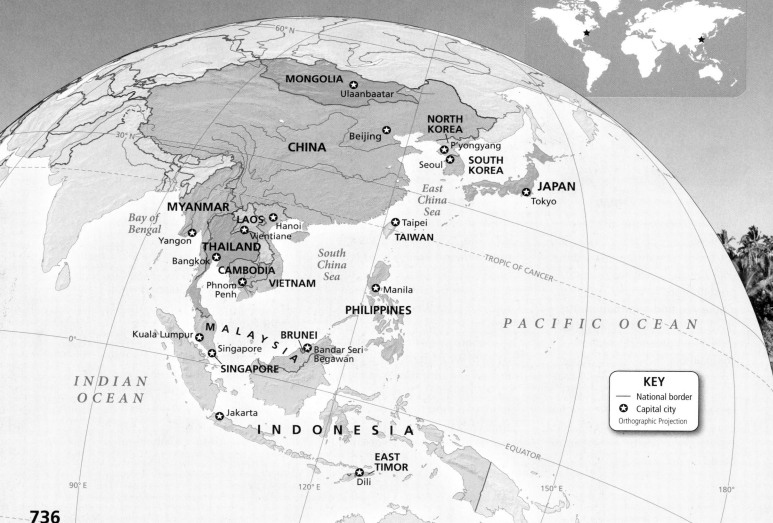

MONGOLIA
Ulaanbaatar

CHINA
Beijing

NORTH KOREA
P'yongyang
Seoul
SOUTH KOREA

JAPAN
Tokyo

East China Sea

MYANMAR
Bay of Bengal
Yangon

LAOS
Hanoi
Vientiane

THAILAND
Bangkok

CAMBODIA
Phnom Penh
VIETNAM

Taipei
TAIWAN

South China Sea

Manila

PHILIPPINES

TROPIC OF CANCER

PACIFIC OCEAN

Kuala Lumpur
MALAYSIA
BRUNEI
Bandar Seri Begawan
Singapore
SINGAPORE

INDIAN OCEAN

Jakarta

INDONESIA

EQUATOR

EAST TIMOR
Dili

90° E   120° E   150° E   180°

60° N
30° N
0°

KEY
— National border
✪ Capital city
Orthographic Projection

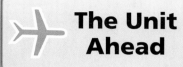

The Unit Ahead

➡ **Chapter 21** China and Its Neighbors

➡ **Chapter 22** Japan and the Koreas

➡ **Chapter 23** Southeast Asia

my **worldgeography.com**

Plan your trip online by doing a Data Discovery Activity and watching the myStory Videos of the region's teens.

my Story

Xiao

Age: 18

Home: Wuxi, China

Chapter 21

my Story

Asuka

Age: 18

Home: Yokohama, Japan

Chapter 22

my Story

Ridwan

Age: 19

Home: Bukittinggi, Indonesia

Chapter 23

Rice fields in Bali, Indonesia

Regional Overview
Physical Geography

T i a n   S h a n
Taklimakan Desert
Kunlun Shan

G o b i

Plateau of Tibet
Mt. Everest
29,035 ft (8,850 m)

H i m a l a y a s

Huang (Yellow) River

North
China Plain

Chang (Yangtze) River

The Himalayas are one of
the many mountain ranges
in East Asia.

Malay Peninsula

Gulf of
Thailand

South China Sea

INDIAN
OCEAN

Java Sea

Active volcanoes lie throughout
the islands of Southeast Asia.

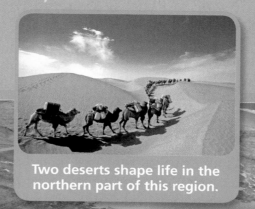

Two deserts shape life in the northern part of this region.

Manchurian Plain

Korean Peninsula *Sea of Japan (East Sea)*

Philippine Sea

Mountains give way to plains in China and, on a smaller scale, in Taiwan, the Koreas, and Japan.

P A C I F I C   O C E A N

Regional Flyover

Beginning your flight in the west, you enter China's airspace high above the Himalayas. Then, you face the high Plateau of Tibet.

To the north of this plateau lie two vast deserts, the Gobi and the Taklimakan. As you fly north over the Gobi Desert, you come to Mongolia, a dry land of deserts, plateaus, and mountains.

Circling south from Mongolia, along the eastern coast of Asia, you see a mountainous peninsula, home to North and South Korea. As you continue south the climate becomes warmer, and soon your eyes glimpse the tropical forests of Vietnam, Laos, Thailand, Cambodia, and the island nations of Malaysia, Singapore, Indonesia, East Timor, Brunei, and the Philippines. As the plane turns north, you pass over the small island nation of Taiwan. When you reach Japan, count the countries you have seen—17!

my worldgeography.com **In-Flight Movie**

 In-Flight Movie

Take flight over East Asia and Southeast Asia and explore the regions from the air.

Regional Overview
Human Geography

Downtown Tokyo is lit up brightly every night.

Where People Live

East and Southeast Asia's physical features have influenced where people in the region live. Many nations in these regions do not have much land that is good for farming or settlement. Not very many people live in the rugged mountains and dry deserts. The dry climate in the north of these regions is particularly challenging. Even in the south, where water is more plentiful, there are many hills and very little land that is flat enough to farm.

As a result, the huge population of these regions is packed into the areas where life is easier—on the plains and along rivers and flat coastal areas. Japan, the Koreas, and many of the nations of Southeast Asia have forested mountains running through their centers, so in those countries people live mainly in valleys and in coastal cities. China and Mongolia both have large plains where people can farm or raise livestock.

This map shows where people live in East and Southeast Asia.

The lights in this satellite photo show electricity use in heavily populated areas of East and Southeast Asia.

MONGOLIA

NORTH KOREA

JAPAN

SOUTH KOREA

CHINA

TAIWAN

MYANMAR

LAOS

VIETNAM

THAILAND

CAMBODIA

PHILIPPINES

PACIFIC OCEAN

BRUNEI

MALAYSIA

SINGAPORE

INDIAN OCEAN

INDONESIA

EAST TIMOR

KEY
· 100,000 people

my World IN NUMBERS

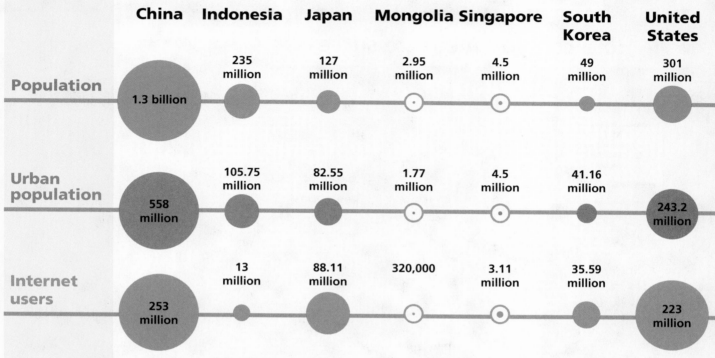

	China	Indonesia	Japan	Mongolia	Singapore	South Korea	United States
Population	1.3 billion	235 million	127 million	2.95 million	4.5 million	49 million	301 million
Urban population	558 million	105.75 million	82.55 million	1.77 million	4.5 million	41.16 million	243.2 million
Internet users	253 million	13 million	88.11 million	320,000	3.11 million	35.59 million	223 million

SOURCE: *CIA World Factbook, Encyclopaedia Britannica*

Put It Together

1. What physical features prevent western China from being heavily settled?

2. Where do many of the rivers in China and Southeast Asia begin?

3. Compare the number of Internet users to the number of urban dwellers. Which country has more Internet users than urban residents?

 Data Discovery

Find your own data to make a regional data table.

Size Comparison

East and Southeast Asia are more than twice as large as the United States but have 7 times the population.

my worldgeography.com Data Discovery

Chapter 21

China and Its Neighbors

How can you measure success?

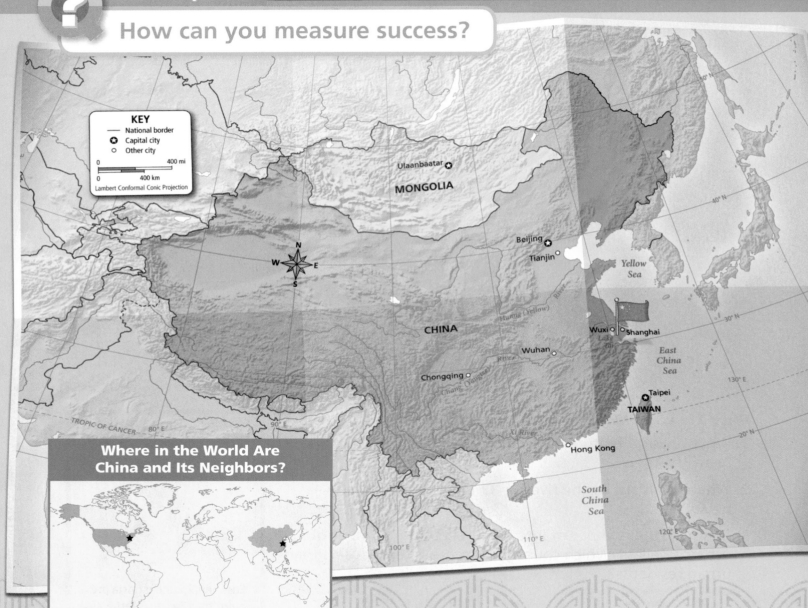

KEY
— National border
✪ Capital city
○ Other city

0 ___ 400 mi
0 ___ 400 km
Lambert Conformal Conic Projection

Ulaanbaatar ✪

MONGOLIA

Beijing ✪
Tianjin ○

CHINA

Huang (Yellow) River

Wuxi ○ ○ Shanghai
Lake Tai

Wuhan ○

Chongqing ○

Chang (Yangtze) River

Xi River

Hong Kong ○

✪ Taipei
TAIWAN

Yellow Sea

East China Sea

South China Sea

TROPIC OF CANCER — 80° E

90° E

100° E

110° E

120° E

130° E

20° N

30° N

40° N

Where in the World Are China and Its Neighbors?

Washington, D.C., to Wuxi: 7,440 miles

my Story

Xiao's Lake

Explore the Essential Question

- at **my worldgeography.com**
- using the **myWorld Chapter Activity**
- with the **Student Journal**

In this section you'll read about Xiao, a young man helping to care for his family. He lives in eastern China. What does his story tell you about the challenges China faces?

Story by Megan Shank for myWorld Online

Xiao lives with his father, mother, grandmother, and older brother in a tiny village near Wuxi (woo shee), an ancient city in the east of China. After learning of his father's diabetes diagnosis, 17-year-old Xiao found a full-time job to help support his family.

Xiao (whose name is pronounced show, as in *shower*) and his brother both work at a factory that produces machines that make ice cream. His mother works at a different factory and tends the family's orange and peach orchard. His father is a part-time driver.

Every morning at 7 A.M., Xiao rides his motorcycle to Wuxi. There are many factories in this area. They have easy access to railways and canals that transport goods to large cities, such as Shanghai. Xiao works 10 hours a day, five days a week. Many local youth leave to make their fortunes, but Xiao wants to stay close to his family.

Life has changed as China has become wealthier. Meat used to be too expensive to eat every day. Thirty years ago, few people could afford a television. Now, most families in Xiao's village own one.

Xiao rides home from work.

my **worldgeography.com** On Assignment

A street in Xiao's village

Xiao's mother prepares dinner in a large wok.

Xiao's family shares these dishes at dinner.

Xiao's mother applies pesticides to the orange trees in the family orchard.

Unlike his parents' generation, which suffered famine and shortages of many goods, Xiao doesn't remember a time when food was scarce.

He does remember when the waters of Lake Tai were clean and clear. Lake Tai is China's third-largest body of fresh water. It is just a five-minute jaunt from Xiao's house. As a boy, he learned to swim there. He collected snails in the lake and had mud fights with friends.

Walking through the family's fruit orchard, it's hard to imagine this place ever smelled like anything other than sun-ripened oranges. Yet in the summer of 2007 a terrible odor crept from the lake across the orchard and into their home.

An algae bloom covered the lake with green slime. The algae bloom was caused, in part, by pollution and pesticides from the farms and factories around the lake. The algae used up the oxygen in the lake. Suffocated fish floated to the surface, belly up.

"You didn't even want to use the water to bathe, much less to drink," says Xiao.

Thirty million people rely on Lake Tai for drinking water. That summer, families in Xiao's village avoided the lake water. They drew water from local wells or bought bottles of water. Bottled water was rushed to Wuxi during the crisis.

Xiao's family shut the windows and put up with the stench. Flies and mosquitoes swarmed.

A factory by the lake is torn down.

Algae and trash float on this small pond near Xiao's home.

Small ponds where neighbors had once washed their fruit and rinsed their rice filled with algae and muck. People started to throw their garbage into these pools, as well.

"If the environment is better, people behave better," says Xiao. "When there's pollution, people throw their garbage where they shouldn't."

The city of Wuxi has started to solve the problem. They hired people to remove the algae. They have also shut down some factories around the lake to reduce the pollution.

Towns are also being bulldozed. Citizens in the village next to Xiao's village were forced to move when the government claimed the area for a park. Xiao has never lived anywhere else and worries the government will make his family move, too.

He has mixed feelings about his parent's use of pesticides and fertilizers in their orchard. He knows these chemicals run off into the lake and cause

more harm. He also knows that the factory where he works may be adding to the pollution. Still, Xiao needs his job. He hopes to save money, marry, and start a family—preferably, he says, by the time he's 23— so there are no easy answers.

"How can you choose between your family and your home?"

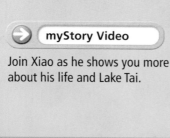

Meet the Videographer

Name Carl Thelin

Favorite Moment Eating dinner with Xiao's family

▶ **myStory Video**

Join Xiao as he shows you more about his life and Lake Tai.

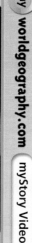

The Communist Party is still important in Mongolia. Candidates from this party have won many elections. Now, though, this party competes with other parties for control of the government.

The new constitution also protects certain freedoms, such as religious freedom. In the past, the communists did not allow people to worship freely. Now, many people are again practicing Buddhism and other religions.

Democracy Grows in Taiwan After China's civil war, Jiang Jieshi left China and set up a government in Taiwan. He created a **single-party state,** that is, a country in which one political party controls the government. Jiang's Nationalist Party controlled the government. In the 1980s, some Taiwanese people began to push the government to become more open.

Finally in 1989, the Nationalists allowed other parties to take part in elections. Like the communists in Mongolia, the Nationalists Party is still important in Taiwan. Now, though, the Taiwanese can choose from more than one party when they vote.

Limited Freedom in China China's leaders have not made major political changes. It continues to be a single-party state. The Chinese Communist Party (CCP) controls the government.

The CCP no longer controls the economy. It does control peoples' lives in other ways. For example, China does not have freedom of the press. That is, journalists are not free to report the news

as they see it. The CCP also blocks many Web sites. Chinese people do not have <u>access</u> to all information on the Internet.

Chinese people also do not have freedom of speech. The government may imprison people who say or do things to oppose the government.

In 1989, tens of thousands of people gathered in Tiananmen Square (tyen ahn mun skwehr) in Beijing. They called for more freedom and changes to the government. They refused to leave the square. China's leaders sent in tanks and troops to break up the demonstration. Thousands of people were killed or wounded.

The government refused to make any of the changes that the protesters had demanded. The freedoms of the Chinese people remain very limited.

Reading Check Is Taiwan a single-party state today?

access, *n.,* ability to be used

Political and Economic Systems: China and Its Neighbors

	China	Taiwan	Mongolia
Political Parties	Single-party system	Several parties	Several parties
Elections	Few elections, very limited	Open elections	Open elections
Freedoms	Freedoms limited by government	Religious freedom, freedom of the press	Religious freedom, freedom of the press
Economic System	Market system	Market system	Market system

Chart Skills

How is China different from Taiwan and Mongolia? How are all three countries similar?

Data Discovery

my worldgeography.com Data Discovery

The skyscaper Taipei 101 towers over Taiwan's capital. ▼

Economic Growth: The Importance of Exports

Trade is important for the economies of all three countries in this region. Taiwan and China have had rapid economic growth. Mongolia struggles to strengthen its economy.

Taiwan: An Asian Tiger Taiwan has been called an "Asian Tiger" because for decades its economy had strong growth. In the mid-1900s, Taiwan began to manufacture more goods. At the time, many people still worked on farms. The country was relatively poor.

People were paid a low **wage,** that is, their pay was low. Factories paid their workers less than factories paid in wealthier countries. As a result, factories in Taiwan could make their products more cheaply. Other countries were happy to buy Taiwan's cheaper goods. Soon, the country was exporting goods. Its economy began to grow quickly.

As money from exports came into the country, Taiwanese people became wealthier and wages increased. The price of making goods in Taiwan went up.

The Taiwanese economy continued to grow even as wages went up. One reason is because the government improved the education system. Better education helped Taiwan to produce new, technologically advanced products, such as chemicals, medicines, and electronics. Taiwan now exports these complex, expensive products. By making this change, the economy continued to grow.

Mongolia's Mineral Resources Early in the 1990s, Mongolia changed to a market economy. This change was difficult. In the past, the Soviet Union gave Mongolia economic support. Mongolia struggled without this help.

Wages are not high in Mongolia, but transportation is difficult. This increased the cost of making goods in Mongolia. The country is landlocked. This means it has no coastline. Moving goods long distances across land is more expensive than shipping them the same distance by sea.

Railroads connect Mongolia to Russia and China. Now, China is one of Mongolia's major trading partners. Mongolia's main exports are its mineral resources. In addition, raising livestock is still important to Mongolia's economy.

With the market economy, Mongolia's economy has grown. More Mongolians now have cellphones and access to the Internet. Still, many people remain poor. The country has not had the strong growth of Taiwan and China.

China's Economic Miracle China's economic reforms began much earlier than Mongolia's. In the late 1970s, the Chinese government told farmers in some areas that they did not have to follow the government's economic plan. The farmers could decide what they wanted to grow. They could sell their harvest and keep the profits. Some farmers figured out how to use their land more efficiently than the government plan. They produced more than before.

Because these farmers were successful, the government expanded the policy. Farmers across the country could make their own decisions. The government also let more people start private businesses. Slowly, the government gave up the command economy.

As with Taiwan, trade became important to China's economic growth. Wages in China continue to be relatively low. Companies make their products cheaply and sell them abroad.

The Chinese government also encouraged foreign companies to come to China. These companies had money to build new factories. Most of these factories are along China's long coastline. Here, it is easy for companies to ship their goods around the world. The companies need many workers. People have moved to coastal cities to find jobs in these factories. Shenzhen is one coastal city where many factories have been built. In 1980, it was a town of 30,000 people. By 2006 it had become a city of more than 8 million people!

Now, China's economy is one of the largest in the world. Toys, clothing, and many other goods sold in the United States are made in China.

Reading Check **Why is trade more difficult for Mongolia?**

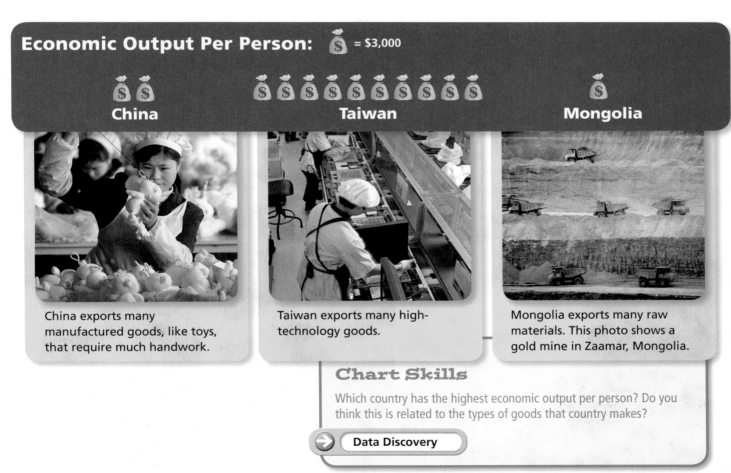

Economic Output Per Person: 💰 = $3,000

China 💰💰

Taiwan 💰💰💰💰💰💰💰💰💰💰

Mongolia 💰

China exports many manufactured goods, like toys, that require much handwork.

Taiwan exports many high-technology goods.

Mongolia exports many raw materials. This photo shows a gold mine in Zaamar, Mongolia.

Chart Skills

Which country has the highest economic output per person? Do you think this is related to the types of goods that country makes?

→ Data Discovery

my worldgeography.com Data Discovery

A More Unequal Society

The economic growth in China has made many people wealthier. Now, more families can afford products such as televisions, refrigerators, and even cars. Still, some people have <u>benefited</u> from this new wealth more than others have.

benefit, *v.,* to help, be of service to

Greater Wealth in the East Trade has helped bring growth to coastal cities. Many factories are located along the south and east coasts. This area produces 60% of the nation's industrial output.

Areas in the west and center of China face many of the same challenges as Mongolia. Companies far from the coast find it expensive to transport their goods. In recent years, the Chinese government has tried to increase investment in the west and center of China. Still, growth there lags behind eastern China.

Many Rural Areas Struggle Many rural communities have also faced difficulties. Under the command economy, the national government provided some services to rural areas. They sent doctors to rural areas to give everyone basic medical care. The **life expectancy,** that is, the number of years that people live on average, rose rapidly.

Now, individuals or local governments often must pay for these services. Less wealthy areas struggle to pay the costs of basic services. For example, some villages do not have enough money to have their own school. Parents, then, have to pay to send their children to a school in a different town. Some parents cannot afford these fees. Children from rural areas are less likely than those from urban areas to go to college and get higher-paying jobs.

Many villages in rural China cannot afford to have their own school. Five small villages share this primary school. Mr. Dai teaches all classes at the school.

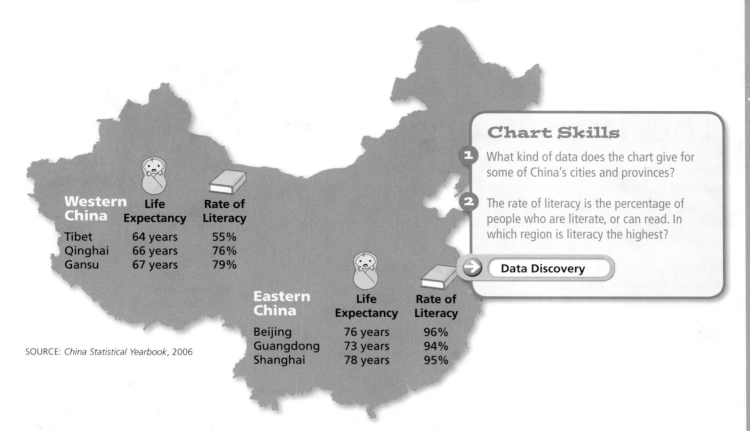

Western China	Life Expectancy	Rate of Literacy
Tibet	64 years	55%
Qinghai	66 years	76%
Gansu	67 years	79%

SOURCE: *China Statistical Yearbook*, 2006

Eastern China	Life Expectancy	Rate of Literacy
Beijing	76 years	96%
Guangdong	73 years	94%
Shanghai	78 years	95%

Chart Skills

1 What kind of data does the chart give for some of China's cities and provinces?

2 The rate of literacy is the percentage of people who are literate, or can read. In which region is literacy the highest?

→ **Data Discovery**

The Floating Population Because there are fewer opportunities for education and employment in rural areas, millions of people have been moving to cities.

These migrants are known as the "floating population." It is estimated at over 140 million people, or one tenth of China's total population. That is nearly half the population of the United States.

This floating population is moving illegally. The Chinese government has a rule allowing people to live only where they are registered, usually their birthplace. The government limits new registration in cities. Migrants who work in a city without registration often cannot receive healthcare or other government services. This is another challenge for people from rural areas as they try to improve life for their families.

Opportunities for Women Traditionally, couples live with the husband's family. The son takes care of his parents as they grow older. Therefore, many parents want to have at least one son.

The one-child policy changes this situation. If a couple has a daughter, they cannot have a son. They will help their daughter to be as successful as possible. Now, many daughters support their elderly parents.

Still, parents who have more than one child may send their son to school and keep their daughter at home to work. More women than men are **illiterate,** that is, more women than men do not know how to read. Women still do not have equal education and job opportunities.

Reading Check Why are migrant workers described as a floating population?

The Three Gorges Dam

China's huge Three Gorges Dam produces clean electricity. This helps the country meet its growing need for energy. In addition to producing energy, the project created thousands of jobs. It also changed the landscape along the Chang River. A 400-mile-long resevoir now extends behind the dam.

THINK CRITICALLY **Examine the diagram below. What are the benefits and drawbacks of building the dam?**

▲ **Relocation**
More than a million people had to move because their homes were covered by the reservoir.

◄ **Lost History**
The rising waters of the reservoir covered many historic sites along the river.

The dam can hold back high waters and help control flooding along the river.

Turbines in the dam produce electricity.

myWorldActivity
Three Gorges Dam

Newly built locks make transport along the river easier.

Environmental Challenges

As the Chinese economy has grown, pollution has become a major problem. China also uses many resources to feed, clothe, and house its large population.

Facing Environmental Problems Chinese cities have some of the worst air pollution in the world. Millions of cars, buses, and coal-burning electricity plants contribute to the smog around Chinese cities.

Water pollution is also a serious problem. Factories and farms dump dangerous chemicals into rivers and lakes near cities. Lake Tai near Xiao's home is one of many lakes affected by this issue.

Drier areas in the north and west are struggling with shortages of water. Factories, farms, and citizens compete to use this limited resource. At times, the Huang River dries up before reaching the sea. The land around Beijing is so dry that sandstorms blow into the city.

China has laws to limit pollution, but local governments do not want to punish polluters too harshly. People would lose their jobs if factories closed down.

Searching for Energy In the past, China could produce all the energy it needed. Now, more energy is needed to run its many new businesses. China has started importing oil. Also, it has been building more coal-burning power plants.

Burning oil and coal makes China's air pollution even worse, so China is looking for cleaner forms of energy. In western China, wind power produces electricity. The Chinese government also built the Three Gorges Dam along the Chang River to produces **hydroelectricity** (hy droh ee lek TRIH suh tee), or electricity made by water power. Building this dam was disruptive and expensive. China's leaders have to balance these costs with the need for new sources of energy.

Reading Check What kinds of environmental challenges does China face?

my Story **Photo**

Xiao, like many Chinese people, boils his water to make it safe to drink.

Section 3 Assessment

Essential Question

How can you measure success?

Key Terms

1. What is a single-party state?

2. What is illiteracy?

Key Ideas

3. Compare and Contrast How has reform been different in China and Mongolia?

4. What is one problem that China faces, and how might China solve it?

Thinking Critically

5. Analyze Cause and Effect What effect does geography have on Mongolia's economic growth?

6. What is one way that China has been successful? Give evidence from the text and from figures to support your point. Go to your Student Journal to record your answer.

Chapter Assessment

Key Terms and Ideas

1. **Discuss** Why are people migrating from villages to cities in China?

2. **Summarize** How has the government of China helped and hurt China's minority groups?

3. **Compare and Contrast** How are men and women treated differently in China?

4. **Explain** What are the important beliefs of Confucianism and Daoism?

5. **Recall** What are some of the main physical features of China?

6. **Compare and Contrast** How do a command economy and a market economy differ?

7. **Describe** How and when did the Mongols conquer China?

Think Critically

8. **Problem Solving** What are some causes of air and water pollution in China? How could you lower pollution in China without forcing many people out of work?

9. **Identify Evidence** What might explain why China's population density is higher than Mongolia's?

10. **Draw Conclusions** Why is it easier for a country to export its goods if wages are low?

11. **Core Concepts: Economics** What three basic questions do economists ask when studying economies? How have the answers to these questions changed for China?

Places to Know

For each place, write the letter from the map that shows its location.

12. **Beijing**

13. **Chang River**

14. **Huang River**

15. **Mongolia**

16. **Shanghai**

17. **Taiwan**

18. **Estimate** Using the scale, estimate the distance between Beijing and Shanghai.

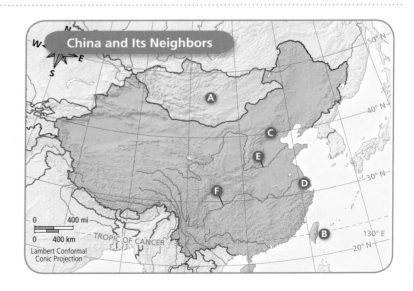

China and Its Neighbors

A Changing China: Who Benefits the Most?
Gather data about the changes taking place in China. Answer the question *How do these changes affect different people in different ways?* Organize your findings and write a report to an economic leader.

21st Century Learning

Evaluating Web Sites

Search for three different Web sites that give information on the Three Gorges Dam. Examine each site and answer the following questions. Create a table to record your answers.
- Who is the source of the information?
- How up-to-date is the information?
- Does the information seem accurate?
- Is the information easy to understand?

Document-Based Questions

Success Tracker™
Online at myworldgeography.com

Use your knowledge of the region and Documents A and B to answer Questions 1–3.

Document A

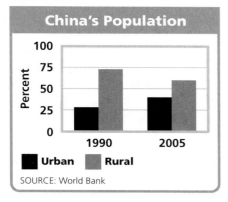

China's Population

SOURCE: World Bank

Document B

" There are no social benefits—all I get is my salary. Hands stop, mouth stops. If I get sick, I just have to keep my eyes open and sit here."

—a migrant worker in urban China

1. Which of the following might explain the change seen in Document A?

   A better health care in rural areas

   B better schools in rural areas

   C better-paying jobs in urban areas

   D natural disasters in urban areas

2. Which of the following best describes the worker quoted in Document B?

   A a member of the "floating population"

   B a person who was born in a big city and has health benefits

   C a government official in a city

   D a farmer in western China

3. **Writing Task** Do you think the situation described in Document B is common? Explain your answer.

Chapter 22

Japan and the Koreas

Essential Question

How much does geography shape a country?

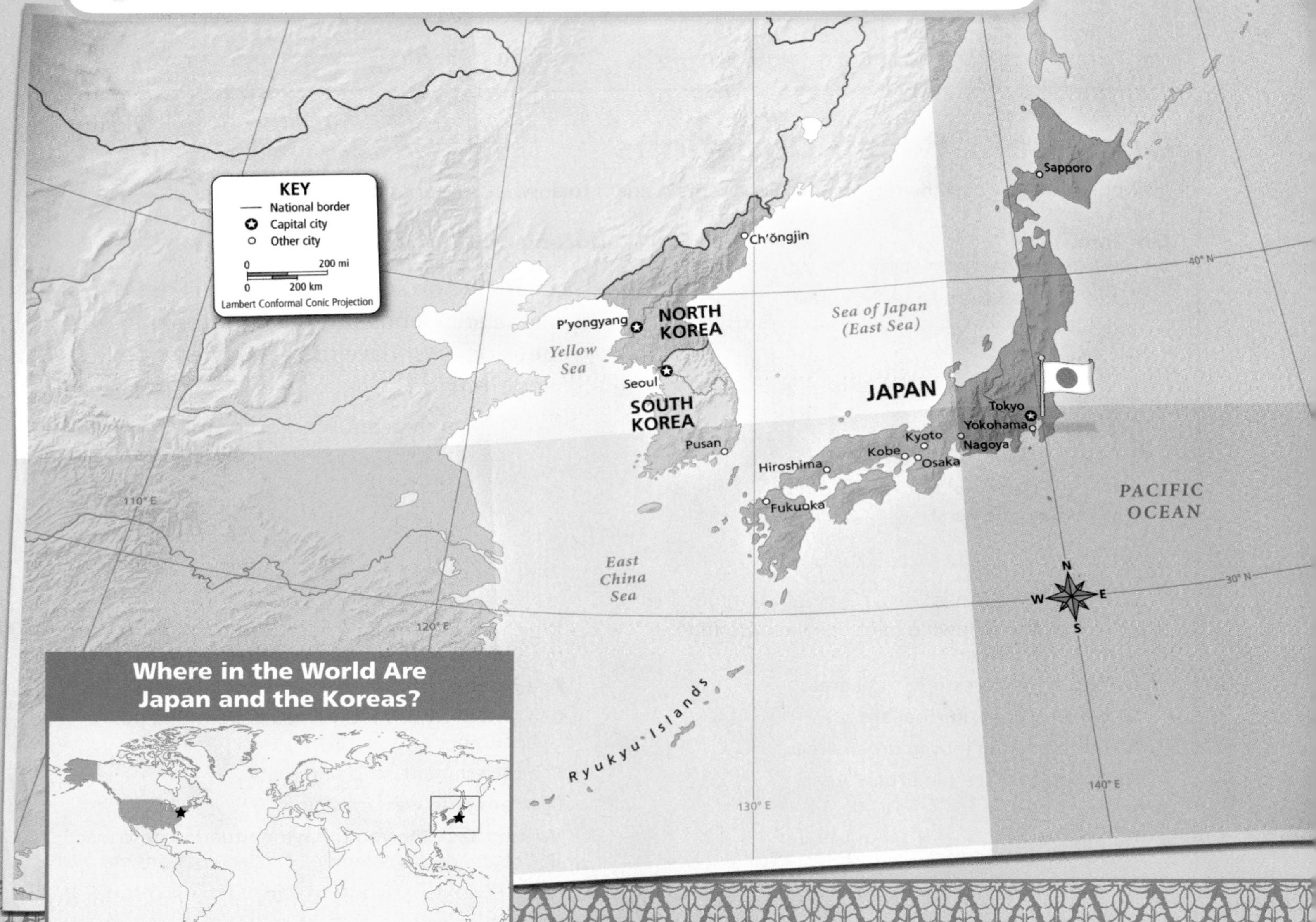

KEY
— National border
✪ Capital city
○ Other city

0   200 mi
0   200 km
Lambert Conformal Conic Projection

Sapporo

Ch'ŏngjin

P'yongyang ✪ **NORTH KOREA**

Yellow Sea

Seoul ✪

SOUTH KOREA

Pusan

Sea of Japan (East Sea)

JAPAN

Tokyo ✪
Yokohama
Kyoto
Kobe
Osaka
Nagoya

Hiroshima

Fukuoka

40° N

30° N

East China Sea

PACIFIC OCEAN

N W E S

Ryukyu Islands

110° E
120° E
130° E
140° E

Where in the World Are Japan and the Koreas?

Washington, D.C., to Tokyo: 6,770 miles

my Story

Asuka: A Girl on the Go

? Explore the Essential Question

- at my worldgeography.com
- using the **myWorld Chapter Activity**
- with the Student Journal

*In this section you'll read about Asuka. She is a senior in high school and lives with her family in Yokohama, Japan. Life has not been easy for Asuka, but that has not stopped her from wanting to make the world a better place to live. **What does Asuka's story tell you about the challenges young people face living in Japan?***

Story by Michael Condon for MyWorld Geography Online

In the bamboo- and -concrete-covered hills of Yokohama, a cluster of identical apartment blocks stands out. The drab, box-shaped buildings have numbers stenciled onto the top of their walls to identify them. On the third floor of one of the apartment buildings, in a small apartment no bigger than an average American living room, lives Asuka. The third-year high school student shares the apartment with her father, her grandmother, her 15-year-old brother, the family's pet turtle, and Max, a pet rabbit.

More than 35 million people live in the Greater Tokyo-Yokohama metropolitan area. This is almost twice as many people as live in Greater New York. With so many people needing housing, space is scarce. Most people live in small apartments. About 2,500 people live in this four-block square area of Yokohama. It is very crowded, and the cost of living in Yokohama is high.

Asuka's grandmother serving dinner in a small kitchen

A crowded bedroom and study area

Standing room only on the train to school

For a single-parent family, it can be a struggle to make ends meet. Asuka's family moved to Yokohama after her parents divorced. She was three years old. To support the family, her father took a job as a salesman in the construction industry. With money short, Asuka also helps out by working up to 20 hours a week after school. She gives one third of her wages to the family and uses the rest to pay her other expenses.

Though her family does not have a lot of money, the 18-year-old high school senior considers herself fortunate. Every day she wakes up at 6:30 A.M., grabs the "bento" lunch box her grandmother has prepared, and heads off to school. She attends a high school in the middle of Yokohama, where she studies international affairs. Her curriculum is demanding. It includes courses in world history, politics, economics, Japanese, English, and Korean.

Asuka has developed a keen interest in politics, economics, and history. She plans to major in these subjects when she goes to college. Asuka thinks it is important to study politics and history because they explain how various countries have developed and the way their governments work. With that knowledge, she believes, "We can improve the living conditions of people and make things better."

A Glocally field trip

Class is just about to begin.

Asuka is a high-energy person. In addition to her studies and her job, she takes part in extracurricular activities. These activities range from volunteer work to playing drums in a rock band. Asuka is also the leader of the school's "Glocally" Club. (The club's name is a combination of the words "global" and "locally.") As part of the club's activities, the students go on field trips to observe war ruins. They also learn how wars affect people and look for ways to achieve peace in the modern world.

The teacher in charge of the club has introduced the students to some serious issues that are far from the minds of the average high school student in most developed countries. Asuka is glad he challenges them to think about real-world issues.

Over the last couple of years, Asuka has also taken part in the Yokohama Student Forum. Last year she became a student leader and put together a forum on child labor—an issue that touches the lives of families across Asia.

Asuka appreciates all the opportunities she has had. "I have [led] a privileged life," she says, "while others are suffering elsewhere." After graduating from college, Asuka says she wants to do something to help others less privileged.

Judging by what she has achieved so far, the promising young student will be sure to put her talents to good use in the future.

myStory Video

Join Asuka as she shows you about her life in Yokohama.

Meet the Journalist

Name Heath Cozens
Favorite Moment My favorite memory was Asuka doing karaoke.

Chapter Atlas

Key Ideas

- Mountains cover much of this region.
- A dense population requires careful use of resources.
- People have adapted to sudden natural disasters.

Key Terms • foliage   • scarcity   • comparative advantage   • interdependent   **Visual Glossary**

 Reading Skill: Label an Outline Map Take notes using the outline map in your journal.

A hiker at the base of Mt. Fuji in Japan ▼

Physical Features

Japan, at the far eastern edge of Asia, is sometimes called the "land of the rising sun." The Japanese see each day's sunrise before most parts of Asia. North and South Korea lie just to the west of Japan.

Japan is a 1,500-mile-long chain of islands made up of four large islands and about 3,000 smaller islands. The countries of North and South Korea together form the Korean peninsula.

Four tectonic plates are close to Japan and the Koreas. The plates are slowly moving together. The result is

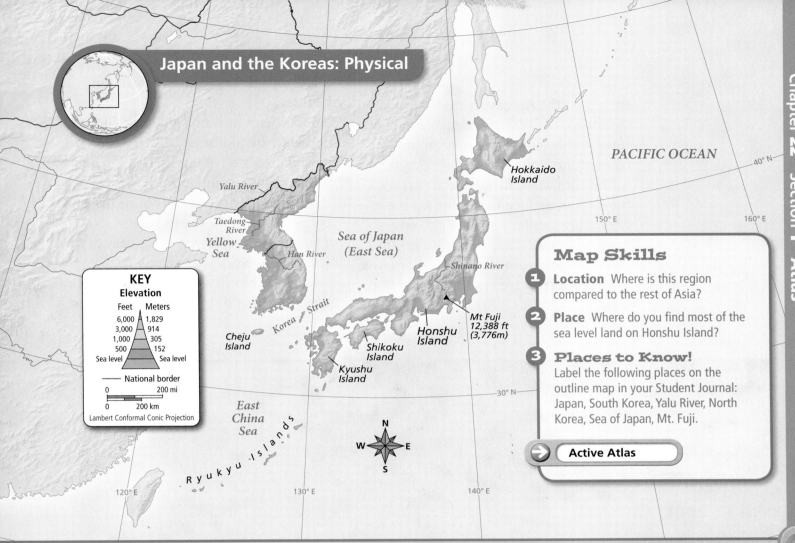

Japan and the Koreas: Physical

PACIFIC OCEAN

Hokkaido Island

40° N

Yalu River

150° E   160° E

Taedong River

Sea of Japan (East Sea)

Yellow Sea

Han River

Shinano River

KEY
Elevation

Feet	Meters
6,000	1,829
3,000	914
1,000	305
500	152
Sea level	Sea level

— National border

0   200 mi
0   200 km

Lambert Conformal Conic Projection

Korea Strait

Cheju Island

Honshu Island

Mt Fuji 12,388 ft (3,776m)

Shikoku Island

Kyushu Island

30° N

East China Sea

Ryukyu Islands

120° E   130° E   140° E

N W E S

Map Skills

1 **Location** Where is this region compared to the rest of Asia?

2 **Place** Where do you find most of the sea level land on Honshu Island?

3 **Places to Know!**
Label the following places on the outline map in your Student Journal: Japan, South Korea, Yalu River, North Korea, Sea of Japan, Mt. Fuji.

→ **Active Atlas**

great pressure that causes earthquakes. Earthquakes that <u>occur</u> under the sea can make huge waves that slam into the towns along the shore. As the Pacific Plate sinks beneath Japan, it melts and is called molten rock. The molten rock then rises to Earth's surface, creating volcanic eruptions. Japan has 108 active volcanoes.

Both North Korea and South Korea are mountainous countries. In both countries, there are a wide coastal plain in the west and smaller plains in the east. South Korea has more flat land suitable for farming than North Korea.

Japan is more rugged than the Koreas. Mountains and hills cover about 70 percent of the country's surface. In Japan and the Koreas, most people live in the valleys and coastal plains. In Japan, the largest level area is on Honshu Island.

The mountains in these countries are popular sites for hiking. Mount Fuji, the highest peak in Japan, is particularly popular. The mountain is a volcano, but it has not erupted for centuries. Thousands of people climb Mount Fuji every year.

Reading Check Why are there earthquakes and volcanoes in Japan and the Koreas?

occur, *v.,* to take place; to happen

my **worldgeography.com** **Active Atlas**

Climate

Japan and the Koreas are mid-latitude countries. The seasonal range of temperatures in this region is similar to the east coast of the United States.

The climate of the northern parts of the Korean peninsula and the Japanese islands are similar to New England and New York State. They have cool summers and long, cold winters. In the fall, Japan's northern forests are bright with red and yellow foliage. **Foliage** is the leaves on the trees.

The southern part of Japan has a climate more like the southeast coastal region of the United States. Winters are mild, and summers are hot and humid.

During the winter, winds blow from central Asia into Korea and across the Sea of Japan. These cold winds are very dry, especially in North Korea.

About three fifths of North Korea's rain falls from June to September. By contrast,

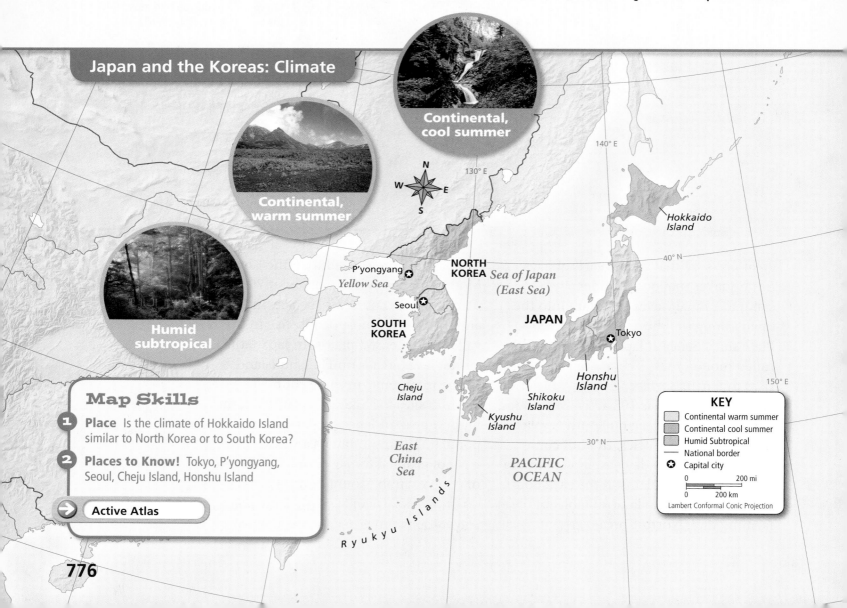

Japan and the Koreas: Climate

Continental, cool summer

Continental, warm summer

Humid subtropical

P'yongyang

Yellow Sea

Seoul

NORTH KOREA

SOUTH KOREA

Sea of Japan (East Sea)

JAPAN

Tokyo

Hokkaido Island

Honshu Island

Shikoku Island

Kyushu Island

Cheju Island

East China Sea

PACIFIC OCEAN

Ryukyu Islands

140° E

130° E

40° N

150° E

30° N

KEY
- Continental warm summer
- Continental cool summer
- Humid Subtropical
- National border
- ⊛ Capital city

0   200 mi
0   200 km

Lambert Conformal Conic Projection

Map Skills

1 **Place** Is the climate of Hokkaido Island similar to North Korea or to South Korea?

2 **Places to Know!** Tokyo, P'yongyang, Seoul, Cheju Island, Honshu Island

→ Active Atlas

the sea brings some moisture all year to South Korea and Japan.

Summer seasonal winds, or monsoons, can drop as much as 80 inches of rainfall a year. They sometimes bring powerful tropical cyclones or hurricanes. In this part of the world, these storms are referred to as typhoons. Because of the warm, moist air, summers are humid in this region.

After a dry winter, the Koreas may experience a spring drought. The heavy summer rains that follow these droughts can cause flooding and mudslides. When this happens, houses are buried, and farmers may lose their crops.

Summer monsoon rainfall supports lush forests. As a result, most of the uplands of Japan and the Koreas are wooded. Particularly in Japan, people have worked hard to preserve their forests. It is one of the few industrialized countries that is heavily forested.

Reading Check **Why are wind patterns important to climate in this region?**

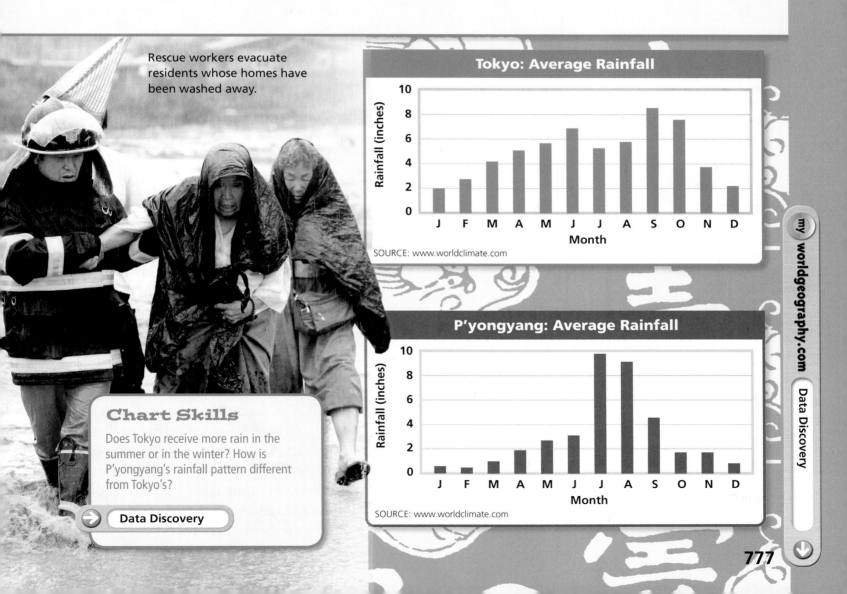

Rescue workers evacuate residents whose homes have been washed away.

Tokyo: Average Rainfall

SOURCE: www.worldclimate.com

P'yongyang: Average Rainfall

SOURCE: www.worldclimate.com

Chart Skills

Does Tokyo receive more rain in the summer or in the winter? How is P'yongyang's rainfall pattern different from Tokyo's?

→ **Data Discovery**

my **worldgeography.com** (Data Discovery)

777

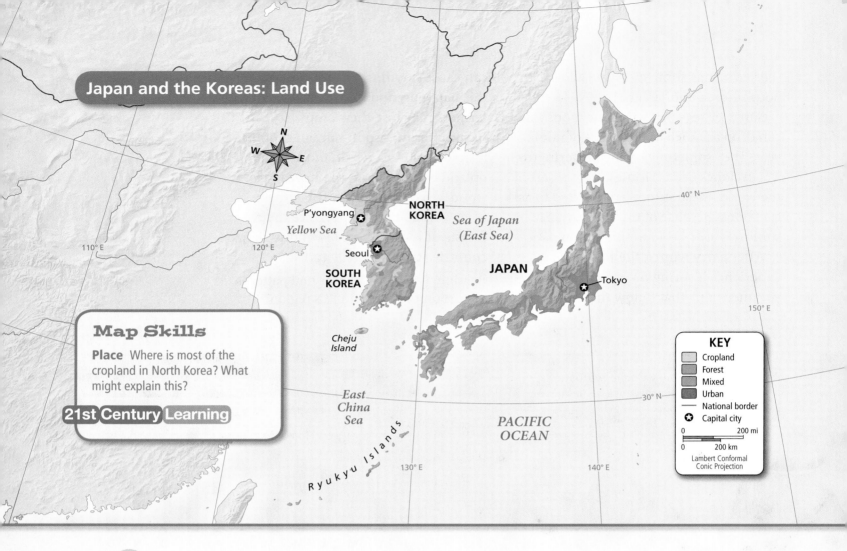

Japan and the Koreas: Land Use

P'yongyang
Yellow Sea
NORTH KOREA
Sea of Japan (East Sea)
Seoul
SOUTH KOREA
JAPAN
Tokyo
Cheju Island
East China Sea
Ryukyu Islands
PACIFIC OCEAN

40° N
30° N
110° E
120° E
130° E
140° E
150° E

Map Skills

Place Where is most of the cropland in North Korea? What might explain this?

21st Century Learning

KEY

- Cropland
- Forest
- Mixed
- Urban
- National border
- ✪ Capital city

0   200 mi
0   200 km

Lambert Conformal Conic Projection

myWorld Activity
Trade Off

Land Use and Natural Resources

With many hills and mountains, the countries of this region face a **scarcity,** or shortage, of flat land. This land is the best location for housing, but it is also needed for farming and industry. As a result, flat land is crowded. Japanese and Koreans must use their land carefully.

Farming the Land Rice is the most important crop in both Japan and the Koreas. With its cool, dry climate, North Korea's farm <u>output</u> lags behind that of South Korea and Japan. Yet, both South Korea and Japan are highly urbanized. Large cities in these two countries take up space. Less land is available for farming. Farmers often must work on difficult, hilly land. Terraces are used to create flat fields on sloping ground. Large tractors are too big to plow the narrow terraces. Instead, rice is planted and harvested by hand or with small machines. In some areas, farmers irrigate the land so that they can plant more than one crop per year on the same land. This type of small-scale rice farming takes a great deal of time and hard work. Farmers do this to make the most of limited land.

output, *n,* the amount of something produced

778

Food Imports and Exports Many other countries can produce farm goods more cheaply than Japan and the Koreas. These other countries have a comparative advantage over Japan and the Koreas in agriculture. **Comparative advantage** is the ability to produce goods at a lower cost than your competitors.

Because farming is costly in Japan and the Koreas, these countries import food. Still, people in this region continue to farm so that they will not be dependent on other countries for all their food.

The sea is also an important resource. Fish products are an important export for North Korea. The ocean currents near Japan create an environment that is good for many kinds of fish. Fish is also an important export for Japan as well as an important part of the Japanese diet.

Scarce Resources Mineral resources are not evenly spread across this region. Both Japan and South Korea have few mineral resources. North Korea, by contrast, is rich in mineral resources including coal, lead, iron ore, copper, gold, and salt.

Scarcity makes countries **interdependent,** which means they depend on each other. Japan and South Korea trade with each other to acquire some of the raw materials they need for industry.

In addition, all three countries need energy resources. Hydroelectricity is one source of energy. Because of the hilly land, there are many fast flowing rivers. These rivers are good for hydroelectric dams because the falling waters carry large amounts of energy that can be used to create electricity.

To meet their energy needs, South Korea and Japan have built nuclear power plants and also produce small amounts oil. Still, it is not enough. These countries must import oil and other resources to meet their energy needs.

Reading Check Which country is richest in mineral resources?

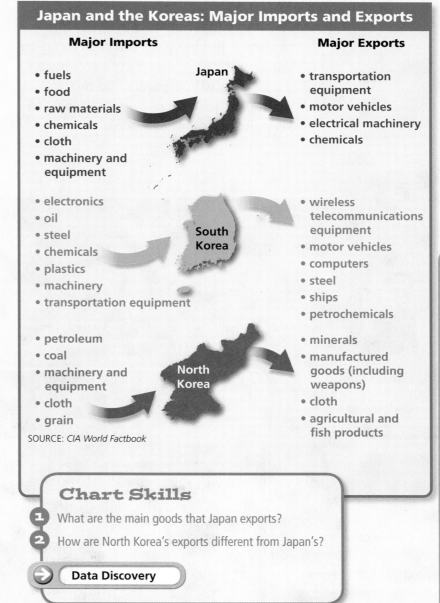

Japan and the Koreas: Major Imports and Exports

Major Imports

Japan
- fuels
- food
- raw materials
- chemicals
- cloth
- machinery and equipment

South Korea
- electronics
- oil
- steel
- chemicals
- plastics
- machinery
- transportation equipment

North Korea
- petroleum
- coal
- machinery and equipment
- cloth
- grain

Major Exports

Japan
- transportation equipment
- motor vehicles
- electrical machinery
- chemicals

South Korea
- wireless telecommunications equipment
- motor vehicles
- computers
- steel
- ships
- petrochemicals

North Korea
- minerals
- manufactured goods (including weapons)
- cloth
- agricultural and fish products

SOURCE: *CIA World Factbook*

Chart Skills

1 What are the main goods that Japan exports?

2 How are North Korea's exports different from Japan's?

→ **Data Discovery**

my World IN NUMBERS

About **10** typhoons pass over Japan each year.

Japan's typhoon season is **6** months long.

Adapting to Challenges

The people of the region have learned to live in a challenging environment. In the past, most buildings in Japan and the Koreas were made of wood. Fires, earthquakes, and floods might destroy them, but these wooden structures could be quickly rebuilt.

Today, the people of Japan and the Koreas use modern technology to build structures that can withstand the forces of nature. Rubber pads under skyscrapers dampen the shock waves of earthquakes. There are also computers that move weights in the base of the skyscrapers to keep the buildings balanced.

Safety Alerts Early warning systems also help people to take safety measures during earthquakes. One system developed in Japan can give people as much as 30 seconds warning. This might not seem like very much time. But every extra second is important when an earthquake is about to hit.

> 66 School children will be able to take shelter under their desks in classrooms if they have five seconds. In fact . . . if we have 10 seconds to prepare for major tremors, we can reduce the number of deaths caused by quakes significantly. 99
> —Yoshinori Sugihara

Tight Spaces

Japan's population density is the third-highest in the world. Skyscrapers fill Japanese cities and underground shopping centers extend for multiple stories underground. Japanese people have found other ways to use space creatively.

The small rooms at capsule hotels are an efficient use of space.

■ 716 ■

→ Culture Close-Up

my Story 📷 Photo

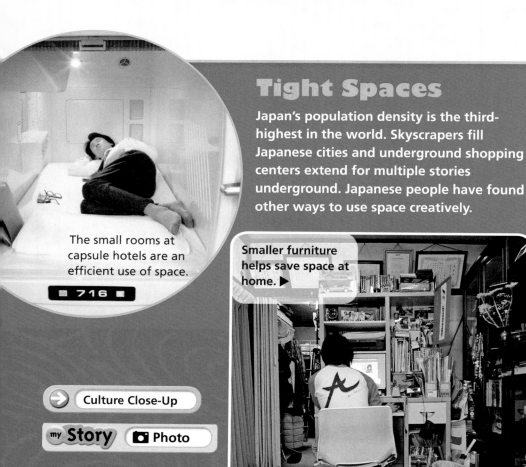

Smaller furniture helps save space at home. ▶

Oshiya or "pushers" pack commuters on to a Tokyo subway train.

Environmental Threats Managing resources is another challenge. With so many people crowded together, it is easy to use limited resources too quickly.

North Korea and South Korea have lost much of their forest land by cutting trees faster than they can grow back. Without tree cover, rain water washes quickly into rivers and streams and flooding becomes worse. As a result, soil needed for farming is washed away.

Overfishing is also a problem in the region. Near Japan, fish were taken from coastal waters too quickly. Now, ships must go far out to sea to find fish.

Intensive use of the land has resulted in serious pollution in all three countries. Factories, cars, and farms create air and water pollution.

While much remains to be done, the people in South Korea and Japan have pushed their governments to make changes. Their governments are working to reduce air and water pollution, find cleaner fuels, and recycle more waste.

The North Korean government has made less progress addressing these problems. The shortage of clean water for drinking and bathing is still a problem in that country.

Reading Check What are two ways people in Japan and the Koreas have adapted to their environment?

Overfishing threatens to drive the tuna fish into extinction. ▼

Section **1** Assessment

Key Terms

1. What is foliage?

2. What does scarcity mean?

3. Use the term *comparative advantage* to describe the products that Japan imports.

Key Ideas

4. How do physical features affect land use in this region?

5. How have Japan and the Koreas used technology to adapt to the forces of nature?

6. What environmental problems have Japan and the Koreas faced?

Think Critically

7. Analyze Cause and Effect How does scarcity make countries interdependent?

8. Compare and Contrast Why does North Korea have less agricultural production than Japan and South Korea?

? Essential Question

How much does geography shape a country?

9. How much does geography affect the problems that countries in this region face? Are there other factors that influence pollution in these countries? Go to your Student Journal and record your answer.

my worldgeography.com   Culture Close-Up

History of Japan and the Koreas

Key Ideas	● Japan and the Koreas all have long histories.	● Korea was divided into two countries, North Korea and South Korea, after the Korean War.	● Japan's economy grew rapidly after World War II.
	● Japan built an empire early in the 1900s but lost this empire at the end of World War II.		

Key Terms • shogun • samurai • Meiji Restoration • Korean War
• constitutional monarchy

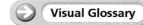 **Visual Glossary**

 Reading Skill: Identify Main Ideas and Details Take notes using the graphic organizer in your journal.

The imperial palace in Seoul, South Korea ▼

The people of Japan and the Koreas have adapted to their environment by building skyscrapers that survive the tremors of earthquakes. These nations have also needed to survive political and cultural tremors, such as wars and invasions. Japan and the Koreas have changed since their beginnings, but they are still standing.

Historical Roots

People have lived in this region for about 30,000 years. Powerful kingdoms have influenced the history of these countries, but each has charted its own course.

Korean Dynasties For thousands of years, kingdoms rose and fell on the Korean peninsula. At times, Chinese empires controlled parts of the peninsula. Ideas from China, especially Confucianism and Buddhism, influenced the Korean kingdoms.

In A.D. 668, the kingdom of Silla conquered the other Korean kingdoms. They pushed the Chinese empire off the peninsula and created a strong government. This dynasty, rulers in the same family, lasted until A.D. 935. After that, a series of dynasties kept the peninsula united for centuries.

Korean Achievements Under the various emperors, a unique society developed. Emperor Sejong called for a new writing system to be created in the 1400s. The system, called Hangul, is still used today. The Koreans also invented moveable metal type. This made printing easier. Korean potters also made delicate porcelain that is valued throughout the world.

Emperors and Shoguns in Japan

Around the time of the Silla dynasty in Korea, Japan became a unified country under an emperor. People believed the emperor was descended from a goddess.

For much of Japan's history, however, the emperors were not strong. Powerful military leaders called **shoguns** controlled Japan's government.

At times, neither the emperor nor the shoguns had complete control over all of the country. Some powerful landowners had their own armies. They granted land to **samurai**, or warrior lords, who supported them. These landowners fought each other to gain power. This created a lot of conflict in Japanese society.

In 1603, a shogun called Tokugawa Ieyasu (toh koo GAH wah ee yay AH soo) came to power. Ieyasu and the Tokugawa shoguns that followed him tried to bring peace to Japan. The Tokugawa brought the powerful landowners under the shogun's control.

The Tokugawa closed the country off from contact with most other countries. They wanted to keep outside forces from disrupting Japanese society.

grant, *v.,* to give

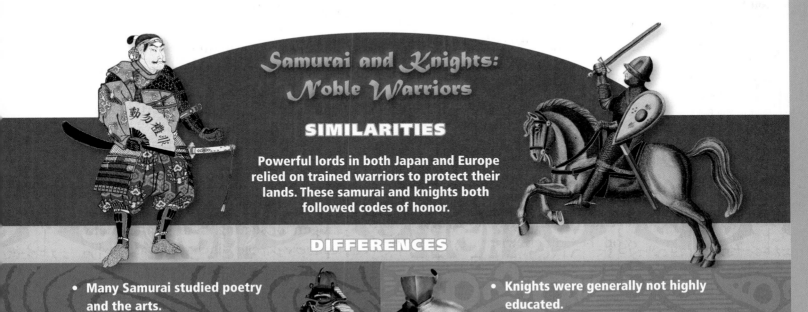

Samurai and Knights: Noble Warriors

SIMILARITIES

Powerful lords in both Japan and Europe relied on trained warriors to protect their lands. These samurai and knights both followed codes of honor.

DIFFERENCES

- Many Samurai studied poetry and the arts.
- Samurai became a closed class under the Tokugawa. They were born into their position.
- Many women of the samurai class learned martial arts.

- Knights were generally not highly educated.
- Any man could become a knight. Knighthood was an honor given by a lord.
- Some women became knights or received training in martial arts.

783

▲ A dinner at the palace of Emperor Meiji. Western-style clothing became popular in the Meiji court.

myWorld Activity
Best of the Best

The Tokugawa created strict divisions between nobles and commoners. People were not allowed to move between these two groups. The nobles were mostly the large landowners and the samurai. The large landowners had the highest status. The highest-ranking commoners were peasants (or small farmers). Below them were craftspeople and merchants. Peasants made up 80 percent of the population.

Before the Tokugawa, Japan had close ties with other countries, particularly China and Korea. Buddhism had spread from Korea into Japan. Many Japanese studied Chinese literature and art. The Japanese writing system was based mainly on the Chinese writing system.

New forms of art developed during the Tokugawa period. The country was prosperous. Wealthy nobles and merchants supported artists who created new styles of theater and painting.

Reading Check How did The Tokugawa try to bring stability to Japanese society?

International Conflicts and Connections

Early in the 1800s, both Japan and Korea were largely cut off from the rest of the world. By the beginning of the 1900s, both nations had been pulled into international conflicts and trade networks.

Early Contact with Europeans Ships from Europe first arrived in Japan and Korea around 1600. Both kingdoms had decided to keep Western merchants and missionaries away. Korea allowed only Chinese and Japanese traders. It attacked American and French ships trying to enter its ports. This isolation, or lack of contact, continued until the mid-1800s in Japan and even longer in Korea.

Changes Come to Japan In 1854, the American commander Matthew C. Perry sailed into a Japanese port despite the Tokugawa ban on foreigners. The Japanese knew that Perry's ship carried powerful weapons. So they accepted the trade agreement that Perry brought from the United States. Soon other nations pushed Japan to sign similar treaties.

Many Japanese people thought that these trade agreements were unfair to Japan. They blamed the Tokugawa shogun for signing these treaties. Many Japanese people felt change was needed to make Japan a more powerful country.

In 1868, new leaders arose and pushed out the Tokugawa shogun. They brought back the emperor, but they told him what to do. This time in Japanese history is called **Meiji Restoration.** It marks the return to power of Emperor Meiji.

The Rise of Japan Japan's new leaders expanded its industry and military. They also increased its power in the region.

In 1910, the Japanese took control over Korea. It was a difficult time for Koreans. They were forced to do hard work in new Japanese industries. They had to learn to speak Japanese, and many were forced to take Japanese sounding names. Japanese control of Korea was harmful to both the Korean people and culture.

Later Japan also invaded other countries. It took over large areas in the north of China as well as Formosa or Taiwan.

When World War II broke out, Japan joined on the side of Germany. Japan soon invaded Southeast Asia. The United States and Japan grew further apart. In 1941, Japan attacked the United States Navy at Pearl Harbor, Hawaii. As a result, the United States entered World War II.

In 1945, the United States dropped atomic bombs on the Japanese cities of Hiroshima and Nagasaki. The resulting casualtes were huge, and Japan surrendered. It lost all the lands it had invaded, including Korea.

Reading Check How did Japan's empire grow and then shrink?

A Japanese fighter plane called a "Zero" ▼

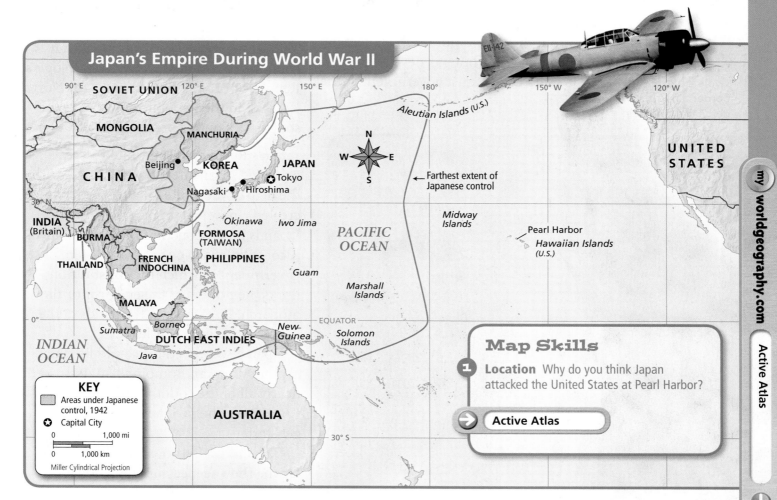

Japan's Empire During World War II

90° E   SOVIET UNION   120° E   150° E   180°   150° W   120° W

EII-142

Aleutian Islands (U.S.)

MONGOLIA   MANCHURIA

Beijing ●   KOREA   JAPAN

CHINA   ☆ Tokyo

Nagasaki ●   ● Hiroshima

UNITED STATES

Farthest extent of Japanese control

30° N

INDIA (Britain)   BURMA   Okinawa   Iwo Jima   PACIFIC OCEAN   Midway Islands   Pearl Harbor   Hawaiian Islands (U.S.)

FORMOSA (TAIWAN)

THAILAND   FRENCH INDOCHINA   PHILIPPINES

Guam

MALAYA   Marshall Islands

0°   Borneo   New Guinea   EQUATOR   Solomon Islands

Sumatra   DUTCH EAST INDIES

INDIAN OCEAN   Java

AUSTRALIA

30° S

KEY
Areas under Japanese control, 1942
☆ Capital City
0   1,000 mi
0   1,000 km
Miller Cylindrical Projection

Map Skills

1 **Location** Why do you think Japan attacked the United States at Pearl Harbor?

→ **Active Atlas**

my worldgeography.com   Active Atlas

Japan and the Koreas Since World War II

After World War II, Japan focused on rebuilding its government and its economy. In Korea, conflict quickly resumed. This conflict would divide a country that had been united for centuries.

The Korean War Japan's control of Korea ended after Japan surrendered at the end of World War II. At that time, the United States occupied the southern part of Korea. The Soviet Union occupied the northern part of the country. The United States and the Soviet Union disagreed about how to unite the two parts of Korea. They asked the United Nations to help, but they could not reach agreement.

Two new governments developed. One was a communist government in the north, which the Soviet Union supported. The other was a democratic government in the south, which the United States supported. Both governments claimed to rule Korea.

North Korea invaded South Korea in 1950. This marked the beginning of the **Korean War**. Hoping to limit the spread of communism, the United States led United Nations troops sent to defend South Korea. The Soviet Union and China aided North Korea.

Neither side won. Instead, they agreed to stop fighting in 1953. The two sides drew a new border. A strip along the border was declared a demilitarized zone, an area that neither army is allowed to enter. The peninsula was split into two countries: the communist Democratic People's Republic of Korea in the north—or North Korea, and the Republic of Korea in the south—or South Korea.

Japan's Recovery The United States occupied Japan after World War II. With the help of the United States, the Japanese created a new system of government. Japan is now a constitutional monarchy. A **constitutional monarchy** is a system of government in which the constitution limits the powers of the emperor or the monarch. Power lies in the hands of the voters, who elect their leaders.

Japan also needed to rebuild its economy after the war. Bombing had destroyed nearly all of the country's industry. The Korean War helped Japan's recovery to get started.

U.S. and U.N. troops were based in Japan. They needed supplies and labor.

occupy, *v.,* to take over, control

South Korean soldiers patrol the border along the demilitarized zone. ▼

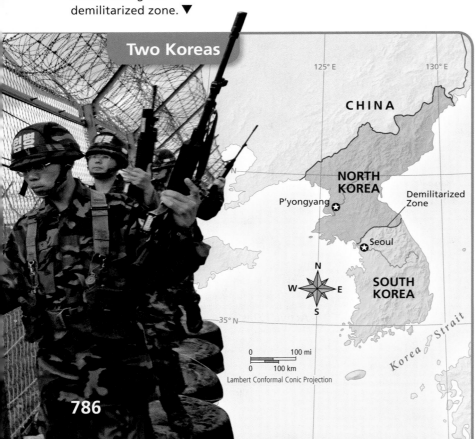

Two Koreas

125° E
130° E

CHINA

NORTH KOREA

P'yongyang ✪

Demilitarized Zone

Seoul ✪

SOUTH KOREA

35° N

Korea Strait

0   100 mi
0   100 km
Lambert Conformal Conic Projection

The Japanese people went to work to meet those needs.

The Japanese built new factories to replace the ones destroyed during the war. These factories had the most modern technology. They produced goods better and cheaper than the old factories.

The Japanese government supported education and job training. It also encouraged people to work hard and save their money. Banks used these savings to make loans to businesses. This helped the economy to grow.

Japan had a well-educated workforce and modern equipment in its factories. Japan produced and exported well-made products such as cars, electronics, and cameras. Those products attracted buyers in many parts of the world. Exports helped Japan's economy grow very quickly for the following 30 years, and the Japanese people grew wealthier.

Reading Check How did the Korean War affect Japan?

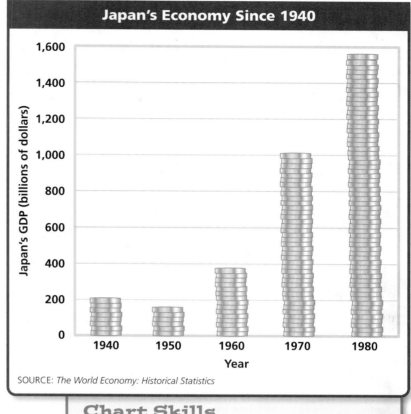

Japan's Economy Since 1940

SOURCE: *The World Economy: Historical Statistics*

Chart Skills

In which decade did Japan's economy grow the most?

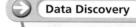
Data Discovery

Section 2 Assessment

Key Terms

1. Who were the shogun and the samurai?

2. What happened during the Meiji Restoration?

3. What is a constitutional monarchy?

Key Ideas

4. How did China influence the culture of Japan and Korea?

5. How did the Tokugawa change Japanese society?

6. Why was Korea divided after World War II?

Think Critically

7. **Draw Inferences** Why might the Koreans have wanted to create their own writing system rather than continuing to use the Chinese system?

8. **Analyze Cause and Effect** What factors helped the Japanese rebuild their economy after World War II?

? Essential Question

How much does geography shape a country?

9. Both Japan and Korea chose to limit contact with outsiders at certain times during their histories. How do you think their geography helped them to do that? Go to your Student Journal and record your answers.

Japan and the Koreas Today

Key Ideas
- South Korea's economy has grown, and its democracy has become stronger.
- North Korea is a communist dictatorship.
- North Korea's nuclear program is a source of conflict in the region.
- Japan has struggled with economic problems in recent years.

Key Terms • limited government   • unlimited government   • dictator
• recession   • Shinto

 Visual Glossary

Reading Skill: Set a Purpose for Reading Take notes using the graphic organizer in your journal.

◄ 63 Building, the tallest building in Seoul, South Korea

Japan and the Koreas have faced challenges in recent years. Yet, the people of South Korea and Japan have a good standard of living. These countries have become more influential in the world. By contrast, North Korea is largely isolated. Its people have suffered severe hardship.

Prosperity and Democracy in South Korea

South Korea has become more democratic over the years. It has also become a world economic power.

Growing Democracy The leaders of South Korea approved a constitution in 1948 and began building a new government. They created a **limited government**, that is, a government with powers that are limited by law. However, the constitution also stated that leaders did not have to follow those limits or protect individual rights if the country faced serious problems.

As a result, South Korea's political system was not always democratic. More than once, the military took over the country. Freedom of speech and freedom of the press was not always protected. In 1987, people began to call for change. Many South Koreans joined huge political protests. That year, the leaders changed the constitution.

Under the new constitution, the government cannot take away freedoms even when there are political or economic troubles. Citizens have more rights. The military is less powerful. It has not taken over the government since those reforms.

Economic Boom After the Korean War, the leaders of South Korea focused on producing industrial goods for export to other countries. The government supported a number of large companies. It helped them get the money and equipment they needed to make more products. The government also improved the education system.

Now, South Korea exports many high-technology goods, such as cell phones and computers. Its economy is one of the largest in the world. People now live more comfortably and have more belongings.

Still, the growth of South Korea's economy has not been stable. The government borrowed large sums of money from abroad. In the late 1990s, the country had too much debt. This hurt the economy. The economy improved, but the government will have to work to avoid this problem in the future.

Daily Life and Culture As the economy has grown, daily life for the people of South Korea has changed. In the past, most Koreans were farmers. Now, most people live in cities. In addition, South Korea now has contact with many countries. This has changed Korean culture. It has also introduced Korean culture to people throughout the world.

For example, the popular Korean sport of tae kwon do has become very popular outside the country. Tae kwon do became an official Olympic sport in 2000. At the same time, the Koreans have become fans of many sports from abroad. Soccer, in particular, is very popular. Almost every town has its own team. Other sports such as baseball, basketball, and volleyball have a wide following.

▲ Winner of a gold medal in tae kwon do, South Korea's Hwang Kyungseon (left) at the Beijing Olympics in 2008

Religious life in South Korea has also changed. Christianity spread rapidly through the country after the Korean War. About one quarter of South Korea's population is Christian. In addition, about one quarter of the population is Buddhist. The Buddha's birthday is a national holiday in South Korea. More than ten thousand Buddhist temples dot the landscape. Both foreign visitors and Koreans study Buddhism at these colorful temples. South Koreans enjoy complete religious freedom.

Reading Check How has the South Korean government changed since the 1980s?

STANDARD OF LIVING:
NORTH AND SOUTH KOREA

	North Korea	South Korea
Ecomonic output per person	$1,800	$27,100
Number of phone lines	1.2 million	24 million
Number of cell phones	0	43.5 million
Undernourished people	36%	1.6%
Life expectancy	64 years	79 years

SOURCE: *CIA World Factbook*, 2008, UN Common Database, 2001

A standard of living measures the health of a country by the goods and services its people can buy.

Chart Skills

From the information in this table, which country has a higher standard of living?

Data Discovery

Repression and Hardship in North Korea

North Korea is very different from South Korea. North Korea is one of the most isolated countries in the world. The people of North Korea face a hard life with little political freedom.

Dictatorship and Isolation North Korea is not a democracy. Its government is an example of an **unlimited government,** which is a government that, by law, may take any action it wants. Kim Jong-il is the country's leader. Kim is a dictator. A **dictator** has total control over the government. Kim Jong-il came to power when his father, Kim Il-sung, died in 1994.

Kim Il-sung rose to power in 1948. He was the leader of the Communist Party. Other parties were not allowed. Communist Party leaders tightly controlled the North Korean people. Like his father, Kim Jong-il is also a Communist and has kept this system.

The government controls the information reported by newspapers, radio, and television. The news supports Kim's policies. In addition, the leadership limits information from the outside world. Very few North Koreans have cell phones or Internet access.

People are not free to express their opinions. People who disagree with the leadership are punished. The North Korean government may have jailed up to 200,000 people for their political actions.

The North Korean government controls cultural and religious life. People cannot worship freely. Only a few churches and temples are allowed in the country.

The government promotes Korean culture by funding museums and the arts. Still, it controls the work of these writers, dancers, and musicians. It can ban any art that goes against the ideas of the leaders. North Koreans have few of the freedoms that South Koreans now enjoy.

▲ Kim Jong-il

Dancers in North Korea perform at a ceremony for the 95th anniversary of Kim Il-sung's birth.

A Crippled Economy North Korea is a communist country with a command economy. The government controls much of the economy and decides what goods are made. Often, it has not managed the economy well. As a result, the economy has not grown.

The leadership has focused on building a strong military. As a result, it does not spend enough to update machines on farms or in factories. Food production has fallen because of shortages of tractors, fertilizer, and fuel.

Natural disasters have added to these problems. Starting early in the 1990s, frequent floods and droughts damaged crops. More than two million people died of starvation in the late 1990s.

Foreign counties have given food <u>aid</u> to help North Koreans survive. Still, the population suffers. The government has focused on keeping control rather than solving its serious economic problems.

A Tense Border Many people in North and South Korea hope the Koreas can be reunited. In recent years, South Korea has given aid, in the form of food, to North Korea. In addition, leaders from North and South Korea have met and agreed to try to improve relations.

However, despite earlier promises not to develop nuclear weapons, North Korea has continued to build them. This has hurt North Korea's relationship with South Korea and many other countries around the world.

World leaders have met with North Koreans and tried to persuade the government to stop developing nuclear weapons. The United States and other countries have pressured North Korea to give up these weapons, but its leaders refuse. Peace and prosperity seem far away for North Korea.

Reading Check Who is the leader of North Korea?

aid, *n.,* help, assistance

my **worldgeography**.com

Data Discovery

791

Challenges and Changes in Japan

Japan's growth in the decades after World War II made it an important economic power. Japan builds many high-technology goods, such as computers and video games. Today, Japan faces new challenges, including slower economic growth and an aging population.

Economic Woes Japan has one of the largest economies in the world. Still, the country's economy has not grown as quickly in recent years.

After the World War II, the Japanese sold more goods abroad. They invested the money they earned to make more advanced products. The Japanese people became wealthier.

At the start of the 1980s, the Japanese economy was doing very well. Each year stock prices went higher and higher. Then in the early 1990s, the Japanese economy started heading downward.

Due to bad bank practices, Japan's economy entered a **recession**, a time when the economy becomes weaker and does not grow. Businesses produced less. They laid off many workers. In 2003, Japan's economy began to improve. In 2008, however, it fell back into recession. Japan continues to face challenges that may make future economic growth difficult.

An Aging Population One of these challenges is supporting a large population of retired people. Japanese people, on average, live longer than people in any other country. They have healthy eating habits and a good healthcare system.

In addition, couples in Japan have fewer children now. As a result, there are

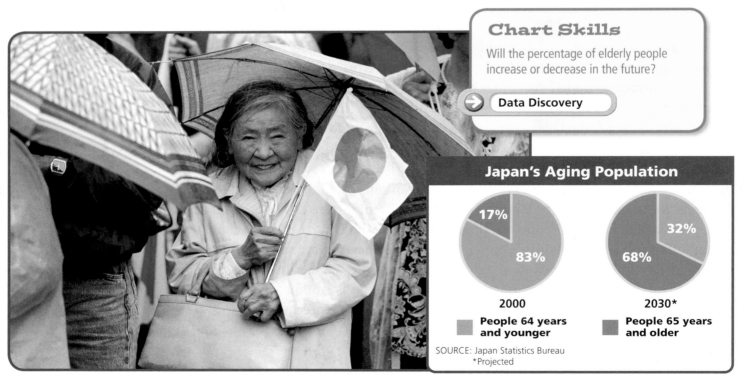

Chart Skills

Will the percentage of elderly people increase or decrease in the future?

→ **Data Discovery**

Japan's Aging Population

17%

83%

2000

32%

68%

2030*

■ **People 64 years and younger**

■ **People 65 years and older**

SOURCE: Japan Statistics Bureau
*Projected

fewer young people to support the elderly population. With fewer young people entering the workforce, Japan may not be able to produce as many goods. Its economy may remain weak.

Some companies in Japan are building new kinds of robots as one way to avoid a possible shortage of future workers. By taking over jobs that people currently do, robots may help keep Japan's economic production high. They can even care for the elderly:

> 66 There are robots [in Japan] serving as receptionists, vacuuming office corridors, spoon-feeding the elderly. They serve tea, greet company guests, and chatter away at public technology displays. 99
>
> —Associated Press

Changing Family Life Most Japanese people now live in cities. People are more likely to live in small family groups than with their extended families.

When the economy was growing quickly, many companies could provide excellent pay and benefits. Often only the husband worked. Wives generally stayed at home to care for children and older family members. Children were expected to study hard to get into college.

These family roles have changed in many families. During the recession, more women found jobs to help support their families. Also, some companies started hiring women as their older employees retired. These companies also encourage women to return to work after having children rather than becoming stay-at-home mothers.

Now, women have more job opportunities, but they still may not be treated equally to men. For example, women may find it difficult to be hired for the highest levels of management in a company.

School life has also changed in Japan. Many schools had classes six days a week to prepare students for difficult college entrance exams. Now, most schools have classes just five days a week.

Yet, the competition to get into the best colleges is as tough as ever. Many students attend extra classes during weekends and evenings in hopes of getting into one of Japan's best universities.

Reading Check How did economic problems change Japanese family life?

In an emergency, this security guard robot can put out a fire. *How might society change if robots could do many jobs that people now do?* ▼

JAPAN'S POPULAR CULTURE

Japan's entertainment industry grew after World War II. People had more time and money for entertainment, such as movies and video games. Japan now has the largest comic book industry in the world, and entertainment is one of Japan's major exports.

CRITICAL THINKING: Why do you think Japanese entertainment has become popular in other countries?

▲ Video games that started in Japan, such as the dancing game above, have become popular across the world.

Manga, or Japanese comics, are reaching a wider audience in the United States. ▼

Sales of Manga in the United States

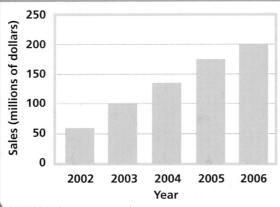

SOURCE: Anime News Network

Shoppers in Tokyo browse manga. ▼

▲ An anime, or cartoon, character from the Japanese video game Dragon Ball Z

This character is from the famous anime series Yu Gi Oh! The show is popular in Japan and also Australia, Germany, and Britain. ▶

myWorld Activity
Political Manga

A Rich Cultural Life

Most people in Japan belong to the same ethnic group and speak Japanese. There are not many immigrants. Yet, like South Korea, Japan is not cut off from the world. It influences and has been influenced by the cultures of many countries.

Spiritual Beliefs More than 80 percent of all Japanese people practice a combination of Buddhism and Shinto. **Shinto** is a traditional Japanese religion. In Shinto, kami are worshiped. Kami are gods or spirits that may live on earth in animals, trees, rocks, or other natural objects.

Today, many Japanese people practice both Buddhism and Shinto. For example, many Japanese people may have a Shinto marriage ceremony. Yet they will choose a Buddhist funeral.

Many traditions and holidays in Japan are connected to one of these two religions. At New Year's celebrations, Japanese people traditionally visit a Shinto shrine to pray to kami for a good harvest in the coming year.

Recent Cultural Borrowing In recent years, Japan has borrowed from the culture of many countries. Cultural imports, such as baseball and soccer, have been popular for many years in Japan.

At the same time, cultures around the world have borrowed from Japanese culture. Japanese martial arts, such as karate, are now popular around the world. So are Japanese foods such as sushi, or raw fish served with rice. Japanese artists have influenced artists in Europe, the United States, and other countries.

Japan has also had a big impact on the world of entertainment. It has had a large video-game industry for decades. Also, Japanese movies and television programs have a wide audience, especially in Asia.

More recently, Japanese anime—or cartoons—and manga—or comics—have attracted more and more fans throughout the world. Japan has added these products to its long list of successful exports.

Reading Check How have Shinto and Buddhism influenced Japanese culture?

Section 3 Assessment

Essential Question

How much does geography shape a country?

Key Terms

1. What is Shinto?

2. What is a limited government?

3. Is Kim Jong-il a dictator? Explain.

Key Ideas

4. Why has North Korea's nuclear program created conflict in the region?

5. How did Japan's economy change beginning in the 1990s?

6. Why is Japan's aging population causing economic problems?

Think Critically

7. **Draw Inferences** Why does the North Korean government limit access to outside information?

8. **Analyze Cause and Effect** What caused South Korea's political system to become more democratic in recent years?

9. How important is geography to the differences between North Korea and South Korea? Go to your Student Journal and record your answers.

Chapter Assessment

Key Terms and Ideas

1. **Explain** During what season do Japan and the Koreas get the most rain? Why is rain heaviest in this season?

2. **Recall** What are some of Japan's and the Koreas important natural resources?

3. **Summarize** What were some of the cultural achievements of the Koreans?

4. **Discuss** What was the Meiji restoration? What changes took place in Japan after this event?

5. **Compare and Contrast** How are the governments of North Korea and South Korea different?

6. **Recall** What were some of the effects of the recession in Japan during the 1990s?

7. **Summarize** What are examples of Japanese culture that have become popular in other countries?

Think Critically

8. **Solve Problems** How has Japan attempted to prepare for earthquakes?

9. **Making Inferences** Under Tokugawa rule, farmers had a higher social status than merchants. Why do you think farming was so highly valued?

10. **Comparing Viewpoints** How does North Korea view culture and the arts? How is this different from Japan?

11. **Core Concepts: Land Use** How does this region's geography create challenges for land use?

Places to Know

For each place, write the letter from the map that shows its location.

12. Japan

13. North Korea

14. South Korea

15. P'yongyang

16. Seoul

17. Mt. Fuji

18. **Estimate** Using the scale, estimate the length of the border between North Korea and South Korea.

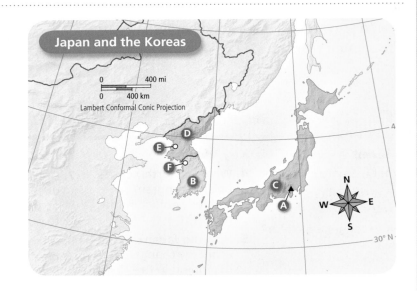

Essential Question

How much does geography shape a country?

Demonstrate Understanding Plan a multimedia presenstation that shows how Japan and the Koreas have adapted to and changed their environment. Make recommendations to the United Nations Environment Programme to help these countries solve environmental problems.

21st Century Learning

Search for Information on the Internet

Search for information on the culture of Japan, North Korea, or South Korea. Then write a report about that country's culture. Include pictures with your report. Be sure to include information on:
- religion
- the arts
- recreation
- food

Document-Based Questions

Success Tracker™
Online at myworldgeography.com

Use your knowledge of Japan and Documents A and B to answer the questions below.

Document A

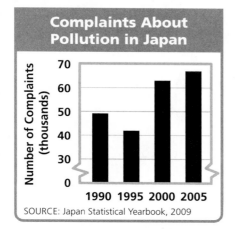

Complaints About Pollution in Japan

SOURCE: Japan Statistical Yearbook, 2009

Document B

" Japan's greenhouse gas emissions [releases] surged [increased rapidly] last year . . . Emissions of carbon dioxide and other greenhouse gases blamed for global warming spiked 2.3 percent to 1.37 billion tons in the 2007 . . ."

—CBS News, November 12, 2008

1. In Document A, which of the following years shows a drop in complaints about pollution?
   A 1990
   B 1995
   C 2000
   D 2005

2. Which of the following BEST describes the information presented in Document B?
   A Pollution decreased in 2007, which was encouraging.
   B Pollution stayed about the same in 2007.
   C Pollution increased a small amount in 2007, which is cause for some concern.
   D Pollution increased sharply in 2007, which is cause for alarm.

3. **Writing Task** Based on Document A and B, did Japan handle its pollution better in the 1990s or in the 2000s? Explain your answer.

myworldgeography.com   Self-Test

Chapter 23

Southeast Asia

Essential Question

What are the challenges of diversity?

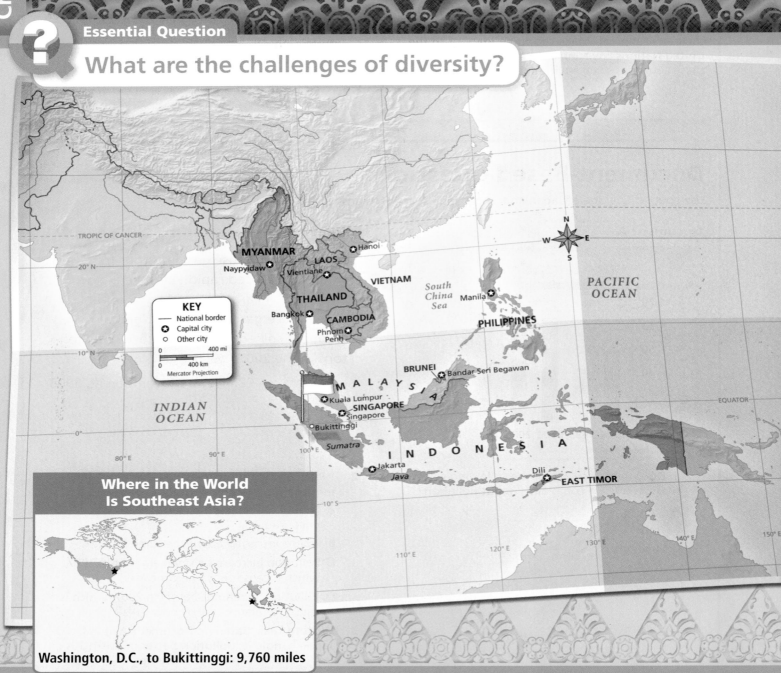

KEY
— National border
⚉ Capital city
○ Other city

0 — 400 mi
0 — 400 km
Mercator Projection

TROPIC OF CANCER

MYANMAR
Naypyidaw ⚉
LAOS
Vientiane ⚉
○ Hanoi
VIETNAM
THAILAND
Bangkok ⚉
CAMBODIA
Phnom Penh ⚉
South China Sea
Manila ○
PHILIPPINES
PACIFIC OCEAN

INDIAN OCEAN

BRUNEI
○ Bandar Seri Begawan
M A L A Y S I A
Kuala Lumpur ⚉
SINGAPORE
Singapore ⚉
Bukittinggi ○
Sumatra
I N D O N E S I A
Jakarta ⚉
Java
Dili ⚉
EAST TIMOR
EQUATOR

Where in the World Is Southeast Asia?

Washington, D.C., to Bukittinggi: 9,760 miles

my Story

A Minangkabau Wedding

In this section you will read about Ridwan, a young man helping his family and friends prepare for his cousin's wedding on the island of Sumatra in Indonesia. What does Ridwan's story tell you about the culture of Southeast Asia?

? Explore the Essential Question
- at **my worldgeography.com**
- using the **myWorld Chapter Activity**
- with the **Student Journal**

Story by Millie Phuah for myWorld Geography Online

Laughing voices drift through the cool air as nineteen-year-old Ridwan works with the men. They are busily moving furniture and cleaning the house where a wedding ceremony will take place. Meanwhile, in the kitchen, dozens of women are preparing chili peppers, onions, garlic, ginger, and a host of other spices. The spices will go into the meat and vegetable dishes of the day-long wedding feast. Although it is still early in the morning, there is not a moment to lose. Soon hundreds of relatives, friends, and neighbors will start arriving to honor the happy couple getting married today.

Ridwan looks out over the rice fields and the sea that surround this village called Bukittinggi, a name meaning "high hill." He can't wait to see his cousin, Nentis, who is the bride, begin her life with Al, her groom.

"Weddings are happy and important events that everyone looks forward to because it's a time for relatives

my worldgeography.com

On Assignment

Bride and groom in one pair of wedding costumes. The photo on the facing page shows them wearing another set of costumes.

Preparing the wedding feast

and friends to get together. Today is especially meaningful to me, not only because my cousin is getting married, but it's also the first time I've attended a Minangkabau wedding," says Ridwan. (The Minangkabau are the main ethnic group in West Sumatra.) "And according to Minangkabau practice, Al is moving into Nentis' home, which belongs to the bride's grandmother."

Minangkabau culture is unique. Minangkabau houses often have upward-curved roofs that look like the horns of a water buffalo. The resemblance is not a coincidence. For centuries the Minangkabau depended on the buffalo for food and to help them plow the rice fields. In fact, the name *Minangkabau* means "winning buffalo." The Minangkabau are also one of the few ethnic groups in the world in which family homes are passed down from mothers to daughters, instead of from fathers to sons.

Nentis starts dressing early, because her wedding costume consists of layers of silk and other fabric woven with gold thread, gold jewelry, and a glittering Minangkabau headdress. Meanwhile, Al dons his suit. He looks like an Indian raja, or king, as he slips on a kris, an ornamental dagger. Such costumes reveal the Chinese and Indian influences that have helped shape Minangkabau culture.

Some wedding guests visit the buffet outside.

Musicians entertain the guests.

Later in the day, as a band plays, the couple moves to the wedding dais, or platform. Everyone lines up to congratulate the smiling pair. It is a long day for the couple as they rise repeatedly to greet new arrivals. During the feast, long-separated relatives laugh and exchange news. Many have traveled from distant parts of Indonesia to be here today.

Traveling and moving away from home are common among the Minangkabau. In fact, Ridwan's parents left Bukittinggi years ago to run a textile shop in East Java. Ridwan helps at his family's textile business and lives in his maternal grandmother's house. The house will one day be passed down to Ridwan's mother and aunt, and then to his sister. When the time comes for Ridwan and his brothers to marry, they will move into their wives' homes. It is the Minangkabau way.

"This is part of Minangkabau culture and I totally accept it, just as all the other men do. It just makes me work harder at my vocation," says Ridwan. "I'd like to further my studies in the Indonesian language and be a theatre performer. My father, of course, hopes I'll take over his business one day, but I think I'll deal with that later," he smiles shyly.

Ridwan returns to his video camera, using modern technology to record an ancient tradition and the scenes that his family will enjoy throughout their lives.

→ **myStory Video**

Join Ridwan as he shows you more about his life.

Meet the Journalist

Name Millie Phuah
Favorite Moment Talking to Ridwan's grandmother

 my worldgeography.com myStory Video ↓

Chapter Atlas

Key Ideas
- Southeast Asia is a region of varied landforms.
- Location and climate affect both agricultural production and natural resources.
- Geography has influenced Southeast Asian history and settlement patterns.

Key Terms • peninsula • archipelago • tsunami • monsoon • typhoon

 Visual Glossary

 Reading Skill: Label an Outline Map Take notes using the outline map in your journal.

Mount Mayon erupts in the Philippines.

Balinese dancers from Indonesia

Physical Features

Ridwan's cousin's wedding took place on the island of Sumatra in Indonesia. Indonesia is one of the 11 nations that make up Southeast Asia. The region has two parts: a mainland and an island area, part of which lies on the Equator.

The mainland of Southeast Asia is a **peninsula**—a land area almost surrounded by water. It extends from the Shan Plateau down to the narrow Malay peninsula. Among the major rivers are the Mekong, the Irrawaddy, and the Red River. These rivers carry rich soil to fertilize the deltas before they empty into the sea.

Southeast Asia: Physical

TROPIC OF CANCER

Irrawaddy River

Shan Plateau

Red River

Gulf of Tonkin

20° N

Chao Phraya River

Annamese Cordillera

Mekong River

Indochina Peninsula

Andaman Sea

10° N

Gulf of Thailand

Philippine Sea

Luzon

South China Sea

Sulu Sea

Mindanao

Strait of Malacca

Malay Peninsula

Celebes Sea

PACIFIC OCEAN

Barisan Mountains

Sumatra

0°

Borneo

EQUATOR

Sulawesi

Maluku Islands

New Guinea

Banda Sea

Java Sea

Arafura Sea

INDIAN OCEAN

Java

Flores Sea

Lesser Sunda Islands

10° S

Timor

Timor Sea

90° E 100° E 110° E 120° E 130° E 140° E 150° E

Map Skills

1 **Location** Read the key. Where are the highest landforms?

2 **Place** What is the longest river in the region?

3 **Places to Know!** Label the following places on the outline map in your Student Journal: Mekong River, Malay Peninsula, Irrawaddy River, Red River.

→ **Active Atlas**

KEY
Elevation

Feet	Meters
10,000	3,048
6,000	1,829
3,000	914
1,000	305
500	152
Sea level	Sea level

—— National border

0 — 400 mi
0 — 400 km
Mercator Projection

The rest of the region is made up of **archipelagoes,** or groups of islands. The sizes of the islands vary greatly, from huge Borneo to tiny islands that may not even appear on some maps. Many island landscapes are breathtaking. Beyond beautiful sandy beaches, mountains and volcanoes tower over narrow coastal plains. Short, fast-flowing rivers run through rain forests filled with great biodiversity, or variety of living things.

Many islands in Indonesia and the Philippines are part of the Ring of Fire, a string of active volcanoes that encircles the Pacific Ocean.

Most of Southeast Asia is part of the Eurasian Plate, which is colliding with the Indo-Australian Plate. When these plates shift deep underground, destructive earthquakes can occur. In December 2004, an earthquake just 150 miles west of the island of Sumatra created a huge **tsunami,** or tidal wave. This tsunami killed more than 230,000 people living around the Indian Ocean. An early warning system has been <u>launched</u> to try to prevent such a disaster from happening again.

Reading Check What are the two main parts of Southeast Asia?

launch, *v.,* to set in operation

my **worldgeography.com** Active Atlas

Climate

Southeast Asia is a region of hot temperatures and abundant rain—perfect conditions for the growth of rain forests. Parts of the mainland and most of the islands have a tropical wet climate. The climate in the northern part of the mainland is humid subtropical. The climate in the rest of the mainland is mostly tropical wet and dry.

Much of the mainland and the islands receive heavy rain. Although occasional dry conditions affect the mainland, most of the islands have no dry season. The islands are near the Equator, so temperatures are hot everywhere.

Every year **monsoons,** or seasonal winds, blow through the region. The summer monsoons carry heavy rain and cause flooding. These winds come in from the Indian Ocean. In the winter, monsoons blow from the Pacific.

Typhoons are storms much like hurricanes. They blow in from the western Pacific between June and November.

Reading Check What are typhoons?

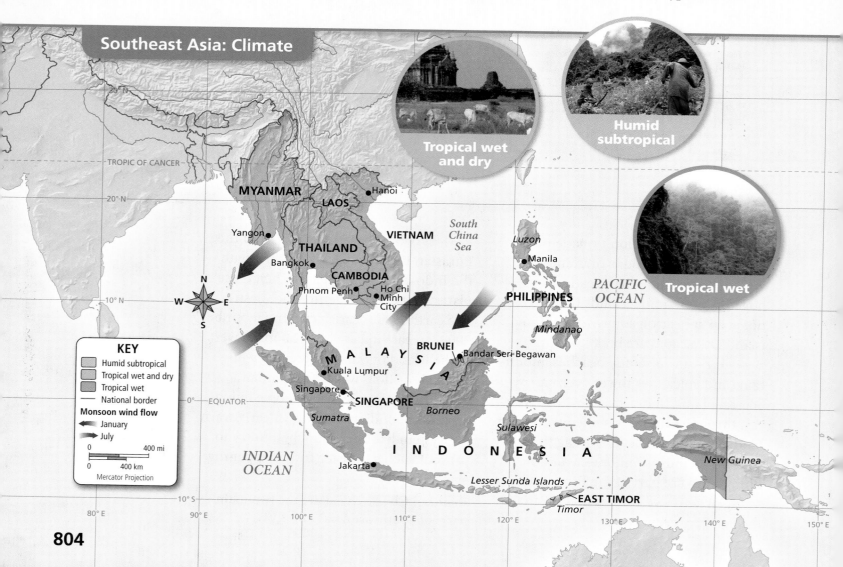

Southeast Asia: Climate

Tropical wet and dry

Humid subtropical

Tropical wet

MYANMAR
- Hanoi
LAOS
Yangon
THAILAND   VIETNAM
Bangkok
South China Sea
CAMBODIA
Luzon
Phnom Penh   Ho Chi Minh City   Manila
PHILIPPINES
PACIFIC OCEAN
Mindanao
BRUNEI
M A L A Y S I A   Bandar Seri Begawan
Kuala Lumpur
Singapore
SINGAPORE   Borneo
Sumatra
Sulawesi
I N D O N E S I A   New Guinea
INDIAN OCEAN
Jakarta
Lesser Sunda Islands
EAST TIMOR
Timor

KEY
- Humid subtropical
- Tropical wet and dry
- Tropical wet
- National border
- **Monsoon wind flow**
  - January
  - July

0   400 mi
0   400 km
Mercator Projection

TROPIC OF CANCER
20° N
10° N
EQUATOR
10° S
80° E   90° E   100° E   110° E   120° E   130° E   140° E   150° E

People and Geography

Geography has shaped the history and culture of Southeast Asia. In the north, mountains separated mainland Southeast Asia from the rest of Asia. Within the region itself, north-south cordilleras, or parallel mountain ranges, isolated early societies. Later, the cordilleras helped define national borders. The rivers that carried rich sediment to the deltas also played an important role, for it was in the <u>fertile</u> river valleys that the first civilizations emerged.

The mostly gentle seas of Southeast Asia allowed trade, much of which traveled through the narrow Malacca Strait. For centuries pirates and kings fought to control the riches of this waterway. Another rich prize lay to the east in the Maluku Islands. Here, in the volcanic soil, grew rare spices such as nutmeg and cloves. At one time, these spices could be found nowhere else on Earth. The spice trade attracted Europeans—who came first to trade and then to colonize.

Reading Check **Where did spices grow?**

fertile, *adj.,* rich, fruitful

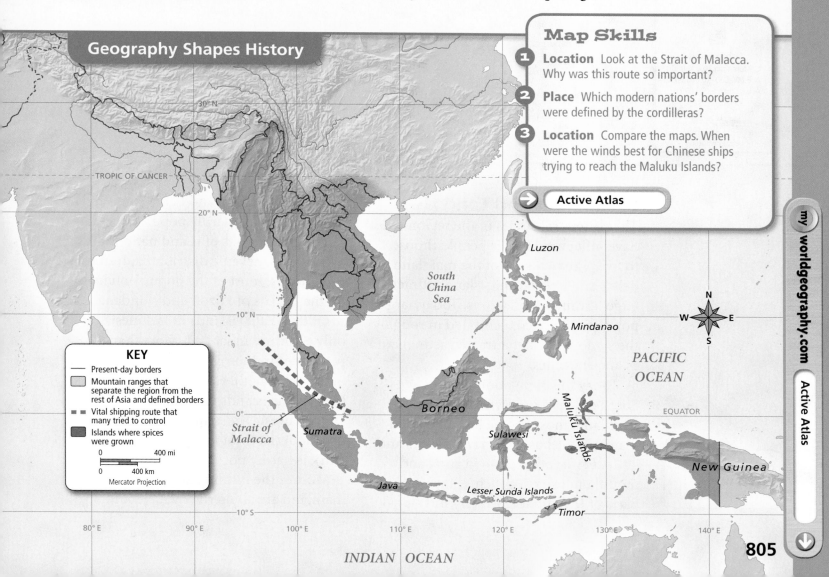

Geography Shapes History

Map Skills

1. **Location** Look at the Strait of Malacca. Why was this route so important?

2. **Place** Which modern nations' borders were defined by the cordilleras?

3. **Location** Compare the maps. When were the winds best for Chinese ships trying to reach the Maluku Islands?

Active Atlas

KEY
— Present-day borders
▢ Mountain ranges that separate the region from the rest of Asia and defined borders
▪▪▪ Vital shipping route that many tried to control
▢ Islands where spices were grown

0 ____ 400 mi
0 ____ 400 km
Mercator Projection

TROPIC OF CANCER

30° N
20° N
10° N
0°
10° S

80° E   90° E   100° E   110° E   120° E   130° E   140° E

Luzon
South China Sea
Mindanao
PACIFIC OCEAN
EQUATOR
Strait of Malacca
Sumatra
Borneo
Sulawesi
Maluku Islands
New Guinea
Java
Lesser Sunda Islands
Timor

INDIAN OCEAN

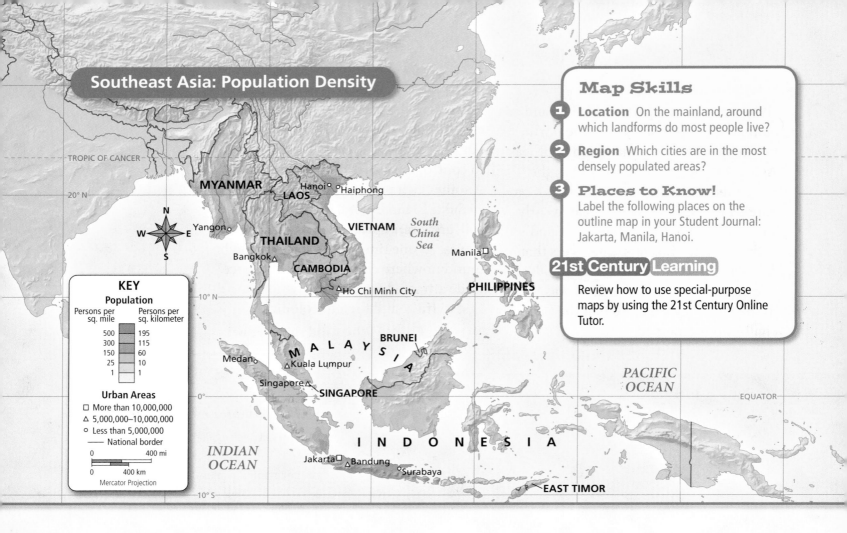

Southeast Asia: Population Density

Map Skills

1 **Location** On the mainland, around which landforms do most people live?

2 **Region** Which cities are in the most densely populated areas?

3 **Places to Know!** Label the following places on the outline map in your Student Journal: Jakarta, Manila, Hanoi.

21st Century Learning

Review how to use special-purpose maps by using the 21st Century Online Tutor.

KEY

Population

Persons per sq. mile	Persons per sq. kilometer
500	195
300	115
150	60
25	10
1	1

Urban Areas

□ More than 10,000,000
△ 5,000,000–10,000,000
○ Less than 5,000,000
— National border

0   400 mi
0   400 km
Mercator Projection

Settlement and Land Use

The natural resources of the region have influenced where people choose to live. The rich soils of the mainland deltas and the volcanic islands attracted large farming populations. Today, large populations are concentrated in roughly the same areas that attracted settlement in ancient times.

Today the population density of Southeast Asia is very uneven. On the mainland, most people live on coastal plains and deltas, or in river valleys and cities. Fewer people live in rural and mountainous areas, such as the northern parts of Myanmar (formerly Burma),

Thailand, Vietnam, and Laos. Some areas of rain forest are hardly populated at all.

The populations of island nations are even more unevenly distributed. In the Philippines, most of the population live on the islands of Luzon and Mindanao.

Of the 17,000 islands in Indonesia, only 6,000 are inhabited. More than 60 percent of Indonesia's population resides on the island of Java. Nearly all the rest lives on the islands of Sumatra, Borneo, and Sulawesi. The easternmost province of Indonesia, Irian Jaya (IRH ee ahn JAH yuh), is hardly populated at all.

Most of the farming areas on the mainland are along river valleys and

myWorld Activity
Why Settle in Southeast Asia?

deltas where plentiful water and good soil allow people to grow rice. Thailand's rice is some of the best in the world. Because Southeast Asia has very little land that is level enough for farming, the peoples of this mountainous region have cleverly altered their landscape to meet their needs. By sculpting the hillsides into steps, or terraces, they have turned mountain slopes into farmland for rice crops. On the higher slopes, cool temperatures provide the perfect conditions for growing tea.

Southeast Asian forests are a great natural resource. Exported lumber from the rain forests is a major source of income for some nations. The lumber is exported mainly to Japan and the United States.

Reading Check Why did large populations develop in the deltas?

Urban Problems

Even though there are many large cities, the region as a whole is mainly rural. However, more people are moving to urban areas in search of jobs and higher living standards. This migration has turned Jakarta, Bangkok, Manila, and Phnom Penh into huge cities with growing urban problems.

The increase in population places great strains on the cities' infrastructures, such as water supplies, electricity, and sewage facilities. Housing, healthcare, and other services also suffer. There are many environmental problems, such as air pollution and traffic congestion. The monsoon rains bring floods that cause sewage overflow and water contamination.

Reading Check What urban problems can be traced to population increases?

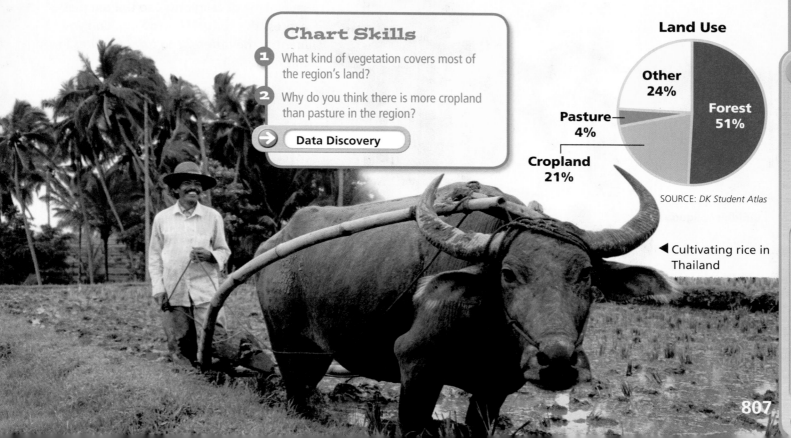

Chart Skills

1 What kind of vegetation covers most of the region's land?

2 Why do you think there is more cropland than pasture in the region?

→ **Data Discovery**

Land Use

Other 24%

Forest 51%

Pasture 4%

Cropland 21%

SOURCE: *DK Student Atlas*

◀ Cultivating rice in Thailand

807

Southeast Asia and the World Today Southeast Asia is once again a center of international trade. The Strait of Malacca is a major global shipping lane. The ports of Singapore, Malaysia, and Indonesia benefit greatly from such traffic. But there are also enormous dangers along the strait. Modern-day pirates have attacked merchant ships. And since the al-Qaeda attack on September 11 and later attacks in Indonesia, there is a new fear. Attacks by militant groups on shipping could endanger the world's oil supply. In the words of one writer,

66 With 60,000 vessels transiting through the Strait each year, carrying half of the world's oil supplies and a third of its trade, the stakes are high in maintaining stability along these sea lanes. 99

—Chietigj Bajpaee

All the countries in the region have the potential for economic growth. Tourism is an important source of income in all of Southeast Asia. Malaysia is developing a high-technology complex near its capital, Kuala Lumpur. This complex is called the Multimedia Super Corridor. Thailand is attempting to develop high-technology industries, but the lack of skilled labor may be an obstacle.

ASEAN, the Association of Southeast Asian Nations, is a trade group working to promote growth and social progress. The organization has reduced regional tariffs and has created a free-trade area.

Today Southeast Asia's problems and strengths are tied to its geography and history. Many of its people, such as the Minangkabau, continue to welcome foreign culture and new ideas. With its ancient traditions of cultural diversity and international trade, Southeast Asia is well positioned to play an important role in the modern world.

Reading Check Why is the Strait of Malacca so important to the world's economy?

my World IN NUMBERS

In 2007, Thailand had a labor force of about **37** million people. In 2008, this figure rose to about **38** million.

myWorld Activity Facing Challenges

Section 3 Assessment

Key Terms

1. Use the following terms to describe Southeast Asia today: secular, military junta, insurgency, separatist group.

Key Ideas

2. What role does Southeast Asia play in the world economy?

3. What kinds of governments exist in Southeast Asia?

4. Why are Southeast Asian rain forests under threat?

Think Critically

5. **Draw Conclusions** Why is religious tolerance valued in Indonesia, where there are so many religious faiths?

6. **Synthesize** Why is it so difficult for Southeast Asian nations to solve environmental problems?

? Essential Question

What are the challenges of diversity?

7. Why has "Unity in Diversity" become the motto of Indonesia? Go to your Student Journal to record your answer.

Chapter Assessment

Key Terms and Ideas

1. **Discuss** How did physical geography determine where people settled in Southeast Asia?
2. **Explain** What kinds of weather conditions do the summer **monsoons** create?
3. **Recall** Which civilizations influenced Southeast Asia?
4. **Explain** How did the ancient Khmer create a food **surplus**?
5. **Summarize** What were the causes and effects of Western colonialism in the region?
6. **Recall** What is the goal of the **insurgency** in the Philippines?
7. **Explain** Why is the Strait of Malacca so important today?
8. **Describe** Which are the richest and the poorest countries in Southeast Asia?

Think Critically

9. **Draw Conclusions** How have the people of Southeast Asia used the environment to meet their needs?
10. **Synthesize** How did geography contribute to the diversity of the region?
11. **Make Inferences** Why did Islam spread through the islands?
12. **Core Concepts: Culture and Geography** How has the environment shaped culture in Southeast Asia?

Places to Know

For each place, write the letter from the map that shows its location.

13. **Mekong River**
14. **Singapore**
15. **Strait of Malacca**
16. **Bangkok**
17. **The Philippines**
18. **South China Sea**
19. **Estimate** Using the scale, estimate the distance between Bangkok and the Philippines.

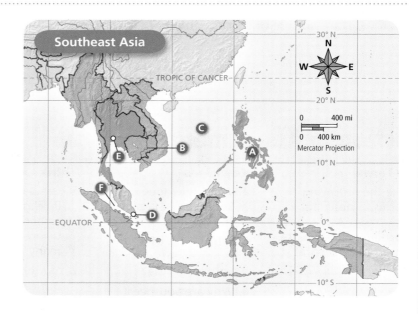

Southeast Asia

myWorld Chapter Activity

Gaining Wealth Through History
Follow your teacher's instructions to investigate the geographical factors that have contributed to the economic success of each historical character. Then rank the characters on an economic assessment scale and explain the reasons for your assessment.

21st Century Learning

Develop Cultural Awareness

Look back over the chapter and make a list of features that make Southeast Asian culture unique. Then consider why each feature might have developed—was it because of geography, climate, or history? Create a table that lists each feature and your theory about its origin.

Document-Based Questions

Success ⭐ Tracker™
Online at myworldgeography.com

Use your knowledge of Southeast Asia and Documents A and B to answer Questions 1–3.

Document A

Vessels Using the Malacca Strait

Vessels (thousands)

- 1999: 43,965
- 2007: 70,718
- 2015*: 120,000

Year

SOURCE: www.earthtimes.org
* Projected

1. What does Document A tell you about shipping in the Strait of Malacca?

 A The number of vessels is decreasing every decade.

 B The number of vessels peaked in the 1990s and then declined.

 C The projected number of vessels will have nearly tripled in a 16-year span.

 D The projected number of vessels will decline sharply by 2015.

Document B

" He who is lord of Malacca has his hand on the throat of Venice."

—Duarte Barbosa describing world trade in the 1400s and 1500s

2. Which of the following best describes the meaning of Document B?

 A The European trading city of Venice depends on goods traveling through the Malacca Strait.

 B The trading city of Venice is being attacked by the lord of Malacca.

 C The cities of Venice and Malacca have little contact with each other.

 D Venice defeated Malacca after a long war.

3. **Writing Task** Use Documents A and B to write a short paragraph explaining the role of the Malacca Strait in world trade.

Plan the City of Tomorrow

Your Mission Study the effects of population change on a city in East or Southeast Asia. Then present a plan for how to manage more growth in your city, including predictions for its future needs.

The skyline of Kuala Lumpur, the capital of Malaysia, is dominated by the twin spires of the Petronas Towers (left). Architects and urban planners designed the building to be a destination for both workers and their families. North of Kuala Lumpur, across the Gulf of Thailand, lies Ho Chi Minh City, the economic center of Vietnam. Historic and elegant, Ho Chi Minh City boasts some 300,000 businesses and contributes as much as 20 percent to the nation's total revenue.

Neither of these cities was planned as an urban success story, yet each is successful for different reasons. Very few cities are planned. Most cities evolve as history, governments, and populations change. As you investigate cities in this activity, consider how their characteristics might be useful when planning the city of tomorrow.

CITY OF TOMORROW

CITY LIMITS

STEP 1

What's in a Name?

The name of the city you are researching may have changed over the years. City names can change, for example, if the country was once a colony that later declared independence. When this happens, large groups of people may move in or out of a region. Investigate the history of your city's name and begin your presentation with this brief overview—it will engage your listeners right from the start.

STEP 2

What's Your Plan?

Your main goal is to improve life for the people of your city. But you need a solid plan. Gather facts and figures about population trends. Identify areas where your city functions well and areas that need improvement. Remember that you are offering a solution for the future and that you can't always predict what will happen. Thus, your plan should offer reasonable expectations for implementing your ideas.

STEP 3

The Big Finale

An effective presentation ends with a summary of what you have already said. If you have any final arguments, make them with confidence. Avoid arrogance. Chances are that your audience will agree with your proposals— after all, they live in this city!—but they may be concerned with the costs associated with your plan. Keep in mind that planning the city of tomorrow begins with understanding cities of today.

Regional Overview

Australia and the Pacific

Australia, New Zealand, and tens of thousands of other Pacific islands are spread across a vast area of ocean to the south and east of Asia. The people of these islands are as diverse as their geography, which includes high mountains, arid deserts, and icy glaciers.

What time is it there?

Washington, D.C.
9 A.M. Monday

Auckland, New Zealand
2 A.M. Tuesday

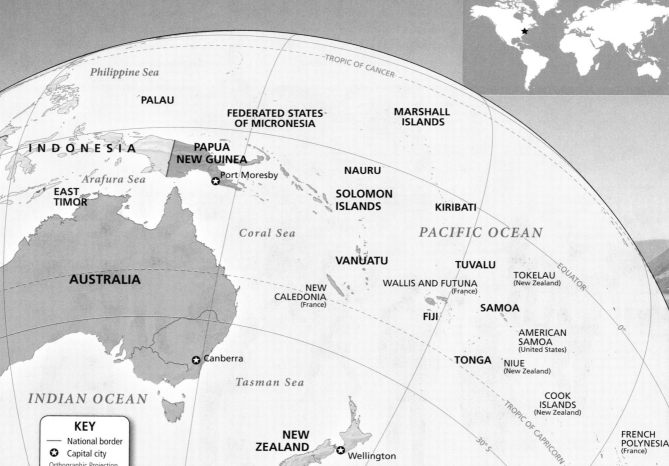

TROPIC OF CANCER

Philippine Sea

PALAU

FEDERATED STATES OF MICRONESIA

MARSHALL ISLANDS

INDONESIA

PAPUA NEW GUINEA

⊛ Port Moresby

NAURU

Arafura Sea

EAST TIMOR

SOLOMON ISLANDS

KIRIBATI

Coral Sea

PACIFIC OCEAN

VANUATU

TUVALU

TOKELAU (New Zealand)

AUSTRALIA

NEW CALEDONIA (France)

WALLIS AND FUTUNA (France)

SAMOA

FIJI

AMERICAN SAMOA (United States)

⊛ Canberra

TONGA

NIUE (New Zealand)

EQUATOR

Tasman Sea

INDIAN OCEAN

COOK ISLANDS (New Zealand)

TROPIC OF CAPRICORN

KEY
— National border
⊛ Capital city
Orthographic Projection

NEW ZEALAND

⊛ Wellington

FRENCH POLYNESIA (France)

30° S

150° E

180°

150° W

➡ **Chapter 24** Australia and the Pacific

The Unit Ahead

my worldgeography.com

Plan your trip online by doing a Data Discovery Activity and watching the myStory Video of the region's teen.

my Story

Jack

Age: 17

Home: Auckland, New Zealand

Chapter 24

New Zealand's South Island has many mountains and thick forests.

Regional Overview
Physical Geography

Most of Australia is very dry. Australians use the continent's dry plains for mining and raising livestock.

Melanesia has many high volcanic islands with fertile soil and mineral resources.

Mount Wilhelm
14,790 ft (4,509 m)

Arafura Sea

Timor Sea

Gulf of Carpentaria

Cape York Peninsula

Coral Sea

Great Barrier Reef

Great Dividing Range

Kimberley Plateau

INDIAN OCEAN

Simpson Desert

Great Artesian Basin

Great Sandy Desert

Darling River

Gibson Desert

Great Victoria Desert

Mt. Kosciuszko
7,310 ft (2,228 m)

Murray River

Nullarbor Plain

Great Australian Bight

Bass Strait

Tasmania

Darling Range

Many Pacific islands are low-lying atolls, islands formed by coral reefs.

P A C I F I C   O C E A N

North Island

—*Cook Strait*

Aoraki (Mt. Cook)
12,316 ft (3,754 m)

South Island

Southern Alps

New Zealand's Southern Alps are home to more than 20 mountains higher than 10,000 feet.

Regional Flyover

You begin your flight at Easter Island, the easternmost settlement in Polynesia. From here you fly west across the Pacific Ocean, traveling over the thousands of high volcanic islands and low coral atolls that form the Pacific islands. These islands are spread out over 116 million square miles of ocean.

Flying low over the ocean, your airplane reaches Papua New Guinea, a nation on the eastern half of the island of New Guinea. Although it is just south of the Equator, Papua New Guinea has peaks high enough to receive snow. As your plane circles back to the southeast, you fly over New Zealand's icy glaciers, tall mountains, and thick rain forests.

Then you travel west across the Tasman Sea to Australia, following the 1,250-mile-long Great Barrier Reef along Australia's northeast coast. Finally you circle south, landing on the deserts of central Australia. Here you find Uluru, or Ayers Rock, an enormous sandstone rock rising about 1,100 feet above the surrounding land.

 In-Flight Movie

Take flight over Australia and the Pacific and explore the region from the air.

my **worldgeography.com**

 In-Flight Movie

827

Regional Overview
Human Geography

People, Land, and Resources

The Pacific region's physical features have shaped where people in the region live. Most Australians and New Zealanders live in dense urban areas near the ocean. Few people live in Australia's dry deserts or in New Zealand's rugged mountains. The population of the smaller Pacific islands is generally more rural. Most people live in small villages.

Some countries in the region have many natural resources. Others are less fortunate. Australia and New Zealand's many resources have led to strong industrial economies. However, the economies of the smaller islands are generally limited by a lack of resources. Most smaller islands have developing economies, and many islanders fish or farm.

Australia and the Pacific: Population Density

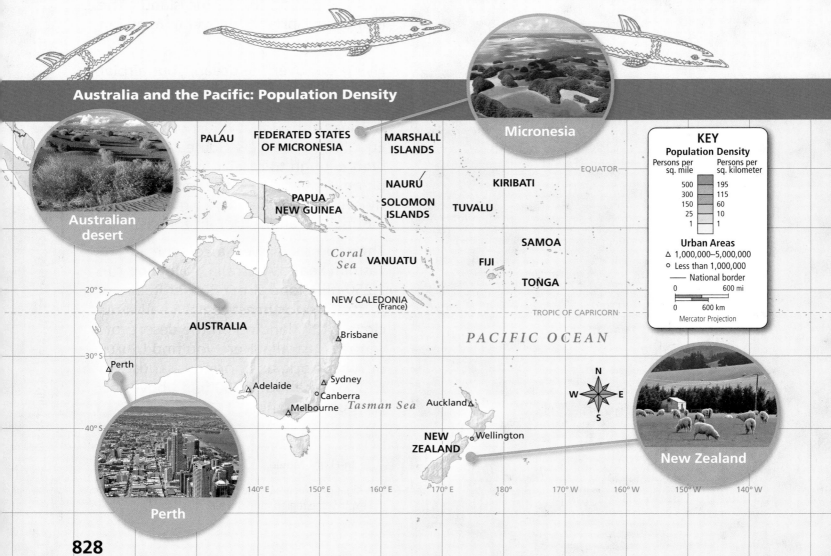

PALAU

FEDERATED STATES OF MICRONESIA

MARSHALL ISLANDS

Micronesia

NAURU

KIRIBATI

EQUATOR

PAPUA NEW GUINEA

SOLOMON ISLANDS

TUVALU

Australian desert

SAMOA

Coral Sea VANUATU

FIJI

TONGA

NEW CALEDONIA (France)

TROPIC OF CAPRICORN

20° S

AUSTRALIA

PACIFIC OCEAN

30° S

Perth

Brisbane

Adelaide

Sydney

Canberra

Melbourne

Tasman Sea

Auckland

40° S

NEW ZEALAND

Wellington

New Zealand

Perth

KEY
Population Density

Persons per sq. mile	Persons per sq. kilometer
500	195
300	115
150	60
25	10
1	1

Urban Areas
△ 1,000,000–5,000,000
○ Less than 1,000,000
— National border

0   600 mi
0   600 km
Mercator Projection

my World IN NUMBERS

	Australia	Federated States of Micronesia	New Zealand	Palau	Tonga	Tuvalu	United States
Population	21 million	108,000	4.2 million	21,000	119,000	9,600	304 million
Population density (people per square mile)	7	397	40	119	430	1,218	86
GDP per capita	$37,300	$2,300	$27,200	$7,600	$5,100	$1,552	$45,800

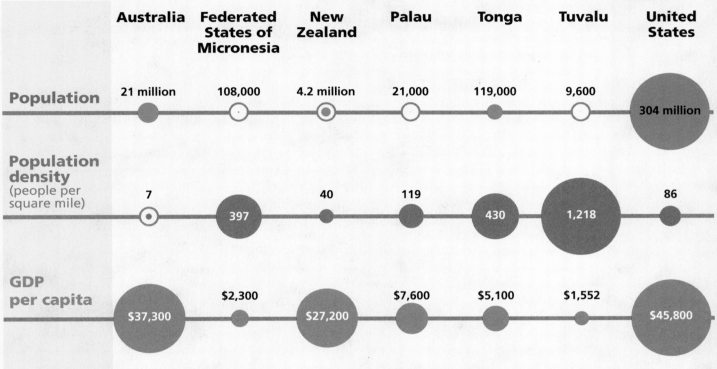

SOURCE: *CIA World Factbook, Encyclopaedia Britannica*

Put It Together

1. What might be the advantages and disadvantages of living on a small Pacific island?

2. Remember that GDP per capita is the total economic output per person in a country. What geographic factors might influence the numbers for this region?

3. What seems to be the relationship between land and population? Between land and economy?

Data Discovery

Find your own data to make a regional data table.

Size Comparison

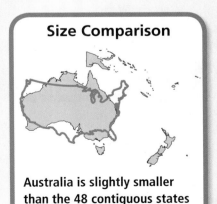

Australia is slightly smaller than the 48 contiguous states of the United States.

my worldgeography.com Data Discovery

Chapter 24

Australia and the Pacific

Essential Question

What makes a nation?

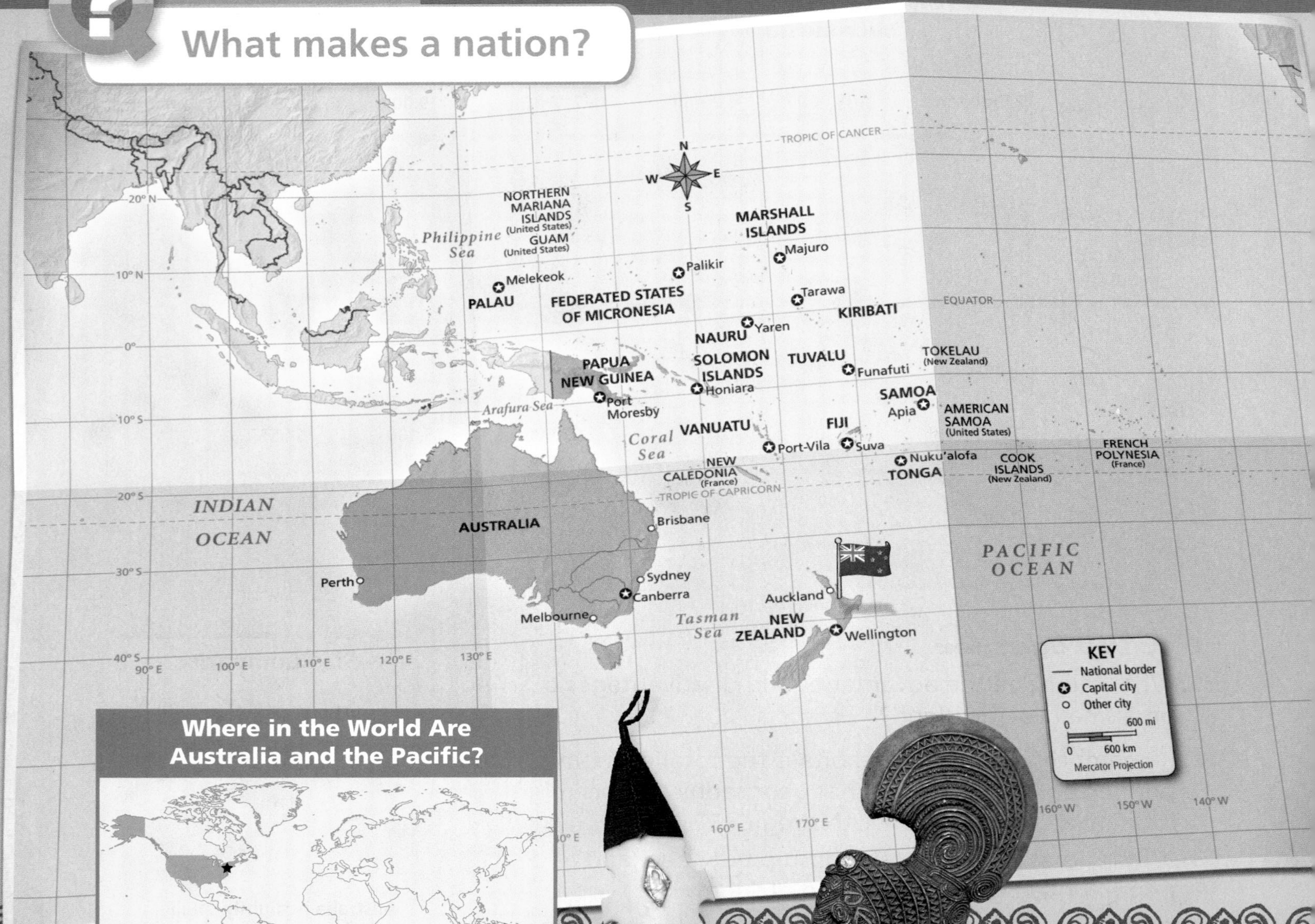

TROPIC OF CANCER
N
W
E
S
20° N
10° N
0°
10° S
20° S
30° S
40° S
90° E
100° E
110° E
120° E
130° E
160° E
170° E
160° W
150° W
140° W
NORTHERN MARIANA ISLANDS (United States)
GUAM (United States)
Philippine Sea
MARSHALL ISLANDS
Majuro
Palikir
Melekeok
PALAU
FEDERATED STATES OF MICRONESIA
Tarawa
KIRIBATI
EQUATOR
Yaren
NAURU
SOLOMON ISLANDS
Honiara
TUVALU
Funafuti
TOKELAU (New Zealand)
PAPUA NEW GUINEA
Port Moresby
Arafura Sea
SAMOA
Apia
AMERICAN SAMOA (United States)
FIJI
Suva
VANUATU
Port-Vila
Coral Sea
NEW CALEDONIA (France)
Nuku'alofa
TONGA
COOK ISLANDS (New Zealand)
FRENCH POLYNESIA (France)
TROPIC OF CAPRICORN
INDIAN OCEAN
AUSTRALIA
Brisbane
Perth
Sydney
Canberra
Melbourne
Tasman Sea
Auckland
NEW ZEALAND
Wellington
PACIFIC OCEAN
KEY
National border
Capital city
Other city
0
600 mi
0
600 km
Mercator Projection

Where in the World Are Australia and the Pacific?

Washington, D.C., to Auckland: 8,620 miles

my Story

Jack Connects to His Culture

In this section, you'll read about Jack, a young man from New Zealand trying to keep in touch with his Maori culture. **What does Jack's story tell you about life in Australia and the Pacific?**

Story by Tui Ruwhiu for myWorld Geography Online

It is early one weekday morning, and 17-year-old Jack is busy getting ready for another day at school. Jack lives in Auckland, New Zealand's largest city. By 7:30, Jack is on the bus for the 50-minute ride to his school, Avondale College.

Jack lives with his two younger brothers and his mother, father, and grandmother. Jack's father is a television actor and comedian. His mother manages the household and works in a television production company.

Jack is part Maori (MAow ree), descended from the original inhabitants of New Zealand. The Maori migrated to New Zealand—which they call Aotearoa (AOW tee AR roh uh)—from other parts of the Pacific region about 1,000 years ago.

Explore the Essential Question
- at **my worldgeography.com**
- using the **myWorld Chapter Activity**
- with the **Student Journal**

Facial expressions like Jack's were often used by Maori to frighten enemies before battle. Today, Maori people make this expression as part of a traditional greeting on important occasions. ▶

my worldgeography.com On Assignment

Jack and his horse

Jack and his brothers

Maori students make up about 8 percent of the 2,600 students at Avondale College. They have their own wharenui (meeting house) and wharekai (dining hall) at school. At breaks, lunchtimes, and after school, Maori students gather at the wharekai to talk and share food with friends.

But Maori people like Jack and his friends once faced many obstacles in New Zealand. During the 1800s, British colonization of New Zealand led to a series of wars with the Maori. Eventually, the British defeated the Maori. Many Maori moved to cities and lost touch with their culture.

Interest in Maori culture has grown since the mid-1900s. Today, many Maori study their language, history, and customs. Jack feels a strong connection to his culture and to his homeland on New Zealand's North Island. "I know the blood of my ancestors is in that soil," he says quietly, "because they gave their lives fighting for that land."

Jack takes a Maori language class at school every day. He hopes to become a skilled Maori speaker like his father, who grew up speaking Maori.

Jack's class practices kapa haka.

Jack's waka ama team

Although Jack went to a Maori-language day care center as a child, his parents decided to send him to English-language schools. English is the language most commonly spoken in New Zealand. At home, the family speaks English.

Jack stays connected to Maori culture in other ways. He is one of the leaders of his school's kapa haka team. Kapa haka is a performance art that combines singing and dancing. It uses parts of traditional Maori songs, dances, and combat techniques.

Each year, New Zealand holds a national competition for high school students of kapa haka. This competition is part of Polyfest, a celebration of Polynesian culture and dance. To prepare for the competition, Jack's kapa haka team practices each day at lunchtime and after school. It also practices for at least one full day each weekend.

Jack is also a member of his school's waka ama team. Waka ama are Maori canoes designed for use on the open ocean. Avondale has male, female, and mixed waka ama teams. Students of all ethnic backgrounds take part in the sport.

Jack plans to continue studying the Maori language and participating in kapa haka after he finishes school. He hopes to increase his understanding of his culture. "If you're interested, it's a lot easier to learn," Jack says. "There are a lot of people out there who have the knowledge. You've just got to be willing to go out and grab it."

myStory Video

Join Jack as he shows you more about his life in New Zealand.

Meet the Journalist

Name Tui Ruwhiu
Favorite Moment Watching Jack's kapa haka team practice

Key Ideas

- The physical geography of Australia and the Pacific region is diverse and unusual.

- The Pacific Ocean includes thousands of islands with different sizes, climates, and resources.

- Climate, location, and resources have affected where and how people live.

 Visual Glossary

Key Terms • Outback • coral reef • atoll • plate tectonics

 Reading Skill: Label an Outline Map Take notes using the outline map in your journal.

Children in Papua New Guinea play in an outrigger canoe designed for ocean travel. ▼

Physical Features

The physical geography of Australia and the Pacific region is diverse. The region has tens of thousands of islands of varying sizes. Each has different resources, climates, and ecosystems. The great distance between these islands and other land areas has helped make them unique.

Australia lies at the southwest edge of the Pacific Ocean between Southeast Asia and Antarctica. It is the largest country in the huge Pacific region. The Pacific region also includes three separate subregions of islands: Melanesia, Micronesia, and Polynesia.

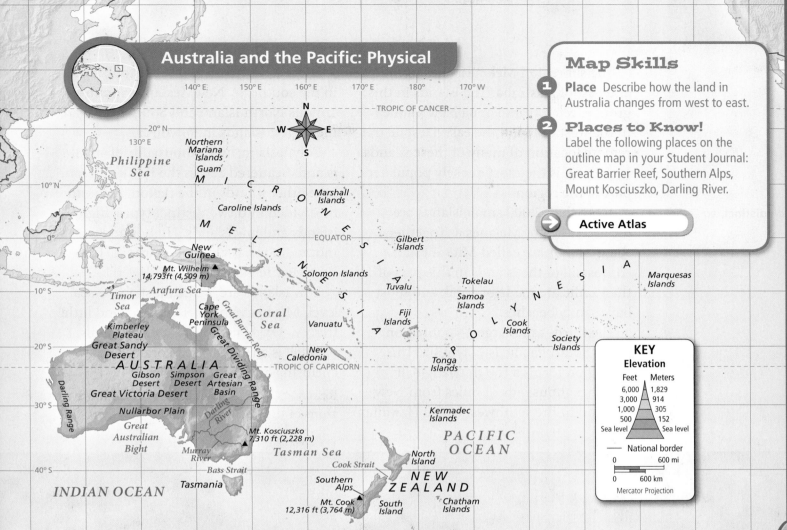

Australia and the Pacific: Physical

Map Skills

1 **Place** Describe how the land in Australia changes from west to east.

2 **Places to Know!**
Label the following places on the outline map in your Student Journal: Great Barrier Reef, Southern Alps, Mount Kosciuszko, Darling River.

→ Active Atlas

KEY
Elevation

Feet	Meters
6,000	1,829
3,000	914
1,000	305
500	152
Sea level	Sea level

—— National border

0   600 mi

0   600 km

Mercator Projection

Australia is completely surrounded by water, just like an island. But because of its large size, it is considered a continent. It is Earth's smallest continent.

Australia has wide, flat stretches of dry land, especially in its central and western portions. The interior of Australia is known as the **Outback,** a sparsely inhabited region with low plateaus and plains. The Outback is home to a large rock formation known as Uluru, or Ayers Rock. Central and western Australia include three large deserts—the Great Victoria Desert, the Great Sandy Desert, and the Simpson Desert. Eastern Australia, on the other

hand, is covered by low mountains, valleys, and a large river system. Australia's coasts also include fertile plains.

Australia's dramatic physical features are not limited to land. The Great Barrier Reef, located off Australia's northeast coast, is the world's largest grouping of coral reefs. A **coral reef** is a formation of rock-like material made up of the skeletons of tiny sea creatures. The Great Barrier Reef is more than 1,250 miles (2,000 kilometers) long. It is home to many different underwater plants and animals. It is also a popular place for surfing and scuba diving.

The subregion Melanesia lies just north and east of Australia. The islands in this group stretch from Papua New Guinea in the west to Fiji in the east. Despite the remote location of many of these islands, Melanesia is the most densely populated part of the region.

distinct, *adj.,* different

More than 2,000 small islands are located north of Melanesia. Together, these islands are called Micronesia. Almost all of the islands in this part of the Pacific are made of coral, and most have sandy beaches.

The third—and largest—subregion in the South Pacific is Polynesia. This subregion forms a rough triangle. It stretches thousands of miles from New Zealand in the southwest to the Hawaiian Islands in the north and to Easter Island in the southeast. New Zealand's mountainous North Island and South Island are the largest islands in Polynesia.

Polynesia includes thousands of small islands scattered across the Pacific Ocean. Like other islands in the region, they can be divided into two <u>distinct</u> types: high islands and low islands. High islands are mountainous, rocky, and volcanic. They have very fertile soil.

Low islands are located just above sea level. Most have poor, sandy soil and little fresh water. Many low islands are atolls. An **atoll** is a ring-shaped coral island enclosing a body of water.

Reading Check What are the three subregions of the Pacific region?

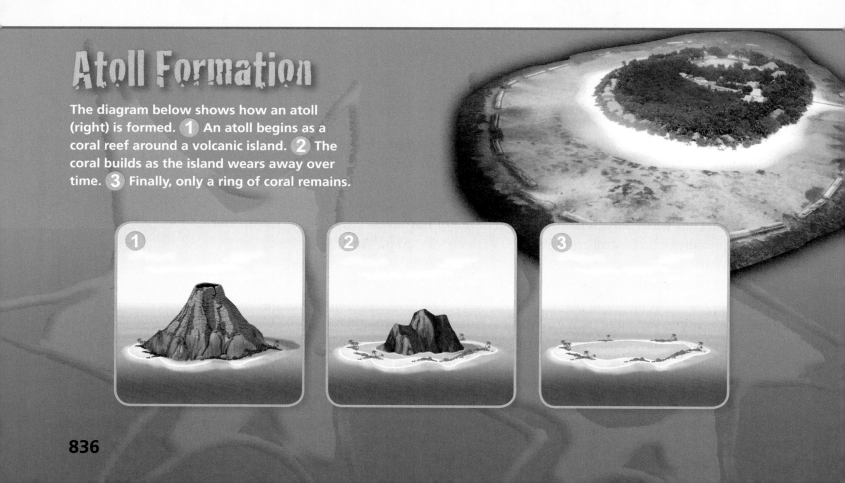

Atoll Formation

The diagram below shows how an atoll (right) is formed. **1** An atoll begins as a coral reef around a volcanic island. **2** The coral builds as the island wears away over time. **3** Finally, only a ring of coral remains.

Plate Tectonics

Plate tectonics helps us understand the forces that have shaped Australia and the Pacific. **Plate tectonics** is the theory that explains how huge blocks of Earth's crust called "plates" move. Hundreds of millions of years ago, the region was part of a giant continent. This ancient continent also included the land that now makes up South America, Africa, and India. Over time, Earth's plates separated. The giant continent slowly broke apart.

Australia and the Pacific include the Indo-Australian and Pacific plates. These two plates move toward each other at a rate of a few inches per year. Although this movement is slow, it has important effects on the region. As the plates <u>collide</u>, they push the ocean floor up above sea level. This creates many islands and volcanoes along the plate boundaries.

Plate movement and volcanic action have formed the two main islands of New Zealand. North Island has a series of high volcanic peaks that tower over green valleys below. South Island's Southern Alps are even higher mountains running along the island's western edge.

The movement of tectonic plates also helps explain the region's unique plant and animal populations. After the region broke away from other areas millions of years ago, its plants and animals were cut off from the rest of the world.

collide, *v.,* to come together

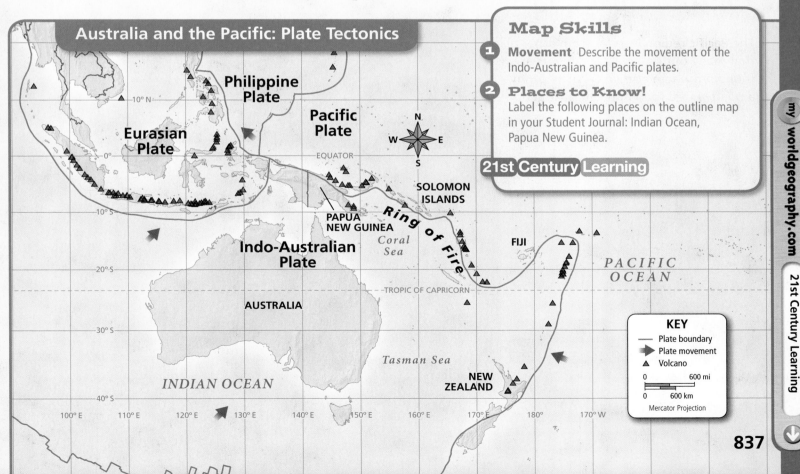

Australia and the Pacific: Plate Tectonics

Philippine Plate

Pacific Plate

Eurasian Plate

EQUATOR

SOLOMON ISLANDS

PAPUA NEW GUINEA

Ring of Fire

Indo-Australian Plate

Coral Sea

FIJI

PACIFIC OCEAN

TROPIC OF CAPRICORN

AUSTRALIA

Tasman Sea

NEW ZEALAND

INDIAN OCEAN

100° E 110° E 120° E 130° E 140° E 150° E 160° E 170° E 180° 170° W

10° N 0° 10° S 20° S 30° S 40° S

N W E S

Map Skills

1. **Movement** Describe the movement of the Indo-Australian and Pacific plates.

2. **Places to Know!**
Label the following places on the outline map in your Student Journal: Indian Ocean, Papua New Guinea.

21st Century Learning

KEY
— Plate boundary
➤ Plate movement
▲ Volcano

0 ——— 600 mi
0 ——— 600 km
Mercator Projection

Over time, small changes have occurred naturally in the region's plants and animals. Because of the area's isolation, these changes have not spread to other places. As a result, Australia and the Pacific islands have many plant and animal species that cannot be found anywhere else in the world.

However, people have brought new plants and animals to the region. In some areas, the spread of nonnative species such as rabbits, snakes, and wild pigs has harmed the region's ecosystems.

Reading Check **How has plate movement affected the region?**

Climate

Weather and climate patterns vary widely across the Pacific region. Even opposite sides of the same island can have very different weather patterns due to differences in elevation, wind, and ocean currents.

Australia Australia's climate changes dramatically from one area to another. Its southeast and southwest coasts have temperate climates. The eastern coast has plentiful rainfall. In far northern Australia, heavy monsoon rains are common in the summer months. A winter dry season follows this wet season. However, most

Pacific Ecosystems

The Pacific region is so far from other places that many of its animals and plants are not found anywhere else on Earth. At right, a boab, a tree found only in Australia.

Koalas sleep for about 19 hours a day.

The platypus is a mammal that lays eggs.

A baby kangaroo lives in its mother's pouch.

of central Australia has arid and semiarid climates. This region has warm temperatures and little rain year-round.

New Zealand and the Pacific Islands
New Zealand has a mild and wet maritime climate. It is cooler than Australia. Most other Pacific islands are located in the tropics. They tend to have tropical wet climates, with heavy precipitation and high temperatures year-round. On some mountainous islands, such as New Guinea, precipitation and temperature vary with elevation. Places at higher elevations usually have less rain and lower temperatures.

Water and Wildfires Although many of the Pacific islands receive heavy rainfall, some places still do not have enough fresh water for drinking or other human use. Low-lying atolls and low, sandy islands can collect very little rainwater.

Wildfires are a serious challenge in dry parts of the region. In Australia, fires can spread rapidly across the countryside during the winter dry season. These destructive fires are made worse by the grasses that grow during the summer wet weather and dry out during the winter.

Reading Check How do climates vary within Australia?

myWorld Activity
Traveling Tips

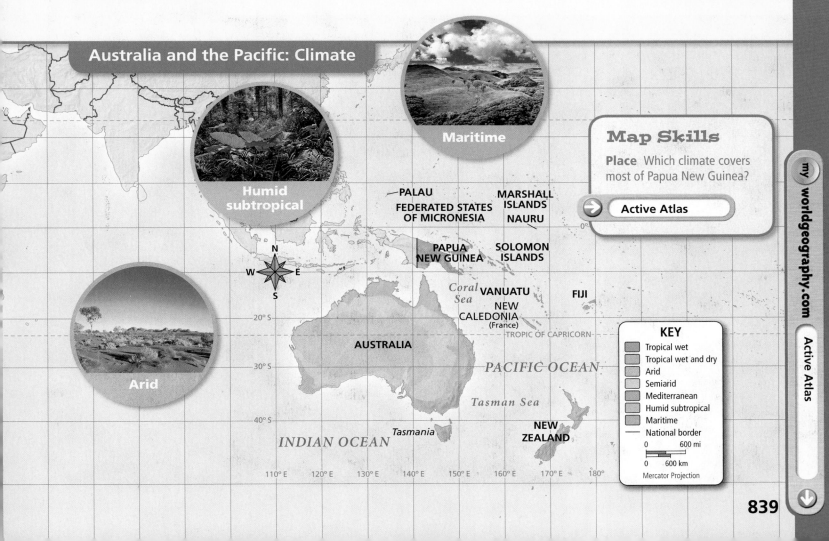

Australia and the Pacific: Climate

Maritime

Humid subtropical

Arid

PALAU
FEDERATED STATES OF MICRONESIA
MARSHALL ISLANDS
NAURU
0°

PAPUA NEW GUINEA
SOLOMON ISLANDS

Coral Sea
VANUATU
NEW CALEDONIA (France)
FIJI
TROPIC OF CAPRICORN

AUSTRALIA

20° S

PACIFIC OCEAN

30° S

Tasman Sea

40° S

Tasmania

NEW ZEALAND

INDIAN OCEAN

110° E   120° E   130° E   140° E   150° E   160° E   170° E   180°

Map Skills

Place Which climate covers most of Papua New Guinea?

Active Atlas

KEY
- Tropical wet
- Tropical wet and dry
- Arid
- Semiarid
- Mediterranean
- Humid subtropical
- Maritime
- — National border

0   600 mi
0   600 km
Mercator Projection

my worldgeography.com | **Active Atlas**

People and Resources

The region's population patterns vary widely. The availability of natural resources also differs from place to place.

Australia and New Zealand Most Australians and New Zealanders live in urban areas. Most Australians live on the country's mild east coast. Nearly 90 percent of the country's 22 million people live in coastal cities such as Sydney and Melbourne. The hot, dry central area of Australia has fewer people.

Most of New Zealand's 4 million people live on North Island. This island includes Auckland and other cities.

Australia is rich in natural resources, including bauxite, iron, and diamonds. It also has energy resources such as coal and natural gas. New Zealand, however, has relatively few mineral resources.

Both Australia and New Zealand have many large farms and ranches. Australia produces cotton, wheat, and sheep, although lack of water is a big challenge

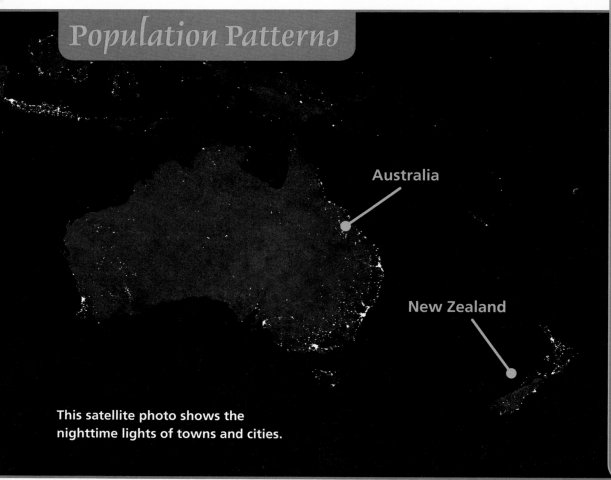

Population Patterns

Australia

New Zealand

This satellite photo shows the nighttime lights of towns and cities.

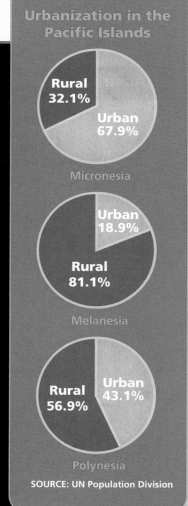

Urbanization in the Pacific Islands

Rural 32.1% · **Urban 67.9%**
Micronesia

Urban 18.9% · **Rural 81.1%**
Melanesia

Rural 56.9% · **Urban 43.1%**
Polynesia

SOURCE: UN Population Division

for farmers and ranchers. Much of central Australia is too dry for agriculture or grazing. Irrigation is very important.

New Zealand's fertile farmland and supplies of fresh water support its successful agriculture. Wool production is important.

Pacific Islands The population of the Pacific islands is generally less urban than that of Australia and New Zealand. Many people live in small villages in hilly regions or on coastlines.

The availability of natural resources varies. Most of the low islands have poor soil, little vegetation, and few mineral or energy resources. As a result, the low islands have relatively small populations.

High islands have fertile soil and many natural resources. Their farms produce bananas, cacao, and other crops. Some high islands also have resources such as gold, copper, and petroleum.

Reading Check How does the availability of resources affect population in the region?

▲ Many Pacific economies rely on natural resources. Above, oil workers drill in Australia.

Section 1 Assessment

Essential Question
What makes a nation?

Key Terms
1. How has the movement of tectonic plates affected the region?
2. Describe Australia's Outback region.

Key Ideas
3. How have Australia's geography and climate influenced where people live?
4. How do high islands differ from low islands?
5. How does the geography of the region vary from one place to another?

Think Critically
6. **Compare and Contrast** How do population and resources vary in different parts of the region?
7. **Draw Conclusions** Why are many Pacific species found nowhere else on Earth?

8. How have climate, location, and resources affected the development of Australia, New Zealand, and the Pacific islands?

History of Australia and the Pacific

Key Ideas
- The Pacific region was one of the last places on Earth settled by people.
- By the late 1800s, Australia and the Pacific were under the control of European and other colonial powers.
- Colonization transformed the region.

Key Terms • Aborigines • Maori • assimilation • ethnocentrism • missionary  Visual Glossary

 Reading Skill: Sequence Take notes using the graphic organizer in your journal.

This Maori woman's chin is marked with the traditional Maori tattoos known as moko. ▼

The Pacific region was one of the last areas on Earth to be settled by people. When European settlers arrived in large numbers in the 1800s, they made the region's native peoples change their ways of life.

Migration and Settlement

People settled the region in three waves of migration, shown on the map in this section. Around 60,000 years ago, the first people settled Australia and New Guinea. By 1,000 years ago, people had sailed across the ocean to New Zealand and other Pacific islands.

Australia The original inhabitants of Australia are known as **Aborigines.** Aborigines lived throughout the continent, but most lived in the temperate southeast part of Australia. Early Aborigines were nomadic. They moved together in small groups, hunting animals and gathering plants. Aborigines had a complex society without chiefs or other formal leaders. They had strong religious convictions about nature, believing that it was their responsibility to care for the land.

The Pacific Islands In Melanesia, the great number of islands led to the development of isolated cultural groups over thousands of years. Most island people relied on the ocean for fishing, but Melanesians also developed agriculture about 10,000 years ago. In Polynesia, kingdoms extended over entire groups of islands.

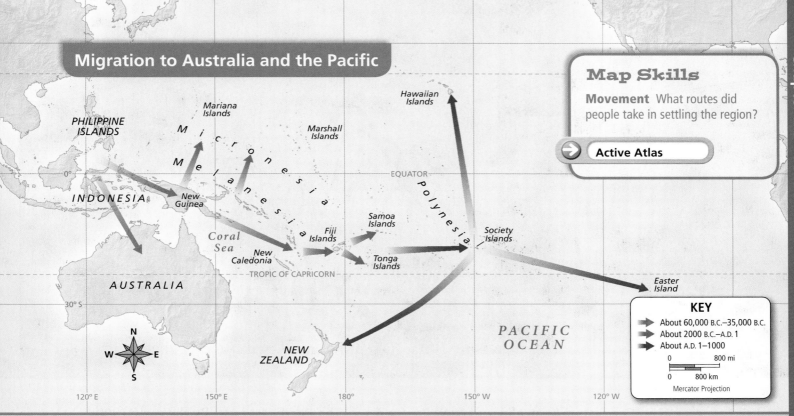

Migration to Australia and the Pacific

PHILIPPINE ISLANDS

Mariana Islands

Marshall Islands

Hawaiian Islands

Micronesia

Melanesia

INDONESIA

New Guinea

EQUATOR

Polynesia

Coral Sea

New Caledonia

Fiji Islands

Samoa Islands

Society Islands

Tonga Islands

AUSTRALIA

TROPIC OF CAPRICORN

Easter Island

PACIFIC OCEAN

NEW ZEALAND

120° E   150° E   180°   150° W   120° W

0°   30° S

Map Skills

Movement What routes did people take in settling the region?

→ **Active Atlas**

KEY
→ About 60,000 B.C.–35,000 B.C.
→ About 2000 B.C.–A.D. 1
→ About A.D. 1–1000

0   800 mi
0   800 km
Mercator Projection

Frequent conflict led people to live in protected settlements. Polynesians often went on long-distance ocean trips.

Like other Polynesians, the Maori lived in small settlements. The **Maori** are the original inhabitants of New Zealand and the Cook Islands. The Maori fished, hunted, and farmed. Chiefs were at the top of Maori society. At the bottom of society were slaves, usually captured during warfare.

The center of Maori society is a marae, an enclosed area of land that includes a meeting house and other buildings. Art is an important part of Maori culture. The Maori carve decorations into their buildings, canoes, weapons, and other objects.

Reading Check How did people settle Australia and the Pacific region?

Exploration and Colonization

In the late 1700s, British explorer James Cook claimed Australia and New Zealand for Great Britain. Cook's expeditions increased European interest in the region.

> 66 In this Extensive Country it can never be doubted but what most sorts of Grain, Fruits, Roots … of every kind would flourish … and here [is food] for more Cattle at all seasons of the year than ever can be brought into this Country. 99
> —James Cook, journal entry, 1770

Colonization Begins British settlement of Australia began in 1788. Many early settlers were convicted criminals who had been <u>exiled</u> to Australia. Colonists farmed and ranched. In 1851, colonists discovered gold, and the British population soared.

exile, v., to force out of one's own home

my **worldgeography.com** Active Atlas

A Changing Region

Lieutenant James Cook was an early British explorer of the region.

British colonization led to conflict with native peoples.

Conflict in Australia and New Zealand
As British colonists forced Aborigines off their lands, fighting broke out. In addition, many Aborigines died from European diseases.

The British also practiced forced assimilation. **Assimilation** is the process by which one group takes on the cultural traits of another. British ethnocentrism led settlers to force Aborigines to adopt British customs. **Ethnocentrism** is the attitude that one's own social or cultural group is better than all others. British colonists took Aboriginal children away from their families and forced them to live in institutions or with white families. This practice continued into the 1960s.

British settlers began to arrive in New Zealand in the early 1800s. They were attracted by New Zealand's harbors and fertile soil. Conflict with the Maori led to a series of wars eventually won by Britain.

strategic, *adj.,* important to military or action plans

The Pacific Islands By the early 1900s, the United States, France, Great Britain, and Japan controlled most of the Pacific islands. Colonizers claimed some islands because of their natural resources. Other islands were taken for their location. For example, the Micronesian islands served as a strategic midpoint between the United States and Japan.

Britain ruled its colonies with colonial governors. Other countries controlled their colonies with military forces or through commercial companies.

Colonizers brought many new ideas and customs. For example, colonizers introduced the concept of owning land instead of using land collectively. Some colonizers were **missionaries,** or people sent to another country by a church to spread its religious beliefs.

Reading Check How did the British treat the region's native people?

844

Left, Aborigines were forced to adopt British ways.
Above, Aborigines protest government policies.

myWorld Activity
Before and After

Independence

Australia and New Zealand gained their independence peacefully in the early 1900s. Today, both belong to the British Commonwealth of Nations, which includes many former British colonies.

Most Pacific islands won independence peacefully in the second half of the 1900s. Independence movements played a role on some islands. In Western Samoa (now Samoa), the nonviolent Mau movement worked for independence, which Samoa won in 1962. Still, not all of the Pacific region has been decolonized. The United States, France, and New Zealand still control some Pacific islands.

Reading Check **How did the region win independence from colonizers?**

Section 2 Assessment

Essential Question

What makes a nation?

Key Terms

1. How did the British policy of forced assimilation affect Aborigines?

2. What did missionaries to the region seek to do?

Key Ideas

3. Why did countries seek to colonize the region?

4. How did people first settle the region?

5. How did the British colonization of Australia and New Zealand affect native peoples there?

Think Critically

6. **Compare and Contrast** How were the region's people alike and different before British colonization began?

7. **Sequence** In what order were Australia and the three subgroups of Pacific islands settled?

8. Does the history of colonization explain the formation of present-day nations in this region? Explain.

Australia and the Pacific Today

Key Ideas
- The region has a great deal of cultural diversity.
- Countries in the region have different forms of government and different levels of economic development.
- Protecting the environment is a major concern for the region's people.

Key Terms • indigenous • coup • secondary industry • primary industry • drought • climate change • nuclear weapon

 Visual Glossary

Reading Skill: Identify Main Ideas and Details
Take notes using the graphic organizer in your journal.

Most Australians, such as the man below, are descended from British settlers. ▼

 Culture Close-up

Australia and the Pacific region are home to many cultures and ethnic groups, such as Jack's Maori people in New Zealand. A shared history and a blend of different cultures and traditions have shaped life in the region. Today, Australia and New Zealand are wealthy, highly developed nations with modern industrial economies. The smaller Pacific islands are less developed, with economies based largely on tourism and the use of natural resources.

People and Culture

Australia, New Zealand, and the Pacific islands include people from many different ethnic groups and cultures. As a result, the population of the region is diverse.

Australia and New Zealand Most Australians and New Zealanders have British ancestors. Since the 1970s, growing numbers of Asians and Pacific islanders have moved to these two countries.

Smaller numbers of Australians and New Zealanders are descended from **indigenous** people, or people native to the region. Only about 1 percent of Australia's 22 million people are Aboriginal. As you learned in Section 2, British settlers and the Australian government mistreated Aborigines for many years. In 2008, the Australian government officially apologized for this unjust treatment of Aborigines.

One Region, Many Cultures

Australia and the Pacific region are home to people from many different cultures. These cultures developed independently because of the great distances separating them.

→ **Language Lesson**

An Aboriginal girl from Australia

A man from Papua New Guinea takes part in a traditional celebration.

Samoan girls wearing woven grass dresses and beaded headbands

Jack, who is from New Zealand, is part Maori.

my **Story** 📷 **Photo**

New Zealand has a larger population of indigenous people: about 8 percent of New Zealand's 4 million people are Maori. Like the Aborigines, the Maori were forced to adopt many British ways of life. Still, Maori culture has survived. In recent years, Maori people have gained more political power. Since the 1970s, the New Zealand government has paid hundreds of millions of dollars to Maori groups to <u>compensate</u> them for having taken Maori land in the past.

In general, Australians and New Zealanders are healthy and well educated, with long average life expectancies. However, many Aborigines and Maori have lower standards of living and levels of education than other Australians and New Zealanders. Government leaders are working to improve the political and economic status of indigenous peoples.

Pacific Islands Over time, Pacific islanders developed many different languages, religions, and customs. European colonization reduced this cultural diversity. For example, Pacific people once practiced hundreds of different religions. Today, most are Christian. Still, most Pacific islanders are indigenous people.

Although modern culture has spread throughout the region, some islanders have kept traditional customs. For example, many Pacific islanders practice traditional forms of art, dance, and music.

Reading Check What is the name of New Zealand's indigenous people?

compensate, *v.,* pay

my worldgeography.com

Culture Close-up

Government

Australia and New Zealand were once British colonies. As a result, both have governments that are similar to the British system of government.

Australia and New Zealand Australia and New Zealand are parliamentary democracies. In these systems, citizens elect representatives to a parliament, or legislature. The parliament then chooses a prime minister as the head of the government. The prime minister and the parliament govern the country.

Australia has six states. As in the United States, these states have a great deal of power to govern themselves. They also have their own legislatures and court systems. New Zealand does not have any provinces or states, but it does have local and regional governments.

Citizens of Australia and New Zealand have rights and responsibilities similar to those of U.S. citizens. For example, Australians have freedom of religion and freedom of speech. There are also differences. Australians who are registered to vote can be fined for failing to vote, for example.

Pacific Islands The Pacific islands have a variety of governments, although most are democratic. A few of these countries have suffered from political <u>corruption</u> or unstable governments. For example, Fiji's military has led four coups since 1987. A **coup** is the sudden, violent overthrow of a government, often by the military.

Reading Check How does Australia select leaders and establish laws?

corruption, *n.,* improper use of power

Queen Elizabeth II of the United Kingdom is the official head of state of Australia, New Zealand, and several other former British colonies. She has little real power, however. ▼

Pacific Governments

Many of the region's countries are parliamentary democracies. Above, a Papua New Guinea man waits to vote in a national election. Left, Australia's Parliament

Economy

The region's levels of economic development vary greatly. While Australia and New Zealand have highly developed market economies, most smaller Pacific islands have developing economies.

Australia and New Zealand Australia's major industries are agriculture, mining, tourism, and manufacturing. Although Australia exports natural resources to many countries in Asia, many Australian businesses are secondary industries. A **secondary industry** involves the use of resources to create new products, as occurs in manufacturing. Australia's highly educated population and advanced technology have helped its industries modernize and succeed. As a result, Australia has a wealthy economy with a high economic output per person.

New Zealand's economy is similar to Australia's, although it is smaller. Services, industry, and tourism are the most valuable elements of New Zealand's economy. New Zealand farmers raise cows and sheep for meat, dairy, and wool products.

Pacific Islands Many island economies rely on primary industries such as fishing. A **primary industry** involves the collection of resources from nature. Agriculture and fishing are important primary industries.

Many islands have joined together in trade and business groups, such as the Pacific Islands Forum. By working together, islanders hope that they can attract international business and tourism to their islands, improving their economies and standards of living.

Reading Check Which countries in the region are wealthiest?

my World IN NUMBERS

The region's countries catch about **1.4** million fish per year—less than **1%** of the world's total fish catch.

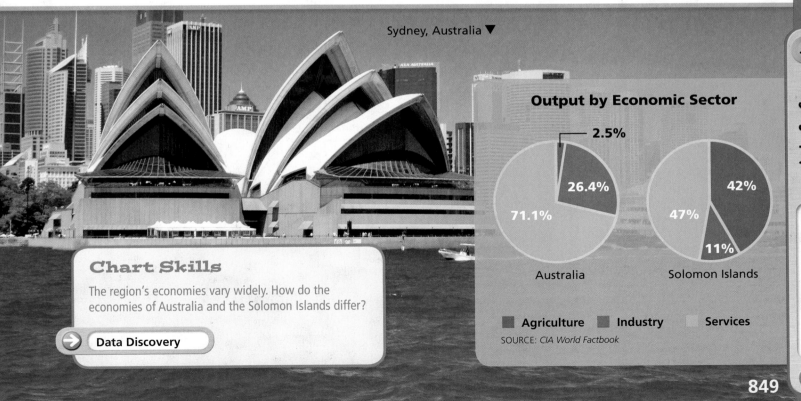

Sydney, Australia ▼

Output by Economic Sector

Australia
- 71.1%
- 26.4%
- 2.5%

Solomon Islands
- 47%
- 42%
- 11%

■ Agriculture ■ Industry □ Services

SOURCE: *CIA World Factbook*

Chart Skills

The region's economies vary widely. How do the economies of Australia and the Solomon Islands differ?

→ **Data Discovery**

my worldgeography.com Data Discovery

Disappearing Islands

myWorld Activity
Take Action on the
Pacific Environment

A melting
Antarctic glacier ▼

In recent years, higher global temperatures have led to the melting of glaciers. Also, as water warms, it expands. Melting ice and expanding water have raised global sea levels. In the Pacific region, many people live close to sea level. For example, Tuvalu is a group of nine tiny islands about 2,500 miles (4,000 kilometers) northeast of Australia. Its highest point is only 15 feet (4.5 meters) above sea level, and most land is just a few feet above the water. As global sea level rises, Tuvalu—with its 9,600 residents—is slowly sinking below the ocean.

THINK CRITICALLY How is the sea level rise affecting Tuvalu?

Effects on Tuvalu

- High tides regularly flood Tuvalu.
- Waves from strong storms can wash completely over Fongafale, Tuvalu's largest island.
- Rising levels of salt water kill Tuvalu's crops and threaten livestock.
- Some residents are making plans to migrate to Australia or other countries in order to flee the rising seas.

Fongafale, Tuvalu

Lagoon

Fongafale

Vaiaku

PACIFIC
OCEAN

Today

Lagoon

Fongafale

Vaiaku

PACIFIC
OCEAN

About 2100

KEY
Island
Reef
Deep Water
o Village

0   1 mi
0   1 km
Lambert Azimuthal
Equal-Area Projection

▲ Parts of Tuvalu flood often, forcing people and animals to adapt.

850

Environment

Pacific economies often depend on the environment. For example, tourism relies on the region's sandy beaches and clear blue water. Agriculture and fishing involve the use of natural resources. Today, people are working to protect the environment and use resources carefully. But the Pacific region still faces environmental challenges.

Drought Australia is the driest inhabited continent. In recent years, many areas of the country have been affected by drought. A **drought** is a long period of extremely dry weather. Drought has caused Australia's farms to produce fewer and smaller harvests.

Climate Change Climate change is another major environmental problem. **Climate change** is a long-term, significant change to a region's average weather. Natural processes can cause climate change. However, many scientists believe that human activity—such as air pollution—is a major factor.

Perhaps the most important effect of climate change in the Pacific region is a rise in sea level. This rise is caused by the melting of glaciers and the warming and expansion of water due to higher global temperatures. Many scientists believe that the sea level will continue to rise in coming years, perhaps by as much as two feet or more by 2100.

Since many of the people in the Pacific region live near sea level, the sea level rise is a serious concern. Even a small rise can affect low-lying areas. Storms can push higher water farther onto land, causing widespread erosion.

Other Issues Some economic activities can cause environmental harm. For example, mining can cause water and soil pollution. In addition, the United States, France, and the United Kingdom tested nuclear weapons in the region from the 1940s to the 1990s. A **nuclear weapon** is a powerful explosive device that can cause widespread destruction. This testing may have harmful long-term effects on the region's people and ecosystems.

Reading Check How is sea level rise affecting the Pacific region?

Section 3 Assessment

Key Terms
1. How is climate change affecting Australia and the Pacific region?
2. What are primary and secondary industries?

Key Ideas
3. Why are the region's people concerned about the environment?
4. Describe the region's economies.
5. Why does the region have such a wide variety of cultures?

Think Critically
6. **Summarize** Summarize the present-day conditions of Australia's indigenous people.
7. **Draw Conclusions** Why might people who live on an island be able to preserve their culture for a long time without change?

Essential Question
What makes a nation?
8. How do governments and economies vary among the region's nations?

851

Antarctica

Key Ideas

- Antarctica is the most remote and least populated continent on Earth.

- Antarctica has a harsh climate.

- People first ventured to Antarctica to claim land and resources, but now the continent is set aside for science.

Key Terms • ice sheet • glacier • iceberg • pack ice • Antarctic Treaty • ozone layer **Visual Glossary**

 Reading Skill: Summarize Take notes using the graphic organizer in your journal.

▲ Adelie penguins on an iceberg off Antarctica

Physical Geography

Covered by a glittering sheet of ice and surrounded by stormy seas, Antarctica is Earth's least populated continent. It is located directly south of Australia, Africa, and South America. It is the coldest and windiest region on Earth.

An Icy Landscape Antarctica is a place unlike anywhere else on Earth. A thick **ice sheet**—a large mass of compressed ice—covers 98 percent of the continent. This ice sheet holds most of the world's fresh water. **Glaciers,** or slow-moving bodies of ice, form in Antarctica's valleys

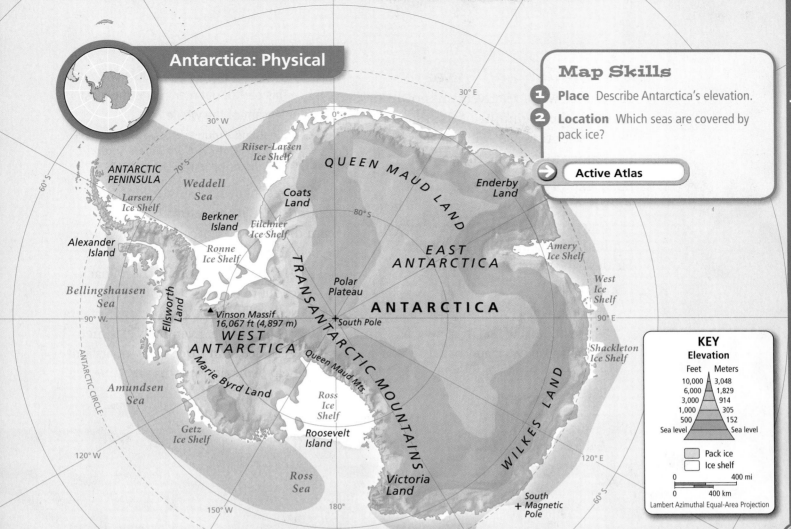

Antarctica: Physical

Map Skills

1 **Place** Describe Antarctica's elevation.

2 **Location** Which seas are covered by pack ice?

→ **Active Atlas**

KEY
Elevation

Feet	Meters
10,000	3,048
6,000	1,829
3,000	914
1,000	305
500	152
Sea level	Sea level

☐ Pack ice
☐ Ice shelf

0   400 mi
0   400 km
Lambert Azimuthal Equal-Area Projection

and flow toward the coast. When glaciers reach the sea, the ice breaks off into **icebergs,** or large floating masses of ice.

In winter, the surface of the sea around Antarctica freezes, forming pack ice. **Pack ice** is seasonal ice that floats on the water rather than being attached to land.

The Transantarctic Mountains divide Antarctica into two regions, a large, flat area called East Antarctica and a smaller region called West Antarctica. At the tip of West Antarctica, the Antarctic Peninsula extends toward South America. The Transantarctic Mountains have glaciers and dry valleys free of snow and ice.

Climate, Life, and Resources Antarctica's interior is a high, dry plateau. It receives little precipitation, less than two inches per year. The snow that does fall does not melt. Instead, it piles up year after year, eventually turning into glacial ice.

Antarctica's mineral resources include coal and iron ore. Its harsh climate limits vegetation to simple plants such as algae and mosses. Penguins, seals, and other animals spend much of their time in the ocean. The seas are home to a variety of fish, whales, and other marine life.

Reading Check How do Antarctica's climate and landscape affect life there?

Exploration and Research

Antarctica was a relatively unknown region at the beginning of the 1900s. Today, scientists use Antarctica as a giant laboratory to examine the natural world.

Early Explorers In 1910, explorers Robert Scott and Roald Amundsen began separate expeditions to the South Pole. Amundsen reached it in December 1911. He described part of the journey:

> 66 Our walk across this frozen lake was not pleasant. The ground under our feet was evidently hollow, and it sounded as if we were walking on empty barrels. First a man fell through, then a couple of dogs … This part of our march was the most unpleasant of the whole trip. 99

–Captain Roald Amundsen, *The South Pole: An Account of the Norwegian Antarctic Expedition in the* Fram, *1910–1912*

Scott reached the Pole a month after Amundsen. On the return trip, Scott's team died in a blizzard. Still, their studies helped advance Antarctic science.

In 1915, British explorer Ernest Shackleton set out to cross Antarctica. His ship was destroyed by pack ice, forcing his team to live on an ice floe. Eventually, the men crossed the ocean in three small boats and found help. Amazingly, everyone survived.

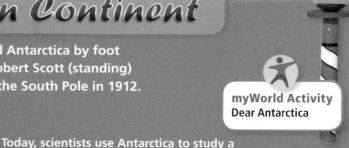

The Frozen Continent

Early explorers mapped Antarctica by foot and dogsled. At left, Robert Scott (standing) and Edward Wilson at the South Pole in 1912.

myWorld Activity
Dear Antarctica

A shelter used by Antarctic explorer Ernest Shackleton in 1907

Today, scientists use Antarctica to study a range of topics. Below, a group of biologists. Right, a marker near the South Pole

Antarctica and Science Early explorers often claimed land in Antarctica. By the 1940s, these competing land claims led to international conflict. In 1959, twelve countries signed the **Antarctic Treaty,** an agreement that preserves Antarctica for peaceful and scientific use. Other protections were adopted in later years.

Today, Antarctica has no permanent human settlement. It does have several scientific research stations scattered across the continent. Scientists from a number of countries study topics such as oceans, glaciers, and climate.

Climate and the Ozone Layer To study climate, scientists drill deep into the ice sheet to gather ice samples. By examining the samples, they can learn more about the climate at the time when the ice was formed. By studying past climates, scientists hope to understand more about how climate might change in the future.

Scientists in Antarctica also study the ozone layer. The **ozone layer** is a layer of the atmosphere that filters out most of the sun's harmful ultraviolet rays. Over time, the ozone layer over Antarctica has grown thinner. This area of reduced ozone, called the ozone hole, allows more ultraviolet radiation to reach Earth. A major cause of the hole in the ozone layer has been certain human-made chemical <u>compounds</u>. Today, most uses of these compounds have been banned. Scientists predict that the ozone layer will eventually recover if this ban is maintained.

compound, *n.,* something formed by two or more parts

Reading Check How do people use Antarctica today?

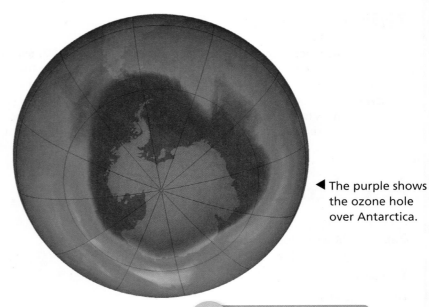

◀ The purple shows the ozone hole over Antarctica.

Section 4 Assessment

Key Terms

1. How does the Antarctic Treaty affect Antarctica?

2. Give short definitions of each of the following terms: ice sheet, glacier, iceberg, and pack ice.

Key Ideas

3. Why is Antarctica the least populated continent?

4. How does Antarctica's climate affect its environment?

5. Why are scientists interested in studying Antarctica?

Think Critically

6. Draw Conclusions How might its geography explain why Antarctica was not explored or settled until relatively recently?

7. Synthesize What challenges might Antarctica face in the future?

Essential Question

What makes a nation?

8. Why have no nations formed in Antarctica?

Chapter Assessment

Key Terms and Ideas

1. **Describe** How does **plate tectonics** explain the creation of volcanic islands in the Pacific?

2. **Recall** How did people settle the Pacific region?

3. **Summarize** What environmental issues does the region face?

4. **Compare and Contrast** Describe population density in Australia, New Zealand, and the Pacific islands.

5. **Paraphrase** Explain **ethnocentrism** in your own words.

6. **Summarize** What do **Aborigines** and the **Maori** have in common?

7. **Recall** How does the **Antarctic Treaty** protect Antarctica?

Think Critically

8. **Draw Inferences** How do you think Australia and New Zealand would be different today if British colonization had never taken place?

9. **Draw Conclusions** How might early explorers' experiences have helped to inspire the Antarctic Treaty?

10. **Synthesize** If drought continues in Australia, how might its population and economy change?

11. **Core Concepts: Climates and Ecosystems** How do you think the introduction of nonnative plant species has affected the Pacific region's ecosystem? What do you think can be done to better protect native species?

Places to Know

For each place, write the letter from the map that shows its location.

12. Great Barrier Reef

13. Papua New Guinea

14. Mount Kosciuszko

15. Darling River

16. Southern Alps

17. Indian Ocean

18. **Estimate** Using the scale, estimate the distance between the northwest tip of Papua New Guinea and the Southern Alps.

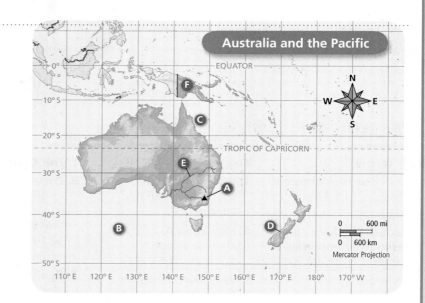

Essential Question

What makes a nation?

Reporting Back: A Voyage to the Pacific Follow your teacher's instructions to investigate geographic features of Australia and New Zealand as a member of explorer James Cook's crew. Work with your team members to collect and organize information on your field of expertise. Then prepare a multimedia presentation on the region to present to the British king.

21st Century Learning

Search for Information on the Internet

Imagine that you work at a U.S. zoo planning an exhibit on Antarctic penguins, leopard seals, and other animals. Use the Internet to research how to create an accurate exhibit. Then use this information to write a brief report. Remember to consider the following:
- Antarctica's climate and landscape
- Antarctica's land and sea temperatures
- the needs of Antarctic animals

Document-Based Questions

Success Tracker™
Online at myworldgeography.com

Use your knowledge of Australia and the Pacific and Documents A and B to answer Questions 1–3.

Document A

Internet Users	
Country	Users per 100 People
Australia	75.1
New Zealand	78.8
Papua New Guinea	1.8
Tonga	3.0
Vanuatu	3.5

SOURCE: United Nations Statistics Division

Document B

" I was definitely not told that I was Aboriginal. What [they] told us was that we had to be white. It was drummed into our heads that we were white … We were prisoners from [the moment] we were born."

—John, an Aboriginal man who was taken away from his family as a child in the 1940s

1. Examine Document A. What can you conclude about Pacific economies based on these data?

    A Australia and New Zealand are less developed than other countries in the region.

    B Australia and New Zealand are more developed than other countries in the region.

    C Countries in the region are equally developed.

    D Smaller countries are more developed than larger countries.

2. Read Document B. What does the quotation describe?

    A climate change

    B forced assimilation

    C migration

    D missionaries

3. **Writing Task** Do you think the situation described in Document B was common? Explain your answer.

Meet the Islanders

Your Mission Working in groups, you will research the indigenous peoples of Australia, New Zealand, and the Pacific islands. Then you will choose a person from one of those groups, research his or her life, and develop a multimedia biography.

One memorable moment of the 2000 Olympic Games in Sydney, Australia, came when Cathy Freeman won the 400-meter race. She was the first person of Aboriginal descent to win an Olympic medal. She took her victory lap proudly waving both the Australian and Aboriginal flags.

Many indigenous groups are found in Australia, New Zealand, and the Pacific islands. The indigenous people of Australia are known as Aborigines. The Maori are the indigenous people of New Zealand. The Pacific islands have a variety of indigenous cultures.

STEP 1

Choose a Subject.

Assign each person in your group to research one of these groups: Aborigines, Maori, and indigenous Pacific islanders. As you learn about these peoples, make a list of well-known or prominent individuals with that heritage. Try to include people from the arts, politics, sports, entertainment, science, and other fields. Share your findings and, as a group, choose one person to be the subject of your multimedia biography.

STEP 2

Research the Subject.

Do additional research on your subject's life and achievements. Divide up the tasks of finding out about the subject's family and childhood, adult life and achievements, historical events from his or her lifetime, and the customs and heritage of his or her ethnic group. Try to find lively details to enhance your presentation. Share your research with your group, and together decide what you will include in the biography.

STEP 3

Make a Presentation.

Plan and present a multimedia biography about your subject. Consider using written materials, photographs, videos, music, and other elements. Your biography should be thorough and focused. It should include interesting details as well as accurate facts. Your presentation to the class may take the form of a multimedia slideshow, a podcast, a radio broadcast, a documentary, or an interactive Web site.

The World: Political

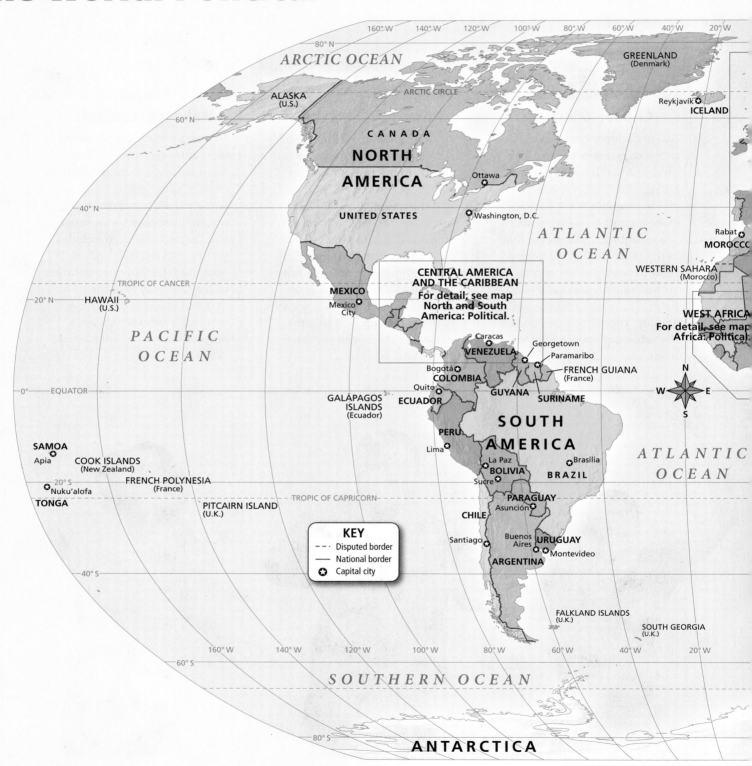

ARCTIC OCEAN

GREENLAND
(Denmark)

ALASKA
(U.S.)

ARCTIC CIRCLE

Reykjavík
ICELAND

CANADA

NORTH

AMERICA

Ottawa

UNITED STATES

Washington, D.C.

ATLANTIC
OCEAN

Rabat
MOROCCO

TROPIC OF CANCER

HAWAII
(U.S.)

MEXICO

Mexico
City

CENTRAL AMERICA
AND THE CARIBBEAN
For detail, see map
North and South
America: Political.

WESTERN SAHARA
(Morocco)

WEST AFRICA
For detail, see map
Africa: Political.

PACIFIC
OCEAN

Caracas

Georgetown

Paramaribo

VENEZUELA

Bogotá

COLOMBIA

FRENCH GUIANA
(France)

GALÁPAGOS
ISLANDS
(Ecuador)

Quito

ECUADOR

GUYANA

SURINAME

EQUATOR

SOUTH

AMERICA

ATLANTIC

OCEAN

SAMOA

Apia

PERU

Lima

Brasília

COOK ISLANDS
(New Zealand)

La Paz

BOLIVIA

BRAZIL

FRENCH POLYNESIA
(France)

Sucre

TROPIC OF CAPRICORN

Nuku'alofa

TONGA

PITCAIRN ISLAND
(U.K.)

PARAGUAY

Asunción

CHILE

KEY

Santiago

Buenos
Aires

URUGUAY

Montevideo

Disputed border

National border

Capital city

ARGENTINA

FALKLAND ISLANDS
(U.K.)

SOUTH GEORGIA
(U.K.)

SOUTHERN OCEAN

ANTARCTICA

20° E 40° E 60° E 80° E 100° E 120° E 140° E 160° E

SVALBARD
(Norway)

ARCTIC OCEAN

EUROPE AND SOUTHWEST ASIA
detail, see maps Europe: Political
and Asia: Political.

ARCTIC CIRCLE

80° N

RUSSIA

60° N

Moscow

ASIA

EUROPE

Astana

KAZAKHSTAN

Ulaanbaatar

MONGOLIA

40° N

UZBEKISTAN Tashkent Bishkek
TURKMENISTAN   KYRGYZSTAN
Ashgabat   Dushanbe
TAJIKISTAN

Beijing

NORTH
KOREA
P'yongyang
Seoul
SOUTH
KOREA

JAPAN
Tokyo

TURKEY

Tunis
TUNISIA
Tripoli

Tehran

Kabul

CHINA

PACIFIC
OCEAN

IRAQ
Baghdad
IRAN AFGHANISTAN
Islamabad
Kathmandu

LIBYA
Cairo
EGYPT

Kuwait
KUWAIT
BAHRAIN Manama
QATAR Doha
Riyadh Abu Dhabi
Muscat

PAKISTAN
New
Delhi
NEPAL
BHUTAN
Thimphu
Dhaka

Taipei
TAIWAN

TROPIC OF CANCER

20° N

AFRICA

Khartoum ERITREA
SUDAN Asmara
CENTRAL N'Djamena
AFRICAN
REPUBLIC

SAUDI
ARABIA

OMAN

UNITED
ARAB
EMIRATES

Sanaa
YEMEN
DJIBOUTI
Djibouti

INDIA

MYANMAR

BANGLADESH
Yangon

LAOS Hanoi
Vientiane
THAILAND VIETNAM
Bangkok CAMBODIA
Phnom Penh

Manila

PHILIPPINES

MARSHALL
ISLANDS
Majuro

NIGER
CHAD

NGERIA

CAMEROON
Bangui
REPUBLIC
OF THE
CONGO

ETHIOPIA

SOMALIA

SRI
LANKA
Colombo
Male
MALDIVES

BRUNEI
Bandar Seri Begawan
MALAYSIA
Kuala Lumpur
Singapore SINGAPORE

PALAU
Melekeok

FEDERATED STATES
OF MICRONESIA

Palikir

KIRIBATI
Tarawa

EQUATOR

0°

UGANDA
Kampala KENYA
Kigali Nairobi
RWANDA
BURUNDI
Bujumbura
DEMOCRATIC
REPUBLIC
OF THE
CONGO
Dodoma

Mogadishu

SEYCHELLES

Victoria

INDONESIA

Jakarta

NAURU
Yaren

razzaville
INDA
(ngola)
shasa
Luanda

Dar es Salaam
TANZANIA

INDIAN

OCEAN

Dili
EAST TIMOR

PAPUA NEW
GUINEA

Port
Moresby

SOLOMON
ISLANDS
Honiara

TUVALU
Funafuti

ANGOLA

MALAWI
ZAMBIA Lilongwe
Lusaka
Harare
ZIMBABWE

COMOROS
Moroni

VANUATU
Port-Vila

FIJI
Suva

NAMIBIA
Windhoek
Gaborone
Pretoria
Bloemfontein
SOUTH
AFRICA
Cape Town

BOTSWANA

MOZAMBIQUE

Antananarivo

MADAGASCAR

MAURITIUS
Port Louis
RÉUNION
(France)

AUSTRALIA

NEW
CALEDONIA
(France)

20° S

Maputo
Mbabane
SWAZILAND
LESOTHO
Maseru

0   2,000 mi

0   2,000 km

Robinson Projection

Canberra

NEW
ZEALAND

Wellington

40° S

20° E 40° E 60° E 80° E 100° E 120° E 140° E 160° E

60° S

SOUTHERN OCEAN

ANTARCTIC CIRCLE

ANTARCTICA

80° S

The World: Physical

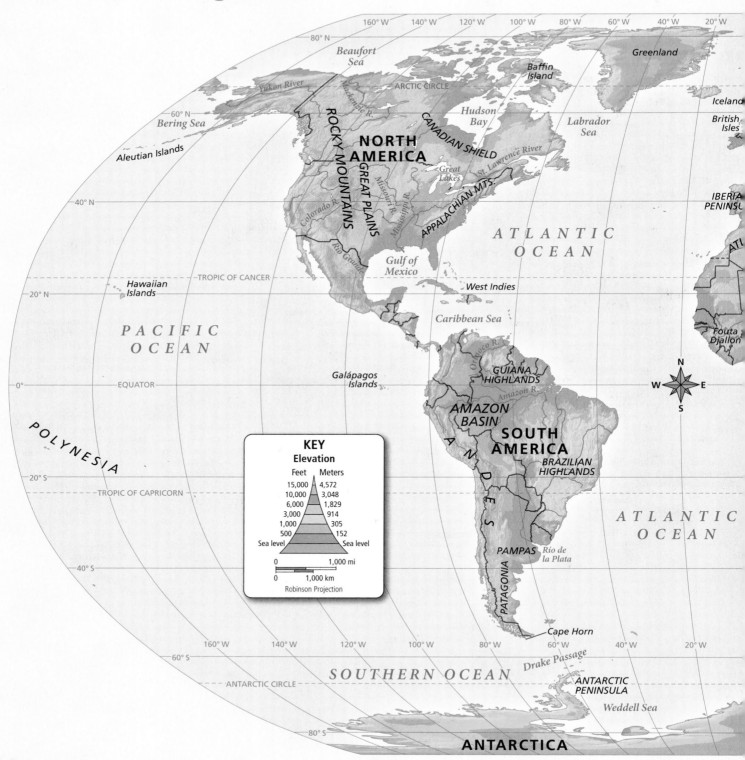

KEY
Elevation

Feet	Meters
15,000	4,572
10,000	3,048
6,000	1,829
3,000	914
1,000	305
500	152
Sea level	Sea level

0　　　1,000 mi
0　　　1,000 km
Robinson Projection

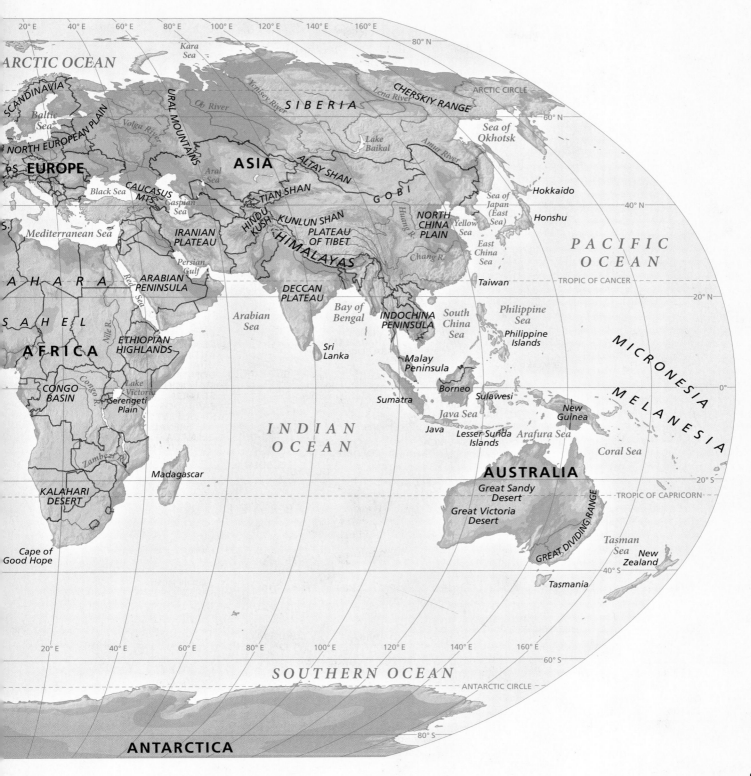

ARCTIC OCEAN

SCANDINAVIA

Baltic
Sea

NORTH EUROPEAN PLAIN

P.S.

EUROPE

Black Sea

CAUCASUS
MTS.

Mediterranean Sea

U.S.

S A H A R A

S A H E L

AFRICA

ETHIOPIAN
HIGHLANDS

CONGO
BASIN

Lake
Victoria

Congo R.

Serengeti
Plain

Zambezi R.

KALAHARI
DESERT

Cape of
Good Hope

Kara
Sea

URAL MOUNTAINS

Ob River

Volga River

Aral
Sea

Caspian
Sea

IRANIAN
PLATEAU

Persian
Gulf

Red Sea

ARABIAN
PENINSULA

Yenisey River

S I B E R I A

ASIA

ALTAY SHAN

TIAN SHAN

HINDU
KUSH

KUNLUN SHAN

PLATEAU
OF TIBET

HIMALAYAS

DECCAN
PLATEAU

Arabian
Sea

Bay of
Bengal

Sri
Lanka

Madagascar

INDIAN
OCEAN

Lena River

CHERSKIY RANGE

ARCTIC CIRCLE

G O B I

Huang R.

NORTH
CHINA
PLAIN

Chang R.

Lake
Baikal

Amur River

Sea of
Okhotsk

Sea of
Japan
(East
Sea)

Hokkaido

Honshu

Yellow
Sea

East
China
Sea

Taiwan

INDOCHINA
PENINSULA

South
China
Sea

Malay
Peninsula

Sumatra

Borneo

Java Sea

Java

Philippine
Sea

Philippine
Islands

Sulawesi

Lesser Sunda
Islands

New
Guinea

Arafura Sea

PACIFIC
OCEAN

TROPIC OF CANCER

M I C R O N E S I A

M E L A N E S I A

Coral Sea

AUSTRALIA

Great Sandy
Desert

Great Victoria
Desert

GREAT DIVIDING RANGE

TROPIC OF CAPRICORN

Tasman
Sea

New
Zealand

Tasmania

SOUTHERN OCEAN

ANTARCTIC CIRCLE

ANTARCTICA

North and South America: Political

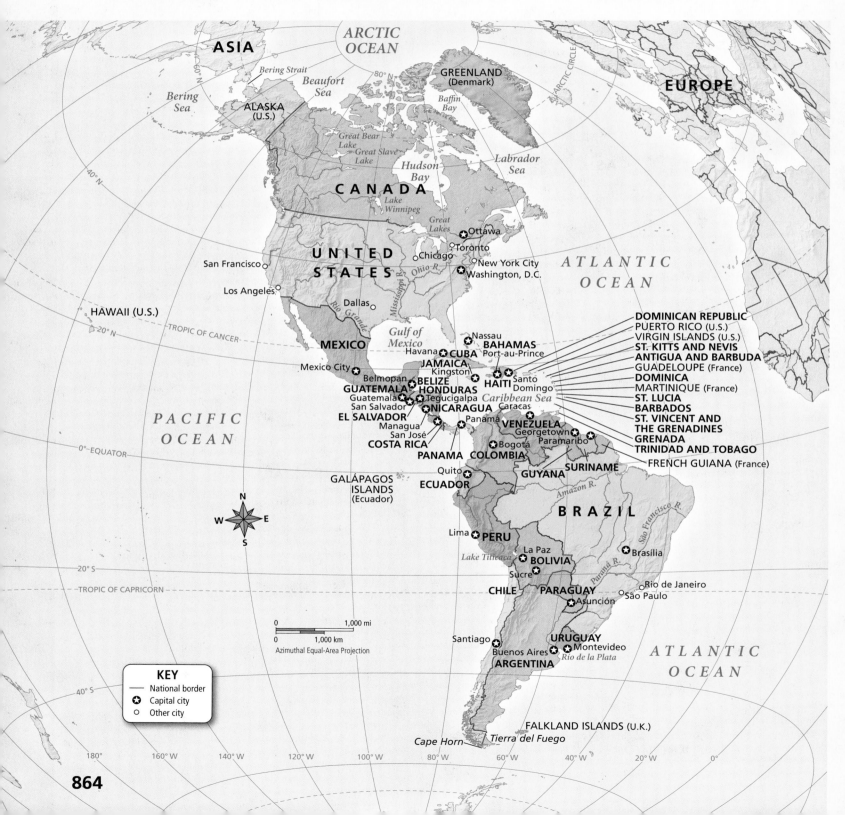

ASIA

ARCTIC OCEAN

Bering Strait

Bering Sea

Beaufort Sea

GREENLAND (Denmark)

Baffin Bay

EUROPE

ALASKA (U.S.)

Great Bear Lake

Great Slave Lake

Labrador Sea

Hudson Bay

CANADA

Lake Winnipeg

Great Lakes

○ Ottawa

○ Toronto

San Francisco ○

UNITED STATES

○ Chicago

Ohio R.

Mississippi R.

⊛ New York City
Washington, D.C.

ATLANTIC OCEAN

Los Angeles ○

HAWAII (U.S.)

TROPIC OF CANCER

20° N

Dallas ○

Rio Grande

Gulf of Mexico

MEXICO

Nassau ○

BAHAMAS

DOMINICAN REPUBLIC
PUERTO RICO (U.S.)
VIRGIN ISLANDS (U.S.)
ST. KITTS AND NEVIS
ANTIGUA AND BARBUDA
GUADELOUPE (France)
DOMINICA
MARTINIQUE (France)
ST. LUCIA
BARBADOS
ST. VINCENT AND
THE GRENADINES
GRENADA
TRINIDAD AND TOBAGO

Havana ○
Mexico City ⊛

⊛ CUBA

Port-au-Prince

JAMAICA

Kingston ○

Belmopan ⊛

BELIZE

⊛ HAITI

Santo Domingo

GUATEMALA
Guatemala ⊛
San Salvador ⊛
EL SALVADOR

HONDURAS
⊛ Tegucigalpa

Caribbean Sea

NICARAGUA

Managua ⊛
San José ⊛

Caracas ⊛

COSTA RICA

Panamá ○

VENEZUELA

Georgetown ⊛
Paramaribo ⊛

PACIFIC OCEAN

PANAMA ⊛

Bogotá ⊛

GUYANA

SURINAME

FRENCH GUIANA (France)

COLOMBIA

0°-EQUATOR

GALÁPAGOS ISLANDS (Ecuador)

Quito ⊛

ECUADOR

Amazon R.

B R A Z I L

N
W E
S

Lima ○

PERU

La Paz ⊛

⊛ Brasília

São Francisco R.

20° S

TROPIC OF CAPRICORN

Lake Titicaca

BOLIVIA

Sucre ⊛

Paraná R.

Rio de Janeiro ○

0   1,000 mi
0   1,000 km
Azimuthal Equal-Area Projection

CHILE

PARAGUAY

Asunción ⊛

São Paulo ○

Santiago ⊛

URUGUAY

⊛ Montevideo

ATLANTIC OCEAN

Buenos Aires ⊛

Río de la Plata

ARGENTINA

KEY

—— National border

⊛ Capital city

○ Other city

40° S

FALKLAND ISLANDS (U.K.)

Cape Horn   *Tierra del Fuego*

180°   160° W   140° W   120° W   100° W   80° W   60° W   40° W   20° W   0°

North and South America: Physical

ASIA

ARCTIC OCEAN

Bering Strait

Beaufort Sea

Bering Sea

Aleutian Islands

Mt. McKinley
20,320 ft. (6,194 m)

Alaska Range

Gulf of Alaska

ROCKY MOUNTAINS

Mackenzie R.

Great Bear Lake

Great Slave Lake

Hudson Bay

Canadian Shield

Lake Winnipeg

Great Lakes

GREAT PLAINS

Missouri R.

Great Basin

Colorado R.

Mississippi R.

Ohio R.

Appalachian Mts.

Coastal Plain

Sierra Madre Occidental

Sierra Madre Oriental

Rio Grande

Baja California

Gulf of California

Gulf of Mexico

Yucatán Peninsula

Cuba

Hispaniola

Greater Antilles

Lesser Antilles

Caribbean Sea

Greenland

Baffin Bay

Baffin Island

Davis Strait

Labrador Sea

Newfoundland

ARCTIC CIRCLE

EUROPE

ATLANTIC OCEAN

Hawaiian Islands

TROPIC OF CANCER

PACIFIC OCEAN

0° EQUATOR

Galápagos Islands

Isthmus of Panama

Orinoco R.

Guiana Highlands

ANDES

AMAZON BASIN

Amazon R.

São Francisco R.

Lake Titicaca

Brazilian Highlands

20° S

TROPIC OF CAPRICORN

ANDES

Gran Chaco

Paraguay R.

Paraná R.

Aconcagua
22,834 ft. (6,960 m)

Pampas

Río de la Plata

ATLANTIC OCEAN

Patagonia

Falkland Islands

Cape Horn

Tierra del Fuego

40° S

KEY
Elevation

Feet	Meters
15,000	4,572
10,000	3,048
6,000	1,829
3,000	914
1,000	305
500	152
Sea level	Sea level

—— National border

0 — 1,000 mi

0 — 1,000 km

Lambert Azimuthal
Equal-Area Projection

80° N

60° N

40° N

20° N

180° 160° W 140° W 120° W 100° W 80° W 60° W 40° W 20° W 0°

865

United States: Political

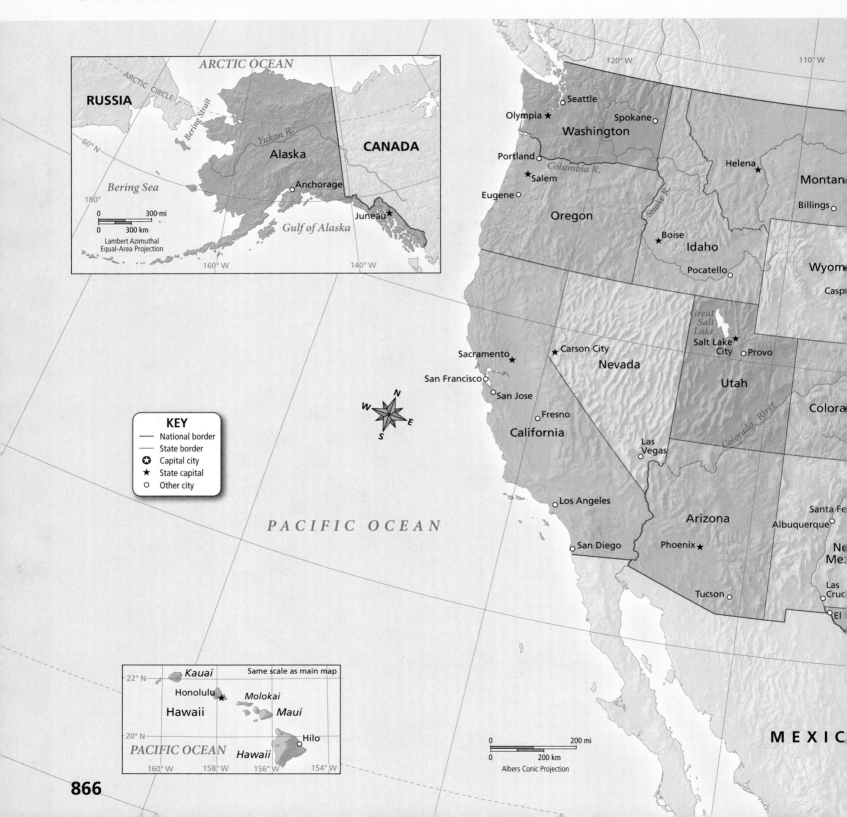

ARCTIC OCEAN

ARCTIC CIRCLE

RUSSIA

60° N

Bering Strait

Yukon R.

Alaska

CANADA

180°

Bering Sea

○ Anchorage

160° W

Gulf of Alaska

Juneau ★

140° W

0   300 mi
0   300 km
Lambert Azimuthal
Equal-Area Projection

120° W   110° W

● Seattle

Olympia ★   Spokane ○

Washington

Portland ○   Helena ★

Columbia R.   Salem ★   Montan

Eugene ○   Billings ○

Oregon   *Snake R.*

★ Boise

Idaho   Wyom

Pocatello ○   Casp

*Great
Salt
Lake*

Salt Lake ★
City   ○ Provo

Sacramento ★ Carson City

San Francisco ○   Nevada   Utah

● San Jose   Colora

○ Fresno

California

Las ○
Vegas   *Colorado River*

KEY
— National border
— State border
⊛ Capital city
★ State capital
○ Other city

Los Angeles ○

Arizona   Santa Fe

Albuquerque ○

PACIFIC OCEAN   San Diego ○   Phoenix ★   Ne
Mex

Las
Cruc

El

22° N   *Kauai*   Same scale as main map

Honolulu ★   *Molokai*

Hawaii   *Maui*

20° N   Tucson ○

PACIFIC OCEAN   *Hawaii*   ○ Hilo

160° W   158° W   156° W   154° W

0   200 mi
0   200 km
Albers Conic Projection

M E X I C

866

CANADA

North Dakota
Bismarck ★
Fargo ○

Lake Superior

Minnesota

South Dakota
Pierre ★
Sioux Falls ○

St. Paul ○
Minneapolis ○

Green Bay

Lake Michigan

Michigan

Lake Huron

Maine

Vermont
Montpelier ★
New Hampshire

★ Augusta
○ Portland

Wisconsin
Madison ★

Grand Rapids
Lansing ★
○ Milwaukee

Detroit

Lake Erie

Lake Ontario

New York
Albany ★
Rochester ○
Buffalo ○

★ Concord
Boston ★
Massachusetts
○ Providence
Hartford ★
Rhode Island

Connecticut

Iowa
Des Moines ★
Cedar Rapids ○

Chicago ○

Fort Wayne

Cleveland ○

Pennsylvania
Harrisburg ★
Pittsburgh ○

New York City

Trenton ★
New Jersey
Philadelphia

Nebraska
Cheyenne
Omaha ○
Lincoln ★

Missouri R.

Illinois
Springfield ★

Indiana
Indianapolis ★
Dayton ○

Ohio
Columbus ★
Cincinnati ○

West Virginia
Charleston ★

Baltimore ○
Washington, D.C.
Annapolis ○
Maryland

Dover ★
Delaware

Platte River

Colorado Springs

Kansas
Topeka ★
Wichita ○

Kansas City ○
Jefferson City ★

St. Louis ○

Frankfort ★
Louisville ○

Kentucky

Richmond ★
Norfolk ○

Virginia

Arkansas River

Missouri

Ohio River

Raleigh ★

Tulsa ○

Oklahoma City ★

Fort Smith ○

Memphis ○

Knoxville ○
Nashville ★
Tennessee

North Carolina
Charlotte ○

Oklahoma

Arkansas
Little Rock ★

Mississippi R.

Tennessee R.

South Carolina
Columbia ★
Charleston ○

Red River

Fort Worth ○○ Dallas

Shreveport ○

Mississippi
Jackson ★

Alabama
Montgomery ★

Birmingham ○

Atlanta ★
Augusta

Georgia
Columbus ○

Savannah ○

ATLANTIC OCEAN

Texas

Louisiana

Mobile ○
Gulfport ○
Baton Rouge ★
New Orleans ○

Tallahassee ★

Jacksonville ○

Austin ★
Houston ○
San Antonio ○

Rio Grande

Gulf of Mexico

Florida
Orlando ○
Tampa ○

Miami ○

867

Europe: Political

KEY
— National border
⊛ Capital city
○ Other city

0   200 mi
0   200 km
Lambert Conformal Conic Projection

ARCTIC OCEAN

Barents Sea

ARCTIC CIRCLE

70° N

Lapland

Reykjavík ⊛ **ICELAND**

White Sea

SWEDEN

FINLAND
○ Tampere

FAROE ISLANDS
(Denmark)

60° N

20° W

NORWAY

Bergen ○

Helsinki ⊛
Gulf of Finland
⊛ Tallinn
○ St. Petersburg

RUSSIA

Nizhni Novgorod ○

Oslo ⊛
Stockholm ⊛
ESTONIA
○ Moscow

Göteborg ○
○ Samara

North Sea

Glasgow ○
UNITED KINGDOM
DENMARK
Copenhagen ○
LATVIA
Riga ○

Baltic Sea
LITHUANIA

Volga R.

IRELAND
Dublin ⊛
Manchester ○
NETHERLANDS
KALININGRAD
(Russia)
Vilnius ⊛
⊛ Minsk

50° N

Birmingham ○
○ Hamburg
BELARUS

London ⊛
The Hague ○
Amsterdam ⊛
Berlin ⊛

English Channel
Brussels ⊛
GERMANY
POLAND
○ Warsaw
○ Kiev

ATLANTIC OCEAN

BELGIUM
○ Frankfurt
Prague ⊛
CZECH REPUBLIC
○ Donets'k

Paris ⊛
LUXEMBOURG
SLOVAKIA
UKRAINE

LIECHTENSTEIN
Vienna ⊛ Bratislava ⊛
Munich ○
FRANCE
AUSTRIA
Budapest ⊛
MOLDOVA
Chişinău ○

Bern ⊛
HUNGARY
Sea of Azov

SWITZERLAND
Ljubljana ⊛
ROMANIA
Caspian Sea

10° W
Lyon ○
Milan ○
SLOVENIA
Zagreb ⊛
○ Timişoara
Bucharest ⊛
Black Sea

Bay of Biscay
CROATIA
Belgrade ⊛
○ Constanţa

Toulouse ○
BOSNIA AND HERZEGOVINA
SERBIA
Danube R.

SAN MARINO
Sarajevo ○
Priština ○
BULGARIA

Marseille ○
MONACO
ITALY
Podgorica ○
Sofia ⊛
○ Istanbul
ASIA

PORTUGAL
ANDORRA
Corsica
Rome ⊛
MONTENEGRO
KOSOVO
Skopje ⊛

○ Madrid
Barcelona ○
MACEDONIA
TURKEY
Ankara ⊛

Lisbon ⊛
SPAIN
Naples ○
VATICAN CITY
Tirana ⊛
ALBANIA

○ Seville
Balearic Islands
Sardinia
Tyrrhenian Sea
Ionian Sea
GREECE

GIBRALTAR
(U.K.)
M e d i t e r
Sicily
○ Valletta
Athens ○

MALTA

30° N

AFRICA

0°
10° E
20° E
30° E
40° E

Europe: Physical

ARCTIC OCEAN

Barents Sea

Kola Peninsula

URAL MOUNTAINS

Iceland

ARCTIC CIRCLE

70° N

White Sea

Norwegian Sea

20° W

60° N

Faroe Islands

Shetland Islands

Kjølen Mountains

SCANDINAVIAN PENINSULA

Gulf of Bothnia

Lake Ladoga

Northern Dvina R.

Volga River

Lake Vänern

Gulf of Finland

Gotland

Baltic Sea

Central Russian Upland

North Sea

Jutland

Sjælland

Ireland

Great Britain

50° N

Thames R.

Elbe R.

NORTH EUROPEAN PLAIN

Vistula R.

Oder R.

Dnieper River

Volga River

English Channel

Rhine R.

Seine R.

Dniester R.

Don River

ATLANTIC OCEAN

10° W

Bay of Biscay

Loire R.

Garonne R.

Massif Central

A L P S

Danube R.

Carpathian Mountains

Sea of Azov

Caspian Sea

Mont Blanc
15,781 ft (4,810 m)

Rhône R.

Po River

Transylvanian Alps

Crimea

CAUCASUS MTS.

Mount Elbrus
18,510 ft
(5,642 m)

Pyrenees

Apennines

Dinaric Alps

Danube River

Black Sea

Meseta

Douro R.

Ebro R.

Corsica

Adriatic Sea

Balkan Mts.

BALKAN PENINSULA

Bosporus

ASIA

IBERIAN PENINSULA

Tagus R.

Guadalquivir R.

Balearic Islands

Sardinia

ITALIAN PENINSULA

Tyrrhenian Sea

Pindus Mts.

Dardanelles

Aegean Sea

Sicily

Ionian Sea

Peloponnisos

M e d i t e r r a n e a n

Maltese Islands

Crete

S e a

AFRICA

30° N

0°

10° E

20° E

30° E

40° E

KEY
Elevation

Feet	Meters
10,000	3,048
6,000	1,829
3,000	914
1,000	305
500	152
Sea level	Sea level

0   200 mi

0   200 km

Lambert Conformal Conic Projection

Africa: Political

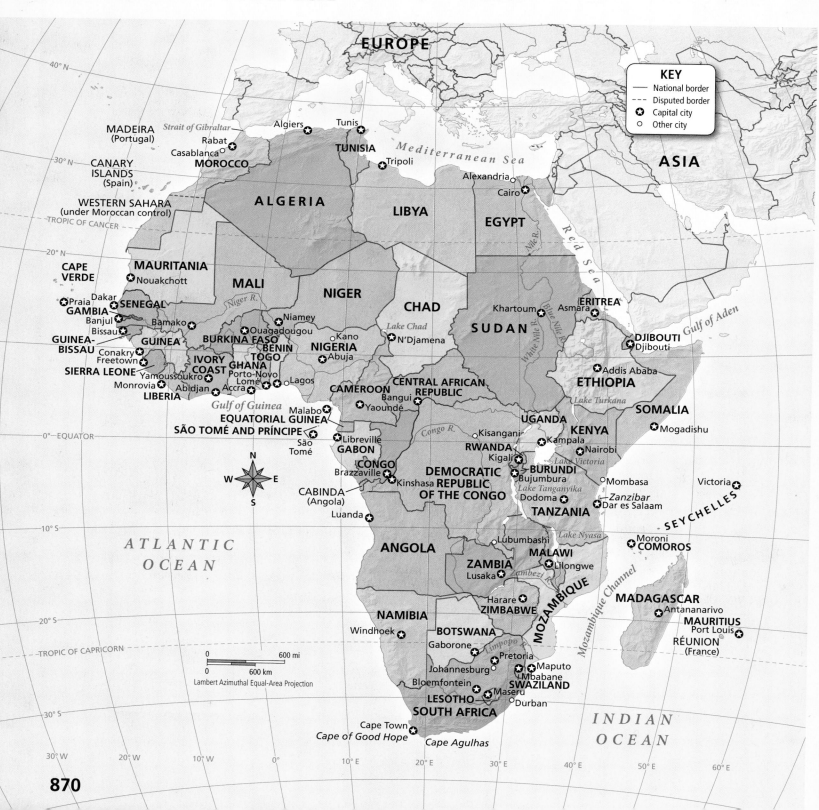

EUROPE

KEY
— National border
--- Disputed border
⊛ Capital city
○ Other city

ASIA

MADEIRA (Portugal)

Strait of Gibraltar

Algiers ⊛   Tunis ⊛
Rabat ⊛   TUNISIA
Casablanca ○   Tripoli ⊛
MOROCCO   *Mediterranean Sea*

CANARY ISLANDS (Spain)   Alexandria ○
                                                             Cairo ⊛

WESTERN SAHARA (under Moroccan control)

ALGERIA   LIBYA   EGYPT

TROPIC OF CANCER

CAPE VERDE

MAURITANIA   *Nile R.*   *Red Sea*

Nouakchott ⊛   MALI   NIGER   CHAD

Praia ⊛ Dakar ⊛   Khartoum ⊛   Asmara ⊛ ERITREA
SENEGAL   *Blue Nile R.*
GAMBIA   Niamey ○   SUDAN   DJIBOUTI
Banjul ⊛ Bamako ⊛   Kano ○   Djibouti ⊛
Bissau ⊛   BURKINA FASO   Ouagadougou ⊛   N'Djamena ⊛   *White Nile R.*
GUINEA-BISSAU   GUINEA   BENIN   NIGERIA
Conakry ⊛   TOGO   Abuja ⊛   Addis Ababa ○
Freetown ⊛ IVORY GHANA   ETHIOPIA
SIERRA LEONE COAST Porto-Novo ⊛   CENTRAL AFRICAN   *Lake Turkana*
Yamoussoukro ⊛ Lomé ⊛ Accra ⊛   REPUBLIC
Monrovia ⊛ Abidjan ○   Lagos ○   CAMEROON   Bangui ⊛   SOMALIA
LIBERIA   Yaoundé ⊛   UGANDA   KENYA
          Gulf of Guinea   Mogadishu ○
                              Malabo ⊛ *Congo R.* Kisangani ○ Kampala ⊛
EQUATORIAL GUINEA   RWANDA   Nairobi ⊛
SÃO TOMÉ AND PRÍNCIPE   São Libreville ⊛   Kigali ⊛ *Lake Victoria*
                             Tomé ○ GABON   BURUNDI   Mombasa ○   Victoria ⊛
0° EQUATOR   CONGO DEMOCRATIC Bujumbura ⊛   SEYCHELLES
                                     Brazzaville ⊛ REPUBLIC Dodoma ⊛ *Lake Tanganyika*
                              CABINDA Kinshasa ⊛ OF THE CONGO *Zanzibar*
                              (Angola)   Dar es Salaam ○
                                                 TANZANIA
                              Luanda ⊛   Moroni ⊛
                                                        Lake Nyasa COMOROS
                                       Lubumbashi ○
ATLANTIC OCEAN   ANGOLA   MALAWI
                                      ZAMBIA Lilongwe ⊛
                                     Lusaka ⊛ *Zambezi R.*   MADAGASCAR
                                                    MOZAMBIQUE   Antananarivo ⊛
                              Harare ⊛   MAURITIUS
                         NAMIBIA ZIMBABWE   Port Louis ⊛
                                                                    RÉUNION (France)
TROPIC OF CAPRICORN   Windhoek ⊛ BOTSWANA
                                                Limpopo R.   *Mozambique Channel*
                                     Gaborone ⊛
0   600 mi   Johannesburg ○ Pretoria ⊛ Maputo ⊛
0   600 km   Mbabane ⊛
Lambert Azimuthal Equal-Area Projection   Bloemfontein ○ SWAZILAND
                                   LESOTHO Maseru ⊛
                              SOUTH AFRICA Durban ○

                         Cape Town ⊛
                         Cape of Good Hope   INDIAN OCEAN
                                   Cape Agulhas

Enlightenment a period during the 1600s and 1700s when scholars studied culture and society by applying reason and natural laws (p. 389)
Ilustración período del siglo XVII al siglo XVIII en que los eruditos estudiaron la cultura y la sociedad a partir de la razón y las leyes naturales

entrepreneur person who organizes and manages his or her own business (p. 454)
empresario dícese de la persona que organiza y maneja su propia empresa

entrepreneurship starting a business (p. 608)
espíritu empresarial el establecimiento de un negocio

epic long poem of adventure and conflict (p. 725)
poema épico poema largo que trata de aventuras y conflictos

equinox point at which, everywhere on Earth, days and nights are nearly equal in length (p. 18)
equinoccio momento en el que la duración de los días y las noches es casi la misma en todos los rincones de la Tierra

erosion process in which water, ice, or wind remove rock and soil (p. 24)
erosión proceso en el que el agua, hielo o viento desgasta la roca y tierra

ethanol sugar cane-based fuel (p. 322)
etanol combustible hecho a base de caña de azúcar

ethics beliefs about what is right and wrong (pp. 92, 628)
ética creencias sobre el bien y el mal

ethnic cleansing attempt to create an area with only one ethnic group by removing or attacking other ethnic groups (p. 458)
limpieza étnica intento de crear un área donde sólo habite un grupo étnico por medio del ataque o el traslado de otros grupos étnicos

ethnocentrism attitude that one's own social or cultural group is better than all others (pp. 541, 844)
etnocentrismo tendencia a valorar la cultura o el grupo social propios por encima de otros

European Union economic and political partnership among member nations (p. 403)
Unión Europea asociación económica y política de países miembros

evaporation process in which a liquid changes to a gas (p. 37)
evaporación proceso en el que un líquido se convierte en gas

exploit take advantage of (p. 812)
explotar aprovecharse de algo o alguien

export good or service produced within a country and sold outside the country's borders (pp. 67, 152)
exportación bien o servicio que se produce en un país y se vende fuera de los confines del país

export economy economy based on exports (p. 317)
economía de exportación economía que se basa en exportaciones

extended family family that includes parents, children, and other family members such as grandparents, aunts, uncles, and cousins (p. 88)
familia extensa familia que incluye a los padres, los hijos y otros parientes como los abuelos, los tíos y los primos

F

family two or more people who are closely related by birth, marriage, or adoption (p. 88)
familia dos o más personas que están estrechamente vinculadas por los lazos de sangre, el matrimonio o la adopción

famine a huge food shortage (p. 759)
hambruna gran escasez de comida

fascism a political system that stresses national strength, military might, and the belief that the state is more important than individuals (p. 397)
fascismo sistema político que enfatiza la fuerza nacional, el poderío militar y la creencia de que el estado es más importante que el individuo

fault seam in Earth's crust (p. 26)
falla quiebra en la corteza terrestre

favela Brazilian slum (p. 315)
favela barrio marginal en Brasil

federal system system of government in which power is divided among central, regional, and local governments (p. 108)
sistema federal sistema de gobierno en el que el poder se divide entre los gobiernos centrales, regionales y locales

Fertile Crescent a region with good conditions for growing crops that stretches from the Mediterranean coast east through Mesopotamia (modern Iraq) to the Persian Gulf (p. 619)
Creciente Fértil región con buenas condiciones para cultivos que se extiende desde las áreas de la costa del Mediterráneo hacia el este por Mesopotamia (que hoy se conoce como Iraq) hasta el Golfo Pérsico

feudalism in medieval Europe, a system in which land was owned by lords but held by vassals in return for their loyalty (p. 358)
feudalismo sistema que se practicó en Europa durante la Edad Media en el que la tierra era propiedad de los señores nobles, quienes se la concedían a vasallos a cambio de su lealtad

First Nations native groups who lived south of the Arctic region in Canada (p. 172)
Primeras Naciones grupos indígenas que habitaron la región al sur del Ártico en Canadá

flood plain flat lands along a river (p. 714)
terreno inundable tierras llanas adyacentes a un río

foliage leaves on trees (p. 776)
follaje hojas en árboles

foreign policy set of goals outlining how a country plans to interact with other countries (p. 110)
política exterior conjunto de metas que describe cómo un país planea interactuar con otros

fossil preserved remain of ancient human, animal, or plant (p. 538)
fósil restos conservados de personas, animales o plantas de la antigüedad

fossil fuel nonrenewable resource formed over millions of years from the remains of ancient plants and animals (pp. 49, 592)
combustible fósil recurso no renovable formado durante millones de años de los restos antiguos de plantas y animales

free market economic market in which businesses operate with few governmental restrictions (p. 216)
libre mercado mercado económico en el cual las empresas operan con restricciones mínimas del gobierno

free trade removal of trade barriers (p. 67)
libre comercio eliminación de las barreras comerciales

French Revolution a political movement that removed the French king from power and formed a republic (p. 391)
Revolución Francesa movimiento politico que derrocó al rey francés y estableció una república

fundamentalism belief that holy books should be taken literally, word for word (p. 607)
fundamentalismo idea que sugiere que las escrituras religiosas deben interpretarse literalmente, al pie de la letra

G

genocide attempt to destroy a whole people (p. 546)
genocidio exterminio de todo un grupo social

geographic information system (GIS) computer-based system that stores and uses information linked to geographic locations (p. 8)
sistema de información geográfica (SIG) sistema computarizado que archiva y usa información relacionada con sitios geográficos

geography study of the human and nonhuman features of Earth (p. 4)
geografía estudio de las características humanas y no humanas de la Tierra

glacier slow-moving body of ice (pp. 415, 852)
glaciar gran masa de hielo que se desliza lentamente

government group of people who have the power to make and enforce laws for a country or area (p. 104)
gobierno grupo de personas de un país o área que tiene el poder de crear y hacer cumplir las leyes

Great Depression worldwide economic slump during the 1930s (p. 396)
Gran Depresión crisis económica mundial durante la década de 1930

Great Rift Valley long, unusually flat area of land between areas of higher ground in eastern Africa (p. 530)
Gran Valle del Rift franja de terreno larga y plana ubicada entre terrenos elevados en África oriental

Green Revolution increase in agricultural production created by improved technology (p. 712)
Revolución verde gran aumento en la producción agrícola debido a avances en la tecnología

griot African musician-storyteller who uses music to track heritage and record history as well as entertain (p. 521)
griot músico y narrador de la tradición oral africana; usa la música para entretener y preservar su historia y cultura

gross domestic product (GDP) total value of all goods and services produced in a country in a year (pp. 64, 426, 572)
producto interno bruto (PIB) valor total de todos los bienes y servicios que produce un país durante un año

gross domestic product per capita a country's GDP divided by the number of people who live in the country (p. 572)

producto interno bruto per cápita PIB de un país dividido por la población del país

gross national product (GNP) annual income of a country's companies and residents (p. 431)

producto nacional bruto (PNB) ingreso anual de las empresas y los residentes de un país

guild association of people who have a common interest (p. 364)

gremio asociación de personas que comparten un interés común

H

hacienda huge farm or ranch in Spain's American colonies (p. 236)

hacienda granja o rancho grande en las colonias españolas en las Américas

hemisphere one half of Earth (p. 5)

hemisferio una mitad de la Tierra

hereditary monarch a ruler from a traditional ruling family who is the son, daughter, or younger relative of the last ruler (p. 635)

monarca heredero soberano perteneciente a una familia gobernante tradicional que es hijo, hija o un familiar joven del soberano anterior

hieroglyphics Egyptian system of writing using pictures and other symbols (p. 565)

jeroglíficos sistema de escritura egipcia que utiliza figuras o símbolos

high latitudes areas north of the Arctic Circle and south of the Antarctic Circle; also known as polar zone (p. 34)

latitudes altas áreas al norte del Círculo Polar Ártico y al sur del Círculo Polar Antártico

hijab concealing, baggy garments worn by many Arab women (p. 611)

hiyab prendas de vestir holgadas que muchas mujeres árabes usan para cubrirse

Hinduism religious system of beliefs and practices that emerged in South Asia (p. 717)

Hinduismo sistema de creencias y prácticas religiosas que emergieron del sur asiático

historian person who studies the past (p. 118)

historiador persona que estudia el pasado

historical map special-purpose map that provides information about a place at a certain time in history (p. 125)

mapa histórico mapa con el propósito especial de dar información acerca de un lugar en un momento determinado de la historia

Holocaust the mass murder of Jews by the Nazis during World War II (p. 399)

Holocausto exterminio masivo de judíos por el régimen nazi durante la Segunda Guerra Mundial

human development index a measure of living conditions using factors such as life expectancy, education, and income (p. 573)

índice de desarrollo humano medición de las condiciones de vida basada en factores como la expectativa de vida, la educación y el ingreso económico

human–environment interaction how people affect their environment and how their environment affects them (p. 7)

interacción humanos–medio ambiente manera en la que los seres humanos afectan su medio ambiente y viceversa

humanism the study of secular, or nonreligious, subjects such as history (p. 375)

humanismo estudio de temas laicos, o no religiosos, como la historia

humid subtropical climate climate with year-round precipitation, mild winters, and hot summers (p. 40)

clima subtropical húmedo clima de precipitación continua durante todo el año, inviernos templados y veranos cálidos

hurricane tropical cyclone that forms over the tropical Atlantic Ocean (pp. 39, 228)

huracán ciclón tropical que se forma sobre el Océano Atlántico tropical

hydroelectric power the power produced by water-driven turbines (p. 202)

energía hidroeléctrica poder que producen turbinas impulsadas por agua

hydroelectricity electricity made by water power (p. 767)

hidroelectricidad electricidad producida por la fuerza del agua

I

Iberian Peninsula Spain and Portugal (p. 434)
Península ibérica España y Portugal

ice age time of lower temperatures when much of the land was covered with snow and ice (p. 447)
edad de hielo período de temperaturas bajas donde gran parte de la tierra estaba cubierta de nieve y hielo

iceberg large floating mass of ice (p. 853)
iceberg gran masa de hielo flotante

ice sheet large mass of compressed ice (p. 852)
capa de hielo gran masa de hielo compacto

illiterate not able to read and write (p. 765)
analfabeta que no sabe leer y escribir

immigrate to migrate into a place (p. 79)
inmigrar llegar a un lugar

immunity natural defense against disease (p. 292)
inmunidad defensa natural contra las enfermedades

imperialism process of creating an empire by taking over other areas (p. 514)
imperialismo creación de un imperio por medio del dominio de otras áreas

import good or service sold within a country that is produced in another country (pp. 67, 152)
importación bien o servicio que se vende en un país pero es producido en otro

incentive factor that encourages people to behave in a certain way (p. 59)
incentivo factor que motiva a la gente a actuar de cierta manera

independence right to rule oneself (p. 236)
independencia derecho de gobernarse a sí mismo

Indian subcontinent land to the south of the Himalayas (p. 708)
subcontinente indio territorio al sur de los Himalayas

indigenous native to a region (pp. 544, 846)
indígena nativo de una región

industrialization growth of machine-powered production and manufacturing (p. 51)
industrialización aumento de la producción a máquina y la manufactura

Industrial Revolution a time in which new technologies transformed manufacturing and changed society forever (p. 392)
Revolución Industrial período en el que nuevas tecnologías transformaron la industria manufacturera en particular y la sociedad en general

infant mortality rate number of infant deaths per 1,000 births (p. 75)
tasa de mortalidad infantil número de muertes infantiles por cada mil nacimientos

inflation general increase in prices (p. 61)
inflación alza general de los precios

infrastructure body of public works, such as roads, bridges, and hospitals, that a country needs to support a modern economy (p. 518)
infraestructura conjunto de elementos o servicios públicos como carreteras, puentes y hospitales que un país necesita para mantener una economía moderna

Institutional Revolutionary Party political party that dominated Mexico's government for much of the 1900s (p. 213)
Partido Revolucionario Institucional partido político que dominó el gobierno mexicano por gran parte del siglo XX

insurgency rebellion (p. 816)
insurgencia rebelión

insurgent rebel (p. 274)
insurgente rebelde

interdependent dependent on one another (p. 779)
interdependiente que depende uno de otro

interest price paid for borrowing money (p. 69)
interés precio que se paga por el dinero prestado

interest group group that seeks to influence public policy on certain issues (p. 113)
grupo de interés grupo que busca influir en la política pública en relación a cuestiones particulares

intertropical convergence zone belt of rising air near the Equator (p. 38)
zona de convergencia intertropical cinturón de aire ascendente cerca del ecuador

Intifada a Palestinian campaign of violent resistance against Israeli control (p. 639)
Intifada campaña revolucionaria palestina en contra del control israelí

investing act of using money in the hopes of making a future profit (p. 69)
invertir usar el dinero con la esperanza de obtener ganancias futuras

irrigate to supply water to (pp. 99, 205, 686)
irrigar aportar agua

Islamism belief that politics and society should follow Islamic teachings (p. 607)
islamismo creencia según la cual la política y la sociedad deben seguir las enseñanzas del islam

Israeli settlements places in the West Bank and Gaza Strip where Israelis have settled (p. 638)
asentamientos israelíes áreas de Cisjordania y la franja de Gaza donde se han establecido los israelíes

isthmus strip of land with water on both sides that connects two larger bodies of land (p. 226)
istmo franja de tierra con agua en ambos lados que conecta dos territorios más grandes

J

jihad Arabic word meaning "struggle" (p. 607)
yihad palabra de origen árabe que significa "luchar por la reforma"

K

Kamchatka Peninsula a peninsula in the Russian far east known for its volcanic activity (p. 471)
Península de Kamchatka península del lejano oriente ruso conocida por su estado volcánico

key section of a map that explains the map's symbols and shading (p. 10)
leyenda sección de un mapa que explica el significado de sus símbolos y áreas sombreadas

KGB the Soviet-era secret police (p. 485)
KGB policía secreta de la era soviética

Korean War war between North Korea and South Korea and their allies during the early 1950s (p. 786)
Guerra de Corea guerra entre Corea del Norte y Corea del Sur, más sus aliados, durante los primeros años de la década de 1950

Kremlin a great complex of Russian official buildings, including palaces, state offices, and churches (p. 478)
Kremlin gran recinto de edificios oficiales rusos que incluye palacios, oficinas del Estado e iglesias

L

Lake Baikal a huge lake in Siberia that is more than one mile deep and holds about 20 percent of Earth's fresh water (p. 471)
lago Baikal gran lago localizado en Siberia que tiene más de una milla de hondo y contiene aproximadamente 20 por ciento del agua dulce de la Tierra

landform shapes and types of land (p. 23)
accidente geográfico formas y tipos de terreno

landlocked cut off from direct access to the ocean (p. 684)
sin litoral sin acceso directo al mar

language set of sounds or symbols that make it possible for people to communicate (p. 90); also, the language of a community or a nation
lenguaje conjunto de sonidos y símbolos que hacen posible la comunicación entre las personas
idioma lengua de una comunidad o una nación

Latin America areas of Middle America influenced by the cultures of Spain, France, or Portugal (p. 271)
América Latina regiones de México, América Central y el Caribe y América del Sur con influencia cultural de España, Francia o Portugal

latitude distance north or south of the Equator measured in degrees (p. 4)
latitud distancia en grados que se mide al norte o al sur desde el ecuador

life expectancy the average number of years a person is expected to live (p. 764)
esperanza de vida número promedio de años que se espera que viva una persona

limited government government structure in which government actions are limited by law (pp. 105, 788)
gobierno limitado estructura gubernamental cuyas acciones están limitadas por la ley

literacy ability to read and write (p. 300)
alfabetismo capacidad de leer y escribir

literature written work such as fiction, poetry, or drama (p. 95)
literatura obras escritas como la ficción, la poesía o el drama

Llanos lowland plains in Colombia and Venezuela (p. 259)
Llanos llanuras de tierra baja de Colombia y Venezuela

897

locator map section of a map that shows a larger area than the main map (p. 10)
mapa localizador sección de un mapa que amplía un área del mismo

loess a dustlike material that can form soil (pp. 416, 747)
loes material polvoroso que puede formar tierra

longitude distance east or west of the Prime Meridian measured in degrees (p. 5)
longitud distancia en grados que se mide al este o al oeste desde el Primer meridiano

lords in medieval Europe, noblemen who gave land to other noblemen in return for services (p. 358)
señores en la Europa medieval, señores nobles que cedían terrenos a otros señores nobles a cambio de sus servicios

low latitudes areas between the Tropic of Cancer and the Tropic of Capricorn; also known as tropics (p. 34)
latitudes bajas áreas entre el Trópico de Cáncer y el Trópico de Capricornio; también se le llama trópico

M

madrassa school that teaches the Islamic religion (p. 695)
madraza escuela que enseña la religión islámica

magma stream of soft, nearly molten rock (p. 26)
magma flujo de roca blanda y casi fundida

Magna Carta document that limited the English king's power (p. 365)
Carta Magna documento que limitaba el poder del rey de Inglaterra

maize corn (p. 206)
maíz choclo

Majlis Iranian legislature (p. 662)
Majlis asamblea legislativa de Irán

majority more than half (p. 596)
mayoría más de la mitad

malaria life-threatening disease spread by mosquitoes and caused by parasites (p. 511)
malaria enfermedad grave causada por parásitos y propagada por mosquitos

Manifest Destiny idea that the United States should expand across the North American continent (p. 149)
Destino manifiesto mentalidad que propone la expansión territorial de los Estados Unidos por todo el continente norteamericano

manorialism in medieval Europe, the economic relationship between a lord and the peasants who worked for him (p. 359)
señorío en la Europa medieval, relación económica entre un señor y sus trabajadores campesinos

mantle thick, rocky layer around Earth's core (p. 22)
manto capa rocosa gruesa alrededor del núcleo de la Tierra

Maori the original inhabitants of New Zealand and the Cook Islands (p. 843)
maorí habitantes nativos de Nueva Zelanda y las islas Cook

maritime having to do with navigation or shipping on the sea (p. 812)
marítimo pertinente a la naútica o la navegación por mar

maritime climate climate that is wet year-round, with mild winters and cool summers (p. 40)
clima marítimo clima que es húmedo todo el año, con inviernos templados y veranos frescos

market organized way for producers and consumers to trade goods and services (p. 60)
mercado intercambio organizado de bienes y servicios entre productores y consumidores

market economy economy in which individual consumers and producers make all economic decisions (pp. 62, 152, 324)
economía de mercado economía en la que los consumidores y los productores toman todas las decisiones económicas

Marshall Plan an economic program initiated by the United States to help Europe recover from World War II (p. 400)
Plan Marshall programa económico iniciado por los EE. UU. para la reconstrucción europea tras la Segunda Guerra Mundial

Mau Mau Kenyan independence movement during the 1950s (p. 542)
Mau Mau movimiento por la independencia de Kenya durante la década de 1950

Maya Native American society living in Central America (p. 234)
Maya sociedad indígena americana que habita en Centroamérica

mechanized farming farming with machines (p. 449)
mecanización agrícola uso de maquinaria en la industria agrícola

Meiji Restoration time period when Japan's Emperor Meiji was returned to power (p. 784)
Restauración Meiji período en el cual el emperador japonés Meiji retomó el poder

mercantilism economic system in which colonies sent raw materials to the mother country; in return, colonists were expected to buy products from the country (p. 293)
mercantilismo sistema económico en el que las colonias enviaban materias primas a la madre patria; a cambio, se esperaba que los colonos compraran los productos del país

merchant trader (p. 693)
comerciante negociante

MERCOSUR trading bloc of the South American countries Brazil, Argentina, Uruguay, and Paraguay, formed in 1991 (p. 299)
MERCOSUR tratado de comercio elaborado en 1991 entre los países sudamericanos de Brasil, Argentina, Uruguay y Paraguay

messiah a leader chosen by God who would restore the Jewish nation and help create God's kingdom in the world (p. 629)
mesías líder enviado de Dios que restauraría el pueblo judío y ayudaría a establecer el reino de Dios en la Tierra

mestizo person of mixed Spanish and Native American ancestry (p. 292)
mestizo persona con ascendencia española e indígena americana

Mexican Revolution armed rebellion in which the Mexican people fought for political and social reform (p. 210)
Revolución mexicana rebelión armada en la que el pueblo mexicano luchó por establecer reformas políticas y sociales

microcredit small loan (pp. 242, 523)
microcrédito préstamo pequeño

middle latitudes areas between the high and low latitudes; also known as temperate zone (p. 34)
latitudes medias (zona templada) áreas entre las latitudes altas y bajas

middle passage voyage across the Atlantic from Africa to the Americas that formed the middle leg of the triangular trade among Europe, American colonies, and Africa (p. 514)
paso central viaje a través del océano Atlántico desde África hasta las Américas que constituía el trayecto medio del comercio triangular entre Europa, las colonias americanas y África

migration movement of people from one place to another (pp. 78, 142)
migración desplazamiento de personas de un lugar a otro

military junta committee of military leaders (p. 816)
junta militar comité de líderes militares

millet self-governing religious community in the Ottoman Empire (p. 659)
millet comunidad religiosa del Imperio Otomano de índole autónoma

minority group making up less than half of a population (p. 603)
minoría grupo que constituye menos de la mitad de una población

missionary a person sent to another country by a church to spread its religious beliefs (p. 844)
misionero persona enviada a otro país por una iglesia con el propósito de diseminar sus creencias religiosas

mixed economy economy that combines elements of traditional, market, and command economic systems (p. 63)
economía mixta economía que combina elementos de los sistemas económicos tradicional, de mercado y dirigida

mixing zone an area where warm and cool water combine and stir nutrients from the ocean floor; fish feed on these nutrients (p. 169)
zona de mezcla área donde la combinación de agua cálida y agua fría revuelve los nutrientes del suelo marino; los peces se alimentan de estos nutrientes

monarchy form of government in which the state is ruled by a monarch (p. 107)
monarquía tipo de gobierno en el que el Estado está regido por un monarca

monotheism the belief in a single God (p. 600)
monoteísmo creencia en un solo dios

monsoon seasonal winds (p. 804)
monzón vientos estacionales

mosque Islamic house of worship (p. 603)
mezquita lugar de culto islámico

movement how people, goods, and ideas get from one place to another (p. 7)
movimiento manera en la que las personas, los bienes y las ideas van de un lugar a otro

mummy a body that has been preserved so it will not decompose (p. 566)
momia cadáver preservado sin descomponerse

music art form that uses sound, usually produced by instruments or voices (p. 95)
música arte que usa sonidos, normalmente producidos por instrumentos o voces

Muslim Brotherhood an Islamist party that opposes the Egyptian government (p. 574)
Hermandad Musulmana partido Islamista que se opone al gobierno egipcio

N

National Action Party Mexican political party that took power in the 2000 presidential election (p. 213)
Partido Acción Nacional (PAN) partido político mexicano que tomó el poder en las elecciones presidenciales del 2000

nationalize government taking ownership of a company (p. 269)
nacionalizar situación en la cual el gobierno toma posesión de una empresa

nation-state state that is independent of other states (p. 107)
estado-nación Estado que es independiente de otros

natural resource useful material found in the environment (p. 48)
recurso natural material útil que se encuentra en el medio ambiente

New France French colony in what is now eastern Canada (p. 173)
Nueva Francia colonia francesa ubicada en lo que hoy se conoce como Canadá oriental

nirvana in Hinduism, a state of understanding that releases the soul from the cycle of rebirth (p. 718)
nirvana según el hinduismo, estado de claridad que libera el alma del ciclo de renacimiento

nomad person who moves from place to place without a permanent home (p. 558)
nómada persona que se desplaza de un lugar a otro sin un hogar permanente

nomadic herder a person who raises livestock for a living and has no settled home but moves from place to place (p. 749)
pastor nómada persona cuyo oficio es criar ganado y que se desplaza de un lugar a otro sin un hogar permanente

nonalignment not becoming an ally of either the United States or the Soviet Union during the Cold War (p. 722)
sin alineación no tener alianzas ni con los Estados Unidos ni con la Unión Soviética durante la Guerra Fría

nongovernmental organization (NGO) group that operates with private funding (p. 549)
organización no gubernamental (ONG) grupo que funciona gracias al financiamiento privado

nonrenewable resource resource that cannot be replaced in a relatively short period of time (p. 49)
recurso no renovable recurso que no se puede reemplazar en un período de tiempo relativamente corto

norm behavior that is considered normal in a particular society (p. 86)
norma comportamiento que se considera normal en una sociedad determinada

northwest passage hypothetical North American passage between the Atlantic and Pacific Oceans (p. 384)
Paso del Noroeste ruta marítima hipotética en Norteamérica que conecta los océanos Atlántico y Pacífico

nuclear family family that consists of parents and their children (p. 88)
familia nuclear familia constituida por los padres y sus hijos

nuclear weapon powerful explosive device that can cause widespread destruction (p. 851)
arma nuclear explosivo de alto poder que puede causar gran destrucción

O

oasis place in the desert where water can be found (p. 557)
oasis lugar del desierto donde se halla agua

oligarchy government in which a small group of people rule (pp. 294, 341)
oligarquía tipo de gobierno en el que un grupo pequeño de personas tiene el poder

one-child policy China's family planning policy; under this law, many married couples are only allowed to have one child (p. 750)
política de hijo único política de planeación familiar china; esta ley permite a muchas parejas casadas tener sólo un hijo o una hija

opportunity cost cost of what you have to give up when making a choice (p. 59)
costo de oportunidad costo de lo que se pierde al elegir una opción

oral tradition community's cultural and historical background, passed down in spoken stories and songs (p. 123)
tradición oral trasfondo cultural e histórico de una comunidad, trasmitido por cuentos hablados y canciones

orbit path one object makes as it circles around another (p. 18)
órbita trayectoria que traza un cuerpo al desplazarse alrededor de otro

Outback a sparsely inhabited region of Australia with low plateaus and plains (p. 835)
outback territorio escasamente poblado de Australia que tiene mesetas y llanuras

outsourcing sending tasks to be done by workers outside a company (p. 731)
subcontratación práctica que consiste en enviar trabajo a trabajadores de otra compañía

overgrazing so much grazing that plants are killed (p. 687)
pastoreo excesivo pastoreo a un nivel tan intenso que causa la muerte de las plantas

ozone layer layer of the atmosphere that filters out most of the sun's harmful ultraviolet rays (p. 855)
capa de ozono capa de la atmósfera que bloquea la mayoría de los nocivos rayos ultravioleta del sol

P

pack ice seasonal ice that floats on water rather than being attached to land (p. 853)
banquisa hielo estacional flotante que no está conectado a la tierra

Pan-Africanism political and social movement that sought to unite black Africans across the globe (p. 516)
panafricanismo movimiento sociopolítico que promueve la hermandad de los africanos de raza negra alrededor del mundo

Pan-Arabism idea that all Arabic-speaking countries should cooperate and join together (p. 569)
panarabismo ideología que promueve la cooperación y unión de todos los países de habla árabe

paramilitary unauthorized armed forces (p. 269)
paramilitar se refiere a un grupo civil con estructura de tipo militar

Parliament British legislature (p. 423)
parlamento asamblea legislativa británica

parliamentary democracy a democracy in which parliament chooses the government (p. 634)
democracia parlamentaria democracia en la que el parlamento escoge al gobierno

partition splitting a country into two states (p. 722)
división separación de un país en dos estados

patricians wealthy aristocrats in ancient Rome (p. 349)
patricios aristócratas adinerados de la antigua Roma

Pax Romana period of stability in the Roman empire under Augustus (p. 351)
Paz Romana período de estabilidad del Imperio Romano bajo el mandato de Augusto

peninsula area of land almost completely surrounded by water but connected to the mainland (pp. 414, 802)
península área de tierra rodeada en su mayoría por agua pero conectada a un territorio más extenso

period length of time singled out because of a specific event or development that happened during that time (p. 118)
período lapso de tiempo resaltado debido a un suceso o desarrollo específico que sucedió durante ese tiempo

permafrost permanently frozen soil (pp. 168, 472)
permafrost tierra permanentemente congelada

perspective a technique that allows artists to portray a three-dimensional space on a flat surface (p. 375)
perspectiva técnica que permite al artista crear un espacio tridimensional en una superficie plana

Pharaoh king of ancient Egypt (p. 565)
faraón rey del antiguo Egipto

philosophy general study of knowledge and the world; Greek for "love of wisdom" (p. 345)
filosofía estudio general sobre el conocimiento y el mundo; en griego significa "amor por la sabiduría"

physical map map that shows physical, or natural, features (p. 12)
mapa físico mapa que muestra las características físicas o naturales

place mix of human and nonhuman features at a given location (p. 6)
lugar combinación de características humanas y no humanas en un sitio determinado

plain large area of flat or gently rolling land (pp. 25, 414)
llanura área extensa de terreno ondulado o llano

plantation large commercial farm (pp. 148, 384)
plantación granja grande con fines comerciales

plate block of rock and soil that makes up Earth's crust (pp. 26, 591)
placa bloque de piedra y tierra que forma la corteza de la Tierra

plate tectonics theory that explains how huge blocks of Earth's crust called "plates" move (pp. 26, 837)
tectónica de placas teoría que explica el movimiento de las placas de la corteza terrestre

plateau large, mostly flat area that rises above the surrounding land (p. 25)
meseta gran extensión de terreno, generalmente plano, que se eleva sobre la tierra circundante

plebeians nonpatrician citizens of ancient Rome (p. 349)
plebeyos ciudadanos de la antigua Roma que no se consideraban patricios

plural society society in which distinctive cultural, ethnic, and racial groups are encouraged to maintain their own identities and cultures (p. 182)
sociedad plural sociedad en la que se fomenta la conservación de la identidad cultural de los distintos grupos culturales, étnicos y raciales

poaching illegal hunting (p. 533)
furtivismo caza ilegal

polar zone areas north of the Arctic Circle and south of the Antarctic Circle; also known as high latitudes (p. 34)
zona polar (latitudes altas) área al norte del Círculo Polar Ártico o al sur del Círculo Polar Antártico

polders areas of dry land reclaimed from lake bottoms or the seabed (p. 431)
pólderes áreas de tierra seca ganadas a los lechos laguneros o marinos

political map map that shows political units, such as countries or states (p. 13)
mapa político mapa que muestra las unidades políticas, como países o estados

political party group that supports candidates for public offices (p. 113)
partido político grupo que apoya a los candidatos que postulan a cargos públicos

pollution waste that makes the air, soil, or water less clean (pp. 53, 419)
contaminación desechos que alteran la pureza del aire, el suelo o el agua

population density measure of the number of people per unit of land (pp. 77, 144)
densidad de población medida del número de personas por unidad de territorio

population distribution spreading of people over an area of land (p. 76)
distribución de población dispersión de las personas a lo largo de un área geográfica

precipitation water that falls to the ground as rain, snow, sleet, or hail (pp. 32, 166)
precipitación agua que cae sobre la tierra en forma de lluvia, nieve, aguanieve o granizo

prehistory time before humans invented writing (p. 119)
prehistoria época anterior a la invención de la escritura

primary industry industry involving the collection of resources from nature, such as fishing (p. 849)
sector primario industria relacionada con la recolección de recursos naturales, como la pesca

primary source information that comes directly from a person who experienced an event (p. 120)
fuente primaria información sobre un suceso que proviene directamente de una persona que experimentó el suceso

privatization individual and private group ownership of businesses (p. 430)
privatización situación en la que individuos o grupos privados son los dueños de las empresas

producer person or business that makes and sells products (p. 59)
productor persona o negocio que fabrica y vende productos

productivity amount of goods and services produced given the amount of resources used (p. 65)
productividad cantidad de bienes y servicios producidos en relación a la cantidad de recursos empleados

profit money a company has left over after subtracting the costs of doing business (p. 60)
ganancias dinero que sobra después que una compañía deduce los costos de operar el negocio

projection way to map Earth on a flat surface (p. 9)
proyección manera de trazar un mapa de la Tierra sobre una superficie plana

prophet a messenger of God (p. 627)
profeta mensajero de Dios

province territory that is under the control of a larger country (p. 175)
provincia territorio que se encuentra bajo la administración de un país más grande

pull factor cause of migration that pulls, or attracts, people to new countries (p. 79)
factor de arrastre causa de la migración que arrastra o atrae a la gente a países nuevos

push factor cause of migration that pushes people to leave their home country (p. 79)
factor de empuje causa de la migración que empuja a la gente a dejar su país de origen

Q

qanat tunnel that provided water to Persian villages by bringing water from an aquifer (p. 652)
qanat túnel que transportaba agua de un acuífero a las aldeas persas

Quran holy book of Islam (p. 600)
Corán libro sagrado del islam

R

rain shadow a dry area that forms behind a highland that captures rainfall and snow (p. 620)
sombra orográfica área árida que se forma detrás de una zona montañosa donde cae lluvia y nieve

recession decline in economic growth for six or more months in a row (pp. 61, 792)
recesión declive en el crecimiento económico por un período continuo de seis meses o más

Reconquista reconquering of Spain by Christians beginning in the 1000s (p. 362)
Reconquista la conquista cristiana de España que comenzó en el siglo XI

referendum vote held to reject or accept a law (p. 301)
referéndum someter una ley al voto para rechazarla o aceptarla

Reformation a religious movement in which calls for reform led to the emergence of non-Catholic, or Protestant, churches (p. 378)
Reforma Protestante movimiento religioso cuya convocación de la reforma de la Iglesia Católica conllevó a la creación de iglesias protestantes o no católicas

region area with at least one unifying physical or human feature such as climate, landforms, population, or history (p. 7)
región área con al menos una característica física o humana que es unificadora, como el clima, los accidentes geográficos, la población o la historia

relative location location of a place relative to another place (p. 6)
ubicación relativa ubicación de un lugar con respecto a otro

religion people's beliefs and practices about the existence, nature, and worship of a god or gods (p. 92)
religión creencias y prácticas de los seres humanos acerca de la existencia, la naturaleza y la adoración de un dios o dioses

remittance money sent to another place (p. 217)
remesa envío de dinero

Renaissance a time of a renewed interest in art and learning in Europe; "rebirth" (p. 374)
Renacimiento período de renovado interés en el arte y el aprendizaje en Europa; "un nuevo nacimiento"

renewable resource a resource that Earth or people can replace (p. 49)
recurso renovable recurso que la Tierra o las personas pueden reemplazar

representative democracy democracy in which people elect representatives to make the nation's laws (p. 273)
democracia representativa democracia en la que el pueblo elige representantes que redactan las leyes de la nación

repressive opposed to freedom (p. 700)
represivo que se opone a la libertad

reservoir storage pool of water (p. 811)
embalse depósito donde se almacena agua

reunification process of becoming unified again (p. 432)
reunificación proceso para volver a unificar

revenue money earned by selling goods and services (p. 60)
ingresos dinero recaudado de la venta de bienes y servicios

revolution circular journey around the sun (p. 18)
revolución vuelta alrededor del Sol

riot noisy, violent public gathering (p. 689)
motín reunión público de carácter violento y ruidoso

Rose Revolution peaceful protests against the results of the 2003 Georgia election (p. 700)
Revolución de las Rosas protestas pacíficas contra el resultado de las elecciones nacionales de Georgia en 2003

rotation complete turn (p. 20)
rotación vuelta completa

rural settlement in the country (p. 80)
rural poblado del campo

S

Sahel a semiarid area that lies between the Sahara and moister regions to the south in northern Africa. (p. 505)
Sáhel área semiárida ubicada entre el desierto del Sahara y las regiones más húmedas al sur del norte de África

salt trade exchange between West Africans selling gold and Arab traders selling salt, beginning around A.D. 750 (p. 513)
comercio de la sal intercambio comercial del oro de África occidental por la sal de los mercaderes árabes, que comenzó alrededor del A.D. 750

samurai Japanese warrior lord (p. 783)
samurái guerrero japonés miembro de la nobleza

Santeria Cuban religion that combines Catholic and West African beliefs (p. 239)
santería religión cubana que combina el catolicismo y creencias de África occidental

satellite image picture of Earth's surface taken from a satellite in orbit (p. 8)
imagen de satélite fotografía de la superficie de la Tierra que tomó un satélite en órbita

satrap Persian governor (p. 657)
sátrapa gobernador persa

savanna parklike landscape of grasslands with scattered trees that can survive dry spells, found in tropical areas with dry seasons (pp. 42, 309, 506)
sabana pradera con árboles dispersos que pueden sobrevivir periodos de sequía; se encuentra en las áreas tropicales que tienen estaciones secas

saving setting aside money for future use (p. 68)
ahorrar reservar dinero para el uso futuro

scale relative size (p. 8)
escala tamaño relativo

scale bar section of a map that shows how much distance on the map represents a given distance on the land (p. 10)
barra de escala sección de un mapa que muestra la correspondencia entre las distancias del mapa y las distancias reales sobre la Tierra

scarcity having a limited quantity of resources to meet unlimited wants (pp. 58, 778)
escasez tener una cantidad limitada de recursos para satisfacer deseos ilimitados

schism split (p. 355)
cisma división

science active process of acquiring knowledge of the natural world (p. 98)
ciencia proceso activo de obtener conocimientos sobre el mundo natural

Scientific Revolution a series of major advances in science during the 1500s and 1600s (p. 388)
Revolución Científica serie de grandes avances científicos durante los siglos XVI y XVII

secede to break away (p. 458)
separarse desprenderse

secondary industry industry involving the use of resources to create new products, such as manufacturing (p. 849)
sector secundario industria relacionada con el uso de recursos para crear nuevos productos, como la industria manufacturera

secondary source information about an event that does not come directly from a person who experienced that event (p. 120)
fuente secundaria información sobre un suceso que no proviene directamente de una persona que experimentó el suceso

secular nonreligious (p. 815)
laico no religioso

secular democracy democracy not based on religion (p. 730)
democracia laica tipo de democracia que no se basa en la religión

secularism idea that government should be separate from religion (p. 574)
laicismo idea que promueve la separación entre el Estado y la religión

sedentary settled (p. 694)
sedentario asentado

semiarid climate dry climate (p. 41)
clima semiárido clima seco

separatist group group of people who want to establish an independent state (p. 816)
grupo separatista grupo de personas que quieren establecer un estado independiente

Serengeti Plain a part of the savanna in Kenya and Tanzania, home to many animals such as elephants and gazelles (p. 532)
Llanura del Serengeti parte de la sabana de Kenya y Tanzania donde habitan animales como elefantes y gacelas

serf a peasant who is legally bound to live and work on land owned by a lord (p. 478)
siervo persona que está legalmente forzada a vivir y trabajar en la tierra de su noble

shah Persian word for king (p. 659)
sah término persa para rey

shamal hot, dry winds that blow across Iran from west to east (p. 651)
shamal viento seco y cálido que atraviesa Irán de oeste a este

Shinto traditional religion that originated in Japan (p. 795)
sintoísmo religión tradicional que se originó en Japón

shogun powerful Japanese military leader who often had more power than the emperor (p. 783)
shogún poderoso líder militar japonés que por lo general tenía más poder que el emperador

Siberia Asiatic Russia (p. 468)
Siberia Rusia asiática

Silk Road series of trade routes that crossed Asia (p. 692)
Ruta de la Seda red de rutas comerciales que atravesaban Asia

single-party state a country in which one political party controls the government (p. 761)
estado de un solo partido país en donde un partido político controla el gobierno

sinkhole depression on the surface of the land caused by the collapse of a cave roof (p. 199)
dolina depresión de la superficie de la tierra causada por el colapso del techo de una cueva

slum poor, overcrowded urban neighborhood (p. 81)
barrio marginal vecindario urbano pobre y sobrepoblado

social class group of people living in simliar economic conditions (p. 89)
clase social grupo de personas que tienen una condición económica similar

social services programs designed to help the poor (p. 325)
servicios sociales programas con el fin de ayudar a los pobres

social structure pattern of organized relationships among groups of people within a society (p. 89)
estructura social patrón de las relaciones organizadas entre los grupos de personas de una sociedad

society group of humans with a shared culture who have organized themselves to meet their basic needs (p. 88)
sociedad grupo de personas con una cultura compartida que se han organizado para satisfacer sus necesidades básicas

Glossary (continued)

solstice point at which days are longest in one hemisphere and shortest in another (p. 18)
solsticio momento en el que la duración de los días es más larga en un hemisferio y más corta en el otro

sovereignty supreme authority (p. 110)
soberanía autoridad suprema

soviet a republic or unit of government under a central communist government (p. 480)
sóviet república o unidad gubernamental bajo un gobierno central comunista

specialization act of concentrating on a limited number of goods or activities (p. 60)
especialización concentrarse en una cantidad limitada de bienes o actividades

special-purpose map map that shows the location or distribution of human or physical features (p. 13)
mapa temático o de propósito particular mapa que muestra la ubicación o distribución de características humanas o físicas

sphere round-shaped body (p. 4)
esfera cuerpo geométrico de forma redonda

spillover an effect on someone or something not involved in an activity (p. 53)
externalidad efecto sobre alguien o algo que no participa en una actividad

standard of living level of comfort enjoyed by a person or society (p. 99)
nivel de vida nivel de comodidad que posee un individuo o una sociedad

staple crop the most important crop produced or consumed in a region (p. 749)
alimento básico el producto alimenticio más importante que se produce o se consume en una región

state region that shares a common government (p. 106)
estado región que tiene un gobierno común

steppes vast areas of grasslands (pp. 471, 685)
estepa territorio extenso de llanuras

stock share of ownership in a country (p. 69)
acción porción de la propiedad de una compañía

strait narrow body of water that cuts through land, connecting two larger bodies of water (p. 649)
estrecho cuerpo de agua angosto que pasa por tierra para conectar a dos cuerpos de agua más grandes

subarctic climate climate with limited precipitation, cool summers, and very cold winters (p. 41)
clima subártico clima de precipitación limitada, veranos frescos e inviernos muy fríos

subduct movement of one part of Earth's crust under another (p. 283)
subducción movimiento de una parte de la corteza terrestre por debajo de otra

subsidence sinking of the ground (p. 272)
hundimiento inmersión de la tierra

subsistence farming farming with little left over to send to market (p. 712)
agricultura de subsistencia tipo de agricultura en el que casi no sobran productos para el mercado

suburb residential area on the edge of a city or large town (p. 51)
suburbio área residencial ubicada en los límites de una ciudad o un pueblo

suburban sprawl spread of suburbs away from the core city (p. 81)
dispersión suburbana extensión de los suburbios lejos del centro de la ciudad

superpower an extremely powerful nation (p. 487)
superpotencia nación sumamente poderosa

supply amount of a good or service that is available for use (p. 59)
oferta cantidad disponible de un bien o servicio

surplus extra (p. 811)
superávit excedente

Swahili Bantu language that has many Arabic elements and words from other languages (p. 545)
swahili lengua bantú que contiene muchos elementos del idioma árabe y palabras de otras lenguas

 T

taiga thick forest of coniferous trees (p. 417)
taiga denso bosque de árboles coníferos

tariff tax on imports (p. 67)
arancel impuesto a las importaciones

technology practical application of knowledge to accomplish a task (p. 65)
tecnología aplicación práctica del saber para ejecutar una tarea

temperate moderate in terms of temperature (pp. 140, 687)
templado de temperatura moderada

temperate zone areas between the high and low latitudes; also known as middle latitudes (p. 34)
zona templada área entre las latitudes altas y bajas; también se le llama latitudes medias

temperature measure of how hot or cold the air is (p. 32)
temperatura medida de cuán caliente o fría se encuentra la atmósfera

terraced farming sculpting the hillsides into different levels for crops (p. 264)
cultivo en terrazas laderas que han sido esculpidas para crear superficies de cultivo niveladas o escalonadas

terrorism use of violence to create fear for political reasons (p. 607)
terrorismo actos violentos destinados a crear un clima de temor para fines políticos

theocracy a government run by religious power (p. 565)
teocracia gobierno en el que rige el poder religioso

timeline line marked off with a series of events and their dates (p. 118)
línea cronológica línea marcada con una serie de sucesos y sus fechas

time zones areas sharing the same time (p. 20)
husos horarios áreas que comparten la misma hora

tornado swirling funnel of wind that can reach 200 miles (320 km) per hour (p. 39)
tornado túnel de aire giratorio que puede alcanzar una velocidad de 200 millas (320 km) por hora

tourism business of providing food, places to stay, and other services to visitors from other places (p. 231)
turismo industria que facilita comida, hospedaje y otros servicios a visitantes de otros lugares

trade exchange of goods and services in a market (p. 66)
comercio intercambio de bienes y servicios en un mercado

trade barrier something that keeps goods and services from entering a country (p. 67)
barrera comercial obstáculos para la entrada de bienes y servicios a un país

traditional economy economy in which people make economic decisions based on their customs and habits (p. 62)
economía tradicional economía en la que la gente toma decisiones económicas de acuerdo a sus costumbres y hábitos

treaty formal agreement between two or more countries (p. 111)
tratado acuerdo formal entre dos o más países

triangular trade three-stage trade pattern that carried goods and enslaved people among Europe, Africa, and the Americas (p. 386)
comercio triangular sistema comercial de tres partes que transportó bienes y personas esclavizadas entre Europa, África y las Américas

tribunes representatives of plebeians in ancient Rome (p. 349)
tribuno representante de los plebeyos de la antigua Roma

Trinity the three persons, or forms, of God according to Christian belief: God the Father, God the Son, and the Holy Spirit (p. 630)
Trinidad dícese de las tres personas o formas de Dios de acuerdo con las creencias cristianas: Dios padre, Dios hijo y Espíritu Santo

tropical cyclone intense rainstorm with strong winds that forms over oceans in the tropics (p. 39)
ciclón tropical aguacero intenso con vientos fuertes que se forma sobre el océano en los trópicos

tropical wet and dry climate climate with a wet season in summer and a dry season in winter (p. 40)
clima tropical húmedo y seco clima de temporada húmeda durante el verano y temporada seca en el invierno

tropical wet climate climate with hot temperatures and heavy rainfall year-round (p. 40)
clima tropical húmedo clima de temperaturas cálidas y lluvia abundante durante todo el año

tropic areas between the Tropic of Cancer and the Tropic of Capricorn; also known as low latitudes (p. 34)
trópico área comprendida entre el Trópico de Cáncer y el Trópico de Capricornio (latitudes bajas)

tsar ruler of imperial Russia; a term used by Byzantine rulers, derived from the Latin *caesar*, or king (p. 478)
zar gobernador del Imperio Ruso; término derivado del latín *césar* o rey, que usaban los gobernadores del Imperio Bizantino

907

tsunami tidal wave (p. 803)
maremoto ola sísmica

tundra area with limited vegetation, such as moss and shrubs (pp. 167, 416)
tundra área con vegetación limitada, como musgos y arbustos

tundra climate climate with cool summers and bitterly cold, dry winters (p. 41)
clima de tundra clima de veranos frescos e inviernos gélidos y secos

typhoon storm much like a hurricane (p. 804)
tifón tormenta parecida a un huracán

tyranny unjust use of power (p. 105)
tiranía uso injusto del poder

U

unitary system system of government in which a central government has the authority to make laws for the entire country (p. 108)
sistema unitario sistema de gobierno en el que un gobierno central tiene la autoridad de hacer leyes para todo el país

universal theme subject or theme that relates to the entire world (p. 94)
tema universal materia o tema que se relaciona con todo el mundo

unlimited government government structure in which there are no effective limits on government actions (pp. 105, 790)
gobierno ilimitado tipo de gobierno en el que no existen límites sobre las acciones del gobierno

Ural Mountains low-lying mountains that separate European Russia from Asiatic Russia (p. 469)
Montes Urales cadena montañosa de poca elevación que separa a Rusia europea de Rusia asiática

urban located in cities (p. 80)
urbano localizado en la ciudad

urbanization movement of people from rural to urban areas (pp. 80, 559)
urbanización desplazamiento de personas de las áreas rurales a las áreas urbanas

urban planning the planning of a city (p. 322)
planeación urbana planeación de una ciudad

urbanized place where most people live in cities (p. 595)
urbanizado lugar donde la mayoría de las personas viven en la ciudad

V

valley stretch of low land between mountains or hills (p. 25)
valle extensión de terreno bajo ubicado entre montañas o colinas

vassals in medieval Europe, noblemen who received land from other noblemen in return for their services (p. 358)
vasallos en la Europa medieval, señores nobles que recibían terrenos de otros señores nobles a cambio de sus servicios

vertical climate zones climate zones in a region that change according to elevation (p. 285)
zonas climáticas verticales zonas climáticas de una región que cambian de acuerdo a la altura

visual arts art forms such as painting, sculpture, and photography (p. 94)
artes visuales expresiones artísticas como la pintura, la escultura y la fotografía

W

wage money paid to an employee (p. 762)
sueldo dinero que se le paga a un empleado

water cycle the movement of water from Earth's surface into the atmosphere and back (p. 37)
ciclo del agua movimiento del agua desde la superficie de la Tierra hacia la atmósfera y viceversa

weather condition of the air and sky at a certain time (p. 32)
tiempo condiciones del aire y el cielo en un momento determinado

weathering process that breaks rocks down into tiny pieces (p. 24)
meteorización proceso que rompe la roca en pedazos muy pequeños

World War I 1914–1918, sometimes called the Great War, the first truly global conflict (p. 394)
Primera Guerra Mundial 1914 a 1918, a veces llamada La Gran Guerra, fue el primer verdadero conflicto global

World War II 1939–1945, second major global conflict (p. 398)
   Segunda Guerra Mundial 1939 a 1945, segundo gran conflicto global

Zionism a movement to create a Jewish state in Jews' historic homeland in Palestine (p. 632)
   sionismo movimiento que busca la creación de un estado judío en el la patria histórica en Palestina de los judíos

Zoroastrianism an Iranian religion that dates back to ancient times (p. 655)
   zoroastrismo religión iraní que data de tiempos antiguos

Index

The letters after some page numbers refer to the following:
c = chart; g = graph; m = map; p = picture; q = quotation.

A

Abdullah II, king of Jordan, 635, 635p
Abkhazia, 690
abolitionists, 318, 886
Aboriginal culture, 91, 842, 844, 845p, 846, 847, 847p, 858, 886
Abraham, 627, 629, 640
absolute location, 6, 886
absolute monarchy, 107, 604
absolutism, 386–387, 386m, 387p, 886
Abu Bakr, 601
acid rain, 170, 419, 419p, 451, 886. See also air pollution
Act of Union (1840), 175, 175p
A.D. See anno Domini
Adamawa Highlands, 871m
adobe, 97c, 147
advertising, 61
Aegean World, 340, 341m
Aeneas, 348
Aeneid (Virgil), 348
aerial photographs, 8, 8p, 886
Aeschylus, 345
Afghanistan, 156, 704m, 861m, 872m
  climate of, 710, 710m, 711
  culture of, 715
  databank, 876
  economy of, 728
  government of, 730
  history of, 714, 723, 723p
  Islam in, 719
  literacy in, 728g
  population of, 726, 726g
  religion in, 725
  Soviet Union and, 723, 723p
  United States and, 723, 729, 730
  women in, 728p
Africa, 861m
  archaeology in, 122p
  human geography, 498–499
  physical geography, 496–497
  physical map of, 863m, 871m
  political map, 861m, 870m
  population density in, 498m
  regional flyover, 497
  regional overview, 494–499
  tourism in, 578–579
  urbanization in, 80
  water resources in, 498, 498m

See also North Africa; Southern and Eastern Africa; West and Central Africa
African Americans, 79, 142, 151
African National Congress (ANC), 543, 886
African Union (AU), 522–523, 549, 575, 886
Afrikaans language, 545
Afrikaners, 545
Afro-Asiatic language, 90
Age of Absolutism, 386–387, 386m, 387p
Age of Empires, 384–386
Age of Exploration, 382–384, 382p, 383m
agora, 346
agriculture, 626, 886
  in Andes and the Pampas, 286, 287m
  in Arabia and Iraq, 594m
  arable land, 750
  in Central America, 230–231
  in China, 749–750, 759, 762
  culture and, 98–99
  free trade and, 242
  plantations, 812, 812g
  pollution and, 232, 242
  in Scandinavia, 425
  in Southeast Asia, 806–807, 807p, 811
  staple crops, 749
  subsistence farming, 519, 519p
  in United States, 141m–142
  in West and Central Africa, 508, 512, 519, 519p
  See also farming; plantations
Agrippina the Younger, 351
Ahaggar Mountains, 871m
ahimsa, 718
AIDS (disease), 522, 537, 537c, 548–549, 886
air circulation, 38, 38p, 39, 39m, 41
air pollution, 53, 851
  in Canada, 170–171
  in Chile, 298
  in China, 767
  in Europe, 407, 419, 419p, 431, 451
  in Mexico City, 204, 204m, 205p
  in South Asia, 727
  in Southeast Asia, 807, 817, 817p
  See also acid rain
Akbar, 719, 720
Aksum kingdom, 539

akyn, 696p, 697, 886
Alabama, 134m, 139, 867m
Alaska, 134m, 138, 139, 141, 149m, 866m
Alaska Range, 139m, 865m, 875m
al-Assad, Bashar, 635, 635p
Alawite Muslims, 625, 886
Albania, 442m, 868m
  databank, 876
  farming in, 449
  government of, 459, 459p
  religion in, 452, 452m
al-Bashir, Omar, 547
Albéniz, Isaac, 436
Alberta, 160m
Alevis, 655
Alexander the Great, 337–339, 337p, 338p, 339p, 343, 346m, 347, 347p, 599p, 600, 657, 718
algebra, 603
Algeria, 552m, 861m
  culture of, 571, 571p
  databank, 876
  economy of, 572–573, 572g
  environmental concerns in, 561
  France and, 568, 568m, 569
  government of, 574
  population of, 558, 559
Algonquin people, 172
Ali, 601
Al-Khwarizmi, 375
Allende, Salvador, 295
alliances, 394
Allied Powers, 398–399, 398m
alphabets, 348, 355, 355p
Alps, 332p, 415, 415m, 869m
al Qaeda, 406, 607, 723, 819
Altaic language, 91
Altay Shan, 873m
Altiplano, 283, 283m, 886
altitude, 35, 201, 886
Amazon basin, 309, 309m, 313, 865m, 886
Amazon rain forest, 322, 322p
Amazon River, 251p, 308–309, 309m
  flooding in, 312–313, 312m, 312p
amend, 301, 886
America, exploration of, 383m, 384–386, 385m
American Revolution, 148–149
American Samoa, 830m
Amnesty International, 111
Amu Dar'ya River, 685, 685m, 686, 694
Amundsen, Roald, 854, 854q
Amundsen Sea, 875m

Amur River, 470
Anabaptist, 379
Anatolia, 648, 649m
Anatolian Plateau, 873m
ANC. See African National Congress
Andean Community of Nations, 300, 300m
Andes and the Pampas, 250p, 862m
  agriculture in, 286, 287m
  atlas of, 278m, 282–289, 283m, 284m, 285c, 287m, 288m
  climate of, 284, 284m
  cultures of, 296–297, 297c
  economy of, 299–300, 300m
  ecosystem of, 285, 285c
  environment of, 298
  fishing in, 286
  governments in, 294–295, 301
  history of, 290–295, 291m, 291p, 292p, 293, 294p
  indigenous people of, 288–289
  languages of, 297, 297c
  literacy in, 300
  mining in, 287, 298
  natural resources of, 287, 287m
  physical features of, 282–283, 282p, 283, 283m
  population density of, 288, 288m
  See also Argentina; Bolivia; Chile; Ecuador; Paraguay; Peru; Uruguay
Andes, 250p, 258, 259m, 261, 862m, 865m
Andorra, 876
Anglican Church, 380
Anglo-Saxons, 356, 365
Angola, 508m, 509, 520, 521, 861m, 870m, 876
animal life
  in Africa, 532–533, 533p
  in Antarctica, 852p, 853
  in Australia, 838, 838p
  in Brazil, 313, 313p
  in Caribbean South America, 261, 261p
  in Mexico, 201
  in Russia, 472
anime, 794, 794p
Ankara River, 470
Annan, Kofi, 547q
anno Domini (A.D.), 119
Antarctica, 8, 8p, 9m, 850, 850p, 851, 860m–861m, 862m–863m, 875m
  animal life of, 852p, 853

climate of, 853, 855
natural resources of, 853
physical features of, 852p,
853m, 852–853
research in, 854–855, 854p,
855p
Antarctic Circle, 34, 34m
Antarctic Treaty, 855, 886
anthropology, 123, 886
Antigua and Barbuda, 231c,
864m, 876
anti-Semitism, 397, 632, 886
apartheid system, 528, 542–
543, 543p, 547, 886
Apennine Mountains, 869m
Appalachian Mountains, 25,
131p, 139, 139m, 862m,
865m
Appalachian Region, 169
appanage system, 477
aqueducts, 207, 351p, 886
aquifer, 622, 623, 652–653, 887
Arabia
Arab culture of, 610, 610p
atlas of, 586m, 590–597,
591m, 592m, 593g, 595m,
596m
economy of, 593, 608–609,
609g
ecosystems in, 594, 594m
history of, 598–605, 598p,
599m, 599p, 600p, 601p,
602m, 603p, 604p, 605p
natural resources in, 592–593,
592m, 608
oil in, 592–593, 592m, 592p,
593g, 604, 608–609, 609g
population density in, 595,
595m
religion in, 596–597, 596m,
596p, 600–603, 600p, 601p,
602m, 606–607, 607p
traditions in, 606–607
water resources in, 594,
594p
Arabian Peninsula, 583p, 590,
591m, 595, 863m, 873m
Arabian Plate, 591, 592
Arabian Sea, 590, 591m
Arabic numerals, 375, 719
Arab-Israeli conflicts, 632–633
arable land, 508, 750, 887
Arabs, 624–625, 624m, 624p
Aral Sea, 685, 699, 699g, 699p
Arawak people, 235, 266
archaeology, 116p, 117, 117p,
122–123, 122p, 538p, 887
archipelagoes, 803, 887
architecture, 94, 94p, 887
of ancient Greece, 345
in Byzantine empire, 356
of Iran, 665, 665p
Muslims and, 361
of North Africa, 567p

in the Renaissance, 374p, 375
of Roman empire, 352
Arctic, 875m
Arctic Archipelago, 165, 165m,
168
Arctic Circle, 33, 33m, 165,
165m, 168, 171, 416, 425
Arctic Ocean, 165m
Argentina, 324, 860m, 864m
agriculture in, 286, 287m
climate of, 284, 284m
culture of, 296
databank, 876
economy of, 299–300, 300,
300m
ethnic groups in, 253c
exports from, 294
government of, 295, 301
history of, 289, 293, 294
immigrants in, 294
physical features of, 283,
283m
population of, 288, 288m
arid climate, 40m–41m, 41, 887
arid zones, 506, 507m
Aristarchus, 345
aristocracy, 341
Aristophanes, 345
Aristotle, 345
Arizona, 134m, 866m
Arkansas, 134m, 867m
Armenia, 480, 680m, 692p,
872m
culture of, 697
databank, 876
ethnic groups of, 690m, 691
history of, 693
natural resources in, 688,
688m
physical features of, 684–685,
685m
poverty in, 698p
religion in, 693
Armenian genocide, 660, 887
arms race, 401
art
of Ancient Greece, 345
Christian, 629p
culture and, 94–95, 94p, 95p
of Iran, 665, 665p
of Japan, 784
of Mexico, 208p–211p, 214
Muslims and, 361
of North Africa, 567p
of North Korea, 790
perspective in, 375, 375p, 377
religion and, 361, 629p
in the Renaissance, 375, 375p,
377, 377p
of South Asia, 725
of Southern Europe, 435,
435p
of West and Central Africa,
521

artifacts, 120, 123, 887
artisans, 364
Aryan people, 717
ascetics, 717
ASEAN. See *Association of
Southeast Asian Nations*
Asia, 861m
earthquakes in, 775, 780
exploration of, 383m, 384,
384p
physical map of, 863m, 873m
political map of, 872m
Russia and, 469, 469m
tectonic plates in, 774–775
urbanization in, 80
volcanoes in, 775
See also *China; Japan; Korea;
North Korea; Southeast
Asia; South Korea*
Asian Tigers, 762, 813
Asoka, 718
Assessment, 100–101, 114–115
Ancient and medieval
Europe, 368–369
Andes and the Pampas,
302–303
Arabia and Iraq, 612–613
Australia and the Pacific,
856–857
Brazil, 326–327
Canada, 184–185
Caribbean South America,
276–277
Central America and the
Caribbean, 244–245
Central Asia and Caucasus,
702–703
China, 768–769
Core Concepts, 14–15, 28–29,
44–45, 54–55, 70–71, 82–83
Eastern Europe, 462–463
Iran, Turkey and Cyprus,
670–671
Israel, 642–643
Japan and the Koreas,
796–797
Mexico, 220–221
Modern Europe, 408–409
North Africa, 576–577
Russia, 490–491
South Asia, 732–733
Southeast Asia, 820–821
Southern and Eastern Africa,
550–551
tools of history, 126–127
United States, 158–159
West and Central Africa,
524–525
Western Europe, 440–441
assimilation, 844, 887
**Association of Southeast
Asian Nations
(ASEAN),** 819, 887
Assyria, 599–600

astrolabe, 119, 119p, 362, 363
astronomy, 207, 600, 602, 887
Aswan High Dam, 560, 569
Atacama Desert, 282, 283m,
284, 284m
Atahualpa, 292
Ataturk, 660, 660p
Athens, 106, 342–347, 344p,
346m
Atlantic Ocean, 36m, 37, 39,
134m, 416, 416m
Atlantic Provinces, 165, 165m
Atlantic slave trade, 514, 887
Atlas Mountains, 556p, 557,
557m, 871m
atmosphere, 23, 887
atoll, 827p, 836, 836p, 887
atomic bomb, 785
Attila the Hun, 353, 694
AU. See *African Union*
Auckland, 840
Augustus, 350–351
Aung San Suu Kyi, 816
Aurangzeb, 721
austerity measures, 269, 887
Australia, 826p, 830m, 861m
animal life of, 838, 838p
atlas, 834–841, 835m, 836p,
837m, 838p, 839m, 840p
climate of, 838–839, 839m
databank, 876
deserts of, 835, 835m
economy of, 849, 849c
ecosystem of, 838, 838p, 839
England and, 385, 843–844
environmental concerns of,
851
ethnic groups of, 846–847,
846p
government of, 848, 848p
history of, 842–845, 843m
human geography, 828–829
indigenous people of, 858
natural resources in, 840–841
physical features of, 834–837,
835m, 836p, 837m
physical geography, 826–827
physical map of, 826m, 863m
plate tectonics and, 837–838,
837m
population of, 828, 840, 840p
regional flyover, 827
regional overview, 824–829
wildfires in, 839
Austria, 376, 387, 390, 428, 433,
433p, 868m, 876
**Austro-Hungarian
empire,** 395, 395m, 433
Austronesian language, 90
**authoritarian
government,** 107, 887
autocracy, 635, 635p, 887
automobile, 99p
Avars, 476

axis, 18, 34, 35, 887
Axis Powers, 398–399, 398*m*
ayatollah, 661, 887
Ayers Rock, 835
Azerbaijan, 680*m*, 872*m*
  climate of, 686*m*, 687
  databank, 876
  economy of, 698
  ethnic groups of, 690–691,
    690*m*, 698
  farming in, 687, 687*m*
  natural resources in, 688,
    688*m*
  physical features of, 684–685,
    685*m*
  religion in, 693
  transportation in, 689
Azikiwe, Nnamdi, 517*p*
Aztec civilization, 119, 119*p*,
  207–208, 207*p*, 208*p*, 209*p*

B

Baath Party, 604, 635
Babur, 719
Babylon, 599, 599*m*, 600
Babylonian empire, 627
Bacon, Francis, 388
Baffin Island, 865*m*
Baganda people, 544
Bagan empire, 811
Baghdad, 602, 602*m*, 603
Bahá'í faith, 655
Bahamas, 231, 235, 864*m*, 876
Bahrain, 596*m*, 597, 603, 604,
  609, 861*m*, 872*m*, 876
Baja California, 198, 199*m*,
  200, 203, 865*m*
Bajpaee, Chietigj, 819*q*
Balboa, Vasco Nuñez de, 384
Bali, 802*p*, 809
Balkan Mountains, 446, 447*m*
Balkan Peninsula, 446, 447*m*,
  458, 869*m*
Baltic Nations. See *Estonia;*
  Latvia; Lithuania
Baltic Sea, 447, 447*m*, 448*m*,
  469*m*
Banco del Sur, 300
Bangkok, 807
Bangladesh, 704*m*, 724, 861*m*,
  872*m*
  climate of, 710, 710*m*
  databank, 876
  economy of, 730
  government of, 730
  history of, 723
  literacy in, 728*g*
  population of, 713, 713*m*,
    726, 726*g*, 727
  religion in, 725

banks and banking
  in Luxembourg, 431
  money management and,
    68–69, 68*c*
  in the Renaissance, 374
  in South America, 300
Bantu language, 545
Bantu people, 539
Baptist Church, 379
Barbados, 864*m*, 876
Barbuda, 231*c*
barter, 60
basin, 884, 884*p*
Bastille, 391
Batista, Fulgencio, 237
bauxite, 230
bay, 884, 884*p*
B.C. See *before Christ*
B.C.E. See *before common era*
before Christ (B.C.), 119
before common era
  (B.C.E.), 119
Beijing, 748, 750
Belarus, 405, 442*m*, 488*m*, 489,
  868*m*
  databank, 876
  history of, 460, 461*p*
  natural resources in, 451
  religion in, 452–453, 452*m*
Belgian Congo, 516, 516*p*
Belgium, 376, 403, 403*m*, 428,
  431, 516, 868*m*, 876
Belize, 233, 226–227, 227*m*, 246,
  247*c*, 247*g*, 864*m*, 876
Benin, 870*m*, 876
Berbers, 567, 571, 571*p*, 887
Berlin Wall, 401, 402, 402*p*, 404,
  405*p*, 432, 887
Bezpalko, 443
Bhutan, 704*m*, 725, 730, 861*m*,
  872*m*, 876
Biafra, 517
bias, 121, 888
Bible (Christian), 630
Bill and Melinda Gates
  Foundation, 157
Bill of Rights (English), 390,
  390*c*, 893
Bill of Rights (U.S), 112
bin Laden, Osama, 607, 723
Bio-Bio River, 287, 287*m*
biodiversity, 52, 229, 888
birth rate, 74, 75, 888
Black Death, 366–367, 366*p*
Black Sea, 469, 469*m*, 470, 649,
  684, 685*m*, 689
Boers, 540, 888
Bolívar, Simón, 268, 268*p*,
  268*q*, 293
Bolivia, 860*m*, 864*m*
  agriculture in, 286, 287*m*
  culture of, 297
  databank, 876

  economy of, 299, 300, 300*m*
  ethnic groups in, 253*c*
  exports from, 294
  government of, 301, 301*p*
  languages of, 297*c*, 297*p*
  literacy in, 300
  mining in, 279–281, 279*p*,
    280*p*, 281*p*
  Native Americans in, 297
  physical features of, 283,
    283*m*
  population of, 288, 288*m*
Bollywood, 725, 725*p*, 888
Bolsheviks, 480, 888
bonds, 69, 888
boom and bust cycle, 318,
  318*m*, 318*p*, 888
Border Air Quality Strategy
  (2003), 170
borders, 72, 73
Borneo, 803, 803*m*, 806
Bosnia, 111*p*
Bosnia and Herzegovina,
  442*m*, 452, 452*m*, 458,
  868*m*, 876
Bosporus Strait, 649
Botswana, 526*m*, 534, 534*m*,
  540*m*, 861*m*, 870*m*, 876
boule, 344*p*
Braga, Wilson, 315*q*
Brahman, 717
Brahmaputra River, 709, 709*m*,
  713
brain drain, 664, 888
Brasilia, 314, 319, 319*p*
Brazil, 860*m*, 864*m*
  animal life in, 313, 313*p*
  atlas, 304*m*, 308–315, 309*m*,
    310*m*, 311*m*, 312*p*, 313*p*,
    314*c*
  Carnival in, 321, 321*p*
  climate of, 310–311, 310*m*
  coffee in, 318–319
  cultural diversity in, 314
  culture of, 320–321, 321*p*
  databank, 876
  economy of, 299–300, 300*m*,
    317, 319, 324, 324*c*
  ecosystem of, 298, 312–313,
    312*m*, 312*p*, 313*p*, 322,
    322*p*
  environmental concerns in,
    322–323, 322*p*, 323*p*
  ethnic groups in, 253*c*, 320,
    321
  farming in, 311, 311*m*, 318,
    318*p*, 324
  flooding in, 312–313, 312*m*,
    312*p*
  government of, 318–319, 325
  history of, 316–319, 316*p*,
    317*p*, 318*m*, 318*p*, 319*p*
  housing in, 315

  hydroelectricity in, 311, 311*m*
  land use in, 51*p*, 311, 311*m*
  language of, 316, 317
  manufacturing in, 324
  myStory, 305–307, 305*p*,
    306*p*, 307*p*
  Native Americans in, 316, 321
  natural resources in, 311,
    311*m*, 324
  physical features of, 308–309,
    309*m*
  plantations in, 318, 318*p*
  population of, 314, 314*g*
  Portugal and, 316, 317–318,
    317*p*
  poverty in, 314–315, 320, 325
  rain forest in, 312–313, 312*p*,
    322, 322*p*
  religion in, 321
  slavery in, 317, 318
  sports in, 305–307, 307*p*,
    308*p*, 320
  trade in, 324
  women in, 319
Brazilian Highlands, 309, 309*m*,
  310–311, 862*m*, 865*m*
brazilwood, 317, 888
Britain
  Berlin Wall and, 401
  Canada and, 174–177, 174*p*,
    175*p*, 176*p*, 177*p*, 178–179,
    178*p*, 179*c*
  currency in, 423
  France and, 148
  India and, 401, 721, 722,
    722*m*
  Iran and, 660
  Iraq and, 603, 604
  North Africa and, 568–569
  population of, 392
  Seven Years' War and, 174,
    174*p*
  Southwest Asia and, 632
  trade in, 423
  World War I and, 395, 395*m*
  World War II and, 398–399,
    398*m*
  See also *England; Great*
    Britain; United Kingdom
British Columbia, 160*m*
British Commonwealth of
  Nations, 845
British North America Act
  (1867), 175*p*, 176, 178
Brooks Range, 875*m*
Bruegel, Pieter, 377
Brunei, 816, 818, 818*c*, 861*m*,
  876
Brunelleschi, Filippo, 375
Brussels, 431
bubonic plague, 366–367, 366*p*
Bucephalus, 337
Budapest, 457*p*

Buddhism, 92*m*–93*m*, 93, 756, 756*p*, 757, 809, 811, 814, 888
in Japan and the Koreas, 784, 789, 795
in South Asia, 717–718, 725
in Southeast Asia, 815
budget, 68, 888
buffalo, 146
Bukhara, 692*p*, 693
Bulgaria, 404, 442*m*, 459, 868*m*, 877
Burkina Faso, 870*m*, 877
Burma, 872*m*, 880. See also *Myanmar*
Burundi, 526*m*, 861*m*, 870*m*, 877
Bush, George W., 156–157, 605
business, 59, 60–61. See also *companies*
butte, 884, 884*p*
Byzantine empire, 354–356, 354*p*, 355*p*, 356*m*, 477, 600, 602, 631, 658, 659*p*

C

Caesar, Julius, 350
CAFTA-DR. See *Central America-Dominican Republic-United States Free Trade Association*
Cailes, Plutarco, 213*p*
Cairo, 559, 567
Calderón, Felipe, 213, 213*p*
calendar, 119, 119*p*, 206, 207
California, 134*m*, 144, 154, 866*m*
caliph, 601, 602, 888
calligraphy, 610, 610*p*
Calvin, John, 379
Cambodia, 861*m*, 872*m*
databank, 877
economy of, 818, 818*c*
government of, 816
history of, 810, 810*p*, 811, 813
Vietnam War and, 813
Cameroon, 508*m*, 509, 522*g*, 861*m*, 870*m*, 877
Canaan, 626, 626*p*, 627
Canada, 128*m*, 860*m*, 864*m*
atlas of, 160*m*, 164–171, 164*p*, 165*m*, 166*m*, 167*m*, 168*p*, 169*m*, 170*g*, 171*c*, 171*p*
Britain and, 174–177, 174*p*, 175*p*, 176*p*, 177*p*, 178–179, 178*p*, 179*c*
climate of, 166–167, 166*m*
constitutional monarchy of, 179
culture of, 182–183, 182*p*, 183*p*
databank, 877

economy of, 170*g*, 171*c*, 177, 180–181
environmental concerns of, 170–171, 171*c*
ethnic groups in, 172–173, 172*p*
First Nations, 161, 172, 173, 182*p*
fishing in, 169–170, 170*p*
France and, 173–174
French Canadian culture in, 86*m*, 87
government in, 176, 177, 178–179, 178*p*, 179*c*
history of, 172–177, 172*p*, 173*p*, 174*p*, 175*p*, 176*p*, 177*p*
human geography, 132–133
hydroelectric power in, 168–169
immigrants in, 133*g*, 176, 176*p*, 182–183, 182*p*
imports and exports of, 181
land use in, 168–169, 168*p*
languages of, 180
literacy rate of, 180
minerals in, 168, 170, 171
myStory, 161–163, 161*p*, 162*p*, 163*p*
NAFTA and, 152, 154, 216, 219
natural resources of, 168–170, 169*m*, 170*g*
parliamentary system of, 179*c*
peacekeeping efforts of, 181, 181*p*
physical features of, 164–165, 165*m*
physical geography, 130–131
pollution in, 170–171
population density of, 167, 167*m*, 176, 182–183
population of, 132*m*
regional overview, 128–133
religion in, 174
rivers in, 168, 168*p*, 169
trade and, 180–181
United States and, 164, 168, 170, 175, 177, 178, 180, 183
World War I and, 177, 177*p*
World War II and, 177
Canada-United States Air Quality Agreement, 170
Canadian Cordillera, 130*m*, 130*p*, 165, 165*m*, 170
Canadian Shield, 131*p*, 165, 165*m*, 168, 170, 862*m*, 865*m*
canals, 226, 227*m*, 237, 599, 755
cannons, 365
canopy, 312, 888
canyon, 884, 884*p*
Cao Dai, 808, 808*p*
Cape Horn, 862*m*

Cape of Good Hope, 863*m*
Cape Town, 540
Cape Verde, 870*m*, 877
capital, 58, 455, 636, 888
capitalism, 62*p*, 485
Capitol, U.S., 108*p*
Caracas, 263, 263*m*, 263*p*
caravans, 567, 692, 694, 888
caravels, 382, 888
cardinal directions, 4, 888
Caribbean, 860*m*
Columbus and, 384
slave trade and, 514
See also *Caribbean South America; Central America and Caribbean*
Caribbean Community (Caricom), 242
Caribbean South America
animals of, 261, 261*p*
atlas, 258–265, 258*p*, 259*m*, 260*m*, 261*p*, 262*m*, 263*m*, 264*p*
climate of, 260, 260*m*
culture of, 270–271, 270*p*, 271*p*
economies of, 275, 275*c*
ecosystems of, 261, 261*p*
environmental problems, 272, 272*p*
ethnic groups in, 265
farming in, 264, 264*p*
governments in, 273–274, 273*p*, 274*p*
history of, 266–269, 266*p*, 267*m*, 267*p*, 268*p*
human settlement in, 262, 262*m*
land use in, 264, 264*p*
Native Americans in, 262, 265
natural resources in, 264, 264*p*
physical features of, 258–259, 259*m*
pirates in, 267, 267*m*, 267*p*
population density of, 263, 263*m*
slavery in, 267
See also individual countries
Carib people, 235, 266
Caricom (Caribbean Community), 242
Carnival, 238, 265, 321, 321*p*, 888
Carpathian Mountains, 446, 447*m*, 869*m*
Carranza, Venustiano, 211
Carthage, 350, 350*m*, 566
Cartier, Jacques, 173
cartograms, 679
cartography, 382, 888
Casas, Bartolome de las, 235*q*
cash crops, 148, 231, 236, 888
Caspian Sea, 469, 469*m*, 470,

649, 651, 676*p*, 684, 685*m*
caste system, 717, 727–728, 888
Castro, Fidel, 237, 237*p*, 241
cataract, 884, 885*p*
cathedrals, 364
Catherine of Aragon, 380, 380*p*
Catherine the Great, 478–479, 479*p*
Catholic Reformation, 380–381, 889
cattle ranching, 231, 286
Cauca River, 258, 259*m*
Caucasus, 680*m*
atlas, 684–691, 685*m*, 686*m*, 687*m*, 688*m*, 689*p*, 690*m*, 690*p*
climate in, 686*m*, 687
cultural diversity in, 690–691, 690*m*, 691*p*
culture of, 696–697, 696*p*, 697*p*
economy of, 698
education in, 695
ethnic groups of, 690–691, 690*m*, 690*p*
farming in, 687, 687*m*
government of, 695, 700–701, 701*p*
history of, 692*p*, 693, 694, 695, 695*p*
land use in, 687, 687*m*
language of, 690, 697, 698
natural resources in, 688, 688*m*
physical features of, 684–685, 685*m*
religion in, 693, 696
Russia and, 695
Soviet Union and, 695, 695*p*
transportation in, 689
water resources in, 689
See also *Armenia; Azerbaijan; Georgia*
Caucasus Mountains, 469, 469*m*, 684, 685*m*, 863*m*, 869*m*, 873*m*
caudillos, 268, 294, 889
Cayenne, 263, 263*m*, 263*p*
C.E. See *common era*
censor, 487, 889
Central African Republic, 522*g*, 861*m*, 870*m*, 877
Central America and the Caribbean, 860*m*
agriculture in, 230, 231
atlas, 222*m*, 226–233, 227*m*, 228*m*, 229*m*, 230*m*, 231*c*, 232*c*
climate of, 228–229
deforestation in, 233
economy of, 237, 241–242, 242*g*

ecosystems of, 228–229, 228*m*

environment of, 232–233

free-trade agreements and, 241–242

government in, 240–241

history of, 234–237, 234*p*, 235*p*, 236*c*, 237*p*

hurricanes in, 228, 229–230, 229*m*

land use in, 230–231, 230*m*, 231*c*

languages of, 239

life expectancy in, 240*c*

literacy in, 240*c*

myStory, 223–225, 223*p*, 224*p*, 225*p*

native cultures in, 234–235, 234*p*, 238–240, 238*p*, 239*p*, 240*c*

physical features of, 226–227, 226*p*, 227*m*

pollution in, 232–233

population density, 229

poverty in, 240

tourism in, 231, 231*c*, 232, 243

tropical rain forests of, 228, 228*m*, 228*p*

volcanoes in, 226*p*

See also names of individual countries

Central America-Dominican Republic-United States Free Trade Association (CAFTA-DR), 242

Central Asia, 680*m*

atlas, 684–691, 684*p*, 685*m*, 686*m*, 687*m*, 688*m*, 689*c*

climate of, 686, 686*m*

culture of, 696–697, 696*p*, 697*p*

deserts of, 685, 685*m*

economy of, 698

education in, 695

environmental concerns in, 698

ethnic groups of, 691

farming in, 686–687, 687*m*

government of, 695, 700–701, 701*p*

history of, 692–693, 692*p*, 693*m*, 694, 694*p*, 695

horses in, 694, 694*p*

human geography, 678–679

land use in, 686, 687*m*

language of, 691, 697, 698

natural resources in, 688, 688*m*

physical features of, 684–685, 684*p*, 685*m*

physical geography, 676–677

regional flyover, 677

regional overview, 674–679

religion in, 691, 693, 696

rivers of, 685, 685*m*

Russia and, 691

Soviet Union and, 691, 695, 695*p*

transportation in, 689

water resources in, 689, 698, 699, 699*g*, 699*p*

See also *Kazakhstan; Kyrgyzstan; Tajikistan; Turkistan; Uzbekistan*

Central Europe. See *Czech Republic; Hungary; Slovakia; Slovenia*

central government, 108

centrally planned economy, 63, 63*p*

Central Russian Upland, 869*m*

Central Siberian Plateau, 873*m*

Central Uplands, 415, 415*m*

Cerrado, 309, 309*m*

Chad, 48*p*, 508, 508*m*, 509, 861*m*, 870*m*, 877

Champlain, Samuel de, 173

Changó, 239

Chang River, 746, 747, 747*m*, 748, 748*m*, 749, 749*m*, 766, 766*p*

chariots, 98*p*

Charlemagne, 356–357, 357*m*, 357*p*

Charles I, king of England, 390

Charter of Rights and Freedoms (Canada), 179

Chavez, Hugo, 269, 273, 273*p*, 274, 274*p*, 275, 277*q*

Chechnya, 483, 485

checks and balances, system of, 349*c*

chemical weathering, 24

Chernobyl, 450*m*, 451, 482

Cherskiy Range, 863*m*, 873*m*, 875*m*

Chiang Kai-shek, 757, 761

Chicago, Illinois, 33*g*, 33*p*

Chihuahuan Desert, 200

Chile, 860*m*, 864*m*

air pollution in, 298

climate of, 284, 284*m*

culture of, 297

databank, 877

deforestation in, 298

economy of, 300

exports from, 294

government of, 295, 301

history of, 289

languages of, 297*c*, 297*p*

literacy in, 300

natural resources in, 287, 287*m*

physical features of, 283,

283*m*

population of, 288, 288*m*

China, 861*m*, 872*m*

agriculture in, 749, 750, 759, 762

atlas of, 742*m*, 746–753, 746*p*, 747*m*, 748*m*, 749*m*, 750*p*, 751*m*, 752*m*

cities of, 750–751, 750*p*

climate of, 748–749, 748*m*

communist government in, 758–759, 758*p*, 761

databank, 877

economic system of, 761*c*

economy of, 758–759, 758*p*, 762–763, 763*c*, 764

education in, 764, 764*p*, 765*c*

environment of, 767, 767*p*

ethnic diversity in, 752–753, 752*m*, 752*p*, 753*p*

government of, 105, 105*c*, 753, 760, 760*p*, 761, 761*c*

Great Britain and, 757

history of, 123*p*, 754–759, 754*p*, 757*p*, 758*p*

Internet and, 99

Japan and, 757, 785, 785*m*

Kazakhstan and, 689

Korea and, 782

land use in, 748–749, 749*m*

languages of, 752*p*, 755

life expectancy in, 764, 765*c*

market economy in, 759

myStory, 743–745, 743*p*, 744*p*, 745*p*

nomads in, 749

one-child policy, 750, 765

physical features of, 746–747, 746*p*, 747*m*

politics in, 761*c*

pollution in, 767, 767*p*

population density of, 749, 750–751, 751*m*, 765

population of, 741

religion in, 753, 756–757, 756*p*

rivers in, 746, 746*p*, 747, 747*m*, 748, 748*m*, 749, 749*m*, 766, 766*p*

Russian Federation and, 489

Silk Road and, 692–693, 692*p*, 693*m*

Southeast Asia and, 808–809, 810

Tibet and, 753

timelines of, 754–755

trade and, 67*c*

women in, 765

Chinese Communist Party, 761

cholera, 537

Chopin, Frederic, 455

Christianity, 92, 92*m*–93*m*

art of, 629*p*

beliefs of, 630, 630*p*

in Byzantine empire, 354–355, 355*p*

Crusades and, 360–363, 360*p*, 361*m*, 362*m*

in Eastern Europe, 452–453, 452*m*, 453*p*

in Egypt, 571

Great Schism in, 355

history of, 629, 629*p*

in Iraq, 597

in Israel, 640, 641*p*

in Korea, 789

in Mexico, 208, 209*p*

in North Africa, 566

in Ottoman empire, 659, 659*p*

in Roman empire, 352–353, 352*m*

in Southeast Asia, 815

in Southern and Eastern Africa, 539, 545, 545*c*, 545*p*

in Southwest Asia, 584, 584*p*, 624*m*, 624*p*, 625

spread of, 356–358

in West and Central Africa, 521

in Western Europe, 418

Christiansen, Ole Kirk, 425*p*

chronology, 118, 889

Churchill, Winston, 399*q*

Church of England, 380

Cicero, 349*q*, 352

circular flow of mixed economy, 63*c*

cities and towns

in China, 750–751, 750*p*

in Middle Ages, 363–364

in North Africa, 559

Silk Road and, 693, 693*m*

in Southeast Asia, 807

suburbs and, 51

in the United States, 142

of West and Central Africa, 510–511, 510*m*

in Western Europe, 426

citizens, 106–109, 112, 113, 113*p*, 155, 180, 212–213, 240, 273, 301, 325, 341–345, 344*c*, 460, 460*p*, 485*c*, 520*p*, 547, 575, 634, 663, 700, 730, 761, 788, 816, 848, 848*p*, 889

in United States, 106, 108, 109, 112, 113

citizenship, 155, 889

in the United States, 112–113, 112*p*, 113*p*

city-states, 106, 341, 889

of Ancient Greece, 341–342, 341*m*, 347

of Italy, 355, 364

Maya, 234
of Sumer, 599
civic life, 113, 889
civic participation, 113, 889
civilizations, 98, 598, 889
civil rights movement, 151, 889
Civil War, United States, 150
class system
in Japan, 784
in Middle Ages, 364
in Roman Republic, 349
of Spanish empire, 292
Cleopatra, queen of Egypt, 566
clerics, 662, 889
climate, 889
of Andes and the Pampas, 284, 284m
of Antarctica, 853, 855
of Australia, 838–839, 839m
of Azerbaijan, 686m, 687
of Brazil, 310–311, 310m
of Canada, 166–167, 166m
of Caribbean South America, 260, 260m
of the Caucasus, 686m, 687
of Central America and Caribbean, 228–229
of Central Asia, 686, 686m
of China, 748–749, 748m
culture and, 711p
of Cyprus, 650m, 651
definition of, 32, 140
of Eastern Europe, 448–449, 448m
of Georgia, 686m, 687
of Greece, 340
Himalayas and, 710, 710m
of Iran, 650–651, 650m, 651c
of Israel, 620–621, 620m
of Jordan, 621
of Lebanon, 620m
of Mexico, 200–201, 200m, 201p
of New Zealand, 839, 839m
ozone layer and, 855, 855p
of Pacific region, 838–839, 839m
of Russia, 470m, 471–472
of South Asia, 710–711, 710m, 711m
of Southeast Asia, 804, 804m
of Syria, 620–621
of Turkey, 650–651, 650m, 651c
types of, 40–41, 40m–41m, 40p, 41p
of United States, 140–141
water and, 36–37, 36m, 37c
of West and Central Africa, 506, 507m
of Western Europe, 416–417, 416m

See also *weather*
climate change, 851, 889
Climate Change Plan (Canada), 171
climate changes, 419, 851
climate graphs, 32, 33g
climate regions, 40–41, 40m–41m
climate zones, 506, 507m
Clinton, Hillary, 157p
Closer Look
ancient Egypt, 565, 565p
ancient Greece, 342–343
Arab culture, 610, 610p
Aral Sea, 699, 699g, 699p
Black Death, 366, 366p
Bollywood, 725, 725p
Brazil economy, 318, 318m, 318p
Canada's history, 174–175
Carnival, 321, 321p
climate and culture, 711p
coffee, 264, 264p
Colombia, 264, 264p
colonization in Africa, 515, 515m, 515p
colonization in Southeast Asia, 812, 812p
cultures of Central America and Caribbean, 239, 239p
Curitiba, 323, 323p
democracy, 344, 344p
economy of Southwest Asia, 637, 637g, 637p
energy choices, 450, 450m, 450p
environment of Southeast Asia, 815, 815p
European Union, 429, 429m, 429p
explorers, 383, 383m, 383p
globalization, 298–299, 298p, 299p
Inca empire, 291, 291m, 291p
Iranian art and architecture, 665, 665p
Iron Curtain, 402m, 402p
Japanese culture, 794, 794g, 794p
Mexico, 201, 208–211, 208p–211p, 218, 218g
Mughal empire, 720, 720p
Russia, 478–479
thirteen colonies, 147, 147m
Three Gorges Dam, 766, 766p
Tuvalu, 850, 850m, 850p
United States economy, 153c, 153p
Venezuela, 274, 274p
water pollution, 232
women in South Asia, 728, 728g, 728p
clothing, 87p, 97c
cloud forest, 229

Clovis, 356
coal energy, 450, 450m, 450p, 451
Coastal Plain, 865m
Coats Land, 875m
coffee, 535, 535p
in Brazil, 318–319
in Colombia, 255–257, 256p, 257p, 264, 264p
in Mexico, 203
Cold War, 400–405, 481, 517, 889
collectivization, 480–481, 889
Colombia, 860m, 864m
atlas, 254m, 258, 259m, 260m, 262m, 263m
climate of, 260, 260m
culture of, 270, 270p, 271
databank, 877
economy of, 275c, 300, 300m
environmental problems of, 272, 272g
ethnic groups in, 253c, 274
government of, 273, 273p
history of, 262, 266, 268, 269
land use in, 264
myStory, 255–257, 255p, 256p, 257p
physical features of, 258, 259, 259m
population density of, 263, 263m
colonialism, 514, 889
colonization, 51, 147–148, 147m, 147p, 235, 889
in Australia, 843–844
in Central America and Caribbean, 235
in India, 721
in Pacific region, 844
in Southeast Asia, 812, 812g
in Southern and Eastern Africa, 540–542, 540m, 541p, 542p
Spain and, 292–293
in West and Central Africa, 514, 515, 515m, 515p, 518
colony, 235, 889
Colorado, 10m, 11m, 134m, 866m
Columbian Exchange, 385c, 385m
Columbus, Christopher, 235, 384
command economy, 63, 63p, 758–759, 758p, 791, 889
commerce, 363
commercial farming, 286, 286p
common era (C.E.), 119
common law, 365
Common Market, 403, 403m
commonwealth, 390
communism, 107, 397, 889

communist government, 107, 397, 397c, 758–759, 758p
capitalism and, 485
in China, 761
in Eastern Europe, 401
failure of, 403–405, 404p, 405p
in Mongolia, 760–761
in Southeast Asia, 813
in Soviet Union, 484–485
Communist Party, 480–481, 481c, 790
Comnena, Anna, 356
Comoros, 877
companies, 60–61, 61p. See also *business*
comparative advantage, 779, 889
compass, 362, 363
compass rose, 10, 11, 12, 890
competition, 60–61, 61p, 890
compromise, 172, 890
confederal system, 108
Confucianism, 756, 756p, 814, 890
Confucius, 756
Congo Basin, 863m, 871m
Congo River, 505, 505m, 516
Congo River Basin, 496p
Congress, U.S., 109
coniferous trees, 42, 42p, 890
Connecticut, 108p, 134m, 147m, 867m
conquistadors, 208, 292, 292p, 384, 890
Constantine, 353, 629, 631
Constantinople, 353, 354, 355, 356, 658, 659p
constitution, 105, 105c, 890
Constitution, U.S., 112, 148–149
constitutional monarchy, 107, 179, 422, 424, 786, 890
consumers, 59, 60–61, 61p, 890
Continental Congress, 148
continental warm summer climate, 40, 40m–41m
continents, 26, 835
Cook, James, 843q, 844p
Cook Islands, 830m, 843
Copernicus, Nicolaus, 388
copper, 534, 534m
Copts, 571, 890
coral reef, 229, 709, 827p, 835, 836, 836p, 890
Cordillera Central, 227, 227m
Cordillera de Mérida, 259, 259m
Cordillera Oriental, 259, 259m
cordilleras, 258, 262, 283, 283m, 805, 805m, 890
Córdoba, 361
core, 22, 890
corruption, 519, 548, 701, 890

Cortés, Hernán, 208, 221q, 384
Costa Rica, 864m
 databank, 877
 ecosystem of, 229
 government in, 240
 life expectancy in, 240c
 literacy in, 240c
 physical features of, 226–227,
  227m
 pineapples and, 230
 tourism in, 232
Council of Clermont, 360
Council of Trent, 380–381
coup, 318, 520, 666, 848, 890
cradle-to-grave system, 424–
 425, 424c, 890
craftspersons, 364
credit and credit unions, 68,
 69, 890
Crete, 340, 341m
Crimean War, 479
criollos, 292, 293, 294, 890
Croatia, 442m, 458, 868m, 877
Crusades, 360–363, 361m, 631,
 890
crust, 22, 26, 890
Cuba, 191m, 864m
 databank, 877
 economy of, 63
 government of, 107, 241
 history of, 237
 physical features of, 227,
  227m
 religion of, 239
cuisine, 457, 890
cultural borrowing, 427, 808,
 890
cultural diffusion, 96–97, 96p,
 97c, 240, 435, 891
cultural diversity, 690–691,
 690m, 690p
cultural exchange, 715
cultural hearth, 96, 342, 716,
 891
cultural landscape, 86, 86p,
 87, 891
cultural mosaic, 178, 891
cultural trait, 86–87, 96, 891
culture, 891
 of Afghanistan, 715
 of Algeria, 571, 571p
 of ancient Greece, 343,
  345–346
 of Andes and the Pampas,
  296–297, 297c
 art and, 94–95, 94p, 95p
 of Brazil, 320–321, 321p
 of Canada, 182–183, 182p,
  183p
 of Caribbean South America,
  270–271, 270p, 271p
 of Caucasus, 696–697, 696p,
  697p
 of Central Asia, 696–697,

 696p, 697p
 climate and, 711p
 definition of, 86–87
 of Egypt, 565, 565p, 570, 571
 environment and, 86p, 87
 families, 88–89, 88p
 food and, 87, 87p
 geography and, 84–101,
  84p, 85p, 86p, 87p, 88p,
  90m–91m, 90p, 91p,
  92m–93m, 92p, 93p, 94p,
  95p, 96p, 97p, 98p, 99p
 of Georgia, 697, 697p
 of Germany, 432
 of Hungary, 457
 of India, 724–725, 724p, 725p
 of Japan, 793, 794, 794g,
  794p, 795
 of Kyrgyzstan, 696p, 697,
  697p
 language and, 90–91,
  90m–91m
 of Latvia, 455, 455p
 of Mexico, 214–215, 214p,
  215p
 of Native Americans, 84p,
  85, 85p
 of North Africa, 570–571,
  570p, 571p
 of Pacific region, 847, 847p
 of Poland, 455
 of Polynesia, 833
 religion and, 87, 92–93,
  92m–93m
 science and, 98–99, 98p, 99c,
  99p
 societies and, 88–89
 of South Asia, 715, 717, 724–
  725, 724p, 725p
 of Southeast Asia, 799–801
 in Southern Europe, 435–436,
  435p
 of South Korea, 789, 789p
 of Sri Lanka, 715
 of Sumatra, 799–801
 technology and, 97, 98–99,
  98p, 99c, 99p
 trade and, 715
 transportation and, 97
 of Turkey, 667
 of United States, 154–156,
  154m, 155p
 of Western Europe, 411–413,
  418
culture region, 86, 86m, 87, 891
cuneiform, 598p, 599
Curitiba, 322, 323, 323p
currency, 60, 403, 423, 437
currents, 36, 36m
cyclones, 39

Cyprus, 644m, 653, 872m
 atlas, 648–655, 649m, 650m,
  652m, 654m, 654p
 climate of, 650–651, 650m
 databank, 877
 ethnic groups in, 654–655,
  654m, 654p
 history of, 658, 658m
 land use in, 652–653, 652m
 physical features of, 648–650,
  649m
 religion in, 654–655, 654m,
  654p
 Turkey and, 668–669, 669m,
  669p
Cyril, 355, 355p
Cyrillic alphabet, 355, 355p
Cyrus the Great, 656
Czechoslovakia
 communism in, 401
 Velvet Revolution in, 404
 in World War II, 398–399,
  398m
Czech Republic, 442m, 868m
 databank, 877
 economy of, 456c
 European Union and, 456
 government of, 456
 religion in, 452, 452m, 453

D

Da Gama, Vasco, 382
dala horse, 425p
Dalit, 728
dance, 84p, 85, 85p, 521
Danube River, 415, 419, 446,
 446p, 447m, 457p
dao, 756–757
Daoism, 756–757, 756p, 891
Darfur, 546, 546m, 546p
Darius III, 337, 339, 347, 656p
Darling Range, 874m
Da Silva, Lula, 325q
Da Vinci, Leonardo, 375, 375p
D-Day, 399
Dead Sea, 619, 619m
death rate, 74, 75, 891
Deccan Plateau, 709, 709m,
 863m, 873m
December solstice, 19
deciduous trees, 42, 42p, 891
decimal system, 719
**Declaration of Human Rights,
 U.N.,** 111
Declaration of Independence,
 148, 390c
deforestation, 52, 509, 509p,
 891
 in Andes and the Pampas,
  298
 in Caribbean South America,
  272, 272g

 in Central America and
  Caribbean, 233
 in Mexico, 205
 in West and Central Africa,
  509, 509p
degree, 4, 891
DeKlerk, F.W., 543
Delaware, 134m, 147m, 867m
Delhi Sultanate, 719
delta, 25, 25p, 557, 884, 885p,
 891
demand, 59, 59g, 891
democracy, 106, 148c, 891
 in ancient Greece, 342–343,
  344, 344p, 434
 in Central Asia and the
  Caucasus, 700
 in India, 724
 in Poland, 454
 representative, 106, 112, 349,
  730
 in Southeast Asia, 816
 in Southern and Eastern
  Africa, 547
 in South Korea, 788–789
 in Turkey, 666–667
**Democratic People's Republic
 of Korea.** See *North
 Korea*
**Democratic Republic of the
 Congo,** 507g, 507m, 547,
 861m, 870m
 databank, 877
 history of, 519–520, 520p, 522
 literacy rate, 522g
 resources of, 508m, 509
demographers, 74, 891
demokratia, 344
demonstration, 700, 701p, 891
Deng Xiaoping, 759
Denmark, 421, 424, 425, 426,
 868m, 877
deportation, 439, 891
deposition, 25, 891
desalination, 594, 594p, 595,
 609, 622, 623, 891
Descartes, René, 388
**desert and desert brush
 ecosystem,**
 42m–43m, 43, 43p
desertification, 75, 509, 510,
 561, 561p, 891
deserts
 in Arabia and Iraq, 594, 594m
 in Australia, 835, 835m
 in Central Asia, 685, 685m
 in Mexico, 200
 in North Africa, 556–557,
  557m
 in Southern and Eastern
  Africa, 531, 531m
 in Southwest Asia, 621
developed country, 64, 64p,
 892

developing country, 64, 64p, 892
development, 64, 548–549, 549g, 892
Dia de la Raza, 214, 214p
diamonds, 534, 534m, 534p
Dias, Bartolomeu, 382
diaspora, 240, 892
Díaz, Porfirio, 210, 210p
dictatorships, 237, 241, 604, 892
   in Andes and the Pampas, 295
   in North Korea, 790, 791p
   in Southern and Eastern Africa, 547
dikes, 431
Dinaric Alps, 446, 447m, 869m
Diocletian, 353
diplomacy, 111, 156, 892
direct democracy, 106, 343, 892
directions, 4
diseases
   Black Death, 366–367, 366p
   Industrial Revolution and, 392, 393
   Native Americans and, 292
   in Russian Federation, 486
   in Southern and Eastern Africa, 527, 537, 537c, 548–549
   in West and Central Africa, 511, 522
disposable income, 485, 892
dissenters, 147, 892
distortion, 9, 9m, 892
diversified economies, 299, 609, 892
diversify, 437, 892
diversity, 97, 892
Djenné, 513
Djibouti, 526m, 861m, 870m, 877
Document-Based Questions
   Andes and the Pampas, 303
   Arabia and Iraq, 613
   Australia and Pacific region, 857
   Brazil, 327
   Canada, 185
   Caribbean South America, 277
   Central America and the Caribbean, 245
   climate and ecosystems, 45
   culture, 101
   Democratic Republic of the Congo, 525
   Eastern Europe, 463
   economics, 71
   Europe, 409, 441
   geography tools, 15
   government, 115

historical maps, 127
human–environment interaction, 55
infant mortality, 525g
Iran, Turkey, and Cyprus, 671
Israel, 643
Japan, 797
John and Abigail Adams, 159q
Kazakhstan, 703
Malacca Strait, 821
Mexico, 221
Middle Ages, 369
North Africa, 577
plates, 29
population and movement, 83
population of China, 769
Roosevelt, Franklin D., 159q
Russia, 491
secondary sources, 127
South Asia, 733
Southern and Eastern Africa, 551
Dome of the Rock, 631p
domestic trade, 67
Dominica, 864m, 877
Dominican Republic, 864m
   databank, 877
   government in, 241
   language of, 239, 239p
   life expectancy in, 240c
   literacy in, 240c
   myStory, 223–225, 223p, 224p, 225p
   physical features of, 227, 227m
dominion, 176, 892
Dominion of Canada, 176
Don River, 470
drainage basins, 505, 505m
Drake, Francis, 382p
Dravidian language, 90
drought, 548, 777, 851, 892
Druze, 625, 892
Dubai, 609
Dürer, Albrecht, 377
Dutch East India Company, 540
Dvina River, 470
dynasty, 754–755, 892

E

Earth
   air circulation and, 38, 38p, 39, 39m
   axis, 18
   climates of, 32–41, 33g, 34m, 35m, 36m, 37c, 38m, 39m, 40m–41m
   directions, 4
   ecosystems of, 42–43, 42m–43m, 42p–43p

forces on, 24–25, 24p, 25m, 25p
hemispheres of, 4m, 5, 5m
inside of, 26–27, 26p, 27m, 27p
latitude, 4–5, 4m
longitude, 5, 5m
rotation of, 20, 20p
seasons of, 18–19, 18p–19p, 35
structure of, 22–23, 22p–23p
study of, 4–7, 4m, 5m
sun and, 18–19, 18p–19p, 20, 20p, 34, 34m, 37, 37p, 38, 38p
surface of, 8–9, 8p, 9m
temperatures of, 34–35, 34m, 35m
time zones, 20–21, 21c
earthquakes, 17, 17p, 26–27, 27p, 415, 803
   in Asia, 775, 780
   in Caribbean South America, 259, 270
   in Central America and Caribbean, 228
   in Mexico, 199
East Asia
   human geography, 740–741
   physical geography, 738–739
   population of, 740m, 740p
   regional flyover, 739
   regional overview, 736–741
East Berlin, 432
Eastern Desert, 871m
Eastern Europe, 442m
   atlas, 446–453, 447m, 448m, 449p, 450p, 451p, 453p
   climate of, 448–449, 448m
   Cold War and, 401
   communism in, 401, 403–405, 404p, 405p
   energy choices in, 450, 450m, 450p, 451
   environmental concerns in, 451
   European Union and, 406
   farming in, 449, 449p
   migration from, 406
   mountains of, 446, 447m, 448–449
   natural resources in, 450, 451
   physical features of, 446–447, 446p, 447m
   religion in, 452–453, 452m, 453p
   See also individual countries
Eastern Ghats, 709, 709m, 873m
Eastern Hemisphere, 5, 5m
Eastern Orthodox Church, 355, 357, 452–453, 452m, 453p, 477
East India Company, 721

East Pakistan, 722–723, 722m
East Slavs, 476–477, 476p
East Timor, 808, 816, 861m, 872m
Ecclesia, 344g
economic development, 64–65, 64p, 65m
economic organizations, 111, 111p
economic regions, 154, 892
economics and economic systems, 62–63, 62p, 63c, 63p, 892
   capital, 58
   command economy, 758–759, 758p, 791
   definition of, 58
   demand, 59, 59g
   entrepreneurs and, 57, 57p, 58, 58p, 62
   factors of production, 58, 58p
   geography and, 56–71
   goods and services, 58, 59, 60
   gross domestic product, 64
   inflation, 61
   labor, 58
   land, 58
   market economy, 152, 759, 761c
   mercantilism, 293c
   money management, 68–69, 68c, 68p, 69p
   opportunity cost, 59
   prices, 59
   process of, 60–61, 60c, 61p
   productivity, 65
   recession, 61, 792
   scarcity, 58
   supply, 59, 59g
   technology and, 65
   theories of, 480, 485
   trade and, 66–67, 66p, 67c
   See also business
economy
   of Algeria, 572–573, 572g
   of Andes and the Pampas, 299–300, 300m
   of Arabia and Iraq, 593, 608–609, 609g
   of Australia, 849, 849c
   of Baltic Nations, 455
   of Bangladesh, 730
   of Belgium, 431
   of Brazil, 317, 318m, 319, 324, 324c
   of Canada, 170g, 171c, 177, 180–181
   of Caribbean South America, 275, 275c
   of Central America and Caribbean, 237, 241–242, 242g
   of Central Asia and Caucasus, 698

of China, 762–763, 763c
of Colombia, 275c
of Czech Republic, 456c
diversified economies, 299, 609
of Egypt, 573
of Europe, 406
of France, 430
of French Guiana, 275p
of Germany, 396, 396g, 396p, 406, 432, 432c
Great Depression and, 151, 396, 396g, 396p
of Greece, 436–437, 437g, 438
of Guyana, 275c
of India, 730–731, 730g, 731p
of Iran, 664
of Israel, 637, 637g, 637p
of Italy, 436–437, 437g, 438
of Japan, 787, 787g, 792
of Jordan, 637g, 637p
of Kenya, 549
of Lebanon, 637g
of Libya, 572–573, 572g
of Mexico, 216–217, 216c, 217m
of Middle America, 192–193
of Mongolia, 762, 763c
of New Zealand, 849
of North Africa, 572–573, 572g
of North Korea, 791
of Pacific region, 849, 849c
of Pakistan, 730
of Poland, 454–455
of Portugal, 436–437, 437g, 438
of Russian Federation, 483, 485
of Saudi Arabia, 609
of Scandinavia, 425
of Slovakia, 456c
of Slovenia, 457
of Solomon Islands, 849, 849c
of South Africa, 549
of South Asia, 728, 730–731, 730g
of Southeast Asia, 818–819, 818c
of South Korea, 789
of Southwest Asia, 637, 637g, 637p
of Spain, 436–437, 437g, 438
of Suriname, 275c
of Syria, 637g, 637p
of Taiwan, 762, 762p, 763c
of Tajikistan, 698
of Turkey, 667–668, 668c, 668p
of United Kingdom, 423
of United States, 152–154, 153c, 153p
of Venezuela, 275c
of West and Central Africa,

518–519, 518p
of Western Europe, 426, 426g
of Yemen, 608
ecosystems, 42–43, 42m–43m, 42p–43p, 52, 892
of Andes and the Pampas, 285, 285c
of Arabia and Iraq, 594, 594m
of Australia, 838, 838p, 839
of Brazil, 312–313, 312m, 312p, 313p, 322, 322p
of Caribbean South America, 261, 261p
of Central America and Caribbean, 228–229, 228m
definition of, 261, 285
of Mexico, 201
of North Africa, 558m
of Pacific region, 838, 839
of South America, 285, 285c
of Southern and Eastern Africa, 532–533, 532m, 533p
of Western Europe, 416–417
ecotourism, 243, 533, 892. See also tourism
Ecuador, 860m
culture of, 297
databank, 877
economy of, 299, 300, 300m
ecosystem of, 285
oil pollution in, 298
population of, 288–289, 288m
education
in Caucasus, 695
in Central Asia, 695
Charlemagne and, 357
in China, 764, 764p, 765c
economic development and, 64
in Germany, 432
Industrial Revolution and, 393
in Japan, 793
in Mexico, 215
Muslims and, 363, 602–603, 607p
in Western Europe, 417, 418
Edward I, king of England, 365
Egypt, 499, 552m, 861m, 870m
ancient, 564–566, 564p, 565p, 566p
Arab-Israeli conflicts and, 632–633
culture of, 565, 565p, 570, 571
databank, 878
economy of, 573
environmental concerns in, 560
farming in, 564, 565, 565p
government of, 565, 569, 569p, 574, 574p
history of, 539, 564–566,

564p, 565p, 566p
human development index in, 573
Israel and, 569, 632–633
landforms of, 25, 25m
myStory, 553–555, 553p, 554p, 555p
natural resources in, 562, 562m
physical features of, 556–557, 557m
population of, 558, 559, 559p
religion in, 566, 566p, 571, 574
Suez Canal, 563
water resources in, 536, 536c, 536m
women in, 553–555, 553p, 554p, 555p
Elburz Mountains, 651
El Dorado, 266, 892
election fraud, 700, 893
electricity, 287, 287m, 389, 393, 523, 766, 766p, 767
elevation, 12, 532, 893
Elizabeth I, queen of England, 372, 380
Elizabeth II, queen of England, 178, 178p, 179, 422, 848p
Ellesmere Island, 168
El Niño, 284, 893
El Salvador, 226–227, 227m, 228, 864m, 878
emigration, 79, 453, 893
emperors, 783–784
empires, 106, 598, 893
employment, 219, 246, 247c, 247g
encomienda system, 235, 893
endangered species, 533
energy sources, 49, 49c, 52, 389
in China, 766, 766p, 767
coal, 450, 450m, 450p, 451
Europe and, 407
in Japan and the Koreas, 779
nuclear, 450, 450m, 450p, 451
in Russian Federation, 485, 487, 488, 488m
in United States, 141, 141m
in West and Central Africa, 523
England, 370m, 422, 423m
Australia and, 385
civil war in, 390
colonies of, 147–148, 147m, 147p, 385
explorations by, 383, 383m
government of, 364p, 365, 390, 423
Hundred Years' War, 365–366, 365p
Industrial Revolution in, 392
myStory, 371–373

Normans in, 364–365
Parliament in, 365
religion in, 380, 380p
in the Renaissance, 376
Spain and, 371–373, 387
Vikings in, 357
See also Britain; Great Britain; United Kingdom
English Bill of Rights, 390, 893
Enlightenment, 148, 209, 389–390, 391, 893
Entekhabifard, Camella, 663q
entrepreneur, 57, 57p, 58, 58p, 62, 392, 423, 454, 608, 609, 893
environment
of Central America and Caribbean, 232–233
of China, 767, 767p
culture and, 86p, 87
ecotourism and, 243
globalization and, 298–299, 298p, 299p
of the Netherlands, 431
population growth and, 75
of Southeast Asia, 815, 815p, 817, 817p
of United States, 145
of West and Central Africa, 508–509, 508m, 509p
See also human–environment interaction
environmental concerns
of Australia and Pacific region, 850–851
of Brazil, 322–323, 322p, 323p
of Canada, 170–171, 171c
of Caribbean South America, 272, 272g
of Central Asia, 698
of Eastern Europe, 451
of Europe, 407
of Japan and the Koreas, 780–781, 781p
of North Africa, 560–561, 560p, 561p
of Russia, 471
of South Asia, 727
of Soviet Union, 482
Environmental Protection Agency (EPA), 47
Epic of Gilgamesh, 599q
Epic of Manas, 681
epics, 599q, 681, 725, 893
equal-area projection, 9, 9m
Equator, 4, 4m, 506, 802
climate and the, 285, 804
precipitation and, 39, 41
Equatorial Guinea, 878
equinox, 18, 19, 893
Erasmus (Dutch humanist), 377
Erie Canal, 142
Eritrea, 526m, 861m, 870m, 878

erosion, 24–25, 53, 893
Essential Question
Ancient and medieval Europe, 336, 347, 359, 367, 369
Andes and the Pampas, 278, 289, 295, 301, 303
Arabia and Iraq, 586, 597, 605, 611, 613
Australia and the Pacific, 830, 841, 845, 851, 855, 857
Brazil, 304, 315, 319, 325, 327
Canada, 160, 171, 177, 183, 185
Caribbean South America, 254, 265, 269, 275, 277
Central America and Caribbean, 222, 233, 237, 243, 245
Central Asia and Caucasus, 680, 691, 695, 701, 703
China, 742, 753, 759, 767, 769
Eastern Europe, 442, 453, 461, 463
Europe, 370, 381, 387, 393, 399, 407, 409
Iran, Turkey, and Cyprus, 644, 655, 661, 669, 671
Israel, 614, 625, 633, 641, 643
Japan and the Koreas, 770, 781, 787, 795, 797
Mexico, 194, 205, 211, 219, 221
Russia, 464, 475, 483, 489, 491
South Asia, 704, 715, 723, 731, 733
Southeast Asia, 798, 809, 813, 819, 821
Southern and Eastern Africa, 526, 537, 543, 549, 551
United States, 134, 145, 151, 157, 159
West and Central Africa, 500, 511, 517, 523, 525
Western Europe, 410, 421, 427, 433, 439, 441
estates, 391
Estonia, 405, 442*m*, 868*m*
databank, 878
government of, 454, 455
religion in, 452, 452*m*, 453
ethanol, 322, 324, 325, 893
ethics, 92, 628, 893
Ethiopia, 499, 526*m*, 861*m*, 870*m*
databank, 878
as developing country, 64
drought in, 548
farming in, 535, 535*p*
government in, 541*p*
history of, 538, 539, 540*m*
religion in, 539
water resources in, 536, 536*c*, 536*m*

Ethiopian Highlands, 497*p*, 863*m*, 871*m*
ethnic cleansing, 458–459, 520, 893
ethnic diversity
in Southeast Asia, 808–809
in United States, 154*m*
in West and Central Africa, 517
ethnic groups
of Australia, 846–847, 846*p*
of Azerbaijan, 698
of Balkan Nations, 458–459
of Brazil, 320, 321
of Canada, 172–173, 172*p*
of Caribbean South America, 265
of the Caucasus, 690–691, 690*m*, 690*p*
of Central Asia, 691
of Cyprus, 654–655, 654*m*, 654*p*
of French Guiana, 274
of Georgia, 698
of Guyana, 274
of Iran, 654–655, 654*m*
of Kyrgyzstan, 698
of New Zealand, 846–847, 847*p*
of Pacific region, 847, 847*p*
of Russia, 474–475
of South America, 252*m*, 253*c*
of Southern and Eastern Africa, 544–545, 546–547
of Southwest Asia, 585*m*
of Suriname, 274
of Turkey, 585*m*, 654–655, 654*m*, 654*p*
of Uzbekistan, 698
ethnocentrism, 541, 542, 844, 893
Etruscan civilization, 348–349
EU. See *European Union*
Euphrates River, 583*p*, 591, 591*m*, 594, 594*m*, 595, 599, 599*m*, 619, 622–623, 623*m*
Eurasia, 414
Eurasian Plate, 591, 592, 803
Euripides, 345
euro, 403, 423, 437
Europe, 356*p*, 360–367, 360*p*, 361*m*, 362*m*, 363*p*, 364*p*, 366*p*, 370*m*, 861*m*
Age of Absolutism, 386–387, 386*m*, 387*p*
Ancient, 337–353
Cold War and, 400–401, 400*p*
colonies in Africa, 514, 515, 515*m*, 515*p*
economy of, 406
Enlightenment in, 389–390
environmental concerns in, 407

famines in, 366
feudalism in, 358–359, 358*c*, 367
Germanic tribes in, 356
Great Depression in, 396, 396*g*, 396*p*
human geography, 334–335
Industrial Revolution in, 392–393, 392*p*, 393*p*
Iron Curtain in, 402*m*
Japan and the Koreas and, 784–785
manorialism in, 359, 367
Middle Ages in, 354–359, 354*p*, 355*p*, 356*m*, 357*m*, 357*p*, 358*c*, 359*p*
migration to, 406
nationalism in, 391
North Africa and, 568–569, 568*m*, 568*p*
Northwestern, 422–427, 422*p*, 423*m*, 424*c*, 425*p*, 426*g*, 427*p*
physical geography, 332–333
physical map of, 863*m*, 869*m*
political map of, 868*m*
political systems in, 397, 397*c*
population density of, 76*m*
regional flyover, 333
regional overview, 330–335
religion in, 379*m*
in the Renaissance, 374–377, 374*p*, 375*p*, 376*p*, 377*p*
Russia and, 469, 469*m*
Scientific Revolution in, 388–389
Southern, 434–439, 434*p*, 435*p*, 436*p*, 437*g*, 438*p*, 439*p*
in Southern and Eastern Africa, 540–542, 540*m*, 541*p*, 542*p*
terrorism in, 406, 406*p*
urbanization in, 80
West Central, 428–433, 428*p*, 429*m*, 429*p*, 430*p*, 431*p*, 432*c*, 433*p*
World War I and, 394–395, 394*p*, 395*m*
World War II and, 398–399, 398*m*
See also *Eastern Europe*; individual countries; *Western Europe*
European Economic Community (EEC), 403, 403*m*, 429
European Space Agency, 275, 275*p*
European Union (EU), 403, 418, 423, 424, 893
Baltic Nations and, 455
Central Europe and, 456
Eastern Europe and, 406

flag and motto of, 434
headquarters, 431
history of, 429, 429*m*, 429*p*
open-border policy of, 427
Poland and, 455
Russia and, 488–489
Southern European countries in, 437
Turkey and, 668
West Central European countries of, 428–429
evaporation, 37, 37*c*, 893
executive branch, 109, 148*c*
exploit, 812, 893
explorer, 383, 383*m*, 383*p*
export economy, 317, 893
exports, 67, 67*c*, 152, 317, 893
of Canada, 181
of Germany, 432, 432*c*
of Japan and the Koreas, 779, 779*c*
of Southeast Asia, 812, 812*g*
of South Korea, 789
of West and Central Africa, 518
extended family, 88, 88*p*, 893

F

factors of production, 58, 58*p*
fado music, 436
Faisal, king of Iraq, 604
Falkland Islands, 295, 864*m*
family, 88–89, 894
famine, 366, 481, 759, 894
Faraday, Michael, 389
farming, 626
in Albania, 449
in ancient Egypt, 564, 565, 565*p*
in Azerbaijan, 687, 687*m*
in Brazil, 311, 311*m*, 324
in the Caucasus, 687, 687*m*
in Central Asia, 686–687, 687*m*
in Eastern Europe, 449, 449*p*
in Georgia, 687, 687*m*
in Japan and the Koreas, 778–779, 778*m*
mechanized, 449
in Mexico, 201, 203, 205, 206, 207, 217
in Middle Ages, 363
in North Africa, 573
in South Asia, 712, 712*g*
in Southern and Eastern Africa, 535, 535*p*
in Soviet Union, 480–481
statistics, 286
terraced farming, 264, 264*p*
See also *agriculture*; *commercial farming*; *plantations*; *subsistence farming*

fascism, 397, 397c, 894
Fatah, 634–635
fault, 26, 894
favela, 315, 894
federal republic, 212
federal system, 108, 894
Federated States of Micronesia, 828, 830m
Ferdinand of Aragon, 362
Fertile Crescent, 619, 626, 894
feudalism, 358–359, 358c, 367, 894
Fiji, 830m, 835m, 836, 848, 861m, 878
Final Solution, 398, 399
Finland, 370m, 424, 425, 426, 868m, 878
fireworks, 755
First Nations, 161, 172, 173, 175, 182p, 894
fishing, 141m, 142
  in Canada, 169–170, 170p
  in Central America and Caribbean, 232–233
  in Japan, 779, 781, 781p
  in Mexico, 203
  in North Korea, 779
  in South America, 286
Five Pillars of Islam, 601, 601p, 606
flamenco dance, 435p, 436
Flanders, 376, 431
floating population, 765
flooding, 27, 30p, 31, 31p, 141, 781, 815, 815p
  in Brazil, 312–313, 312m, 312p
  in North Africa, 560
flood plain, 714, 884, 885p, 894
Florence, 374, 374p
Florida, 134m, 144, 149m, 867m
fold trap, 592, 592p
foliage, 776, 894
food
  cultural diffusion and, 97c
  culture and, 87, 87p
  of Hungary, 457
  of South Asia, 725
foreign policy, 110–111, 110p, 111p, 156–157, 156c, 894
forests, 807
  canopy, 506
  of Southeast Asia, 817
  of West and Central Africa, 506
  of Western Europe, 416
Formosa, 785, 785m
fossil, 123, 538, 538p, 894
fossil fuels, 49, 49c, 592–593, 592m, 894
Fouta Djallon, 871m
Fox, Vicente, 213, 213p
France, 370m, 428p, 868m

absolutism in, 387
in Africa, 540, 540m
Algeria and, 568, 568m, 569
Britain and, 148
Canada and, 173–174
colonies of, 385
databank, 878
economy, 430
Enlightenment in, 391
European Union and, 403, 403m
explorations by, 383, 383m
French Guiana and, 273
French Revolution, 391, 391p
government of, 387, 430
Great Depression and, 396
history of, 430
Hundred Years' War, 365–366, 365p
Mexico and, 210
name of, 356
North Africa and, 568–569, 568m, 568p
in the Renaissance, 376
Seven Years' War and, 174, 174p
Southwest Asia and, 632
Spain and, 209
United States and, 149
Vikings in, 357
World War I and, 395, 395m
in World War II, 398–399, 398m
Francis I, king of France, 376
Franco, Francisco, 397, 436
Franks, 356
Frederick II, ruler of Prussia, 390
free market, 62, 216, 894
free trade, 67, 425, 819, 894
  in Brazil, 314, 324
  in Europe, 403, 403m
free-trade agreements
  agriculture and, 242
  in Central America and Caribbean, 241–242
  NAFTA, 152, 154, 180, 216, 219
  in South America, 299–300, 300m
Free Trade Area of the Americas (FTAA), 219
French Canadian culture, 86m, 87
French Guiana
  atlas, 254m, 258, 259m, 260m, 262m, 263m
  climate of, 260, 260m
  culture of, 270, 271, 271p
  economy of, 275c
  ethnic groups in, 265, 274
  European Space Agency and, 275, 275p

government of, 273, 273p
history of, 267
land use in, 264
physical features of, 258, 259, 259m
population density of, 263, 263m
French Polynesia, 830m
French Revolution, 391, 391p, 894
FTAA. See *Free Trade Area of the Americas*
Fujimori, Alberto, 301
Fulani people, 62, 62p
fundamentalism, 607, 894
fur trade, 173, 173p, 174

G

G-8. See *Group of 8*
Gabon, 870m, 878
Gadsden Purchase, 149m
galaxy, 18
Galen, 352
Galileo Galilei, 388, 389p
Gambia, 870m, 878
Gandhi, Indira, 722
Gandhi, Mohandas, 718, 721, 721p, 721q, 722, 728
Ganges River, 709, 709m, 711, 713, 713m
gasoline, 421
gauchos, 289, 289p, 294, 296
Gaul, 350, 350m, 356
Gautama, Siddhartha, 718, 756
Gaza Strip, 614m, 618, 625, 632–633
  conflict and the, 638–640, 638m, 639p, 640p
  government of, 634, 635
GDP. See *gross domestic product*
Geneva Conventions, 111
Genghis Khan, 694, 755
Genoa, 374
genocide, 894
  in Darfur, 546, 546m, 546p
  in Rwanda, 547
geographic information systems (GIS), 8, 894
geography, 895
  climate and, 32–41, 33g, 34m, 35m, 36m, 37c, 38m, 39m, 40m–41m

culture and, 84–101, 84p, 85p, 86p, 87p, 88p, 90m–91m, 90p, 91p, 92m–93m, 92p, 93p, 94p, 95p, 96p, 97p, 98p, 99p
definition of, 4
directions, 4
economics and, 56–71
ecosystems and, 42–43, 42m–43m, 42p–43p
history and, 714, 714m
human-environment interaction, 47–53, 47p, 48p, 49c, 50m, 51p, 52p, 53p
latitude, 4–5, 4m
longitude, 5, 5m
population and movement, 72–81, 72p, 73p, 74g, 75p, 76m, 76p, 77p, 78p, 79p, 80p, 81c, 81p
themes of, 6–7
tools of, 2–15, 4p, 5m, 6p, 7p, 8p, 9m–13m
trade and, 66–67, 66p, 67c
  See also *Earth*
geology, 17
Georgia (Asia), 480, 680m, 872m
  climate of, 686m, 687
  culture of, 697, 697p
  databank, 878
  ethnic groups of, 690, 690m, 690p, 698
  farming in, 687, 687m
  government of, 700–701, 701p
  history of, 693
  physical features of, 684–685, 685m
  transportation in, 689
Georgia (U.S.), 134m, 139, 147m, 867m
Germanic tribes, 356
Germany, 428, 868m
  culture of, 432
  databank, 878
  division of, 401, 402m
  economy of, 396, 396g, 396p, 406, 432, 432c
  European Union and, 403, 403m
  government of, 107, 391
  immigrants in, 433
  Japan and, 785
  Jewish people in, 397–398, 398p, 399
  Nazi Party in, 397–399, 397c, 398m
  religion in, 380
  in the Renaissance, 376, 377
  reunification of, 404, 405p
  Rhine-Ruhr region, 421, 421m
  Thirty Years' War, 380

World War I and, 395, 395*m*
World War II and, 398–399, 398*m*
gers, 751, 751*p*
Ghana, 870*m*
  databank, 878
  empires in, 512*m*, 512*p*, 513
  history of, 516, 520, 520*p*
  myStory, 501–503
  population of, 510, 510*m*
Gilgamesh, 599*q*
GIS. See *geographic information systems*
Giza, 566
glaciers, 168, 415, 447, 850, 850*p*, 851, 852–853, 884, 885*p*, 895
glasnost, 482, 484
global economy, 423, 438
global grid, 5, 5*m*
globalization, 298–299, 298*p*, 299*p*, 549
global positioning system (GPS), 3
global warming, 727
globe, 8, 8*p*
Globe Theatre, 377*p*
GNP. See *gross national product*
Gobi, 747, 747*m*, 748, 863*m*
Godunov, Boris, 478
Golan Heights, 618, 620*m*, 623, 633
gold, 512*p*, 513, 534, 534*m*
Golden Hind, 382*p*
Golden Horde, 477*p*, 478
goods and services, 58, 59, 60
Gorbachev, Mikhail, 404, 405*p*, 482, 482*p*, 484
Gordian knot, 339, 339*p*
Goths, 476
government, 894
  of Afghanistan, 730
  of Albania, 459, 459*p*
  of Algeria, 574
  of ancient Egypt, 565
  of ancient Greece, 341, 342–343, 347
  of Andes and the Pampas, 294–295, 301
  of Arabia and Iraq, 604
  of Australia, 848, 848*p*
  of Austria, 433
  of Bangladesh, 730
  of Belgium, 431
  of Bhutan, 730
  branches of, 109, 109*p*
  of Brazil, 318–319, 325
  of Brunei, 816
  of Bulgaria, 459
  of Cambodia, 816
  of Canada, 176, 177, 178–179, 178*p*, 179*c*
  of Caribbean South America, 273–274, 273*p*, 274*p*

  of Caucasus, 695, 700–701, 701*p*
  of Central America and Caribbean, 240–241
  of Central Asia, 695, 700–701, 701*p*
  of China, 105, 105*c*, 753, 758–759, 758*p*, 760, 760*p*, 761, 761*c*
  citizenship and, 112–113, 112*p*, 113*p*
  of Colombia, 273, 273*p*
  colonial, 147–148, 147*m*, 147*p*
  communist, 480–481, 481*c*, 758–759, 758*p*, 760–761
  constitutional monarchy, 179, 422, 424, 816
  of Cuba, 107
  of Czech Republic, 456
  definition of, 104
  democracy and, 148*c*, 434
  of East Timor, 816
  economic systems and, 62–63, 62*p*, 63*c*, 63*p*
  of Egypt, 569, 569*p*, 574, 574*p*
  of England, 364*p*, 365, 390
  in the Enlightenment, 390–391
  of Estonia, 454, 455
  of Ethiopia, 541*p*
  foreign policy, 110–111, 110*p*, 111*p*
  forms of, 107
  of France, 387, 391, 430
  of French Guiana, 273, 273*p*
  of Georgia, 700–701, 701*p*
  of Germany, 107, 391
  of Greece, 434
  of Guyana, 273, 273*p*
  of Hungary, 457
  of India, 730
  of Indonesia, 816
  of Iran, 662–663, 662*p*, 663*p*
  Islamic, 607
  of Israel, 634–635, 634*p*
  of Italy, 391
  of Japan, 786–787
  of Jordan, 635, 635*p*
  of Kazakhstan, 700
  of the Koreas, 786, 786*m*
  of Kyrgyzstan, 697, 701*p*
  of Laos, 816
  of Latvia, 454, 455
  of Lebanon, 635, 635*p*
  of Libya, 574
  limited government, 105, 105*c*, 788
  of Lithuania, 454, 455
  of Malaysia, 816
  of Mexico, 212–213, 212*p*, 213*p*

  in Middle Ages, 364–366, 364*p*, 365*p*
  military junta, 816
  of Mongolia, 758–759, 758*p*, 760–761, 761*c*
  of Morocco, 574, 575, 575*p*
  of Myanmar, 816
  of Nepal, 730
  of New Zealand, 848
  of North Africa, 574–575, 574*p*, 575*p*
  of North Korea, 107, 107*p*, 790–791, 791*p*
  oligarchy, 341, 347, 816
  origins of, 104, 104*p*
  of Pacific region, 848, 848*p*
  of Pakistan, 730
  parliamentary system, 240
  in Persian empire, 657
  of Philippines, 816
  of Poland, 454–455
  political structures, 108–109, 108*p*, 109*p*
  powers of, 105, 105*c*
  principles of, 108
  Protestant Reformation and, 379–380
  of Romania, 459
  of Roman Republic, 349, 349*c*
  of Russia, 479–483, 480*p*, 481*c*, 482*p*
  of Russian Federation, 483, 484, 486–487
  of Saudi Arabia, 107, 604
  of Scandinavia, 424–425
  of Singapore, 816
  single-party state, 761
  of Slovakia, 456
  of Slovenia, 457
  of Somalia, 548
  of South Africa, 547, 548*p*
  of South Asia, 730
  of Southeast Asia, 813, 816
  of Southern and Eastern Africa, 547–549
  of South Korea, 788–789
  of Soviet Union, 404, 481–482
  of Sri Lanka, 730
  of Sudan, 547
  of Suriname, 273, 273*p*
  of Switzerland, 433
  of Syria, 635, 635*p*
  systems of, 107–108
  of Taiwan, 761, 761*c*
  of Turkey, 666–667
  of Turkmenistan, 700, 700*p*
  of Ukraine, 460, 460*p*
  of United Kingdom, 107, 422–423
  of the United States, 105, 105*c*, 106, 108, 148–149, 148*c*
  unlimited, 790

  of Venezuela, 273, 273*p*, 274, 274*p*
  of Vietnam, 816
  of West and Central Africa, 514, 515, 515*m*, 515*p*, 516–517, 516*p*, 517*p*, 518, 519–520, 520*p*
  of Zimbabwe, 547
  See also *political systems*
GPS. See *global positioning system*
Granada, 362
Grand Banks, 169
Grand Canal (China), 755
Granicus River, 337
grasslands, 504, 506
Great African Rift Valley, 619
Great Artesian Basin, 874*m*
Great Barrier Reef, 835, 835*m*
Great Basin, 865*m*
Great Britain, 422
  Africa and, 540, 540*m*, 542, 542*p*
  Australia and, 843–844
  Central Asia and, 695
  China and, 757
  Cyprus and, 668
  Falkland Islands and, 295
  New Zealand and, 844
  See also *Britain; England; United Kingdom*
Great Depression, 151, 177, 396, 396*g*, 396*p*, 895
Great Dividing Range, 863*m*, 874*m*
Greater Antilles, 865*m*
Great European Plain, 414, 415*m*
Great Hungarian Plain, 447, 447*m*
Great King, 656
Great Lakes, 134*m*, 168, 169
Great Leap Forward, 759
Great Plains, 131*p*, 141, 141*m*, 144, 170, 865*m*
Great Pyramid, 566, 566*p*
Great Rift Valley, 530–531, 531*m*, 871*m*, 895
Great Sandy Desert, 835, 835*m*, 863*m*, 874*m*
Great Schism, 355
Great Victoria Desert, 835, 835*m*, 863*m*, 874*m*
Great Wall of China, 754*p*–755*p*, 755
Great War. See *World War I*
Great Zimbabwe, 539, 539*p*
Greco-Roman culture, 351
Greece, 415, 868*m*
  ancient, 340–347, 340*p*, 341*m*, 342*p*, 343*p*, 344*p*, 345*p*, 346*m*, 347*p*, 351, 599*p*, 600

city-states of, 341–342, 341*m*, 347
climate of, 340
Cyprus and, 668
databank, 878
economy of, 436–437, 437*g*, 438
in European Union, 437
government of, 341, 344*c*, 347, 434
physical features of, 340, 341*m*
religion in, 345, 435
slavery in, 346, 347
trade in, 342–343, 439, 439*p*
women in, 346, 347
Greek Orthodox Church, 435, 655. See also *Eastern Orthodox Church*
Greenland, 421, 860*m*, 864*m*
Green Revolution, 712, 895
Greenwich, England, 5, 5*m*, 21
Greenwich Mean Time, 21
Gregorian calendar, 119
Grenada, 864*m*, 878
griot, 521, 521*p*, 895
gross domestic product (GDP), 64, 679, 895
of Australia, 849
of North Africa, 572–573, 572*g*
of Southeast Asia, 818, 818*c*
of Southern Europe, 437*g*
of Western Europe, 426, 426*g*
gross national product (GNP), 431, 895
Group of 8 (G-8), 487
Guardian Council, 662
Guatemala, 246, 247*c*, 247*g*, 864*m*
databank, 878
as developing country, 64*p*
earthquakes in, 228
government in, 240–241
history of, 237
land-reform laws in, 242
language of, 239, 239*p*
life expectancy in, 240*c*
literacy in, 240*c*
native cultures in, 238*p*, 239
physical features of, 226–227, 226*p*, 227, 227*m*
volcanoes in, 226*p*, 227, 227*m*
Guiana Highlands, 259, 259*m*, 309, 309*m*, 862*m*, 865*m*
guild, 364, 895
guillotine, 391*p*
Guinea, 870*m*, 878
Guinea-Bissau, 870*m*, 878
Gulf Coastal Plain, 199, 199*m*
Gulf of Aden, 590, 591*m*
Gulf of California, 194*m*, 198, 199*m*

Gulf of Mexico, 199, 199*m*, 202, 202*m*
Gulf of Oman, 590, 591*m*
Gulf Stream, 36*m*, 37
gunpowder, 363, 365, 384, 755
Gupta empire, 718–719
Gutenberg, Johannes, 376, 376*p*, 377
Guyana, 860*m*, 864*m*
atlas, 254*m*, 258, 259*m*, 260*m*, 262*m*, 263*m*
climate of, 260, 260*m*
culture of, 270, 271
databank, 878
economy of, 275*c*
environmental problems of, 272
ethnic groups in, 265, 274
government of, 273, 273*p*
history of, 267
land use in, 264
physical features of, 258, 259, 259*m*
population density of, 263, 263*m*
Gypsies. See *Roma ethnic group*

H

hacienda, 236, 895
Hagia Sophia, 659*p*, 666*p*
Hainan, 748
Haiti, 864*m*
databank, 878
deforestation in, 233
as developing country, 64
government in, 241
history of, 236
language of, 239, 239*p*
life expectancy in, 240*c*
literacy in, 240*c*
population of, 75*p*
religion of, 239
Hamas, 634–635, 640
Hamlet **(Shakespeare),** 377
Hammurabi's Code, 104*p*
Han dynasty, 756, 757
Han ethnic group, 752, 752*m*, 752*p*
Hangul writing system, 783
Hanseatic League, 376
Harappa, 716
Hastings, Battle of, 365
Havel, Vaclav, 404, 404*q*
haveli, 711*p*
Hawaii, 16*p*, 17, 17*p*, 26–27, 26*p*, 134*m*, 138, 139, 399, 785, 785*m*, 836, 866*m*
hazardous waste, 47
HDI. See *human development index*
healthcare, 157
hemispheres, 4*m*, 5, 5*m*, 895

Henry the Navigator, 382
Henry VIII, king of England, 372, 380, 380*p*
hereditary monarchy, 635, 635*p*, 895
Herodotus, 345
hieroglyphics, 895
in ancient Egypt, 565, 565*p*, 566*p*
in Olmec civilization, 206
high island, 836
high latitudes, 34, 34*m*, 895
high technology, 426, 819
hijab, 611, 895
Hildegard of Bingen, 358
hill, 25, 884, 885*p*
Himalayas, 677*p*, 708–709, 708*p*, 709*m*, 738*p*, 746, 747*m*, 863*m*, 873*m*
climate and, 710, 710*m*
cultural exchange and, 715
history and, 714, 714*m*
Himalchal Pradesh, 708
Hinduism, 92*m*–93*m*, 93, 239, 809, 811, 814, 895
Islam and, 719, 721, 729
literature of, 725
in South Asia, 717, 717*p*, 725
Hindu Kush, 709, 709*m*, 863*m*, 873*m*
Hiroshima, 785
Hispaniola, 227, 227*m*, 865*m*
historians, 895
of ancient Greece, 345
anthropology, 123
archaeology, 122–123, 122*p*
measuring time, 118–119, 118*p*, 119*p*
women, 356
historical maps, 124–125, 124*m*, 125*m*, 127, 895
historical sources, 120–121, 120*p*, 121*p*
Hitler, Adolf, 397–399
Hmong ethnic group, 808
Hobbes, Thomas, 389, 389*q*
Ho Chi Minh, 813
Ho Chi Minh City, 822
Holland. See *Netherlands*
Holocaust, 399, 432, 453, 632, 896
Holy Land, 360, 361, 631
Holy Roman Emperor, 356
Holy Roman Empire, 370*m*
Holy See, 878
Homer, 342
Homo erectus, 538, 538*p*
Honduras, 864*m*
databank, 878
fishing in, 233
hurricanes in, 229, 229*m*

native people in, 233
physical features of, 226–227, 227*m*
Honshu Island, 775, 775*m*
Horace, 352
horses, 146
in Central Asia, 694, 694*p*
in Middle Ages, 363
Native Americans and, 96
House of Commons, 179–180, 423
House of Lords, 423
housing, 315, 711*p*
Huang River, 746, 747, 747*m*, 767
Hudson Bay, 165, 165*m*, 174
Hudson Bay Company, 174
human development, 65, 65*m*
human development index (HDI), 573, 896
human–environment interaction, 7, 896
land use, 50–51, 50*m*, 51*p*
natural resources and, 48–49, 48*p*, 49*c*, 52–53
pollution and, 53
technology and, 53
humanism, 375, 377, 896
humanitarian organizations, 111, 111*p*
human rights, 487
human settlement, 262, 262*m*
Humboldt Current, 284, 286
humid subtropical climate, 40, 40*m*–41*m*, 896
Hundred Years' War, 365–366, 365*p*
Hungary, 357, 442*m*, 457*p*, 868*m*
culture of, 457
databank, 878
food of, 457
government of, 401, 457
history of, 404
religion in, 452, 452*m*, 457
in the Renaissance, 376
Huns, 476, 694
hunter-gatherers, 290
hurricanes, 27, 30*p*, 31, 31*p*, 39, 140, 200, 201, 228, 229–230, 229*m*, 804, 896
Hus, Jan, 378
Hussein, Saddam, 157, 597, 604, 605
Hutu people, 544, 547
hydroelectricity, 202, 287, 287*m*, 523, 766, 766*p*, 767, 896
in Brazil, 311, 311*m*
in Canada, 168–169
in Japan and the Koreas, 779
in Mexico, 202, 202*m*

I

Ibadism, 597
Iberian Peninsula, 415*m*, 434, 862*m*, 869*m*, 896
Ibo people, 517
ice age, 447, 896
icebergs, 853, 896
ice cap ecosystem, 42*m*–43*m*, 43, 43*p*, 171
Iceland, 415, 424, 426, 426*g*, 860*m*, 868*m*, 878
ice sheet, 852, 896
ice shelf, 875*m*
Idaho, 134*m*, 866*m*
igapo, 313
Igbo people, 517
Ignatius of Loyola, 381
Illinois, 33*g*, 33*p*, 134*m*, 867*m*
illiterate, 765, 896
immigrants and immigration, 79, 896
  in Argentina, 294
  in Canada, 176, 176*p*, 182–183, 182*p*
  cultural diffusion and, 97
  in France, 430
  in Germany, 433
  in Italy, 438–439, 438*p*
  naturalization and, 112, 112*p*
  from North Africa, 563
  in Norway, 427
  in United Kingdom, 423
  in the United States, 78*p*, 79, 79*p*, 142, 144, 150–151, 155–156
  in Western Europe, 427, 427*p*
  See also *migration; movement*
immunity, 292, 896
imperialism, 394, 514, 515, 515*m*, 515*p*, 896
imports, 67, 67*c*, 152, 896
  of Canada, 181
  of Japan and the Koreas, 779, 779*c*
  of Southern Europe, 436
  of West and Central Africa, 518
Inca empire, 122*p*, 290, 290*p*, 291, 291*m*, 291*p*, 292, 384
incentives, 59, 896
independence, 236, 896
India, 384*p*, 678*p*, 704*m*, 726*p*, 861*m*, 872*m*
  Britain and, 401, 721, 722, 722*m*
  caste system in, 727–728
  climate of, 33*g*, 33*p*, 710, 710*m*, 711
  colonization of, 721
  culture of, 724–725, 724*p*, 725*p*
  databank, 878
  democracy in, 724, 730

economy of, 730–731, 730*g*, 731*p*
  government of, 730
  Islam in, 719–721
  literacy in, 728*g*
  myStory, 705–707, 705*p*, 706*p*, 707*p*
  Pakistan and, 729, 729*m*
  partition of, 722–723, 722*m*
  physical features of, 709, 709*m*
  population of, 713, 713*m*, 726, 726*g*
  religion in, 725
  timeline of, 720
  trade in, 721, 730*g*, 731
  urbanization in, 81, 81*p*
  women in, 728*p*
Indiana, 134*m*, 867*m*
Indian Ocean, 590, 591*m*, 709, 709*m*
Indians. See *Native Americans*
Indian subcontinent, 708, 896
indigenous people, 239, 808, 846, 896
  of Andes and the Pampas, 288–289, 297
  of Australia and Pacific region, 858
  of Canada, 161
  of Southern and Eastern Africa, 544–545
  See also *Native Americans*
Indo-Australian plate, 803, 837, 837*m*
Indochina Peninsula, 863*m*, 873*m*
Indo-European languages, 90
Indo-Gangetic Plain, 714, 714*m*
Indonesia, 861*m*, 872*m*
  culture of, 799–801, 802*p*
  databank, 878
  economy of, 818, 818*c*, 819
  government of, 816
  myStory, 799–801, 799*p*, 800*p*, 801*p*
  physical features of, 803, 803*m*
  population of, 741, 806, 806*m*, 817
  religion in, 809, 815
Indus River, 709, 709*m*
Indus River Valley, 716–717
industrialization, 51, 896
  in Andes and the Pampas, 294–295
  in Kenya, 542
Industrial Revolution, 75, 99, 150, 392–393, 392*p*, 393*p*, 480, 896
infant mortality rate, 75, 896
inflation, 61, 897
infrastructure, 518, 541, 897

Inquisition, 362, 378
***Institutes of the Christian Religion* (Calvin),** 379
Institutional Revolutionary Party (PRI), 213, 897
insurgents and insurgency, 274, 816, 897
interdependent, 779, 897
interest, 69, 897
interest group, 113, 897
Interior Plains, 165
intermediate directions, 4
International Monetary Fund (IMF), 111
international trade, 67, 67*c*, 111, 180–181
Internet, 155
  China and, 99
  cultural diffusion and, 97
  evaluating sources on, 15, 121, 463, 734–735, 769
Interstate Highway System, 186–187
intertropical convergence zone (ITCZ), 38, 506, 897
Intifada, 639, 897
Inuit people, 161, 162, 163, 173, 183*p*
invention, 755
investments, 69, 69*p*, 897
Ionia, 340, 341*m*
Iowa, 134*m*, 867*m*
Iran, 570, 644*m*, 861*m*, 872*m*
  Arab conquest of, 658
  art and architecture of, 665, 665*p*
  atlas, 648–655, 649*m*, 650*m*, 651*g*, 652*m*, 653*c*, 653*p*, 654*m*, 655*p*
  Britain and, 660
  climate of, 650–651, 650*m*, 651*c*
  databank, 879
  earthquakes in, 650
  economy of, 664
  ethnic groups in, 654–655, 654*m*
  government of, 662–663, 662*p*, 663*p*
  history of, 656–661, 656*p*, 657*m*, 657*p*, 658*m*, 661*p*
  Iraq and, 605
  irrigation in, 652–653
  Kurdish people in, 654–655
  land use in, 652–653, 652*m*, 653*c*
  oil in, 652, 653, 653*c*, 653*p*
  physical features of, 648–650, 649*m*
  population of, 652
  religion in, 654–655, 654*m*, 658
  revolution in, 661, 661*p*
  Russia and, 489, 660

terrorism and, 664
  United States and, 661, 664
  voting rights in, 663
  women in, 663
Iran-Iraq War, 605
Iraq, 156–157, 861*m*, 872*m*
  agriculture in, 594
  Arab culture of, 610, 610*p*, 611
  Arab-Israeli conflicts, 632–633
  atlas of, 586*m*, 590–597, 591*m*, 592*m*, 593*g*, 595*m*, 596*m*
  Britain and, 603
  databank, 879
  economy of, 593, 608–609, 609*g*
  ecosystems in, 594, 594*m*
  ethnic groups in, 596
  government in, 604, 605
  history of, 598–605, 598*p*, 599*m*, 599*p*, 600*p*, 601*p*, 602*m*, 603*p*, 604*p*, 605*p*
  Iran and, 605
  Kuwait and, 605
  natural resources in, 592–593, 592*m*, 608
  oil in, 592–593, 592*m*, 592*p*, 593*g*, 604, 605, 608–609, 609*g*
  population density in, 595, 595*m*
  religion in, 596–597, 596*m*, 596*p*, 597, 600–603, 600*p*, 601*p*, 602*m*, 606–607, 607*p*
  rivers of, 599, 599*m*
  traditions in, 606–607
  water resources in, 594, 594*m*, 594*p*
  women in, 611
Ireland, 370*m*, 422, 868*m*
  currency in, 423
  databank, 879
  economy of, 426, 426*g*
  trade in, 423
  Vikings in, 357
Irian Jaya, 806
iron, 534, 534*m*, 539
Iron Curtain, 402*m*, 402*p*
Iroquois people, 172, 172*p*
Irrawaddy River, 802, 803*m*
irrigation, 99, 99*c*, 205, 897
  in Central Asia, 686
  in Egypt, 565
  in Iran, 652–653
  See also *water resources*
Isabella of Castile, 362
Islam, 92, 92*m*–93*m*, 607
  in Afghanistan, 719
  in Arabia and Iraq, 596*m*, 597, 606–607, 607*p*
  beliefs of, 601, 601*p*
  in Byzantine empire, 355–356
  calendar of, 119

in the Caribbean, 239
in the Caucasus, 693
Crusades and, 360–362, 361m, 363
in Eastern Europe, 452–453, 452m, 453p
fundamentalism, 607
Hinduism and, 719, 721, 729
history of, 360, 598, 600–603, 631
in India, 719–721
in Iran, 658
in North Africa, 567, 567p, 570, 570p
in Pakistan, 719, 719p
in South Asia, 715, 719–721, 719p, 725
in Southeast Asia, 809, 812, 815
in Southern and Eastern Africa, 539, 545, 545c
in Southwest Asia, 584, 584p, 624m, 624p, 625
in Tibet, 752
in West and Central Africa, 521
women and, 606
Islamic law, 631, 661, 662
Islamism, 607, 897
islands, 26, 884, 884p
Israel, 563, 570, 614m, 872m
Arabs in, 625
atlas, 618–625, 619m, 621m, 622m, 623p, 624m
climate of, 620–621, 620m
conflicts in, 632–633, 638–640, 638m, 639p, 640p
databank, 879
economy of, 637, 637g, 637p
Egypt and, 569
government of, 634–635, 634p
history of, 627, 627p, 632–633
myStory, 615–617, 615p, 616p, 617p
parliamentary democracy in, 634
physical features of, 618–619, 619m
population density of, 621m
religion in, 624–625, 624m, 624p, 640
settlements in, 638–639
standard of living in, 636
trade in, 636, 640–641, 641
United States and, 633
water resources in, 622–623, 622m, 623p
Israeli settlements, 638–639, 897
Istanbul, 356, 649, 658m, 659p, 666p, 667, 667p
isthmus, 226, 884, 884p, 897
Isthmus of Panama, 290, 865m

Itaipu Dam, 287m, 287p, 311
Italian Peninsula, 869m
Italy, 403, 403m, 415, 868m
culture of, 435–436, 435p
databank, 879
economy of, 436–437, 436p, 437g, 438
in European Union, 437
fascism in, 397
government of, 391
immigrants in, 438–439, 438p
population of, 419
religion in, 374p, 435
in the Renaissance, 374, 376
trade centers in, 364
in World War II, 398–399, 398m
See also *Roman empire; Roman Republic*
ITCZ. See *intertropical convergence zone*
Ivan III, prince of Russia, 478
Ivan the Terrible, 477p
Ivory Coast, 509, 509p, 870m, 879

J

Jagdeo, Bharrat, 273, 273p
Jainism, 718
Jakarta, 807
Jamaica, 864m
databank, 879
mining in, 230
physical features of, 227, 227m
religion of, 239
tourism in, 231, 232
Jamestown, Virginia, 147, 385
Jani festival, 455, 455p
Japan, 770m, 861m, 872m
art in, 784
atlas of, 770m, 774–781, 774p, 775m, 776m, 777g, 777p, 778m, 779c, 780p, 781p
China and, 757, 785, 785m
class system in, 784
climate of, 776–777, 776m, 777g, 777p, 780
constitutional monarchy of, 786
culture of, 793, 794, 794g, 794p, 795
culture regions, 87
databank, 879
as developed country, 64p
economic system of, 63
economy of, 787, 787g, 792
education in, 793
emperors of, 783–784
energy resources in, 779
environmental concerns in,

780–781, 781p
Europe and, 784–785
farming in, 778–779, 778m
fishing in, 779, 781, 781p
government of, 786–787
history of, 783–787, 783p, 784p, 785m, 787g
hydroelectricity in, 779
imports and exports in, 779, 779c
Koreas and, 785, 785m, 786
land use in, 51p, 778
language of, 91
Meiji Restoration, 784
mountains in, 774p, 775, 775m
myStory, 771–773, 771p, 772p, 773p
natural resources in, 778–779, 778m, 779c
physical features of, 774–775, 774p, 775m
pollution in, 781
population density in, 780, 780p, 792–793, 792c
population of, 741
religion in, 784, 795
rivers in, 779
sports in, 795
United States and, 784, 785, 786–787
women in, 793
World War II and, 151, 398–399, 398m, 785, 785m
Java, 806, 806m, 810, 811, 817
Jericho, 626
Jerusalem, 361, 361m, 614m, 627, 640
Jesus, 353, 629, 629p
Jewish Diaspora, 627, 632
Jewish people, 597
calendar of, 119
in Central Asia, 698
differences among, 624–625
in Germany, 397–398, 398p, 399, 432
Holocaust and, 399, 432, 453, 632
in Middle Ages, 367
in North Africa, 571
in Ottoman empire, 659
religious tolerance and, 390
in Western Europe, 418
Jiang Jieshi. See *Chiang Kai-shek*
jihad, 607, 897
Joan of Arc, 365
John, king of England, 364p, 365, 422
John and Abigail Adams, 159q
John of the Cross, 381
Jordan, 614m, 872m
Arab-Israeli conflicts, 632–633
atlas, 618–625, 619m, 621m,

622m, 624m
climate of, 621
databank, 879
economy of, 637g, 637p
government of, 635, 635p
history of, 632–633
physical features of, 618–619, 619m
population density of, 621m
religion in, 625
standard of living in, 636p
water resources in, 622m, 623
Jordan River, 619, 619m, 622m, 623
Joseph II, ruler of Austria, 390
Juárez, Benito, 209–210
Judaism, 92, 92m–93m
beliefs of, 628, 628p
in Eastern Europe, 452–453, 452m, 453p
history of, 352–353, 626–627, 627p
in Israel, 640, 641p
in Southwest Asia, 584, 584p, 624–625, 624m
Judea, 352–353, 627, 629, 631
judicial branch, 109, 148c
June solstice, 18
justice system, 344p, 349, 815
Justinian, 354, 354p
Justinian's Code, 354
Jutland, 869m

K

Kaaba, 600, 601, 610, 610p
Kabila, Joseph, 520
Kabila, Laurent, 519–520
Kahlo, Frida, 214
Kalahari Desert, 531, 531m, 871m
Kalahari Plain, 871m
Kaliningrad, 470
Kamchatka Peninsula, 469m, 471, 873m, 897
Kami, 795
Kansas, 134m, 143m, 867m
Kara-Kum Desert, 676p, 676m, 685, 685m, 873m
Karimov, Islom, 697
karma, 717
Kashmir, 722, 722m, 724, 725, 729
Kazakhstan, 488m, 489, 680m, 861m, 872m
culture of, 697
databank, 879
economy of, 698
government of, 700
land use in, 686, 687m
natural resources in, 688, 688m
oil in, 689c

physical features of, 685, 685m
transportation in, 689
water resources in, 689, 699, 699g, 699p
Kemal, Mustafa, 660, 660p
Kentucky, 134m, 867m
Kenya, 526m, 861m, 870m
 animal life in, 533
 databank, 879
 economy of, 549
 ecosystem of, 532, 532m, 533
 ethnic groups of, 544
 European rule in, 540, 540m
 independence of, 542
 literacy rates in, 549g
Kenyatta, Jomo, 542
Ketuvim, 628
keys, 10, 11, 897
KGB, 485, 897
Khamenei, Ayatollah Ali, 662p
Khatami, Mohammed, 663
Khazars, 476
Khmer empire, 811
Khmer ethnic group, 808, 811
Khmer Rouge, 813
Khomeini, Ayatollah Ruhollah, 661, 661p, 662
Khrushchev, Nikita, 482
Khyber Pass, 714, 714m
Kiev, 476p, 477
Kievan Rus, 357, 476p, 477
Kikuyu people, 542, 544
Kilauea volcano, 16p, 17, 17p, 26–27, 26p
Kimberley Plateau, 874m
Kim Il-sung, 790
Kim Jong-il, 790, 791p
Kingdom of Guatemala, 235, 236
Kingdom of Judah, 627
King of Kings, 656
Kiribati, 861m, 879
Kjølen Mountains, 869m
kleroterion, 344p
Knesset, 634
knights, 358, 358c, 359, 360p, 365, 783c
Koch, Robert, 393
Kola Peninsula, 869m
Kolyma Range, 873m, 875m
Koreas, 770m
 atlas of, 770m, 774–781, 774p, 775m, 776m, 777g, 777p, 778m, 779c, 780p, 781p
 China and, 782
 climate of, 776–777, 776m, 777g, 777p
 energy resources in, 779
 environmental concerns in, 780–781, 781p
 Europe and, 784–785

farming in, 778–779, 778m
government of, 786, 786m
history of, 782–783, 782p, 784, 785, 786, 786m
hydroelectricity in, 779
imports and exports in, 779, 779c
Japan and, 785, 785m
land use in, 778–779, 778m, 779c
language of, 91, 752p
natural resources in, 778–779, 778m, 779c
physical features of, 774–775, 775m
precipitation in, 777, 777g
religion in, 784
Soviet Union and, 786
writing systems of, 783
See also North Korea; South Korea
Korean peninsula, 774
Korean War, 786, 786m, 897
Kosovo, 442m, 868m, 879
Kremlin, 478, 897
Kuala Lumpur, 819, 822, 822p
Kunlun Shan, 863m
Kurdish people, 596–597, 603
 in Iran, 655
 in Syria, 624
 in Turkey, 645–647, 645p, 646p, 647p, 654–655, 668
Kuril Islands, 472
Kush, 539
Kuwait, 861m, 872m
 databank, 879
 ethnic groups in, 596
 government of, 604
 history of, 603
 Iraq and, 605
 oil in, 592, 592m, 604
 religion in, 596m, 597
 water resources in, 594, 594m
Kyoto Protocol, 407
Kyrgyzstan, 680m, 694p, 861m, 872m
 culture of, 696p, 697, 697p
 databank, 879
 ethnic groups of, 698
 government of, 697, 701p
 literature of, 681
 myStory, 681–683, 681p, 682p, 683p
 natural resources in, 688, 688m
 physical features of, 685, 685m
 water resources in, 689

L

labor, as factor of production, 58
Labrador, 160m

Lake Atitlán, 227, 227m
Lake Baikal, 469m, 471, 897
Lake Chad, 505, 505m
Lake Maracaibo, 259, 264, 272
Lake Nasser, 560, 560p
Lake Tai, 744–745, 767
Lake Victoria, 531, 531m
land, as factor of production, 58
landforms, 23, 25, 25p, 898
landlocked, 684, 689, 898
land reform, 242
landslide, 27
land use
 in Brazil, 311, 311m
 in Canada, 168–169, 168p
 in Caribbean South America, 264, 264p
 in the Caucasus, 687, 687m
 in Central America and Caribbean, 230–231, 230m, 231c
 in Central Asia, 686, 687m
 in China, 748–749, 749m
 in Cyprus, 652–653, 652m
 human-environment interaction and, 50–51, 50m, 51p
 in Iran, 652–653, 652m, 653c
 in Japan and the Koreas, 778–779, 778m, 779c
 in Kazakhstan, 686, 687m
 in South Asia, 712, 712g
 in Southeast Asia, 806–807, 807c
 in Turkey, 652–653, 652m
 in Venezuela, 264
language, 898
 of Andes and the Pampas, 297, 297c
 Bantu, 539, 545
 of Brazil, 316, 317
 in Byzantine empire, 355
 of Canada, 180
 of the Caucasus, 690, 697, 698
 of Central America and Caribbean, 239
 of Central Asia, 691, 697, 698
 of China, 752p, 755
 cultural diffusion and, 97c
 culture and, 90–91, 90m–91m
 of Hungary, 457
 of Korea, 752p
 of Luxembourg, 431
 of Mexico, 214
 of Morocco, 570
 of New Zealand, 833
 of North Africa, 563, 567, 570, 571
 of Russia, 474
 of Southern and Eastern Africa, 545
 of Southern Europe, 434
 of Tibet, 752p

Turkic, 691
 of United Kingdom, 423
 of Western Europe, 265, 417–418, 418m
Laos, 861m, 872m
 databank, 879
 ethnic diversity in, 808
 government of, 816
 history of, 813
 population of, 806, 806m
Laozi, 757q
Late Middle Ages, 374
Latin America, 271, 898
Latins, 348
latitude, 4–5, 4m, 6, 34, 34m, 898
Latium, 348
Latvia, 405, 442m, 868m
 culture of, 455, 455p
 databank, 879
 religion in, 452, 452m
lava, 26, 26p, 775
law, 109, 148c
 common law, 365
 Justinian's Code, 354
 Roman, 349, 351
 See also justice system
League of Nations, 150p, 603, 632
Leakey, Louis and Mary, 122p
Lebanon, 566, 614m, 872m
 Arab-Israeli conflicts, 632–633
 atlas, 618–625, 618p, 619m, 620m, 621m, 622m, 624m
 climate of, 620m
 databank, 879
 economy of, 637g
 government of, 635, 635p
 history of, 632–633
 physical features of, 618–619, 619m
 population density of, 621m
 religion in, 624, 624m, 630p
 standard of living in, 636, 636p
 war in, 633
 water resources in, 622, 622m
legislative branch, 109, 148c
Lenin, Vladimir, 480, 480p
Leningrad, 474
Leo III, Pope, 356
Leo X, Pope, 380
Lesotho, 526m, 861m, 870m, 879
Lesser Antilles, 865m
Leviathan (Hobbes), 389, 389q
Liberia, 508m, 509, 861m, 870m, 879
Libya, 552m, 861m, 870m
 databank, 879
 economy of, 572–573, 572g
 environmental concerns in, 560–561
 government of, 574

natural resources in, 562, 562m
population of, 558, 559
Libyan Desert, 871m
Liechtenstein, 428, 868m, 879
life expectancy, 898
in Central America and Caribbean, 240c
in China, 764, 765c
economic development and, 64
in North Africa, 572
in South America, 328
limited government, 105, 105c, 788, 898
Limpopo River, 531, 531m
literacy, 898
in Afghanistan, 728g
in Andes and the Pampas, 300
in Bangladesh, 728g
in Canada, 180
in Central America and Caribbean, 240c
economic development and, 64
in India, 728g
in Mexico, 215
in Pakistan, 728g
in Southern and Eastern Africa, 549g
in Tunisia, 573
in West and Central Africa, 522g
literature, 95, 95p, 898
of Ancient Greece, 345
Hindu, 725
Muslims and, 361
in the Renaissance, 377
in Roman empire, 352
Lithuania, 370m, 442m, 868m
databank, 879
government of, 454, 455
history of, 405
Livia, 348p, 351
Llano, 259, 259m, 898
loan, 69
local government, 108
location, theme of, 6
locator map, 10, 898
Locke, John, 390
loess, 416, 747, 898
logging, 142
London, 77p, 334p, 423, 426
longbow, 365, 365p
longitude, 5, 5m, 6, 898
lord, 358, 358c, 359, 898
Louisiana, 30p, 31, 31p, 134m, 867m
Louisiana Territory, 149, 149m
Louis XIV, king of France, 387, 387p
Louis XVI, king of France, 391

L'Ouverture, Toussaint, 236
Low Countries, 431, 431p
Lower Canada, 175
lower class, 89
low island, 836
low latitude, 34, 898
Lukashenko, president of Belarus, 460
lumber, 807
Luther, Martin, 378–379, 380
Lutheran Church, 379, 380
Luxembourg, 403, 403m, 428, 431, 868m, 879
Luzon, 806

M

Maasai people, 544
Maastricht Treaty (1992), 403
Macedonia, 337–339, 442m, 458, 868m, 879
Machu Picchu, 122p, 291m, 291p
Madagascar, 526m, 533, 861m, 870m, 880
madrassas, 692p, 695, 696, 898
Magdalena River, 258, 259m
magistrates, 344p
magma, 26, 898
Magna Carta, 364p, 365, 390c, 422, 898
Magyars, 357, 476
Mahabharata, 717
Maijuna tribe, 2p, 3, 3p
Maine, 134m, 139, 147m, 867m
maize, 206, 898
Majlis, 662, 898
majority, 596, 898
majority rule, 108
Malacca Strait, 805, 805m, 811, 811m, 812, 819, 821
malaria, 511, 522, 537, 898
Malawi, 526m, 861m, 870m, 880
Malay Peninsula, 815, 873m
Malaysia, 815, 861m, 872m
databank, 880
ethnic diversity in, 808, 816c
global trade and, 819
government of, 816
high-technology in, 819
Maldives, 709, 709m, 724, 861m, 880
Mali, 513, 513p, 521, 870m, 880
Malta, 370m, 868m, 880
Maluku Islands, 805, 805m, 812
Manaus, 314
Mandela, Nelson, 543, 543p
manga, 794, 794g
Manifest Destiny, 149, 149m, 898
Manila, 807
Manitoba, 160m
manorialism, 359, 367, 898

Mansa Musa, 513
mantle, 22, 898
manufacturing, 324
Maori culture, 123p, 831–833, 831p, 832p, 833p, 842p, 843, 844, 847, 847p, 899
Mao Zedong, 757, 759
maps and mapping
Earth's surface and, 8–9, 9m
keys, 10, 11
physical, 10, 10m, 12, 12m
political, 13m
projections, 9, 9m
reading, 10m, 11, 11m
road maps, 11, 11m
special purpose, 13m, 124–125, 125m
types of, 12–13, 12m, 13m
Map Skills, 14m, 28, 44, 54, 82
ancient Europe, 341m, 346m, 350m, 352m
Andes and the Pampas, 283m, 284m, 287m, 288m, 302m
Antarctica, 853m
Arabia and Iraq, 591m, 592m, 595m, 596m
Australia and the Pacific, 835m, 837m, 839m, 843m
Brazil, 309m, 310m, 311m
Canada, 165m, 167m, 169m
Caribbean South America, 259m, 260m, 262m
Central America and Caribbean, 227m, 228m, 230m, 244m
Central Asia and Caucasus, 685m, 687m, 688m, 690m, 693m
China, 747m, 749m, 751m, 752m, 768m
Eastern Europe, 447m, 448m, 452m, 458m
Europe, 379m, 383m, 386m, 395m, 398m, 402m
Iran, Turkey, and Cyprus, 649m, 650m, 652m, 654m, 658m
Israel, 619m, 621m, 622m, 624m, 638m
Japan and the Koreas, 775m, 776m, 778m, 785m
medieval Europe, 356m, 357m, 361m, 362m
Mexico, 199m, 200m, 202m, 204m
North Africa, 557m, 558m, 562m, 568m
Russia, 469m, 470m, 473m, 474m, 488m

South Asia, 709m, 710m, 713m, 714m, 718m, 722m, 729m
Southeast Asia, 803m, 805m, 806m, 811m, 820m
Southern and Eastern Africa, 531m, 532m, 534m, 536m, 540m
United States, 139m, 141m, 143m, 144m, 149m, 158m
West and Central Africa, 505m, 507m, 508m, 510m, 524m
Western Europe, 415m, 417m, 418m, 420m, 421m, 423m, 440m
marae, 843
Marathon, Battle of, 347
March equinox, 18
Marco Polo, 382, 688q
Maria Theresa, empress, 387
Marie Byrd Land, 875m
maritime climate, 40, 40m–41m, 899
maritime trade, 812
market, 60, 899
market economy, 62, 152, 324, 759, 761c, 762, 899
Maroons, 265
Marshall Islands, 830m, 861m, 880
Marshall Plan, 150p, 400, 899
Martel, Charles, 356
Marx, Karl, 480
Marxism, 480
Mary I, queen of England, 372
Maryland, 134m, 147m, 867m
Massachusetts, 134m, 147m, 867m
Massif Central, 869m
mathematics, 602, 603
in ancient Greece, 345
in India, 719
Muslims and, 361, 375
Mau Mau, 542, 899
Mau movement, 845
Mauritania, 510, 510m, 870m, 880
Mauritius, 526m, 861m, 870m, 880
Mauryan empire, 718, 718m
Maya people, 207, 207p, 214, 899
calendar of, 119
culture of, 234–235, 234p, 239
history of, 122p
Mbeki, Thabo, 548p
Mecca, 513, 600–601, 601p, 602m, 610, 610p
mechanical weathering, 24
mechanized farming, 449, 899
medicine, 361. See also *diseases*

medieval period. See *Middle Ages*
Medina, 119
Mediterranean brush ecosystem, 42*m*–43*m*, 43, 43*p*
Mediterranean climate, 40, 40*m*–41*m*
Mediterranean Sea, 350, 350*m*, 415, 415*m*, 416, 416*m*, 620, 649
Medvedev, Dmitry, 487*q*
Meiji Restoration, 784, 899
Mekong River, 802, 803*m*
Melanesia, 826*p*, 835, 835*m*, 836, 858, 863*m*
  history of, 842, 843*m*
  population in, 840*c*
Melbourne, 840
Mennonite Church, 379
Mercado Común del Sur, 324
mercantilism, 293*c*, 317, 899
Mercator projection, 9, 9*m*
merchants, 364, 693, 899
MERCOSUR, 299–300, 300, 300*m*, 324, 899
meridian, 5
Meroë, 539
mesa, 884, 884*p*
Mesopotamia, 599–600, 599*m*, 656
messiah, 353, 629, 899
mestizo people, 288–289, 292, 297, 899
Methodist Church, 379
Methodius, 355, 355*p*
Metís people, 161
metropolitan areas, 144, 899
Mexican Cession, 149*m*
Mexican Plateau, 198–199, 199*m*, 201
Mexican Revolution, 210, 899
Mexico, 190*p*, 246, 247*c*, 247*g*, 860*m*, 864*m*
  art of, 208*p*–211*p*, 214
  atlas, 194*m*, 198–205, 198*p*, 199*m*, 200*m*, 202*m*, 203*c*, 204*m*, 205*p*
  climate of, 200–201, 200*m*, 201*p*
  Constitution of, 210–211, 212
  culture of, 214–215, 214*p*, 215*p*
  databank, 880
  economy of, 216–217, 216*c*, 217*m*
  ecosystems of, 201
  education in, 215
  emigration from, 73
  employment in, 219
  farming in, 201, 203, 205, 206, 207, 217
  fishing in, 203
  France and, 210

  government of, 212–213, 212*p*, 213*p*
  history of, 122*p*, 149*m*, 206–211, 206*p*, 207*p*, 208*p*–211*p*
  hydroelectricity in, 202, 202*m*
  language of, 214
  literacy in, 215
  Mexican Revolution, 210
  myStory, 195–197, 195*p*, 196*p*, 197*p*
  NAFTA and, 152, 154
  Native Americans in, 206, 214, 215
  natural resources of, 202–203, 202*m*, 203*p*
  oil production in, 152, 202, 202*m*, 203*c*, 203*p*, 216
  physical features of, 198–199, 199*m*, 226, 227, 227*m*
  political parties in, 213
  population of, 73, 204–205, 204*m*, 205*p*, 214
  poverty in, 217
  religion in, 208, 209*p*, 215
  Spain and, 208–209, 209*p*, 214, 384
  tourism in, 216
  trade and, 180, 216, 218, 218*g*, 219
  United States and, 216, 219
Mexico City, 194*m*, 199
  history of, 208, 208*p*
  pollution in, 204, 204*m*, 205*p*
Michelangelo, 375
Michigan, 134*m*, 867*m*
microcredit, 242, 523, 730, 899
Micronesia, 836, 858, 861*m*, 863*m*
  databank, 880
  history of, 842, 843*m*, 844
  population of, 828, 840*c*
Middle Ages, 374
  early, 354–359, 354*p*, 355*p*, 356*m*, 357*m*, 357*p*, 358*c*, 359*p*
  high and late, 360–367, 360*p*, 361*m*, 362*m*, 363*p*, 364*p*, 365*p*, 366*p*
Middle America
  economy of, 192–193
  employment in, 246, 247*c*, 247*g*
  human geography, 192–193
  physical geography, 190–191
  regional flyover, 191
  regional overview, 188–193
middle class, 89, 364
Middle Colonies, 147*m*, 148
Middle East, 570–571
middle latitudes, 34, 899
middle passage, 514, 899
migration, 78–79, 78*p*, 79*p*, 899
  to Australia and Pacific region, 842–843, 843*m*

  Bantu, 539, 545
  in China, 765
  to Europe, 406
  reasons for, 79
  from Russian Federation, 486
  to South America, 252*m*
  in Southeast Asia, 807, 808
  in United States, 142–144
  See also *emigration; immigration; movement, theme of*
militarism, 394
military coup, 666
military junta, 816, 900
Milky Way, 18
millet, 659, 900
Minangkabau ethnic group, 799–801, 809, 812
Mindanao, 806, 809
Ming dynasty, 755
mining
  in the Andes, 287, 298
  in Bolivia, 279–281, 279*p*, 280*p*, 281*p*
  in Canada, 168
  in Jamaica, 230
  in Southern and Eastern Africa, 534–535, 534*m*, 534*p*
Minnesota, 134*m*, 867*m*
Minoan civilization, 341
minority, 603, 900
minority groups, 571
minority rights, 108
Miri, Emmanuel, 511*q*
Miskito people, 233
missionary, 844, 900
Mississippi, 134*m*, 867*m*
Mississippi River, 134*m*, 139, 139*m*
Missouri, 134*m*, 867*m*
mixed economy, 63, 63*c*, 900
mixing zone, 169, 900
Mobuto, Joseph, 516, 516*p*, 519
Mogadishu, 539
Mohammed VI, king of Morocco, 575
Mohenjo Daro, 716
Moldavia, 370*m*
Moldova, 405, 442*m*, 451, 460–461, 461*p*, 868*m*, 880
Monaco, 428, 880
monarchy, 106*p*, 107, 900
monastery, 358
money, 403, 423, 437
  definition of, 68
  economics and, 60
  management of, 68–69, 68*c*, 68*p*, 69*p*
Mongol Empire, 694
Mongol ethnic group, 477, 603, 755, 811
Mongolia, 861*m*, 872*m*
  climate of, 748, 748*m*

  databank, 880
  economy of, 758–759, 758*p*, 761*c*, 762, 763*c*
  government of, 758–759, 758*p*, 760–761, 761*c*
  history of, 754, 755, 757, 758–759
  nomads in, 749, 755, 759
  physical features of, 747, 747*m*
  politics in, 761*c*
  population of, 741, 751, 751*m*
  religion in, 757
Mongolian Plateau, 873*m*
monk, 358
monotheism, 352, 600, 900
monsoons, 710–711, 777, 804, 804*m*, 815, 815*p*, 900
Montana, 134*m*, 144, 866*m*
Montenegro, 442*m*, 458, 868*m*, 880
Montesquieu, Charles-Louis, 390
Montreal, 182
Montserrat, 227, 227*m*
Morales, Evo, 297, 301, 301*p*
More, Thomas, 377
Morocco, 552*m*, 860*m*, 870*m*
  databank, 880
  environmental concerns in, 561*p*
  government of, 574, 575, 575*p*
  language of, 570
  natural resources in, 562, 562*m*
  physical features of, 556–557, 556*p*, 557*m*
  population of, 558, 559, 559*p*
  religion in, 570*p*, 571
  women in, 575
Moscow, 471, 473, 474, 474*m*, 477*c*
Moses, 627, 627*p*
mosque, 603, 665, 665*p*, 900
mosquito, 511, 537
mountain grassland and brush ecosystem, 42*m*–43*m*, 43, 43*p*
mountain pass, 885, 885*p*
mountains, 2*p*, 25, 26, 885, 885*p*
  of Brazil, 309, 309*m*
  of Central America and Caribbean, 227, 227*m*
  of Eastern Europe, 446, 447*m*, 448–449
  of Japan, 774*p*, 775, 775*m*
  of South Asia, 709, 709*m*
  in Southeast Asia, 805, 805*m*
  of Western Europe, 414, 415, 415*m*
Mount Fuji, 774*p*, 775, 775*m*

Mount Girnar, 716p
Mount Kenya, 532
Mount Kilimanjaro, 530p, 531, 531m, 532, 871m
Mount Mayon, 802p
Mount Olympus, 345
movement, theme of, 7, 72p, 73, 73p, 900. See also *immigration*
Mozambique, 526m, 540m, 861m, 870m, 880
Mubarak, Hosni, 574
Mugabe, Robert, 547
Mughal empire, 719–721, 720, 720p
Muhammad, 119, 600–602, 631, 640, 658
multiculturalism, 182
Multimedia Super Corridor, 819
mummy, 566, 566p, 900
Mumtaz Mahal, 721
Muscovy, 477p
music, 95, 95p, 900
  of Algeria, 571, 571p
  of Arabia and Iraq, 610, 610p
  of Southern Europe, 436
Muslim Brotherhood, 574, 574p, 900
Muslim empire, 602–603, 602m
Muslims
  in Arabia and Iraq, 596–597, 596m, 596p
  Crusades and, 631
  in Israel, 640
  mathematics and, 375
  See also *Islam*
Mussolini, Benito, 397
mutual funds, 69
Myanmar, 861m, 872m
  databank, 880
  economy of, 818, 818c
  environment of, 815, 815p
  ethnic diversity in, 808
  government of, 816
  population of, 806, 806m
  See also *Burma*
Mycenaean civilization, 341
mystic, 381
myStory
  Alexander the Great, 337–339, 337p, 338p, 339p
  Bolivia, 279–281, 279p, 280p, 281p
  Brazil, 305–307, 305p, 306p, 307p
  Canada, 161–163, 161p, 162p, 163p
  Central America and Caribbean, 223–225, 223p, 224p, 225p
  China, 743–745, 743p, 744p, 745p

Colombia, 255–257, 255p, 256p, 257p
Egypt, 553–555, 553p, 554p, 555p
England, 371–373
Ghana, 501–503, 501p, 502p, 503p
India, 705–707, 705p, 706p, 707p
Indonesia, 799–801, 799p, 800p, 801p
Israel, 615–617, 615p, 616p, 617p
Japan, 771–773, 771p, 772p, 773p
Kyrgyzstan, 681–683, 681p, 682p, 683p
Mexico, 195–197, 195p, 196p, 197p
New Zealand, 831–833, 831p, 832p, 833p
Palestinians, 615–617, 615p, 616p, 617p
Russia, 465–467, 465p, 466p, 467p
Saudi Arabia, 587–589, 587p, 588p, 589p
South Africa, 527–529, 527p, 528p, 529p
Spain, 371–373
Spanish Armada, 371–373
Sumatra, 799–801, 799p, 800p, 801p
Turkey, 645–647, 645p, 646p, 647p
Ukraine, 443–445, 443p, 444p, 445p
Vietnamese-Americans, 135–137, 135p, 136p, 137p
West and Central Africa, 501–503, 501p, 502p, 503p
Western Europe, 411–413, 411p, 412p, 413p
mythology, 345
myWorld in Numbers
  Africa, 499
  Albania, 449
  Arabia and Iraq, 608
  Argentina, 253, 294
  Australia, 829
  Black Death, 367
  Bolivia, 253
  Bollywood, 725
  Brazil, 253, 315, 317
  Britain, 392
  Canadians, 173
  Central Asia, 679
  China, 749
  Colombia, 253
  Costa Rica, 193, 230
  democracy, 457
  East Asia, 741
  Egypt, 499

Ethiopia, 499
Europe, 335
farming, 286
fishing, 849
France, 335, 430
Haiti, 193
Honduras, 193
immigrants in United States and Canada, 133
India, 715, 725
Indonesia, 809
Iran, 652
Italy, 335
Ivory Coast, 511
language in Central Asia and Caucasus, 697
Mexico, 193, 219
Middle America, 193
mosquito net, 511
Nigeria, 499
Pacific region, 829
population in cities, 840
religions, 625
Russia, 335, 487
Russian language, 691
South Africa, 499
South America, 253
South Asia, 679
Southeast Asia, 741
Southwest Asia, 585
Spanish language, 265
Suez Canal, 563
Sweden, 335
Tanzania, 533
Thailand, 819
tropical rain forest, 228
typhoons in Japan, 780
Ukraine, 335
United Kingdom, 335
Venezuela, 269
world populations, 792
World War II, 151

N

NAFTA. See *North American Free Trade Agreement*
Nagasaki, 785
Nagorno-Karabakh, 691
Namib Desert, 531, 531m, 871m
Namibia, 520, 526m, 861m, 870m
  databank, 880
  European rule in, 540m
  farming in, 535
  independence of, 542
Naples, 370m
Napoleon Bonaparte, 209, 317, 391
Napoleonic Wars, 391
Nasser, Gamal Abdel, 569, 569p

National Action Party (PAN), 213, 900
nationalism, 394, 405
  in Europe, 391
  in North Africa, 568
  in Southeast Asia, 812
  in Soviet Union, 482
  in Turkey, 666
nationalize, 269, 900
nation-state, 107, 900
Native Americans, 146–147, 146p, 149
  in Andes and the Pampas, 289, 290–292, 290p, 291p
  in Bolivia, 297
  in Brazil, 316, 321
  in Caribbean South America, 262, 265
  in Central America, 233, 234–235, 234p, 238–240, 238p, 239p, 240c
  dance, 84, 85, 85p
  diseases and, 292
  encomienda system, 235
  horses and, 96
  language of, 91
  in Mexico, 206, 214, 215
  slavery and, 235–236, 235p
  Spain and, 267
  trade and, 385
NATO. See *North Atlantic Treaty Organization*
natural disaster, 27
natural gas, 202, 202m, 451, 592–593, 592m, 653
natural hazard, 27
naturalization, immigrants and, 112, 112p
natural resources, 900
  of Andes and the Pampas, 287, 287m
  of Antarctica, 853
  of Arabia and Iraq, 608
  of Australia, 840–841
  of Brazil, 311, 311m, 324
  of Canada, 168–170, 169m, 170g
  of Caribbean South America, 264, 264p
  of Central Asia and Caucasus, 688, 688m
  definition of, 48
  of Eastern Europe, 450, 451
  human–environment interaction and, 48–49, 48p, 49c, 52–53
  of Japan and the Koreas, 778–779, 778m, 779c
  of Mexico, 202–203, 202m, 203p
  of New Zealand, 840–841
  of North Africa, 562, 562m
  of Pacific region, 841, 841p

of Russia, 472–473, 473m
of South Asia, 712
of Southern and Eastern Africa, 534–535, 534m, 535p, 536, 536m
of United States, 141, 141m
of West and Central Africa, 508–509, 508m
of Western Europe, 417, 417m, 419
Nauru, 830m, 861m, 880
Navajo culture, 84p, 85, 85p
navigation, 389
Nazarbayev, Nursultan, 700
Nazca Plate, 283
Nazi Party, 397–399, 397c, 398m
Ndebele people, 545p
Neblina Peak, 309, 309m
Nebraska, 134m, 867m
Nehru, Jawaharlal, 722
Nepal, 704m, 725, 730, 861m, 872m, 880
Netherlands, 387, 403, 403m, 428, 431, 431p, 868m
in Africa, 540, 540m
databank, 880
explorations by, 383, 383m, 385
Nevada, 85, 134m, 866m
Nevi'im, 628
New Brunswick, 160m
New Caledonia, 830m
Newcomen, Thomas, 389
New Deal, 151
New England, 147–148, 147m, 147p, 385
Newfoundland, 160m, 170p
New France, 173, 900
New Guinea, 830m, 839, 839m, 872m
New Hampshire, 134m, 147m, 867m
New Jersey, 134m, 147m, 867m
New Mexico, 85, 134m, 139, 866m
New Orleans, 30p, 31, 31p
New Testament, 630
Newton, Isaac, 389
New York, 134m, 142, 147m, 819, 867m
New York Stock Exchange, 69p
New Zealand, 827p, 830m, 861m, 874m
climate of, 839, 839m
databank, 880
economy of, 849
ethnic groups of, 846–847, 847p
government of, 848
Great Britain and, 843–844
history of, 843, 843m, 844, 845
indigenous people of, 123p

language of, 833
myStory, 831–833, 831p, 832p, 833p
natural resources in, 840–841
physical features of, 835m, 836, 837, 837m
plate tectonics and, 837, 837m
population of, 840, 840p
NGO. See nongovernmental organizations
Niagara Falls, 168
Nicaragua, 864m
databank, 880
history of, 237
native people in, 233
physical features of, 226–227, 227m
volcanoes in, 190p
Nicholas II, tsar of Russia, 479, 480
Niger, 62, 62p, 507g, 507m, 861m, 870m, 880
Niger-Congo language, 90
Niger Delta, 508m, 509
Nigeria, 499, 861m, 870m
agriculture in, 519p
databank, 880
ethnic diversity in, 517
history of, 516–517, 517p
oil in, 519
population of, 510, 510m
resources of, 508, 508m, 509
Niger River, 504p, 505, 505m
Nile River, 25, 25m, 531, 531m, 536, 536m, 557, 557m, 562
Nile River Valley, 564
Nilo-Saharan language, 91
Ninety-five Theses, 378, 380
nirvana, 718, 900
Niyazov, Saparmurat, 700, 700p
Nkrumah, Kwame, 516, 520
Nobel Prize, 430
nomadic herder, 749, 900
nomads, 558, 684, 694, 695, 900
Arabian, 600
in China, 749
in Mongolia, 749, 751, 751p, 755, 759
in West and Central Africa, 508
nonalignment, 722, 901
nongovernmental organizations (NGOs), 549, 901
nonprofit organization, 61
nonrenewable resource, 49, 49c, 901
nonviolence, 718
norm, 86, 901
Normans, 357
North Africa, 552m
art and architecture of, 567p

atlas, 556–563, 556p, 557m, 558m, 559p, 560p, 561p, 562m
Britain and, 568–569
culture of, 570–571, 570p, 571p
deserts in, 556–557, 557m, 561, 561p
economy of, 572–573, 572g
ecosystem of, 558m
environmental concerns in, 560–561, 560p, 561p
Europe and, 568–569, 568m, 568p
farming in, 573
flooding in, 560
France and, 568–569, 568m, 568p
government in, 574–575, 574p, 575p
history of, 564–569, 564p, 565p, 566p, 567p, 568m, 568p, 569p
language in, 563, 567, 570, 571
life expectancy in, 572
Middle East and, 570–571
minority groups in, 571
nationalism in, 568
natural resources in, 562, 562m
oil in, 562, 562m, 573
physical features of, 556–557, 556p, 557m
population of, 558–559, 559p
poverty in, 572
religion in, 566, 567, 567p, 570, 570p
standard of living in, 572
tourism in, 573
trade in, 563, 567
urbanization in, 559
water resources in, 562
in World War II, 398–399, 398m
North America, 860m
colonies of, 385
historical map of, 124m
physical map of, 862m, 865m
political map, 864m
slave trade and, 514
urbanization in, 80
See also Canada; United States
North American Free Trade Agreement (NAFTA), 152, 154, 180, 216, 219
North Atlantic Current, 36m, 37
North Atlantic Treaty Organization (NATO), 401, 431, 459, 487

North Carolina, 134m, 147m, 867m
North China Plain, 747, 747m, 863m, 873m
North Dakota, 134m, 867m
North European Plain, 447, 447m, 449, 863m, 869m
Northern Hemisphere, 4m, 5, 34, 34m, 35, 506
Northern Ireland, 422, 423, 423m
Northern Mariana Islands, 830m
Northern Renaissance, 376–377, 376p, 377p
North Indian Plain, 677p
North Island, 836, 837, 837m, 840
North Korea, 770m, 861m, 872m
art in, 790
atlas of, 770m, 774–781, 774p, 775m, 776m, 777g, 777p, 778m, 779c, 780p, 781p
climate of, 776–777, 776m, 777g, 777p
databank, 879
economic system of, 63, 63p
economy of, 791
energy resources in, 779
environmental concerns in, 780–781, 781p
farming in, 778–779, 778m
fishing in, 779
government of, 107, 107p, 790–791, 791p
history of, 782–783, 782p, 784, 785, 786, 786m
hydroelectricity in, 779
imports and exports in, 779, 779c
land use in, 778–779, 778m, 779c
natural resources in, 778–779, 778m, 779c
nuclear weapons and, 791
physical features of, 774–775, 775m, 779
religion in, 790
South Korea and, 786, 786m, 791
standard of living in, 790c
United States and, 791
North Korean Six-Party Talks, 487
North Pole, 4, 4m, 5, 875m
Northwest Europe, 422–427, 422p, 423m, 424c, 425p, 426g, 427p
Northwest Passage, 173, 384, 901
Northwest Territories, 160m
Norway, 415, 868m

Index (continued)

databank, 880
economy of, 426, 426g
government of, 424
high technology in, 426
immigrants in, 427
population density of, 76p
Nova Scotia, 160m
Novorossiysk, 470
Nubia, 539
Nubian Desert, 531, 531m
nuclear energy, 450, 450m, 450p, 451, 482, 664, 779
nuclear family, 88, 88p, 901
nuclear weapons, 401p, 489, 664, 791, 851, 901
Nullarbor Plain, 874m
Nunavut, 160m

O

OAS. See *Organization of American States*
oasis, 556–557, 600, 901
Obama, Barack, 109p, 157, 157q
oceans, climate and, 36–37, 36m, 37c
Octavian, 350
October Manifesto, 479
Odoacer, 353
Odyssey (Homer), 342
Ohio, 134m, 867m
oil, 152
    in Arabia and Iraq, 592–593, 592m, 592p, 593g, 604, 605, 608–609, 609g
    in Central Asia and Caucasus, 688, 688m
    in China, 767
    in Iran, 652, 653, 653c, 653p
    in Kazakhstan, 689c
    in Mexico, 202, 202m, 203c, 203p, 216
    in North Africa, 562, 562m, 573
    pollution and, 46p, 47, 47p, 298
    in Scandinavia, 425
    in Southwest Asia, 641, 672, 673g
    in Venezuela, 269, 277q
    in West and Central Africa, 508m, 509, 519
    in Western Europe, 417m
    See also *petroleum*
Oklahoma, 134m, 867m
Old Testament, 630
Olduvai Gorge, 122p
oligarchy, 294, 341, 347, 816, 901
Olmec civilization, 206, 207p
Olympic Games, 345
Oman, 591, 591m, 861m, 872m

databank, 881
government of, 604
history of, 603, 604
religion in, 596m, 597
one-child policy, 750, 765, 901
Ontario, 160m
OPEC. See *Organization of Petroleum Exporting Countries*
open-border policy, 427
opium, 757
opportunity cost, 59, 901
oral tradition, 123, 901
Orange River, 531, 531m
orbit, 18, 901
Oregon, 134m, 149m, 866m
Organic Law of the Environment, 272
Organization for Security and Cooperation in Europe (OSCE), 432
Organization of African Unity, 522
Organization of American States (OAS), 275
Organization of Petroleum Exporting Countries (OPEC), 604
Orinoco Delta, 261
Orinoco River, 266
Orozco, José Clemente, 214
orthodox, 357
OSCE. See *Organization for Security and Cooperation in Europe*
Ottawa, 161–163, 161p, 162p, 163p, 179
Ottoman empire, 370m, 603, 631, 632, 695
    history of, 658–660, 658m, 659p
    World War I and, 395, 395m
Ottoman Turks, 356
Outback, 835, 901
outsourcing, 731, 901
overgrazing, 687, 901
ozone hole, 855, 855p
ozone layer, 855, 855p, 901

P

Pacific Coastal Lowlands, 199, 199m
Pacific Islands Forum, 849
Pacific Ocean, 134m, 830m, 835m
Pacific Plate, 775, 837, 837m
Pacific region
    atlas, 830m, 834–841, 834p, 835m, 836p, 837m, 838p, 839m, 841p

economy of, 849, 849c
ecosystem of, 838, 839
environmental concerns of, 850–851
ethnic groups of, 847, 847p, 858
government of, 848, 848p
history of, 842–845, 842p, 843m, 844p–845p
human geography, 828–829
indigenous people of, 858
migration to, 842–843, 843m
natural resources in, 841, 841p
physical features of, 834–837, 834p, 835m, 836p, 837m
physical geography, 826–827
physical map of, 874m
plate tectonics and, 837–838, 837m
population of, 840c, 841
regional flyover, 827
regional overview, 824–829
water resources in, 839
pack ice, 853, 901
pagan, 357
Pahlavi, Reza, 660–661
Pakal (Maya leader), 122p
Pakistan, 704m, 861m, 872m
    climate of, 710, 710m
    databank, 881
    discrimination in, 728
    economy of, 730
    government of, 730
    history of, 714
    India and, 729, 729m
    Islam in, 719, 719p, 725
    Kashmir and, 724
    land use in, 712, 712g
    literacy in, 728g
    partition of, 722–723, 722m
    population of, 713, 713m, 726, 726g
    religion in, 719, 719p, 725
Palau, 828, 830m, 861m, 881
Palawan, 809
Palestine, 360, 631, 632
Palestine Liberation Organization (PLO), 639
Palestinian Authority, 634, 639
Palestinian people, 615–617, 615p, 616p, 617p, 623
Palestinian Territories, 618, 624, 626, 636, 640
Pampas. See *Andes and the Pampas*
PAN. See *National Action Party*
Pan-Africanism, 516, 902
Panama, 864m, 865m
    colonization in, 235
    databank, 881
    ecotourism in, 243

history of, 237
physical features of, 226–227, 227m
urbanization in, 80, 80p
Panama Canal, 226, 227m, 237
Pan-Arabism, 569, 902
Pantanal, 309, 309m
Papal States, 370m
paper, 363
Papua New Guinea, 830m, 835m, 836, 841p, 847p, 848p, 861m, 874m, 881
Paraguay, 311, 324, 860m, 864m
    agriculture in, 286, 287m
    climate of, 284, 284m
    culture of, 297
    databank, 881
    economy of, 299–300, 300m
    exports from, 294
    population of, 288, 288m
paramilitaries, 269, 902
Paris, 430
Parliament, 365, 390, 390c, 422–423, 902
parliamentary democracy, 634, 635, 635p, 848, 902
parliamentary system, 179, 179c, 240
Parmenio, 339
Parthenon, 345
partition, 722–723, 722m, 902
Passover, 627
Pasteur, Louis, 393
Patagonia, 283, 283m, 862m, 865m
Patil, President, 728p
patricians, 349, 902
Paul (follower of Jesus), 629
Paul III, Pope, 380
Pax Romana, 351, 902
Peace Corps, 157
Pearl Harbor, 785, 785m
peasants, 359, 359p, 363
Pedro I, emperor of Brazil, 318
Peloponnesian Wars, 345, 347
peninsula, 414, 802, 884p, 885, 902
peninsulares, 268, 292, 293
Pennsylvania, 134m, 147m, 867m
People's Court (Ancient Greece), 344p
perestroika, 482, 484
Pérez, Carlos Andrés, 269
Pericles, 343q
period (time), 118, 902
permafrost, 168, 472, 902
Perón, Eva, 295p
Perón, Juan, 295
Perry, Matthew C., 784
Persia, 655, 656. See also *Iran*

Panama, 864m, 865m
    colonization in, 235
    databank, 881
    ecotourism in, 243
climate of, 838–839, 839m
culture of, 847, 847p

Persian empire, 600, 602, 656–657, 656*p*, 657*m*, 657*p*, 695
Persian Gulf, 590, 591, 591*m*, 605, 605*p*, 641, 649
Persian Wars, 347
perspective, 375, 377, 902
Peru, 3, 384, 860*m*, 864*m*
  climate of, 284, 284*m*
  culture of, 297
  databank, 881
  economy of, 299, 300, 300*m*
  ecosystem of, 285
  environment and, 298
  government of, 294, 301
  history of, 292–293
  languages of, 297*c*, 297*p*
  literacy in, 300
  physical features of, 122*p*, 283, 283*m*
  population of, 288, 288*m*
pesticides, 232, 242
Peter the Great, 478–479, 478*p*
Petition of Right, 390
petroleum, 49, 52, 202, 202*m*, 203*c*, 203*p*. See also *oil*
Petronas Towers, 822
phalanx, 338*p*, 348
pharoah, 565, 902
Philip II, king of Macedonia, 337
Philip II, king of Spain, 372, 386–387
Philippines, 802*p*, 861*m*, 872*m*
  databank, 881
  government of, 816
  physical features of, 803, 803*m*
  population of, 806, 806*m*
  religion in, 809, 815
philosophy, 345, 902
Phnom Penh, 807
Phoenicia, 566, 626
physical map, 10, 10*m*, 12, 12*m*, 902
Picasso, Pablo, 435
Pico Duarte, 227, 227*m*
pineapple, 230
pirates and piracy, 267, 267*m*, 267*p*, 548, 548*p*, 819
Pizarro, Francisco, 292, 384
place, theme of, 6, 902
plains, 25, 414, 415, 415*m*, 885, 885*p*, 902
Plains Indians, 146
planets, 18
plantations, 142, 148, 231, 318, 318*p*, 384, 385, 902
Plata Basin, 286
plateau, 25, 25*p*, 504, 591, 746, 747*m*, 884, 885, 902
Plateau of Iran, 863*m*, 873*m*
Plateau of Tibet, 863*m*, 873*m*
plates, 26, 27, 27*m*, 227, 591, 902

plate tectonics, 26, 837–838, 837*m*, 902
Platiensis, Michael, 367*q*
platinum, 534
Plato, 345
plebeian, 349, 902
PLO. See *Palestine Liberation Organization*
plural society, 182, 902
Plymouth Colony, 147, 385
poaching, 533, 903
Poland, 370*m*, 442*m*, 454*m*, 454*p*, 478, 868*m*
  culture of, 455
  databank, 881
  democracy in, 454
  economy of, 454–455
  European Union and, 455
  government of, 454–455
  natural resources in, 451
  religion in, 452, 452*m*, 453*p*
  Solidarity in, 404, 404*p*
  World War I and, 395, 395*m*
  World War II and, 398–399, 398*m*
polar zone, 34, 34*m*, 903
polder, 431, 903
political map, 13*m*, 903
political party, 113, 213, 903
political structures, 108–109, 108*p*, 109*p*
political systems, 106–107, 106*p*, 107*p*
  communism, 480–481, 481*c*
  in Europe, 397, 397*c*
  See also *government*
pollution, 419–420, 419*p*, 903
  in Brazil, 322, 322*p*
  in Canada, 170–171
  in Central America and Caribbean, 232–233
  in Central Asia, 698
  in China, 767, 767*p*
  in Eastern Europe, 451
  in Egypt, 560
  in Europe, 407
  human–environment interaction and, 53
  in Japan and the Koreas, 781
  in Mexico City, 204, 205*p*
  oil spills, 46*p*, 47, 47*p*
  population growth and, 75
  in South Asia, 727
  in Southern and Eastern Africa, 535
  in Venezuela, 272
  See also *air pollution; water pollution*
Polynesia, 835*m*, 836, 862*m*
  culture of, 833
  history of, 842–843, 843*m*
  population in, 840*c*
population
  of Australia, 828, 840, 840*p*

  of Britain, 392
  of Canada, 132*m*
  of China, 741
  of East Asia, 740*m*, 740*p*
  of Egypt, 558, 559, 559*p*
  of Federated States of Micronesia, 828*m*
  of Indonesia, 741
  of Iran, 652
  of Japan, 741
  measuring, 74–75, 74*g*, 75*p*
  migration and, 78–79, 78*p*, 79*p*
  of Mongolia, 741
  movement of, 72*p*, 73, 73*p*
  of New Zealand, 840, 840*p*
  of North Africa, 558–559, 559*p*
  of Pacific region, 840*c*, 841
  of Palau, 828*m*
  of Singapore, 741
  of Southeast Asia, 740*m*, 740*p*
  of South Korea, 741
  of Tonga, 828*m*
  of Turkey, 652
  of Tuvalu, 828*m*
  of United States, 132*m*, 741
  urbanization and, 80–81, 80*p*, 81*c*, 81*p*
  world, 74, 74*g*
population density, 77, 903
  of Africa, 498*m*
  of Andes and the Pampas, 288, 288*m*
  of Arabia and Iraq, 595, 595*m*
  of Brazil, 314, 314*g*
  of Canada, 167, 167*m*, 176, 182–183
  of Caribbean South America, 263, 263*m*
  of China, 750–751, 751*m*, 765, 765*c*
  definition of, 144
  of Europe, 76*m*
  of Germany, 432
  of Israel, 621*m*
  of Japan, 780, 780*p*, 792–793, 792*c*
  of Jordan, 621*m*
  of Lebanon, 621*m*
  of Mexico, 204–205, 204*m*, 205*p*, 214
  of the Netherlands, 431
  of Russia, 474–475, 474*m*
  of South Asia, 712, 712*m*, 726–727, 726*g*, 726*p*
  of Southeast Asia, 806–807, 806*m*, 817
  of Syria, 621*m*
  of United States, 144, 144*m*

  of West and Central Africa, 510–511, 510*m*
  of Western Europe, 419–421, 420*m*, 421*m*
population distribution, 76–77, 76*m*, 77*p*, 903
population growth, 75, 75*p*
Portugal, 370*m*, 868*m*
  Brazil and, 316, 317–318, 317*p*
  culture of, 435–436, 435*p*
  databank, 881
  economy of, 436–437, 437*g*, 438
  in European Union, 437
  explorations by, 382, 383, 383*m*
  slave trade and, 540
poverty
  in Armenia, 698*p*
  in Brazil, 314–315, 320, 325
  in Central America and Caribbean, 240
  in Jordan, 636*p*
  in Mexico, 217
  in North Africa, 572
  in South America, 300
  in South Asia, 713, 730
  in West and Central Africa, 522, 523
precipitation, 32, 39, 41, 903
  in Canada, 166, 166*m*
  definition of, 166
  in Japan, 777, 777*g*
  in the Koreas, 777, 777*g*
prehistory, 119, 903
President, U.S., 109*p*
press, freedom of the, 761
PRI. See *Institutional Revolutionary Party*
prices, 59, 61
primary industry, 849, 903
primary source, 120–121, 120*p*, 903
Prime Meridian, 5, 5*m*, 21
prime minister, 179, 179*c*, 240
Prince Edward Island, 160*m*, 176
printing press, 99, 99*c*, 376, 376*p*, 377, 378
privatization, 430, 437, 903
producer, 59, 60–61, 60*c*, 61*p*, 903
productivity, 65, 903
profits, 60, 903
Prohibition of Mixed Marriages Act, 542
projections, 9, 9*m*, 903
propaganda, 397
prophet, 627, 903
Protestant Reformation, 372, 378–380, 379*m*, 380*p*
province, 175, 903
Prussia, 370*m*, 387, 390

Ptolemy, 352
public health organization, 110, 110p
Puerto Rico, 239, 239p
pull factor, 79, 903
Punic Wars, 350
Punjab, 725
push factor, 79, 903
Putin, Vladimir, 483, 485, 486–487
pyramids, 566, 566p
Pyrenees Mountains, 869m

Q

qanat, 652–653, 903
Qatar, 861m, 872m
   databank, 881
   ethnic groups in, 596
   government of, 604
   history of, 603
   oil in, 592, 592m
Qin dynasty, 123p, 755
Qing dynasty, 757
Quaker Church, 379
Quebec, 86m, 87, 160m, 172, 174–175, 180p, 182p
Quebec Act (1775), 174–175
Quebec City, 173
Quechua language, 239, 297c, 297p
Quechua people, 289
Queen Maud Land, 875m
Quran, 600, 600p, 601, 607, 607p, 903

R

Race Day, See *Día de la Raza*
racial discrimination, 151
railroad, 142, 541
Raï music, 571, 571p
rain forest, 2p, 804, 807
   in Brazil, 312, 312p, 322, 322p
   mapping the, 3
   in Mexico, 201, 201p
rain shadow, 620, 620p, 904
The Ramayana, 725
Rastafarianism, 239
Rawlings, Jerry, 520
recession, 61, 792, 904
Reconquista, 362, 904
Red Cross, 110p
Red River, 802, 803m
Red Sea, 590, 591m, 619
reefs, 229
referendum, 301, 904
Reformation, 378, 452, 904.
   See also *Protestant Reformation*
refugees, 546, 546m, 546p
region, theme of, 7, 904

regional government, 108, 108p
Reign of Terror, 391, 391p
reincarnation, 717
relative location, 6, 904
religion, 904
   in ancient Egypt, 566, 566p
   in Ancient Greece, 345
   in Arabia and Iraq, 596–597, 596m, 596p, 600–603, 600p, 601p, 602m, 606–607, 607p
   in Armenia, 693
   art and, 361, 629p
   in Azerbaijan, 693
   in Bali, 809
   in Balkan Nations, 452–453, 452m, 453p
   in Brazil, 321
   in Canada, 174
   Cao Dai, 808, 808p
   in Caribbean, 238–239
   Catholic Reformation, 380–381
   in the Caucasus, 693, 696
   in Central America, 239
   in Central Asia, 691, 693, 696
   in China, 753, 756–757, 756p
   Confucianism, 756, 756p, 814
   culture and, 87, 92–93, 92m–93m
   in Cyprus, 654–655, 654m, 654p
   Daoism, 756–757, 756p
   definition of, 92
   dissenters and, 147
   in Eastern Europe, 452–453, 452m, 453p
   in Egypt, 571, 574
   in England, 380, 380p
   in Europe, 379m
   in France, 430
   in Germany, 380
   Greek Orthodox Church, 435
   in Hungary, 457
   in Indonesia, 809
   in Iran, 654–655, 654m, 658
   in Israel, 624–625, 624m, 624p, 640
   in Italy, 435
   in Japan, 784, 795
   in Korea, 784
   in Lebanon, 630p
   Maya, 235
   in Mexico, 208, 209p, 215
   in Mongolia, 757
   monotheism, 352
   in Morocco, 570p, 571
   in North Africa, 566, 567, 567p, 570, 570p
   in North Korea, 790
   in Philippines, 809
   Protestant Reformation, 378–380, 379m, 380p

Roman Catholic Church, 357, 435, 809
   in Roman empire, 352–353, 352m
   in Russia, 475
   in Saudi Arabia, 606–607, 607p
   separation of church and state, 148–149
   in South Asia, 715, 717–718, 717p, 724, 725
   in Southeast Asia, 808–809, 808p, 811, 814–815
   in Southern and Eastern Africa, 539, 545, 545c
   in South Korea, 789
   in Southwest Asia, 585m, 624–625, 624m, 624p
   in Soviet Union, 453
   technology and, 99
   in Tibet, 752
   timeline of, 632
   traditional, 92m–93m, 93
   in Turkey, 654–655, 654m, 654p, 655p
   in Vietnam, 814–815
   in West and Central Africa, 513, 521
   in Western Europe, 418
   See also *Buddhism; Christianity; Crusades; Hinduism; Islam; Jainism; Judaism; Sikhism*
religious tolerance, 390
remittance, 217, 904
Renaissance, 374–377, 374p, 375p, 376p, 377p, 904
renewable resource, 49, 49c, 904
representative democracy, 106, 112, 273, 349, 730, 904
repressive, 700, 904
Republic of Biafra, 517
Republic of Korea. See *South Korea*
Republic of the Congo, 522, 522g, 861m, 870m, 877
reservation, 149
reservoir, 811, 904
resurrection, 629, 630
reunification, 432, 904
revenues, 60, 904
revolution, Earth, 18, 904
Revolutionary War. See *American Revolution*
Rhine River, 415, 419, 420
Rhine-Ruhr region, 421, 421m
Rhode Island, 134m, 147m, 867m
Rhodes, 340, 341m
Rhodes, Cecil, 541p, 541q
rice, 778

Ring of Fire, 27m, 803
Rio de Janeiro, 314, 316
Rio de la Plata, 282, 283m
riot, 689, 904
Rivera, Diego, 208p–211p, 214
river blindness, 537
rivers, 885, 885m
   of Arabia, 591, 591m, 594, 594m
   of Canada, 168, 168p, 169
   of Central America and Caribbean, 227, 227m
   of Central Asia, 685, 685m
   of China, 746, 746p, 747, 747m, 748, 748m, 749, 749m, 766, 766p
   of Iraq, 591, 591m, 594, 594m, 599, 599m
   of Japan and the Koreas, 779
   of Russia, 469m, 470
   of South Asia, 709, 709m
   of Southeast Asia, 802, 803, 803m, 805
   of Southern and Eastern Africa, 531, 531m
   of United States, 139, 139m
   of West and Central Africa, 504p, 505, 505m
   of Western Europe, 415, 419, 424
road maps, 11, 11m
road system, 657
Robespierre, 391p
Robinson projection, 9, 9m
robots, 793, 793p
Rocky Mountains, 25, 130m, 130p, 139, 139m, 862m, 865m, 875m
Roma ethnic group, 439
Roman calendar, 119, 119p
Roman Catholic Church, 355, 435, 809
   in Central America and Caribbean, 238–239
   Inquisition, 362
   in Mexico, 208, 209p, 215
   Protestant Reformation and, 372, 378–380, 379m, 380p
   women in, 358
Roman empire, 124m, 350–353, 350m, 351p, 352m, 658
   in the Caucasus, 693
   Judea and, 627, 629, 631
   Persian empire and, 600
Romania, 404, 442m, 459, 868m, 881
Romanov Dynasty, 478–479, 478p, 480
Roman republic, 348–350, 348p, 349c
Rome, 348. See also *Roman empire; Roman republic*

Roosevelt, Franklin D., 120q, 151, 159q
Rosas, Juan Manuel de, 294
Rose Revolution, 700–701, 701p, 904
rotation, 20, 20p, 904
Rousseau, Jean-Jacques, 390
rule of law, 357
runoff, 232
rural area, 80, 81c, 904
Russia, 405, 464m, 861m, 868m, 872m
  animal life in, 472
  atlas, 468–475, 469m, 470m, 471p, 472g, 473m, 474m, 475p
  Caucasus and, 695
  Central Asia and, 691
  climate of, 470m, 471–472
  Communist Party in, 480–481, 481c
  databank, 881
  environmental concerns in, 471
  ethnic groups in, 474–475
  European Union and, 488–489
  Five-Year Plans, 480–481
  government in, 479–483, 480p, 481c, 482p
  history of, 395, 397, 476–483, 476p, 477p, 478p, 479p, 480p, 481c, 482p, 483m
  human geography, 334–335
  Iran and, 660
  Kazakhstan and, 689
  language in, 474
  myStory, 465–467, 465p, 466p, 467p
  natural resources of, 472–473, 473m
  physical features of, 468–471, 469m
  physical geography, 332–333
  population density of, 474–475, 474m
  regional flyover, 333
  regional overview, 330–335
  religion in, 475
  rivers of, 469m, 470
  Russian Revolution, 395, 397, 480
  timeline of, 476–477
  transportation in, 472g, 472p, 473
  tsars in, 478–480, 478p
  vegetation in, 471, 472
  volcanoes in, 471
  westernization of, 478–479
  World War I and, 395, 395m, 480
  See also *Russian Federation; Soviet Union*
Russian empire, 370m

Russian Federation
  alliances of, 487–488
  China and, 489
  disease in, 486
  economy of, 483, 485
  energy in, 487, 488, 488m
  government of, 483, 484, 486–487
  human rights in, 487
  Iran and, 489
  migration from, 486
  NATO and, 487
  Putin and, 485, 486–487
  standard of living in, 486, 486c
  See also *Russia; Soviet Union*
Russian Orthodox Christians, 475
Russian Plain, 469, 469m
Russian Revolution, 395, 397, 480
Rus tribe, 476p, 477
Rwanda, 110p, 520, 526m, 861m, 870m
  animal life in, 533p
  databank, 881
  ethnic groups of, 544
  genocide in, 547

S

Sabato, Ernesto, 301q
Sadat, Anwar, 569
Safavid empire, 658m, 659
Sahara, 496p, 504, 531, 531m, 556–557, 557m, 863m, 871m
Sahel, 505, 505m, 506, 508m, 509, 510, 863m, 871m, 904
Saint-Domingue, 236
Saint Kitts and Nevis, 864m, 881
St. Lawrence River, 165, 165m, 168, 168p, 169
Saint Lucia, 864m, 881
St. Petersburg, 470, 471, 474, 474m, 478, 479p
Saint Vincent and the Grenadines, 864m, 881
Saladin, 361
Salamis, Battle of, 347
salt trade, 512p, 513, 905
Samoa, 830m, 845, 847p, 881
samurai, 783–784, 783c, 784, 905
San Francisco, 26
San Marino, 881
San Martín, José de, 293, 294q
San Salvador, 228
Santander, Francisco de Paula, 268
Santeria, 239, 905
São Paulo, 311, 314
São Tomé and Principe, 881

Sargon, king of Sumer, 599
Sarkozy, Nicolas, 273, 273p
Saskatchewan, 160m
Sassanian empire, 657
satellite images, 8, 8p, 905
satraps, 657, 905
Saudi Arabia, 861m, 872m
  Arab culture of, 610, 610p, 611
  databank, 881
  economy of, 593, 608–609, 609, 609g
  ecosystems in, 594, 594m
  ethnic groups in, 596–597, 596m, 596p
  government of, 107, 604
  history of, 598–605, 598p, 599m, 599p, 600p, 601p, 602m, 603p, 604, 604p, 605p
  oil in, 152, 592, 592m, 604, 608–609, 609g
  religion in, 596–597, 596m, 596p, 600–603, 600p, 601p, 602m, 606–607, 607p
  traditions in, 606–607
  water resources in, 594, 594m, 594p
  women in, 587–589, 587p, 588p, 589p, 611
savanna, 42, 42m–43m, 42p, 259, 309, 506, 905
  in Africa, 532, 532m, 533p
savings, 68, 905
Savonarola, Girolamo, 378
scale, 8, 905
scale bar, 10, 11, 905
Scandinavia, 332p, 357, 416, 416m, 424–428, 424c, 863m
  agriculture in, 425
  cradle-to-grave benefits, 424–425, 424c
  government of, 424–425
  See also *Denmark; Finland; Iceland; Norway; Sweden*
Scandinavian Peninsula, 415, 415m, 869m, 875m
scarcity, 58, 778, 779, 905
schism, 355, 905
science, 905
  in ancient Greece, 345
  in Antarctica, 854–855, 854p, 855p
  culture and, 98–99, 98p, 99c, 99p
  in Roman empire, 352
scientific method, 388, 389, 389c
Scientific Revolution, 388–389, 905
Scotland, 357, 422, 423, 423m
Scott, Robert, 854, 854p
sea level, 35, 619, 850, 850m, 850p, 851

Sea of Galilee, 619, 619m, 622m, 623
season, 18–19, 18p–19p, 35
secede, 458, 905
secondary industry, 849, 905
secondary sources, 120–121, 121p, 127, 905
secular, 815, 905
secular democracy, 730, 905
secularism, 574, 905
secular state, 666
sedentary, 694, 905
seed culture, 811
Sejong, emperor of Korea, 783
Selassie, Haile, 541p
Seljuk Turks, 360
Sembene, Ousmane, 523q
semiarid climate, 40m–41m, 41, 905
Senegal, 521, 521p, 870m, 881
Seoul, 782p, 788p
separation of church and state, 379
separation of powers, 148c
separatist groups, 816, 905
September equinox, 19
September 11th attacks, 156, 723, 819
Serbia, 395, 395m, 442m, 458, 868m, 881
Serengeti Plain, 497p, 531m, 532, 871m, 905
serfdom, 390, 478, 479, 481, 905
service industries, 154
Seven Years' War, 174, 174p
Seychelles, 861m, 881
Shackleton, Ernest, 854, 854p
shah, 659, 660–661, 905
Shah Jahan, 720, 721
Shakespeare, William, 377
shamal, 651, 906
Shanghai, 740p, 750, 750p
Sharia law, 815
Shenzhen, 763
Shevardnadze, Eduard, 700
Shia Muslims, 596m, 596p, 597, 601, 603, 625, 655, 659
Shi Huangdi, 754p, 755
Shinto religion, 795, 906
Shiva, 716p
shogun, 783, 906
Siberia, 468, 469m, 471, 474, 863m, 906
Sierra Leone, 508m, 509, 522, 870m, 881
Sierra Madre, 190p, 227, 227m
Sierra Madre Occidental, 199, 199m, 865m
Sierra Madre Oriental, 199, 199m, 865m
Sikhism, 92m–93m, 93, 719, 721, 725

Silk Road, 602, 692–693, 692p, 693m, 694, 715, 906

Silla Kingdom, 782

Simpson Desert, 835, 835m

Sinai Peninsula, 557, 557m, 569

Singapore, 808, 813, 816p, 861m, 872m
  databank, 881
  economy of, 818, 818c
  ethnic diversity in, 816c
  global trade and, 819
  government of, 816
  population of, 741, 817

single-party state, 761, 906

sinkhole, 199, 906

Sino-Tibetan language, 90

Siqueiros, David Alfaro, 214

slavery, 79, 149–150
  in ancient Greece, 346
  in ancient Rome, 351
  in Brazil, 317, 318
  Native Americans and, 235–236, 235p
  trade and, 236, 386, 514, 514p, 539, 540

sleeping sickness, 511, 522, 537

Slovakia, 442m, 868m
  databank, 881
  economy of, 456c
  European Union and, 456
  government of, 456
  religion in, 452, 452m

Slovenia, 442m, 457, 458, 458m, 868m, 882

slum, 81, 906

Sochi, 470

social class, 89, 717, 906

social services, 325, 906

social structure, 89, 89c, 906

society, 88–89, 906

Socrates, 345

soil, 24, 53

solar energy, 49, 53

Solidarity, 404, 404p, 454

Solomon Islands, 830m, 849c, 861m, 882

Solon, 342

solstice, 18, 19, 906

Somalia, 526m, 861m, 870m
  databank, 882
  farming in, 535
  government in, 548
  independence of, 542

Songhai empire, 513, 513p

Sonoran Desert, 200, 201

Sophocles, 345

Soufriere Hills Volcano, 227, 227m

South Africa, 111p, 499, 526m, 861m, 870m
  animal life in, 533
  apartheid system, 528, 542–

543, 543p, 547
  databank, 882
  economy of, 549
  ecosystem of, 533
  ethnic groups in, 527–529, 527p, 528p, 529p, 544
  European rule in, 540, 540m
  farming in, 535
  government of, 547, 548p
  independence of, 543
  language of, 545
  literacy rates in, 549g
  myStory, 527–529, 527p, 528p, 529p
  natural resources of, 534, 534m

South America, 248m, 860m
  atlas of, 278m, 282–289, 283m, 284m, 285c, 287m, 288m
  climate of, 284, 284m
  cultures of, 296–297, 297c
  ecosystems of, 285, 285c
  fishing in, 286
  free-trade agreements of, 299–300, 300m
  history of, 290–295, 291m, 291p, 292p, 293, 294p
  human geography, 252–253
  industrialization in, 294–295
  life expectancy in, 328
  migrations to, 252m
  oil production in, 152
  physical features of, 282–283, 282p, 283m
  physical geography, 250–251
  physical map of, 862m, 865m
  political map of, 864m
  population density of, 288, 288m
  poverty in, 300
  regional flyover, 251
  regional overview, 248–253
  slave trade and, 514
  See also *Andes and the Pampas; Caribbean South America*

South American Plate, 283

South Asia, 704m
  art of, 725
  atlas, 708–715, 708p, 709m, 710m, 711p, 712g, 713m, 714m
  caste system in, 717, 727–728
  climate of, 710–711, 710m, 711m
  conflicts in, 729, 729m
  culture of, 715, 717, 724–725, 724p, 725p
  economy of, 728, 730–731, 730g
  environmental concerns of, 727

farming in, 712, 712g
  food of, 725
  governments in, 730
  history of, 714, 714m, 716–723, 716p, 717p, 718m, 719p, 720p, 721p, 722m, 723p
  housing in, 711p
  human geography, 678–679
  Islam in, 715, 719–721, 719p
  land use in, 712, 712g
  mountains of, 709, 709m
  natural resources in, 712
  physical features of, 708–709, 708p, 709m, 714, 714m
  physical geography, 676–677, 714, 714m
  population density of, 713, 713m, 726–727, 726g, 726p
  poverty in, 713, 730
  regional flyover, 677
  regional overview, 674–679
  religion in, 715, 717–721, 717p, 724, 725
  rivers of, 709, 709m
  women in, 728, 728g, 728p
  See also *Afghanistan; Bangladesh; Bhutan; India; Nepal; Pakistan; Sri Lanka*

South Carolina, 134m,147m, 867m

South Dakota, 134m, 867m

Southeast Asia
  agriculture in, 806–807, 807p, 811
  air pollution in, 807, 817, 817p
  atlas of, 798m, 802–809, 802p, 803m, 804m, 805m, 806m, 807c, 808p
  China and, 808–809, 810
  cities and towns of, 807
  climate of, 804, 804m
  culture of, 799–801
  economy of, 818–819, 818c
  environment of, 815, 815p, 817, 817p
  ethnic diversity in, 808–809, 809p
  government in, 813, 816
  history of, 805, 805m, 810–813, 810p, 811m, 812g
  human geography, 740–741
  independence of, 812
  land use in, 806–807, 807c
  migration in, 807, 808
  physical features of, 802–803, 803m
  physical geography, 738–739
  population density of, 806–807, 806m, 817
  population of, 740m, 740p
  regional flyover, 739

regional overview, 736–741
  religion in, 808–809, 808p, 811, 814–815
  rivers of, 802, 803m, 805
  tourism in, 819
  trade in, 805, 805m, 810–812, 811m, 812g
  volcanoes in, 738p
  World War II in, 812
  See also *Brunei; Cambodia; East Timor; Indonesia; Laos; Malaysia; Myanmar; Philippines; Singapore; Thailand; Vietnam*

Southern and Eastern Africa
  animal life in, 532–533, 533p
  atlas of, 526m, 530–537, 530p, 531m, 532m, 533p, 534m, 535p, 536m, 537c
  climate of, 548
  conflicts in, 546–547, 546p
  deserts of, 531, 531m
  development in, 548–549, 549g
  diseases in, 527, 537, 537c, 548–549
  ecosystems of, 532–533, 532m, 533p
  ethnic groups in, 544–545, 546–547
  governments in, 547–549
  history of, 538–543, 538p, 539p, 540m, 541p, 542p, 543p
  indigenous people of, 544–545
  languages of, 545
  literacy rates in, 549g
  mining in, 534–535, 534m, 534p
  natural resources of, 534–535, 534m, 535p, 536, 536m
  physical features of, 530–531, 531m
  pollution in, 535
  religion in, 539, 545, 545c
  trade in, 539, 540
  water resources in, 535, 536, 536c
  See also *individual countries*

Southern Colonies, 147m, 148

Southern Common Market, 299–300, 300m, 324

Southern Cone, 294, 299

Southern Europe, 434–439, 434p, 435p, 436p, 437g, 438p, 439p

Southern Hemisphere, 4m, 5, 34, 34m, 35, 506

South Island, 836, 837

South Korea, 770m, 861m, 872m
  atlas of, 770m, 774–781,

774p, 775m, 776m, 777g,
777p, 778m, 779c, 780p,
781p
climate of, 776–777, 776m,
777g, 777p
culture of, 789, 789p
databank, 879
economy of, 779, 779c, 789
energy resources in, 779
environmental concerns in,
780–781, 781p
farming in, 778–779, 778m
government of, 788–789
history of, 782–783, 782p,
784, 785, 786, 786m
hydroelectricity in, 779
Korean War and, 786, 786m
land use in, 778–779, 778m,
779c
natural resources in, 778–779,
778m, 779c
North Korea and, 791
physical features of, 774–775,
775m
population of, 741
religion in, 789
rivers in, 779
sports in, 789, 789p
standard of living in, 790c
South Ossetia, 690
South Pole, 4, 4m, 5
Southwest Asia, 861m
deserts of, 621
economy of, 637, 637g, 637p
ethnic groups in, 584–585,
585m
government in, 104, 104p
human geography, 584–585
mandates in, 632
oil in, 641, 672, 673g
physical geography, 582–583
regional flyover, 583
regional overview, 580–585
religion in, 585m, 624–625,
624m, 624p
See also *Arabia; Iraq; Israel;
Jordan; Lebanon; Syria*
sovereignty, 110, 906
soviet, 480, 906
Soviet Union
Afghanistan and, 723, 723p
Caucasus and, 695
Central Asia and, 691, 695
Cold War and, 400–405, 517
collapse of, 403–405, 404p,
405, 405p, 482
communism in, 397, 480–481,
481c, 484–485
Eastern Europe and, 401
environmental concerns in,
482
farming in, 480–481
government of, 404, 481–482
Koreas and, 786

nationalism in, 482
religion in, 453
United States and, 481
in World War II, 398–399
See also *Russia*
Spain, 370m, 868m
absolutism in, 386–387
class system of, 292
Colombia and, 266
colonies of, 235, 292–293
conquistadors, 292, 292p
culture of, 435–436, 435p
databank, 882
economy of, 436–437, 437g,
438
encomienda system, 235
England and, 371–373, 387
in European Union, 437
explorations by, 383, 383m,
384
fascism in, 397
France and, 209
Incan culture and, 290, 291p,
292
mercantilism and, 293c
Mexico and, 208–209, 208p,
209p, 214, 384
Muslims in, 361–362
myStory, 371–373
Native Americans and, 146,
267
Reconquista, 362
in South America, 297
Spanish Armada and, 371–
373, 387
terrorism in, 406, 406p
Spanish American War, 150p
Spanish Armada, 371–373, 387
Sparta, 346–347, 346m
specialization, 60, 906
special-purpose map, 13m,
124–125, 124m, 125m, 906
speech, freedom of, 112, 155,
761
sphere, 4, 906
spice trade, 384, 805, 805m,
812
spillover, 53, 906
sports
of Ancient Greece, 345
in Brazil, 305–307, 307p,
308p, 320
in France, 430p
in Japan, 795
in South Korea, 789, 789p
in West and Central Africa,
521
Sri Lanka, 704m, 861m
culture of, 715
databank, 882
government of, 730
history of, 723
physical features of, 709,
709m

religion in, 725
Stalin, Joseph, 480–481, 695p
standard of living, 99, 906
in Israel, 636
in Jordan, 636p
in Lebanon, 636, 636p
in North Africa, 572
in North Korea, 790c
in Russian Federation, 486,
486c
in South Korea, 790c
staple crop, 749, 906
state, 106, 906
steam engine, 99c, 389, 392
steppe, 471, 685, 685m, 686,
906
stocks, 69, 69p, 906
strait, 649, 884p, 885, 906
subarctic climate, 40m–41m,
41, 907
**subarctic forest
ecosystem,** 42, 42m–43m,
42p
subducted, 283, 907
subsidence, 272, 907
subsistence farming, 286,
286p, 519, 519p, 712, 907
suburban sprawl, 81, 907
suburbs, 51, 81, 907
Sudan, 526m, 861m, 870m
conflicts in, 546
databank, 882
farming in, 535
government in, 547
history of, 539, 540m
language of, 545
literacy rates in, 549g
water resources in, 536, 536c,
536m
Sudd, 531, 531m
Suez Canal, 563, 569
sugar cane, 236, 324
Suharto, 816
Sulawesi, 806
**Suleiman the
Magnificent,** 659
sultan, 719
Sumatra, 799–801, 803, 803m,
806, 811
Sumer, 598p, 599, 599m
sun, Earth and the, 18–19,
18p–19p, 20, 20p, 34, 34m,
37, 37p, 38, 38p
Sun King, 387, 387p
Sunni Muslims, 596, 596m,
596p, 597, 601, 603, 607,
625, 655
Sun Yixian, 757p
superpower, 487, 907
supply, 59, 59g, 907
Supreme Court, U.S., 109, 109p
Supreme Leader, 662
Suriname, 860m, 864m
atlas, 254m, 258, 259, 260,

260m, 263m
climate of, 260, 260m
culture of, 270, 271, 271p
databank, 882
economy of, 275c
environmental problems of,
272
ethnic groups in, 265, 274
government of, 273, 273p
history of, 267
land use in, 264
physical features of, 258, 259,
259m
population density of, 263,
263m
surplus, 811, 907
Swahili language, 545, 907
Swaziland, 526m, 540m, 861m,
870m, 882
Sweden, 370m, 424, 425, 868m,
882
Swiss Confederation, 370m
Switzerland, 343, 428, 433,
868m, 882
Sydney, 840, 849p
Sydykova, Zamira, 701p
Syr Dar'ya River, 685, 685m,
686
Syria, 569, 614m, 872m
Arab-Israeli conflicts, 632–633
atlas, 618–625, 619m, 621m,
622m, 624m
climate of, 620–621
databank, 882
economy of, 637g, 637p
government of, 635, 635p
history of, 631, 632–633
Kurdish people in, 624
physical features of, 618–619,
619m
population density of, 621m
religion in, 625
water resources in, 622–623,
622m
Syrian Desert, 619, 619m, 620

T

tae kwon do, 789, 789p
Tagore, Rabindranath, 814q
taiga, 417, 472, 907
Taiwan, 785, 785m, 861m, 872m
climate of, 748, 748m
databank, 882
economic system of, 761c
economy of, 762, 762p, 763c
government of, 761, 761c
history of, 757
industry in, 749
physical features of, 747,
747m
politics in, 761c
population of, 750–751, 751m

Index (continued)

Tajikistan, 680*m*, 684*p*, 861*m*, 872*m*
  databank, 882
  economy of, 698
  ethnic groups of, 691
  physical features of, 685, 685*m*
  water resources in, 689
Taj Mahal, 720*p*, 721
Taklimakan Desert, 747*m*,748, 873*m*
Taliban, 156, 723, 729, 729*m*
Talmud, 628
Tamazight, 571
Tamerlane, 477*p*
Tanakh, 628, 630
Tanzania, 526*m*, 530*p*, 533, 861*m*, 870*m*
  databank, 882
  ecosystem of, 532, 532*m*
  ethnic groups of, 544
  history of, 538, 540*m*
tariffs, 67, 438, 819, 907
Tasmania, 874*m*
taxes and taxation, 351
technology, 426, 819, 907
  culture and, 97, 98–99, 98*p*, 99*c*, 99*p*
  economic development and, 65
  human-environment interaction and, 51, 53
  Industrial Revolution and, 392–393, 392*p*, 393*p*
  in Middle Ages, 363
  religion and, 99
  transportation and, 98*p*–99*p*
tectonic plates. See *plate tectonics*
Tehran, 664, 664*p*
telecommunications, 437
temperate, 140, 687, 907
temperate forest ecosystem, 42, 42*m*–43*m*, 42*p*
temperate grassland and brush ecosystem, 42, 42*m*–43*m*, 42*p*
temperate zones, 34, 34*m*, 416, 416*m*, 907
temperature, 32, 34–35, 34*m*, 35*m*, 41, 907
Temple of Inscriptions, 122*p*
temples, 345, 627
Ten Commandments, 627, 628
Ten-Day War, 457
Tennessee, 134*m*, 867*m*
Tenochtitlán, 208, 208*p*
Teresa of Avila, 381
terraced farming, 264, 264*p*, 778, 907
terrorism, 156, 607, 819, 907
  in Europe, 406, 406*p*

  Iran and, 664
  United States and, 723
Texas, 108, 134*m*, 141, 144, 149*m*, 867*m*
Thailand, 861*m*, 872*m*
  agriculture in, 807, 807*p*
  databank, 882
  ethnic diversity in, 808
  high-technology in, 819
  history of, 812
  labor force of, 819
  population of, 806, 806*m*
Thar Desert, 873*m*
theocracy, 565, 662, 907
Thermopylae, 347
Thirty Years' War, 380
Three Gorges Dam, 766, 766*p*, 767
Thucydides, 345
Tiananmen Square, 760*p*, 761
Tian Shan, 863*m*, 873*m*
Tiber River, 348
Tibesti Mountains, 871*m*
Tibet, 749, 752, 752*p*, 753
Tibetan Plateau, 746, 747*m*
tidal waves, 415, 803
Tigris River, 583*p*, 591, 591*m*, 594, 594*m*, 595, 599, 599*m*
time, measuring, 118–119, 118*p*, 119*p*
timeline, 907
  of Arabia and Iraq, 603
  Chinese dynasties, 754–755
  of India, 720
  religion, 632
  of the Roman empire, 353
  of Russia, 476–477
  of the United States, 150*p*
  using, 118, 118*p*
  of West and Central Africa, 513
time zone, 20–21, 21*c*, 907
Timor-Leste, 882
tin, 534, 534*m*
Tito, Josip Broz, 458
Togo, 870*m*, 882
Tokelau, 830*m*
Tokugawa Ieyasu, 783–784, 783*c*
Tombouctou (Timbuktu), 513
Tonga, 828*m*, 830*m*, 882
Torah, 628, 628*p*
tornadoes, 27, 39, 39*p*, 907
Toronto, 182, 182*p*
tourism, 907
  in Africa, 578–579
  in Austria, 433, 433*p*
  in Central America and Caribbean, 231, 231*c*, 232, 243
  in France, 430
  in Mexico, 216
  in North Africa, 573

  in Portugal, 437
  in Southeast Asia, 819
  in Southern and Western Africa, 533
  in United Kingdom, 424
  See also *ecotourism*
towns. See *cities and towns*
trade, 907
  agreements, 111
  in ancient Greece, 342–343
  in Arabian Peninsula, 600
  barter, 60
  Canada and, 180–181
  Crusades and, 362–363, 362*m*
  cultural traits and, 96–97
  culture and, 715
  definition of, 66
  geography and, 66–67, 66*p*, 67*c*
  in Greece, 439, 439*p*
  historical maps and, 125*m*
  in India, 721, 730*g*, 731
  Industrial Revolution and, 392
  in Israel, 636, 640–641, 641
  in Mexico, 180, 216, 218, 218*g*, 219
  in Middle Ages, 362–363, 362*m*
  in Muslim empire, 602, 602*m*
  NAFTA and, 152, 154, 216
  in North Africa, 563, 567
  in Persian empire, 657
  in the Renaissance, 374–375, 376
  in Roman empire, 351
  slave, 236, 386, 514, 514*p*
  in South America, 299–300, 300*m*
  in Southeast Asia, 805, 805*m*, 810–812, 811*m*, 812*g*
  in Southern and Eastern Africa, 539, 540
  in Sumatra, 811
  in Turkey, 667–668, 668*c*, 668*p*
  types of, 67, 67*c*
  in United Kingdom, 423
  in West and Central Africa, 512–513, 514
  See also *free-trade agreements*
trade barriers, 67, 907
trade winds, 228, 229
traditional economy, 62, 62*p*, 908
Trajan, emperor of Rome, 350*p*
Transantarctic Mountains, 853, 853*m*, 875*m*
Transdniestria, 461

transportation,
  in Central Asia and Caucasus, 689
  culture and, 97
  in Industrial Revolution, 392
  population distribution and, 77
  in Russia, 472*g*, 472*p*, 473
  technology and, 98*p*–99*p*
  in Western Europe, 421, 421*m*
Trans-Siberian Railroad, 472*g*, 472*p*, 473
Transylvanian Alps, 446, 447*m*, 869*m*
treaty, 111, 908
Treaty of Tordesillas (1494), 317
Treaty of Versailles, 395, 397
trees, 42, 42*p*
triangular trade, 236, 386, 514, 514*p*, 908
tribunes, 349, 908
tributary, 885, 885*p*
Trinidad and Tobago, 239, 864*m*, 882
Trinity, 630, 908
trireme, 342, 342*p*
Trojan War, 348
tropical cyclones, 39, 908
tropical or subtropical forest ecosystem, 42, 42*m*–43*m*, 42*p*
tropical or subtropical grassland ecosystem, 42, 42*m*–43*m*, 42*p*
tropical rainforest, 504
  of Central America and Caribbean, 228, 228*m*, 228*p*
  deforestation and, 233
  of West and Central Africa, 506, 507*m*
tropical wet and dry climate, 40, 40*m*–41*m*, 506, 507*m*, 908
tropical wet climate, 40, 40*m*–41*m*, 506, 507*m*, 908
Tropic of Cancer, 34, 34*m*, 200
Tropic of Capricorn, 34, 34*m*
tropics, 34, 34*m*, 36, 908
Trudeau, Pierre, 180
tsar, 478–480, 478*p*, 908
tsetse belt, 537
tsetse fly, 510*p*, 511, 537
tsunamis, 415, 803, 908
tundra, 166*m*, 167, 416, 416*m*, 471, 908
tundra climate, 40*m*–41*m*, 41, 908
tundra ecosystem, 42*m*–43*m*, 43, 43*p*
Tunisia, 552*m*, 557*m*, 566, 573*p*, 870*m*
  databank, 882

government of, 575
literacy in, 573
natural resources in, 562, 562*m*
population of, 558, 559
religion in, 567
Turkey, 570, 644*m*, 861*m*, 868*m*,
    872*m*
    atlas, 648–655, 648*p*, 649*m*,
        650*m*, 651*g*, 652*m*, 653*c*,
        654*m*, 654*p*
    climate of, 650–651, 650*m*,
        651*c*
    culture of, 667
    Cyprus and, 668–669, 669*m*,
        669*p*
    databank, 882
    earthquakes in, 650
    economy of, 667–668, 668*c*,
        668*p*
    ethnic groups in, 654–655,
        654*m*, 654*p*
    European Union and, 668
    government of, 666–667
    history of, 658–659, 658*m*,
        659*p*, 660, 660*p*
    Kurdish people in, 645–647,
        645*p*, 646*p*, 647*p*, 654–655,
        668
    land use in, 652–653, 652*m*
    myStory, 645–647, 645*p*,
        646*p*, 647*p*
    nationalism in, 666
    oil in, 653
    physical features of, 648–650,
        649*m*
    population of, 652
    religion in, 654–655, 654*m*,
        654*p*
    as secular state, 666
    trade in, 667–668, 668*c*, 668*p*
    water resources in, 623
    women in, 667
    See also *Ottoman empire*
Turkic languages, 691
**Turkish Republic of Northern
    Cyprus,** 669
Turkmenistan, 676*p*, 680*m*,
    861*m*, 872*m*
    databank, 882
    government of, 700, 700*p*
    natural resources in, 688,
        688*m*
    physical features of, 685,
        685*m*
    water resources in, 689
Tutsi people, 544, 547
Tuvalu, 828, 830*m*, 850, 850*m*,
    850*p*, 861*m*, 882
Twelve Tables, 349
**Twenty-first Century
    Learning**
    analyze media content, 83,
        115, 221, 277, 492–493, 551,
        643

communication, 409
community awareness, 29
creativity, 369
cultural awareness, 127, 185,
    245, 613, 703, 821, 858–859
cultural differences, 441
effective presentations, 45,
    303, 822–823
evaluate Web sites, 15, 463,
    734–735, 769
generate new ideas, 578–579
Internet information, 55, 71,
    159, 327, 328–329, 491, 577,
    733, 797, 857
make a difference, 672–673
research aid organizations,
    525
solve problems, 246–247, 671
work in teams, 101, 186–187
typhoon, 804, 908
tyranny, 105, 105*c*, 908

U

Uganda, 520, 526*m*, 861*m*,
    870*m*
    AIDS in, 549
    animal life in, 533*p*
    databank, 882
    ethnic groups of, 544
    population of, 75*p*
    water resources in, 536, 536*c*,
        536*m*
Uighur ethnic group, 752,
    752*m*, 753, 753*p*
Ukraine, 405, 442*m*, 478, 481,
    488*m*, 489, 868*m*
    databank, 882
    government of, 460, 460*p*
    myStory, 443–445, 443*p*,
        444*p*, 445*p*
    natural resources in, 451
    religion in, 452–453, 452*m*,
        453*p*
    Vikings in, 357
Ulaanbaatar, 748
Uluru, 835
unemployment, 180, 728. See
    also *employment*
**Union of Soviet Socialist
    Republics (USSR).** See
    Soviet Union
unitary system, 108, 908
United Arab Emirates, 592,
    592*m*, 593*g*, 872*m*
    databank, 882
    economy of, 609
    ethnic groups in, 596
    government of, 604
    history of, 603
    water resources in, 594, 594*m*
United Kingdom, 868*m*
    databank, 883
    economy of, 426, 426*g*

government of, 107, 422–423
immigrants to, 423
languages of, 423
population of, 420, 420*m*
tourism in, 424
See also *Britain; England;
    Great Britain*
United Nations (UN), 111,
    111*p*, 150*p*, 181, 181*p*, 433
    Balkan Nations and, 459
    formation of, 401
    Korean War and, 786, 786*m*
    Rwanda and, 547
**United Provinces of Central
    America,** 236
United States, 128*m*, 860*m*,
    864*m*
    Afghanistan and, 723, 729,
        730
    agriculture in, 141, 142
    atlas, 134*m*, 138–145, 139*m*,
        140*m*, 141*m*, 143*m*, 144*m*
    Canada and, 164, 168, 170,
        175, 177, 178, 180, 183
    Caribbean and, 237
    cities and towns in, 142
    citizenship in, 102*p*, 103,
        103*p*, 112–113, 112*p*, 113*p*
    climate of, 140–141, 140*m*
    Cold War and, 400–405, 517
    culture of, 154–156, 154*m*,
        155*p*
    databank, 883
    democracy in, 343
    as developed country, 64
    economic system of, 63
    economy of, 152–154, 153*c*,
        153*p*
    environment in the, 145
    ethnic diversity in, 154*m*
    foreign policy, 156–157, 156*c*
    France and, 149
    government of, 105, 105*c*,
        106, 108, 148–149, 148*c*
    history of, 146–151, 147*m*,
        147*p*, 149*m*, 175, 396, 813
    human geography, 132–133
    immigration in, 73, 78*p*, 79,
        79*p*, 133*g*, 142, 144, 150–
        151, 155–156
    Interstate Highway System,
        186–187
    Iran and, 661, 664
    Iraq and, 156–157, 605, 605*p*
    Israel and, 633
    Japan and, 784, 785, 786–787
    landforms of, 25, 25*p*
    Mexico and, 216, 219
    migration in, 142–144
    myStory, 135–137, 135*p*,
        136*p*, 137*p*
    NAFTA and, 152, 154, 216,
        219
    nation-states and, 107

natural resources of, 141,
    141*m*
North Korea and, 791
Panama Canal and, 237
physical features of, 138–139,
    139*m*
physical geography, 130–131
physical map of, 12*m*
political map of, 13*m*, 134*m*,
    866*m*–867*m*
population density of, 144,
    144*m*
population of, 132*m*
regional overview, 128–133
regions of, 142–143, 142*p*,
    143*m*, 143*p*
Soviet Union and, 481
special-purpose map of, 13*m*
terrorism and, 723
timeline, 150*p*
trade and, 67*c*
Vietnamese Americans, 135–
    137, 135*p*, 136*p*, 137*p*
World War I and, 395
World War II and, 151, 398,
    399
universal theme, 94, 908
Universal Time (UT), 21
unlimited government, 105,
    105*c*, 790, 908
uplands, 414, 415, 415*m*
Upper Canada, 175
upper class, 89
Uralic language, 91
Ural Mountains, 414, 469,
    469*m*, 863*m*, 869*m*, 873*m*,
    908
uranium, 534, 534*m*
urban area, 80–81, 80*p*, 81*c*,
    81*p*, 908
urban continent. See *Western
    Europe*
Urban II, Pope, 360*q*
urbanization, 80–81, 80*p*, 81*c*,
    81*p*, 595, 908, 909
    in Kenya, 542
    in North Africa, 559
urban planning, 322, 323,
    323*p*, 908
Uribe Vélez, Álvaro, 273*p*
Uruguay, 324, 860*m*, 864*m*
    agriculture in, 286, 287*m*
    climate of, 284, 284*m*
    culture of, 296
    databank, 883
    economy of, 299–300, 300*m*
    exports from, 294
**U.S.-Chile Free Trade
    Agreement,** 300
USAID, 157
USSR. See *Soviet Union*
Usumacinta River, 227, 227*m*
UT. See *Universal Time*
Utah, 134*m*, 866*m*

Utopia (More), 377
Uzbekistan, 680*m*, 872*m*
  culture of, 697
  databank, 883
  ethnic groups of, 698
  natural resources in, 688,
    688*m*
  physical features of, 685,
    685*m*
  water resources in, 689, 699,
    699*g*, 699*p*

V

Valdivian Forest, 298
valley, 25, 25*p*, 885, 885*p*, 909
Vancouver, 182
Vandals, 353
Vanuatu, 830*m*, 861*m*, 883
Vargas, Getúlio, 319
varzea, 313
vassal, 358, 358*c*, 909
Vatican City, 435, 868*m*, 878
Vedas, 717
vegetation, 471, 472
Venetiaan, Ronald, 273, 273*p*
Venezuela, 860*m*, 864*m*
  atlas, 254*m*, 258, 259*m*,
    260*m*, 262*m*, 263*m*
  climate of, 260, 260*m*
  culture of, 270, 271, 271*p*
  databank, 883
  economy of, 275*c*
  environmental concerns of,
    272, 272*g*
  ethnic groups in, 265, 274
  government of, 273, 273*p*,
    274, 274*p*
  history of, 266, 268, 268*p*,
    269, 293
  land use in, 264
  oil in, 269, 277*q*
  physical features of, 258, 259,
    259*m*
  pollution in, 272
  population density of, 263,
    263*m*
Venice, 355, 363*p*, 364, 370*m*,
    374
Vermont, 134*m*, 867*m*
vertical climate zones, 285,
    285*c*, 286, 909
Vespucci, Amerigo, 384
viceroys, 235, 292
Victoria Falls, 497*p*, 531, 531*m*
Vietnam, 822, 861*m*, 872*m*
  databank, 883
  environment of, 815, 815*p*
  government of, 816
  history of, 810, 813
  religion in, 808, 808*p*, 814–
    815

Vietnamese-Americans, 135–
    137
Vietnam War, 813
Vikings, 357, 425, 425*p*, 476–
    477
Virgil, 348, 352
Virginia, 147*m*, 385, 867*m*
Visigoths, 353, 356
visual arts, 94, 94*p*, 909
Vladimir, prince of Russia, 477
Vladivostok, 470, 473, 474*m*
Volcán de Fuego, 227, 227*m*
volcanoes, 16*p*, 17, 17*p*, 26–27,
    26*p*, 415, 803, 884*p*, 885
  in Asia, 775
  in Central America, 226*p*,
    227, 227*m*
  in Mexico, 199
  in Nicaragua, 190*p*
  in Pacific region, 837
  in Russia, 471
  in Southeast Asia, 738*p*
Volga River, 469*m*, 470
Volta, Alessandro, 389
voodoo, 239
voting, 113
  in Brazil, 319
  in Iran, 663
  in Mexico, 213

W

wage, 762, 909
Wahhabism, 607
Wales, 422, 423, 423*m*
Walesa, Lech, 454
Wallonia, 431
warfare, 365, 365*p*, 367
War of 1812, 175
Warsaw, 454*p*
Warsaw Pact, 401
Washington, 134*m*, 866*m*
Washington, D.C., 6–7, 6*m*–7*m*,
    134*m*, 867*m*
water cycle, 37, 37*c*, 909
water pollution, 53
  in China, 767, 767*p*
  crops and, 232
  in Western Europe, 419–420,
    419*p*, 431
water resources, 23
  in Africa, 498, 498*m*
  of Arabia and Iraq, 594,
    594*m*, 595, 595*m*
  in Central Asia and the
    Caucasus, 689, 698, 699,
    699*g*, 699*p*
  climate and, 36–37, 36*m*, 37*c*
  in Israel, 622–623, 622*m*, 623*p*
  in Jordan, 622*m*, 623
  in Kazakhstan, 699, 699*g*,
    699*p*
  in Lebanon, 622, 623*m*

  in North Africa, 562
  in Pacific region, 839
  in Southern and Eastern
    Africa, 535, 536, 536*c*
  in Syria, 622–623, 623*m*
  in Turkey, 623
  in Uzbekistan, 699, 699*g*,
    699*p*
  See also *irrigation*
Watt, James, 389
weather, 32, 140, 909. See also
    climate
weathering, 24–25, 909
Weddell Sea, 875*m*
Wellington, 830*m*
Wesley, John, 379
West and Central Africa, 860*m*
  African Union, 522–523
  agriculture in, 508, 512, 519,
    519*p*
  arts of, 521
  atlas of, 500*m*, 504–511,
    504*p*, 505*m*, 506*p*, 507*m*,
    508*m*, 509*p*, 510*m*
  cities and towns of, 510–511,
    510*m*
  climate of, 506, 507*m*
  corruption in, 519
  disease in, 511, 522
  economy of, 518–519, 518*p*
  empires in, 512–513, 512*m*,
    513*p*
  environment of, 508–509,
    508*m*, 509*p*
  ethnic diversity in, 517
  government of, 514, 515,
    515*m*, 515*p*, 516–517, 516*p*,
    517*p*, 518, 519–520, 520*p*
  history of, 512–517, 512*m*,
    512*p*, 513*p*, 514*p*, 515*m*,
    516*p*, 517*p*
  literacy in, 522*g*
  myStory, 501–503
  natural resources of, 508–509,
    508*m*
  Pan-Africanism in, 516
  physical features of, 504–505,
    505*m*
  population density of, 510–
    511, 510*m*
  poverty in, 522, 523
  religion in, 521
  timeline, 513
  trade in, 125*m*, 512–513, 514
  trade routes, 125*m*
  war in, 522
  See also *Africa*; individual
    countries
West Bank, 614*m*, 618, 620, 623,
    625, 626, 632–633
  conflict and the, 638–640,
    638*m*, 639*p*, 640*p*
  government of, 634, 635

West Berlin, 432
West Central Europe, 428–433,
    428*p*, 429*m*, 429*p*, 430*p*,
    431*p*, 432*c*, 433*p*
Western Europe
  air pollution in, 419, 419*p*
  atlas of, 410*m*, 414–421,
    415*m*, 416*m*, 417*m*, 418*m*,
    420*m*, 421*m*
  cities and towns of, 426
  climate of, 36*m*, 37, 416–417,
    416*m*
  Cold War and, 401
  culture of, 418
  ecosystems of, 416–417, 416*m*
  education in, 417, 418
  high technology in, 426
  immigrants in, 427, 427*p*
  languages of, 417–418, 418*m*
  natural resources of, 417,
    417*m*, 419
  physical features of, 414–415,
    415*m*
  population density of, 419–
    421, 420*m*, 421*m*
  religion in, 418
  water pollution in, 419–420,
    419*p*
  See also individual countries
Western Ghats, 709, 709*m*, 711,
    873*m*
Western Hemisphere, 5, 5*m*
Western Sahara, 552*m*, 562*m*,
    575
West Germany, 403, 403*m*
West Pakistan, 722–723, 722*m*
West Siberian Plain, 333*p*, 468,
    469, 469*m*, 873*m*
West Virginia, 134*m*, 867*m*
wheel, 98*p*–99*p*, 99*c*
white nights, 425
wildfire, 839
Wilkes Land, 875*m*
William and Mary, 390
William the Conqueror, 364–
    365
Wilson, Woodrow, 150*p*, 151*q*
wind, 38–40
  energy, 49, 53, 53*p*, 767
  patterns, 140
windmills, 431, 431*p*
Wisconsin, 134*m*, 867*m*
women
  in Afghanistan, 728*p*
  in ancient Greece, 346, 347
  in Brazil, 319
  in Byzantine empire, 356
  in China, 765
  in Egypt, 553–555, 553*p*,
    554*p*, 555*p*
  historians, 356
  in India, 728*p*
  in Iran, 663

in Iraq, 611
in Japan, 793
in manorialism, 359
in Middle Ages, 364
in Morocco, 575
Muslim, 606
in Roman Catholic Church, 358
in Roman Empire, 351
in Saudi Arabia, 587–589, 587p, 588p, 589p, 611
in South Asia, 728, 728g, 728p
in Turkey, 667
in Yemen, 590p
working class, 89
World Bank, 111, 111p
World Health Organization, 110p
world maps, 860m–861m, 862m–863m
World Trade Center, 156, 819
World Trade Organization (WTO), 180
World War I, 395m, 632, 909
in Arabian Peninsula, 603
Canada and, 177, 177p
Europe and, 394–395, 394p, 395m
Ottoman empire and, 660
Russia and, 480
World War II, 398–399, 398m, 909

Canada and, 177
in Germany, 432
Holocaust and, 632
Japan and, 151, 785, 785m
in Southeast Asia, 812
United States and, 150p, 151
writing systems
in ancient Egypt, 565, 565p
in Arabia and Iraq, 598, 598p, 600
civilizations and, 98
Etruscan, 348
in Korea, 783
Mayan, 234, 234p
Phoenician, 626
prehistory and, 119
WTO. See *World Trade Organization*
Wycliffe, John, 378
Wyoming, 134m, 141, 144, 866m

X

Xenophon, 345
Xerxes, 347
Xhosa people, 527–529, 527p, 528p, 529p, 544

Y

Yale people, 173

Yangtze River. See *Chang River*
Yazidis people, 597
Yekooche people, 173
Yellow River. See *Huang River*
Yeltsin, Boris, 482p, 483
Yemen, 861m, 872m
agriculture in, 594
databank, 883
economy of, 608
history of, 603, 604
population density in, 595, 595m
religion in, 596m, 597
women in, 590p
Young Turks, 660
Yucatán Peninsula, 199, 199m, 207, 214, 865m
Yugoslavia, 395, 395m, 457, 458, 458m, 459
Yukon, 160m

Z

Zaire, 516, 516p, 519–520, 520p, 547
Zambezi River, 531, 531m
Zambia, 526m, 540m, 861m, 870m, 883
Zanzibar, 539, 539p
Zapotec group, 214
Zedillo, Ernesto, 213
"Zero" plane, 785p
Zeus, 345

Zimbabwe, 520, 526m, 540, 540m, 542, 547, 861m, 870m, 883
Zionism, 632, 909
Zoroastrianism, 655, 655p, 657, 909
Zulu people, 544

Acknowledgments

The people who made up the **myWorld Geography** team—representing composition services; core design, digital, and multimedia production services; digital product development; editorial; editorial services; materials management; and production management—are listed below.

Leann Davis Alspaugh, Sarah Aubry, Deanna Babikian, Paul Blankman, Alyssa Boehm, Peter Brooks, Susan Brorein, Megan Burnett, Todd Christy, Neville Cole, Bob Craton, Michael Di Maria, Glenn Diedrich, Frederick Fellows, Jorgensen Fernandez, Thomas Ferreira, Patricia Fromkin, Andrea Golden, Mary Ann Gundersen, Christopher Harris, Susan Hersch, Paul Hughes, Judie Jozokos, Lynne Kalkanajian, John Kingston, Kate Koch, Stephanie Krol, Karen Lepri, Ann-Michelle Levangie, Salena LiBritz, Courtney Markham, Constance J. McCarty, Anne McLaughlin, Rich McMahon, Mark O'Malley, Alison Muff, Jen Paley, Gabriela Perez Fiato, Judith Pinkham, Paul Ramos, Charlene Rimsa, Marcy Rose, Rashid Ross, Alexandra Sherman, Owen Shows, Melissa Shustyk, Jewel Simmons, Ted Smykal, Emily Soltanoff, Frank Tangredi, Simon Tuchman, Elizabeth Tustian, Merle Uuesoo, Alwyn Velásquez, Andrew White, Heather Wright

Maps

XNR Productions, Inc.

Illustration

Kerry Cashman, Marcos Chin, Dave Cockburn, Jeremy Mohler

Photography

FRONT MATTER **Pages vi–xxix, Bkgrnd sky,** Image Source/Getty Images; **vi–vii,** Image Source/Getty Images; **vii, T,** ZZ/Alamy; **viii, L,** Jim Sugar/Corbis; **R,** GoGo Images Corporation/Alamy; **viii–ix,** Image Source/Getty Images; **ix,** Superstock/age Fotostock; **x,** Jeff Greenberg/PhotoEdit; **xii–xxiii, All,** Pearson Education Inc.; **xxx, Bkgrnd,** Michele Falzone/JAI/Corbis; **LT,** Pearson Education, Inc.; **TM,** Pearson Education, Inc.; **RT,** Pearson Education, Inc.; **xxxi, RM,** iStockphoto.com.

CORE CONCEPTS **Pages xxxii–1, Bkgrnd sky,** Image Source/Getty Images; **xxxii, L,** Shutterstock; **LM,** Jim Sugar/Corbis; **M,** Fabian Gonzales/Alamy; **RM, All** Canada Photos/Alamy; **R,** Gavin Hellier/Getty Images; **1, L,** Reed Kaestner/Corbis/JupiterImages; **LM,** Gavin Hellier/Getty Images; **RM,** Todd Gipstein/Corbis; **R,** Digital Vision/Getty Images; **2, LT,** Shutterstock; **RT,** Photo courtesy of Jason Young; **B,** Beth Wald/Aurora/Getty Images; **LB,** Harley Couper/Alamy; **3, LT,** Photo courtesy of Jason Young; **RT,** Photo courtesy of Jason Young; **4, LM,** Mike Agliolo/Corbis; **6,** Saul Loeb/AFP/Getty Images; **8, RT,** Silver Burdett Ginn; **LM,** Bill Curtsinger/National Geographic Stock; **16, RT,** Jim Sugar/Corbis; **LT,** Shutterstock; **M,** Jerry Driendl/Getty Images; **17, RT,** Stephen Alvarez/Getty Images; **Inset,** Courtesy of Tamsen Buriak; **LT,** Hyogo Prefectural Government/epa/Corbis; **24,** Goodshoot/Corbis; **25, RT,** Shutterstock, Inc.; **RM,** Digital Vision/Alamy; **26, L,** Jim Sugar/Corbis; **27, RM,** Hyogo Prefectural Government/epa/Corbis; **RB,** AP Photo/Ric Francis; **30, RT,** NOAA; **M,** David J. Phillip/AP Images; **LT,** NASA/Corbis; **31, RT,** Photo courtesy of Airin McGhee; **LT,** Alex Brandon/Newhouse News Service/Landov; **TM,** Smiley N. Pool/Dallas Morning News/Corbis; **32, LB,** Paul Zahl/National Geographic/Getty Images; **33, LT,** M. Spencer Green/AP Photo; **RB,** Indranil Mukherjee/AFP/Getty Images; **39, B,** Wave RF/Photolibrary; **40,** Francisco González/age Fotostock; **41, RT,** JTB Photo/JTB MEDIA CREATION, Inc./Alamy; **RB,** James L. Stanfield/National Geographic Stock; **42, T,** Fabian Gonzales/Alamy; **LM,** Joseph Sohm-Visions of America/Getty Images; **TM,** John Glover/Getty Images; **LB,** Jake Rajs/Getty Images; **M,** David Ball/Getty Images; **42–43, B,** Macduff Everton/Corbis; **43, TM,** Radius Images/Photolibrary; **M,** Mike Tittel/Getty Images; **T,** Ruth Tomlinson/Getty Images; **LM,** Ron Sanford/Photo Researchers; **RB,** Bill Curtsinger/National Geographic Stock; **46, LT,** Jon Holloway/Stock Connection; **RT,** Marilyn Humphries/The Image Works; **M,** Ashley Cooper/Picimpact/Corbis; **47, RT,** Photo courtesy of Lauren Hexilon; **TM,** Frank Perry/AFP/Getty Images; **LT,** Atlantide Phototravel/Corbis; **48, LM,** Melanie Stetson Freeman/The Christian Science Monitor/Getty Images; **B,** vario images GmbH & Co.KG/Alamy; **50–51, All,** Pearson Education, Inc.; **52, B,** Paul Hanna/Reuters/Corbis; **53, RT,** All Canada Photos/Alamy; **56, RT,** San Rostro/age Fotostock; **LT,** Alexey U/Shutterstock; **B,** Jim Russi/age Fotostock; **57, RT,** Photo courtesy of Chris Krestner; **TM,** Imagebroker/Alamy; **LT,** J.R. Bale/Alamy;

TM, James A. Isbell/Shutterstock; **58, LB,** LWA/Getty Images; **BM,** Ariel Skelley/Blend Images/Corbis; **BM,** fotog/Getty Images; **RB,** Getty Images; **59, RT,** Brigitte Sporrer/zefa/Corbis; **62, B,** Dennis MacDonald/PhotoEdit; **M,** Bruno Morandi/age Fotostock; **63, T,** Reuters/KNS Korean News Agency; **64, LB,** Gavin Hellier/Getty Images; **RB,** Mike Cohen/Shutterstock; **66, B,** SuperStock/age Fotostock; **67, LB,** The Seattle Times/Newscom; **RB,** Photo by Wang Kai/ChinaFotoPress/Newscom; **68, LB,** Ed Kashi/Corbis; **69, RT,** Hou Jun/Newscom; **72, M,** Reed Kaestner/Corbis/JupiterImages; **LT,** DDCoral/Shutterstock; **RT,** Mark Gabrenya/Shutterstock; **73, RT,** Photo courtesy of Ludwig Barragan; **TM,** Pearson Education, Inc.; **LT,** Steven Senne/AP Images; **74–75, B,** Shutterstock; **75, RT,** ©2008 by Ira Lippke/Newscom; **LB,** Thony Belizaire/AFP/Getty Images; **76, B,** Travelpix Ltd/Getty Images; **77, B,** PCL/Alamy; **78, LT,** Private Collection/The Bridgeman Art Library; **B,** Bettmann/Corbis; **79, RT,** Jack Kurtz/Newscom; **80, LT,** Paul Almasy/Corbis; **LB,** iStockphoto.com; **81, RT,** Bettmann/Corbis; **RB,** Fly Fernandez/zefa/Corbis; **84, B,** Interfoto/Alamy; **RT,** Sylvain Grandadam/age Fotostock; **LT,** Sergei Bachlakov/Shutterstock, Inc.; **85, TM,** Photo courtesy of Joanna Baca; **RT,** mikenorton/Shutterstock; **RT,** Photo courtesy of Joanna Baca; **86, LT,** Gavin Hellier/Getty Images; **LB,** Pearson Education, Inc.; **BM,** Pearson Education, Inc.; **RB,** Pearson Education, Inc.; **87, All,** Pearson Education, Inc.; **88, LM,** Glenda M. Powers/Shutterstock; **B,** GoGo Images Corporation/Alamy; **89, RB,** Rubberball/Getty Images; **RM,** Kuzma/Shutterstock; **RT,** Silver Burdett Ginn; **TM,** Kokhanchikov/Shutterstock; **TM,** Lebedinski Vladislav/Shutterstock; **M,** George Doyle & Ciaran Griffin/Getty Images; **M,** Pearson Education, Inc.; **TM,** Cecile Treal and Jean-Michel Ruiz/Dorling Kindersley; **90, LT,** Pearson Education, Inc.; **LT,** Pearson Education, Inc.; **LM,** Pearson Education, Inc.; **LM,** Pearson Education, Inc.; **LB,** Pearson Education, Inc.; **LB,** dbimages/Alamy; **91, RT,** Pearson Education, Inc.; **RT,** Pearson Education, Inc.; **RM,** Rubberball/age Fotostock; **RM,** Jaime Mota/age Fotostock; **RB,** Pearson Education, Inc.; **RB,** Pearson Education, Inc.; **94, LT,** Carp (1848). Woodcut by Taito/The Granger Collection, New York; **B,** Jarno Gonzalez Zarraonandia/Shutterstock; **95, BM,** Hellestad Rune/Corbis Sygma; **T,** Bob Krist/eStock Photo; **96,** Stephane De Sakutin/AFP/Getty Images; **97, TM,** Dmitry Kosterev/Shutterstock; **RT,** Dave King/Dorling Kindersley; **RM,** Luchschen/Shutterstock; **RB,** Dorling Kindersley; **BM,** Owen Franken/Corbis; **RB,** James Marshall/Corbis; **98, L,** Alistair Duncan/Dorling Kindersley; **LB,** Michael Holford/Dorling Kindersley; **RB,** Bruce Forster/Dorling Kindersley/Courtesy of the National Historic Oregon Trail Interpretive Center; **99, TM,** Swim Ink 2, LLC/Corbis; **RB,** Matthew Ward/Dorling Kindersley; **102, RT,** Kim Sayer/Dorling Kindersley; **B,** Tom Sliter/The Stennis Center for Public Service Leadership; **RT,** Phil Sandlin/AP Images; **103, LT,** Reuters/Hans Deryk; **RT,** Photo courtesy of Anne Marie Sutherland; **104, LB,** Art Resource/Musée du Louvre; **RB,** Spc Katherine M. Roth/HO/epa/Corbis. All Rights Reserved; **105, L,** Todd Gipstein/Corbis; **R,** Imaginechina via AP Images; **106, R,** Pool/Anwar Hussein Collection/Getty Images; **L,** Karel Prinsloo/AP Images; **107,** John Leicester/AP Images; **108, T,** Kim Sayer/Dorling Kindersley; **M,** L. Clarke/Corbis; **B,** AP Photo/Douglas Healey; **109, M,** White House Photo Office; **T,** Wally McNamee/Corbis; **B,** The Collection of the Supreme Court of the United States; **110,** Alan Gignoux/age fotostock; **111, B,** Kote Rodrigo/EFE/Corbis; **T,** Karel Prinsloo/AP Images; **112, B,** Jeff Greenberg/PhotoEdit; **T,** William Whitehurst/Corbis; **113, RB,** Wally McNamee/Corbis; **116, RT,** Jim Zuckerman/Corbis; **LT,** Digital Vision/Getty Images; **B,** El Comercio Newspaper, Dante Piaggio/AP Images; **117, RT,** Photo courtesy of Brian McCray; **LT,** Ira Block/National Geographic/Getty Images; **TM,** University of Oregon/AP Images; **118, LB,** The British Museum/Dorling Kindersley; **LB,** O. Louis Mazzatenta/National Geographic Stock; **RB,** Ivonne Wierink/Shutterstock; **M,** Giles Stokoe/Felix deWeldon/Dorling Kindersley; **119, RT,** Image Asset Management Ltd./Alamy; **M,** Andy Crawford/Dorling Kindersley, Courtesy of the University Museum of Archaeology and Anthropology, Cambridge; **RB,** Getty Images/De Agostini Editore Picture Library; **120, LB,** Bettmann/Corbis; **LM,** Bettmann/Corbis; **121, RB,** Hulton Archive/Getty Images; **L,** The Granger Collection, New York; **122, LT,** Sean Hunter/Dorling Kindersley; **B,** Martin Gray/National Geographic Stock; **R,** Robert F. Sisson/National Geographic Society; **123, LB,** O. Louis Mazzatenta/National Geographic Stock; **LB,** Anders Ryman/Corbis.

UNIT 1: **Pages 128–133, T, Bkgrnd sky,** Image Source/Getty Images; **129, L,** Pearson Education, Inc.; **R,** Pearson Education, Inc.; **Bkgrnd,** Ray Juno/Corbis;

Acknowledgments (continued)

343, RB, Peter Hayman/The British Museum/Dorling Kindersley; RB, Paul Harris/Dorling Kindersley; 344, M, DEA/G. DAGLI ORTI/Getty; RT, Gianni Dagli Orti/Corbis; 345, RT, Nick Nicholls/The British Museum/Dorling Kindersley; 346, LM, Hoberman Collection/Corbis; 348, L, Réunion des Musées Nationaux/Art Resource, NY; 350, LT, John Heseltine/Dorling Kindersley; 351, B, Franck Guiziou/Hemis/Corbis; 353, RT, PoodlesRock/Corbis; 354, LB, Cameraphoto Arte, Venice/Art Resource, NY; 355, RB, Museum of History of Sofia, Sofia, Bulgaria/Archives Charmet/Bridgeman Art Library; 357, RT, Gianni Dagli Orti/Corbis. All Rights Reserved; 359, RT, Réunion des Musées Nationaux/Art Resource, NY; 360, LB, Geoff Dann/Dorling Kindersley; 361, RT, Werner Forman/Art Resource, NY; 363, RB, SIME s.a.s/eStock Photo; 364, L, Bridgeman Art Library; LB, Bettmann/Corbis; 365, RB, Snark/Art Resource, NY; 366, M, Bettmann/Corbis; LB, *The Dance Macabre* (detail, 1485), Artist unknown, Fresco. L'Oratorio dei Disciplini/SuperStock; LT, Frank Greenaway/Dorling Kindersley; L, maxstockphoto/Shutterstock.

CHAPTER 9: Pages 370–373, All, Pearson Education, Inc.; **374,** Philip Gatward/Dorling Kindersley; **375, RM,** *The Last Supper* (1495–1498), Leonardo da Vinci (1452–1519). Fresco. Santa Maria della Grazie, Milan/A.K.G., Berlin/SuperStock; **RB,** Dorling Kindersley; **376, LT,** Ellen Howdon/Dorling Kindersley, Courtesy of Glasgow Museum; **T,** FPG/Getty Images; **RT,** Pearson Education, Inc.; **377, M,** Dorling Kindersley; **RB,** Adrea Pistolesi/Getty Images; **380, BM,** *Portrait of Henry VIII* (16th century), Hans Holbein the Younger, Oil on canvas. Belvoir Castle, Leicestershire. The Bridgeman Art Library Ltd.; **LB,** Portrait of Catherine of Aragon (1485–1536), 1st Queen of Henry VIII (1825), from "Memoirs of the Court of Queen Elizabeth," watercolor and gouache on paper. Private Collection/The Bridgeman Art Library; **382, Bkgrnd,** Joel W. Rogers/Corbis; **383, RT,** Reuters New Media Inc./Corbis; **BM,** James Stevenson/Dorling Kindersley, Courtesy of the National Maritime Museum, London; **RB,** Clive Streeter/Dorling Kindersley, Courtesy of The Science Museum, London; **LT,** Dorling Kindersley; **384, LB,** *Padshahnama: Europeans Bring Gifts to the Shah Jahan.* The Royal Collection, Her Majesty Queen Elizabeth II; **385, RT,** Chas Howson/The British Museum/Dorling Kindersley; **386, LB,** Erich Lessing/Art Resource, NY; **387, RM,** *Louis XIV, King of France* (1701), Hyacinthe Rigaud. Oil on canvas, 277 x 194 cm. Louvre, Paris, France. Photo: Herve Lewandowski. Louvre, Paris, France. Réunion des Musées Nationaux/Art Resource, NY; **388, LB,** Martin Jones/Corbis; **389, LT,** The Granger Collection, New York; **T,** Shutterstock; **391, RB,** Reduced model of a guillotine (18th century), French School, wood and metal. Musée de la Ville de Paris, Musée Carnavalet, Paris, France, Giraudon/Bridgeman Art Library; **RT,** Getty Images/De Agostini Editore Picture Library; **BM,** Musée de la Révolution Française, Vizille, France/The Bridgeman Art Library; **392, TM,** Lebrecht Music & Arts Photo Library; **RT,** The Francis Frith Collection/Corbis; **393, RT,** Underwood & Underwood/Corbis; **LT,** Musée National de l'Education, Rouen, France/The Bridgeman Art Library; **394, B,** Bettmann/Corbis; **396, LB,** Hulton-Deutsch Collection/Corbis; **397, RB,** Dorling Kindersley; **398, LT,** Andy Crawford/Dorling Kindersley/Imperial War Museum, London; **399,** PhotoDisc/Getty Images; **400, B,** Bettmann/Corbis; **401, RT,** U. S. Navy/Photo Researchers; **402, RB,** AP Images; **B,** Bettmann/Corbis; **404, BM,** Bettmann/Corbis; **LB,** Bettmann/Corbis; **405, L,** The Punch Cartoon Library; **R,** Str Old/Reuters; **406, T,** Peter Dejong/AP Images; **LT,** Peter Dench/Corbis; **407, T,** Dorling Kindersley.

CHAPTER 10: Pages 410–413, All, Pearson Education, Inc.; **414, Bkgrnd,** Sylvain Grandadam/age Fotostock; **B,** J. D. Heaton/age Fotostock; **416, RM,** iStockphoto.com; **M,** Dhoxax/Shutterstock; **T,** Pierre Jacques/Hemis/Corbis; **M,** Bo Zaunders/Corbis; **RB,** Rick Price/Corbis; **RB,** Gavin Hellier/Robert Harding World; **419, L,** Lawson Wood/Corbis; **RM,** Simon Fraser /Photo Researchers; **422,** Dallas and John Heaton/Stock Connection; **425, M,** Pearson Education, Inc.; **RB,** Erik Svensson and Jeppe Wikstrom/Dorling Kindersley; **R,** David Lomax/Robert Harding/Getty Images; **426,** Annie Griffiths Belt/Corbis; **427,** Ken Straiton/Corbis; **428, LB,** Patrick Müller © Centre des monuments nationaux, Paris; **429, T,** Britta Jaschinski/Dorling Kindersley; **B,** Prentice Hall School; **RB,** Le Segretain Pascal/Corbis Sygma; **RM,** Perrush/Shutterstock; **430,** AP Photo/Cristophe Ena; **431,** Bjorn Svensson/Photolibrary; **432,** George Hammerstein/Solus-Veer/Corbis; **433,** Fancy/Veer/Corbis; **434,** Dorling Kindersley; **435,** Pearson Education, Inc.; **RM,** Bob Sacha/Corbis; **RB,** iStockphoto.com; **436,** massimo Borchi/Corbis; **438, RB,** Reuters/Susana Vera (SPAIN); **439,** George Christakis/epa/Corbis.

CHAPTER 11: Pages 442–445, All, Pearson Education, Inc.; **446, Bkgrnd,** Erich Lessing/Magnum Photos; **LB,** Stefano Pensotti/age Fotostock; **448, LB,** Per Karlsson—BKWine.com/Alamy; **LB,** Jaroslaw Grudzinski/Shutterstock; **449, M,** Dean Conger/Corbis; **B,** AFP/Getty Images; **450, RB,** Zaichiki/Alamy; **RB,** Reuters/Vasily Fedosenko; **RM,** AP Photo/CTK, David Veis; **LM,** iStockphoto.com; **LB,** Photoshot Holdings Ltd./Alamy; **451,** Stan Kujawa/Alamy; **453, TM,** Idealink Photography/Alamy; **RT,** ziontek/Dabrowski-KPA/Zuma Press, © 2004 by Wziontek/Dabrowski-KPA (Newscom TagID: zumaphotos661194) [Photo via Newscom]; **LT,** AP Photo/Hidajet Delic; **LT,** Martin Bureau/AFP/Getty Images; **454, LB,** Steven May/Alamy; **455, RB,** imagebroker/Alamy; **456, B,** Petr Josek Snr/Reuters; **457, B,** Carlos Nieto/age Fotostock; **459, B,** Getty Images/De Agostini Editore Picture Library; **460, RT,** Viktor Drachev/AFP/Getty Images; **461, LT,** East News/Getty Images; **RT,** AFP Photo/Daniel Mihailescu/Newscom.

CHAPTER 12: Pages 464–467, All, Pearson Education, Inc.; **468, Bkgrnd,** Sergey Yakovlev/Shutterstock; **LB,** David Turnley/Corbis; **470, R,** isoft/iStockphoto.com; **M,** Dean Conger/Corbis; **L,** Superstock; **471,** Gerd Ludwig/Corbis; **472,** Sovfoto/Eastfoto; **475, R,** Gideon Mendel/Corbis; **L,** Pearson Education, Inc.; **476, L,** Werner Forman/Art Resource, NY; **R,** Erich Lessing/Art Resource, NY; **477, L,** Jeremy Horner/Corbis; **R,** *Ivan the Terrible* (20th century), English School, Gouache on paper. Private Collection/© Look and Learn/The Bridgeman Art Library; **478, L,** The Art Gallery Collection/Alamy; **R,** The Granger Collection, New York; **479, LB,** David South/Alamy; **LT,** The Gallery Collection/Corbis; **RB,** Réunion des Musées Nationaux/Art Resource, NY; **480,** Photos 12/Alamy; **481,** Charles & Josette Lenars/Corbis; **482, L,** Gianni Giansanti/Sygma/Corbis; **R,** Peter Turnley/Corbis; **484,** Iain Masterton/Alamy Images; **485, L,** Peter Turnley/Corbis; **R,** AntonioDiaz/Shutterstock; **486,** Vasily Fedosenko/Reuters/Corbis; **487,** Lystseva Marina/ITAR-TASS Photo/Corbis; **489,** Gleb Garanich/Reuters/Corbis.

UNIT 4 CLOSER: Page 492, B, Shutterstock; **LB,** Shutterstock; **RT,** Shutterstock; **RT,** Shutterstock; **492–493, Bkgrnd,** Shutterstock; **493, R,** European Communities, 1995–2009; **R,** Shutterstock.

UNIT 5: Pages 494–499, T, Bkgrnd sky, Image Source/Getty Images; **495, LT,** Pearson Education, Inc.; **TM,** Pearson Education, Inc.; **RT,** Pearson Education, Inc.; **B,** Stellapictures/JupiterImages; **496, T,** Radius Images/JupiterImages; **B,** Matthew Septimus/Getty Images; **497, T,** Gavin Hellier/Photolibrary; **B,** Roger De La Harpe/Photolibrary; **M,** Eric Isselée/Shutterstock; **498,** Hugh Sitton/zefa/Corbis; **499, All** Pearson Education, Inc.

CHAPTER 13: Pages 500–503, All, Pearson Education, Inc.; **504,** Bruno Morandi/Getty Images; **506,** Bruno Morandi/Getty Images; **507, LM,** Pearson Education, Inc.; **L,** Nigel Bean/naturepl.com; **RM,** Atlantide Phototravel/Corbis; **R,** Bruno Fert/Corbis; **509, Inset,** Bruce Dale/National Geographic/Getty Images; **Bkgrnd,** Keira McKee/Alamy; **510,** Martin Dohrn/Photo Researchers, Inc.; **512,** Frans Lemmens/Corbis; **513, L,** John Webb/The Art Archive; **R,** Joan Pollock/Alamy; **514,** Courtesy of the Wilberforce House Museum, Hull/Dorling Kindersley; **515, T,** National Archives Image Library, UK/Dorling Kindersley; **B,** Popperfoto/Getty Images; **516, L,** Bettmann/Corbis; **R,** AFP/Getty Images; **517,** AP Images; **518,** Gideon Mendel/ActionAid/Corbis; **519,** Jacob Silberberg/Getty Images; **520, L,** AFP/Getty Images; **R,** George Osodi/AP Images; **521, Cloth,** Dorling Kindersley; **LT,** Comstock Images/Jupiter Unlimited; **RT,** Paul Almasy/Corbis; **LB,** Studio Patellani/Corbis; **RB,** Philippe Lissac/Godong/Corbis; **523,** Pearson Education, Inc.

CHAPTER 14: Pages 526–257, Ksenia Khamkova/iStockphoto.com; **526, B,** Pearson Education, Inc.; **527, T,** Pearson Education, Inc.; **B,** Pearson Education, Inc.; **528–529, All,** Pearson Education, Inc.; **530, Bkgrnd,** SuperStock; **B,** Steve Outram/Mira.com; **533, L,** Tim Laman/Getty Images, Inc.; **L Inset,** meoita/Fotolia; **M Inset,** Beckman/Dorling Kindersley; **R Inset,** Oleg Znamenskiy/Fotolia; **R,** Image Source/Photolibrary; **534, L,** Ian Murphy/Getty Images; **M,** Charles O'Rear/Corbis; **R,** Kulka/zefa/Corbis; **535, Bkgrnd,** franco pizzochero/age Fotostock; **B,** F.A.O. Food and Agriculture Organization of the United Nations; **536, T,** Reza/Webistan/Getty Images; **TM,** Peter Martell/AFP/Getty Images; **BM,** Andrew Holt/Getty Images; **B,** Jenny Matthews/Alamy; **537,** Liba Taylor/Corbis; **538, T,** David Boyer/National Geographic/Getty Images; **B,** Gallo Images/Corbis; **539, B,** Peter Groenendijk/age Fotostock; **541, RT,** The Granger Collection, New York; **LT,** The Granger Collection, New York; **B,** Bettmann/Corbis; **542,** Bettmann/Corbis; **543,** David Turnley/Corbis; **544,** PCN Photography/PCN/Corbis; **545, T,** Patrick Robert/Sygma/Corbis; **B,** Lindsay Hebberd/Corbis; **546,** Alfred De Montesquiou/AP Images; **548, B,** AFP Photo/HO/U.S. Navy/Jason R. Zalasky/Newscom; **T,** epa/Corbis; **549,** Wolfgang Schmidt/Peter Arnold, Inc.